P9-DVO-065

☆☆☆☆☆☆☆☆☆☆☆☆☆☆☆☆☆☆☆☆☆☆☆☆☆☆☆☆☆☆☆☆☆☆

"We have recently learned much of the Negro's mistreatment, but the trials of a single man, when recounted as vividly as Sammy Davis, Jr.'s are in his lengthy autobiography, renew and redoubled the shock. The image which emerges from YES I CAN is vivid. We see a man of immense drive and vitality, spontaneous, clever, generous, sophisticated about people (and loyal to those he likes), aggressive, egotistical, tough-tender.... And his confessions are in good taste—he neither conceals nor belabors the lurid details. Nor does he use them for secondary gains: the book is honorably free of mere scandal-mongering, of calculated humble-pie, of weaknesses unveiled only to offset dramatically his later virtue.... In describing his relationship with May Britt, Davis conveys the full dimension of American racial hatred. Threatened with violence, heaped with abuse (sample letter before their wedding: Dear Nigger Bastard, I see where Frank Sinatra is going to be best man at your abortion...), they react with a courage so free of self-pity that in the same breath you want to cheer them and curse the maniacs who pursue them. 'Dear God,' Sammy Davis, Jr. asks, 'will it ever end? Will I ever be able to live like everybody else?' It is the rhetorical question."

—Martin Duberman
The New York Times Book Review

☆☆☆☆☆☆☆☆☆☆☆☆☆☆☆☆☆☆☆☆☆☆☆☆☆☆☆☆☆☆☆☆☆☆

☆☆☆☆☆☆☆☆☆☆☆☆☆☆☆☆☆☆☆☆☆☆☆☆☆☆☆☆☆☆☆☆☆☆☆

☆☆☆☆☆☆☆☆☆☆☆☆☆☆☆☆☆☆☆☆☆☆☆☆☆☆☆☆☆☆☆☆☆☆☆

☆☆☆☆☆☆☆☆☆☆☆☆☆☆☆☆☆☆☆☆☆☆☆☆☆☆☆☆☆☆

"*An extraordinarily frank and full autobiography*...exceptional on several grounds... so rich in impressions and reactions it is difficult to single out specific incidents.... It boldly confronts taboo issues.... Most importantly, the book has been set down with a minimum of depersonalization by his collaborators.... This is Sammy Davis, Jr. telling the story of his life in his own unmistakable style—dynamic, cocky, flamboyant, naïve, defiant.... The most vivid, candid, unsparing show-biz autobiography since that of Ethel Waters."

—John Barkham
Philadelphia Bulletin

YES I CAN
was originally published by
Farrar, Straus and Giroux.

☆☆☆☆☆☆☆☆☆☆☆☆☆☆☆☆☆☆☆☆☆☆☆☆☆☆☆☆☆☆

Silhouette from a photograph
by Milton H. Greene

YES
I
CAN

THE STORY OF SAMMY DAVIS, JR.

BY SAMMY DAVIS, JR., and JANE and BURT BOYAR

ILLUSTRATED WITH 32 PAGES OF PHOTOGRAPHS

A POCKET CARDINAL EDITION
PUBLISHED BY POCKET BOOKS · NEW YORK

YES I CAN: THE STORY OF SAMMY DAVIS, JR.

Farrar, Straus and Giroux edition published September, 1965

A Pocket Cardinal edition
1st printing.........August, 1966

This Pocket Cardinal® edition includes every word contained in the
original, higher-priced edition. It is printed from brand-new
plates made from completely reset, clear, easy-to-read type.
Pocket Cardinal editions are published by Pocket Books, a division of
Simon & Schuster, Inc., 630 Fifth Avenue, New York, N.Y. 10020.
Trademarks registered in the United States and other countries.

L

We ain't what we oughta be,
we ain't what we wanta be,
we ain't what we gonna be,
but thank God we ain't what we was.

MARTIN LUTHER KING

YES
I
CAN

The Story of

SAMMY DAVIS, JR.

PROLOGUE

THEY LIKED ME.

The audience was leaning in to me, nodding, approving, catching every more I was making, and as I finished big with "Birth of the Blues" their applause was like a kiss on the lips.

It was November of 1954, we were playing the New Frontier in Las Vegas, and after twenty-six years we were finally getting off the ground, starting to make our move. People were beginning to hear about The Will Mastin Trio and "the kid in the middle." They weren't exactly hysterical about us yet, but everybody knew it was going to happen for us any day—we were contenders and they were rooting us in.

The applause kept building. I looked out at the people, absorbing what they were giving me, wishing I never had to walk off that stage and leave them. I smiled "Thank you." Not for the applause. For making it possible for me to walk through the world through the front door.

I changed out of my stage clothes and Charley handed me my gold cigarette case, polished and filled. I nodded ceremoniously. "You are indeed a gentleman's gentleman and I shall speak of you to the King." I gave him a shot on the arm, "I've gotta go by the room to pick up some things. See you in the car in an hour."

As I stepped out the stage door the glow from the casino was lighting up the desert, and as the doors swung open and people came out, the sound of money, laughs, and music poured past them as if there was just too much hilarity inside to stay bottled up. It was out of my way but I felt like walking through there for the sheer joy of knowing I could.

The deputy sheriff standing just inside gave me a big "Hi'ya, Sam." I waved and kept moving through all the ac-

1

tion, past a wall of slot machines, the dice tables, black jack . . . "Hi'ya, Sammy" . . . "Swingin' show, Sam." . . . "Here, make room for Sammy."

"Thanks, not tonight. Gotta run into L.A. Catch y'tomorrow."

I loved the way the crowds opened up for me and I circled the room twice, getting loaded on the atmosphere they'd kept us away from the other times we'd played Vegas, when there'd been a law against me, when it had been "Sorry, but you're not allowed in the casino—you understand." While the other acts had laughs and gambled, we went back to the colored side of town and we "understood." But now we didn't have to understand, and the joy of it swept through me every time I walked through that door.

Two of the chorus chicks standing at the roulette table waved and made room for me between them. I had no desire to gamble, but people were gathering around to watch my action. I dropped five one-hundred-dollar bills on the table. "On the red, please." An excited murmuring rose around me. "Sammydavis . . . Sammydavis . . . Sammydavis . . ." The chicks were grinning, digging the big-time move. The dealer spun the wheel. I shook my fist at him. "If you yell 'black' at me there's gonna be a race riot." It got a laugh. I lit a cigarette and as I took the first drag the ball clicked into the red six. The dealer matched my money with a huge stack of chips and pushed it all back to me. I split my winnings, slid one pile to each of the girls, and playing it Cary Grant-on-the-French Riviera, with a little bow and "Thank you for bringing me luck, ladies," I turned and rode away on their gasps.

Walking along the corridor to my room, I intensified the satisfaction by the bittersweet of contrast, concentrating on the emotionless face, remembering the matter-of-fact voice: "You people can't stay here. You'll have to find a boarding house in the—uh, on the other side of town." Now they wanted us enough so they were breaking their rules, we were bigger than Jim Crow. They were paying us $7,500 a week, the best money we'd ever made, but that was the least of the payoff. It was as though a genie had materialized out of show business and said, "You're going to be a star and anything you want is yours; now you're as good as anybody," and he'd handed us a solid gold key to every door that had ever been slammed in our faces.

I sat on an easy chair in my living room, absorbing the acceptance, smoking a cigarette, enjoying the luxury of the suite and the picture of myself in the middle of it.

I showered and called Room Service for a hamburger. There was a knock at the door. One of the chorus kids was standing there wearing skin-tight blue jeans. I laughed. "They've got crazy Room Service here." She laughed too. She didn't understand the joke but she laughed anyway. That was a part of it all. When you're making it you get laughs with "Good morning."

Charley was waiting in the car in front of the hotel. "Baby, you drive the first half while I catch a few hours' sleep." I climbed into the back seat and got comfortable. As the car rolled down the Strip toward the highway I saw the big neon sign flashing my name across the desert. I could smell the brand new leather as I rested my face against it and I kissed that expensive seat with all the love I had for everything it represented.

I was glad to take over the driving. Nobody's invented booze that'll give you a kick like the first few times you drive your first Cadillac convertible. I pulled onto the highway and let the car swallow up the road. The sun was coming up over the mountains and I saw the night leaving and the day growing bigger, brighter every minute. It was one of those magnificent mornings when you can only remember the good things —as though nothing bad has ever happened. I was actively aware that the edge of the window was exactly the right height for my left elbow. My fingers fit perfectly into the ridges around the steering wheel, and the clear desert air streaming in through the window was wrapping itself around my face like some gorgeous, swinging chick giving me a facial.

I turned on the radio, it filled the car with music and I heard my own voice singing "Hey, There." Oh, God! What are the odds against turning on the radio to the exact station at the exact moment when a disc jockey is playing your first hit? For a second I was afraid that life was getting so good that something would have to happen to take it all away. But the car, the suite in Vegas, the hit record—and all they symbolized, were the start of a new life, and nobody had given it to me, so there wasn't anybody who could take it away. It had all come from show business and as long as God let me keep my talent it would keep on coming. We were building and any day now we'd really break wide open and I'd be a star. A real goddam *star*! And nobody could ever again tell me, "Here, this is your corner of the world. Stay there." And that would be it, that would be goddam *it*!

We were on a double lane highway with two lanes going each way. A green car passed me, the first car I'd seen in ten minutes. At another time I might have raced it, but I didn't need that jazz any more. I was on my way to record my first movie sound track. It wasn't really being in pictures but it was closer than I'd ever gotten before. I visualized myself driving through the gate at Universal in my own Cadillac convertible. The guard was tipping his hat, "Good morning, Mr. Davis. They're waiting for you on sound stage Number One."

The green car was slowing down but it wasn't pulling over to the right like they had to stop for a flat or something; they were pulling over to the left. I knew there were women in it because I'd noticed their hats. Whoops, stay away from them. I moved into the right lane fast but as I did she started moving into it, too, but not all the way, she was straddling the two lanes. Now what the hell is she trying to do? Oh, she's not going to make a U-turn on the parkway! Or is she? Why else would she be slowing down? She must have missed her turn-off. Well go on, baby, if you're gonna do it then do it. I got way over to the right to give her all the room she'd need but still she didn't move. She stayed in the middle . . . then a little left . . . a little right . . . now it looked like she wanted to stop. Make up your mind, lady. She cut sharp to the left, hooking out to make a wide U-turn, then stopped, stretched out across both lanes like a roadblock. I had no choice but to use the oncoming lane to swing around her. I started to make my move but suddenly several cars were coming toward me. I was boxed in. I hit my brakes. Only a second ago she had seemed to be a mile away. I was jamming on the brake with all my strength and pulling back on the wheel as though hoping I could pull the car to a stop with my two hands. I knew I was going to hit her. I cut the wheel as hard as I could toward her rear fender trying at least not to make it broadside where the driver was sitting. . . .

The grinding, steel-twisting, glass-shattering noise screamed all around me. I had no control. I was just there, totally consumed by it, unable to believe I was really in an automobile crash. I saw the impact spin her car completely around and hurl it out of sight, then my forehead slammed into my steering wheel.

As I felt pain and saw my hand moving I was stunned by the knowledge that I was still alive.

I heard Charley moaning in the back. Thank God, he was alive too. I felt blood running down my face and into my eyes like it had a couple of times in the army when I'd been hit over the head. I could hardly see but I knew I'd be okay as soon as the blood cleared away.

I was afraid to see what had happened to Charley. When I turned around he was trying to get up off the floor. "Charley? You okay?" I opened my door and got out to help him. I reached into the back seat and took hold of his arm. When he stood up I could see his jaw hanging loose and blood coming out of his mouth. "Oh, God! I'm sorry, Charley. Please forgive me! I'm sorry. . . ."

Cars were stopping and people were running out of a diner and gas station. Someone said, "It's Sammy Davis." I started up the road to see what had happened to the women, but a soldier stopped me. "They're all right over there. We better get you to a hospital."

"I'm okay. My friend's hurt." I pulled the soldier over to Charley. He had both hands in front of his mouth and the blood was pouring through his fingers. I put my arm around him. "It's gonna be all right . . . don't worry. It'll be okay. . ." He looked up at me and made a horrible choking sound, trying to speak. He pointed to my face, closed his eyes and moaned. I reached up. As I ran my hand over my cheek I felt my eye hanging there by a string. Frantically I tried to stuff it back in, like if I could do that it would stay there and nobody would know, it would be as though nothing had happened. The ground went out from under me and I was on my knees. "Don't let me go blind. Please, God, don't take it all away. . . ."

People were picking me up and carrying me and putting

me somewhere but I couldn't see, I couldn't move. I was half-awake, half-asleep, hanging somewhere between the past and the future. But there was no future any more. All the beautiful things, all the plans, the laughs—they were lying out there, smashed just like the car. The doors were going to close again. The people who'd been nice when I was somebody would turn away from me. None of them were going to say "Hi'ya, Sam" any more.

I heard a siren. There was movement under me and I knew I was in an ambulance. Can it really happen this way? Twenty-six years of working, and taking it, and reaching— was all that for nothing? Can you finally get it and blow it so fast? Was that little touch all there was for me? For my whole life? I'm never going to be a star?

They're going to hate me again.

part
I

1

I Was Born In Harlem On December 8, 1925. My father was the lead dancer in Will Mastin's *Holiday in Dixieland,* a vaudeville troupe in which my mother, Elvera "Baby" Sanchez, was a top chorus girl. Good jobs were scarce so she remained in the line until two weeks before I was born. Then, as soon as she was able to dance, she boarded me with friends in Brooklyn, and continued on the road with my father and the show.

My grandmother, Rosa B. Davis, came out from Harlem to see me and wrote to my father, "I never saw a dirtier child in my life. They leave Sammy alone all day so I've taken him with me. I'm going to make a home for that child."

I heard my father call my grandmother "Mama" so I called her Mama, and this was appropriate because by the time I could speak I thought of her as that.

Mama was housekeeper for one family for twenty years, cooking, cleaning, ironing, and raising their children and me at the same time.

One day she returned to the nursery school at which she'd been leaving me. The nurse was surprised. "We thought you were on your job, Mrs. Davis."

"Something told me get off the streetcar and see what you're doing with my Sammy. Now I find you put these two other children in his carriage with him and you got Sammy all scrooched up in a corner of his own carriage. I bought that carriage for Sammy. Paid cash for it. Now you got him so he can't stretch out in his own carriage. Get those kids out of Sammy's carriage."

She began taking me to work with her. On her days off she took me to the park and put me on the swings. Nobody else could push or touch me. When her friends saw us coming they snickered, "Here comes Rosa Davis and her Jesus." Mama's reply was, "He's a Jesus to me."

When I was two my parents had a daughter, Ramona, whom they sent to live with my mother's family while they stayed on the road. Six months later they separated. My mother joined another travelling show, Connie's Hot Chocolates, and my father came home to get me.

"Sam, this child's too young to go on the road."

"Hell, Mama, I'm his father and I say he goes on the road. I ain't leaving him here so's Elvera can come in and take him away. 'Sides, I want my son with me."

When the train moved into the tunnel and I couldn't see Mama anymore I stopped waving and settled back in my seat. My father started taking off my coat, my leggings and my hat. "Where we goin', Daddy?"

He smiled and put his arm around me. "We're goin' into show business, son."

Our first stop was the Pitheon Theatre in Pittsburgh. I was backstage with my father all day, but at night he left me at the rooming house with a chair propped against the bed and often I didn't see him again until the next afternoon. Will Mastin came in every morning, bathed me in the sink and made my breakfast, Horlick's malted milk, which he mixed with hot water from the tap. We were great friends. He spent hours making funny faces at me and I loved making the same faces right back at him. One afternoon I was in the dressing room playing with the make-up, trying to use the powder puffs and tubes and pencils on my face the way I always saw my father and Will doing it. Will was watching me. "Here, let me show you how to do that." I sat on his chair while he put blackface on me. Then he took a tube of clown white, gave me the big white lips and winked, "Now you look like Al Jolson." I winked back. He snapped his fingers like he'd gotten an idea, and sent for our prima donna who sang "Sonny Boy." "Next show," he told her, "take Sammy on stage, hold him in your lap and keep singing no matter what happens."

As she sang, I looked over her shoulder and saw Will in the wings playing our game, rolling his eyes and shaking his head at me and I rolled my eyes and shook my head right back at him. The prima donna hit a high note and Will held his nose. I held my nose, too. But Will's faces weren't half as funny as the prima donna's so I began copying hers instead: when her lips trembled, my lips trembled, and I followed her all the way from a heaving bosom to a quivering jaw. The people out front were watching me, laughing. When we got off, Will knelt to my height. "Listen to that applause, Sammy, some of it's for you." My father was crouched beside me, too, smiling, pleased with me. "You're a born mugger, son, a born mugger." He and Will both had their arms around me.

When we arrived at our next town Will began giving out meal tickets to the troupe. Once an act had its name up on a theater, there were restaurants in show towns that would give food on credit. They'd issue a meal ticket good for a week's food and we'd settle with them on payday. Will gave my father his ticket and then put one in my pocket. "Here you are, Mose Gastin. You got a meal ticket coming to you same as anyone else in the troupe."

I took it out of my pocket and held it. "Okay, Massey." I couldn't say Mastin. Why he called me Mose Gastin or where he got that name I don't know.

Will built up a new show called *Struttin' Hannah from Savannah.* Curvy, sexy Hannah was struttin' from Savannah to New York. On the way, she'd pass a house with a picket fence, see me playing in the yard with a pail and shovel and do a slinky Mae West kind of walk over to me. "Hi, Buster. Any place around here where a lady can get a room?" She'd turn to me and roll her eyes, but the audience could only see me wildly rolling my eyes back at her. "Hey, are you a little kid or a midget?" Then she'd wink, also without the audience seeing it, and I'd wink back hard and long.

Between shows I'd stand in the wings watching the other acts, like Moss and Fry, Butterbeans and Susie, The Eight Black Dots, and Pot, Pan & Skillet. It never occurred to me to play with the pail and shovel, they were my props, part of the act, and I didn't think of them as toys. At mealtime, I'd sit with my father, Will, and the other performers, listening to them talk show business, hearing about the big vaudeville acts that played the Keith "time." Keith was far over our heads.

11

Shows like ours, Connie's Hot Chocolates and McKinney's Cotton Pickers played small time like TOBA and Butterfield but there was no end of stories to be heard about the great acts who worked the big time.

We always rented the cheapest room we could find, and my father and I shared the bed. He'd turn out the light and say, "Well, good night, Poppa." Then I'd hear a scratching sound. I'd sit up, fast. "What's that, Daddy?"

"I didn't hear nothin'."

The scratching would start again. I'd be suspicious. "Lemme see your hands."

"Fine thing when a kid don't trust his own daddy." He'd hold both hands in the air and I'd lie down, watching them. The scratching would start again.

"Whatsat, Daddy? Whatsat? Lemme see your feet, too."

He put his feet in the air along with his hands. "Now how d'you expect a man to sleep like this, Poppa?" The game was over then and I'd snuggle in close to him where it was safe.

We were playing the Standard Theater in Philadelphia when he said, "Good news, Poppa. There's a amateur dance contest here at the theater day after we close. Course, there's sixteen other kids'd be against you. And all of 'em older'n you. You suppose you c'd beat 'em?"

"Yes."

I was only three but I'd spent hundreds of hours watching Will and my father work, and imitating their kind of dancing. They were doing a flash act—twelve dancers with fifteen minutes to make an impression or starve. The other kids in the contest were dancing in fox-trot time but when I came on, all the audience could see was a blur—just two small legs flying! I got a silver cup and ten dollars. My father took me straight over to A. S. Beck's shoe store and bought me a pair of black pumps with taps.

We hung around Philadelphia hoping to get booked, but our money ran out and my father had to call Mama for a loan. She told him, "That's no life for Sammy if you gotta call me for money. I'm sending you fare to bring him home."

He told Will, "Guess she's right. This ain't no life for a kid. Trouble is, I can't bring myself to leave him there and travel around without him now. I'll just have to get me a job around home doin' somethin' else." I saw tears in my father's

12

eyes. "I'll always wanta be in show business, Will. It's my life. So anytime you need me, just say the word."

Massey picked me up and hugged me. "Be a good boy, Mose Gastin. And don't worry. We'll be working together again someday."

Mama was waiting up for us when we got home. I put on my shoes and ran into the front room to show them to her. My father proudly explained how I'd won them to her. Mama turned on her player-piano and I did my routine. She smiled. "My, oh my! You're a real dancer now." She shook her head at my father. "You buy him shoes when you don't have money for food. I always knew you was smart."

My father left the apartment every morning and came back at dinner time, but after a week he was still without a job. "I couldn't bring myself to look for nothin' outside of show business, Mama. I'll do it tomorrow. I really will."

But each day it was the same thing. He was spending his time hanging around backstage with the dancers at the Odeon Theater. When he came home he'd just stare out the window, shaking his head. "I can dance circles around them guys. I'm over them like the sky is over the world, and they're making $150 a week."

Before I was born he'd driven cabs in New York, shined shoes, cooked, pulled fires on the Erie Railroad, and run an elevator at Roseland Dance Hall. Then he'd won some Charleston contests, met Will, and from then on there was only one way of life for him.

One night he looked over and saw Mama and me dancing. That was the first thing that brightened him up. "Mama, just whut'n hell do you call what you're doin' with him?"

"We're doin' the time step."

He laughed. "Hell, that ain't no time step."

Mama snapped back. "Maybe so, but we like it. And if Sammy likes it, then anything to make him happy."

I couldn't stand the way he was laughing at me. I tried harder to do it the way he'd shown me but he kept shaking his head. "Damnedest thing how he can do some tough ones and can't do the easiest of all. Here, lemme show you again." He did a time step. "Now you do it." I tried to copy it. "Hell, you ain't doin' nothin'." I kept trying, harder and harder but I couldn't get it right. He said, "Here, looka this."

He showed me his airplane step and some of the really hard steps I'd seen him and Will do in the act. "Some day maybe you'll be able to do that, too, Poppa." Then he went back to the window.

I heard Mama laughing excitedly. "Look at your son flyin' across the room."

I was doing a trick of his with one hand on the floor, the other in the air and my two feet kicking out in front of me. He snapped out of his melancholy and almost split his sides laughing. The harder he laughed the harder I kicked. He bent down and put his face right in front of mine. "Betcha I can make you laugh, Poppa." He made a very serious face and stared at me. I bit my lips and tried desperately to keep a straight face, but that always made me die laughing.

He lost interest in me again and went back to the window, staring at the street, leafing through an old copy of *Variety* which he'd already read a dozen times. Suddenly he smacked the arm of the chair and stood up. "Mama, I'm wiring Will to send me a ticket. I'm in the wrong business here."

She snapped, "You ain't in *no* business here."

"Maybe so, but it's better to go hungry when you're happy than to eat regular when you're dead. And I'm good as dead out of show business."

A few days later a letter arrived Special Delivery from Will. My father pulled his suitcase out from under the bed. I ran to the closet for my shoes and put them in the suitcase alongside his. He took them out and I held my breath as he stared at them, balancing them in one hand. Then he slapped me on the back, put them in the suitcase and laughed. "Okay, Poppa, you're comin' too."

Holding hands we half-walked, half-danced toward Penn Station, smiling at everybody.

"Where we goin', Daddy?"

"We're goin' back into show business, Poppa!"

2

WE RARELY REMAINED IN ONE PLACE MORE THAN A WEEK or two, yet there was never a feeling of impermanence. Packing suitcases and riding on trains and buses were as natural to me as a stroll in a carriage might be to another child. Although I had travelled ten states and played over fifty cities by the time I was four, I never felt I was without a home. We carried our roots with us: our same boxes of make-up in front of the mirrors, our same clothes hanging on iron pipe racks with our same shoes under them. Only the details changed, like the face on the man sitting inside the stage door, or which floor our dressing room was on. But there was always an audience, other performers for me to watch, always the show talk, all as dependably present as the walls of a nursery.

We arrived in Asheville, North Carolina, on a Sunday, and Will gave everybody the day off. We were doing the three-a-day, from town to town, so most of our troupe spent the time catching up on sleep, which was also the cheapest thing they could do. I wasn't tired so I wandered into the parlor of our rooming house. Rastus Airship, one of our dancers, was reading a paper, and Obie Smith, our pianist, was rehearsing on an upright. I started doing the parts of the show along with him. Rastus left the room and came back with Will and my father and I did the whole hour-and-twenty-minute show for them, doing everybody's dances, singing everybody's songs, and telling all the jokes. People were coming in from other rooms and from the way they were watching me I knew I was doing good. When I finished our closing number, Will said, "From now on you're going to dance and sing in the act." My father picked me up, "Damned if he ain't," and carried

15

me around the room introducing me to everybody we'd been living with for the past year. "This is my son. Meet my son, Sammy Davis, Jr."

She was much prettier than any of the girls in our show. I started to shake hands with her but she knelt down and hugged me and when she kissed me her eyes were wet.

"You cryin'?"

She touched her eyes with a handkerchief. "I'm happy to see my little boy, that's all."

My father told me this was my mother and that I wouldn't be doing the show that night so I could spend time with her. Then he left us alone in the dressing room.

I looked up at her. "I can dance."

"No kidding. Let's see."

I did one of my father's routines but she started crying again. "Don't you like the way I dance?"

"Darling, I love everything you do. I know that dance and you did it real good. As good as your daddy."

That was more like it. I did half our show for her. Then we went outside and she held my hand while we walked.

"You like show business, Sammy?"

"Yes."

"You happy?"

"Yes." From the moment we'd left the theater all I could think of was my father and Will would be doing the show without me.

She asked, "How'd you like a nice ice cream soda?"

"No, thank you."

We came to a toy store. "Let's go in and buy you a present." I didn't want a present. I just wanted to get back to the theater, but she bought me a ball. Outside, she said, "Let's see you catch it, darlin'." I'd never done it before and I put my hands up too late and it hit me on the cheek. It didn't hurt but it scared me. I just watched it rolling away.

"Get it, Sammy."

"I don't want it." I was sorry as soon as I'd said it.

We walked a few more blocks. "Is there anything you'd like to do?" I didn't tell her, but she understood.

I ran ahead of her into the dressing room. My father was putting on his make-up. "You do the show yet, Daddy?"

"Nope. You're just in time."

I ran for my costume. My mother started to leave but I grabbed her skirt. "Don't go."

As I danced I saw her watching me from the wings, and smiling. She liked me and I hadn't even done my tricks yet. When I went into them I could only see her out of the corner of my eye, but she wasn't smiling any more. I wasn't able to turn around again and when I got off she was gone.

My father picked me up. He was hugging me very tight, patting my back, as he walked toward the dressing room. "Your mother had to leave, Poppa. She said to tell you she loves you."

For no reason I could understand I started to cry.

Mama smiled at the truant officer, "Yes sir, I'll bring him over tomorrow." But when he'd gone she told me, "You're five years old and they want you at the school but I don't want you to go. You'll meet all classes of children and I don't want you playing with nobody's children."

From then on she watched at the window for truant officers. The first time she spotted one she told me, "Sammy, now we're gonna play a game called Fool the School. There'll be a knock on this door but just sit in your chair and don't make a sound. We can wait long as he can knock." Mama stayed at her post near the window until she saw him go down the street. Then, she put a roll of music on the piano and we danced to celebrate how we'd fooled him.

That night, she told my father, "You gotta get him a tutor when you're on the road 'cause the bulls are going to lock me up sure if they catch me!"

I stayed around the apartment listening to the radio while my father and Will were at the booking offices looking for work. Sometimes I sat at the window watching the kids skating or throwing a ball around but I had no desire to join them. I didn't think of things like skating and football or any of the sports kids played, nor did I miss them. They just didn't fit into my life.

Whenever they could, Will and my father found someone around the theater to tutor me in how to read and write. We'd go into the dressing room between shows and work, and nobody else was allowed in until it was time to dress for the next show.

We moved from New England into the Midwest, working steady, covering most of Michigan in theaters, burlesque houses, and carnivals, changing the size of the act to as many as forty people depending on what the bookers needed. We were in Lansing doing a "Four and a Half"—Will, my father, two other dancers, and me as the half—when a woman came storming backstage with the theater manager. "There he is. It's shameful." She was pointing at me. She knelt down and put her arms around me. "Everything's goin' to be all right now," and, glaring at Will and my father, "You Fagins! You should be in jail for what you're doing to this poor, suffering child."

I had no idea what a Fagin was, but I knew for sure that I wasn't suffering. My dancing was getting better, the audiences liked me, and I was always with my father and Massey—I had everything I wanted.

The manager paid Will off that night. "Sorry, but I can't fight her. She's too big. If she says the kid's too young to be on the stage then he's too young even if he was fifty."

Will asked, "How about if Sammy don't work?"

He shook his head. "With the kid you're a novelty, but I'm up to my ears in straight dance acts."

Weeks passed as we hung around the parlor of our rooming house hoping for some booker to call, but my benefactor was powerful enough to have closed off all of Michigan to us and all we heard was the landlord telling us: "You owe me twenty-eight dollars now."

We went to dinner at our usual restaurant and Will looked at the menu hanging on the tile wall.

"The Special is beef stew."

"That's what I want," I said.

My father went to the steam table and brought back a Special. I'd half-finished it when I noticed that they weren't eating. "Our stomachs are a little upset, Poppa. But you clean your plate. You needs food to stick to your ribs in this kind of weather."

They watched me eating my stew and the roll that came with it. My father snapped his fingers. "Hey, Will, maybe a cup of soup'd do our stomachs some good." He finished his soup and crackers. Then he wet his finger, ran it around the inside of the cracker paper and licked off the crumbs that stuck to it. He took a small piece of my roll. "Maybe I'll just mop up a little of your gravy, Poppa, to see if it's fresh cooked."

The next night the Special was chicken and rice but they only had coffee.

"You still sick, Daddy?"

"I'm just not up t'snuff, Poppa."

"Massey, too?"

"Now Poppa, just eat your dinner and don't worry none 'bout us. It's just bein' out of work and not doin' nothin' for so long, well, we older men don't need food 'less we uses up the energy at somethin'.'"

The landlord sprang out of the parlor just as we hit the stairs. "No point tryin' to get into y'r rooms. You're locked out! I'm holding your things 'til you pay up."

Will was stunned. "In all my years in show business nobody ever had to hold my clothes to get paid. . . ."

"Well, I'm holding 'em now. I'm sick of you show business deadbeats. Maybe you wanta go through life happy-go-lucky without doing a day's work t'get a day's pay, but I'm a businessman and I mean t'be paid for my room. If you're not here with my money in a week I'll sell your things for junk. Now get outa here before I have y'locked up."

We stood on the sidewalk outside the rooming house. The temperature had dropped below freezing. Will said, "We'll go over to the railroad station. It'll be warm there."

While I slept on a bench wrapped in my father's overcoat they took turns walking around the waiting room pretending to use the telephone and asking the station patrolman questions like: "You mean there's no train out of here 'til morning?" so we wouldn't be arrested for vagrancy.

My father was shaking me, gently. "Wake up, Poppa. They're lockin' up for the night. We'll go over to the bus station." When that closed at midnight we started walking, looking for any place that would be warm and open, stopping in doorways every few minutes for a break from the fierce wind. Finally we saw a building with a lighted sign, and we ran until we were in front of a small hotel.

My father said to Will, "Lemme handle this." He sauntered

over to the room clerk. "Good evening. I'd like to rent two of your best suites for the night."

The clerk didn't look up at him. "We don't have rooms for you people."

My father was pointing toward me. "Look, I have a six-year-old boy—can we at least stay in the lobby?"

"You can't stay here."

"How 'bout if we just leave the boy for a few hours? It's freezing cold outside."

My father patted my head. "They don't like show people here, Poppa." He picked me up. "How'd you like a free ride?" He unbuttoned his overcoat and closed it around the two of us.

Outside, a woman came running up to us. "Excuse me, my name is Helen Bannister. I was in the lobby and saw what happened. I'm on my way home and you're welcome to come with me, if you like."

She cooked bacon and eggs and as we all sat around the table Will explained that we were in show business and told her about the trouble we were having. She said, "I have an extra room you can use until you get on your feet."

Two days later Will burst into the house holding up a handful of money. "We're booked in Atlanta, Georgia, and I've got an advance." He tried to pay Miss Bannister at least for our food, but she wouldn't accept anything. "What happened to you the other night was inexcusable. I'm embarrassed by it. We're not all like that. I'm happy that I was able to help you."

As we left my father said, "Once a year we oughta say the name of Helen Bannister. That lady saved our lives."

We were playing a roadhouse in Hartford, Connecticut. My father said, "Tell y'what, Poppa. We got the day off, whattya say we take in a movie?"

Halfway through the picture he leaned over and whispered, "You stay here and watch the picture, son. I'll just be next door at the bar gettin' me a few skull-busters. Be back for you like always."

The picture was going on for the third time when I felt his hand on my arm. "You ready to go now, Poppa?"

We stopped for dinner, then he took me back to the hotel. "See you later, Poppa. I've got some things to do."

I knew he was going out drinking. He'd been doing it for some time.

The next day, in the dressing room, I asked Will why. "Your daddy's lonely, Sammy, that's all it is. There's no one he cares about and it makes him feel bad. The whiskey makes him feel better."

"Don't he care about me?"

"He cares the whole world about you, Sammy. But he needs a woman to love, too. You'll understand some day. . . ." He took hold of my hand and made me stand up. "Take off your clothes and hang them up. Never sit around in what you wear on the stage. We've always had the name of the best-dressed colored act in the business and we're gonna keep that name."

I undressed immediately, embarrassed because I'd known better. One is about all we ever had of anything but you'd never see wrinkles in our pants or make-up on our shirts and we shined our shoes every time we came off so they were ready for the next show.

As I started my big number my father slipped out into the audience and on cue, a half-dollar flew toward me and clanged noisily onto the stage. I danced to it, picked it up, flipped it in the air, caught it, put it in my pocket and nodded. "Thank you," without losing a beat, and it started raining money.

My pockets were so heavy with coins that I could hardly dance in our closing. When we got to the dressing room I dumped the money onto a table, "Hey, Poppa, this looks like our best night yet." He stacked the nickels, dimes, and quarters. "Twelve eighty-five! You realize this is as much as we get in salary for a whole night's show?" He swung me in the air, laughing. "You're the breadwinner, Poppa. Damned if you ain't. You, I, and Will are gonna bust loose tonight. We'll put on our best clothes, go over to the Lobster Restaurant and have us some real full-course dinners."

Our party was going full blast when my father was suddenly very drunk. I tried not to let him see I'd noticed but he snapped, "Why're you lookin' away from me?" All the laughter was gone and he was glaring across the table at me. His eyes narrowed. "You're holdin' out money!" Before I could deny it he slapped me and I fell off the chair. "I'll teach you to cheat your own father. . . ." I lay on the floor waiting for something to happen. I opened my eyes and looked up. He was standing over me, crying, his arms hanging loose at his sides, staring at me, shaking his head like he couldn't believe what he'd done. He knelt down, picked me up, and carrying me in his arms walked out of the restaurant hugging and kissing me. "Oh God, I'm sorry, Poppa. I didn't mean it. Honest I didn't mean it."

"I didn't hold out money, Daddy."

"I know, Poppa, I know."

In the middle of my big number the next night I saw him watching me from his place behind me. He looked sadder than I'd ever seen him. I kept trying to let him see me smiling at him so he'd know it was okay.

When we got off Will took me aside. "You didn't have your flash tonight. And you weren't dancing, neither. Now I know you're troubling and you're worried about Big Sam, but you can't take any thoughts onstage with you except the show you're doing. That's the first rule of show business. Always be thinking when you're out there or the audience'll start to out-think you and then you'll lose them."

I knew I'd done badly. "I'm sorry I lost 'em, Massey."

He put his arm around me. "We all have troubles sometimes, Mose Gastin, but those people out front don't want to know 'em. No matter how bad you're hurting, leave your troubles here in the wings, and come on smiling."

I'd seen a lot of show business by standing in the wings watching the other acts in theater after theater and I couldn't fail to learn from them. I'd been on the stage for almost four of my seven years and I was developing a feeling for "timing." I could watch other acts perform and anticipate when a gesture, a fall, or an attitude would or would not work. I remembered everything I saw. If anyone in our troupe missed a cue or forgot a line I'd remind Will and he'd have it put back in.

I was seven and we were in New York when Will started taking me with him to the booking offices. "I want you to listen carefully to everything that's said, Sammy. There's two words in show business, 'show' and 'business,' and one's important as the other. The dancing and knowing how to please the audience is the 'show' and getting the dates and the money is the 'business.' I know you like to dance and sing and be on the stage in front of the people but if you don't get money for it, then you ain't doing nothing but having a good time for yourself. You have to know how to make deals, which to take and which to let go by."

The man behind the desk, Bert Jonas, said to me, "You're learning the business from the right man. Follow his ways. His handshake is all the contract anybody needs." He looked at Will. "I've got a great spot for you with Minsky in the Liberty Theater here on Forty-second street but I didn't realize Sammy was still so small. I'm afraid he's going to be a problem. The Geary Society's got that law that no kid under sixteen can sing or dance on the stage."

My father laughed slyly. "Don't give no thought to that, Bert. We been workin' Sammy under the cork. We blacks him up, he's got a Jolson suit and we bills him as "Silent Sam the Dancing Midget' and the way he dances there's no chance of anyone catching wise."

As we started to leave, my father gazed longingly at the large diamond ring Mr. Jonas was wearing, and sighed wistfully, "One day I'm gonna have me a ring just like that."

Two women and three cops climbed onstage, over the footlights. My father yelled, "It's the Geary Society. Go to Mama." I slipped between the cops and was halfway home before I stopped running. As soon as I was with Mama, surrounded by the safety of our apartment, I burst into tears.

Mama looked me in the eyes. "What's wrong, Sammy? Somebody hit you?" I shook my head and sat down in my chair. "Then why you crying?" I didn't say anything. "Well, wash up for dinner and stop crying because if there's nothing wrong then there's no need to be crying." I walked toward the bathroom. "Sammy, where's your father?"

I couldn't keep it from her any longer. "I don't know, Mama. We were doin' the act when some cops came . . ."

Will walked in and Mama turned on him. "Mastin, is Sam in jail?"

"Well—uh, yes, Mrs. Davis."

"What'd he do?"

"Well, it's a long story. . . ."

"I think it's a short story. I told him don't take Sammy downtown on that stage. That's a burlesque theater you're in and he's right in the center of attraction with people packed in on both sides waitin' to see those naked girls and this little child. . . ."

An hour later, my father came in smiling, but one look at Mama and he sat down and stared at the floor.

"So you finally got yourself locked up, Sam. That's lovely. That's fine things to show a little child. That's really good bringin' up."

"Come on, Will, we better get outa here." He turned to me, "Start gettin' your stuff together."

I stood up. Mama snapped, "Don't you do it, Sammy." I sat down again, fast. "Sam, where do you think you're going?"

"Hell, Mama, they wants me in front of a judge tomorrow, so I'm gettin' as far outa New York as I c'n get. And I'm taking my son with me."

"You ain't takin' Sammy nowhere, or I'll have the Thirty-second Precinct bulls on you. You got no booking, you got no money, you got no nothing. You think I'm gonna let you take this child running from the bulls, wandering to beg food with no place to sleep? Not while I'm willing and able to work. I don't want him hungry and naked."

"Mama, you got no say. Sammy's my son and I say he comes with me."

"Well, he ain't going to be your son. I'm takin' him from you. And from Elvera." She put her arms around me. "You'll have to kill me before I let him go with you like this!"

The judge glanced around the courtroom. "Where's the mother?"

Mama stood up. "No tellin' where she is, y'honor. She's chorus girling somewhere."

"Who are you, madam?"

"I'm the child's grandmother, Mrs. Rosa B. Davis, sir."

"Oh yes. I received a telephone call from your employer. I'm told you're a fine woman and you have a nice little boy. She said you've cared for her children for years and she feels you're capable of raising this boy, too."

"Yes, Judge, I love him and I can do it. I want to give him a home like a child should have and keep him out of show business where he doesn't eat every day and sometimes has no place to sleep, but I can't do that 'less he's mine."

Back at the apartment Mama laid down the law to Will and my father. "You heard with your own ears. The judge said his own father and mother ain't capable of raising him and he gave Sammy to me. Legal! So, from now on, you can't just pack up Sammy and go to this place and that place and just leave me a note."

My father didn't say anything. He just looked miserable. Will cleared his throat. "Uh—Mrs. Davis, I just got us a fine booking up in Boston next week. Naturally it's your say if we can take Sammy along with us."

Mama looked at me and stroked my head. I wanted desperately to go with them. After awhile she said, "All right, Sammy. I know you want to sing and dance and be in show business more than anything, so you can go. Mastin, you and Sam sit there and listen to me tell you how you'll take care of this child. You won't let him eat no hot dogs, and no hamburgers neither. Give him chicken and be sure and give the leg, not the breast, it's too dry. And don't let him eat close to the bone. And when he says he's had enough don't you tell him 'There's food on the plate.' Let him leave it. He'll eat as much as he wants and that's enough. And don't give him no pork chops. You and Sam can eat all the pork you want and all the pigtails but don't you give none to Sammy. If you can't get him chicken legs, then give him a piece of beef. Don't you upset his stomach. If he gets sick on the road, you won't have the money to call a doctor and you'll kill my child."

"All right, Mama, we'll do just like you say."

She handed him a bottle of Scott's Emulsion. "Always keep a bottle of this and give it to him three times a day 'til he's sixteen. There'll be times you don't have heat in the room and this'll keep him from catching cold. . . ."

After dinner Mama gathered up the dishes and washed them. I helped her dry them. She seemed tired. "You work hard, don't you, Mama?"

"Yes, I do."

"I work hard, too."

"But you make more money than me. Let me ask you something, Sammy. Does your father take your money to a table where he puts it down and sometimes he can't pick it up?"

"Sure, Mama, he gambles."

"That's what I thought."

"But he gives me what I want."

"While you're on the road—you ever been hungry?"

"No. Daddy and Massey been hungry, but never me."

She nodded, satisfied. "But the first day you come home and tell me you been hungry then that's the end of show business. And don't let nobody sew up nothing for you or put patches on you. You understand what I'm talkin' about? If there's a little hole in your stocking, then you tear it and make it such a big hole that nobody can sew it up for you. You don't need to wear nothing mended. I'll always buy you whatever clothes you need. You're my little boy now, Sammy, and I love you like I always loved you and I'll always be here 'til you don't need me no more."

I tugged at my father's arm as he, Massey, and I approached Grand Central Station. "Where we goin', Daddy?"

"We're goin' to the railroad station."

"But where else we goin'?"

He winked at Will. "Well, let's see . . . from there we're catchin' the smokey to Boston."

"I *know* that, but where else?"

He hoisted me onto his shoulders, laughing. "We're goin' back into show business, Poppa. Back into show business."

3

My Father Came Into The Dressing Room And Before he even said hello to me he spoke to Will, "I just got word that Timmy French give up the ghost. Let everybody go and he's runnin' a elevator at some hotel."

Will sat down and slowly twirled his hat on the tip of his finger. It slipped and fell to the floor but he didn't reach down to pick it up. He spoke, but to neither of us, "Timmy had a good show."

There was a silence in the room, the same sad and hopeless kind of quiet that I'd been hearing since we'd come to town. Vaudeville was dying. Wherever we went, for meals, or between shows in the Green Room, backstage, there was none of the usual atmosphere of clowning around that had always been so much fun. Everybody seemed afraid and they spoke only of acts that had been forced to quit the business.

A performer from the next dressing room looked in and saw me brushing our high silk hats. "Not much point in that," he said, "there's hardly anyone out front to see 'em. They're all across the street at the goddam talkies."

I put down the hat, half finished. Will turned to me. "Sammy, brush that hat 'til it gleams." He was speaking with controlled anger. "And remember this like it's your Bible. If there's one person or one thousand sitting out there, you gotta look as good and work as hard for that one man as you would for the one thousand. Never sluff off an audience. They paid their money and you owe them the best you got in you."

My father and Will burst into Mama's in the middle of the afternoon. "C'mon, Mose Gastin, you're gonna be in the talkies." My father took my suit out of the closet. "Ethel Waters is doin' a two reeler called 'Rufus Jones for President' and you've gotta audition 'cause they're looking for a seven-year-old who c'n sing and dance to play Rufus. And that's gonna be you."

We filmed it at the Warner studios in Brooklyn. The idea of the picture was that Rufus Jones falls asleep on his mother's lap and dreams he's elected President. When Rufus Jones attended a Cabinet meeting, there were signs saying "Check Yo' Razors at the Door." He appointed a "Secretary in Charge of Crap Shooting" and a Secretary of Agriculture to "Make sure the watermelons come in good and the chickens is ready fo' fryin'."

I made another movie right after it with Charlie Chaplin, Jr., who was about my age. His mother, Lita Grey, starred in it. On the last day of shooting she told my father, "Mr.

Davis, the way more vaudeville houses are changing over to movie theaters every day you soon may have no place left to do your act. I adore Sammy. If you'll agree to let me adopt him legally, I'll take him to Hollywood and I promise you I'll make him a star."

Mama made the decision. "Sammy's *my* son now and I don't want nobody telling me I can't see my own son."

"That's how I feel," my father said. "We come up together as pals. Movies'd only pull us apart."

I went downstairs to the candy store below our apartment to buy comic books. Some kids from the neighborhood were sitting at the table in the back. I walked over to them. "Hi." They were looking at cards with pictures on them. I watched for a while. "What're those?"

One of them looked up. "You kiddin'?" I didn't answer. "Boy, anyone don't know what these is must be pretty dumb."

"Well, it ain't dumb just 'cause I never saw somethin' before!" I looked around the table hoping to find someone who'd agree with me but they all just shook their heads like I was too stupid to live. I was dying to walk away but I knew if I said, "Well, so long," nobody'd answer.

"These're baseball cards, dopey! Where y'been all your life?"

The most any of them had was about a dozen. I had a ten dollar bill in my pocket. The bubble gum the cards came in was a penny apiece. I bought a hundred of them.

They all stopped talking. I played it big, pulling the cards out of the packages, piling them into one tall stack. The boy who'd first called me dumb came over and looked eagerly at my cards. "Y'wanta trade?"

"Sure. Whattya wanta trade?"

He picked out three. "I'll take these."

"Okay, but what'll you give me for 'em?" I didn't care but I didn't want to look dumb again. He handed me three of his cards and I looked at them as if I knew one from the other.

"Fair 'nuff?" he asked. I nodded. He shouted, "Trade's off 'n no trades back!" and all the other kids burst out laughing. He grinned. "Boy, you really are dumb. Anybody who'd give up a Babe Ruth or a Lou Gehrig for less'n five cards—boy, that's the dumbest thing I ever saw."

This time I even felt dumb. I ran out of there leaving my cards on the counter. I closed the door to my room and played a record, loud, so Mama couldn't hear me crying. I sat on my bed, mad at myself for running out like that and for letting them get the best of me in the first place. And to make it worse I hadn't gotten the comic books. I hated to face them again but they weren't going to keep me from getting what I wanted.

I picked out *Superman, The Flash, Batman* and about twenty others. They were watching me from the table. I had four singles but I gave Mr. Peterson a five dollar bill. They came closer. "Where'd you get all that money?"

"I made it."

"Aww, how'd you ever make five dollars?"

"Dancing."

"Yeah? What kinda dancin' you get five dollars for?"

I put the magazines down and looked him right in the eye. "This kind." I did some of the fanciest tricks I knew and I didn't stop until they were all gaping at me. One of them shrugged. "Well, I guess you c'n dance, but that don't say you get paid no five dollars for it."

I laughed in his face. "Five dollars? I wouldn't even walk out on a stage for only five dollars. Sometimes I make more'n a hundred dollars a week."

"A hundred dollars? You're lyin' through your teeth! My old man's ten times as big as you and he does a man's work loadin' a truck and *he* don't make no hundred dollars."

"Just the same that's what I make."

"How'd you go to school travellin' like you do?"

"I don't hafta go t'school. I work." I knew as I said it that it would kill them.

One of them said, "Here's the cards y'left here before." Another looked enviously at the comic books under my arm. "Y'think I could see those after you're finished with 'em?"

"Sure! Here, you guys can have these." I picked out twenty more for myself and paid for them. "Well, I gotta go upstairs." They walked me to Mama's door.

I saw them every day but by the end of the week they were kidding about me again, only now they did it behind my back. Then the next day they started getting nice again. They were waiting in the front of the store for me. "The new *Batman* and *Superman* come in. You gonna be buyin' 'em, Sammy?"

I stared from face to face. I nodded. "I'll buy 'em when I feel like it." They were as disappointed as I'd wanted them to be and they left the store to play some stupid game out on the street. I watched them go, not caring if they liked me or not any more, knowing how I could make them like me again if ever I wanted to.

Some of the girls my age were sitting at the table having cokes. I tried to concentrate on the comic books in the rack but I could hear them giggling and I could feel them looking at me. My ear itched. After I scratched it the back of my neck itched, but I didn't go for it. When I turned around one of them smiled, "Hi."

As I walked toward them they all scrambled for a piece of yellow paper they'd had on the table, like they were trying to hide it, but it tore apart and they all got hysterical and ripped the pieces smaller and dropped them under the table. Then they ran past me holding their hands over their mouths so I wouldn't see them laughing.

I got under the table and gathered up all the pieces of yellow paper.

I laid them out on my bed like the parts of a jigsaw puzzle. Eventually I got enough of it together so I could see that it was a picture one of them had drawn, a picture of me. I closed the bedroom door and worked for an hour putting the last pieces in place. I stood in front of the bed looking at it. The face was like mine, except the nose was flattened almost completely across it. She'd drawn my head the same size as the whole rest of my body and made it look like I was only about two feet tall. And she'd made my arms so long that my fingers hung down to my shoes. On the bottom it said, "Ugly!"

I tore each piece of paper into such tiny slivers that nobody could ever put them together again, and I threw them into the toilet, flushed it and watched them go down. A few pieces fluttered back up and I flushed it three more times.

I looked at myself in the mirror. My head wasn't that big. Maybe it was a little bigger than it ought to be, and my arms weren't that long, either. I was short, though. Shorter than any of those girls. I turned, looking at myself from all different angles. I hated the way I looked.

I saw Mama in the mirror, watching me, and I had a feeling she'd been there for a while. "Mama, whattya think of how this suit fits me?" She stroked my head. "The suit's nice, but I like what's in it. That's really something good t'look at."

I fell into her arms and cried.

I didn't go back to the candy store any more. I preferred playing pinochle with my father and listening to him talk show business, and I couldn't wait until we got back on the road. Nobody in show business had ever said I was dumb, or ugly.

One night as I was dealing the cards he asked, "You got any money, Poppa?" I shook my head. He sighed. "Well, I'm out too, so we'll hafta play Smut."

He got a bag of cinders from the chimney and mixed them with a jar of vaseline. "Now, this is smut. And the way we play is, if you lose then I gets to smear it all over your face and you gotta sit there with it on you for a hour and let everybody see you."

"Do I get to smear the smut on you?"

"Hell, yes, Poppa. If you wins. This is a fair game. What's good for one is good for all."

Soon I was sitting there with smut on my face, hating it with all my heart. Night after night, it was always the same. Then, one night I was way behind when I noticed he was dealing me seconds. I jumped up. "You're cheating, Daddy. I saw you, I saw you . . ."

He sat there righteous and fatherly. "That's right. And I'm mighty glad you caught me." I looked at him suspiciously. "Yes, son, I been doin' it for your own good. I been cheatin' you so's to teach you the tricks of the game. That way when you grows up and I'm not around t'protect you there won't be nobody can suck you into a crooked game without you knowin' it. I'm doin' you a favor, son, so sit down and let's finish up."

I sat down and he did me a favor for another three hands. Then he smeared the smut on me.

We'd used some of the movie money to buy a victrola, and I spent hours every day winding the machine and listening to the big names—Cab Calloway, Chick Webb, the Dorseys, Duke Ellington, and Jimmy Lunceford. I played a Chick Webb record for Mama and told her I wanted a set of traps like he played, but she didn't understand and she bought me a toy drum. With that as a start I built a set of traps with bottles, tin pans, half-filled glasses of water and anything else that would make the sounds I wanted, and sat in the front room playing along with Chick Webb, trying to capture all his licks.

My father came roaring in. "Hell, Mama, *damn!* He don't never stop playin'. He's drummin' and the neighbors are goin' knock knock knock—he's gotta cut it out!"

"You don't like it? Move out. Sammy's got to practice."

"Practice for *what?* To be in a show business there ain't gonna be?" He slammed his door. Mama turned to me and smiled. "Sammy, you just keep practicin'."

At last, Will arrived at the apartment with the news we'd been waiting for. Mama rushed in from the kitchen, a bunch of greens in her hand. "What's all this ruckus about?"

Will took off his hat. "We're booked, Mrs. Davis. Six weeks firm and maybe more after that." We all sat around him while he explained, "I've been trying to fight the talkies, trying to sell the bookers on how much show business we can put on a stage with our big shows, but I had to face up to the fact of the talkie being the attraction today. What the theaters need is small acts that can do the vaudeville half then go back out and give 'em another eight or ten minutes while the stagehands are setting up the sound horns for the talkie. It's gotta be a simple act with no props and scenery, but fast and flashy enough to hold the audience even with the work going on. And that's us. I've cut down to just the three of us." Then the excitement left his face and he turned away. "There's no more *Holiday in Dixieland,* no more *Shake Your Feet* or *Hannah from Savannah* . . . I'll miss our big shows . . . those were really shows." He looked at me and smiled. "How come nothing's ever what it was 'til it's gone?" I knew I wasn't expected to understand or answer. He smacked his knee. "Well, that's all past now. The business has changed, so we're changing with it."

4

I COULDN'T READ MUCH BUT I KNEW MY NAME WHEN I saw it and this was the first time I'd ever seen it on the front of a theater. Will read the sign out loud: "Will Mastin's Gang, Featuring Little Sammy." I asked, "What's 'featuring' mean?" My father said, "That means you're something worth seeing. Ain't many eight-year-old kids got their name out front like this."

Will said, "From now on it's just the three of us. We're a trio and we'll split our money three ways. You're an equal partner now, Sammy, and we're counting on you. Your daddy and me will open strong to form the impression. Then you've got to go out there and keep 'em going. Start strong to get them, then pace yourself so you hold them, but save yourself for your big finish. There's only two things to remember in show business: making an impression and leaving them with it." He put his arm around my shoulder. "Do your best, Mose Gastin, but don't ever worry 'cause whatever you do your daddy and me'll come on and it'll be okay."

The three of us shook hands and went inside to dress for our first show.

I was in the middle of my big number when a drunk began heckling me. I kept dancing but it threw me so badly that I lost all my flash and only went through the motions until my number was over. I closed the dressing room door against the mild applause, half of what I usually got, and burst into tears. I didn't know what the drunk had been saying but I knew I'd done a bad show because of him, and the audience hadn't liked me enough. I couldn't face my father or Will. When they came in, I stuck my head into my lap and kept crying. My father patted my shoulder. "No need to cry, Poppa. Not over one fool drunk."

"They didn't like me."

"Well that just shows they don't know nothin'." He picked me up in his arms and wiped my face with his handkerchief. Will said, "Sammy, something good happened to you tonight. You gave a bad performance, but now you'll never let yourself get thrown that way again. One thing you can't ever forget: if anybody out there gets to you, ignore him and wait 'til you can make a clean exit."

My father rubbed his chin thoughtfully. "I'd say I'm kinda in the mood for the glen plaid with the pearl gray shirts." He'd chosen our best clothes for our first look around Joplin, Missouri. Will and I nodded and we started getting dressed. The three of us always dressed identically. My clothes were exact miniatures of theirs, with breast pocket handkerchief, vest, gold watch and chain, spats and a cane. My father set the pearl stick-pin into my necktie and we went downstairs to the bulletin board where there was always a card with the name of a nearby restaurant that had good food.

My father nudged me and Will. "Look who's here." Vern and Kissel, a good act, and friends of ours, were coming up the stairs from the Green Room. They were on their way to eat, too, so we all went together. "How you been makin' out against the talkies?" . . . "Great. We just played some time for Dudley in Detroit." . . . "Hey, you guys look like ready money. . . ." We walked down the street, happy to be working, talking show talk, laughing all the way to the restaurant. It was a big square room with a completely round counter. "Sammy's a full partner now and pullin' his weight. Wait'll you see him doin' my African Zulu Charleston Prance . . ."

The counterman smiled, "Evening folks. You niggers'll have to sit on the other side."

The counter-top was painted white halfway around and brown on the other half. He was pointing to the brown section.

Vern said, "But we're together . . ."

"Sorry, bub, you ain't together in here. Black 'n white don't sit together in here even if you're brothers." He grinned, "Although 'tain't likely."

Vern was on his feet. "Let's get out of here."

The muscle in Will's cheek was moving up and down. He looked at his watch. "No point in spoiling your meal. If we leave here you won't have time to find some place else."

The counterman shrugged. "Fact is it's no different elsewhere 'n these parts so you might as well make do."

My father stood up, took my hand, and he, Will, and I moved over to the brown side. Vern and Kissel moved to the seats next to us on the white side where the line ended. The counterman nodded. "That'll do fine." Nobody said much anymore. We finished eating very quickly and went back to the theater.

Vern and Kissel were talking to the stage manager. They were angry, pointing down the street, but I couldn't hear what they were saying. My father and Will stood with me on the stairs waiting for them. The stage manager was listening and shaking his head. Then he hit the palm of his hand with his fist, strode over to the bulletin board, tore the restaurant's sign down and came over to us. "I'm damned sorry about this Mr. Mastin, Mr. Davis. . . ."

My father said, "I'd as soon not discuss it now." He moved his eyes toward me. They walked away and all of them stood near the door talking low. I inched up a little closer, but Will saw me and took my hand. "C'mon, Sammy, we'll go upstairs and get ready for the show." My father called out, "I'll be right up, Poppa."

Will didn't say a word as we got undressed.

"Massey?"

"Yes, Sammy?"

"What's goin' on?"

Again the muscles of his face tightened and started moving. "Nothing for you to be worrying yourself over."

"I'm not worryin'. I'm just wonderin' what happened. We were havin' fun and then everybody got mad and now downstairs they're talkin' about it. . . ."

"Talk-ing, Sammy. Say the word the way it's supposed to be said. Don't be lazy."

"What's a nigger?"

35

Will walked over to his make-up chair and sat down. "That's just a nasty word some people use about us."

"About show people?"

"No. It's a word some white people use about colored people. People like us whose skin is brown."

"What's it mean, Massey?"

He faced me. "It don't mean nothing except to say they don't like us."

"But Vern and Kissel like us, don't they?"

"Yes. But show people are different. Most of 'em don't care about anything except how good is your act. It's others I'm talking about. Some of the people outside—someday you'll understand. . . ."

My father walked in. "Don't you even think about it, Poppa. That man was just jealous 'cause we're in show business and he's gotta be pushin' beans all his damned life. Don't you even give it a thought."

I started getting dressed but I was all the more confused. Vern and Kissel were in show business and he hadn't called them niggers. The way Will and my father were so angry and hurt I knew the word must have meant just us and it must have been terrible. The closest I could come is that somehow it meant we were different from other people in a way that was bad. But that didn't make any sense at all. I wasn't any different from anybody else.

"Betcha I can make you laugh, Poppa."

My father was crouched in front of me making his poker face. I fought it, as I always did, but within a minute I was rolling on the floor, laughing.

My father handed me a package. "Play this on your machine, Poppa, and see how a *headliner* sounds." It was Louis Armstrong's new record: "I'll Be Glad When You're Dead You Rascal You." I played it a dozen times and then tried to sing it making his sound. My father was lying on the bed reading a newspaper. He jumped up and got Massey from the next room. I did it again, thrilled by how much they liked it.

"Don't that hurt your throat, Poppa?"

"Feels fine."

Will said, "Then that goes into the act." He smiled, "I'll introduce you as Satchmo himself, and you'll come running

36

on carrying the brass trumpet and big white handkerchief like he does."

Bill Robinson was playing at the Plymouth Theatre while we were in Boston. He and Will were the best of friends since a poker game years before when somebody pulled a gun on him and Will saved his life. Between our shows Will brought me along to the Plymouth so I could stand in the wings and watch. I'd heard about "Bojangles" all my life but I'd never seen him work and it was shocking to see how different his dancing was from ours or any I'd ever seen. We'd exhaust ourselves trying, arms and legs flying six ways to the moon and come off limp and wet. But Mr. Robinson had his hands in his pockets and he was going up and down a flight of stairs and around the stage like he was taking a stroll set to music. He wasn't even trying to get the audience, yet I'd never seen anyone go over so big. As he came off and passed by me I knew I'd just seen the biggest dance act in the business, but his face wasn't even damp.

He brought us back to his dressing room, took off his jacket, handed it to his valet, and put on a beautiful robe with his initials on it. His valet opened a curtain in front of a clothes rack. I stared at the floor beneath it. I had never seen so many shoes in one place in my life.

"Whose are those?"

Mr. Robinson was eating a pint of ice cream. "They're mine, kid."

I counted them. There were twenty-five pairs of shoes. I couldn't take my eyes off him. After a while he turned to me, "Lemme see you dance, kid." Will nodded that it was okay and I did my whole routine.

"That's good. But make it so the people can understand it. Make it look easy."

As we walked back to the rooming house Will said, "Mose Gastin, you just met the biggest in the business." He stopped walking. "When Bill Robinson plays the Palace he gets *thirty-five hundred dollars a week*. That's as big as anyone can get."

Bill Robinson was his own style, but we had to fight for our lives every time the lights went up. We knew that we were booked on the strength of our reputation as a clean act that could be depended on for fast and furious flash dancing. Probably fifty per cent of our flash came from our dread of the word "Cancelled." There were no unions and at the whim of a theater manager any show could be our last. We played theaters where if an act wasn't going over someone out front would yell, "The hook! Get the hook!" and a giant hook would swoop out from the wings and drag the performer off the stage. As he went off the audience splattered him with fruit and rotten eggs. Sometimes it was a hundred-pound sandbag that swung down and knocked the performer off his feet in the middle of his act. Hook or sandbag, what made this man get up off the floor and try again at another theater is one of the unanswerables about show people, but they dragged better performers off those stages than many who are stars today.

By the time I was fifteen we'd crossed the country twenty-three times and played so much time in Canada that we were considered residents of Montreal. In 1941 we were booked into the Michigan Theater in Detroit with Tommy Dorsey, to pinch hit for his regular opening act, Tip, Tap & Toe.

A fellow in his twenties, standing near the bulletin board backstage, walked over to us and held out his hand, "Hi'ya. My name's Frank. I sing with Dorsey."

I knew Frank Sinatra's work because he was the vocalist on most of my Tommy Dorsey records. I stood in the wings at each performance, eating up Dorsey's music. The audiences loved Frank. He had an entirely different style from other band vocalists. He did his numbers easy and simple and he sang the words so that they weren't just an excuse for him to be singing the melody.

He and I went out for sandwiches a few times between shows, or we sat on the dressing room stairs talking show business. After three days Tip, Tap & Toe got to town and we moved on.

We had a ninety-dollar LaSalle in which we'd been travelling, and often sleeping, and with no bookings we headed toward New York.

Mama was watching us from her window one flight up, shaking her head, calling out, "Here come the gypsies!" I ran up the stairs two at a time and threw my arms around her. She kissed me quickly. "We can have our hellos in a minute.

First go down and tell your father to park that junk away from in front of my house."

I stood in line at the box office of the Paramount Theater watching expensively dressed men paying for tickets as though it meant nothing to them. Then it was my turn. I asked to see the manager and when he came out I smiled, "Do you recognize performers?" He passed me by the ticket taker, but as always, I felt like a moocher for bumming my way in.

After the show I walked up Broadway. A crowd of fans were gathered outside the stage door of the Loew's State. I could feel the anxiety in the air, like nothing mattered to them except getting a look at the person who was going to walk out of that door. Then the door opened and Bob Hope stepped out and was swallowed up by the crowd until I couldn't see his beautiful clothes any more or the smile on his face like all this was coming to him and he expected it. I watched him get into a beautiful new car and drive away and I pictured the kind of a place he must be going to, with elevator men and everybody calling him "Sir" and bringing him letters and flowers and anything he wanted.

I hardly felt like I was in the same business. I took the subway uptown and I ran the few blocks from the station, eager to get home and ask my father, "Do you think we'll ever make the Big Time?"

I was leaning across the kitchen table, looking straight at him. He shook his head slowly, "I don't know, Poppa. If it's meant for us to make it then I guess we'll make it."

I kept looking at him, needing more, wishing he'd said, "Yes, we'll make it," or even, "No. Not a chance." Anything would have been better than an answer that told me nothing.

He knew I was waiting, hoping, knowing how small-time we were. He looked at me. "Betcha I c'n make y'laugh, Poppa."

At dinner, Mama said, "You know my friend, Mrs. Martin, Sammy? Well, Mrs. Martin's daughter is a nice girl and I told her all about you and she'd like to go on a date with you."

I'd never asked a girl for a date. They'd made it clear what they thought about my looks. But with the arrangements made I was dying to go.

My father fixed my tie which I'd already fixed ten times, and slipped me an extra five. Mama asked, "Where are you taking her?"

"Down to the Capitol to see the show." She nodded, properly impressed.

I picked up my girl at her apartment down the street and told her mother, "Don't worry, Mrs. Martin. I'll take good care of her. We're going by taxi."

I slapped down the money for our tickets and bought us some candy. The stage show was just starting and it was a good one. But when the movie went on I couldn't relax and enjoy it because I was too involved in trying to get up enough nerve to reach over and hold her hand. I still hadn't made my move by the time the movie ended but I didn't care— at least the ordeal was over.

On our way out, she stopped to go to the ladies' room. We were standing in front of a water fountain in the lobby. "I'll wait right here," I said. There was another boy standing there and I smiled at him, wanting him to know that I was waiting for a date, too.

Twenty minutes passed and she didn't come back. Maybe I'd misunderstood, maybe she was waiting someplace else, but I didn't dare get out of sight of the water fountain. I asked an usher if he could find out if she was in the ladies' room. He came back and told me she wasn't.

I was tired and hungry but I'd told her mother I'd take care of her and I'd said I'd wait for her. I stood there for two hours.

Then I saw my father talking to the ticket taker, pointing to me. I ran out to him and explained what had happened. He nodded. "Come on, Poppa. Mama's waiting to give you dinner."

"How'd you know to come down here for me?"

"Mrs. Martin come by the house."

"How'd Mrs. Martin know? Is she all right, Dad?"

"She's okay."

"Well, what happened? Why'd she go?" He didn't want to tell me but I kept asking.

"Look, Poppa, she ain't nothin'. She met some kids in the

ladies' room and she got so excited seeing them that she was halfway home before she remembered you was waitin' for her."

We sat on the subway and I bit my lips and clenched my fists in my pockets refusing to cry. "She'd have remembered me if I was good looking."

He put his arm around me. "Hell, that's plain ridiculous!" I looked at his handsome face. How could he understand? "Listen, Poppa, she's just a dumb kid that's got no brain. Lookit how stupid she's gotta be to do a damn fool thing like that."

Nothing could change the fact that I had been so unimportant to her that she couldn't even remember I was waiting for her. And I'd stood there all that time.

I closed my eyes . . . I was headlining the Paramount. She was sitting up front waving at me, hoping I'd notice her. When I came off, the manager thanked me and handed me a thousand dollars . . . I stepped out the stage door . . . the street was crowded with kids screaming for me. I signed a few autographs and pushed my way to my limousine and smiled at my beautiful wife sitting inside happy to be waiting for me. My chauffeur opened the door . . . she handed a piece of paper through the window, "Oh, please, Mr. Davis. May I have your autograph?" There were tears in her eyes, "Don't you remember me?" I smiled and signed my name. I motioned to the chauffeur and we drove away.

The train stopped. We were back in Harlem at 140th Street and Eighth Avenue. My father was saying, "Come on, Poppa. Let's go home."

Mama called from the kitchen, "That you, Sam? Wash up for dinner." I heard him answer, "Just gimme a minute to hang up all these clothes."

I turned off my record player and went through the kitchen, into the bedroom. "Where'd you get money for new clothes, Dad?"

He smiled, then opened the closet. It was empty except for the hangers, each with nothing but a pawn ticket hanging from it. "There's my gray sharkskin, my pin stripe with the English vest, my . . ." He closed the door. "Hell, Poppa, it'll pass for a wardrobe 'til we got somewhere to go in 'em."

Our fortunes had hit such a lasting low that we'd been home for five months without getting even a one-nighter. The people Mama worked for had moved out of town and she couldn't find another job. For the first time in our lives we were on relief, waiting helplessly for the checks to arrive, hoping every day that Will would come running up the stairs and say, "We're booked."

My father did an elaborate sniffing of the air. "Smells like turkey 'n dumplings tonight, Mama." She gave him a look and put the bowl of neckbones and greens on the table, the same meal we'd had every night for eight weeks because Mama could buy neckbones at five pounds for eight cents. There was a knock on the door and she smiled, "That'll be Nathan." ·

There he was, hat askew on his head, hanging drunkenly to the door frame to keep from falling down. He staggered into the front room, weaving and stumbling. We all watched him until he found a chair to collapse into, then my father gave him a round of applause. "Not bad, Nat. It ain't what you'd call good, but it ain't bad neither."

Nathan Crawford, a lifelong friend of my father was, besides the relief checks, our main means of support. He and my father had grown up together in North Carolina and Nathan had settled in New York where he was a foreman in a plant making pipe racks for the garment industry. Once a week he arrived at Mama's and turned over half of his thirty-five-dollar-a-week salary as if she were his own mother. He wanted nothing in return. He sat around for awhile or stayed for dinner. Occasionally he dropped in during the week, but every Friday at five o'clock he arrived weaving and spinning. The ridiculous part of it is that Nathan never touched a drop in his life. He's just a big ham who loves doing a drunk act. He'd "sober up" as soon as he hit the chair and stay that way until the next week.

The handwriting on the wall was saying, "You're out of the business." Months passed and we went nowhere but to the pawnshop until everything we owned was there except our radio, the last link between us and show business.

My father and I killed our evenings sitting in the kitchen near the stove, listening to the radio and playing pinochle, with him still trying to cheat me as though we were playing for $100,000 a hand. I looked forward all day to Jack Eigen's celebrity interview program from the lounge of the Copacabana. I never tired of listening to the celebrities. When they talked show business they weren't dreaming as we always were. These people were making movies, hit records, doing radio, and starring on Broadway. Eigen's slogan, or catch-phrase, was "I'm at the Copa, where are you?" That killed me. And almost every time he said it I threw down my cards and shouted back, "I'm in my goddamned hole in Harlem, that's where I am." But I kept listening, trying to forget we weren't working, that we were nobodies.

With vaudeville dead and even the Palace running movies, variety acts like ours were moving into nightclubs, and *the* top-drawer club was the Copacabana. Everything else was either the way up or the way down.

I lost interest in the pinochle and listened to Jimmy Durante describing his new home in Hollywood, then George Raft talking about the picture he'd just made . . . and the sound of people laughing and clinking glasses in the background . . . Joe E. Lewis was just passing through New York and he'd dropped in for a drink and to say hello. . . .

I asked my father, "You think we'll ever play it?"

His answer was the same as always, "Hell, I dunno. If we're meant to play it, we'll play it."

We listened to them talking about "the glamorous Copa" and the fabulous homes stars had just bought or were building, with swimming pools and golf courses. I couldn't even swim, but oh God how I wanted just to see a home with a swimming pool. I looked around our railroad flat with the windows closed in the back room to keep out the smell of the garbage that people threw out of their windows. I snapped off the radio. "Come on, Dad." He knew where I wanted to go. We did it all the time. We only had fare for one way so we whistled as we walked. It took us a while to get there but we had nothing but time.

It was a freezing night, but we stood in the doorway of a building at 15 East 60th Street, directly across from the Copa, watching the people going inside, the doorman helping them out of their limousines and cabs, tipping his hat, holding the door open for them until they disappeared inside, laughing. Why shouldn't they laugh? They had everything, importance, clothes and jewelry like I'd never seen anywhere but in movies. God, they were beautiful.

We waited to see them again when they came out. I clenched my fists. "Someday I'll play that place, so help me God. I'm gonna have Mama there and when we go home, there won't be a goddamned empty icebox. And I won't have to wait 'til Easter to buy a new suit. I'll buy them whenever I want them, ten at a time . . . I'm gonna be a star."

Then, all the way home on the A train, I wondered—will I ever be a star?

The music stopped abruptly: "We interrupt this program for an urgent news bulletin: The Japanese Air Force has just bombed Pearl Harbor. President Roosevelt is expected to issue a declaration of war . . . The United States is at war with Japan . . ." I put down the piece of birthday cake I was holding and looked from face to face around the room at my Uncle Bubba's place where we were celebrating my sixteenth birthday on Sunday, a day early. "We repeat, the Japanese have just bombed Pearl Harbor. President Roosevelt is expected to issue a declaration of war. . . ."

My father whistled down a cab and we headed for the Army recruiting office in Times Square. The cab fare was unimportant. Money had no meaning any more. For the first time in my life and probably my father's, something was more important than show business. We were gripped by patriotism and there was nothing else to do but join the Army. I loved my country not so much for anything in particular it had given me, but for the most fundamental reason: it was mine. And maybe I took extra pride in it because being an American was the only big-time thing I had going for me.

"What about Massey, Dad? You think he'll join up, too?"

My father roared hilariously, "Will? Hell, he was too old for World War *One*."

I sat back in the cab totally involved in being "the young man about to leave his loved ones," and the ride to Times Square was a montage of movie scenes: I was marching with thousands of men singing "You're a Grand Old Flag." Pat O'Brien was my Captain and Spencer Tracy was the chaplain in our outfit. Between 125th and 42nd streets I won my wings in the Army Air Force, and I saw myself zooming off on dangerous missions, bombing enemy ships and dog-fighting with Zeros. As we stood outside the recruiting office at the end of a long line, I pictured myself coming home on leave to show Mama my Army Air Force uniform with the peaked cap, the glamorous one that everyone knew was worn only by flyers because it had soft edges for ear phones to be worn over it. . . .

The Master Sergeant said, "You're too young. Come back in two years." He told my father, "Overage. Sorry. Next man. . . ."

We were playing the Fortune Club in Reno when I was ordered to report to the Presidio of Monterey, the induction center for the San Francisco area. I showed the notice to my father. He sat down on the bed and didn't even try to smile. "Well, Poppa, I guess this is it." Will was shaking his head, as though unable to believe it was really happening. "We're splitting up the act."

All in all it had been sixteen happy years of sometime-eating but always thinking and working together as a unit. Now we were breaking with a way of life we loved. Certainly show business had not chosen us or held out its arms and lavishly rewarded our love, but even the hard times had been good times, at least in retrospect, and there was never a moment when one of us regretted that we chose to stick it out.

The rent didn't get paid but Will and my father spent $150 on a gold wrist watch for me, with a stop-watch built into it, a chronograph, the kind the Air Force was using. I'd been dying to own one for a year and they must have borrowed the money to buy it. Will said, "We always had the name of the best-dressed colored act in show business. Can't let 'em think different about us in the Army."

At six o'clock Saturday morning the three of us were standing outside the induction center making our awkwardly manly goodbyes. My father said, "Now, Poppa, you're goin' in a boy but you'll come out a man. You'll meet all kinds of people but just do your job like you're supposed to and nobody can bother you. That's all I got to say 'cept I know you'll do good and we'll be waitin' for you when you come back."

A whistle sounded. Will said, "Okay, Mose Gastin, you're

on. Just treat it like show business. Give 'em the best you got."

It was like I had two fathers. I hugged and kissed Will and turned to my dad. I grabbed him with all my strength and kissed him goodbye. "So long, Poppa. I'm proud of my boy." He tried to smile. "Don't forget about when the other guy's dealin' the cards. Ain't no one can fool you if you're watchin'. I taught you all the tricks. . . ."

I grinned and gave him a shot in the arm. Reluctant to go, yet for the lack of knowing what else to say that might keep me there a few more minutes, I checked the time on my wrist watch which I'd polished almost every hour in the last few days. The dial was a blur. I kept telling myself I'm a man going into the Army and I'm going to fly a plane. I'd looked forward to this day but now it struck me how much I didn't want to leave my father and Will, that it was going to be the first night in my life I hadn't been with either them or Mama.

"Hey, Poppa? Betcha I c'n mak y'laugh."

There was his old poker-face, dead serious, not moving a muscle, with two big tears rolling down his cheeks. The whistle blew again, impatiently. I walked away from them, forcing myself not to look back.

5

A PFC WAS SITTING ON THE STEPS OF A BARRACKS, SEWING an emblem onto a shirt. I walked over to him. "Excuse me, buddy. I'm a little lost. Can you tell me where 202 is?"

He jerked his head, indicating around the corner. "Two buildings down. And I'm not your buddy, you black bastard!" He turned back to his sewing.

The corporal standing outside 202 checked my name against a list on a clipboard. "Yeah—well, you better wait over there awhile 'til we figure out what to do with you."

I was at the Infantry's Basic Training Center at Fort Francis E. Warren in Cheyenne, Wyoming.

I sat on the steps where he'd pointed. Other guys were showing up and he checked them off his list and told them, "Go inside and take the first bunk you see." I looked away for a moment and heard him saying, "Sit over there with Davis."

A tall, powerfully built guy dropped his gear alongside mine. "My name's Edward Robbins." We shook hands and he sat down next to me. One by one, men were arriving and being sent inside. They kept on coming but no one else was told to wait with us. Then, finally, there was no point in hoping against the obvious. It was clear that we were the only ones being held outside while all the white guys were going right in.

The corporal went inside. We were sitting in front of a screen door so even though he lowered his voice I could hear every word he was saying. ". . . look, we got a problem. Those niggers out there are assigned to this company. I'm gonna stick 'em down there. You two guys move your gear so I can give 'em those last two bunks."

Another voice said, "Hey, that's right nexta me. I ain't sleepin' near no dinge."

"Look, soldier, let's get something straight right off. I'm in charge of this barracks and . . ."

"I ain't arguin' you're in charge. I'm only sayin' I didn't join no nigger army."

Embarrassed in front of each other, Edward and I looked straight ahead.

". . . what about the can? Y'mean we gotta use the same toilets as them?"

"That's right, soldier. They use the same latrine we all use. Now look, we got no goddamned choice. They used t'keep 'em all together, but now for some goddamned reason they sent 'em here and we just gotta put up with 'em. . . ."

It was impossible to believe they were talking about me.

"Yeah, but I still ain't sleepin' nexta no nigger."

"What the hell's the army need 'em for? They'll steal ya blind while ya sleep and there ain't one of 'em has any guts. They're all yeller bellies . . ."

"Awright, knock it off. I don't want 'em any more than you do but we're stuck with 'em. That's orders."

They weren't even trying to keep their voices down any more.

There was the sound of iron beds sliding across the wooden floor. The corporal beckoned from the doorway. "Okay, c'mon in and I'll assign you your bunks. Let's go," he snapped, "on the double." We picked up our gear and followed him through the door. I felt like a disease he was bringing in.

There were rows of cots on both sides with an aisle down the center. The guys were standing in groups. They'd stopped talking. I looked straight ahead. I could feel them staring as we followed the corporal down the aisle. He pointed to the last two cots on one side. "These are yours. Now, we don't want no trouble with you. Keep your noses clean, do as you're told, and we'll get along." He walked away.

I looked around the barracks. The bed nearest to ours was empty. All the cots were about two feet apart from each other except ours, which were separated from the rest by about six feet—like we were on an island.

A few of the men sort of smiled and half-waved hello. Some wouldn't look over at us. The nearest, a tall, husky guy who must have been a laborer or an athlete, kept his back turned.

A sergeant came in and from the center of the barracks announced, "I'm Sergeant Williams. I'm in charge of this company and I . . ." His glance fell on the space between the beds. He turned to the corporal. "What the hell is that?"

The corporal quietly explained how he'd handled things. Sergeant Williams listened, then spoke sharply: "There is only one way we do things here and that's the Army way! There will be exactly three feet of space, to the inch, between every bed in this barracks. You have sixty seconds to replace the beds as you found them. *Move!*"

He came over to me. "What's your name, soldier?"

"Sammy Davis, Jr."

"Of all the men in this barracks did you arrive first or tenth or last or what?"

"About in the middle."

"Did you choose this bunk?"

"Well, no, I was told . . ."

He looked around. By this time the barracks had been re-ar-ranged. "All right, Davis. Move your gear one bunk over." He turned to Edward. "You do the same."

He addressed us all. "No man here is better than the next man unless he's got the rank to prove it."

I sat on the end of my bunk, the shock gone, immense anger growing within me until my legs were shaking and it was impossible for me to keep them still. I couldn't give them the satisfaction of seeing how they'd gotten to me. I saw one of the other guys polishing his boots. That was a good idea. The boots were a brand new, almost yellow leather and we'd been told to darken them with polish. I took off my watch and laid it carefully on the bed. I opened my shoe shine kit, took out the polish and brush, and began rubbing the polish into the leather, doing the same spot over and over, concen-trating on it, working so hard that I could blank out every-thing else from my mind. Suddenly another pair of boots landed at my feet. "Here, boy, you can do mine, too."

I looked up. It was the guy who had the bed next to me, and he'd already turned away. I grabbed for the boots, to throw them at his head—but I didn't want to make trouble, not on my first day in camp. I put them down beside his bed.

He looked at me, surprised. "Hey, boy, don't get me wrong, I expected t'give you a tip. Maybe two-bits for a good job."

"I'm no bootblack. And I'm no boy, either."

"Whoa now, don't get so uppity, boy. Hell, if you don't wanta make the money it's okay by me." He shrugged and walked over to Edward. "Here y'are, boy. You can do 'em."

"Yes suh! Glad t'do 'em, suh."

"Well, that's more like it. Glad somebody around here knows his place. And you don't have to call me sir. Just call me Mr. Jennings. Y'see in the Army you only call the officers 'sir.'"

"Yes, suh, Mr. Jennings and my name is Edward. Anything you needs. . . ."

I wanted to vomit. I was alone in that barracks.

Jennings was talking to a couple of the other guys. "This may work out okay. One of 'em's not a half-bad nigger." He came by Edward's bunk with three more pairs of boots. Edward's face fell for a second but he brightened up right away. "Yes, suh, you just leave 'em here and I'll take care of 'em."

"You oughta thank me for settin' up this nice little business for you."

"I *do* thank you." He smiled broadly. "Oh, yes suh. I thanks you kindly."

Edward was avoiding my eyes. Eventually he looked up and moved his head just the slightest bit. For a split second he opened up to me and I saw the humiliation he was enduring because his fear of trouble was stronger than his need for dignity. I hoped he'd look up again so I could let him know I was sorry I'd judged him and forced him to let me look inside him and see the pain and weakness that was his right to hide.

Perhaps this was how he had to live, but I wasn't going to take it from anybody. I wasn't going to let anybody goad me into fights and get myself in trouble, either. I was going to mind my own business and have a clean record.

Jennings flopped onto his bunk. He sat up, reached over and took my watch off my bed. "Say, this ain't a half-bad watch." He looked at me suspiciously.

"Put it back."

"Hold on, now. My, but you're an uppity one." He stood up. "Hey, Philips . . . catch!" He tossed the watch across the barracks. I ran to get it back but just as I reached Philips he lobbed it over my head to another guy who threw it back to Jennings. I ran after it, knowing how ridiculous I looked getting there just as Jennings threw it over my head again, that I shouldn't chase after it, that I was only encouraging them, but I was afraid they'd drop it and I couldn't stop myself.

"Atten*shun!!!*" Every head in the barracks snapped toward the doorway. Sergeant Williams walked straight to Jennings. "What've you got there?"

Jennings opened his hand and showed him my watch. "Whose is it?"

Jennings shrugged.

"It's mine."

Sergeant Williams brought it to me. Jennings grinned. "Hell, Sarge, we were just kiddin' around. I was only showing the watch to the guys."

"You're a wise guy, Jennings. In the Army we respect another man's property. You just drew K.P. for a week." He
left the barracks.

Jennings looked at me with more hatred than I had ever
seen on a man's face. "You just wait. I'll fix you for this,
black boy."

Hours after lights-out I lay awake trying to understand.
How many white people had felt like this about me? I
couldn't remember any. Not one. Had I just been too stupid
to see it? I thought of the people we'd known—agents, managers, the acts we'd worked with—these people had all been
friends. I know they were. There were so many things I had
to remember: the dressing rooms—had we been stuck at the
end of corridors off by ourselves? Or with the other colored
acts? That was ridiculous. Dressing rooms were always assigned according to our spot on the bill. And the places we
stayed? They *were* almost always colored hotels and rooming
houses, but I'd never thought of them like that. They were
just *our* rooming houses. But, did we *have* to go to them?
Didn't we just go to them because they knew us and because
they were the cheapest? Or wasn't that the reason? Sure there
were people who hadn't liked us, but it had always been
"Don't pay attention, Poppa, he's just jealous 'cause we got a
better act." Or, "They don't like us 'cause we're in show
business." And I'd never questioned it. In the last few years
I'd known there was prejudice and hate in the world. I remembered several times Will telling me, "Someday you'll understand." But I didn't understand and I couldn't believe I
ever would.

The physical grind of basic training wasn't as rough on
me as on some of the others because as a dancer I was in good
shape. I didn't even mind the food. I'd had far worse and far
less.

Most of the men in our barracks gave me no problems,
either because they didn't care, or because after a day of Basic
they were too tired to worry what the hell I was. But there
were about a dozen I had to look out for. They clustered
around Jennings and their unity alone was enough to intimi-
date anybody who might have wanted to show friendliness
toward me. When that group wasn't around, the others

would be pleasant, but as soon as one of them showed up, it was as if nobody knew me. The sneers, the loud whispers, the hate-filled looks were bad enough, but I didn't want it to get worse. I tried to keep peace with Jennings without Tom-ing him as Edward was doing. I hoped that if I was good at my job he'd respect me, but when I was good on the rifle range he hated me all the more. If I was bad he laughed at me. I found myself walking on eggs to stay out of his way, casually but deliberately standing on a different chow line, always finding a place at one of the tables far away from him in the mess hall.

I was dressing, fastening the strap on my watch before evening mess and it slipped off my wrist and fell to the floor next to Jennings' bed. Before I could reach it he stood up and ground it into the floor with the heel of his boot. I heard the crack. He lifted his foot, smiling coyly, "Oh! What *have* I gone and done? Sure was foolish of you to leave your watch on the floor. Too bad, boy. Tough luck."

The glass was crushed and the gold was twisted. The winding stem and the hands were broken off and mangled. I put the pieces on the bed and looked at them, foolishly trying to put them together again.

"Awww, don't carry on, boy. You can always steal another one."

I looked at him. "What've you got against me?"

"Hell, I ain't got nothin' against you, boy. I like you fine."

I knew I shouldn't just take it from him like this. I knew I should swing at him or something, but I was so weakened from the hurt of it that I couldn't get up the anger.

I wrapped the pieces in some paper and put it in my pocket. Maybe it could still be fixed.

Overnight the world looked different. It wasn't one color any more. I could see the protection I'd gotten all my life from my father and Will. Yet, I couldn't thank them for it. I appreciated their loving hope that I'd never need to know about prejudice and hate, but they were wrong. It was as if I'd walked through a swinging door for eighteen years, a door which they had always secretly held open. But they weren't there to hold it open now, and when it finally hit me it was worse than if I'd learned about it gradually and knew how to move with it.

Sergeant Williams walked out of the mess hall with me. "I was looking over the service records and I see that you were in show business. We have shows at the service club every Friday. If you'd care to help out I'm sure it would be appreciated, and perhaps you might enjoy doing it."

After the show, I was standing backstage with one of the musicians, a guy from another company, and I suggested we go out front and have a coke.

He said, "Maybe we better go over to the colored service club. You don't want trouble, do you?"

"Trouble? I just entertained them for an hour. They cheered me. Hey, look, God knows I don't want trouble but there's gotta be a point where you draw the line. Now I don't know about you, but I'm thirsty and I'm goin' in for a coke."

A few of the guys who'd seen the show saw us walking in and pulled chairs up to their tables, making room for us. Jennings was at a table with four of his buddies. They looked over at me and smiled or smirked, I couldn't be sure which. I sat with a group from our barracks and it was the happiest hour I'd spent in the Army. I luxuriated in it. I had earned their respect; they were offering their friendship and I was grabbing for it.

After an hour or so I said good night and headed for the door. As I passed Jennings' table he stood up. "Hey, Davis, c'mon over here and let's get acquainted." He was smiling, holding out his hand. It would have been satisfying to brush him off, but if he was trying to be friendly it seemed better to accept it and keep peace. "Well, I was going back to the barracks. . . ."

"Hell, you got time for one little drink with us." He pulled out a chair for me. "Man, where'd you learn t'dance like that? I swear I never saw a man's feet move so fast. By the way, you notice I ain't callin' you 'boy.' "

"Have a beer, Davis." One of the guys pushed a bottle toward me. "Here y'are," Jennings said, "here's one nobody touched."

"If you don't mind I'd rather have a coke."

"Hey, old buddy, you're in the Army. It's time you got over that kid stuff. You gotta learn to drink like a man. Try it. You're gonna like it."

The others were watching me. One of them grinned. "Yeah, you oughta learn to drink if you're gonna be a soldier."

Jennings said, "Listen, you're gonna insult me in a minute. Any man who won't drink with me . . ."

"Okay, I'll try it."

"That's better. Now I'll tell you how to drink beer. It can't be sipped like whiskey or a coke. To really get the taste of beer you've gotta take a good long slug."

The others nodded and raised their bottles. Jennings said, "Here's to you." I picked up my bottle to return their toast. I had it halfway to my mouth when I realized it wasn't cold. It was warm. As it came close to my nose I got a good whiff of it. It wasn't beer.

"Hell, don't smell it, man! Drink it!"

I took another smell and all at once I understood the smiles, the handshakes, the friendliness from Jennings. Somebody had taken the bottle empty into the men's room and came back with it filled.

Jennings was saying, "Come on, drink up, boy . . ."

I put the bottle on the table. The faces in front of me zoomed in like a movie close-up and I could see every line, every bead of perspiration, every blink of their eyes. The noise in the room was growing loud then low, loud then low. Suddenly I snapped out of it.

"Drink it yourself, you dirty louse."

Jennings roared with laughter. "Hell, he even curses like a coke drinker, don't he?"

I tried to stand up but my chair wouldn't move. Jennings had his foot behind a leg of it, trapping me. The old hate was back in his face. "You wanta live with us and you wanta eat with us and now you came in here and you wanta drink with us. I kinda thought you loved us so much you'd wanta . . ."

I felt a warm wetness creeping over the side of my shirt and pants. While he'd been talking he had turned the bottle upside down and let it run out on me. I stared at the dark stain spreading over the khaki cloth, stared at it in unbelieving horror, cringing from it, trying to lean away from my wet shirt and wet pants. My pocket was so soaked I couldn't put my hand in for my handkerchief.

Jennings jumped up, pointing to me, jeering loudly,

"Silly niggers can't even control themselves. This little fella got so excited sittin' with white men—look what he did to himself."

I was out of the chair and on top of him. I had my hands on his throat with every intention of killing him. I loved seeing the sneer fall from his face and be replaced by dumb shock as I squeezed tighter and tighter, my thumbs against his windpipe. He was gasping for breath. In a desperate effort he swung around fast, lifting me off the floor. My own weight dragged me off him and I flew through the air and crashed into one of the tables. Within seconds the area was cleared as though we were in a ring together.

Until this moment it hadn't been a fight, it had been an attack by 115 pounds of rage propelled by blind impulse. I hadn't known it was going to happen any more than Jennings had. The weeks of taking it, the time of looking for peace, of avoiding trouble, had simply passed, and it just happened, like a pitcher overflows when you put too much into it.

But we both knew it was going to be different now: he was a foot taller than me and half again my weight, or more, and without the advantage of surprise I was like a toy to him. He was taking his time, grinning to his friends, caressing the knuckles of one hand with the palm of the other. He raised his fists and began circling, licking his lips, anticipating the pleasure he was going to take out of me.

I flew into him with every bit of strength I had. His fist smashed into my face. Then I just stood there watching his other fist come at me, helpless to make myself move out of the way. I felt my nose crumble as if he'd hit an apple with a sledge hammer. The blood spurted out and I smelled a dry horrible dusty smell.

"Get up, you yellow-livered black bastard, you stinking coon nigger . . ." I hadn't realized I was on the floor. I got to my feet and stumbled toward him. He hit me in the stomach and I collapsed. I was gasping for breath but no air was coming in and I was suffocating. Then suddenly I could taste air, and the figures in front of my eyes straightened out and became people again. I got up and went for him. He was methodically hitting me over and over again, landing four to every one of my punches, but they weren't hurting me any more, they were just dull thuds against my body. Then his fist was beating down on the top of my head like a club. Someone shouted, "Don't hit 'im on the head, Jen. Y'can't hurt a nigger 'cept below the forehead." He kept pounding me and I felt myself slipping to the floor again. I grabbed his shirt with one hand to keep myself from falling so I could hit him in the face with my other hand. I had to stay on my feet and keep hitting him, nothing else mattered, and I was glad to trade being hit ten times by him for the joy of feeling my fist smash into his face just once. I hung on and kept hitting him and hitting and hitting. . . .

A guy named O'Brien, from my barracks, was holding a wet cloth against my face. "You'll be okay," he said. "The bleeding's stopped."

We were outside. I was propped up against the side of the PX. It was very quiet. Another guy was there. Miller. They were part of the group that always avoided trouble with Jennings. He smiled. "You might feel better to know that you got in your licks. I think you closed one of his eyes and you definitely broke his nose. He's wearing it around his left ear." I started to laugh but a shock of pain seared my lips. My head was pounding like it was still being hit. I opened my mouth carefully to ask how long I'd been out.

O'Brien said, "Take it easy." He grinned and showed me the cloth he was wiping my face with. "You ripped his shirt when you fell and you had part of it in your hand. You had a death grip on it even after you went out."

They walked me back to the barracks. Sergeant Williams was waiting in the doorway. He shook his head in disgust. "Very smart! Well, get over to the infirmary with Jennings." He walked into his bedroom.

I had sent Jennings to the infirmary. What beautiful news. Gorgeous! Miller and O'Brien were waiting to take me there. I shook my head and thanked them. I wasn't going to give Jennings the satisfaction of seeing me in the infirmary, not if my nose fell off entirely.

Lights were out but on the way to my bunk some of the guys stopped me and told me that when I'd fallen off Jennings he was starting to stomp me but Miller and O'Brien had stepped in and pulled him away. I realized that I'd broken the barracks into two groups: the haters, and the guys in the middle who didn't care enough to take sides or who didn't want to get involved. It had never occurred to me that some might swing over to my side. But when Miller and O'Brien saw that I was down and Jennings was *still* kicking me they had to get involved, and say, "Hey, wait a minute. This is ridiculous. Nobody's *that* bad."

I got into bed and it was delicious. I tried to turn over on my stomach but the bruises were murder. Still, as much as I hurt, as awful as it had been, the worst pain wasn't so bad that I wouldn't do it again for the dignity I got from hitting back.

Jennings had beaten me unconscious and hurt me more than I'd hurt him, but I had won. He was saying, "God made me better than you," but he lost the argument the minute he had to use his fists to prove it. All he'd proven is that he was physically stronger than me, but that's not what we were fighting over.

I'd never been so tired in my life, but I couldn't sleep. I hated myself for those weeks of sneaking around trying to avoid trouble. I'd been insane to imagine there was anything I could do to make a Jennings like me. I hadn't begun to understand the scope of their hatred. I was haunted by that voice yelling, "Y'can't hurt 'im 'cept below the forehead." My God, if they can believe that then they don't even know what I am. The difference they see is so much more than color. I'm a whole other brand of being to them.

There was so much to think about. How long would I have gone on not knowing the world was made up of haters, guys in the middle, Uncle Toms . . . I couldn't believe I was going to spend the rest of my life fighting with people who hate me when they don't even know me. But I kept hearing that voice and I knew I'd hear it again, out of another mouth, from another face, but spouting the same ignorance. I tried to stay awake to think it out, but my head was throbbing and the room began tilting to the left, then the right. . . .

. . . "Come on, Davis. Out of the sack." Sergeant Williams was leaning over me, tilting the bed. "I told you to go to the infirmary last night. You're a damned fool. I'm putting you on sick call this morning and you will report over there immediately after Mess. That's an order." Everybody else was outside for morning muster. I'd slept right through reveille.

I looked across the mess hall. Jennings had a strip of tape across his nose and his left eye was so swollen that he wouldn't be opening it for a week. The guys were buzzing and pointing at us and I made three trips back to the food counter for things I didn't want, just so that he could see me with no tape on my face, practically dancing there, as though I'd been to a health farm all month.

I had been drafted into the Army to fight, and I did. We were loaded with Southerners and Southwesterners who got their kicks out of needling me, and Jennings and his guys never let up. I must have had a knockdown, drag-out fight every two days and I was getting pretty good with my fists. I had scabs on my knuckles for the first three months in the Army. My nose was broken again and getting flatter all the time. I fought clean, dirty, any way I could win. They were the ones who started the fights and I didn't owe them any Queensberry rules. It always started the same way: a wise guy look, a sneer—once they knew how I'd react, they were constantly maneuvering me into more fights. To them it was sport, entertainment, but for me the satisfaction which I had first derived diminished each time, until it was just a tiresome chore I had to perform. Somebody would say something and my reaction would be, oh, hell, here we go again. But I had to answer them. Invariably, I'd walk away angrier than when the fight had started. Why should I have to keep getting my face smashed? Why should I have to fight to break even? Why did I always have to prove what no white man had to prove?

I kept in touch with my father and Will by phone. They'd tried doing a double, but all their material was geared to three people, so eventually they put a girl in the act. Then for a while they had a roller skater named Joe Smythe working with them. "We're makin' ends meet, Poppa. They ain't what you'd call huggin' and kissin' but we're gettin' by killin' time 'til the day you come home. So do your job in the army and then get back as fast as you can." I never bothered to tell them what my job in the Army was exactly.

The guy in front of me finished with the wash basin and as I moved forward, a big Texan grabbed me by the T-shirt and yanked me back so hard that I stumbled clear across the room, hit the wall, and fell down.

"What's *that* for?"

He drawled, "Where I come from niggers stand in the back of the line."

I got up, gripped my bag of toilet articles and with all the strength I had, hit him in the mouth with it. The force and shock knocked him down. I stood over him, fists ready. But he sat on the floor making no attempt to get up. Blood was trickling out of his mouth. He wiped it away with his towel, then looked up at me. "But you're still a nigger."

Sergeant Williams was standing in the doorway. He motioned for me to follow him to his room and closed the door. "Sit down, Davis." He offered me a cigarette and I took it. "That's not the way to do it, son. You can't beat people into liking you!"

What the hell was he talking about? Or maybe I knew. The moment I'd heard, "But you're still a nigger," I'd known that this was not the way to fight.

"Okay, you've punched your way across the camp. What've you proven? Have you stopped the insults? After you beat them up did they respect you any more?"

"Look, Sergeant, I'm not bucking for camp boxing team, but when a guy insults me what should I do, curtsy and tell him thanks?"

"You've got to fight a different way, a way that you can win something lasting. You can't hope to change a man's ideas except with another, better idea. You've got to fight with your brain, Sammy, not your fists."

It seemed as though I passed the Texan a hundred times each day, and I was haunted by that mocking voice telling me, "But you're still a nigger." He never said another word to me, but his eyes were saying it in the way they passed over me—as though I wasn't there.

We finished Basic and took our physicals for overseas duty. I was rejected because of an athletic heart. The doctor explained, "A lot of people have them and live long, useful lives. If you get enough sleep and don't overtax yourself, you'll be fine." I applied twice more and was turned down each time for the same reason.

I didn't qualify for any of the Army's specialist schools

59

where I might have bettered myself. My lack of education closed everything to me. They didn't know what to do with me so somebody sent down an order, "Put him through Basic again," probably hoping that by the time I came out I'd be somebody else's problem. When I came out I was sent right back again, like a shirt that hadn't been done right. Four times.

I was depressed and disgusted with myself. Outside a club or a theater I was totally unequipped for the world, just another uneducated laborer doing every lousy job in the camp.

I was on latrine duty and I passed Sergeant Williams' room. The door was open and I saw him stretched out on his bed, reading. He must have had a hundred books in there. "Are these your books, Sergeant? I mean, do you own them all?"

"Yes. Would you like to read one?"

I shrugged. I wanted to but I'd never read a book in my life and I was afraid of picking something totally ridiculous and making a fool of myself.

Sergeant Williams closed his book and sat up. "You'll get a lot more out of them than you do from those comic books you read."

He chose a book and gave it to me. "Start with this one. You may not enjoy it right away but stick with it."

It was *The Picture of Dorian Gray* by Oscar Wilde. I began reading it early that evening. After taps, I went into the latrine where the lights stayed on and sat on the floor reading until after midnight. When I got off duty the next day I bought a pocket dictionary at the PX and started the book from the beginning again, doing my reading in isolated places so people wouldn't see me looking up words.

When I'd finished it I gave it back to Sergeant Williams and we discussed it. He handed me three more and told me in what order to read them and we had long discussions about each one as I finished it. He took a book from his shelves, *The Complete Works of Shakespeare*. I looked at him. "You have to be kidding with that. Now you're going too far. I mean, I never spent a day in school in my life."

His voice had a slight edge to it. "I never said you should be ashamed of no schooling. But it's not something to be proud of, either."

He gave me Carl Sandburg's books about Lincoln, books by Dickens, Poe, Mark Twain, and a history of the United States. I read *Cyrano de Bergerac*, entranced by the flair of the man; by the majesty of speeches I read aloud in a whisper, playing the role, dueling in dance steps around the latrine; imagining myself that homely, sensitive man, richly costumed in knee breeches, plumed hat, a handkerchief tucked into my sleeve, a sword in my hand. I feasted on the glory of the moment when, making good his threat, he drove the actor from the stage, and, as the audience shouted for their money back, tossed them his last bag of gold and admitted to Le Bret, "Foolish? Of course. But such a magnificent gesture." And it was. Glorious! I put my hand in my pocket, and, clutching a fistful of silver, I slipped out into the night, swor din hand, to drive the actor from the stage. Then, as fops and peasants alike shouted for their money back I bowed and hurled my handful of coins into the air. They landed, clanging against the side of the barracks. A light went on. A voice yelled, "Corporal of the guard." I ran like hell.

The more education Sergeant Williams gave me, through his books and our discussions, the greater a hunger I developed for it. When I ran out of his books I found others at the Post Library and then reread the ones he had.

6

As I Got Offstage At The Service Club, A Fellow standing in the wings came over to me. "That was one hell of a show you just did. Will you come out front and have a drink with me?" He offered his hand. "My name is George M. Cohan, Jr."

We sat down together and he said, "You've heard about

the big show every camp's going to be doing for the inter-camp competition? Well, with all the stuff you know and with my dad's special material, which I know backwards, I'll bet we could get that assignment. You know as well as I do that all the guys who'll be trying for it will just be using stuff out of the Special Services books. But with us writing our own, something fresh, we couldn't miss. Whatya think?"

"Well, naturally, I'd love to do it."

"Great. The General has the say. As long as I know you want to try for it with me, I'll make an appointment to see him about it."

He told me, a few days later, that the General would let us do an audition at the Officers' Club. Using a few pros we found around camp and a few semi-pros, we put together a small scale version of what we had in mind. I did an impression of Frank Sinatra that night, with the bow tie and the corny business of him being so weak and skinny that he had to hold onto the microphone. The General sent for us as soon as we'd finished and told us to be in his office the next afternoon. He wanted to hear the rest of our ideas.

A WAC Captain, his adjutant, sat in on the meeting and as we described our show she found enough stumbling blocks to build a wall around the entire camp and she said she'd let us know in about a week.

Outside, George said, "Well, she's the power as far as our show is concerned. We've got to butter her up, or she'll kill it entirely."

We dreamed up excuses to go to her office and always brought along bunches of flowers that we'd picked. George and I became as well known in Headquarters as the General. The Captain was getting to like us and it seemed as if she was swinging over to our side, so we doubled our efforts.

I stopped off to leave a bundle of new material we'd worked out. She said, "Tell me something about yourself, Davis. You were a professional performer?"

"Yes, Captain. Since I was three."

"Where did you perform?"

As I spoke she leaned back in her chair, listening to every word I was saying, waving away the clerks who occasionally tried to speak to her. Her interest triggered a stream of show talk and "the old days" poured out of me, until I began to feel like an old vaudevillian.

She smiled, "When I heard your ideas in the General's office they seemed so professional that frankly I doubted you'd be able to execute them. But now that I understand your background, and from what I know of George, I'm convinced you and he are more than up to the job. I'd like you two to work out a budget for scenery, props, and costumes and drop it off here as soon as you can." She walked me to the door, shook hands with me and smiled. "I probably shouldn't say this but you boys have quite an edge over the others. We should have the official word for you by Friday."

Leaving, I felt like doing a Fred Astaire number, tap dancing across the tops of the long row of desks leading to the front door. I was a specialist. Show business had given me something to offer the Army.

By Thursday afternoon when George and I left the Captain's office after dropping off a two-pound box of candy, our final and most glorious effort, he, the Captain, and I were almost buddies, and as the door closed behind us George sighed, "All we can do now is wait and hope. Keep your fingers crossed."

As I started toward my barracks, a couple of Headquarters clerks called out to me. One of them, a PFC with a heavy Southern drawl, smiled, "The Captain told us to take you to meet her over at Building 2134."

I grinned, "Her wish is my command." I walked with them, wondering why she hadn't just told them to bring me back to the office. Maybe she wanted me to look at a warehouse of props and scenery they'd used in other shows. We'd gone about half a mile, to a semi-deserted part of the camp, to barracks that weren't in use. I followed the PFC into 2134. One of the men closed the barracks door behind us. They shoved me into the latrine. Four others were in there, obviously waiting for us.

"Sorry, nigger, but your lady love won't be here."

"What is this?"

"This ain't nothin' but a little meeting some of us in the office thought we oughta have with you." They took hold of my arms. The PFC spit in my face. I tried to reach up to wipe it away but I couldn't move my arms. He saw me trying to reach for it. "Oh, I'm sorry. Here, I'll wipe it for you." He slapped me across the face, then backhanded me.

The seven of them crowded around me. The PFC was breathing heavily and a vein in his forehead was pulsing quickly. "We've been watching you makin' eyes at the Captain for a week now, and we decided we oughta have a little talk with you."

"Making eyes? Wait a minute . . ."

He hit me again. "Niggers don't talk 'less they're spoken to." He punched me in the stomach and I collapsed, hanging by the arms from the two guys who were holding me. "Now, like I was sayin', we just get so sick to our stomachs seein' you playin' up to her, and bringin' her flowers, and tryin' to make time, that we thought you'd appreciate us explaining a few things. Not to say the Captain would give an ape-face like you the time of day, but we figured we should smarten you up some so you won't keep makin' such a fool of yourself.

"Now, what you gotta learn is that black is black and it don't matter how white it looks or feels, it's still black, and we're gonna show you a little experiment to prove it so's you won't think we're trying to fool you none."

One of the others was stirring a can of white paint. Two of them ripped my shirt open and tore it off my back. The PFC had a small paint brush, like an artist uses, which he dipped into the paint can. They held me in front of a mirror. He wrote, "I'm a nigger!" across my chest. Then he wrote something on my back. When he was finished with that he took a larger brush and began to cover my arms and hands with white paint. I watched the brush going back and forth over the hair on my arms until every strand was covered and plastered down.

"Now," he said, "we're gonna let this paint dry so we can finish our experiment proper. So while we're waiting, you c'n give us a little dance."

They let go of my arms. My legs felt like cardboard buckling under me. The door out of the latrine was completely blocked. Two of them were in front of it and the other five were surrounding me.

"Come on, Sambo, give us a little dance!"

I just stood there, dazed, looking at them. My mouth was bone dry. My throat was closed. I tried to talk but no words would come out. The PFC said, "Guess he don't understand English." They held me again while he picked up the brush and wrote on my forehead, grinning, taking great pleasure in his work, doing it slowly, carefully. When he finished they dragged me back to the mirror. He'd written "Coon" in white paint that was starting to drip into my eyebrows.

"Now listen," he said, "you gotta understand me. When I tell you we wanta see you dance for us then you gotta believe we wanta see you dance. Now we're trying to be gentlemen about this. We figured you don't teach a hound nothin' by whipping him, so we're trying to be humane and psychological with you, but if we're takin' all this trouble on your education then you gotta show a little appreciation and keep us entertained durin' all this time we're givin' up for you. So, come on, Sambo, you be a good little coon and give us a dance."

They let go of my arms again. I couldn't move a muscle. The PFC punched me in the stomach. "Dance, Sambo." When I got my wind back I started moving my feet and tapping, staring incredulous and numbed.

"That's better, Sambo. Keep it going. And a little faster. . . ."

I danced faster, stumbling over my own legs.

"Faster, Sambo, faster. . . ."

I moved as fast as I could. As I got near the PFC, he hit me in the stomach again. "Didn't you hear me say faster, Sambo?" They made me keep dancing for at least half an hour, until I couldn't raise my feet off the ground.

"Okay, that's enough of that. You're not that good." He turned to the others. "I really thought we were gonna have us a treat, didn't you?" They all nodded and acted disappointed. "Well, guess we can't be mad 'cause you don't dance good. Anyway we gotta get back to your education."

I could feel the paint tightening on my skin.

"Now, we figure you've got the idea you're the same as white 'cause you're in a uniform like us and 'cause you dance at the shows and you go in and sit down with white men and because you think you got manners like a white man with your flowers and candy you give our women. So we gotta explain to you how you're not white and you ain't never gonna be white no matter how hard you try. No matter what you do or think you can't change what you are, and what you are is black and you better get it outta your head to mess around with white women.

"Now lookit your arm. Looks white, don't it? Well, it ain't. Watch and see." He poured turpentine on a rag and began wiping my arm in one spot. When my skin showed through the paint he grinned. "There. Y'see? Just as black 'n ugly as ever!"

He rubbed some turpentine on his own arm. "See the difference? No matter how hard I keep rubbin', it's still white. So, like I said, white is white and black is black." He poured the rest of the turpentine down the drain.

"Okay, you ugly little nigger bastard. We're lettin' you off easy this time. I mean we coulda been nasty and painted all the rest of you, but we figured you're a smart nigger and you'll get the idea fast, so because we're peace-lovin' fellas we don't wanta hurt you none, so we didn't do that. Now we're gonna be leaving you here but remember that we did you this big favor, see? And if you should decide to tell anybody anything 'bout our little lesson, well first of all we'd just have to admit we caught you makin' passes at the Captain and that sure wouldn't do neither of you no good, and then besides that we'd have to find you again and give you another lesson 'cept we'd have to try harder to make you understand, like maybe open up your skin a trifle and show you it's black under there, too. So just take our little lesson in the spirit we meant and we're willin' to let bygones be bygones and you'll stay away from the Captain. Right? Okay, Sambo, we'll be goin' now. Just try to remember everything we told you and we won't have no call to teach you no more lessons."

Then I was alone. I looked at myself in one of the mirrors. I wanted to crawl into the walls and die. I sat down on the floor and cried.

I looked at the part of my arm they had cleaned with turpentine. I rubbed the skin and watched it change color under the pressure, then darken as the blood flowed through again. How could the color of skin matter so much? It was just skin. What *is* skin? Why is one kind better than another? Why did they think mine made me inferior?

I stayed there for an hour, maybe two hours, I don't know, I lost track of time, trying to understand it. Why should they want to do this to me? I thought of a hundred questions—but no answers. I'd have given my life to hear my father say, "Hell, Poppa, they're just jealous of our act." I wanted to believe anything but that people could hate me this much.

The more the paint hardened the more it drew on my skin. It was starting to pull the hairs on my arms and it itched terribly. I couldn't think of any place where I could find some turpentine. I tried to wipe some of the paint off with toilet paper but it tore and stuck to the paint and only made it worse. I had to get back to the barracks. I dreaded being seen. Some of the guys would laugh and some would feel sorry for me and one would be as bad as the other. But I wanted Sergeant Williams to see me. I wanted to hear him tell me again, "You've got to fight with your brain." I wanted him to see how wrong he'd been. Or I wanted him to give me an answer.

It was already dark. I'd missed evening formation. Most of the camp was in the Mess Halls, so it was easy to sneak behind buildings back to the barracks. It was empty. I got my towel and aftershave lotion and went into the latrine. I poured half a bottle on the towel and rubbed until it hurt but it didn't help at all. There were voices outside, Sergeant Williams and some of the guys. I hid in the shower, praying they wouldn't come in. When I heard the other guys' steps going toward their bunks I ducked out and into Sergeant Williams' room.

He pulled me inside and closed the door. "Who did it?"

I shook my head.

"Don't be a fool. You don't have to fear them. They'll be court-martialed and sent to the stockade for years. Nobody can get away with this."

I wasn't afraid. I just wanted it to be over. I'd get no satisfaction out of putting them in jail. If they were arrested there'd be a trial and everybody in camp would know about it. I just wanted to forget that it ever happened.

There was no pity in his face—just sadness. Not only for

me but for the depth of what he with his wisdom could read into what had happened.

He left the room, cautiously, so nobody would see me, and sent someone to the motor pool for turpentine. Then he locked the door, soaked his towel, and began wiping the paint off my skin. For the next hour and a half he didn't say one word. I sat there naked to the waist until he was finished. Then he gave me soap and a brush and sent me to the shower room.

Bits of paint clung to my pores. I stood under the hot water brushing them out, rubbing until rashes of blood trickled to the surface, brushing, harder and harder, until I'd scraped the last speck of white out of my skin.

It wasn't lights out yet but I got into bed. The guys were talking on all sides of me. I pulled the blanket over my head, trying to hear nothing. All I could think was, nobody, nobody in this world is ever going to do this to me again. I'll die first.

The band was in the middle of the overture. George made room for me to peek through the curtain. The General was sitting in the first row. The house was packed.

For the first time in eighteen years of performing I didn't want to go on. I scanned the faces waiting to be entertained. The Texan from my barracks was in the third row. How can you run out and smile at people who despise you? How can you entertain people who don't like you?

George was holding out his hand. I put mine in his and he smiled, "Buddy, after they see our show I'm worried they're going to want us around for ten years." The music was two bars away from my cue. I took a deep breath and rushed on. I did my opening number, forcing myself to concentrate on the one thing I was out there to do: entertain the audience.

As I was taking my bow, enjoying the applause, absorbing the payoff for a month of night-and-day work, I glanced over to where the Texan was sitting. He wasn't applauding. Our eyes met and I caught something in his face that I'd never seen there before. It wasn't warmth or respect—he was trying to show no recognition at all. At that moment, I knew that because of what I could do on a stage he could never again think "But you're still a nigger." Somehow I'd gotten to him. He'd found something of me in six minutes of my performance which he hadn't seen in the barracks in all those months.

My talent was the weapon, the power, the way for me to fight. It was the one way I might hope to affect a man's thinking.

I was bowing to the audience and smiling only by the reflex developed through years of hearing a sound and reacting to it, but my awareness of any outside happening was overwhelmed by the birth of potency surging through my being.

The same man who had caused the question had provided the answer. The man who had shown me that my fists could never be enough was showing me how to fight with whatever intelligence and talent God had given me.

We played the show for a week and when I was on that stage it was though the spotlight erased all color and I was just another guy. I could feel it in the way they looked at me, not in anything new that appeared in their faces, but in something old that was suddenly missing. While I was performing they forgot what I was and there were times when even I could forget it. Sometimes offstage I passed a guy I didn't know and he said, "Good show last night." It was as though my talent was giving me a pass which excluded me from their prejudice. I didn't hope for camaraderie. All I wanted was to walk into a room without hearing the conversation slow down, and it was happening. I was developing an identity around camp and it was buying me a little chunk of peace.

I was transferred into Special Services and for eight months I did shows in camps across the country, gorging myself on the joy of being liked, killing myself to give back as much as they were giving me. I combed every audience for haters who'd come in by mistake or because there was nothing else to do, and when I spotted them I was able to give my performance something even more than I usually had, an extra burst of strength and energy, an ability that came to me because I had to get those guys, I had to neutralize them and make them acknowledge me, and I was ready to stay onstage for two hours until I saw one of them turn to his buddies and say, "Hey, this guy's not bad," or until I caught an expression that confirmed the power I knew I had. I dug down deeper every day, looking for new material, inventing it, stealing it, switching it—any way that I could find new things to make my shows better, and I lived twenty-four hours a day for that hour or two at night when I could give it away free, when I could stand on that stage, facing the audience, knowing I was dancing down the barriers between us.

I wished I'd made it person to person. The manager of the Chetwood, a small hotel in Los Angeles, seemed to be taking an hour to get them to the phone. Finally I heard the receiver being picked up.

"Poppa? That you?"

"I'm out of the Army, Dad. I'm taking the next train."

". . . cut it out, Will. How c'n I hear what he said with you askin' what he said—"

"Sammy? This true?"

"Hello, Massey. Yes, it's true. Get my clothes cleaned and pressed, I'm coming back into the act."

I paid the operator for the overtime and left the PX. I walked around the camp, remembering my first day in Cheyenne, waiting outside the barracks. Now that I was leaving the Army I had a detached feeling about it, almost as though it had happened to someone else. But it was me all right, and I wasn't about to let myself forget it.

Prejudice had been forced on me and crammed down my throat. I'd gone into the Army like a kid going to a birthday party, and I'd seen it. They'd taught me well all that my father and Will, with the help of show business, had so carefully, lovingly, kept from me.

I'd learned a lot in the Army and I knew that above all things in the world I had to become so big, so strong, so important, that those people and their hatred could never touch me. My talent was the only thing that made me a little different from everybody else, and it was all that I could hope would shield me *because* I was different.

I'd weighed it all, over and over again: What have I got? No looks, no money, no education. Just talent. Where do I want to go? I want to be treated well. I want people to like me, and be decent to me. How do I get there? There's only one way I can do it with what I have to work with. I've got to be a star! I have to be a star like another man has to breathe.

Almost everybody in the coach was asleep in their seats but I was wide awake all the way to Los Angeles, planning what I was going to tell my father and Will. A new life was starting and it was going to be a different one. There could be no picking up where we left off. No more, "We'll make it if we're meant to."

They were waiting for me in the Los Angeles station. They'd had no way of knowing what train I was on so they'd met them all until I arrived. Their clothes were wrinkled from sitting around the station half the night and they were dead tired, but they looked great to me.

At the Chetwood, I got out of my uniform and changed into one of my old suits. It fit perfectly. My father was sitting on the bed. He was looking at my wrist. "Where's your gold watch, Poppa?"

I still had it wrapped in paper. When he saw the smashed, twisted parts, he looked at me, hurt, heartbroken. "How'd that happen?"

What would be gained by making him suffer through the stories about Jennings and the others? They were just history now.

He was staring at the watch, probably remembering how he and Will had gone into hock to buy it. "Gee, Poppa, you shoulda looked after a watch like this. It's valuable."

He could never know how valuable it had been. "I'm sorry, Dad. But it wasn't my fault. It got smashed on maneuvers."

I was silent for a few minutes, lost in thoughts of Jennings and the others like him, loathing them, yet grimly grateful to them for wising me up. My father was studying me, his eyes shadowed, questioning. His voice was quiet. "It wasn't no fun, huh, son?"

I shrugged a denial. "It was the Army," and I turned away. "Hey, Poppa?"

I looked around.

"Betcha I c'n make you laugh."

He put on his poker face and stared at me solemnly. I was suddenly terribly depressed, remembering how that had never failed to send me into hysterics and obscure any problems we had. All my life we'd just laughed and looked away from trouble.

The poker face grew even more solemn.

I forced a smile, then a laugh, but there was a terrible, frustrated look in his eyes as he, too, realized that it just couldn't work any more.

Will came in and my father smiled as though he'd been waiting for him. "Poppa, here's your homecomin' surprise. We're set to go back to work as a trio. At four hundred a week."

Will nodded. "The way it come about is that we bumped into an old pal of ours, Arthur Silber. You won't remember, but we worked the same bills together 'til vaudeville went under. Today he's the biggest independent agent in the West. Soon as we hung up from your call we went over and saw him and he signed us for a big show he's putting together for the Japanese-American troops in Hawaii. We leave for Honolulu in ten days."

My father said, "Only drawback is we gotta go up in a plane to get there. Fact is we almost canceled out when we heard about it, but four hundred a week and a connection like Arthur Silber ain't something to fool with."

I stood up. "Look, I've got no eyes for flying, either, but I'll fly or swim to Hawaii. I don't care what we've got to do, we're going to make it this time. Big. We're going all the way."

We shook hands three ways and went out for dinner. They asked me about the Army and I told them the kind of stories they wanted to hear. They got a thrill out of hearing that I knew George M. Cohan, Jr., and I described the show we'd done. As I talked, I had to work half from memory, half from imagination. It was all yesterday, and all I could concentrate on was tomorrow.

part

II

7

Being In Front Of Audiences, Each Of Which Was Going to lift us closer and closer to the top, was a joy. We left Hawaii with almost a thousand dollars saved. I wanted to enjoy every indication of progress so in the cab from the airport to Los Angeles I asked my father, "How about us moving into a better hotel?"

He looked at me like, yeah, let's live, and told the driver, "Make that the Morris over on Fifth Street."

We ran up the stairs, hardly feeling the weight of our bags, and stopped at my room. I pulled the string on the light bulb hanging from the ceiling. It was the first room of my own I ever had. It was freshly painted and it had a private bathroom with a toilet and sink. My father glanced around happily. "Makes our old places look like San Quentin." He started down the hall to his own room and called back to me, "Here's the showers."

Toward the end of the week Mr. Silber said, "I'm sorry things aren't working out as fast as I'd expected. I hate to suggest it but I can put you into the Cricket Club here in L.A."

Will asked, "What's the money like?"

I stood up. "Massey, that's the least of it. Who the hell's gonna see us at the Cricket Club? My God, we played better places than that before I went into the Army."

Mr. Silber nodded sympathetically. "I know you did. And it's only $250 a week, but at least it'll pay the rent 'til things get rolling."

The door to my room was opening. The hotel manager's head appeared, then he pushed the door the rest of the way and stepped in, holding a passkey hanging by a chain from a wooden block. My father was behind him in pajamas and bathrobe. The manager left, shaking his head.

I took off my earphones and turned off the Woody Herman record I'd been listening to.

"Poppa, what in hell's goin' on here? The guy at the desk come by my room and says he's been knockin' at your door for ten minutes and he was gonna open your room to quiet you down." He looked at the drums I was holding between my knees. "When'd you start playin' bongos?"

"I picked 'em up this afternoon."

"What for?"

"I don't know, I figured I oughta know how to play 'em, maybe they'll work into the act somewhere. I'm sorry they got you out of bed. I was using earphones so nobody'd hear the record, and I thought I was tapping the drums quietly."

He sat on the bed. "You feel like playin' a little pinochle? Unless you're tired?"

"How the hell can I be tired?" I lit a cigarette and paced the room. "I don't get it, Dad. It's two weeks since we closed the Cricket and still not a word from Mr. Silber."

"He talked to Will today and it ain't a case of him not tryin'. The fact is clubs ain't fallin' all over themselves fightin' t'book us."

"You go back to bed, Dad. I don't feel much like playing cards."

He stood up. "It's almost five, Poppa. I wouldn't mess with the drums no more tonight."

I flopped on the bed and stared at the ceiling. I felt like a diesel engine with no track.

The glare of the sun forced my eyes open. I changed out of my wrinkled clothes and went to a cafeteria. The steam table was loaded with eggs, ham, bacon, sausage, cereals, hash, french toast, pancakes. I stopped in front of the pancakes. They were thin and crisp at the edges and little bottles of maple syrup were stacked alongside them. A delicious aroma came wafting up to me. I waited for the counterman, getting hungrier by the second, imagining myself digging into a stack of them . . . the counterman was coming toward me. I could picture him finding out what I wanted and thinking of "Little Black Sambo" and all the goddamned pancakes he ate, and smiling like "They all love pancakes and watermelon." I pointed to the ham and eggs.

I looked around a penny arcade, listening to the sound of rifle shots and an occasional ping! when somebody hit a duck, hating the kinship between myself and the guys loafing around there, killing time. I went into one of the Record Your Own Voice booths, dropped in a quarter and did Billy Eckstine singing "Little White Lies." The green light went off. I dropped in another quarter and tried Louis Armstrong doing the same song. It was tougher making his sound with a song I'd never heard him do. I played around with Edward G. Robinson's big speech from *Little Caesar* and listened to it play back. I liked it. I sang the number one song, "Five Minutes More," in my own voice. When I opened the curtain about a dozen people were standing there, grinning. I smiled, embarrassed as hell, and beat it.

I lugged my record player down the hall to my father's room and played "Five Minutes More," watching him, noticing how he cocked his head when I made the high note.

"That's not bad singin', Poppa, not bad at all. 'Course, it'd help if you could do it where you won't pick up the sound of cars goin' by."

"Very funny." I looked at my watch and turned on the radio. The music came pouring out and I sat there absorbing what sounded like a hundred pieces playing the Axel Stordahl arrangement, swelling, softening, opening a path for Frank Sinatra's voice to come through singing "I'm going to buy a paper doll that I can call my own . . ." I dropped my do-it-yourself record on the floor, listening, appreciating the professionalism, the way all that music served as no more than a frame for his voice, a frame he didn't seem to even notice was there. He sang free, unencumbered, as easy as if he were in a shower, yet all the elements fit and came together in a bigtime sound that gave me chills.

When the chorus started doing a Lucky Strike Extra, I reached for the dial knob. "Dad, you wanta hear something unbelievable? Watch this." I switched from station to station and the same voice came out, ". . . five minutes more, only five minutes more, only five minutes more in your arms . . ."

My father leaned back in his chair and sighed. "Yeah, Poppa, he's what you calls *big*!"

He was "Frankie," "The Voice" and the "Bow Tie," he was "loved and idolized by millions." I read every word I could find about his records, his pictures, his long-term deals, his personal appearances, his homes, his friends, the big openings he made bigger just by appearing. Everyone he knew, everything he did was big, lavish and spectacular. He personified the word "star."

"Poppa? You sittin' there eatin' yourself up over how he's doin'?"

"Oh, come on, Dad. He's too big to envy. But I just can't help thinking we were on the same bill with him when nobody knew him either. Now look where he is, and we haven't budged one goddamned inch. Why can't it happen for us, too? Okay, not like it did for him, but *something*, a decent club, a few good theaters, at least a *chance*. . . ."

The announcer was signing off the air. "Your Hit Parade has been broadcast from the NBC studios in Hollywood." I turned it off. "I'm going down there to see him next week."

"Hell, he ain't about to remember you and you ain't gonna get nowheres near him, anyway. It's plain ridiculous."

"I know he won't remember me, but I want to watch him work."

My best chance for a ticket was in the servicemen's line, so I got my army uniform out of a box, ironed it, and wearing my Ruptured Duck, the honorable discharge emblem, I went down to NBC three hours early to be sure I'd get in.

After the show I hurried around the corner to the stage door. There must have been five hundred kids ahead of me, waiting for a look at him. When he appeared, the crowd surged forward like one massive body ready to go right through the side of the building if necessary. Girls were screaming, fainting, pushing, waving pencils and papers in the air. A girl next to me shouted, "I'd faint if I had room to fall down." She got her laugh and the crowd kept moving. I stood on tiptoe trying to see him. God, he looked like a star. He wasn't much older than a lot of us but he was so calm, like we were all silly kids and he was a man, sure of himself, completely in control. He acted as if he didn't know there were hundreds of papers being waved at him. He concentrated on one at a time, signing it, smiling, and going to the next. He got to me and took my paper. He used a solid gold pen to sign his name. I thanked him and he looked at me. "Don't I know you?"

"Well, we were on the bill with you in Detroit about five years ago."

"What's your name?"

"Sammy Davis, Jr."

"Didn't you work with your old man and another guy?"

"That's us. Remember?" Oh, God! Obviously he remembered.

"Yeah, sure. I hate 'Sammy.' I'll call you Sam. Why don't you come back next week and see the show? I'll leave a ticket for you." The kids were pressing toward him, shoving papers in his face for autographs. He touched me on the arm. "See y'next week, Sam." He turned back to them and was absorbed by the crowd.

I was looking for a box office when an NBC guard walked over to me. "Hey, you! The end of the line."

"But Frank Sinatra left a ticket for me." As I said it I was struck by how ridiculous it sounded.

The guard was giving me a "Yeah, sure" look, but he took me over to the Guest Relations desk. They went through a stack of envelopes. There was nothing for me.

I was almost out the door when a uniformed page came running up to me and asked my name. He looked at an envelope. "Then this must be for you." It had one word on it. "Sam."

He ushered me through a private door to a seat in the front row of the reserved section. And after the show he removed me from the line that was moving slowly up the aisle. "Mr. Sinatra would like you to come to his dressing room."

It was at least five times the size of my room at the Morris, with a bed, easy chair, a couch, icebox, bar, and phonograph. I could see into the tiled bathroom. It had a stall shower and a bathtub, and the rich, thick towels were initialed FS. Someone gave me a coke. Important-looking people were coming in.

"Beautiful show, Francis . . ."

". . . that last song, Frank."

"You were in great voice, baby, great!"

They must have been sponsors or NBC executives and they

introduced themselves to me as if I must be somebody because I was in there, too.

He had the aura of a king about him and that's how people were treating him. Anything he said made them laugh. And me, too. Half the talk was inside jokes about the business, jokes I didn't begin to understand, but just being there was so exciting that everything he said seemed wonderful and funny. I kept thinking, "I can speak to Frank Sinatra and he'll answer me." But I couldn't think of anything clever enough to say so I just watched him, smiling and laughing at his every word.

He didn't say anything directly to me and I was beginning to wonder if he remembered who I was and that he'd sent for me, but as he was leaving he turned to me. "Hey, Sam. Maybe next week you'll come around and watch rehearsal." He put his arm around my shoulder and we walked out the stage door together and into the mob of screaming kids. He was reaching for his gold pen to sign autographs. He smiled at me and spoke over the uproar around us, "So long, Sam. Keep in touch."

Will said, "Glad you're back, Sammy. I was just telling Big Sam nothing's happening and there's no sense just sitting here not even making expenses, so I called Joe Daniels and he's set us for a tour of the North at $250 a week."

"But, Massey, it's the same lousy dead end—we'll be *buried* there. Who'll see us?"

I looked up, knowing that I'd hurt him, that there was nothing else he could do and he'd expected me to be glad just to be working. "I'm sorry, Massey, you're right."

He spoke softly. "Sammy, there's nothing lousy about being booked twenty out of twenty-one weeks."

My father came into the dressing room and flopped onto a chair. "Well, I covered every street downtown. Nothin'!" He started taking off his shoes, rubbing his feet. "Tomorrow I'll go back over to Mrs. Clark's and see if she's expectin' anything to open up. Meantime, guess we'll have to sleep in here."

Will asked, "You mean there's nothing in the whole city of Spokane?"

"There ain't that many colored rooming houses to start with."

"What about a hotel?"

"Ain't a single colored hotel around."

Colored side of town? Colored rooming house, colored hotels? Colored, colored, colored! And the way they were accepting it, so matter of factly. "Whattya mean *colored* rooming house? Why must it always be colored rooming houses and colored hotels . . . ?"

"Now Poppa, you know better'n this."

"I do like hell! Why do we always have to be pushed in a corner somewhere? Why do we have to live *colored* lives?" I was out of my chair, pacing our dressing room. "Y'mean we have to let people say, 'You're colored so you gotta sleep in your dressing room'? Where, Dad? Where do we sleep? On the goddamned floor?"

"Now Poppa, that's how it is and there ain't no use fightin' it. That's how people are."

"Nobody has to tell me about people. I got the word. I found out how they are. And it ain't 'cause they're jealous we're in show business." He backed up, hurt. As I was saying it I was sorry, but the heat was pouring out of my body. "I'll get us a room. In the whitest goddamned hotel in town."

As I spun through the revolving door, I glanced at the clean lobby, the uniformed bellboys and the elevators. This is the kind of place I'm going to stay in. I sauntered up to the front desk and practically yawned, "I'd like three single rooms for the next ten days. We're appearing in the show downtown . . . "

"I'm terribly sorry, sir, but we're entirely filled. There isn't a vacancy. As a matter of fact, the manager had to turn his own personal suite over to a guest, a steady guest who arrived unexpectedly."

He's really turning me down. I'd known it would happen, yet I hadn't really *believed* it would.

". . . swamped. Truly swamped. Busiest we've seen it in . . ."

I didn't want his room any more but I couldn't back down now. My air of "show biz" and world traveller had disappeared and I stood there, frozen, staring at him. A moment before it had been impersonal, I was just a nuisance to be handled as he'd probably handled others before me, but I wasn't taking the gentle way out, playing the game, smiling: "Well, thank you very much," like I'd tried and lost; and now he began perspiring around his forehead, doing "nervous hotel clerk" bits, coughing, looking around for the assistant manager and pretending to check the list of rooms. I guess this is what I'd wanted—to make it hard for him, to embarrass him. But there was no satisfaction.

The revolving door seemed so much heavier as I pushed my way to the outside.

". . . nervy nigger wanted a room. Some crust." A bellboy was telling the story to the doorman and he didn't care a bit that I'd heard him. "Go on," he said, "get outta here. Go back where you belong." The face wasn't grinning or leering or mocking, it just looked at me with the kind of contempt you have for something you dispose of with a D.D.T. spray gun.

All the strength in the world was in my body as I hurtled toward that face and hit it.

I was sitting on the ground smelling that awful, dry, dusty smell like I had when Jennings broke my nose. The doorman helped me up. I nodded my thanks and walked back to the theater. I should have been embarrassed returning like this after all my big talk, but all I could think was that my nose was broken and I had to keep the blood from staining my shirt.

My father and Will were waiting for me outside the stage door. There was nothing to say.

We made beds on the floor out of canvas tarpaulins, used our overcoats for blankets, and I made a pillow out of a rolled up pair of pants. All I'd accomplished was to get my damned nose broken so that for at least two weeks I'd be limited in what I could do onstage. I'd slid back and tried to hit an idea with my fists. I couldn't make that mistake again. Every drop of my physical and mental strength had to be concentrated on just one thing.

At breakfast I told Will: "I'd like to put in impressions of Jimmy Cagney and Durante and Edward G. Robinson."

He put down his coffee cup. "Sammy, what's the matter with you? You want to do impressions of *white* people?"

"Why not?"

"You just can't." He was shaking his head. "They'll

think you're making fun of them. No colored performer ever did white people in front of white people."

"But I did them in the Army and they went over great."

"That's a whole other story. Those soldiers are hungry for shows plus the fact of getting 'em free, but this is show business and when the people put down their money they don't want to sit there wonderin' if you're trying to insult 'em. You just stick with Satchmo and B and Step 'n Fetchit. Don't fool with those others, not for white audiences. I've watched what'll go over and what won't for nearly forty years and you can't get away with something like that."

"Massey, I won't argue with you. You're the boss of the act. But it seems to me that all that should matter is if they're good or not."

"I don't mean t'say I told you so, but you also thought we wouldn't have t'sleep on the floor of our dressing room 'cause it wasn't right. Sammy, what's right and what's wrong don't always have say over what is."

In Seattle, after our fourth show, the musicians would sit in with a college band run by a kid named Quincy Jones. I went along with them and we played, sang, and experimented with new things until dawn.

There was a note under my door when I got home one morning. "Wake me whenever you come in. Don't worry. Everything's fine. Will."

I heard the springs of his bed creak, then his slippers swooshing across the floor. He opened the door, rubbing his eyes, smiling. "Go get Big Sam."

I looked from one to the other. "Okay, now we have a pajama party. What's it all about?"

Will said, "We're booked as the opening act at El Rancho Vegas in Las Vegas, Nevada, for five hundred dollars a week." He smiled, pleased. "Mose Gastin, *now* let me hear you say we're going to be buried."

The trade papers were bursting with news about Las Vegas. It was starting to become a show town. El Rancho and the Last Frontier were the first luxury hotels and there was talk about new hotels being planned to go up near them.

My father was heating coffee on the hot plate. "The word is they're payin' acts twice as much as anywheres else. Free suites and food tabs." Will said, "They're out to make it the number one show town." I listened to them like I was watching a ping-pong game. ". . . flyin' customers in . . ." "*Variety* says . . ." "The whole business is watching what's happening in Vegas."

I walked over to Will. "Massey, I'm going to do those impressions."

He got out of bed and stared out the window. I knew by his long silence that he wasn't going to fight me. Finally, "Sammy, I don't think you can get away with it. Still, you're a third of the trio and you've seen a lot of show business so I won't stop you. I'm just going to hope you're right."

I looked around backstage while we waited to rehearse. The band was the biggest we'd ever worked with, the floor of the stage was springy and slick, the lighting was the most modern I'd ever seen. I was standing next to the stage manager. I asked, "Do I have it right about our rooms, that they're a part of our deal here?"

The manager came over to us as we finished rehearsing. "Sorry. We can't let you have rooms here. House rules. You'll have to find a place in the—uh, on the other side of town."

I picked up our suitcases. "Let's go, Dad, Will."

The hotels we'd passed in the town itself looked awful compared to El Rancho but even they were out of bounds to us. The cab driver said, "There's a woman name of Cartwright over in Westside takes in you people."

It was Tobacco Road. A three- or four-year-old baby, naked, was standing in front of a shack made of wooden crates and cardboard that was unfit for human life. None of us spoke.

The driver sounded almost embarrassed. "Guess y'can't say a lot for housing out here. Been hardly any call for labor round these parts. Just a handful of porters and dishwashers they use over on the Strip. Not much cause for you people t'come to Vegas."

The cab stopped in front of one of the few decent houses. A woman was standing in the doorway. "Come right in, folks. You boys with one of the shows? Well, I got three nice rooms for you."

When she told us the price Will almost choked. "But that's probably twice what it would cost at El Rancho Vegas."

"Then why don't you go live at El Rancho Vegas?"

"Pay her the money, Massey. It's not important."

Will counted out the first week's rent. My father smiled sardonically at her. "Looks like if the ofays don't get us, then our own will."

"Business is business. I've got my own troubles."

My father followed me into my room. "Not half bad." I nodded and started unpacking. He sat down and I could feel him watching me. I threw a shirt into a drawer and slammed it closed. "All right, Dad, for God's sake what is it?"

"*That's* what it is. Exactly what you're doin', eatin' yourself up, grindin' your teeth. Y'can't let it get t'you, Poppa. I know how you feels. But the fact is, when it comes time to lay your head down at night what's the difference if it's here or in a room at El Rancho?"

"Dad, I don't give a damn about their lousy rooms, I really don't. Right now, the only thing in this world that I want is their stage!"

As I danced, I did Satchmo. I shuffled across the stage like Step'n Fetchit. Then I spun around and came back doing the Jimmy Cagney walk to the center of the stage and stood there, facing my father and Will, doing Cagney's legs-apart stance, the face, and then "All right . . . you dirty rats!" For a moment there was no sound from out front—then they roared.

In the wings Will smiled warmly. "I'm glad I was wrong, Sammy." My father laughed and hugged me. "Poppa, you was *great!*" He put me down. "Whattya say we get dressed after the next show and go look around the casino. I got fifty dollars that's bustin' t'grow into a hundred."

We went out the stage door and around the building. The desert all around us was as dark as night can be but the casino was blazing with light. The door opened and as some people came out there was an outpour of sounds such as I'd never before heard: slot machines clanging, dealers droning, a woman shrieking with joy—and behind it all, a background of the liveliest, gayest music I'd ever heard. As I held the door open for my father, my head went in all directions to slot machines, dice tables, waiters rushing around with drinks, a man carrying a tray full of silver dollars.

I saw a hand on my father's shoulder. A deputy sheriff was holding him, shaking his head.

We rode to Mrs. Cartwright's in silence. They got out of the cab and I continued on downtown where there was a movie theater, where for a few hours I could lose myself in other people's lives.

A hand gripped my arm like a circle of steel, yanking me out of my seat, half-dragging me out to the lobby. "What're you, boy? A wise guy?" He was a sheriff, wearing a star badge and the big Western hat. His hand came up from nowhere and slapped across my face. He'd done it effortlessly but my jaw felt like it had been torn loose from my head. "Speak up when I talk to you!"

"What'd I do?"

"Don't bull me, boy. You know the law."

When I explained I'd just gotten to town and had never been there before, he pointed to a sign. "Coloreds sit in the last three rows. You're in Nevada now, not New York. Mind our rules and you'll be treated square. Go on back and enjoy the movie, boy."

I had no choice but to go in. A Mickey Rooney picture was on. After a while I glanced up to catch a song he was doing and I looked away, still steaming. Then I looked up again and I forgot the cop and the theater and the rules and I was dancing across the campus in a college musical. An hour later I was Danny Kaye git-gat-gattling my way through the Army. Then the lights went on and I was sitting in the last row of an almost empty movie theater, and again I was a Negro in a Jim Crow town.

I went back to Mrs. Cartwright's and slammed her dirty, gouging door and swore to myself that someday it would be different. I tried reading but I couldn't keep my mind on the book. I felt closed in so I went out for a walk but the sight of all the poorness drove me back to my room. I stared out the window at the glow of the lights from the Strip in the distance until it faded into the morning sun.

I should have been tired the next night but as eight o'clock drew near I was vibrating with energy and I couldn't wait to get on the stage. I worked with the strength of ten men.

We did our shows and went out to get a cab to Mrs. Cartwright's. I looked away from the lights of the casino but I couldn't avoid hearing the sounds. Night after night I had to pass that door to get a cab. Once, between shows, I stood around the corner where nobody would see me, and waited for the door to open so I could catch the short bursts of gaiety that escaped as people went in and came out. I sat on the ground for an hour, listening and wondering what it must be like to be able to just walk in anywhere.

My father looked into my room, smiling. "Hey, Poppa, you wanta come out and wrap yourself around some of the best barbecue you'll ever taste? Then after lunch we could look in on the bar. It's a real nice place. They got a Keeno game goin' and we can double our money." He was selling me, as he had been every day for a week.

"Thanks, Dad. You go ahead."

"Hell, son, come on and get some laughs outa life."

"I'm happy, Dad."

"No you ain't."

"The hell I'm not."

"The hell you is. You sit here all day listening to them records when already you sound more like them people than they do. Then you're blowin' the horn. . . ."

"And I'm getting pretty good. Here, listen. . ."

"I know." He tapped on the wall, causing a hollow knocking sound, and smiled. "This ain't exactly made outa three-foot-thick cement." He sat down on the bed. "Poppa, you do impressions, you dance, you play drums and trumpet, but you don't know doodly squat about livin'. You're not havin' your fun."

"I will, Dad. Bet your life on it. I will!"

He gave me a frustrated look. "Okay, son. I don't know how t'help you. So just tell me. . . ."

I watched him walking down the street toward the commercial section of Westside. There were a few decent places over there and under other conditions I could have enjoyed them, but the idea that I was being told, "That's your side of town, stay there," that those were the only places I was allowed in, made it impossible for me to go near them.

He looked back and saw me in the window and waved, offering me a chance to change my mind. I waved back and he turned and kept walking. I picked up the trumpet and started playing.

There was no bus or train out of Vegas until morning but I gladly paid fifty dollars to a musician for a lift into L.A. an hour after we closed. He dropped me a block from the Morris and I walked toward the hotel. Everywhere I looked were the dregs of Los Angeles, as if every pimp and dope peddler in town had suddenly moved onto Fifth Street. I reached the Morris but kept walking, faster, almost running. I saw an empty cab and ran into the street to flag him down.

When we'd gone a few blocks, I began to feel the pressure easing, and I didn't have to hold my breath any more.

"Made up your mind yet, buddy?"

"Yes. The Sunset Colonial, please." Lots of performers stayed there and I knew they'd take me. It was on Sunset Strip, in Hollywood, and it was more expensive but I knew that no matter what I had to do—or do without—I was never going back to Fifth Street.

I went over to the Frank Sinatra show and sent my name in. I was "the kid" to him and he let me watch rehearsals every week. I sat around the studio, absorbing everything that was happening, inhaling the atmosphere of the Big Time like it was clean, delicious, fresh air.

I figured if I spent my time at places where show people hung out, maybe I'd make a connection that could do us some good. There was a club called Billy Berg's where I could get Cokes at the bar. Mel. Tormé came in all the time. He had the Mel-Tones and he was dating Ava Gardner. I made it my business to meet him and we became friends. Frankie Laine sang there every Sunday night for twenty dollars at the jam sessions. We'd sit at the bar and he'd have a beer and say, "I'm just waiting for that break to come along."

Through Jesse Price, a drummer, I made a connection at Capitol Records and got a contract for fifty dollars a side.

Will shrugged. "You sure didn't get yourself much of a deal. The thing to have is a royalty, something that'd come to about a nickel apiece for every record they sell."

"Massey, when I'm Bing Crosby I'll ask for royalties. Right now what I want is this opening."

At the studio, I listened to the band running through the

music: thirty-two bars of clichés, with all the musical riffs lifted from other people's hits. The conductor was swinging his baton with all the enthusiasm of a guy painting a house, and the band of staff musicians who ground out one session after another for no-names like me was playing like I was number 428. I knew I was lucky just to be getting the chance but I couldn't help hearing the contrast between this and the fresh, vital sound of the Hit Parade band.

Mama's kitchen was the warmest room because it had no windows, but even so, my father and I wore overcoats and had the oven on low. The refrigerator, unplugged to save electricity, was open, scrubbed clean, and empty except for some ads my father had clipped from magazines: pictures of a roast beef, eggs, butter, sausage, and a bottle of milk.

It was 1946 and everybody else was rich and happy, tearing up their ration stamps and ordering their first new cars in five years. We, however, were bringing down the National Prosperity Average. We'd left L.A., plodding our way across the country, barely making expenses at the same old clubs, finally limping into New York and up to Harlem where Mama was still on relief. We were a great big help, starving on occasional one-nighters and listening to Jack Eigen telling us he was at the goddamned Copa.

Nathan Crawford's factory had laid off a lot of men and forced him to take a cut to twenty-five dollars a week, but still he came stumbling into Mama's place every Friday, doing his drunk act and giving her at least ten or fifteen dollars, never letting on how rough things were for him. We watched it week after week, unable to find sufficient words to say to this man who was actually keeping Mama alive.

My father was tapping *Variety* with the back of his hand. "Accordin' to this, the Chicago clubs are usin' acts by the hundreds. I heard the same thing from some of the boys. The sayin' is 'You can burp and get booked.'"

"It's a long walk, Dad." I was skimming through *Metronome*, hoping maybe Capitol had taken an ad.

I took *Variety* out of my father's hands, stood up, and bowed. "*Metronome* has picked me, your son and heir, as 'The Most Outstanding New Personality of the Year.' Plus,

'The Way You Looked Tonight' has been chosen Record of the Year."

He read it and we screamed with laughter. He took an iron washer out of his pocket. It was the size of a quarter and we'd been using them to get cigarettes out of machines. He stood, ceremoniously. "Mr. Davis, I presents you with the first Iron Record ever given out in music. It's a honor which means: you sings good even if you sells bad."

I went downtown to *Metronome* to thank them, hoping they'd write more about me. I saw Barry Ulanov and George Simon, the editors, and sure enough they said they'd like to do a story on me, but they suggested I ask Billy Eckstine, who was playing the Paramount, to pose for a picture with me to give the story name value. He was a friend of the family and it was embarrassing to ask this kind of a favor, but I called him.

He posed with me the next afternoon between shows and I started to leave. "Thanks a lot, B. I really appreciate it."

"Thanks for what? C'mon up and sit with me awhile." I followed him to the star dressing room, we had coffee and he asked how things were going for us.

There was no point in trying to kid him. He'd know we had to be in trouble or we wouldn't be taking the one-nighters. "No good. We just can't seem to get off the ground. I'm getting some good writeups on the records but they're not selling."

"You meeting the rent?"

"We're hungry, B."

He shook his head compassionately. "It's rough."

I thought about asking him for a loan. Pride is great but Mama and my father were at home with an empty icebox and not twenty cents between them, and I knew it would be like twelve times Christmas if I came back with a few dollars for food. "B, if you could lend me five dollars, I'd sure appreciate it."

He looked at his watch, a gold and diamond one that must have cost $500. "Come on downstairs and watch the show."

I stood in the wings waiting for him to go on. I shouldn't have asked him. Maybe he was broke, or maybe he just didn't want to lend me any money. It seemed that it would be nothing to him but you never know about people when it comes to money. He'd been great about taking the picture but that hadn't cost him anything. What the hell, why shouldn't he have done it? Not that he needed it, but it couldn't hurt him any to have his picture in *Metronome* again. He was on-stage and I could see the spotlight bouncing off a diamond ring he was wearing. We could eat on that for a year . . . he's got a helluva nerve keeping me on the string like this for a few lousy dollars, humiliating me, making me stand here like a moocher. It's a lesson I won't forget: keep your problems to yourself unless you know the guy you're telling them to is going to help you. I started to walk out, to show him I didn't need him. But I did need him.

I watched him work. He was everything I was not: tall and good-looking and sure of himself, and he had every right to be. He was a giant in the business, as hot as the news yet to come, and they were packing the place to see him. Everything he wore was made to order for him and it all had its own style. He reeked of success. And the way he handled himself. What a pro!

As he came off I said, "Great show, B. Thanks a lot for the picture. I've gotta cut and get uptown, now."

"Here, wait a minute, you forgot this."

I left, hating myself for misjudging him, disgusted with myself for being so nowhere that I had to bum a few dollars from a man I didn't even know that well. When I was on the street I took it out of my pocket. It was a hundred-dollar bill. He'd known we were in trouble, but he had the sensitivity not to show it by offering me money. Instead he'd opened the subject so I could ask him if I chose to.

We hit Chicago laughing and scratching and ready to go. Will went out every day, from club to club, agent to agent, but we might as well have been out of town. People were standing in line for entertainment but after two months of stagnating at the old Ritz Hotel on Chicago's South Side we still hadn't been able to get on a stage.

Ossie Wilson, an old friend of my father's, was keeping us off the streets, standing for the ten dollars a week rent on our rooms. He was running poker games and depending on whether he won or lost, we ate or starved. He hit a losing streak for eight days and the only thing Will, my dad, and I had to eat was a Mr. Goodbar apiece and a So-Grape. Occasionally his girl friend brought us the leftovers from their dinner, but after another week he was still on a losing streak and it reached the point where we were down to filling ourselves with water. The pain of hunger was almost matched by the excruciating frustration of idle hours, of knowing all the entertainment we had welled up inside us, while the radio taunted us with all the sounds of the life for which we were so starved. Night after night we listened to interview shows hysterical with the atmosphere of a nightclub boom, and we sat there endlessly wondering how it was possible we couldn't get into it.

The Ritz was a real theatrical hotel and the three of us sat around the lobby every day with other performers like in a scene from a corny MGM musical. Will pointed to a newspaper ad. "I see where Dick and Gene Wesson opened downtown." My father looked at it. "Damned fine billing, too." A pleasant nostalgia crossed his face. "Remember back in the thirties when we were workin' the 'World's Fair Vanities' through Maine, Massachusetts, and Canada . . ." Will's face relaxed into the same happy memories. He folded the paper. "I'm happy to see the boys making it so big. They had plenty of hard times getting there."

I looked around the lobby at groups of performers clustered together having the same kind of talks, convincing themselves that it could still happen to them too, like gamblers in a roulette game, hanging on, staying in, waiting for the wheel to spin again. I couldn't stand the sight of all that failure lumped together. "I'm going upstairs."

My father stood up, too, and spoke loudly, for effect. "Yeah, might as well go get washed up for dinner."

I turned on the radio hoping, as usual, that I'd hear one of my records. I listened to Frankie Laine's "That's My Desire" for about the tenth time that day. The same man who used to sing at Billy Berg's, the same talent, the same style, but from one month to the next he'd become a star, gone from $20 a Sunday to $5,000 a week. The disc jockey said, "That's it, folks, the biggest selling piece of wax in America today. And here he is in person, *Frankie Laine*. Frankie, how does it feel to be sitting on top of the world?"

I snapped off the radio. "We've gotta get the hell out of this town. We can't just sit around mildewing in the damned lobby. If we've got any sense at all we'll go see the Wessons. My God, we've got roots with these people. Let's ask 'em outright if they'll lend us enough to get us out of town."

Will was shaking his head. "I don't want to do that."

"Massey, pride is fine and wonderful but it's past the point of being ridiculous. It's suicide not to try."

Into the pocket they went and gave us a hundred dollars. And that wasn't enough. The Wessons' manager, Sam Stefel, also managed Mickey Rooney, who'd just come out of the Army and was putting together a show to tour the RKO circuit. They called Stefel in Boston and got him to use us on the bill as the opening act.

8

MICKEY ROONEY WALKED INTO THE GRAND BALLROOM of the Copley Plaza Hotel at twelve o'clock sharp. Will nudged me and pointed to his watch. "Now that's a pro for you." I got a light-headed feeling when I saw him come in with that go-go-go walk, just like he did in the movies. He faced the company and said, "Hi, my name is Mickey Rooney!" Then he started shaking hands saying hello to us one by one.

I thought: it's nice of him not to take the attitude that he's a big star and everybody knows who he is; it was so warm for somebody that important and that famous to say, Hi, I'd like to meet you and this is my name. I liked it. Yeah. When I make it, when I can walk into a room and everybody will know who I am just by looking at me, then I'll say, "Hi, my name is Sammy Davis, Jr. . . ."

He was standing in front of me, his hand out.

"Hi, my name is Sammy Davis, Jr." Oh, God! I tried to recover. "My name's Sammy, Mr. Rooney."

"The name is Mickey." He looked at me and shook his head. "Damn! I *never* find anybody who's shorter than me. *Everybody's* taller. Even you. And you're a midget!"

He ran through a single he was going to be doing, then the production numbers with the girls, songs from the MGM musicals he'd made with Judy Garland. I'd seen every one of them, I had the albums and I knew every sound by heart, but seeing him doing them in person, so close, without the help of music, lights, costumes, nothing but his talent . . . he was incredible. The entire cast stood up to applaud him. After rehearsal he told Mr. Stefel, "I want Sam to work with me in the act." He turned to me, "What can you do besides the dancing?"

"I play drums, a little trumpet, I do some impressions. . . ."

"You're kidding! Who do you do?"

"Well, I've been doing Danny Kaye. The 'Melody in 4F' thing."

Sam Stefel cut in, "*You'll* do all the impressions, Mickey. They were hired to dance."

"Sam, what are you bitching about? Let the kid do it."

Stefel was firm. "We don't need it. We bought a dance act and we want a dance act. You'll do all the impressions and that's final."

On opening night, Mickey came to our dressing room and motioned for me to come out in the hall. "Look, Sam, about that Danny Kaye impression, at least sneak it in tonight till we can make it a regular thing. Do it over your dance for the first show when the critics are there so they'll get to see it." He ducked down the stairs before I could thank him.

I told my father and Will about it. "My God, what a generous, thoughtful thing."

The curtain went up on the big opening production number: twenty Roxyettes, hands on each other's hips like a train, the classic number they'd done at the Roxy, with tail lights hanging from each of their behinds. Will went on dressed as a porter, and I came out swinging a lantern, shouting, "Train leaving on Track 29. All aboarddd!!!" It was a six-minute scene, and the next spot on the bill was our dance number.

The tempo of the first notes of our music was a fast and furious rat-a-tat machine gun speed, and we never slowed down for the ten minutes we were on. And in the middle of it, I was doing Danny Kaye's git-gat-gattle better than I'd ever done it. We worked so desperately that it was like our feet never touched the ground until we were in the wings. We went back for our bow and were rushing off when Mickey walked on. He was the first man I ever saw walk onto a stage without being introduced. There was no announcer doing a "well, folks, here he is . . . Mickey Rooney!" When they saw him, the applause doubled but he didn't acknowledge it, as though it were all for us. He called me back and I did a little step with him. He was pointing me up, showing his fans that he liked me so that automatically they'd like me, too.

I was going to bed at four in the morning when the landlord pounded on my door. He was half-asleep and burning mad. "There's a damned fool on the phone who keeps saying he's Mickey Rooney. I hung up on him twice but he keeps calling back. Now you get down there and tell him if he calls again. . . ."

Mickey was tremendously excited. He had the reviews and he read them to me, not what they said about him, he skipped over that and read only what they'd written about us. "The best dance act to hit Boston in years." "Berry Brothers, Nicholas Brothers better forget it!" "The kid in the middle is funny!"

I stood in the wings watching every show Mickey did, soaking up his tremendous knowledge of the business, totally awestruck by his talent. He was the multi-talented guy who had to do everything: sing, dance, comedy, impressions, drums, trumpet, everything! And he did them all well. Nor could anybody out-act Mickey when he wanted to act. He'd do a vignette and make the people cry or laugh as he chose. Show after show I watched him devastate audiences with his talent and his energy. Mickey was the performer I admired more than any in the world.

Between shows we played gin and there was always a record player going. He had a wire recorder and we ad-libbed all kinds of bits into it and wrote songs, including an entire score for a musical.

Mickey was upstairs in his dressing room and I was downstairs when I heard him shout: "Sam! Get your tail the hell up here!"

I made the stairs three at a time. "What's the matter, Mickey, what's wrong?"

He was leaning against the wall. "Tell me something, are you going to play a little gin or not?" He dealt the cards. "I cleared it with Sam for you to do more of the impressions. Do about four minutes of them." He smiled. "And slip in a little trumpet when you do Louis Armstrong."

He kept encouraging me to build up our act and he made it possible by clearing more and more time for me onstage.

As we left the theater one night he looked at the sign out front, "The Mickey Rooney Show" with pictures of him in different poses, and told Sam Stefel, "I want some of those pictures out. Instead of them, put 'The Will Mastin Trio, starring Sammy Davis, Jr.'"

He was taking space away from himself to make room for me. I tried to thank him but he cut me off. "Let's not get sickening about this."

On Christmas Eve we were playing Cleveland, and Mickey took over a banquet room and threw a party for the troupe. We all brought gifts, mostly gags and corny toys, and the party was really moving when a voice shouting "Hey!" cut through the laughter. A guy, obviously from another party in the hotel, wearing a pointed party hat with a string under his chin, staggered into the room, and leaning against a chair with one hand, holding a glass in the other, stared at me, my father and Will. "What the hell's goin' on here with niggers and white women?"

Mickey was out of his chair, sailing across the room and on top of the guy, slugging him. It took four of us to pull him off. He sat down, depressed.

The presents hadn't been given out yet but he said, "Okay, folks, that's it. The party's over."

As they said good night to Mickey, they looked at me consolingly, but it was impossible for them to understand the worst of it, the humiliation of knowing that because of me everybody's Christmas had been ruined.

We were going into our last month of the tour when Mickey told me, "We've got to close for a month or so. MGM wants me to do another Andy Hardy thing. But when that's finished I'm going to do a script called *Killer McCoy*. It's a remake of the old Robert Taylor picture *The Crowd Roars* and I want you as the fighter. I think you could play the hell out of it. I'll talk to them as soon as I get out there."

Our trio played two weeks in Reno. Mr. Silber and his son Arthur came out and I spent every spare minute with Art working out fake fights, stunt-man style, with grunts, groans and falling over tables, all the things I'd have to know for the picture.

When we picked up the tour Mickey had no news on the picture yet. We were back in our routine of song writing, playing gin between shows, and me standing in the wings at every performance. There were so many tangible things I could get from watching Mickey work: the use of a topical joke, using the people in the show for various effects, the little "class" touches that he had. But his greatest power was his ability to "touch" the audience. When Mickey was on-stage, he might have been pulling levers labeled "Cry!" and "Laugh!" He could work the audience like clay, molding them the way he wanted them. But it wasn't only because he's a fine actor, there was something more, and night after night I tried to understand it.

I asked my father, "How do you *touch* an audience?"

He said, "Well, I been in this business all my life and there's only one way. You go out there and you do your show the best you can and if you're good you'll touch 'em and if you're bad they'll know it."

Will didn't understand either. They tried to give me answers but they were as much as saying, "A bird flies by flapping his wings." But how does he flap them that makes it different than when I flap my arms? How come I don't fly, too? How did Mickey get inside of every person who watched him so that he wasn't just another performer to them? What was it about him that made them open up and care so much?

We were at the Loew's State in New York, our last stop on the tour, and Mickey and I were playing gin in his dressing room. "Sam, about the picture. I heard from them last night. It's out." I kept shuffling the cards, trying not to react and make it tougher for him. He said, "I could give you a lot of crap about it, but honest-open MGM doesn't want to use you. They fought it tooth and nail. They don't know you and they don't know if you can act." He looked at me with sadness.

"I don't think they want a colored fellow. They told me, 'Use a Mexican kid, it's less problems.' "

I walked uptown after our last show that night. Knowing Mickey I could imagine how he'd fought for me with his position as he had with his fists but still, someone who'd never met me, never seen me, could throw the whole dream down the drain by saying, "Use a Mexican kid. It's less problems." It wasn't "How good is he?" There was no "Let him do a screen test." Just plain, cold "No. He's a problem."

I went into the bedroom, closed the door and sat down on the bed, rubbing the skin on my hand, staring, wondering.

Before I was aware that I was on my feet I'd jumped up and hit the wall with all my strength. My fist crashed through the thin plaster between rooms. When I took it out I could see Mama through the hole I'd made. She was looking at the wall, shaking her head helplessly, not knowing what was wrong, nor asking.

The last curtain had fallen. Mickey and I walked downstairs together and said good-bye on the street outside the stage entrance. I watched him walking toward the limousine that was waiting for him. At the car door he hesitated, then turned and came back. "Listen, Sam—about that lousy deal on the picture. I tried everything. You know that, don't you? A few years ago it couldn't have happened, but I'm not too well-entrenched any more. The truth is the Hardy picture isn't doing so well. The day of the series pictures like *Kildare* and *Hardy*—it's over. I'm not King of the Box Office any more. Andy Hardy's dead." He nodded grimly. "I made the mistake of going into the Army. I guess the times have passed me by."

"Aw, come on, Mick, you're still the most talented man in the world."

"Talent isn't enough." He was silent for a moment, then he shrugged, put out his hand again and smiled. "So long, buddy. What the hell. Maybe one day we'll get our innings."

We were booked right into the Strand Theatre on Broadway with Billie Holliday and Count Basie. Will came up to Mama's the day before the opening. "I just stopped by the theater and they said we gotta cut down to twelve minutes."

I slammed my fork onto the table. "The hell with that! Let someone else cut their act. We're doing twenty minutes."

"Now, Sammy, don't talk foolish. We're only the opening act. We can't get away with trying to run the whole show. . . ."

"Will's right, Poppa. We gotta go out there and give 'em twelve minutes like they want and not look for no trouble."

"Trouble? I just want to be seen."

"Who'll see us if we get canceled after the first show, Sammy?"

"Nobody'll cancel us if we're good enough."

We did twenty minutes. The audience was still applauding. Billie Holliday was waiting to follow us and I was embarrassed to face her, but she smiled and took my arm. "Come on, little man, you'd better carry me on or they'll never calm down."

One look at the house manager's face and I knew Will had been right, and now, as the axe was about to fall, I couldn't believe my own nerve.

"Where the hell do you guys get off disobeying my orders? What kind of a honky-tonk do you think this is?"

Will stepped forward. "We're sorry. We really are. We'll cut it right down to twelve minutes. . . ."

"Well, you're damned good'n lucky you went over so big. Keep the act as is and we'll cut eight minutes somewhere else."

I felt like an animal, fit and ready for the jungle, more powerful, more able to meet the world than I'd ever felt in my life. Will mopped his brow like "phew" and my father fell into a chair and sighed, "We sure got lucky that time." I was reeling drunk from the success of it. I felt like I was a man and they were kids. "That wasn't luck! Let me tell you something, Dad, Will. This is how it's gonna be for us from now on. We're gonna take what we want. We can be the dirtiest bastards in the world as long as we've got what that audience wants."

"Wait a minute, Sammy . . ."

"Wait nothing. What we just saw is how life is. If you 'make it' you can have anything! But if you don't you can be the nicest guy in the world and they won't book you to play the men's room at intermission. Well, I'm gonna make it. And when I do what'll you bet they'll like me? They'll like me even if they hate my guts!"

Neither of them said another word. They were looking at me as though seeing me for the first time. I think I was seeing myself for the first time. And I liked it. I liked not "taking it" and I liked winning.

We left the Strand on an express train and rode it right into the yards. After weeks of waiting around for poverty we wound up in Boston at a sailor haven called The Silver Dollar Bar for $110 a week. We floundered around New England making a round trip back to the world of two-dollar hotel rooms and deadly dull dates which I'd really believed we'd seen for the last time, as far away from "New York" as we'd ever been.

I watched Will and my father dancing, working like dependable machines, smiling, giving the audience everything they had. Then, in the wings, the smiles were gone, their faces expressionless. A performer knows above all things that he must convince the audience he's a winner. So he bounces on—always laughing. But when he spends his life on a treadmill, each night planning how he'll bum a meal or sneak into his boarding house unseen by the landlord, the onstage enthusiasm fades the moment the spotlight dims.

I tried to understand what had gone wrong. When you've never had a break you can say, "All we need is that one big break." But Mickey had been our break, he'd given us every opportunity, so there could be no saying, "Wait'll the big bookers get a load of our act." They'd seen us, the critics had seen us, and the people had seen us. And they'd all liked us. But as soon as we were off they forgot we'd ever happened.

We laid off at Mama's and every morning we'd go downtown to a booking office. When a call came in for an opening dance act, we were one of ten or twenty or a hundred who could fill the bill, so we'd sit there hoping it was we who had the strongest connection. And I was beginning to understand that's how it was going to be all our lives. We weren't an attraction that drew people to a theater, we were just a prop, a tool to open another man's show fast and lively, interchangeable with countless others just as fast and just as lively. We were one of a million like us in a world that was buying tickets to see one-of-a-kind.

When United Booking had closed for the day Will and my father went to dinner. I left them at the Paramount Building and walked up Broadway. People were streaming out of the office buildings and theaters and I was swallowed up by the thousands of bodies swarming around me, pushing past me. I was so tired of being lost in the crowd, just another face with no name, the performer nobody remembers the minute he steps off the stage.

Lucky Millander's band was doing the stage show at the Strand. A colored comedy act was just going on as I sat down. They were pros, funny as hell and I was laughing, but I wasn't enjoying myself. Something was bothering me. I listened to them saying, "Ladies and Gen'men, we's gwine git our laigs movin', heah." They were talking "colored" as Negro acts always did. I'd heard it a thousand times before, but for the first time it sounded wrong. They were labeling themselves. I watched them doing all the colored clichés, realizing that we were doing exactly the same thing. We'd always done them. They were an automatic part of our personalities onstage. It was the way people expected Negro acts to be so that's the way we were. But now it was like I was seeing it for the first time and I almost couldn't believe my ears. Why don't they say, "Gentlemen"? Why must it be "Gen'men"? Isn't there a way to give people laughs without doing it at our own expense? Must we downgrade ourselves? Must we be caricatures of cotton field slaves? We don't all pull barges up the Mississippi. Can't we entertain and still keep our dignity?

If a white man ever said "Yassuh" to me I'd climb all over him. But how could I logically resent it from him when we were doing it ourselves, contributing a means for their mockery by characterizing all Negroes as good-natured, lazy, shuffling illiterates who carried razors, shot craps, lied, and ate nothing but watermelon, fried chicken and black-eyed peas?

I went from theater to theater, wherever there were colored acts. They were all shuffling around, "Yassuhing" all over the stages. Does the public really want this? It doesn't seem possible. If the joke is funny won't they still laugh if we call them "Gentlemen"? They don't expect every Jew to have a long nose and a heavy accent; not every Irish performer has to do "Pat and Mike" jokes so why must every Negro be an Uncle Tom?

Then I saw the trap of it: they were making no personal contact with the audiences. None! And how could they even *hope* to with their real personalities camouflaged, buried beneath ten feet of "Yassuh, gen'men"?

I studied the acts and saw that most Negro performers work in a cubicle. They'd run on, sing twelve songs, dance, and do jokes—but not to the people. The jokes weren't done like Milton Berle was doing them, to the audience, they were done between the men onstage, as if they didn't have the right to communicate with the people out front. It was totally the reverse of the way Mickey played, directly to the people, talking to them, kidding them, communicating with them.

By a lifetime of habit by *tradition,* I too had been cementing myself inside a wall of anonymity. It didn't matter how many instruments I learned to play, how many impressions I learned to do, or how much I perfected them—we were still doing *Holiday in Dixieland*—still a flash act. That was how we set ourselves up so that was how the audience would see us.

I strode the floor of Will's room for hours, explaining everything I'd seen, everything I felt and wanted to do. He was gazing past me. "Okay, Sammy. The only thing is I've been doing an act one way all my life, the way I know, and making a living. Only a fool would throw away what he's lived on for forty years. But I won't stop you from trying new things if you believe in them. Maybe you're right that we've been sneaking in the impressions instead of framing them to get the most out of them. Take a straight eight minutes in the middle of the act and use it however you want. But your father and me'll do what we know and always did."

We were up North playing Portland when Will received a wire.

OPEN CAPITOL THEATRE NEW YORK NEXT MONTH, FRANK SINATRA SHOW. THREE WEEKS, $1250 PER. DETAILS FOLLOW. HARRY ROGERS." We passed that telegram back and forth like three drunks working out of the same bottle.

My father was gazing at it, "I ain't lookin' no gift horse in the mouth, but I'm damned if I can figure how come us?"

Will shrugged. "Frank Sinatra always has a colored act on the bill with him."

"Yeah, Will, but why *us?* I mean, with all the power-house acts around like Moke and Poke, Stump and Stumpy, the Nicholas Brothers, the Berry Brothers. . . ."

"We're as powerhouse as the next and I guess Harry Rogers did a good job of agenting."

I stopped listening and counted the days on a calendar. We had three weeks to get ready. I could feel myself on the stage with our new act, smooth, organized, everything displayed to give it the best possible chance to go over—and at the Capitol Theater with Frank Sinatra where the *world* would have a chance to see us!

Alan Zee, the general manager of the Capitol, came over to us at rehearsal. "You ran sixteen minutes. Gotta cut it. Too long. Drop the jokes, drop the impressions, all we want is the flash dancing. Just give me six minutes. No more."

I ran after him. "Is there any chance of taking a little time out of Lorraine and Rogman?"

He kept walking. "Just cut your act. Don't worry about anybody else's."

"But, Mr. Zee . . ." He went through a door and closed it behind him.

My father and Will walked over to me. "What the hell, Poppa. You'll get another chance." He put his arm around me. Will said, "Sure you will." He hesitated. "I know how you feel, Sammy, but I hope you know that you can't get away with what you did at the Strand. Not here. Not for $1250 a week."

I nodded. "I know, Massey."

On opening day, a Pinkerton man made a break in the line of kids so we could slip through and in the stage door. I put on my make-up and got into the zoot suit I'd had made. The waistline of the pants came up to my chest and the legs were like balloons around the knees, tapering down skintight at the ankle where they zippered closed. The coat was tight at the waist but the shoulders measured three and a half feet across and I had to walk sideways through narrow doorways. I had a four-foot dangle chain, and I'd changed the style of the day, slightly, by adding a cowboy hat for laughs. A guy in a short-sleeved shirt came in. "You Sam? Mr. Sinatra would like you to come by his dressing room."

Frank Sinatra came out of a second room, dressed in his shirt and tie, his valet behind him helping him into his jacket. "Hi'ya, Sam, good to see you. How's your family?" As we walked toward the wings he smiled. "Glad we're working together."

The house lights were down, the orchestra played the first bars of "Night and Day," the pit rose with Skitch Henderson conducting, the curtains opened, Frank Sinatra was onstage and the kids began stamping their feet, screaming hysterically and leaping up and down as though the seats were hot. He sang three numbers to get the show started. Then he said, "We've got three cats here who really swing and they're all too much but keep your eye on the little cat in the middle, because he's my boy! Here they are, 'The Will Mastin Trio and Sammy Davis, Jr.'"

Frank took me completely under his wing. He didn't just say, "Well, you're working and that's fine." He had our names up out front, he was wonderful to my family, and he had me to his dressing room between almost every show. If I was there at dinner time he'd take me out to eat with him. Every time we stepped through the stage door there were hundreds of kids waiting for him, and it took us half an hour to walk the twenty feet across the sidewalk to his limousine. They even screamed at me, "Oh! You touched him. Let me touch you." Day after day they were in line for tickets at six in the morning, holding bags of sandwiches, and they wouldn't come out until late at night.

I stood in the wings at every performance watching him work. He'd walk to the microphone like he had nothing better to do, arriving there at exactly the moment his cue came up. As he rolled through a song I could see him almost smiling as he got to certain phrases, knowing the bobby-soxers were going to swoon as he sang them, and they did, on cue as if he'd pressed a button. His effect on the audience was awesome: they held their breaths during the quiet moments of a song as if they'd rather stop breathing than break the spell. They were completely involved with him, reacting to every shading of his voice, finding meaning in every gesture. Like Mickey, he was touching them, taking a mass of people and making them care.

"Pretty great, isn't he?"

Sidney Piermont, the head of all Loew's booking, was standing beside me. I whispered back, "He's unbelievable, Mr. Piermont."

We walked toward the dressing rooms together. "Your trio is doing a fine job."

"Thank you very much, sir."

"Don't thank me," he smiled, "I fought against hiring you." He saw that I didn't understand. "You were booked strictly because Frank insisted on you. When I was lining up the show I asked him who he wanted. He said, 'Get Skitch to put the band together.' Then, for the opening act I suggested the Berry Brothers and he said, 'Yeah, fine. No, wait a minute. There's a kid who comes to my radio show when he's in town, he works with his family, his name is Sam something. Use him.' I tried to figure out who he meant. 'You don't mean Will Mastin's kid?' He said, 'Yeah, that's them.' I was totally against it. I told him, 'I know they worked the Loew's State with Mickey Rooney and the kid did a lot of time onstage, but they're unknowns, why gamble on them?' Frank insisted, so I said, 'All right, Frank, if you want 'em you got 'em. How much do you want to give them?' 'Make it $1250.' Well, that was ridiculous. I argued, 'We can get the Nicholas Brothers for that kind of money and they've even got a movie going for them. They're hot.' He said, '$1250. That's it. I don't want the Nicholas Brothers. I want Sam and his family.'"

Frank had never even hinted at it. Just, "Glad we're working together." Like it was a surprise to him, too.

He invited the cast to a Thanksgiving dinner the day before closing. He had a basement rehearsal hall converted into a party room and his mother sent over pots and pots of delicious homemade Italian food. We were eating our heads off when somebody yelled, "Hey, Sammy, do the thing for Frank like you did for us." I'd been playing around with an impression of him. I hadn't done one since the Army but being with him all the time I was able to catch the physical things he does, his hands, his mouth, and his shoulders, as well as the voice.

He said, "Let's see it, Sam." He had no idea what it was and I was afraid he'd be offended. But he laughed, "Beautiful, beautiful. It's a scream. Listen, I want to talk to you tomorrow."

The next afternoon in his dressing room he asked, "Why don't you sing?"

"Well, I sing when I do impressions, but as far as straight singing goes I made a few sides, but Capitol's melting 'em down for candles. I don't have a style of my own."

"Let me hear some of the impressions." I did a few and he began shaking his head. "You're ridiculous if you don't put those in the act. And you definitely should sing. Straight. You've got the voice, work on it, develop a style. And you should do as many of those impressions as you can. Do them all." He frowned. "You should have been doing them here. You wasted three weeks of important exposure."

There was no point explaining that they'd been cut.

After the closing show, the members of the company came to his dressing room to say goodbye. I stood off to the side thinking how a star of Frank's stature had taken the time and thought to help me. We were so many miles apart in every way that it was hard to imagine why he would reach out for me as he had. When the last of them were gone I tried to let him know how grateful I was.

He gave me an "are you kidding?" look and we shook hands. "So long, Sam, I'll be seeing you." He looked me straight in the eye. "Anything I can ever do for you—you've got yourself a friend for life."

I nodded the best thank-you I could and went for the door. He called out, "Hey, Charley." I turned. He was smiling. "Take care of yourself, Charley. And remember—if anybody hits you, let me know."

9

"This Is Where We Oughta Be, Massey." I handed him an article about Celebrity Night at Slapsie Maxie's, a club in Los Angeles owned by Ben Blue and Sammy Lewis. "We've got the act now and this is the showcase we need. Everybody in the business would see us."

We hit the stage at Slapsie Maxie's like Joe Louis went for Schmeling, the second time. My father and Will stepped back, I did Satchmo, Lionel Barrymore, Edward G. Robinson, Cagney, Jimmy Stewart, Sinatra and Danny Kaye—and I did them directly to the audience. Our music came in over the applause, my father and Will moved forward and as we swung into our closing number our normally frenzied dancing was frantic.

The audience, mostly show people, was giving us a tremendously warm ovation and I wanted to do something more than just stand there bowing and smiling our thanks.

I stepped forward. They were quieting down to listen to me. I felt the cold of the mike against my hands. I'd never before spoken a word onstage that hadn't been prepared in advance, but they were waiting. "Ladies and gentlemen, you can't imagine what this means to my father and . . ." I couldn't possibly say "Mr. Mastin" or "our friend Will." I said, "my father, my uncle and me."

We were booked for two weeks. I'd just come off stage when I caught a look at myself in the dressing room mirror. I looked again, staring at my zoot suit. It was horrible! I'd thought of it as a timely costume which got big laughs but I was doing exactly what I despised in other Negro performers —making people laugh *at* me. I was saying, "Gen'men" with those clothes just as loud and clear as if I'd come shuffling on singing "Old Black Joe." I tore it off my body, unable to get out of it fast enough, and dropped it in the trash can.

A few nights later, a middle-aged woman came backstage and said, "I just had to meet you to tell you that when you first came onstage I thought, 'There's the most unattractive man I've ever seen.' But fifteen minutes after you started performing I thought you were beautiful." She turned and left.

Something had happened during my performance. I must have touched this one woman. I must have gotten through to her enough so she couldn't see anything but what I was trying to do as a performer. I wanted to ask her a dozen questions. Maybe she'd be able to tell me when I'd changed and maybe I could analyze why. I searched for her in the audience every night but she never came back. I was lifted to the skies by the knowledge that it was within me to touch an audience, but after all the wondering and testing and trying, it was killing not to know what thing or combination of things had accomplished it for me.

The stage manager handed me a cablegram. "THE REVIEWS WERE GREAT. KEEP IT UP. FRANK."

I showed it to Will and my father, then looked at it again, seeing that it had come all the way from Spain, realizing that almost a year had passed since the Capitol. And what a rotten year it had been for him. His radio shows were off the air and his records had begun dropping on the charts. For no logical reason he'd cooled off and his career was in a serious decline. I hung the cablegram on the dressing room mirror. "Can you imagine a guy like this? With all his troubles. . . ."

Our name was getting around, people were starting to say, "Hey, y'oughta catch that new act at Slapsie Maxie's," and we were actually attracting a few customers. We'd taken the job for $200 a week, just to be seen, but we closed riding such a crest of good talk and publicity that when we signed for our next date, the Golden Gate Theater in San Francisco with Buddy Rich and his band, our price went to $550 a week and stayed there as we played our way across the country to New York.

I saw Buddy Rich standing on Broadway outside the Brill Building. He introduced me to the fellow he was with, Marty Mills, and nodded toward the second-floor windows of the Brill Building that said "Mills Music" in gold letters. "Marty's plugging songs for his old man. C'mon with us. We're going over to Mel's rehearsal." Perry Como had a fifteen-minute TV show every night on CBS and Mel Tormé and Peggy Lee were his summer replacements. I felt very "inside" going over there to drop in on a friend's rehearsal.

Marty, Buddy and I were together constantly. We formed a club, a very secret organization. Marty was X1-69, Buddy was X2-69 and I was X3-69. We'd call each other on the phone and say, "Hello, X1? This is X2. We're meeting in front of the Paramount at 12:30."

Marty found four old police badges in a pawnshop. We each had big gold "Chief Inspector" badges. The fourth was silver. Buddy said, "C'mon, let's go over and show Mel."

It was a silly time in our lives. We were grown men in our twenties, but we walked into the studio wearing our badges Secret Service style, concealed behind our lapels. Mel was just finishing a number. We walked over to him and flashed them.

"Hey, how about me?"

Buddy was firm. "Sorry, Mel, you can't join."

Marty agreed. "We'd like to have you, kid, but it's very secret."

I said, "Hey, wait a minute, X1 and X2, let's have a conference on this." We walked away and did a whole arguing bit, with shaking our fists, looks of horror and mistrust, and a lot of whispering. It was no more incredible that Mel was holding up rehearsal awaiting the verdict than that we were actually doing this whole thing in the first place.

Buddy gave him the official word. "Okay, Mel. You made it!"

"Hey, wow! I'm in the club?"

"From now on you're X4-69." We shook hands ceremoniously and Buddy handed him our extra badge.

Mel's face dropped. "But this one's silver."

Marty patted him on the arm. "Well, you're not really in yet, Mel. You're on probation and we're watching you."

We left the rehearsal and wandered over to Times Square. The Shriners were in town and the Astor Hotel had uniformed private detectives all over the lobby. Buddy approached one of them. "Pretty crowded, huh? They're giving us a rough time on the force, too." He flashed his badge. "Grab a smoke. I'll take over for you." The guard was delighted and went down to the men's room.

On Eighth Avenue we passed a fruit peddler, flashed the badges, grabbed apples, and walked away.

We went to a movie at the Capitol and got out around two in the morning. Marty said, "Let's go over to Lindy's for a sandwich."

I copped out. "I don't have much money with me. . . ."

"We don't need money. I just sign my dad's name."

We were almost in front of the place so I had to come right out with it. "Look, X1, I don't know how they're gonna feel about me in there."

"Are you kidding? Listen, I've been eating in there all my life."

The lights outside the restaurant were off. "Hey, it looks like they're closed."

"They're still open for the steady customers. The door-man'll let us in."

Through the glass door I caught sight of Milton Berle sitting at the head of a long table directly in front of the entrance. He had a big cigar in his hand and he was telling a story or something. He really looked like what he was: the idol of the hour, the King of Television holding court, with everybody laughing hysterically at every word he said. I nudged Marty. "Look."

He took it very casually. "Berle's in here every night. That's the Comics' Table. It's a regular thing for the comics and press agents and writers." He knocked on the door. The doorman appeared from inside, spotted me, and waved us away. Marty rapped the door again. It opened a crack. "We're closed."

Marty said, "You're out of your mind." The doorman was looking straight at me as he said, "I told you we're closed to you."

Marty turned purple. He banged on the glass door with his fist and shouted, "Tell Mr. Lindy that Marty Mills will never be back again."

We stood on the sidewalk watching the doorman walk away from us. "Look, I'll catch you guys tomorrow."

Buddy said, "Come on. We'll go to the Bird 'n Hand and have some coffee."

"No, really, I'm a little tired."

He grabbed my arm and pointed to the restaurant only two doors away. "How tired can you be?"

We sat at the counter staring silently at menus. I heard the revolving door turn and in the mirror over the counter I saw a man in a baggy tuxedo hurrying toward us. He tapped Marty on the shoulder. "Mr. Mills, I'm sorry about what happened. It was that damned doorman . . . please come back. I have a table all ready for you."

Marty looked at me to see what I wanted to do. Obviously the headwaiter wasn't concerned over my feelings. He was worried about offending a good customer. On the other hand I didn't want to make problems for Marty. He answered for me, "We've already ordered, thanks." As the headwaiter left Buddy called after him, "By the way . . . you apologized to the wrong man."

Marty was looking at me, a world of disbelief and compassion in his face. "Sammy, I'm sorry." All the certainty of our fun times was gone from his voice. "Jesus. I knew it went on, but I never figured New York. . . ."

I wanted desperately to play it like it didn't bother me. "Baby, keeping us out of restaurants and hotels is the national pastime. It's bigger than baseball."

He kept looking at me as though he couldn't accept the fact that it had happened. "Is it always like this?"

I shrugged. "Only when I'm colored. Listen, I'm starved . . ." I used the menu as a prop and as I stared into it I knew I'd have broken my arms to have prevented it from happening—they were my friends and I wanted them to like me, not pity me—yet I was strangely glad that they saw what it was like.

The club was meeting at Mel's apartment. "Well, do I get my gold badge yet?"

Buddy looked at me and I looked at Marty, who hung his head a little. "Gee, Mel, I hate t'tell you this—but frankly the reports haven't been good."

Mel made a face. "Very funny. Boy, you guys are a scream. Big deal with your gold badges." He opened a closet and took out a western holster which he buckled around his waist and tied down to his leg. Then the gun was in his hand pointed at us. Then it was spinning around his finger, forward, backward, and into the holster. He drew three more times, faster than I'd ever seen it in the movies. When he figured we were sufficiently impressed, he unbuckled the holster and started to put it back in the closet.

I ran over to him. "Can I see the gun?" My hand dropped six inches. I hadn't expected it to be so heavy. "Is this real?"

"It's a single action Colt .45. Put it on."

I buckled it on and reached for the gun but I misjudged where the butt was and my hand went right over it. I went for it again. This time I got it out and I started spinning it around on my finger.

Mel said, "Forget the fancy stuff. First learn to draw it right."

"But you've gotta admit I wasn't so bad for the first try."

"Except it wasn't cocked, baby. You'd be a dead man."

I was so tickled with the way I had it spinning around my finger that I looked up. "Hey, this is a breeze." As I searched his face for a little approval the gun slipped off the end of my finger and fell to the floor with a humiliating thud. Mel made a whole Laurel and Hardy scene out of picking it up, spinning it on his finger casually, expertly, then looking at me with patient disgust. "Would you like to learn the right way? Or did you just come up here to break my gun?"

I kept at it, working in front of a mirror until I made a fairly decent draw. He sighed, "You're hooked!"

When we were leaving, he asked, "Well what about my gold badge?"

Buddy shook his head. "You're not ready yet, Mel."

"Whattya mean I'm not ready? You saw the way I handle a gun."

Buddy nodded and patted him on the shoulder. "That's true, kid, but it's a little flashy for our kind of work."

I caught Mel's reaction, and the joke, at least for me, lost its humor. I had a strong desire to give him my own gold badge so he wouldn't feel left out. But I did nothing. At that moment I felt that I was in a small way exactly what was wrong with the world and that I was everything I hated. But still I did nothing.

My father tugged gently at the shirt cuff concealed under the sleeve of his best suit. "Always show a little linen, Poppa."

"You're looking like Saturday night at Small's, Dad."

He fixed his tie. "Well, son, you might as well know. I met myself a nurse, name of Rita Wade—I calls her Peewee 'cause she's real little and neat. I'm takin' her for dinner soon as she gets off duty." He turned. "What're you doin' tonight?"

"Nothing much, just going over to the Copa to catch Frank Sinatra."

"The Copa?" His forehead wrinkled. "Listen, Poppa . . ."

"It's okay, Dad. Buddy Rich invited me. He's a hip guy,

right? He must know it's okay or he wouldn't have brought it up."

I spent twenty minutes getting a perfect knot on a ten-dollar tie I'd bought at Saks Fifth Avenue that afternoon, and although the subway downtown was half empty I stood all the way so I wouldn't crease my suit. I was in front of the Copa entrance at a quarter to eleven, staring across the street at the doorway I'd stood in so many times with my father.

Buddy and his friends pulled up in a cab. As we got to the steps the doorman stopped us. "Wait a minute. Only people with reservations." He rushed in front of us. "Hey, didn't you hear me?"

"I'm Buddy Rich and I have a reservation."

He shook his head. "You better wait here while I check." He was back in a few minutes. "They don't know anything about a reservation for you." He gave me a meaningful look, then turned to Buddy. "Maybe if you go away and come back in a little while they'll be able to find it."

Buddy blew. "Wait a minute, fat face! Are you saying that if we come back without our friend we'll get a table? 'Cause if you're saying it I want to hear it."

The doorman's face reddened. "I didn't say that. Now look, don't make trouble. We're not looking for trouble. Go away peacefully . . ."

Buddy's arm was back, cocked to swing, but I stopped him. "Come on, let's go." We walked away. I couldn't face him.

"Look, this is ridiculous. You guys go in. Why should you miss Frank's show? I really wish you'd . . ."

He grabbed my arm. "If you say that again I'm going to belt you. C'mon, we'll find a movie or something."

We walked silently toward Fifth Avenue. As we reached the corner I looked back at the big awning that said "Copacabana." I felt Buddy's hand on my shoulder. "To hell with those bastards. You'll dance on their tables someday."

My father was waiting up for me in the kitchen. "How'd it go?"

"They didn't let us in. Good night, Dad." I went into the bedroom and began undressing. It was hot as hell but I closed the window to keep out the smell of the garbage that people threw out their windows and which piled up in the courtyard. I heard his steps coming into the room.

113

"Look, Poppa, they never did want us in them places and they never will and it kills me seein' you gettin' yourself hurt over somethin' you oughta know by now."

"Any word from Will yet?"

"Yeah, but you ain't gonna do no celebratin' over that news, neither. We're set to play the Flamingo in Vegas. Will signed 'cause they upped us to $750-plus pickin' up our fare out. We can't afford to turn down that kinda money, Poppa."

I turned around. "Dad, I'll play the Governor's mansion in Alabama if it'll help us get off the ground a little faster! *Anything* to change the way we've gotta live. I've gotta get away from it! I've *got* to!"

He was looking at my hand, at the necktie I hadn't realized I'd been holding in my fist, crumpling it into a wrinkled mess. He shook his head slowly, sadly. "Sammy . . . you ain't gonna get away from it 'til you die."

Buddy said, "I talked to Frank last night. He wants you to call him." I looked up from my coffee. He nodded. "Certainly. I told him." He pointed to the phone booth. "Eldorado 5-3100."

Frank didn't even say hello. His opening line was, "Tonight, you are coming to the club. I'm making the reservation and you're walking in there alone."

"Look, Frank, I'd rather not. I appreciate . . ."

"That's *it!* We don't discuss it. Just be there." His voice softened. "When something is wrong it's not going to get right unless you fix it. I know it's lousy, Charley, but you've got to do it."

I walked slowly toward the Copa. Sure, Frank had made the reservation, but what if they forgot to tell the doorman I was coming? And even if it goes smoothly, if I get in and get a table—at best, forcing my way in where I'm not wanted is even more degrading than being turned away. They're wrong not to want me but they'll sure as hell have a right to hate me for pushing my way in. I walked past the entrance intending to just keep going, but I could never face Frank if I backed away. His decline had grown worse and he needed the Copa far more than they needed him, but despite that he was fighting for me.

I walked up the three front steps. The doorman stood on

the sidewalk, watching. I pulled open the door and walked in. I was braced to be facing people but I found myself alone in a vestibule. I paused, then pushed open the next door.

There was a hatcheck room in front of me and I wished I had a hat to give them so I could have a minute to look around and get my bearings. I saw people standing around a bar to the right of me. I couldn't see anything but a mirror on the left so I took a guess and turned right. A captain smiled too brightly. "Good evening, *sir*. A drink at the bar?"

"No, thank you. I have a reservation for the show."

"The show is downstairs." He smiled indulgently.

There were two groups of people ahead of me downstairs. The headwaiter asked for their names, checked them off on a list, and sent them to their tables. I stepped forward but before I could give my name he snapped his fingers and a captain appeared, telling me, "Right this way, sir." Obviously they'd had no trouble recognizing me.

I felt as if I were a bundle of dirty laundry being taken through the dining room. He left me at a table and as I began to get my bearings I realized I was so far back that I could better see what was happening in the kitchen than on the stage. A captain was standing over me. "Your order, sir."

"I'll have a coke—a cola, please."

The stares, like countless jabs against my skin, were coming from every direction. I lit a cigarette, and took a long drag, breathing the smoke out gently, holding the cigarette delicately at the tips of my fingers, trying to do all the suave Cary Grant moves I'd just seen in "Mr. Lucky." Two guys were coming across the room straight toward me. I put the cigarette into the ashtray. A hand moved forward. "Sam? We're friends of Frank. He said you wouldn't mind if we sat at your table. . . ."

As we talked it was clear they were close friends who'd seen the show more than once. Frank had wanted me to walk in by myself, leaning on nobody, but he had sent them to sit with me so I wouldn't feel like I was alone on an island.

The waiter brought my coke and I reached for it but he beat me to it, pouring it elaborately, his patronizing smile informing me that he understood I wasn't accustomed to being served.

There were cards on all the tables with Frank's picture on

them, and brochures with pictures of the stars who played there every year. They were all wearing the Copa Bonnet, a hat made of fruit. The brochure described it as "the laurel wreath of achievement in nightclub circles, awarded only to entertainers who had reached the peak." I looked at the pictures of the stars who were wearing it, smiling like they had the whole world in their pockets. I wondered what you had to accomplish before you could get that kind of acceptance. One of Frank's friends laughed. "Pretty ridiculous looking hat they got 'em wearing, huh?"

I smiled. "Yeah." I could see how a hat made out of grapes and oranges could look silly, but to me it seemed like a crown.

When I asked the waiter for my check he said, "Mr. Sinatra has taken care of it." We went up to Frank's dressing room. He took me aside and put his arm around my shoulder. "You did something good, Charley."

The subway lurched from side to side and I swayed with it as though all the muscles and nerves in my body had been stretched until they'd snapped and were hanging limp like broken rubber bands. For the first time I could remember, I loved that ride uptown and I nestled into the restful, anonymous cheapness of it, and where it was taking me. Usually I saw just the seamy side of Harlem and resented being glued to the poverty and second-bestness of everything, but now I yearned for the peace it offered, the release from watching every move I made and from being watched. I knew I was thinking wrong, that it was everything I hated and I tried to bring myself out of it. "I've been to the Copa." I kept repeating it until I heard it screaming in my ear, roaring back at me in time with the wheels. "I've been to the Copa . . . been to the Copa . . . been to the Copa . . ." But all I felt was like I'd bought a brand new Cadillac convertible—for a hundred thousand dollars.

At breakfast I lit a cigarette with a match from the Copacabana. My father spotted them instantly. "Hey! How'd you get them? Were you inside?" I nodded. "Damn!" He laughed, giddily. "What's it like? Anything like we figured?"

"It's unbelievable! You go downstairs and a guy in a black coat is waiting with the reservations list. He turns you over to a guy in a red coat who takes you to your table. Then a guy in a blue coat takes your order and a waiter in a white jacket brings it to you. And when you're finished along comes a maroon jacket who takes away the dishes. . . ." He was hanging on every word.

Later, I went into the front room and looked out the window, staring downtown, toward Lindy's and the Copa—two in one week—understanding for the first time what lay ahead, and that it was worse than an insult or a fight, it was a pressure chamber, and the further I moved out into the world, the thinner the air would become. Buddy and Marty were just the start, I'd make other friends, and every time they'd breeze into a restaurant for a sandwich I'd be holding my breath, waiting.

I stood at the window for a long time, watching people moving but going nowhere—people who'd never tasted anything but the leftovers, seeing Harlem again as it is, a corner of New York like all the Harlems are, just used-up corners of the country, the carpet under which every city sweeps its problems. I looked at the people who stay "uptown" under that carpet where prejudice does not seek them out. Obviously, they could accept the peace and be content just to hear Jack Eigen describe the Copa, but I was glad I'd seen it for myself.

I went downstairs to the candy store and called Marty. He said, "Hello, X-3. Whattya say we case X-4's rehearsal this afternoon?"

I went downtown.

In Vegas, for twenty minutes, twice a night, our skin had no color. Then, the second we stepped off the stage, we were colored again.

I went on every night, turning myself inside out for the audience. They were paying more attention and giving us more respect than ever before, and after every performance I was so exhilarated by our acceptance onstage that I really expected one of the owners to come rushing back saying, "You were great. To hell with the rules. Come on in and have a drink with us." But it never happened. The other acts could move around the hotel, go out and gamble or sit in the lounge and have a drink, but we had to leave through the kitchen, with the garbage, like thieves in the night. I was dying to grab a

117

look into the casino, just to see what it was like, but I was damned if I'd let anyone see me like a kid with his nose against the candy store window. I wanted to believe "If they don't want me then I don't want them either," but I couldn't help imagining what it must be like to be wanted, to be able to walk into any casino in town. I kept seeing the warmth in the faces of the people we'd played to that night. How could they like me onstage—and then this?

My father spent his time around the Westside bars and casinos but I went to my room trying to ignore the taunting glow of light coming from the Strip, bigger and brighter than ever, until finally the irresistible blaze of it drew me to the window and I gazed across at it knowing it was only three in the morning, which is like noon in Las Vegas, feeling as wide awake as the rest of the town which was rocking with excitement. I pictured myself in the midst of it all, the music, the gaiety, the money piled high on tables, the women in beautiful dresses and diamonds, gambling away fortunes and laughing.

It took a physical effort to tear myself away from the window. I forced it all out of my mind and kept telling myself: Someday . . . listening to records and reading until I was tired enough to fall asleep, always wondering when "someday" would be.

Mr. Silber said, "Well, this is it. Ciro's." None of us said a word. "Janis Paige will be headlining and I can get you the opening spot. Herman Hover caught the act at Slapsie Maxie's and he likes it. He won't meet your price of $550—the most he'll go for is $500—naturally I told him we'd take it."

Will said, "He'll meet our price or we don't play it."

"Massey, you can't be serious?"

"I am. We're not starving. No point taking a cut just to work a place."

"A *place!*? This is *Ciro's,* for God's sake."

"Then they can afford to pay $550."

"Well, if fifty lousy dollars means that much to you then take it out of my cut. I'll gladly . . ."

"It's not the money. It's the idea of the thing. If you cut your price in business then what've you got? If we was hungry it'd be something else."

118

I couldn't believe it. To throw away an opportunity like this over fifty dollars. But he was like a rock, and to make it worse, my father agreed with him. "I'll quit show business before I'll go in there for $500. Herman Hover was a dancer for Earl Carroll when I was and he knows we can outdance him every minute of the day." ·

I was panicking. "What the hell has *that* got to do with it? He's not a dancer any more. He owns the best club out here and we need to play it."

Late the next afternoon Mr. Silber called Will. "It's all set. He'll go for the $550."

When we signed the contracts we learned that Mr. Hover, well aware of the importance of his club to an act like ours, knew he could get plenty of others to come in at his price, or less. Finally Mr. Silber had said, "Okay, Herman. Don't tell them and I'll pay the other $50." Mr. Hover said, "All right, you win! If you believe in them that much I'll go for the $550." He sighed. "What else do you want me to do for them?" "Nothing," Mr. Silber smiled, "they'll do the rest."

10

WE HAD A MONTH TO GET READY. WE FOUND A TAILOR who'd make us three suits for only a hundred dollars down. We picked out a beautiful plaid and ordered dinner jackets with black satin lapels and black pants.

I went over the act piece by piece. Our construction was sound. My father and Will would go on, then I'd come out and do the opening with them, we'd do individual dances and then I'd swing into the impressions. I'd open with Frank Sinatra. I could really hook the audience with that one because I could do funny physical bits as well as the voice, so I'd have twice as much going for me. Then I'd do Nat

Cole, Frankie Laine, Mel Tormé, The Ink Spots, Al Hibbler, Vaughn Monroe, and close with Louis Armstrong. He was the only one to end on because it was the strongest impression and it would be hard to follow with another singer. Then I'd switch to movie stars. I'd been using a big cigar as a prop for Edward G. Robinson and it always got a laugh. I wanted a bigger one for a bigger laugh. I found a private cigar maker in downtown L.A. and paid him five dollars to roll me a four-teen-inch cigar.

I'd noticed in Vegas that half of the first impression was wasted because the audience wasn't ready for it. I went through the newspapers looking for a current event on which I might be able to hang a topical joke to use as a bridge be-tween the wild dancing and the impressions so the audience would be settled down and prepared for the quieter stuff.

On the afternoon of the opening we went to the club for rehearsal with the band. The sign out front said "JANIS PAIGE" then, underneath in smaller letters, "The Will Mas-tin Trio."

The stage manager said, "I'll show you where you'll be dressing." We followed him upstairs. "We've only got space for one real dressing room so naturally it goes to the star. The other acts always change up here." We were in the attic where they stored the signs and extra tables. One corner of it was fixed up with a light, a mirror and a clothes tree. The three of us burst out laughing. We wouldn't have cared if it had been a phone booth but it was funny—a part of the glamour of Ciro's the public didn't see.

"By the way," he said, "under no conditions can you take more than two bows. Even if the audience calls you back. It's in Miss Paige's contract."

Dick Stabile, the band leader, also introduced the acts. He told us, "Nobody pays any attention to opening acts here but I'll gag it up a little and get their attention for you."

It was Academy Awards night so there was going to be only one show, at midnight. I had dinner early, then went back to the hotel and took a nap and a long hot bath until finally it was time to go back to the club.

Will said, "You two go on upstairs. I'll be along in a min-ute. I want to look around here a bit."

My father and I went ahead. There was still almost an

hour to kill but we began dressing leisurely. Will came up-stairs at a run. "Well, I've seen it all now." He was out of breath from excitement. "I walked around backstage and took a peep out front and you oughta see what's going on. This place is loaded with the biggest names in the business from Martin and Lewis right on down the line. They all came over from the Academy Awards."

I'd known it was going to be a pretty big opening because Janis Paige was very "in" with the Hollywood group, but I should have realized that with half of Hollywood out on the town Ciro's was the logical place for them to wind up their evening. "What's it like down there, Massey?"

"Elegant! We never played anything like this before, I can tell you that. It's got the French menus and the captains in tails and the customers are dressed to the teeth. This place is about as high class as you can get, and they got the highest class prices, too. I saw one of those menus . . ."

He was still talking but I leaned back in my chair and be-gan picturing it for myself. I could imagine the stars sitting in the audience when we came out. I could hear them applaud-ing us and yelling for more. . . .

There is never a night that a supporting act opens anywhere that he, she, or they don't think, "This is the night. This is the time we hit that stage and the audience won't let us off. They'll stand up and cheer and no act will be able to follow us. Then, tomorrow night *we'll* be the star attraction, the Headliners, and we'll close the show. And from then on, we'll be stars." This is the dream of every supporting act just as every Broadway understudy fancies the night Ethel Merman will be caught in a blizzard in Connecticut and she'll have to go on in her place, and she'll be so great that the critics will cheer "Better than Merman!" and columnists will rush to their papers to report "A star is born!" It happens only once in a thousand openings, to only one out of thousands of performers —just often enough to keep the dream alive in all the others.

But the kind of applause that would make that happen, the kind that was thundering in my imagination couldn't possibly come just from doing a dance or sounding like Jimmy Stewart. There had to be that extra thing, the communication be-tween performer and audience that's so strong he gets right inside of them and they like him personally, they feel for him.

I tried to picture myself in front of the audience, touching the people, manipulating their emotions the way I'd watched Mickey and Frank do over and over again—but how?

My father was dressed and standing against the wall, absorbed in his own thoughts.

"Dad, how do you touch them?"

He looked up and gave me what I'd gotten so many times before, the helpless look, the groping for words and explanations that simply were not his to give and then finally, "Well —you give 'em your best and—well that's all you can do, son."

I was sorry I'd asked and again put him in the position of being unable to come through for me. I nodded like "I guess that's it," but we both knew it wasn't and I leaned back in the chair, wondering, "What *is* it? How do you touch them?"

Will said, "We better go down, now." At the bottom of the stairs, we took a final look at each other. My father reached down and picked a piece of lint off my pants. Then he stood there for a second looking at me, smiling. "You think we're too high class for the room, Poppa?"

As we got backstage I could hear the nightclub sounds: hundreds of forks and knives scraping dinner plates, cups sliding onto saucers, a thousand swirling ice cubes clinking against the sides of glasses, the hiss of soda bottles being opened, the like-no-other-sound of champagne corks popping, the slooshing of the bottles sliding into buckets of ice, cigarette lighters clicking open, hundreds of voices talking and laughing—the place was packed.

We were so nervous we were doing bits with each other to break the tension, the corniest lines in the world. "Hey, Massey, you nervous?"

He shrugged. "I ain't nervous."

"Well, maybe *you* ain't nervous but yo' knees sho' is."

My father asked, "*You* nervous, Poppa?"

"Hell, I ain't nervous 'bout nothin'."

He rolled his eyes. "Well, you better *git* nervous 'cause we's in a *lotta* trouble . . ."

We were lapsing into the deepest Amos 'n' Andy talk, something Negroes do among themselves when they're nervous but happy. Maybe there's a psychological reason behind it, perhaps it makes us feel safe, closer to our roots. I

122

don't know. But there are times when "colored talk" serves the moment as nothing else can.

The musicians were putting our music on their stands. Dick Stabile began our introduction. "Ladies and gentlemen, I think you're going to be knocked out by these guys who are coming on now. I played their music this afternoon and they're something to watch. Here they come . . ." He hit the first few notes of "Dancing Shoes," our opening number. Once again this was *the* important show, it was all the shows we would ever do in our lives. My father and Will moved out into our opening number and they were never better. Eight bars later I joined them and we might have been barefoot on hot sand, our feet weren't on the stage as much as they were in the air. We'd started probably faster than any act this crowd had ever seen and we kept increasing the pace, trying as we never had before. We finished the opening number, and characteristic of colored acts we didn't wait to enjoy the applause before we were off and dancing again, first Will, then my dad and then me. We were fighting for our lives and our frenzy of movement got to the audience from the moment we started until soon it was like they were out of breath trying to keep up with us. The applause was great when my father and Will finished their numbers. Then they stepped back. As I introduced the impressions my speech was perfect. I did Sinatra and they screamed. I went through the rest of the singers, and by the time I finished Satchmo they were pounding the tables so hard I could see the silverware jumping up and down. I switched into the movie stars, first Bogart, then Garfield—suddenly I felt the whole room shifting toward me. They were no longer just sitting back watching, amused. From one second to another they'd become involved with me. They were reacting to everything, catching every inflection, every little move and gesture, concentrating, leaning in as though they wanted to push, to help. I was touching them. It was the most glorious moment I'd ever known— *I was really honest to God touching them.*

We swung into our dances again, never letting them catch up with us or grow tired of anything, switching and changing the pace like broken field runners going the whole hundred yards.

When we finished, after being on for forty minutes, they

wouldn't let us stay off. It was as though they knew something big was happening to us and they wanted to be a part of it. They kept applauding, and began beating on the tables with knives and forks and their fists, screaming for us to come back. My father and Will stood in the wings, hesitating. We'd already taken our two bows but a man with a gun couldn't have held me back. I looked at my father. "To hell with her contract. I ain't gonna miss this for *nobody!!!*" We went out twice more. They kept shouting for an encore. I'd already done every impression I'd ever tried. But we had to do something so I did Jerry Lewis which I had never done before. The sight of a colored Jerry Lewis was the absolute topper. It was *over*. When I heard that scream I knew we'd had it. There was nothing we could do that would top that!

We'd taken eight bows. I was hugging Massey and my dad, half-laughing, half-crying. "I touched them, Dad, I touched them!" He understood. "Yes, Poppa, you touched 'em. And they reached out and touched you, too." He was right. Oh, God, he was right. They really had!

Janis Paige was in the wings waiting to go on to close the show, giving us glares like the world has never seen. She was so upset she sang off key for fifteen minutes. She couldn't even get their attention. It was strictly our night, there was a post-pandemonium atmosphere out there and she was just one girl coming on to sing after three strong, hungry men had just given the show of their lives. No one could have followed us then.

We stayed up until eight o'clock and the three of us went out and bought every newspaper and trade paper that had just come out. We brought them back to Will's room. I turned to Herb Stein's review in the *Hollywood Reporter* and read out loud: "Once in a long time an artist hits town and sends the place on its ear. Such a one is young Sammy Davis, Jr. of the Will Mastin Trio at Ciro's." Paul Coates' column in the *Mirror*: "The surprise sensation of the show was the Will Mastin Trio, a father-uncle-son combination that is the greatest act Hollywood has seen in some months . . . left the audiences begging for more." And *Daily Variety*: "The Will Mastin Trio is a riotous group of Negro song and dance men whose enthusiasm, brightness, and obvious love for show business combine to form an infectious charm which wins the audience in a flash . . . walloping success. . . ."

Will was reading the Los Angeles *Times*. "Listen to this from Walter Ames' column: 'The Will Mastin Trio, featuring dynamic Sammy Davis, Jr., are such show-stoppers at Ciro's that star Janis Paige has relinquished the closing spot to them.' "

It was almost nine o'clock. We called Mr. Silber. "It's true," he said. "I thought you'd be sleeping or I'd have called you. Starting tonight you close the show. It would be impossible to continue the way it was. Naturally she keeps top billing but Hover's putting your name in the same size letters. That's a big concession because her contract guarantees her name to be fifty per cent larger than the supporting act, but it was the only thing to do."

He congratulated each of us. To me he said, "You've earned what's happened and nobody could be happier for you than I am. I know how you guys worked to get to this point. I know how hard it's been."

I was shocked to hear myself saying, "It wasn't that bad." Only a few weeks before we had been in Vegas feeling abused, hurt, and angry. At that time I could have made a list of every bug-infested mattress we'd slept on for ten thousand nights. I knew every heartache, frustration, and pain, every brush-off which had tormented us for twenty-three years. They had scarred deep, and forgetting them seemed as impossible as undoing them. But as we sat in Will's room reading those reviews the novocaine of success had already begun numbing our memories, making the past indistinct until miraculously there were no yesterdays.

A quiet tension filled the dressing room as we got ready. I nudged my father. "Hey, wouldn't it be funny if last night never really happened and *tonight* is the opening?"

As we hit the stage I could feel something going for us that we'd never had before. The audience was presold by word of mouth and the reviews, we weren't starting from scratch any more, we didn't have to get lucky and strike that one moment in a million when you go off like a Roman candle. We had only to confirm what they'd heard, and it's a lot easier

125

to please the public when the experts have already said you're good.

The night before, we'd gotten our strength from sheer desperation. This was still in evidence. We worked with everything we had, as hard, maybe harder but with the added power of knowing we belonged. We weren't trying to kill the ball any more and we gave an absolutely flawless performance.

I was hanging my jacket on a hook in our "dressing room" when I heard someone clearing his throat. Jerry Lewis was banging his fist against the wall. He grinned. "I'd knock on the door if you had one. May I come in?"

"Mr. Lewis! Of course. Please!" I pulled up a chair and almost pushed him into it.

"Don't give me a Mister. I'm a Jerry not a Mister. How can we be friends if we're misters and you'll call me up 'Hello, Mister, let's have dinner tonight.' " He smiled. "I came back because I love the act and if you don't mind I'd like to give you a little advice."

"Mind? My God. Are you kidding? Please do."

He shouted, *"Get outa the business!"* He jumped up and kicked me. "I don't *need* such competition, I don't *want* it, I was doing fine. Who asked you to come along?" I broke up. The idea of him sitting in our ridiculous dressing room and doing bits with me was too much.

After a while he said, "But I really do have a few suggestions. Now listen, you shouldn't hit me in the mouth from what I'll tell you 'cause it's only good I mean you. Okay? Samele, you're a great performer, but you're making some mistakes. I'll tell you what I saw and maybe you'll change a few little shtick, it'll be nice, it'll be better for the act the people should like you even more." He reached into his pocket and took out a wad of notes. "First of all, you talk too good."

My back went up. "That's how I speak. What do you expect me to say, 'Yassuh ladies an' gen'men'? Look, I appreciate your interest, but not all Negroes talk that way . . ."

"Ah hah! You promised you wouldn't make an angry. But I'll forgive you. Just listen to yourself. You don't talk that way now, in here with me. You talk nice, like a regula fella. But I know Englishmen who don't talk as good as you did onstage with such an accent. Sam, people don't go for that English crap, not from you and me."

He'd said, "You and me." He wasn't putting us down as another Negro act that should shuffle around and say, "Yassuh, folks." He was speaking as one performer to another.

"I don't mean you should come on and do Amos and Andy. I just mean you talk *too* good! Let's face it, American you are, but the Duke of Windsor you ain't!"

"I'm not sure I know what you mean."

"Sammy, you walk on and you say, 'Ah, yes, hello there, ladies and gentlemen.' That's an English actor! Forget it. Nobody is gonna like a guy who sings and dances and tells jokes as good as you and who talks that good, too. You want mass appeal! You can't afford to make the average guy feel like he's an illiterate. You've got to bring yourself down. Not colored, but a little less grand . . ." His "Jerry Lewis" character was gone, there was no comic dialect. "When you figure they like you, when you've got them, and they're thinking: 'Hey, this guy's okay, he's like me,' *then* you can switch it and talk good. When they figure you're just a simple kind of a bum, then surprise them with it. But save it, hold it back, let it work for you."

As he spoke I realized I'd been saying things like "Ladies and gentlemen, at this time, with your very kind permission we have some impersonations to offer. We do hope you'll enjoy them." I sounded like a colored Laurence Olivier. In trying to elevate myself I had gone from one extreme to the other. And there was no honesty in it, I wasn't leveling with the audience. It was phony. Luckily I hadn't done enough of it to stifle whatever they saw in me that they liked, but I could see that if I kept it up eventually my personality could become buried beneath an English accent just as surely as it had been buried beneath "Yassuh."

Jerry was pointing out things only another performer could see. Nobody else had ever done this for me. Nobody whose opinion I could respect above my own had ever sat in the audience with a pad on his knee and made notes, trying to help me.

"Y'know something? Tonight you didn't make a single mistake. Not one. Last night—a few, but tonight your performance was letter perfect."

I smiled. "Well, I guess we got lucky."

He was shaking his head. "That's terrible! You've got to make some mistakes on that stage. Sure you know your act perfectly, but you can't have the satisfaction of looking like such a pro. Some things you should make look like they never happened before. The greatest thing that can happen for the guy sitting out front is if he can go home and say, 'Wow, I saw Sammy Davis at Ciro's and did he have his troubles: the mike went dead, the piano fell apart but he kept on performing and he was great.' If he can do that then he feels like he's been a part of something. You've gotta break up every now and then, maybe blow a lyric—something! If you do they'll root for you all the more.

"Also, in the impressions where you use props, like a hat or the big cigar, you've been handing them to your father and your uncle. That's awful. What are they, prop men? Don't hand them your stuff with that gracious 'Thank you, Dad, thank you, Will,' like you're some kind of a big deal and they're your servants. Get your own cigar. Get your own hat. And put them down yourself when you're finished with them."

He was so right. From the audience's point of view, it had to look like "This kid's making his father and his uncle wait on him. What an ingrate! They put him in show business and look how he's using them." The audiences would have to resent it. We'd done it because it kept the pace moving. In the old days it hadn't mattered, but from now on it was a different audience. They were more show-wise, more discerning. In the past no one was ever offended by me handing Will my hat and taking a cigar from my father. Or, had they been?

Jerry said, "In all these things, find a happy medium. Just keep them in mind and you'll know how to do them."

"This is the greatest advice I ever got in my life. I just don't know how to thank you."

He was on his feet, glaring at me. "You wanta thank me? Then like I said in the first place, get outa the business. *That'll* be a thank you." We shook hands and he smiled. "Let's see each other."

Jeff Chandler and Tony Curtis came backstage with Byron Kane, a radio actor I'd known since the Sinatra rehearsals, and as soon as we met it was Instant Pals. They came by almost every night. Tony was dating Janet Leigh who was already a big star, but he was still getting the corny parts in the corny pictures like *The Prince Who Was a Thief* and he'd just changed his name again, from Anthony to Tony. Jeff had been a radio actor but now he was the fair-haired boy at Universal and getting hotter every day. The four of us were together constantly at Byron's apartment or at Jeff's house, playing records and charades, sitting around the pool for hours talking movies, often daydreaming about Tony, Jeff, and me doing one together.

Whenever any of the buddies came in I sent a message to the maître d', "Give me the check for that table. And send over a bottle of champagne." My cut of our $550 minus Mr. Silber's 10 per cent was $165 but by the end of the first week I owed the club $280 for the checks I'd picked up. How Big Time can you get? I didn't care. Money was just around the corner.

I was two weeks behind in my rent at the Sunset Colonial. I dreaded bumping into the manager and getting his withering deadbeats fish-eye, so I was doing some of the world's great sneak-ins and sneak-outs. But one day there was no escaping him. I went straight for him. "I'm sorry I haven't been able to stop by and take care of my bill . . ."

"Mr. Davis. Please! I'm embarrassed that you even mentioned it. I can imagine how busy you've been." He put his arm around my shoulder and walked me to the elevator. "Whenever it's convenient." He winked. "We know you're good for it."

I rode upstairs marveling. "Oh, daddy, what a life this is gonna be! It was slow in coming, but wow."

I was the star of the hotel. People who'd brushed by me a hundred times before now wanted to stop and talk. The shocker was a chick named Mikki something. Whenever I'd passed her in the hall and tried to be civil the best I could get back was frostbite. But a week after the opening I saw her in the lobby and damned if she wasn't maneuvering herself to be standing right where I had to walk, giving me an ear-to-ear and a from head-to-toe—all that was missing was R.S.V.P. I was the same guy she wouldn't look at last week. I had the same face girls had always laughed at, the same broken nose but now that it was in the papers every day it was okay. Fame creates its own standards. A guy who twitches his lips is just another guy with a lip twitch—unless he's Humphrey Bogart. Certainly I was no Bogart. It was only a few days since we'd caught on, but people knew it was happening and already I had begun changing in their eyes.

I ran into her twice the next day. She was tall and had a figure like forget-it, with long legs and shiny golden hair hanging below her shoulders. She looked like she should star in a movie called "Goddess of the Sun" and each time I saw her she all but handed me the key to her room. I smiled politely and ran. I'd have given anything to make a move—anything but "everything." All I needed was a nice little racial scandal to make everything blow up in my face. I had a lot of catching up to do, I wanted wine, women, and swinging by the yard, but the Sun Goddess was too much of a threat to everything yet to come. I'd have my chicks, all right, but I'd get them from downtown. Safe ones.

As I came out of Ciro's a woman handed me a pen and a piece of paper. "Can I have your autograph, Mr. Davis?" I was caught completely off balance, but I wrote something to her and signed my name while she stood there beaming at me. I handed it to her glorying in the moment, trying to act cool. She thanked me and I gave her a little Doug Fairbanks bow. "My pleasure, I assure you."

She squinted at the paper. "I can't read what you wrote here." As I watched her puzzling over my childish scribbling the image of myself as the suave movie-star type shattered.

I took a cab straight to the hotel. I sat at the desk in my room writing "All my best, Sammy Davis, Jr." I wrote it over and over again, working until it was light outside, trying to make something I wouldn't have to be ashamed of.

Our two weeks were up and Herman Hover held us over for six more as the headliners. We moved our things into the star dressing room and our name went up on top out front.

Abe Lastfogel, the head man at the William Morris Agency, one of the real powers in show business, came backstage to see us. "You're doing wonderfully well. It's time for you to have proper representation."

They knew every facet of the business, they knew how to negotiate and they, if anybody, would know how to construct our bookings so that every move we made would be one step closer to the Copa. Will signed with them and immediately their men in cities all over the country began lining up dates for us. Within a week we were set for six months: they got us out of a $750 booking we'd made in Chicago and put us into the Chez Paree, the biggest club there, for $1250 a week; then on the bill with Jackie Miles at the Riviera across the bridge from New York; Buffalo, and a tour with Jack Benny which would bring us back to Los Angeles to be on the Eddie Cantor Colgate Comedy Hour.

We closed Ciro's after eight weeks of excitement and capacity crowds which we alone had attracted. My one regret was that Mama was three thousand miles away and the closest I could bring her to it all was some envelopes of press clippings and a few long-distance phone calls. I could practically see her nodding her head and smiling as she said, "Well, Sammy, you finally got your break like I always knew you would."

But as I thought about it later that wasn't exactly true. The classic fallacy of show business is the statement, "Someday you'll get your break and then it'll be all velvet for you." It's a lovely dream but untrue. You can be ready for your break and not get it or you can get your break and not be ready for it. Nobody could have convinced me I wasn't ready when I came out of the Army. And, playing on the bill with Mickey and with Frank and with Count Basie and Billie Holliday at the Strand, being seen in Vegas and at Slapsie Maxie's—those had all been breaks. But there was no mystery about why we'd gone back into the dirt after each of them. Something had been missing until the night we opened at Ciro's.

I saw, as I never had before, the importance of *everything* that happens on the stage. Everything the audience sees, hears and senses about you contributes toward forming an image which makes the difference between just another performer or somebody with whom the audience becomes involved, somebody they care about.

Most of what I read about us after the opening indicated that the people liked the relationship between my father, Will and me: the two vaudevillians who knew the business backwards and the kid they'd taught it to. They liked the contrast between the old show business and the new. Maybe they also understood our feelings for the business, maybe they caught our desperation to make good—there's no way of knowing all the things which contributed to create the image of us that they liked. Little by little we had changed our clothes, our jokes, our manner—everything. Whatever we were on the stage had evolved through the years until on opening night at Ciro's the combination of circumstances was finally right and it all fell in place, like when the three cherries on a slot machine all come up at once.

11

EVERY HEAD IN THE CANDY STORE TURNED AS I WALKED in. Mr. Peterson put down a sundae he was making and rushed over to wait on me. Apparently Mama had been casually dropping our $1500 salary, and in our neighborhood $1500 a week was more successful than anyone had ever been. I'd never thought about this aspect of success, but I enjoyed the moment. I liked them staring at me like "Gee, he's making it big."

As I was paying for the newspapers I looked up and above the counter I saw my picture, clipped from the *Amsterdam News* and posted on the wall.

"H'lo Sa . . . Mr. Davis."

It was the guy who'd beaten me out of the baseball cards. I hadn't thought about any of those kids in years. He seemed grateful that I remembered him and he called over a couple of his buddies. "This is my friend Sammy Davis, Jr. He used to dance for us right in this store when he was just getting started." I went right along with him, arm around the shoulder and "Yes, we're old pals." I was killing him with kindness, and he knew it, but he couldn't get mad at his old pal, the local celebrity. Maybe he preferred to believe I meant it.

When I left I should have had the traditional empty feeling of pointless triumph. But I'd loved every second of it and I felt just great!

I spread the newspapers on my bed. I'd never seen an ad like it before. It was a letter to the public:

"A young man by the name of Sammy Davis, Jr. will be opening at the Riviera on Thursday. He's not head-lining, and not many people know his name yet, but they will. I think that my many years of presenting the finest acts in show business give me the right to assume that I know talent when I see it, and in my opinion Sammy Davis, Jr. is the most talented, most versatile, and ex-citing young performer to come along in many years . . ."

It was signed by Bill Miller.

It was hot as hell in my bedroom. I opened the window. When I had it halfway up the smell of garbage whacked me in the throat and I remembered. I slammed it down and went into the front room. I wanted to call Marty Mills but we had no phone. I tried to take a bath but there was no hot water. Everything seemed smaller, more overcrowded, shabbier, than it used to be. I looked out the window at a bunch of kids coming down the street and I knew instantly which one's mother worked for the richest family. I stared around me at everything I'd almost forgotten, hating it, yet glad to be re-minded.

I lit a cigarette to help kill the last few minutes before we went on. It seemed as though every performance we had ever done had been driven by fear. At each degree of progress along the way I had felt: "If we can just make it tonight." But then at the next plateau there was a new reason to be afraid. I took a last drag and ground my cigarette hard into the wooden floor. We stood in the wings listening to our in-troduction, waiting for our cue, all but crouched like runners waiting for the gun. My father held up his crossed fingers and we ran on.

They sat forward like we'd pulled a string. By the time the last notes of our music were playing they were shouting and banging spoons against the tables. They were friends and the fighting was over. For tonight.

Jack E. Leonard and Red Buttons, strangers, came to the dressing room. Red said, "We just wanted to say hello and tell you to keep it going—you've got a great act." Fat Jack said, "Yeah, your act is a bitch." He glared at me. "But, if our friendship is to continue you'll have to become a headliner very soon because I need a bigger dressing room to hang around in and I'm not going on a diet just to hang around with you."

I thanked them for coming back. Fat Jack snapped, "It was your pleasure, I assure you." His voice softened. "Just keep swinging this way. You can't miss." He started out the door, blocking it completely, and I heard him growl, "Don't stand there with your arms folded, Ed, or somebody'll bury you." He turned into the corridor and Ed Sullivan stepped in.

When finally the room emptied, we closed the door and the three of us collapsed into chairs. "Do you guys realize: a man sits out front, likes the act, says hello for two minutes and bam! we're on the Ed Sullivan show with millions of people seeing us from coast to coast?"

My father was shaking his head, dazed. "I'll betcha John D. Rockefeller don't make twenty-five hundred dollars in six minutes."

I sat in the dressing room rereading Robert Sylvester's review in the New York *Daily News:* "The best, fastest, and most furious young entertainer to come along in some time is a twenty-six-year-old named Sammy Davis, Jr. Sammy works with his old man and his uncle Will Mastin in the latter's trio at Bill Miller's Riviera. As the old saying goes, God made Sammy as ugly looking as He could and then hit him in the face with a shovel. But the young Samuel doesn't need any beauty because he sure has got everything else. . . ."

I stared at my face in the mirror. I guess I'd gotten used to it.

If I didn't have to stand still in front of the microphone, if I used a hand mike with a long cord, I could keep moving around the stage and dazzle them with so much motion that it would draw their attention away from my face. . . .

That night as we came off my father smacked me on the back. "Hey, Poppa, that's a helluva style you found yourself."

I closed the dressing room door. "Y'know, Dad, Massey, I've been thinking, I've got some ideas, things we need."

Will hung up his coat. "Like what?"

"Well, the first thing is our own conductor."

"Have you any idea what it'd cost to have our own man?"

"Massey, please, hear me out. I've got a lot going for me—I dance, I do jokes, impressions, and I play the instruments, right? If one thing dies I could keep switching until I find the thing that'll entertain them. But I'm wasting my versatility by being tied to a routine, I'm not getting the most mileage out of it if I can't use each thing when it'll work best. Now, if I had my own conductor, a guy who knows the act backwards, then, as soon as I see what I need I'd give him a cue and wham, we'd swing right into what I need *when* I need it. Tonight was the perfect example. When I got to the impressions the people just weren't ready for them."

"Well . . . They hadn't quite settled down as much as would've been best. But once you got started . . ."

"Meanwhile I completely lost the value of the first two or three guys I did. I was dying to switch our order and do the drums in that spot and *then* the impressions. But I was stuck to the way the band had rehearsed it. It's ridiculous! I can't do the same show for a dinner crowd that I do for the hard drinkers. Every audience is different, what's great one night dies the next, so I've got to have the flexibility to give them exactly what they want at that moment. But I can't know what it'll be until I get out there and feel them."

Will put up his hands "Hold on, now, and let's come down to facts. I'm not saying it wouldn't be dandy to have our own man. But a good conductor comes high, maybe four or five hundred a week. We've gotten by all our lives without one. . . ."

"We can't just 'get by' any more. The people aren't going to excuse the rough edges like they did when we were coming up. We're right on the brink of being headliners and if we're gonna get inside then we've gotta come in like we rate it. We need the little touches, the professionalism."

"You said there was a couple of things? What else?"

"A press agent. Now before you tell me I'm crazy, take Buffalo, we've got only two weeks there, right? So, we should have a good man arrive ahead of us with his hands full of our New York reviews—someone like Jess Rand, the kid who works for the press agent here—he should hit every newspaper and radio and TV guy around, setting up interviews and appearances, everything he can. Then I get to town a few days early, I make six or seven stops a day and by the time we open, the papers are full of us."

Will was smiling. "Sammy, you're not crazy. You're just ahead of yourself."

"Massey, let's be honest, take five hundred away from the four thousand we'll be making in Buffalo and you *know* we've lived on a lot less than $3500 a week. Hey, do you realize what a guy like Jess Rand could do with a human interest thing like that? 'The same act that got $40 a week and a meal returns to Harry Altman's Town Casino at $4000 per week just a few years later!' Can't you see it in the papers?"

"I can. But I'd rather see it in the bank. Now's the time for us t'put some aside in case something happens and we don't keep working."

"No! You're dead wrong. Now's the time to put on the pressure and use everything we've got so that nothing *does* happen except us getting bigger."

He was shaking his head, sitting there like an adding machine. I'd made no impression on him at all.

I stood in the wings rooting for Jackie Miles to get big laughs. We were a tough act to follow, particularly for a guy who did his soft, quiet type of humor. The Janis Paige story had spread throughout the industry and plenty of headliners didn't want us on the bill with them. Jackie was tremendously "hot" and easily in a position to tell Bill Miller, "Hey, cut those guys down to twelve minutes. I worked a long time to get where I am. I don't have to work that hard— to follow an act like that!" But we were told that he'd said to Bill Miller, "Give 'em their heads. Let the kid do as much time as he wants."

Jess Rand came backstage with Danny Stradella. He was about my height and he seemed so young that it was hard to imagine him the owner of Danny's Hideaway, a restaurant that was constantly mentioned in the columns as a celebrities' hangout. He was tremendously warm and invited me to come there for dinner. He insisted. "Make it tomorrow night before the show, will you? Bring Jess. He'll show you where it is."

I met Jess at Hanson's drugstore at six o'clock and we took a cab across town toward East 45th Street. He said, "I've got great news, chicky. I set up an interview for you with the Associated Press."

"I'm sorry, Jess. What'd you say?"

"I got you an interview with the Associated Press."

"Sounds great. Does Danny's have a doorman?"

"Sure. What afternoon this week can you make it?"

"Make what?"

"Listen, this is a fantastic break. It'll run in hundreds of papers."

". . . Jess, I'm sorry. I've got some things on my mind. Can we talk about it later? Maybe at dinner?"

"Well, sure . . . anything wrong?"

"No, everything's swinging." We rode a few blocks in silence. "Jess? What's it like inside?"

"Inside what?"

"Danny's."

"Oh. Well, it's sporty—celebrity pictures on the walls, no menus, good food, steaks and Italian, very homey."

"Hey, wouldn't it be a shakeup if Danny forgot he invited us?"

"You kidding?"

"Well, he might've been a little high last night."

"Naah."

The doorman held the door for us. I spotted Danny standing at a little desk. He rushed over and grabbed my hand. "I'm glad you could make it." He walked me to a table in the front corner. A young guy with a cane and the Herbert Marshall walk came over. Danny said, "This is Cliff Cochrane, my press agent." We shook hands and he said, "I hear you're doing great across the river. The whole town's talking about you guys."

A heavy-set, red-faced man was coming straight at me. My stomach tightened. About three feet away, he began smiling.

"Mr. Davis, may I shake your hand? I was at your opening the other night and I never enjoyed anything so much."

I finished my main course and asked for a check. Pete the headwaiter came over. "Compliments of Mr. Danny." On the way out I thanked him but he brushed it off. "Cut it out, willya? Thank *you* for coming in." He put his arm around my shoulders and walked us to the door. "Now, don't be a stranger. Please, I want you to think of this as your home away from home—y'know what I mean?"

Danny and Marty Mills caught the late show that night and drove me back to New York. Marty said, "How about a sandwich?"

The last thing I wanted was to be the cause of an incident somewhere. Especially in front of Danny. He thought of me as a winner. . . .

He was saying "Let's go over to Longchamps, at 59th and Madison. They're open all night. Most of the kids from the shows drop in. We'll have some laughs."

As we reached the East Side I asked them to let me out at 61st Street. "I'll meet you in a little while. There's something I've gotta do."

"We'll wait for you in the car."

"No, please. You guys go ahead. Everything's fine, no problems."

They had to think I was crazy but they dropped me at Fifth Avenue and 61st. I started walking toward a dark building as if I really had something to do there. When they were out of sight I looked for a phone so I could call Longchamps and leave word I couldn't make it. But I was repulsed by the indignity of backing away. It was the defeat of everything I wanted. I killed twenty minutes walking around the block, and headed for the restaurant. At least if it's a turnaway maybe nobody'll see it.

I looked through the plate-glass window. Marty was sitting at the table talking to someone, but his eyes were glued to the entrance. By the time I went through the revolving door he was at my side, leading me to our table. Four showgirls from the Riviera were sitting there with Danny. I pointed to a table for two right next to it. "Let's you and me take this one." I didn't wait for him to answer. He shrugged, not understanding, but he sat with me.

Danny gaped at us. "What the hell are y'doing?"

I gave it a Jack Benny reading. "I *hope* you won't take it personally but I can't sit with those girls. They're only in the chorus and I'm a *star!* I mean, you understand—" The girls laughed and I played it like I had something private to tell Marty and somehow I got lucky and Danny wasn't insulted. Or, maybe he understood.

In the middle of our spot on the Sullivan show the coaxial cable broke for the first time in television history and every screen in America was blacked out. Only the sound remained on. We didn't find out about it until we were off the air. My father and Will, everybody, treated it like it was a disaster. But to me it seemed that it had worked *for* us. Ed Sullivan told us he'd book us again, which was gravy, and the next day's papers were full of stories about what had happened, they ran my picture captioned "The Mystery Guest," "The Invisible Man?" and "The Little Man Who Wasn't There," and people all over the country were saying, "Some guy was on Ed Sullivan's program when the picture went off and I'd have sworn it was James Cagney and Humphrey Bogart talking to Edward G. Robinson. You never heard anything like it. . . ." It drew more attention and caused more talk about us than there could possibly have been if everything had gone smoothly.

Passing the musicians' rehearsal room between shows, I was stopped by the sound of somebody noodling on the clarinet, real music, creative, sensitive, a man daydreaming through a horn. It was Morty Stevens. A guy I'd thought of as just a hack in a show band was a musician when he wasn't tied down to corny arrangements of popular songs. He saw me and stopped, and self-consciously began drying the reed.

I sat down next to him. "You ever do any arrangements? I mean original stuff? I've been thinking about doing some straight singing in the act. If I could get the right arrangement of 'Birth of the Blues' it would work beautifully for me. You want to take a shot at it?"

"And how! I'd love to hear you do some straight singing. You do everybody else and you sound better than they do."

"Crazy. Here's the way I picture doing it—I don't want to tell you how to arrange . . ."

"Go ahead."

"Well, the thing is I don't want to stand there like 'Hey, look at me, I'm a singer.' First of all that's not what people come to see me for, and secondly I don't kid myself I'm about to be a Frank Sinatra. So I've got to do it like no straight singer would. I want the freedom to move with it, to drop in a few dance steps if I feel I need them, maybe switch to impressions in the chorus, and instead of bluesy like Harry Richman does it, I want it to be loud enough and exciting enough to shatter the glassware."

Three days later he played it for me on the piano in the rehearsal room, and I couldn't believe what I was hearing. He was such a quiet guy but the arrangement went like a mad man. As I listened he suddenly became somebody I wanted to know better. The one thing I really respected was talent and he had it coming out of his ears. He'd taken my basic ideas of how I wanted to perform it and developed it with a complete understanding of my voice and my kind of performing, tailoring it for me so that I could really go with it.

My father sailed his hat across the dressing room onto the hook. "Wow, what a number! Hell, they was still stuck to the ceiling five minutes after you'd done it."

Will nodded. "That's a great piece of material."

"Yeah, but it's too powerful to do in the middle of the act. I was left hanging with stuff that wasn't nearly strong enough to follow it. I'll have the band change the order around. It'll be fantastic for the closing. Damn! If we'd had our own conductor tonight I'd have cut off the last five minutes and gone off on all that excitement! Massey, we've *got* to get our own man! We can't put it off any longer."

"We can put it off 'til we've got the money to pay for one."

"We've gotta *find* the money for this. Take it out of my piece, I don't care where it comes from, I'm going to talk to Morty Stevens about coming with us."

"*Morty Stevens?* What's he ever done but one song?"

"He hasn't done much but I think he's good. Really good. Okay, so he doesn't have the experience of an older guy but that also means I won't be up against: 'Well, this is how it's always been done.'"

Will almost laughed. "He ain't no conductor. Anyway, this is a colored act. We don't need no white people in it."

I jumped out of my chair. "Whattya mean this is a colored act? It's not a colored act or a white act. It's just a plain 'act.'"

Will was out of his chair, too. "I'm the boss of this act and what I say goes and don't you forget it! This is a colored act and it's gonna stay a colored act until I die."

"For God's sake, Will, what's the difference? If he's good he's good. That's all we should think about."

"Don't tell me what I should think about. My thinking kept you in food and clothes all your life and it got us up to $1500 a week and more to follow. . . ."

I had to get out of there. I wandered around the parking lot and kicked a few tires. He had sixty years of one-way thinking and nothing I could say was going to change him.

He was sitting in his chair, staring at the wall. He looked up as I came in and I put out my hand. "I'm sorry, Massey."

"I'm sorry, too, Sammy. I guess sometimes I lose track of how you're a full-grown man. I don't intend for it to come out like I'm the boss and you gotta do it my way. You've a right to your say same as Big Sam and me."

Milton Berle was at center ringside, watching, appraising, as performers will. Occasionally his head would nod like he was saying to himself, "Yeah, that's good," and I put extra steam into everything I did, because as a performer his little nods or the lack of them told me far more than a layman's applause.

I dressed quickly, knowing that he'd give us the courtesy of stopping back to say hello.

After we'd spoken about the performance for a few minutes, he said, "Hey, you talk pretty good!" But he didn't mean it entirely as a compliment. In going for articulation I had slipped into the British thing again, but by this time I was practically the Prince of Wales and he was warning me against it. There was no excuse for making the same mistake again.

Berle lit a cigar. "Lemme suggest something to you.

Y'know the line you did when the drunk heckled you? The way you're doing it now, it's 'If you're ever in California, I hope you'll come by my house and take some drowning lessons in my pool.' It's a cute line, but you're not getting the most out of it. Switch it around. Frame it as a straight invitation, like, 'If you're ever in California, sir, I do hope you'll come by and use my pool.' A guy has been heckling you and you say something nice to him? This confuses the audience, and they're waiting. *Now* you hit him with the punch line: 'I'd love to give you some drowning lessons!' The element of surprise has to get you a bigger laugh. Also, the joke phrase is 'drowning lessons' so let those be the last words. You can't follow them with 'in my pool,' or you're stepping on your own laugh. You force them to pause to listen and if they can't laugh the second they want to you'll lose part of it."

"I'm not about to argue with *you* on how to do a line."

"If you do I'll break your arm. There's one other thing. When you get a guy who starts throwing lines at you like that, don't go for him right away. Ignore him the first couple of times. Let the audience become disgusted with him so that by the time you finally belt him they'll be rooting for you and you almost can't miss."

He stood up to leave and we shook hands. "I can't thank you enough, Mr. Berle—"

"The name is Milton. Listen, I'm going down to Lindy's. You feel like a sandwich?"

Danny had been coming by every night. He was waiting for me in his car with Marty and Cliff. "You guys better go without me tonight. I'm sorry, but Milton Berle asked me to join him at Lindy's."

Marty gave me a wink. Danny said, "Hey, that's pretty good."

I sighed, "Yes, it's a little sit-around-and-have-a-sandwich. Just us stars."

He smiled. "I'll give you a star—right between the eyes. See you tomorrow at dinner."

The doorman at Lindy's spotted Berle's limousine pulling up, rushed to the curb, opened the door and I stepped out. Milton gestured for me to go ahead of him and I spun through the revolving door. He introduced me to the guys who'd been waiting for him, and made a place for me next to him. Everybody at the table focused attention on me. "Caught the act," "tremendous," "where do you play after the Riviera?" They were press agents, personal managers, comedy writers, all Broadway pros who were on close terms with a lot of stars and they knew I was just a "kid who's moving up" but they treated me almost as if I were already there, giving me far more attention and acceptance than I really rated. It seemed that as much as the world loves a winner it reaches out all the more for a contender.

Suddenly Berle stood up and shouted at me. "Okay, out! out! I don't need you to steal my audience."

As we left there an hour later Milton offered me a lift but the world was beautiful and I felt like walking in it. I headed downtown, crossed 51st Street and as I passed the Capitol Theater, I thought about Frank. I'd read that he was in town and I was wondering where he was staying and how I could get in touch with him, when I looked across the street and there he was. I started to run after him and call out to him but I stopped, my arm in the air. He was slowly walking down Broadway with no hat on and his collar up—and not a soul was paying attention to him. This was the man who only a few years ago had tied up traffic all over Times Square. Thousands of people had been stepping all over each other trying to get a look at him. Now the same man was walking down the same street and nobody gave a damn. God, how could it happen?

I thought maybe he'd rather not see me. I couldn't take my eyes off him, walking the streets, alone, an ordinary Joe who'd been a giant. He was fighting to make it back up again but he was doing that by himself, too. The "friends" were gone with all the presents and the money he'd given them. Nobody was helping him. He was walking slowly—a hundred people must have passed him in those few minutes—dozens of them must have been fans who'd screamed for him only a few years ago, but now nobody knew who he was or cared. I was dying to run over to him, but I felt it would be an intrusion. Or, maybe I felt too much for him to want to see him this way.

I didn't want to walk any more.

I stood in the wings watching Jack Benny's performance

every night. I think he's the only man in the world who can do nothing but gaze at the people and make them laugh. His legendary genius for timing was the next thing to hypnosis. He'd mold a theater full of people into a little ball and hold them in his hand. And when he was ready—only when he was ready, he would open his hand and as much as say, "Okay, now you laugh."

Almost always, they roared. But by not setting himself up like "Here comes the joke, folks," by carefully not preparing them for anything hilarious, if a joke didn't work he was never left in the position of having to do desperation lines like "I know you're out there 'cause I can hear you breathing" or, "But, seriously, folks . . ."

I saw my mistake in presenting the impressions by saying, "Ladies and gentlemen, Jimmy Cagney." If on a particular night I didn't sound exactly like Jimmy Cagney I was in trouble. Without intending to, I'd been creating a "watch this!" atmosphere, setting myself up as Charley Impressionist and I had to be great or I was dead.

I tried it differently. I said, "These are just in fun, they're satirical impressions of people I dig," implying that I was just doing them for laughs rather than "Look how much I sound or look like somebody." And I could feel it paying off before I'd finished the first one. No one knows better than I the impressions I do very well, the ones I do badly and the ones which are just passing. But now when I did one that was just passing, it got laughs instead of polite applause, and when I threw a good one the audience screamed. The whole answer was in how I set it up in their minds and the impressions began working better for me than ever before.

The most influential people in the industry throughout the world are Jack's close friends and he made a point of seeing to it that I was at dinner with him or in his dressing room to meet them. "These are the people you'll be dealing with soon, and I want you to know them as friends, first."

Being with Benny was invaluable, but there was also relative obscurity in the shadow of a performer of his magnitude. There was certainly no shame, in being second to him. He was a "King" and just being with him offered a glory of its own, but it came a year too late and by the time the tour dropped us in Los Angeles I was eager for us to be out on our own again.

At dress rehearsal the director said, "We're running three minutes over, Eddie." I began thinking which of our numbers to cut. Mr. Cantor glanced at the list of songs and dances. "Kill my second number."

Before we went on the air he said, "After your act you and I'll have some fun together onstage, for three minutes."

My father, Will, and I took our bows. They went off and I stayed on to join Mr. Cantor. They were still applauding when he came on. He hugged me and took a handkerchief from his pocket and blotted my face, beaming at me like a proud father. We hadn't planned what we were going to do for our three minutes so I just followed his lead, and he was such a great pro that we could have ad-libbed another ten minutes with no trouble at all.

In his dressing room after the show I noticed a gold chain with a gold capsule attached to it. He saw me examining it. "That's a mezuzah, Sammy, a holy Hebrew charm. We attach them to the doorposts of our homes or wear them for good luck, good health, and happiness. There's a piece of parchment rolled up inside and on it are twenty-two lines of Deuteronomy, a prayer for the protection of the home."

"Do you have to be Jewish to wear one?"

"I'm sure the sentiment is what counts. I don't suppose God cares very much which floor we do our shopping on, just as long as we go to His store. Keep that, Sammy. I'd like you to have it."

I opened my shirt and hung it around my neck. "Is there anything I'm supposed to do with it—I mean a special prayer?"

"Only what's in your heart. In our religion we're not confined to many rituals. That's a basic part of our belief—that every man should have the freedom to face God in his own way."

Frank called me at the Sunset Colonial. "Bogie's having some people over. I want you to meet him."

The butler escorted us to the living room. Bogart nodded to Frank the way you do to a close friend and shook hands with me. "Glad to see you. Come on in." He took me over to

Lauren Bacall. "This is my wife."

She smiled. "I'm glad to meet you. I saw you on the Cantor show and you're marvelous."

Bogart said, "Come on and meet the people." He began steering me around the room. "Mr. Davis, Mr. Tracy. This is the kid I saw on television, Spence, he's been doin' me and if he keeps it up he's gonna get a knuckle sandwich . . . Say hello to the Grants . . . Mr. and Mrs. Stewart . . . Miss Hepburn . . . Mr. and Mrs. Gable . . . Miss Garland . . . okay, now make yourself at home."

I tried to seem at ease and at home drinking a coke, listening to the conversations, but I found myself gazing like an idiot. There was something so incredible about being in a private home, watching four people casually chatting like anybody would at a party—except they were Jimmy Stewart, Katherine Hepburn, Spencer Tracy and Judy Garland.

I couldn't take my eyes off Frank. The dignity and the guts of the man! By all standards of show business success he was as down as anybody could be, yet, as he moved around in this incredible group of movie giants, he stood as tall as any of them.

He'd starred in half a dozen big pictures that had been completely built around him, and he'd lost it all. But, he had the strength to start all over again completely from scratch. He'd just signed to make *From Here to Eternity*, accepting a secondary role, without any singing, ready to try for a whole new career as an actor. Being down in the business hadn't licked him as an individual. Maybe the whole world was saying he'd had it, but he didn't hear them or care. He was a total individual, measuring himself against nothing but his own standard.

I went into a coffee shop for breakfast. The counterman smiled "Afternoon, Mr. Davis." I didn't know him. He began sponging the counter in front of me, even though it had seemed spotless. "I saw you on the Eddie Cantor show. You were real fine." A man two seats away from me raised his coffee cup, "Enjoyed you a lot. The whole family did."

In over twenty years of playing nightclubs and theaters nobody had ever before recognized me, cold, like that. But the right presentation on just one television show had done it.

Will was waiting for me at the Morris office. The head of

the nightclub department said, "I've got great news for you. Sam Bramson just called from the New York office. You're hot as a pistol in Pittsburgh. They're completely sold out for your entire engagement. The club started getting calls the night of the Cantor show and they had to close reservations in forty-eight hours. That show was fantastic for you."

"Do you think we'll get another shot?"

"We're almost sure of it. He was tremendously pleased with you."

I stopped at a newsstand and bought a pile of papers and movie magazines. I picked up my mail at the front desk and as I started toward the elevator the door slid open and there was the Sun Goddess in a pair of white sharkskin slacks that fit like they'd been painted on. The elevator closed behind her and she was coming straight for me, smiling. The best thing was to keep it light—do jokes with her. I shook my head. "You could be arrested for looking like that." *Exactly* the wrong thing to say.

Her smile expanded. "Well, you *can* be friendly."

Oh God, that voice! She made Marilyn Monroe sound like a bus driver. Where the hell was the damned elevator?

"I saw you on television the other night. You were wonderful."

The elevator opened and I did one of those great suave walkaways, crashing right into a guy who was coming out. I rolled off of him, fell against the edge of the door and stumbled into the elevator like a graceful drunk, mumbling, "Well, s'long, nice t'have met you." As the door closed she was gaping at me like I was out of my mind.

I stared out the window thinking about the rules of society. If she were colored and gave me openings like that—but she isn't. What'd I need her for? There was nothing about her that was any better than most of the girls I was making it with.

I started going through my mail to get my mind off her. I opened a manila envelope from NBC and took out a stack of letters and a note: "Dear Mr. Davis, Enclosed please find letters addressed to you in care of the Colgate Comedy Hour. We will forward any further viewer mail."

I cleared the bed of everything but my fan mail, stretched out comfortably, lit a cigarette and ceremoniously

147

opened the first letter. "Dear lousy nigger, keep your filthy paws off Eddie Cantor he may be a jew but at least he is white and dont come from africa where you should go back to I hope I hope I hope. I wont use that lousy stinking toothpaste no more for fear maybe the like of you has touched it. What is dirt like you doing on our good American earth anyway?" There was no signature.

I fell back on the pillow, soaking wet. How could someone who'd never met me hate me so much that he'd take the trouble to write this? Why?

I opened a few others. The same. I threw the letters in a corner. All I wanted to do was forget them and the bastards who wrote them. I was an idiot to let them bother me. The hell with them.

I turned the pages of a fan magazine trying to lose myself in the Hollywood Hills, Bel Air, and Beverly Hills, trying to imagine myself owning one of those beautiful homes with a swimming pool and a convertible parked in the driveway. I stopped at a picture of a girl stretched out on a diving board. The shape was unmistakable. The Sun Goddess. I should have known that anyone who looked like her could only be out here trying to get into the movies. I thought of the big hellos she'd given me in the lobby and her incredulous stare as the elevator door closed. I really *must* be out of my mind. I turned down *that?* For what? To stay in good with people who call me nigger?

I felt stupid. I hated myself for thinking I could stand in the middle of the road without getting hit by a truck. How did I wind up there, anyway? What the hell had happened to me since I got out of the Army? I'm the guy who wasn't going to let anybody tell me how to live. But they'd started telling me and I'd listened instead of spitting in their eyes the way I should have. I'd played it safe. I wanted to be a star, so I'd as much as made a deal: "You let me 'make it' and I'll play the game." But suddenly I had an 8 x 10 glossy of the guys I'd made the deal with, whose rules I was following. I could never satisfy the people I'd been trying to appease. How could I not offend them by what I do when my very existence was offensive to them? There could be no end to it. Don't be seen at the same tables with white people. Stay away from white women. Don't touch Eddie Cantor. What next? I wanted to make it, but if that was the price, it was too high. If I'd just thought it out, I'd have known it couldn't work. It was spelled out for me right in the Bible. "What shall it profit a man if he shall gain the world and lose his own soul?" I'd sold my dignity. Worse still, I'd sold it to people who never believed I had any. And it was no less humiliating that I was the only one who knew what I had done.

I looked for her last name in the magazine. I could feel my hand getting moist on the phone while I waited for the operator to connect me with her room. What the hell was I going to say? She definitely must think I'm a lunatic by now . . .

"Hello?"

"Uh—hi! This is Sammy Davis, Jr. . . ."

"Well, *hello!*"

"I didn't think you'd be in your room!"

"Oh? Is that why you called?"

"Look, I know you must think I'm some sort of a nut, but —well, y'see, I was in a big hurry before . . ."

"I got that impression."

"What I called about is, well—I thought it would be nice if . . ."

"I can't hear a word you're saying, Sammy. We must have a very bad connection. I'm in 418, why don't you stop by and tell me?"

I walked slowly down the hall toward her room. I stopped a few feet away to make sure the coast was clear. I could feel the skin on my face tightening. I knocked lightly. There was no answer. I knocked again, hard!

I heard her telling me, "The door is open."

The guy at the Morris office said, "There's been an avalanche of 'em. To the station, to Cantor, the sponsor . . ." The bundles of letters covered his desk. I looked at one, addressed to Eddie Cantor: "Where do you get off wiping that little coon's face with the same handkerchief you'd put on a good, clean, white, American face?"

"Well, I guess this finishes us with the Cantor show."

The Morris guy said, "It's a damned shame. But the sponsors don't want bad public opinion. Even from bigots. They've warned Cantor that if anything like this happens again they'll take him off the air."

"What about other shows?"

He shook his head, grimly sympathetic. "We might as well face the facts. These things don't stay secret very long."

There was nothing more to talk about. My father asked, "Y'want a little lunch, Poppa?"

"No, Dad. I don't feel like anything. You and Massey go ahead." I left them and took a cab downtown.

The driver was staring at me in his mirror. When he stopped at a light he turned around for a better look. "I *thought* I saw you on television." He smiled, "You're okay."

"Thanks." We were approaching a movie theater. "Let me out here, will you, please?"

When I got back to the hotel there were five phone messages from the Morris office. I used the booth in the lobby.

"We've been trying to reach you all afternoon. Where've you been?"

"I don't know. I went to a movie. What's wrong?"

"Cantor called, Cantor himself. He wants to negotiate a contract for you to be on all the rest of his Colgate shows for the season. I guess he's not a guy that pushes easily. God knows what went on between him and the sponsor but what counts is that he's got three shows left for the year and you're on all of them at three thousand each."

Long after I'd hung up I was still sitting in the phone booth. The man was a pro before I was born and he knew exactly what he was doing when he told me, "We'll have some fun on the stage together," but he'd done it anyway because he wanted to point me up, obviously not worrying that some people might not like it.

How could you figure it? Here there were people going out of their way to kick me in the face with nothing to gain by doing it, then along comes a man like Eddie Cantor with everything to lose, but he deals himself into my fight and says, "They'll have to kick me, too."

The sign on the hotel said "No Niggers—No Dogs." I squeezed the prongs of the shade together, pulled it down and leaned back in my Pullman seat. Everybody'd assured us: "Miami Beach? You'll have no problems there. It's like New York."

Sure!

But the date was serving my purpose: it was the height of the season, every celebrity from New York was in Miami Beach and if you were a top act then this is where you should be playing.

Arthur Silber, Jr., had come along as company. He put down his magazine and glanced out of his window. "Hey, we're coming to a station. I wonder where we are."

I raised my shade and looked out. "We're in a lotta trouble, that's where we are."

He grinned. "Whattya mean *we*, colored boy?"

I did an elaborate lean-back and pointed out the window to a sign: "Everybody Welcome but The Nigger and The Jew."

He swallowed hard. "Well, yeah, Kingfish, like you was saying, we's in a lotta trouble."

Morty Stevens pushed open the door of the club car and did the railroad walk down the length of it: legs apart for balance, hands out to steady himself on the chairs he passed. The train lurched and dropped him into the seat next to me. "You ready to start talking about the show?"

"Baby, I've been sitting right here. While you were stuffing yourself in the dining car the only conductor I saw was a guy who asked me for a ticket."

"Gee, I'm sorry. I didn't realize . . ."

"Hey, hold it. I was just doing bits with you."

We worked out physical cues, like a fast tapping of my foot for "Birth of the Blues" and "handlebar cues," the handlebar being the type of talk I'd start doing with the audience. As soon as Morty'd hear the first few words he'd know which number I wanted.

He asked, "What'd you think of the new arrangement I did?"

"I dug it like Walter Pidgeon dug Greer Garson." He began smiling with pleasure. "But I have one question: how do I stand on a stage and sing 'How Are Things In Gloccamorra?' "

He blinked, aware for the first time of the ludicrous picture. "Well—I just thought of the music and I knew it would be great for your voice . . ."

"Yeah, baby, but what about this little brown suit I wear? You think I need a guy to stand up and yell, 'Hey, folks, it's a colored elf!' "

"I never thought about it like that."

"Baby, Old Sam has come to the rescue and saved your arrangement from oblivion by a master stroke of savoir faire. I can take the curse off me coming on like Charley Irish by doing an introduction like: 'Ladies and gentlemen, I've been requested to do a certain song but before I even tell you what it is I want you to know I'm not too thrilled about doing it. This song wasn't exactly written with me in mind, but a customer asked for it and I want to please, so I hope you'll bear with me.' Something like that."

"Hey, that's great. Then the handlebar'll be when you start copping out."

"I'll *start* to sing it but if I get into trouble you may hear Barry Fitzgerald finishing it.

"Look, for years I've been forced to go down a straight track even when I saw the bridge was out. But now that I've got you it's like all of a sudden there's a steering wheel: I see trouble? wham, I fling you the cue and off we go in a different direction. So let's develop antennae for each other, a private radar going between us. Let's get these cues memorized so good that when you're sleeping if the guy in the next room starts tapping his foot you'll start conducting 'Birth of the Blues.'"

The redcaps passed us by, grabbing for white people's luggage. We watched one straining under a load of suitcases, followed by the people who owned it, a thick woman in a frilly cotton dress that was fighting to reach around her, and a man in a shiny blue suit with brown shoes. My father sighed, "Trouble with some colored people is they're plain prejudiced. Now that redcap's gonna catch himself a white two-bits and he ain't never gonna know it coulda been a colored five-spot."

Will said, "No point waiting all day. We'll carry our own."

Arthur, Morty, and I were bringing up the rear. As we neared the end of the platform a heavy set cab driver rushed past us, bumped into Will from behind, and knocked the suitcases out of his hands. "Outa my way, niggah." Will stood motionless, struggling to regain his shattered dignity. I lunged after the cab driver but a hand caught my arm. Will was looking into my eyes. "That won't get us nothing, Sammy. But, thank you." He let go of my arm and picked up his bags.

There was a big sign on the wall of the station building: "WELCOME TO MIAMI." Inside, to the left and right, were the waiting rooms: "WHITE," "COLORED."

The Lord Calvert was a first-rate, second-class hotel in the heart of the Negro section of the city of Miami. Eddie Compadre, one of the bosses of the Beachcomber, looked around my room. "Everything okay?"

"Yeah, sure, it's fine. Everything's crazy."

He handed me a car key and pointed out the window to a bright red, brand-new Corvette in the parking lot. "That's yours as long as you're here. Only white cabs can cross the bridge from Miami onto the Beach and they aren't allowed to ride colored guys." He was telling it to me fast, like a man jumping into cold water. "Here, I got you these cards from the Police Department. There's a curfew on the Beach for all colored people and they can arrest you unless you show 'em this card which explains you got a right 'cause you're working there. . . ."

"But there's a desegregation law!"

He looked at me, sympatico. "Not if they don't wanta enforce it. But you'll be in the club most of the time anyway and naturally the place is yours."

The Beachcomber was owned by Sophie Tucker and Harry Richman but it was run for them by Eddie and two other professional club operators. Harry Richman MC'd the shows and I met him backstage as I was coming in on opening night. He said, "I hear you do a great job with 'Birth of the Blues.' Give 'em hell, cousin. That song was good to me."

Arthur came into the dressing room and handed me a newspaper. "There's a guy peddling this in front of the club." The headline was "NIGGER ON THE BEACH" and the story was titled, "Stamp Out Sammy Davis, Jr." It said, "The black people are an un-American disease which threatens to spread all over the Beach . . ."

"Baby, do me a favor, will you? Go out front and see what Eddie can do about this."

It was a six-page hate-sheet and as I sat down to read it my father said quietly, "You're gonna wrinkle your pants, Poppa. No point upsettin' yourself over fools like that, son. C'mon, we gotta go on now, anyway." The chorus kids and the back-

153

stage guys were giving me sympathy looks like "How can he possibly do a show now?"

I did three encores. Arthur was waiting in the dressing room when we got off. "Well, the guy is gone, but who do you think chased him? Only Milton Berle. I'm walking outside with Eddie when Berle gets out of a car. He hears the guy shouting 'Nigger on the Beach,' walks over, takes one look at the headline and smashes the guy in the mouth, a shot that knocks him right off his feet. The papers go flying in the air and Berle is kicking them into a mud hole. The guy gets up and runs like a thief. Berle! He was beautiful. Everybody starts applauding but he didn't even look around."

Eddie came back after the second show. "Whattya say we bum around with some of the guys? We'll have some laughs." I knew he was trying to make me feel that I didn't have to run back to the hotel. He took me to a few jazz spots where I was tuned in half to the music and half to the people around us, looking for a raised eyebrow, listening for a comment. Nobody said anything but they didn't have to, the pressure was there.

I fell into bed, exhausted, and lay staring into the darkness above me until I became aware of the ceiling turning white with the first rays of morning sun.

I woke up around two o'clock and went down to the pool area. The hotel was jumping: Nat Cole and Sugar Ray Robinson were there and the ball clubs were in town for winter training so the Campanellas and Jackie Robinson were there, too. Arthur was in the swimming pool riding Roy Campanella's kids around on his shoulders. When Arthur and Monty had checked in with us there'd been a few remarks and some suspicious looks, but now nobody seemed to be giving them a second thought.

I was enjoying the crowd of chicks around me until one of them sighed, wistfully, "Gee, I sure wish I could see your show." I was embarrassed to be playing a club that wouldn't let me in either if I weren't starring there, and I would never do it again, but I wasn't sorry. Every important date like Miami Beach was bringing me one step closer to the top. Someday they'd want me so badly that I'd be in a position to demand they open the doors to everybody or I won't play.

I made a date with her for that night and we hit all the colored clubs, had laughs, champagne, and everywhere we went the MC introduced me from the stage. I got back to the room around six in the morning, dead tired, but unable to sleep any better than the night before. I kept telling myself what a swinging night it had been, but it was no good, I'd had a million laughs but no fun. It should have been, and it would have been if it wasn't being forced down my throat.

Eddie asked me to join him every night. Sometimes I went with him, sometimes I went back to the Calvert. It didn't matter. There was a hole in the laughs at each end.

Will closed the dressing room door. "I'm calling a meeting of the Trio. Eddie wants us back next season. He's offering . . ."

"The next time I'm playing Miami Beach, is never! Not 'til they let colored people come in as customers. I don't care how much the money is, I don't want it!"

He was smiling. "I already told him no." He waved away my apology. "I'm only telling you so you can enjoy that we're in a position to pick and choose. And, as long as we're all in the mood you'll be glad to hear I turned down another Vegas deal. They're up to $7500, but they still won't give us rooms in the hotel."

"They must be crazy wanting us that badly but expecting us to live in a slum."

"You won't believe the nerve they got. They know we won't go live in Westside any more, so they came up with a compromise, a new thing some of the colored acts have been taking." He was shaking his head incredulously. "They offered us three first-class fully-equipped trailers parked on the hotel grounds."

"Did the Morris office say anything about the Copa?"

"No. Jules Podell who owns the Copa doesn't move fast. He isn't ready to come up with an offer yet."

It only takes 336 hours for two weeks to end. I finished our last show with "Birth of the Blues" as an encore. Harry Richman was calling me back for another bow when someone yelled, "Now *you* sing it, Harry."

He shook his head. "Friends . . . you and I have had a lot of good times through all the years we've been together, and

I'm not reluctant to say that it's been a lot of years. I remember the day somewhere along the line a man came to me and handed me a piece of paper, a song, and I had no way of knowing then that those thirty-two bars of music would turn out to be the best friend I ever had." He put his arm around my shoulder. "For the last two weeks I've been watching this youngster putting all of his heart and soul into what he's been giving you and I've been trying to think of a way to let him know what an oldtimer like me feels when he sees someone like him come along. The only way I have is to give him something I love. So I'm turning 'Birth of the Blues' over to my young friend, Sammy Davis, Jr. He's going to go a long way and I want him to take my song along with him. I'll never sing it again, Sammy. It's yours and I hope it's as good to you as it's been to me."

I knew that at that moment he meant it, just as I knew that the next day when I was gone he'd be singing it again. But I appreciated it for the gorgeous piece of show business shmaltz that it was.

I packed my dressing room things and Arthur helped me load them into the Corvette. When we'd squeezed all my stuff in he appraised the remaining space. "Even *you* can't fit in there now."

"Then, baby, how about if you run them back to the hotel and come back and get me? I can use the time to say goodbye to Eddie and some of the guys inside."

By four o'clock the bartender had locked up the liquor and everybody was gone except me and the night man who was making his last rounds. I called Arthur at the hotel but his room didn't answer. At a quarter to five, I said, "There's no point in your staying to lock up. I can wait outside. He's sure to be along any minute."

I sat on the curb trying to remember exactly what I'd said to Arthur. He couldn't possibly have misunderstood. He must have had a flat or run out of gas or something. A taxi was cruising up the avenue. I stood up and waved to him. He slowed down and called out, "Sorry. Can't ride you." Another cab slowed down but as he got a closer look he stepped on the gas. I watched his tail-lights disappear. There was another cab coming. I shouted, "I'll pay you double. I have no other way to get home. . . ."

I started walking. It must have been fifteen minutes before I saw another one. I had to try again. I rushed out into the street and held my arm up. He stopped about ten feet in front of me. I was suddenly blinded by a huge beam of light. A man ordered, "Stand right where you are." He touched my chest, waistband and back pockets. "What're you up to? You know you've got no right being here."

"I'm Sammy Davis, Jr." He had one hand resting on the butt of his gun. "I have a card . . ."

"Let's see it." I moved my hand slowly to my inside pocket and drew my wallet out. He looked at the card. "Well why're you sneaking around here at *this* hour?"

"I've been waiting for my friend. He was supposed to pick me up. I don't know what happened to him."

He took his hand off the gun and led me over to the car. He leaned in and told his partner, "He's in the show. Says he's waiting for somebody to pick him up."

"Well, what're we gonna do with him? He can't stay here."

"Officer, if you'll call Eddie Compa—"

"Easy, boy. We'll handle this."

The other one said, "What're we wasting our time for? Get him in the car. We'll leave him at the bus stop."

They put me between them. As we drove, the first one talked past me to the other. "I think he's the one my kid saw on television."

"What's he do?"

"I guess he tap dances. I know my kid likes him, and I think I read somewhere that he gets five thousand smackers a week for being here."

"Where'd you read bull like that?"

"One of the papers. I don't remember."

"You didn't read that, you dreamed it. Five thousand a week! Hell! *I'd* get up and do a dance for that much."

They were pulling over to a street corner. "Officer, couldn't you take me somewhere so I could call my friend?"

"No need for that. A bus'll be along in an hour or so. But don't you go walking nowhere or we'll have to lock you up. Just sit on that bench 'til the bus comes and everything'll be fine."

I walked over to the bench and sat down. They didn't

drive away. One of them waved his arm out the window. "Hey, c'mere a minute, boy."

I walked to the car. He handed me a slip of paper and a pencil.

"Put your autograph on here for my kid."

As they drove away, I lit a match and looked at my watch. It was 5:20. An hour and a quarter later it was light out and the bus stopped at the corner.

Mama sat in a big easy chair in my dressing room at the Apollo Theater on 125th Street, holding court as she did every day for dozens of people from our neighborhood. I sat on the arm of her chair while the women stood around giggling, trying to think of things to say. "I knew you when your grandma used to wheel you in a carriage, Sammy. We'd say, 'Here come Rosa Davis and her Jesus.'" She smiled at Mama. "Guess you always knew he'd turn out to be something, didn't you, Rosa?" Mama gave her a silent, blasé nod which as much as said, "You see I did, so why do you ask such foolish questions?"

Sometimes I stayed off in a corner so I could just enjoy watching her. I knew she was bursting with happiness, but she just sat there, arms folded, her mink jacket draped over the back of her chair, nodding graciously, occasionally smiling and accepting the attention she was getting with all the dignity of a queen completely at home on a throne.

I'd taken a room at The America on West 47th Street, and on my way uptown one morning I left the cab a block early so I could stand across the street from the theater, looking at the long line of people waiting to buy tickets for our early show. A truck went by carrying a billboard for *The Barefoot Contessa*. As hot as we were, *that* would be the capper. *Ava Gardner*, in person, on 125th Street. I went back to the dressing room and looked up the phone number of the Drake Hotel.

I looked out at the jam-packed theater. "Ladies and gentlemen, I'd like you to meet a lady who took the trouble to come up here from downtown. This lady is the brightest light in all of Hollywood . . ." They were looking around, sensing it was going to be someone big. I kept building the suspense. "She is in town to publicize her newest motion picture, *The Bare-*

foot Contessa . . ." Then the buzzing really started and they were turning back and forth with question-mark looks, having mental arguments with themselves, like, "He can't mean Ava Gardner. It must be someone else in the picture . . ." "Well, who else could it be?" "Hell, this cat ain't about t'get no Ava Gardner to come uptown—is he?" I kept building it, and every word was like I was pumping air into a balloon. When they were all but leaning out of their seats I paused and laid it on them: "Ladies and gentlemen, Miss *Ava Gardner!"*

There was utter stillness. The Love Goddess of the World was walking toward me, a smile on her face, diamonds in her hair, swathed in a skin-tight gown which was not just revealing, but elegant—and at the same time so sexy it was frightening.

The audience started whistling and shouting. She put her arm around my waist and they exploded, stamping and jumping up and down in their seats until I could actually feel the theater rocking! Never before had a star of this magnitude come to Harlem and they were going out of their minds, and I was thinking, "I can die right now because I ain't *never* gonna see an audience this excited again!"

Ava was smiling as cool as ice cream, knowing what this would mean to me, playing it right to the hilt for me with her arm still around my waist, best-of-friends style.

I finally had to put up my hands for quiet but it took a full five minutes before they settled down enough for Ava to say, "I can't tell you how wonderful it is to be here, and how grateful I am for your very generous reception. I know that we share a mutual respect for this great entertainer who so kindly invited me to come here. Incidentally, I'm in a picture called *The Barefoot Contessa* and if you don't mind, I'd love to take my shoes off . . ." She kicked them off and that started it all over again. When they quieted down she spoke for a few more minutes, waved good-bye and did one of those tippy-toe walks off on the balls of her feet. Every eye in the place was watching her very feminine departure and I summed up what everybody was thinking. "Well—if you're gonna be a girl, *be a girl!"*

She was waiting in my dressing room with her escort, William B. Williams, and a guy from United Artists. "Ava, I can't tell you how grateful I am. You wanta talk about making somebody a big man?"

William B. asked, "How about a little drink?"

The street outside the stage door was entirely blocked with people standing on stoops, on cars and literally climbing up lamp posts for a look at her. With the help of twenty policemen who'd rushed over on a riot call, we were finally able to get through to her limousine.

We had a drink at the Shalimar, a nearby bar. They were going on to Birdland and asked me to join them but I knew that word of this evening had already spread all over Harlem and I wanted to stick around and take some bows. I went over to the Baby Grand and gorged myself on admiration.

Jess Rand, who'd been working for us since before Miami, called me at the hotel, excited. "Sam, the editors at *Our World* heard about Ava Gardner coming up to the Apollo and they said if you can get her to pose for a picture with you they'll use it for the cover of their Christmas issue. They want you dressed up like Santa Claus standing near her while she sits in a chair with a pencil like she's making up a Christmas list. Her studio wants to build her in the Negro market, so they're writing a by-line story for her to okay called 'Why I Dig Sammy Davis, Jr.'—it goes into why she thinks you're such a great performer, and all that kinda jazz."

"Well, if the studio wants it then why don't *they* ask her?"

"Chicky, they're tickled silly she's making the p.a. tour to promote the picture and they're not asking any extra favors. But they figure if it came from you it would be like a personal thing. . . ."

She was waiting for us in her suite. A press agent from United Artists neutralized me with the Santa Claus suit and two photographers took pictures for twenty minutes. When we were ready to leave I thanked her. "But you don't wanta give me that autographed picture you promised me at least a year ago, right?"

She laughed. "I only have those glossies the studio sends out. But we can take a picture together right now if you like."

We posed for a few shots of us talking together. The guy from United Artists happened to be standing so that half of him was sure to be in the picture but I didn't ask him to move away, I felt enough like Charley Fan already. When the photographer was through I told him, "Baby, lemme have that roll of film, will you?"

"I'll develop it for you."

"Well, look, please be careful. Don't let it get into the wrong hands. It could make trouble for her."

"I'll process these shots myself. Nobody'll even see them."

I felt foolish. Here I was telling another Negro to be careful, as if he didn't understand.

Will, my father, and I went up to Mama's to say good-bye. Nathan Crawford was there but he was a different Nathan. There was no drunk act, no laughs. His face lit up when he saw us but a minute later he was down in the dumps. When he left the room my father asked, "Mama, what's wrong with Nat?"

"He's been laid off his job, Sam."

"But he was foreman!"

"Well, he got to be an *old* foreman so they fired him six months ago and he can't find work."

When he came back my father took out his wallet. "Look, Nat, I been keepin' track of the money you been lendin' Mama all these years and now that we're doin' good I'd like t'give you a thousand down on it. I can't give you all we owe you, not right off . . ."

"No, Sam, that money wasn't a loan. But seeing as how you're doing big and meeting so many people, well, maybe you know somewhere I could get a job?"

My father snapped his fingers. "Hell yes. Us. Now that we're startin' to build we need a good all-around man like you to help us."

"Well, I *could* look after your clothes and things for the show . . ."

Will smiled. "How much time you need to pack?"

"Ten minutes."

"Grab a cab to your place on the expense account. We'll be by for you in half an hour."

His steps on the wooden staircase sounded like a kid running a stick against iron bars. We looked down to the street and saw him hurrying out of the building, waving both hands to stop a passing cab. He jumped in, stuck his head out the window, looked up at us and waved. The old smile was back.

Mama was pleased. I pulled her over to the couch and sat down next to her. "I've got something special to tell you. Do you remember that place we used to listen to on the radio? The one Dad and I used to go downtown to look at all the time?"

"You mean where they wouldn't let you in to see Frank Sinatra?"

"That's the one. The Copacabana. Well, we're coming back to New York in one month and we're opening there."

She didn't let me down. Her face expressed all the "of course" I'd hoped it would. Then, just the faintest doubt. "You're really going to be working there?"

"*Starring* there. Will signed a contract today. For five thousand a week. We got in on April first as the headliners! The top act! This is the beginning, Mama. Once we make it at the Copa—from then on we're on our way and there ain't nothing can stop us. You'll come out to California with us, and we'll have a house of our own . . . we'll be so big that everybody'll treat us good . . . we're really going to have everything."

12

I Sat At A Table On The Upper Level Of The Copacabana. A hard light from two large, bare bulbs illuminated the room which was a mass of plain wooden tables with chairs stacked on top of them. A man was pushing a vacuum cleaner between the tables, and another was washing the mirrored walls of the staircase. I ran my hand over the unfinished wood table top. I wasn't surprised that the Copa was just a nightclub, but that I'd never before thought of it as one. All these years it had been an intangible, a place without definition. I'd feared and lived in awe of it but now being there to work, seeing it without its illusion-making white table cloths, its shiny black ash trays, the silver, the glassware, and the beautiful people, it was just another room where people come to be entertained. Okay, it was *the* club and they were *the* people but still they were only people.

Morty was running through our opening number with the band. They were playing it well—loud and flashy the way it was supposed to be. I listened carefully to music I'd heard a thousand times but suddenly I didn't like it. It was jarring me. I disliked what it was saying.

When they finished the number, I walked over to Morty. "Baby, can I talk to you for a minute?" He gave the guys a break and we sat down at a table. "Morty, I want to change the opening number."

"Not for tomorrow night?"

"I'm sorry. I know it's a hell of a thing to ask at the last minute, but please don't fight me on it. I don't care if I have to pay ten guys to stay up all night copying new music—I can't use that opening number."

"But what's wrong? I don't understand. What would you rather have?"

"I don't know. I only know that I don't want to come running onto this stage tomorrow night the way we always have. I don't want to come on with panting and puffing and fighting for my life like 'Is this good enough, folks?' I want to do something that no Negro dance act has ever done before. From now on I'm going to *walk* onto the stage."

I waited for him to say something, hoping I wouldn't have to draw a picture, to explain, ". . . with dignity. I'm a Headliner. I want to walk on like a gentleman."

He was looking past me, thinking. Then he said, "There's a number from *Street Scene*. It's soft, New Yorky, and it has an importance to it." He hummed it.

"That's perfect. Start off with twelve bars of what you were just rehearsing, to get their attention, then drop into *Street Scene* and I'll walk on."

"I'll ask the guys to ad-lib it right now. See if you like the way it sounds."

As I sat there listening to it I felt like a Headliner.

My father and I left our hotel at six-thirty Thursday night and I told the cab driver, "The Copacabana." As we turned off Madison Avenue into 60th Street I said, "Driver, stop on the other side of the street." My dad and I got out and walked over to our old doorway. I didn't have to explain what I was doing. He could appreciate the corny "show business" mood of the moment. We were five or six hours earlier than we used to be, and it was ten years later. My father was staring across the street and back through the years as I was. I remembered the hundred times he'd said, "If we're supposed to play it, we'll play it." I remembered Buddy saying, "You'll dance on their tables someday." I remembered the doorman's face when he was chasing me away, and the captains with their "This way, *Sir*." I tried to remember something pleasant about those years, but it seemed that the first real happiness to come out of all that time was this ten-minute period when I stood there looking back on it.

My father put his arm around my shoulder and we walked across the street.

People were pouring into the dressing room, grabbing for my hand, reaching out to smack me on the back. "Tremendous!" "Great opening." "You were fantastic." But their words were shrouded by what I knew to be true. We hadn't made it. We'd stayed on for an hour and twenty minutes and I'd never tried harder in my life, I'd thrown everything I had at them, I'd dug down deeper than ever but I hadn't been able to find that extra half ounce that lifts the show off the ground. They'd given us strong applause, but they'd only been thanking us for a good, solid performance. They hadn't been cheering us for a great one.

People were filling the room, smiling, shouting how well we'd done, but I couldn't focus on their faces or listen to what they were saying. All I could hear was the big hollow where the applause had ended just below the level I had hoped for. I'd blown it. I had wanted to explode them through the roof with my performance but I hadn't done it.

Our dressing room was a suite in the Hotel Fourteen above the Copa. I was taking my shirt off in the bedroom when Sam Bramson came in with some other men from the Morris office. "You were great, Sammy. They were calling for more even after you left." I looked into their eyes as they continued praising our performance and I could see they meant it. Sam patted me on the shoulder. "Get some rest before the next show." I was grateful to him for that. I could have listened all night if it had been true or if I thought they could convince me I was wrong, but nobody knew better than I exactly how well I'd done. They closed the door behind them and I fell on the bed doing cop-outs to myself: it was the first time in a new room, I was nervous, it was a lousy audience, the music wasn't right. But the music was perfect and there's no such thing as a bad audience if there's a great performance. And what if it was a new room? I'm supposed to be a pro.

I heard the door open and Jess Rand whisper, "You sleeping, chicky?" I kept my eyes closed until I heard him shut the door softly behind him.

I went over every move I'd made, trying to understand what had gone wrong. It could be only one thing: I'd run scared and tried to kill the ball. I'd been out for blood and I'd stood offstage waiting for my cue, thinking, "I'm gonna give them a performance like the world has never seen." I'd reached so deep and desperately and belted so hard, I'd been so involved with making my performance letter perfect, that I all but forgot the audience. I never created a relationship with them. It was inexcusable. For years I had known the importance of touching the audience and I had finally started doing it. Now, when it counted more than ever—I hadn't done it.

I had one more chance. The top people in the business always waited for the second show. If I could just get across to *them* . . . but I couldn't remember what it feels like to touch the people. Or how to do it. I'd never really known how. I could control the rest of my performance, but this was nothing I could try to do, it was something intangible that happened by itself between me and the audience. What if it never happens again?

The door opened. "You sleepin', Poppa?"

"No, Dad. C'mon in."

He handed me a slip of paper. "Ronnie, the maître d' downstairs just sent up this list of celebrities that's here for the second show, in case you wants t'introduce 'em. This way you won't leave nobody out."

I looked at the first few names, Milton Berle, Red Buttons, Jackie Miles, Eddie Fisher. . . . Just what I need. I crumpled it up. "Dad, this is very efficient, but where the hell would I get off asking people like this to stand up and take a bow? Maybe for the next opening. If there ever is one."

"Whattya mean if there ever is one?"

"Nothing, Dad. Just talk. Anybody in the other room?"

"No, they all cleared out."

I went into the living room and poured a coke. Will was rattling around like I was. "Well, Massey, this is the big one. . . ." I was hoping for support from his steadfast attitude that it was just another show, but he nodded, "Sure is."

I went back into the bedroom and sat on the bed. I turned on the television set and tried to get involved in a movie. After a while I noticed Will getting dressed. I looked at my watch. Page and Bray, the opening dance act, were about to go on. Then there'd be a production number, then Mary Small, then another production number, then us. I had about an hour, but I started dressing so I could be downstairs early. Maybe another feel of the room would help.

Jules Podell was standing near the cash register in the kitchen. He beckoned to me and I walked over.

"Have a drink, kid."

"Thanks, Mr. Podell. I'll have a coke."

His eyes narrowed. "Kid, I said have a drink! It'll do you good." He rapped the bar hard with his heavy star-sapphire ring. "Bring us two scotches." He didn't even look up to see if the bartender was there. He knew he would be. Two shot glasses were placed in front of us and filled. Mr. Podell raised his. "Good luck."

I reached for mine. He growled. "What the hell are you shaking about?"

"Well, you know, opening night nerves, I guess. . . ."

"What's there to be nervous about? You've *got* the job!" I couldn't believe my ears but damned if he wasn't yelling at me. "What the hell do you think I hire? Amateurs? If you didn't belong here, you wouldn't be here. Do you think you'd be starring at the Copacabana if you were a bum! Let me tell you something, kid. Don't worry about them out there. The hell with 'em. The only one you gotta worry about is me. And my contract with you says you're a *star!*" He shrugged and threw out his hands. "So what's there to be nervous

166

about?" Then, his eyes, which had looked like two steel balls, softened, his jaw relaxed, his face lit up with an angelic smile and his voice was like a kid on his first date asking his girl, "Will y'have another drink?"

The first one had gone down so easily I didn't even feel it, but one was enough and he didn't push me for a second one. I heard applause. The last production number had ended. Morty was probably already out there and Nathan would be setting up the drums and putting my dancing shoes under the piano. Mr. Podell put out his hand. He was rough and gruff and hard as nails, yet he'd shown untold warmth and understanding in those few minutes.

I walked over to my father and Will. We hugged each other. None of us spoke—we'd said it all a hundred times in the last few weeks and there was nothing left to say.

We stood at the top of the three steps leading toward the stage. I watched a man squeezing himself between tables, hurrying to get back to his seat. The tables all had large cards with our names and pictures on them. The stage was dark. I closed my mind to everything.

The announcer was saying, "Ladies and Gentlemen, the Copacabana proudly presents: *The Will Mastin Trio . . .*" Morty brought the band in on the button, stinging the audience with loud, sharp notes, the stage lights came up full, my father and Will slapped the stage with their opening steps and stood back exactly on beat as Morty stopped the music dead. Every sound and movement in the room stopped with it. He let the absolute silence hang in the air for a full two seconds, he dropped into "Street Scene" and the announcer said, "Featuring *Sammy Davis, Jr.*" The audience was turning around, looking, anticipating, applauding in welcome. I waited for three bars—and I walked onto the stage.

The time I was onstage might have been a minute or an hour or my lifetime, it was as unreal, as immeasurable as a dream which covers a year but takes only seconds to happen. There were no clocks in the world, no tomorrows, no yesterdays. I was welded to the emotions of the audience. Suddenly the bond between us was snapped by a tentative crackling of applause answered by a sharp burst from across the room. Another picked it up and it began spreading, gaining urgency, ripping through the stillness like something wild breaking loose, rolling toward me with such force that I couldn't hear the music playing or the words I was singing—only that monumental roar growing and growing and finally wrapping itself around me, penetrating until it filled every inch of my being.

My head fell to my chest. My arms hung limp at my sides. When I could look up I saw a wall of people rising all around us; table by table they were getting to their feet, standing and applauding us. I was unable to feel my feet on the floor or the fingers I knew I was digging into my palms, or hear anything except one vast, magnificent roar that went on and on and on. I looked at my father and Will and the tears were pouring out of their eyes as they were from mine. After more than twenty years of performing together this was the climax, the ultimate payoff. I lost count of the bows we took and the encores we did before I was stumbling offstage, exhausted, stunned, crying for joy.

Mr. Podell had me by the arm, half-leading, half-carrying me toward the kitchen, waving to my father and Will to follow. The whole kitchen staff in aprons, the waiters, the bus boys, over a hundred people, gathered around us. Mr. Podell led them in three cheers and said, "From now on, Sammy, you wear the Copa Bonnet."

I heard my voice saying, "Thanks, boss," and it startled me. I'd never called any man boss. Then he was walking me back to the elevator. "Y'see what I told you? There's no amateurs headlining at the Copa." He gave me an affectionate shot on the back that flung me into the elevator and almost flattened me. I looked back in time to see him beaming like an angel as the doors closed.

The hall to our dressing room was jammed with people I'd never even met, waiting in line to get in. Jess Rand cleared an aisle through them for me. My father came rushing out of the bedroom. "Earl Wilson wants five minutes with you—he's in the other room. And Danny Stradella said come down to the Lounge soon as we're dressed 'cause he's throwing a party for us." The phone was ringing. I heard Jess saying, "You'll have to call back. He just got offstage and he can't talk to anybody. . . ."

As I walked into the Lounge a captain came straight for me. "Right this way, Sammy." He cleared an aisle for me through the crowd. Someone touched me on the arm. "Sam-

my, will you sign this for me, please?" "My pleasure, ma'am."
. . . "Sammy, I met you in Miami. I'm a friend of Eddie C."
"Nice to see you again, sir." The captain came back for me.
"Please, folks, let him through." . . . "Great show, Sammy.
Listen, my daughter's too shy to ask, but would you sign this
menu for her?" The captain fought his way back to me. "This
way, Mr. Davis." When we finally made it to the table he
shrugged. "I'm sorry. I tried to bail you out."

"Don't give it a thought, baby. Can't brush the paying
customers." Danny's table covered the entire length of the
room and was loaded down with bottles of liquor and champagne. I leaned over to my father. "Would you believe that it
just took me twenty minutes to walk across this room?"

I searched my pockets for a cigarette but I'd left them upstairs. A captain said, "I'll send the girl right over, Mr.
Davis." She appeared instantly, opened them, offered one to
me, and put the rest of the pack on the table. . . . She knows
I'm a star and I haven't got time to open my own cigarettes
any more. Crazy! I handed her a ten. "Keep it, darling." At
once a match flared and a flaming lighter materialized from
behind me: a waiter and a captain were competing for my
cigarette.

A captain was standing near Mama, waiting for her order.
When he came to me I handed him a ten. He was surprised.
"Thank you, Mr. Davis." I smiled. Don't thank me, baby.
You're one of a thousand lousy things that drove me so hard
that I'm sitting here now and you're taking Mama's order. "Are
you sure I can't bring you something? Maybe a little soup?"

"Bring him a steak!" The captain nodded and hurried
away. Mr. Podell was beaming. "You've gotta keep up your
strength, kid." The quartet on the bandstand started playing
"Birth of the Blues," dedicating it to me. A woman came
by. "Can I have your autograph, Sammy?" A waiter put a
steak in front of me. I signed the menu she'd handed me.
"Sammy, my children are going to get a big kick out of this.
They're big fans of yours." "Thank you, ma'am. Give them
my best, please." I reached for my fork and knife but someone
else was waiting. My father was winking at me, smiling. They
were surrounding me, holding out papers and pens. Danny
pushed his way through the crowd. "Hey, give him a break.

169

He's tired. He just did two shows. Let'm eat his meal."
"That's okay, Danny. Thanks." I reached for another pen.

At 3:30 I thought: If I got up and left now—that would be a class move.

As I walked toward the door, the band hit "Birth of the Blues" and everybody started applauding me. I turned, waved, and went through the door.

"Taxi, Mr. Davis?" The doorman whistled for a cab and rushed to open its door for me. I gave him a ten. He tipped his hat. "Good night, Mr. Davis." And looking to see that my feet were safely inside, closed the door as though it were made entirely of glass.

As the cab pulled away I reached for a cigarette and was aware that for the first time all evening there was no one there trying to light it for me. I leaned back in the seat thinking about the standing ovation—the sight and the sound of it. I closed my eyes and concentrated, hoping I could feel like I was still in the middle of it all. I could remember the faces and the sound of the applause, but I couldn't feel it any more.

As we approached the America, the only things moving were my cab and a cop walking slowly from door to door trying the locks. There was nobody in the lobby except the night man behind the desk. I looked into my box. Empty.

I opened the door to my room and turned on the light— took one step inside, turned off the light, stepped back into the hall, and closed the door.

Waiting for the elevator I tried to think of an excuse I could give for coming back to the Copa. I unstrapped my wristwatch and slipped it into my pocket. I rang for the elevator again. It's a definite back-to-the-party-to-find-my-watch and I'll let 'em talk me into staying for a cup of coffee. Then I can bring Danny and some of the guys back here. I must have been out of my mind. These Star bits are great, but I'm not about to spend my opening night alone.

I caught a cab cruising up the street. "Baby, the Copacaboo. And I'll double the fare if I make my plane. And don't worry about the traffic lights, just stop when they're red 'cause the commissioner's a pal of mine."

The Copa was dark! The driver said, "I had a feeling they'd

170

be closed. They gotta close at the dot of four. All the ginmills do."

"Then, swing around the corner to Longchamps on Madison and 59th."

"I'll save you the trip. They don't stay open late no more. I had a fare there just the other night."

"Well—look, start driving over toward Times Square. I'll let you know where to stop." The cab headed downtown, past Lindy's. Closed. "Boy, it's like New York's become a ghost town."

He nodded. "Yeah, everybody goes to sleep early these days. I figure it's the taxes. People have to work harder for a living. . . ."

I got out at 42nd Street and walked west. I passed a movie that looked good but the box office was closed. There was an usher standing outside wearing a red uniform jacket with gold braid and epaulets, and wrinkled gray tweed pants.

"I thought these theaters stayed open all night."

"Only 'til four o'clock. Say, aren't you Sammy Davis, Jr.?"

"Yes."

"That's what I thought."

We stood there staring at each other for a minute. I walked a few blocks, stopped for a hamburger and walked back to the hotel.

Daylight was just beginning to show. I tried the television set but it was too early. I dropped my coat and tie on the bed and looked out the window. A garbage truck was coming down the street. I lit a cigarette and watched the men emptying trash cans into the back of it.

I covered my head with the pillow to block out the sound of the phone but then I made the mistake of listening to hear if it was still ringing.

"It's one o'clock, Mr. Davis."

"Mmmmmmmm . . . call me back in five minutes, will you?"

"Okay. Congratulations about last night. The papers say you were fabulous."

I sat up. "Thanks. Will you send them up? All of them. And see if I can get some coffee and a sweet roll. But have him bring the papers first."

171

After I'd read and absorbed every word of the reviews, I called Will's room. "Massey? You see the papers, yet?"

"We couldn't ask for anything more, could we?"

"They're fantastic! Listen, I wanted to speak to you last night but it got a little wild. The light cues weren't picked up on the split second and it hurt some of the laughs. I think the only way we're going to get what we want is by having our own man."

"Well, the truth is we could use a man to do that and to handle a lot of other things, too—transportation, props, setting up. I think I know just the man we oughta get. Big John Hopkins. The fella who used to be Nat Cole's road manager. I'll take care of it."

I smiled, remembering the dates we'd played on the bill with Nat, how John always needled me for standing in the wings watching Nat work. It was always: "Bet you wish you could sing like him, huh?" and I'd say "John, one of these days I'll be a star and you'll be working for *me*."

Will's voice brought me back to the present. The all-business tone was gone. "Mose Gastin? How's it feel being a star?"

As I hung up I shifted my eyes from the cardboard coffee cup to the waxed paper the Danish had come in, to the wooden spoon I'd used to stir my coffee, to the open closet half-filled with unexciting suits, empty wire hangers, a dozen or so ties lumped together on the single hook. To the right of the newspaper reviews a hole in the gray blanket had been mended with white thread, the wallpaper across the room had buckled, probably from the heat of the uncovered radiator. I was laughing out loud. I *didn't* feel like a star, but I sure was going to.

I leafed through the classified directory to "Hotels." Abruptly I was aware of being colored. I skimmed the list. The Warwick. They catered to a lot of show people, it was a first-class hotel, good location. I wrote the number on a piece of paper, "Circle 7-2700."

I opened the window and waited for a gust of air to grope its way in. I sat down at the phone and stared at my hand on the receiver . . . there's only one way to find out. I lifted the phone and gave the number to the operator.

172

"This is Sammy Davis, Jr. Do you have a suite available for me? For about four weeks."

I went to Will's room, told him I was moving to the Warwick, got a fistful of cash and hit the stores.

I glanced at the bolts of fabric along the wall of Cye Martin's shop. He saw me and rushed from the back. "Sammy, that show you did last night—I never saw anything like it. I mean—what can I tell you?"

"Thanks. Look, baby, I'd like to see Rocco. I've got an idea I want to go over with him."

Rocco was cutting the shoulder of a jacket. "Oh? You're not going to stop when a star comes in? You won't put down the scissors, right?"

He took one last snip and put it down. "Mr. Davis, how are you? What can I do for you?"

"I want you to make me some suits with three buttons down the front, a center vent . . ."

"But we're making the two button Hollywood lounge suit with side vents. Nobody's wearing the three button suits any more."

"I don't care about that. I'd like to have three button suits with center vents."

When I'd chosen the fabrics I asked Cye, "How long does it take to make a suit?"

"I can have these for you in—three weeks."

"No, what I want to know is, how long does the process take? I mean the actual cutting and sewing. How many hours?"

"Oh. Well, it takes maybe eight hours for a fitting to be ready, then after that there are corrections . . . figure another twenty hours to make the finished garment."

"But in my case we don't need a fitting 'cause he's got my pattern perfect from the last time, right? Fine. Then, today is Friday so that means I can have five suits by Wednesday, right?"

"Sammy! I couldn't begin to do it in less than two weeks. The men go home after eight hours."

"I'll pay them to stay overtime."

"Bubbula, be patient. Can't you wait?"

"No. I've waited all my life. I'm through waiting."

"Well, how about if I give you three on Wednesday?"

"Give me at least five on Wednesday and the rest by Saturday."

"Okay." He was mopping his brow. "It can't be done but I'll do it if I have to glue 'em together."

"Cye, you're one of the great men of our time. Now don't let me down, baby. Get them to me on Wednesday at the Warwick Hotel."

I stood outside Sulka, sizing up the marble front and the elegant window displays. A distinguished looking man came out, a maroon box under his arm. I pushed the door open.

A salesman smiled warmly. "Mr. Davis! I'm one of your greatest admirers. What may I show you?"

"Everything."

"Splendid." I followed him to the tie department and he handed me a basket. "Just drop your selections in here."

"Why, thank you. Well, here we go gathering nuts in May . . ." I picked out a few ties. "I love the quality of these but I wish they weren't quite so wide."

"Why don't you let me take you upstairs, show you our silks and make them to order for you? There's no extra charge and that way you'll have them exactly the length and width you'd like." He smiled and led me to the elevator. "While we're upstairs I'll show you our robes and pajamas."

"Excellent. Do you by any chance have pajamas that're cut a little slim? I'd love to avoid the balloony pants."

"We can easily make them to your specifications."

"You mean with a fitting? For pajamas? *Marvelous*. And while we're at it, let's do something a little different. How about a nice double-breasted pajama, cut exactly like a suit, except no pockets in the pants. . . ."

The clerk at Alfred Dunhill of London, Ltd., lifted the large silver lighter gently off the glass shelf. "We call it the 'Standard Unique.' It's a fine lighter, sir."

"I love it. I'll take two of them, please. And may I see those cigarette boxes . . . and that pipe with the curved stem. Yes, that's the one. A bit like Sherlock Holmes, isn't it? I'll take that. And will you show me that set over there, the one with a pipe for each day of the week. Charming idea. One can never grow tired of the same pipe that way. Can one? Now what tobacco would you recommend for me as a starter?"

Big John Hopkins was in the dressing room with Will

and Nathan when I got there. "Mr. Davis," he laughed, "I believe you're the gentleman who called for a road manager. Now I've worked for some very fine acts like Nat 'King' Cole, Lionel Hamp . . ."

I wanted to play it cool but I couldn't. "Well? Didn't I say you'd be working for me someday?"

John roared like a laughing lion, picked me up like I was a glass of water and swung me around in the air. "You were right, Boss! And I'm glad I'm here to see it." He put me down and shook his head. "What's been happening to you! Good God Almighty! Did you see where Lee Mortimer called you a miracle?" He took a newspaper clipping from his pocket.

"John, you're working for a very big star now. I mean—really, I couldn't possibly begin to read *everything* that's written about me."

He laughed in my face. "Hell, you can't con me with that bored jazz. You musta already read it. I knew you when your little bottom was hangin' out and it ain't been that long since then."

When I came back between shows a vaguely familiar looking man, carrying a little black suitcase, was waiting for me. "Sammy, my name is George Unger and I'm glad to meet you. I've been around show business all my life and I never saw a performer like you." He opened the combination lock on the suitcase and began taking out platinum and gold watches, diamond rings, gold cigarette cases . . . "Whattya like, Sammy?"

Now I placed him. He sold jewelry to a lot of show people and I seemed to remember him in Frank's dressing room at the Capitol. He kept pulling things out of the suitcase. I picked up a heavy gold money clip with a twenty-dollar gold piece mounted on it.

"Y'like that?"

"Yeah, it's pretty crazy. How much is . . ."

"Put it in your pocket."

"But how much?"

"What're you worrying about? Put it in your pocket." He moved around the room giving away gold chains and key rings to everyone there.

"Are you kidding with all this? Look, George, I appreciate the gesture, but I'd really rather pay."

"Will you stop it, please? Now cut it out or you'll embarrass me."

I put the money clip in my pocket. "Okay. It's ridiculous but I'd never want to embarrass a nut who's trying to give me a present." I browsed through some of his things. "I'm in the market for a good watch."

He showed me a Patek Philipe, then a platinum Vacheron-Constantin. "Here. Look at this one if you can stand it. It's the thinnest watch in the world. Go to a jewelry store and price the same watch at $1150. It's yours for nine hundred."

"I'll take it. Can I pay you at the end of the week?"

"No! You can't pay me 'til the end of the year. Maybe not even 'til *next* year."

"Now wait a minute, you've gotta be kidding."

He threw his hands in the air. "What is it with you? I'm making statements of fact and you're asking me am I kidding. Now be a good fellow. You like something? Take it! You got any presents you have to buy people? Take 'em now. If you don't see 'em here, tell me what you want and I'll bring 'em around. I've got 'em at the store. And stop annoying me about money."

"George, you're out of your mind but if that's how you want to play, it's okay with me. I dig this kind of a game. Listen, do you have a diamond ring . . . a stone about this big, set in platinum or white gold?"

He reached into the suitcase. "You mean something like this?"

I stood up and held it under the light of a table lamp, turning it slightly, watching the sparks flash from its facets, remembering the ritual that took place every time we'd gone to Bert Jonas' office, hearing my father's words echoing back through the years: "One of these days I'm gonna have me one just like that, Bert. . . ."

Unger was saying, "Try it on."

I swirled my bathrobe like a cape, and flourished Will's gold-headed cane like a sword at Unger. I held the ring high. "So, Richelieu . . . you believed your traitorous intrigue, your treacherous theft of the Queen's eleventh diamond stud would prevent her attendance at His Majesty's celebration? You hoped to cause a royal rift, eh? But, foul fool, you are foiled again for I shall return the missing diamond to Her

Majesty and within moments she will make her appearance at
the Royal Ball for all of France to see. Your villainy has failed.
Once again power has slipped through your fingers and I give
you your life only because it will amuse Her Majesty to wit-
ness you choking to death on your own traitorous laughter."

"Richelieu?" Unger was gaping at me. "What Richelieu?
I'm a happy Hungarian trying to make a living. Will you try
on the ring, please?"

I sat down on the couch. "No, baby. It's for somebody else.
Be sure to put it in a nice box, will you?"

"Sure."

"Hey, listen. One more thing. Have you got a solid gold
pen? With a heavy point? Something I could use for signing
autographs?"

Standing at a window in my suite at the Warwick, looking
out over the city, I felt as though I were in a scene from a
John Garfield movie.

I opened the ribbon on the Dunhill box. The lighters were
in flannel bags. I set one on the coffee table and put the other
in the bedroom on my night table. I distributed the cigarette
boxes, set the pipes up in the bedroom, and started on the
Sulka boxes.

Wearing a pair of maroon silk pajamas with white piping,
the matching robe and black velvet slippers, I sat down at the
phone and lit my Saturday pipe, waiting for Room Service to
answer. "Good morning. This is Sammy Davis, Jr. I'd like to
order some breakfast. . . ."

Morty Stevens called me late in the afternoon.

"Baby, I hope you've got something very important to
say. You interrupted me right in the middle of putting
away my gold garters. Now if you have any class at all you'll
get off the phone and be over here in fifteen minutes."

He walked in and blinked at the sight of me.

"Just a little something Sulka whipped up for me." I took
him on a tour of my closet and dresser drawers.

"You're joking with all this . . ."

"Don't get hysterical, baby. Just some of the little niceties
of life. Hey, whattya say we call Room Service? We can
watch television and have dinner right here. How about
steak, salad, and coffee?"

177

"Great."

I got Room Service on the phone. "Darling, this is Sammy Davis, Jr. I'd like to order some dinner. . . . Oh? . . . Why, yes, fine. Thank you."

Morty was looking at me when I hung up. "How come you didn't order?"

"Baby, I wish you had a little more class. How can you order dinner until they send up a Captain with the menu?"

We were finishing our coffee when Jess Rand called. "I've got some wild news for you. I arranged for you to have a layout in *Look* magazine."

"Beautiful."

"You're damned right. I set up a dinner for tomorrow night with the photographer, Milton Greene."

"You're kidding. He's like an idol of mine in photography."

"Well, anyway, *Look* assigned him to shoot you at the Copa, during the show. But he wants to get together with you first."

The operator buzzed me back as soon as I hung up. "Mr. Davis, did you want service on the line?"

I rested the phone back on its cradle, and turned slowly. "Morty, from now on when you call, it may take a while to get me." I crossed my legs and puffed on my pipe. "You'll have to give your name and then the operator'll have to tell me who it is and . . . well, who knows, I mean I can't be expected to be in a telephone mood *all* the time."

Will closed the dressing room door. "Sammy, I want a word with you. You and your father are spending money like you're plain drunk."

"I can't talk about what my dad's doing. That's his business."

"Then we'll just talk about you. The way you're buying clothes and jewels and records and hi-fi sets all over the place and spreading yourself out in a hotel suite . . . why, you're acting like you believe the mint is working overtime just for you."

"Don't you think maybe you're exaggerating it just a little bit?"

"Am I? Why, you must've spent five thousand dollars this week alone."

"So what? It's only a week's salary."

It's *five* weeks' salary. Sure we're making $5000 a week

but we're splitting it three ways and we're *supposed* to only take a thousand a week apiece in salary and put the rest aside for agents and taxes and expenses. But this week alone you've already borrowed three thousand from me in cash, plus you drew your salary, plus I know you've got a whole lot of charge accounts because you've been letting them send the bills to the Morris office. Now I told them to go ahead and pay 'em, but you gotta cut down. I'm afraid to see what it totals up to."

"What's the difference? So it'll take me a few weeks to catch up. How many weeks a year will we be playing New York anyway? Look, I'm having a little splurge. I can cut down when we hit the smaller towns where they don't have these kind of stores. And by then I'll have everything I need, anyway."

"I certainly hope so. You've got to start thinking some about the future."

"I am thinking about the future."

"When you buy yourself ten suits at a time?"

"That's right. I'm a *star!* And I've got to *look* like one. When I walk down the street I want people to say, 'Hey, that's Sammy Davis, Jr.' I don't want to look like the guy next door who blends in like he isn't there. Nobody goes to clubs to see the guy next door and I can't be a star just the few hours we're on the stage. I can't turn it on and off like a light. I've got to feel like a star every minute I'm awake."

"Sammy, what's the name of that comic who was sitting outside?"

"What's the difference?"

"*That's* the difference! You don't even know his name and you gave him a hundred dollars."

"Massey, he's a performer and a good one, too. If he needed a few bucks badly enough to have to ask for it well, I'm sorry, but I couldn't turn him down."

"I'm not saying don't help people. But you're overdoing it. Why, the word'll get around there's a damned fool at the Copa handing out money and he doesn't even want to know your name!"

"Maybe. But it would've been a long walk back to South Side if the Wessons hadn't helped us in Chicago. And I can't forget what it was like when I had to ask B and he came through for us."

"I can't forget it either, Sammy. And it could happen again. That's why you've gotta be more careful with your money."

"Oh, come on, Massey. It's not going to happen again. We've made it for sure this time, and we're going to keep on making it. My God, we've got enough offers to keep us working two hundred weeks this year. *Nothing* can stop us now!"

"The only thing that sure is money in the bank! Don't you see that you've been working the Copa for nothing?"

"How do you figure *that*?"

"You've got nothing left, so you've worked for nothing."

"The way I see it you're the one who's working for nothing. Look at that suit you're wearing. It's the same one you wore four years ago. And you're still living in the cheapest room you can get at the America, right? We're making $5000 a week and what've you got to show for it? A bank book?"

"That's what I work for."

"Well, it's not what *I* work for. The money has never been my payoff for a week's work. Never! When we were starving from one town to another I wasn't thinking, 'Someday I'll have a pile of money.' I was thinking, 'Someday we'll make it and I'll live like a human being. I'll go where I want to go and I'll be able to do anything I want to do!' I've got no complaints about this week. I've got everything I wanted out of it."

"Poppa? What's got six legs and is big in Harlem?" He was stretched out on a bed in the dressing room holding a copy of the *Amsterdam News*, waiting for an answer.

"I'll bite."

"Us."

I gave him a look, and took the paper he was offering. "Damn! I've heard about hometown boys making good but this is ridiculous!"

He smiled happily, his hands clasped behind his head, tapping his toes together thoughtfully. "Yeah. I'd've figured we'd have t'knock off the whole Ku Klux Klan t'come home in this kinda style."

The cab dropped me at 125th Street and Seventh Avenue, and I went into the Baby Grand. Nipsey Russell introduced me from the stage, finished MC'ing the show, and sat down with me, smiling, "Welcome to the small time."

"Still no bites from downtown?"

He shook his head. "Still playing the back of the bus."

"A guy with your talent . . ."

"Thanks, Sammy, but they just don't want me. Maybe someday. 'Til then I'm not complaining. I work steady. I've got wine, women, and the thin-skinned sensitivity of an armadillo."

"It's wrong, Nips. You've got something to offer."

"That's the funny part of it, isn't it? The mountain comes to Mohammed." He gestured around the room which was seventy per cent filled with white people.

It was time for his next show. I sat at the table alone, listening to the sharp, often brilliant, comedy he was doing. Laugh for laugh he could stand against almost any of the big name comedians. He wasn't doing "my wife is so fat that—" He was really saying something. I tried to understand why acts like ours could get booked "downtown" but he couldn't. It was obvious. We came in dancing. Without planning it that way we offered something they would accept from a Negro. Nat Cole came in singing. They'd accept that, too. Louis Armstrong was a jazz musician. The same thing. But a humorist was different. They weren't ready for an articulate man who could face them on their own level and offer ideas.

I left the Baby Grand and started walking west on 125th Street. Some kids spotted me and fell in alongside of me. "You're Sammy Davis." I nodded and smiled. He nodded, satisfied, and they kept walking with me. We passed an all-night barber shop and a guy came to the door with shaving cream on his face. "Hey, Sammy, whattya say?"

I waved back. "Whattya say, baby!"

I stopped at a barbecue stand and ordered some ribs. A crowd started gathering. "You're top man at the Copa, huh, Sammy?" "You really know movie stars?" "You read about yourself in the papers?" "Hey, Sammy, there ain't nothing you can't have, right?"

Every question was asked with a smile and the hope that the answer was yes. They were catching every move I made, digging my clothes, the jewelry—but without envy of me as an individual, as much as a wistful wondering what it was like.

They clustered around me, their faces impassioned by what I represented: I was the guy who'd broken out, I'd made it downtown. They'd seen us on television and read about us at Ciro's, The Chez, Miami, and the Riviera, and now the Copa. They knew we were making it in the white man's world, and if you were making it there then you were something else.

The crowd parted for me at my first step forward. They followed me to the sidewalk as a cab pulled up. I waved good-bye, got in, and told the driver, "The Warwick on 54th Street, baby."

"Anything you say, Sammy."

I turned around and waved again to the crowd that was still standing at the curb watching me go downtown.

What had once been a simple matter of my father, Will and me packing two or three suitcases and leaving town unnoticed, now took on the proportions of a troop movement. On closing night I handed out gold watches engraved "Thanks, Sammy Jr." to the captains and key staff guys at the Copa. The next day Jess left for the coast by plane. We were going to rent a house in Hollywood, so Mama went in Will's car with him, my father, Peewee, and Nathan. Morty and I left by train, and John took off in a truck we'd bought, loaded with drums, vibraphones, props, sound equipment, stage wardrobes, a box of photography equipment, tape recorder, hi-fi sets, a crate of records, and a 280-pound box of music.

13

THE REAL ESTATE BROKER DROVE ME STRAIGHT TO THE colored section of Los Angeles.

"Nothing up in the hills, in the Hollywood section?"

"Well—you see—uh . . ."

"I see."

"Mr. Davis, try to understand. If you were buying it would be a lot simpler. An outright sale—well, these things can be handled. But renting presents certain additional problems. . . ."

Obviously I wasn't big enough yet. "Will you take me back to the Sunset Colonial, please."

"But don't you want to see any of these?"

"I don't have to."

I was never again going to live in a ghetto. Not even if the wall around it were made of solid gold.

I took a cab to my father's apartment. "I'm sorry, Mama. You'll just have to stay here with Dad and Peewee for a little while until I can work this out somehow."

My father spoke softly. "Sammy, they ain't about to let you have a house up there in the hills. Not to buy, not to rent. No way. So, why tear yourself apart over it? You can't change these things."

There was nothing to be accomplished by arguing with him.

We were booked as summer replacements for Eddie Cantor's Colgate shows, so we spent the summer playing clubs around L.A. and San Francisco. I'd started recording for Decca and "Hey There," one of my first sides with them, was starting to appear on all the record charts.

Tony, Janet, and Jeff were buddies I could be with endlessly and my friendship with Frank was becoming really precious to me. I could relax with him more than I had in the early days, but I was still "the kid" to him and he was still "Sinatra" to me. He took me up to the Bogarts' a few times and those were always beautiful evenings. Bogart might have been color blind. He decided on somebody with his second level of understanding. There was no "he's a this" or "he's a that." Bogart got to know a man before he decided if he liked him or not.

I was dating anyone I wanted to, not "white girls" or "colored girls"—girls! If I saw one I liked and got the nod and she happened to be white there'd be a voice saying, "Hold it. She's trouble." Then there was another voice that answered. He was the swinger. "Go, baby. If she wants you and you

want her then damn the torpedoes and full speed ahead. *Go.*"
And I went, playing both sides of town, each with its little
extra kick: on one side, the satisfaction of knowing that nobody was telling me how to live, on the other, peace of mind
and the joy I got out of the fantastic attention my own people
were giving me. I hit those hot downtown bars empty handed,
but when I left I was the Pied Piper of the Sunset Colonial,
heading home with the freshest, best-looking tomatoes in
the whole grocery store skipping along behind me.

Then the summer was over. The bed, every chair and every
table in my room was loaded with clothes. I sat down on a
suitcase in the middle of it all, exhausted by the sight of it
and the thought of going through this scene all the way across
the country. A beautiful thought crossed my mind. A valet. A
gentleman's gentleman: "Judson, I'll be traveling in the gray
mohair. You can pack all the rest, baby. I'm going out now.
See you at the train."

The phone rang. "Sammy, I'm at the Morris office and
something just came up. How fast can you get down here?"

"I'm in the middle of packing, Massey, I'm not dressed."

"Then *get* dressed. You'll be glad you did."

The receptionist led me to the room where Will and my
father were waiting with one of the agents from the nightclub
department.

Will said, "We're playing Vegas. We'll be working the
Old Frontier and we'll be *living* at the Old Frontier! In the
best suites they got!"

"You mean right in the hotel?"

"And free of charge besides, and that includes food and
drink *and* $7500 a week."

I resented the excitement I felt over it. "I don't know,
Massey, I just don't know if anything's worth crawling in
there like 'Gee, sir, y'mean you'll really let us live at your
goddamned hotel?' "

"Sammy, we're not crawling to nobody."

The Morris guy smiled. "*Crawling.* It's not good business to
pass up an attraction that'll bring people to the tables. To
get you now, they'll break their necks, let alone a ridiculous
custom."

"When do they want us?"

"They're asking for November." He looked at a sheet of

paper on his desk. "That means you play Detroit, Chicago, Atlantic City, Buffalo, Syracuse, Boston, and then into Vegas. That's twelve straight weeks with no day off except for traveling. . . ."

I wasn't looking for days off. If Vegas could open up to us like that then it was just a matter of time until the whole country would open up and I couldn't wait to hit the road and sing and dance my head off toward that moment.

It was a gorgeous crisp November morning as I stepped off the train in Las Vegas. My father and Will were waiting for me on the platform. I searched their faces. "Well?"

My father made a circle with his thumb and forefinger. "The best."

"No problems?"

Will shook his head. "They're bending over backwards."

I put my arms around both their shoulders and we walked through the station.

They stopped in front of a beautiful, brand new Cadillac convertible. I looked at my father. "Damn! You musta hit a eight-horse parlay to get your hands on this baby!"

He tossed me the key. "Well, seein' as you like her, she's yours. Will and me bought it for you as a sorta advance birthday present." I took a slow walk around the car and stopped in front of the "S.D.Jr." they'd had painted on the door. "Well, climb in, Poppa, and let's see if she drives."

They slid in alongside me and I put the top down. "Might as well let 'em see who owns this boat." I put it in gear and we rolled away from the station. I ran my fingers over a clear plastic cone which jutted out from the center of the steering wheel, enclosing the Cadillac emblem. "I don't know how to thank you."

Will said, "Don't thank us, Sammy. Thank show business. That's where it all come from."

I couldn't get serious if my life depended on it. We stopped for a light and I pulled out the ash tray. "Hey, fellas, whatta we do when this gets filled up?"

My father came right in on cue. "We throws this car away and gets us a *new* one."

Will smiled. "You boys keep doing old jokes like that and we'll be back riding buses."

185

As we got onto the Strip, I slowed down. "We just drive straight up to the front entrance, right?"

My father laughed. "Like we own the place." He was as giddy as I had been a minute before. "We don't even have t'bother parking the car. They got a man standin' there just to do that and all you do is slip him a silver dollar and he tips his hat and says, 'Thank you, sir.'"

As we approached the hotel I saw the big sign out front, "THE WILL MASTIN TRIO featuring SAMMY DAVIS, JR." I turned into the driveway and pulled up in front of the entrance. A doorman hurried over and opened my door. "I'll take care of it for you, Mr. Davis." I gave him a five and he tipped his hat. "Thanks, Mr. Davis." A bellman came over. "Take your luggage, Mr. Davis?" I pointed to a cab just pulling up. "It's in that one, baby. My valet will give it to you."

The door closed and we were alone in a huge, beautiful suite. I collapsed onto the bed, kicking my legs in the air. "I don't *never* wanta leave this room! I'd sign a contract to stay here for the rest of my *natural!*" I got up and looked around. There was a large basket of flowers in the living room. The card read: "Welcome to the Old Frontier" and was signed by the manager.

My father was standing behind a bar in the corner of the room. "Glasses, ice, soda, cokes, scotch, bourbon . . . hell, they didn't slip up on nothin'."

"Well, I guess this is about as First Cabin as anyone can ever hope to go."

Charley Head, the man I'd hired in L.A., came in leading four bellmen carrying my luggage. I walked my father and Will to the door. "How about your rooms?"

"Almost the same layouts. Right down the hall."

I inspected the suite while Charley started unpacking. "Pretty nice, huh, baby?"

He didn't look around. "I'll let you know when I see where they put me."

Oh God, I hadn't thought about that. "Well, look, you let me know, and if it's not okay you'll stay in here with me." He just kept unpacking. I could imagine how he felt. "Let me help you, baby, and we'll get it done faster."

Morty was rehearsing the band. I sat in the back of the room listening, and checked John out on the lights.

When Morty gave the guys a break I called him aside, "Baby, I'll open with 'Birth of the Blues.'"

"You're joking! What'll you go off on?"

"We'll use 'Fascinating Rhythm.' Look, we throw away all the rules here. The plotting of a show for a Vegas audience is different than anywhere else. For openers, the hotels are all but giving away the best shows that money can buy, so the average cat who comes in to see us has been in town for a few days and he's already seen maybe six or eight of the biggest names in the business. This same guy may never see a live show from one end of the year to the next when he's home but after a few days here he's Charley-Make-Me-Laugh. Now, above and beyond that, plus the normal nightclub distractions, if I don't hook that guy right from the start and hang on to him I'm dead, because he'll be watching me but he'll start wondering if when he leaves maybe he should try ten the hard way. So, it's like when we make records: we do or die in the first eight bars." He whistled softly. "And on top of that, where in a normal club if I start off a little slow I can always stay on until eventually I get 'em and they leave saying, 'Hey, isn't it nice the way he does those long shows,' in Vegas the headliner has exactly fifty-two minutes, including bows. They're in the gambling business here and everything's timed down to the split second: there's no dancing after the shows and your check is collected before the show breaks. Those doors lead into the casino and they want the people to walk through them *on time!* There are just so many minutes in each day and the hotel anticipates a certain amount of gambling revenue for each one of them. I can't steal any of that time to make sure I come off smelling like a rose. They pay me to bring customers *to* the tables, not to keep them away. So, watch me extra carefully for the cues, baby, 'cause once I'm out there it's fight-for-your-life time."

As we stood in the wings listening to them shouting for more my father cocked his head and sighed, "I hope the word don't spread that we're bad for the heart." The three of us walked arm in arm back to the dressing rooms. "You gonna take a look around the casino, Poppa? Maybe take yourself a few bows?"

"I don't know, Dad. I'll see."

I put on a black mohair suit, a gray and black striped tie, my platinum watch, folded a handkerchief into my breast pocket and took a last look in the mirror. I took out the handkerchief and went downstairs.

I stood outside the casino, afraid. A security guard passed me. "Anything I can do for you, Sammy?" I shook my head. A few people coming out spotted me. "Great show, Sammy . . . Wonderful!"

I lit another cigarette. I took two drags, stamped it out, pushed the door open and walked in.

The deputy sheriff standing just inside said, "Hi'ya, Sammy."

I smiled back and kept walking. I was right in the middle of all the sounds I'd heard before and they took form even wilder and more feverish than I'd imagined them. People were playing blackjack and roulette and shooting craps with a deadly serious hilarity, dropping coins into hundreds of one-armed bandits which lined every wall and the sound was like we were inside a huge, tin piggy bank and somebody was shaking all the money around.

There was an empty seat at one of the blackjack tables. The faces around the table seemed pleasant enough, but how would they react to me sitting down to gamble with them?

I broke a hundred dollar bill at the cashier's window. The seat was still open. I went over to one of the machines and dropped a silver dollar in the slot. If I win, I go to the table. I pulled the handle and watched the spinning figures slow to a halt . . . cherries . . . cherries . . . orange. There was a sharp click and silver dollars poured out.

The dealer was in the middle of a hand as I put my money on the table and pulled up the chair. Someone said something about me but I couldn't catch what it was. I kept my eyes on the green cloth. People were gathering around. I looked up. They were smiling.

I pushed a silver dollar forward and played my first hand. I won. I let the two dollars ride—and won again. I pulled back my winnings and kept playing for two dollars. A woman at the end of the table smiled. "I loved your show." The dealer glared at her. "Would you like another card?" She giggled nervously and looked back at her hand. I lit a cigarette and he slid an ash tray toward me. He jerked his head toward the nightclub. "I hope you're as lucky in here as you are in there." The man next to me said, "That's not luck. That's talent." A cocktail waitress came by. "Would you like a drink, Mr. Davis?" "I'd love a coke, thank you."

I began to feel some of my audience drifting away. I handed the dealer a hundred dollar bill. "I'll take some of those five-dollar chips, baby." Without counting them I pushed a stack of blue chips forward. Someone said, "Yeah. Go, Sammy. Break the bank." I won. I let it all ride. A woman yelled, "Arnold, come over here. Sammy Davis is playing. Hurry, Arnold." The dealer was all but handing me the chips in a shovel. He looked at the mountain of them spilling over the whole table in front of me. "You want twenty-five-dollar chips for these, Sammy?" "No thanks, baby. These are doing fine for me." The crowd was three deep around the table now. I pushed the whole pile forward. "Shoot the works."

"Oh my God, Arnold, will you look what he's doing?" "It's peanuts to him. Do you know what he makes a week?"

The dealer flipped the cards around the table as casually as if he were dealing to silver dollars. The crowd was silent. The ace of diamonds slid face up in front of me. I opened my down card. The jack of hearts. There was a roar behind me as if I'd just gone off on "Birth of the Blues." Arnold's wife was going out of her mind and people were pounding me on the back as the dealer stacked hundred dollar-chips against my bet and then added half again, the bonus for blackjack.

I wasn't going to top that moment. I pulled the mass of chips toward me and dropped a handful of them into the dealer's shirt pocket. "Thanks, Sammy." A woman moaned. "You're not stopping, are you?" I smiled. "It's a definite quit while I'm ahead." As the crowd opened up for me I heard, "Hurry. Sit there, Arnold. It's a lucky seat."

I walked through the casino, both hands holding the bundle of chips against my chest . . . "Hey, Sammy, y'want some help gettin' rid of those?" . . . "How much you sock 'em for, kid?" . . . "The rich get richer, don't they?" . . . A deputy rushed ahead of me to help me with the door.

Outside, alone, I had to fight an urge to throw the chips in the air like confetti. It was such a joke. Such a big, fat joke.

On my way to breakfast, I passed a couple of the chorus kids sunbathing around the pool. I did bits with them for a few minutes, had some coffee, wandered over to the casino and sat at the bar drinking a coke and watching the action. A middle-aged guy with a swinging-looking blonde raised his glass and smiled. "You're the greatest, Sammy."

The bartender said to me, quietly, "Now there's a guy who lives. Hits town every Friday like clockwork. But with a different wife every week."

The manager sat down on the stool next to me. "Sammy, I hope you won't mind, but I'd consider it a favor if you'd try not to spend too much time around the pool."

I looked him in the eye, waiting for "It's not that *we* mind but you know how people are. . . ." A woman was screaming "Jackpot! Jackpot!"

He said, "You saw what happened in the casino when you played last night. There were shooters playing ten times as big as you were, but nobody paid any attention to them. Whenever a star sits down at a table he draws a crowd. And it's fine, no harm there. But if you hang around the pool during the day you'll attract crowds there, too, and frankly we'd just as soon not have you pull them away from the tables. Naturally, if you feel like a swim, fine, but we'll appreciate it if you'll keep it down to a minimum."

The pulse in my forehead began slowing down to normal again. I smiled. "I don't know how to swim anyway. Besides, I've already got my tan."

I walked around, found a blackjack table that looked good and ran $500 into a twenty-five-dollar chip. I dropped it into the dealer's shirt pocket and stood up. "Thanks, Sammy. Tough luck."

"I'll get even tonight, baby."

He smiled and continued shuffling the cards.

I stopped at a dice table and watched a comic I knew from the coast. "How y'doing, baby?"

He made a wry face. "Great. I got here in an $8000 Cadillac and I'm leaving in an $80,000 bus!"

190

I grinned at the old joke, did one back at him, and wandered around a while longer doing all the Vegas clichés. As I walked toward the steam room I knew I should be concerned over losing $500 in ten minutes, but I just couldn't feel it.

I was dressing after the second show when one of the boy dancers came into the dressing room. "No party tonight?"

"Sorry, baby. Gotta run into L.A. I'm doing the sound track for *Six Bridges to Cross*."

He looked at my rack of clothes and stroked the sleeve of a gray silk. "Crazy-looking threads."

I lifted the suit off the rack and handed it to him. "Wear it in good health."

"Hey, Jesus, no—I didn't mean—"

"No big deal, baby. I'd like you to have it."

I heard him down the hall. "You won't believe what Sammy Davis just did. I was standing in his dressing room looking at this suit . . ."

I felt like Frank had always looked—like a star to my fingertips.

As I stepped out of the dressing room, someone grabbed my arm. "Whattya say, chicky?"

"Jess, you nut. When'd you get in?"

"Ten minutes ago. How's it going?" He walked outside with me.

"We're doing all the business in town and it's been the ball of all time."

"What've you been doing?"

"I do what everybody else does." I stopped at the sound of my own words, gripped by the understanding of their meaning. I snapped myself out of it. "Listen, here's the skam. I'm driving to L.A. to do the sound track for *Six Bridges*, I'll be back tomorrow, sixish, we'll grab some steam, then it's a little din-din, and you can catch the show." I tapped him on the arm. "Meanwhile, grab a chick, have some booze, sign my name, and I'll see you tomorrow."

I took the long way around to my room, through the casino, just for the sheer joy of walking through it. The deputy sheriff standing just inside the door gave me a big "Hi'ya, Sammy." I waved back and kept moving through all the action. Some guys at a dice table made room for me. "Come on in, Sammy. We've got a hot shooter."

"Thanks. Can't tonight. Gotta run into L.A. Catch y'tomorrow."

I browsed through my clothes. Something sporty . . . gray flannel slacks and a cashmere jacket, and maybe a plain black silk shirt. Perfect. Not "Hollywood," just casual. Very "cinema."

I took out a pair of levis and a sweater to wear in the car and called Room Service for a hamburger.

I'd just finished showering when there was a knock on the door. One of the chorus chicks was standing there, smiling.

"Hey, this hotel has crazy room service." She laughed. I told her, "Darling, I sent Charley around to say there'd be no party tonight. I have to go into L.A."

"I know." She stepped in. "But he said you weren't leaving 'til three. I thought maybe you'd like some company while you were getting dressed." I watched her disappear into the bedroom. The doors weren't only opening, they were swinging!

Charley was waiting in the car. I climbed into the back seat and stretched out. The big neon sign in front of the hotel was flashing my name on and off and I lay there enjoying a delicious drowsiness. As we turned off the Strip and onto the highway I said, "Keep it under fifty, baby. Let's break this car in so smooth that she'll sing ballads." I felt around my chest for my mezuzah. I sat up. Maybe the chain had opened. I reached inside my shirt, around my waist, but it wasn't there. I distinctly remembered taking it off to shower, but I couldn't recall putting it back on again. It must have slipped off the dresser, and with the chick there and in the hurry of leaving, I hadn't noticed. I was tempted to turn around and go back for it, but we'd been traveling at least twenty minutes and it would mean losing an hour.

I lay back watching the stars through the window. There were three particularly bright ones in a row, like magnificent diamond studs on a black velvet vest. The desert air was sweet and clear and it seemed a shame that all that beauty had always been there to be enjoyed but when I'd most needed this kind of contentment I'd never had the peace of mind to be able to find it; somehow, it had never looked the same through the windows of a bus. I closed my eyes. The rolling of the car increased my drowsiness, and I let myself sink deeper and more comfortably into it.

14

WHY DO THEY ALWAYS SAY HOSPITAL SHEETS ARE COOL and crisp? They were hot and sticky. And I didn't have to ask "Where am I?" I sensed it or smelled it or remembered it. The room was very dark, I turned my head from one side to the other but there wasn't a crack of light—a bulb, the moon—nothing! It was too dark just to be night. I must have been near an open window because I felt a gust of air pass over me, hot and thick like it never is at night. I heard cars moving outside. Slowly. A lot of them. I could hear a radio soap opera playing, people talking in a daytime tone and walking carelessly down the corridor. There definitely was daylight around me. I just couldn't see it.

I grabbed for my legs but my arms wouldn't move. My hands could feel iron bars on both sides of me and if I had hands then I had to have arms. I kicked my legs and heard them swishing against the bedsheets. I banged my feet together so hard that they hurt. Thank God I had feet. There was terrible pressure around my head. I stretched my neck toward my hands to feel what was wrong.

"Don't touch your bandages, Mr. Davis. Everything is all right."

It was a woman's voice. I fell back against the pillow. Oh, God. I can't see, I can't move, and everything-is-all-right-Mr. Davis. "Are you a nurse? Am I blind?"

"Don't worry. Everything's going to be fine."

"But I can't see! Am I blind?"

"You have bandages over your eyes. You were in a bad automobile accident."

"*Please!* I know that. Just tell me yes or no. *Am I blind?*"

"No. You're not blind."

Naturally she'd say that. They wouldn't let a nurse break it to me. Not like this, not the second I wake up.

"If you promise not to pull at your bandages I can take the straps off your arms now."

"Thank you." I felt my legs. They were okay. There was a small bandage on the palm of my right hand. I put my hands to my face, slowly, so she wouldn't think I was pulling at the bandages. I started touching them at the top of my head but I couldn't feel my skin until I got to my mouth. I was wrapped up like a mummy.

I turned my head toward the sound of footsteps coming into the room. "Good morning, Mr. Davis. I'm Doctor Hull. How are you feeling?"

I nodded, waiting. He wasn't saying anything and I was suddenly afraid he would. "Look doc, I know this sounds like a B-movie, but, where am I?"

"This is the Community Hospital at San Bernardino. You were operated on last night."

"You operated on me?"

"Yes."

"Doctor, please—will I be able to dance? Am I . . , blind?"

"You're not blind. You're going to see. You'll be able to dance and sing and do everything you ever did. But I removed your left eye."

I distinctly heard the words, but the tone—it was like "Shall we have lunch?" Nobody could be so casual as to say, "Ho hum, I took out your eye."

"Mr. Davis, losing an eye isn't as tragic as it seems when you first hear it."

He really *had* said it.

"Try not to touch the bandages."

I dropped my hands. I felt like an idiot. Here a man tells me he took out my eye and I'm checking to see if he's kidding.

"You're handling it very bravely."

"Doc, you'd better tell me some more about it 'cause I'm about to be the scaredest brave man you ever saw."

"We'll discuss it in detail when you're rested, but for the moment what it amounts to is that you struck your left eye against the pointed cone in the center of your steering wheel. When you were brought here yesterday morning . . ."

Yesterday? If a whole night went by, then what happened in Vegas? Who did the show?

". . . the doctors on duty felt that although the eye was severely damaged there was still a possibility of saving it, so they called me because I specialize in this sort of operation. When I examined you I agreed that it might be saved. However, from the amount of damage done, the best you'd ever have had in that eye would be ten per cent vision. Although that would seem to justify saving it, we've learned that the damaged eye pulls, or leans, so heavily on the good one that eventually the healthy eye is weakened and the patient suffers what we call 'sympathetic blindness.' As a result, in a few years you might have had almost no sight at all and for that reason I recommended the removal . . ."

The bed was turning and I grabbed for the bars . . . I don't have to hold on, I can't fall off. The bed isn't really moving. I took deep breaths, trying to fight the nausea.

"With one perfectly healthy eye you'll have excellent vision. As for appearance, you'll have an artificial eye and eventually no one but you will know the difference."

"A glass eye?"

"We don't use glass any more. They're made of plastic. In any event you'll be wearing a patch for a while."

"Aha. Floyd Gibbons, eh?"

His hand was on my arm. "That's the spirit. I know it's a tremendous shock to find that you have only one eye, but the eye is lost and that cannot be changed. You can take the attitude that everything else is lost, too—and it will be, or you can take the attitude that you still have one perfect eye. You can see. You have both legs and both arms. You have a relatively small adjustment to make before resuming a completely normal life. Try not to think of what you've lost but of how much you still have."

Suddenly I was exhausted. I felt myself falling asleep as he spoke.

My father was holding my hand between both of his. Will was on the other side of the bed, patting my shoulder.

"Hi, Dad, Massey. Where's Mama?"

"I'm right here, Sammy."

"How y'doing, Mama?"

"I'm fine."

"When'd you hear about it, Dad?"

"Well, Will here was sleepin' when it come over the radio and someone got him up and told him. I guess I was kinda good-timin' it downtown, but he found me and we caught the first plane out and got a car here from L.A."

"You flew?"

"We didn't know what shape you was in. The radio didn't say nothing but that it was a bad crack-up." He was squeezing my hand hard. "And what reason've I got to live without you, Poppa?"

Mama snapped, "Sam! You won't do him no good that way."

I asked, "Hey, how about Charley?"

"He's down the hall. His jaw's broke and he lost all his teeth, upper and lower, but he'll be okay."

"What happened in Vegas? I mean, the show?"

"Jeff Chandler went on for you last night, Poppa. He called here after the first show and he said when you wakes up to tell you the people was sitting at their tables and cryin' just thinkin' about what happened to you."

I couldn't help smiling over what an emotional "show biz" scene that must have been. But it was odd to picture myself the reason for it. I wondered who'd have come to my funeral if I'd been killed. "Massey? What about our name? Is it still up?"

"Well, it was up when we left there. . . ."

My mind was shooting off in ridiculous directions. I visualized them hiring one act after another—the best, Frank, Dean and Jerry, all of them—but the audience was just sitting on their hands and saying, "Nobody's as good as Sammy Davis was," and the hotel owners onstage announcing, "The club is closed until Sammy can come back," and all the columns would write what a beautiful gesture that was. Sure!

Sentiment's fine but you sweep it out in the morning with the cigarette butts and you hire a new act or there'll be no customers at those crap tables.

My father had walked across the room and he must have been holding his hands or a handkerchief against his mouth so I wouldn't hear him crying. Somebody kept trying to light a match and Will was clearing his throat. I was glad I couldn't see their faces.

"Well, folks—I guess this wraps us up." I waited, hoping somebody might say it didn't make any difference, that we'd be as strong as ever. But nobody said it and I'd have laughed if they had. What chance was there? Sure, they'd cry for me on one dramatic night. People always cry at funerals. Then they go home and forget you. They sure as hell aren't going to be laying down their money to see any one-eyed dancers. A one-eyed colored dancer who sings, tells jokes, and makes people sick.

The nurse broke the silence. "I think you'd better let him rest now."

What a lousy joke. What was there to rest for? I remembered telling Will: "You don't understand, Massey. Nothing can stop us now."

The nurse was buckling the straps on my arms. I could hear her putting up the sides of the bed so I wouldn't fall. It seemed so pointless.

"Nurse?"

"I'm right here."

"What's that smell? Flowers?"

"It's all the flowers in San Bernardino. We can't bring any more into the room or you'll suffocate. But there's a line of baskets leading from the door all the way down the hall. You've cleaned out the shop downtown. They can't fill the rest of the orders 'til tomorrow. You've also gotten over five hundred telegrams."

"I don't even know five hundred people. You don't have to do cheer-up bits with me."

She took my hand and ran it against a stack of envelopes that must have been a foot high. "We've got eight bundles like this one. I'll tell you the truth. I knew you were in show business but I had no idea you were such a celebrity."

197

"There's gotta be a mistake. Will you read me the names on the flowers?"

I waited while she pulled up a chair and started reading. "Betty and Charles Schuyler . . ."

"Darling, I told you something was wrong. That's not for me. I don't know anyone by that name."

"It's addressed to Sammy Davis, Jr. The card says, 'Though we have never met you, our hearts and prayers are with you. Have courage. Betty and Charles Schuyler.' "

What a beautiful thing! Total strangers go to the trouble and expense of sending me flowers.

She continued, then went through the telegrams, reading off names of governors of states, mayors, movie and TV producers, stars, bit players, headwaiters, and vaudeville performers I hadn't seen or heard of in years. But mostly they were from total strangers.

The door opened and I heard somebody coming in. "Well, chicky, this was a great little publicity stunt you dreamed up."

"Jess?"

"Yep. I thought you'd like to know that you've won the hearts of a grateful Hollywood for knocking Eddie and Debbie off the front pages. Even Korea couldn't do *that*."

"Baby, slow up a minute. Are you saying I've been on the front pages?"

"What's the matter? Don't they read the papers around here?"

"Jess, there's been a few other things going on. Like, for openers, I lost an eye."

"I'm hip. Well, then lemme be the first to tell you. You've made page one clear across the country for two days running. But I mean with pictures, stories, the whole bit. The wire services haven't been off my phone since it happened. Every ten minutes it's 'Send us pictures, send us background' . . ."

"Jess, if this is your idea of a gag . . ."

"Chicky, it's emmis! You're the hottest thing in the business. The coverage has been fantastic and it's all sympathetic. Real sob stuff like 'Can the little man with the big talent survive this blow to his career?' . . . 'Just as his dreams of a lifetime were being fulfilled . . .' You know the kinda jazz. Look, Florence Nightingale out at the desk said I could only stay for a minute so I'll leave these clips for you. You can read 'em tomorrow when they take the Invisible Man costume off you."

My father said, "It's almost nine o'clock. Let's see what Winchell's got to say."

I hadn't even known it was Sunday. I waited while he tuned in the radio, listening for the wireless ticker and the staccato voice that had meant Sunday night at nine for as long as I could remember. We'd done it last Sunday and here we were doing it again, the same as always. It seemed impossible that I'd lost an eye in between.

"Good evening, Mr. and Mrs. North and South America and all the ships at sea. Let's go to press! New York: a 22-story building in the heart of . . ." I felt like Charley Ham lying there listening for my name, hoping he might mention me. "Wall Street . . . Chicago . . . Buenos Aires . . . Hollywood . . ." The importance of the news dwindled to a small-time actor's wedding. Then they started the commercial. I lost an eye and my whole damned career, how could he not have mentioned me?

"Hell, Poppa, I kinda figured he mighta said something 'bout you."

"Come on, Dad. I'm yesterday's news. It's already been in the papers. What's there for him to say about it?"

"And now back to Walter Winchell!"

"This is your New York correspondent winding up another edition with a word of advice to young Sammy Davis, Jr., in a hospital somewhere in San Bernardino, California. Sammy: if you can hear me . . . never forget that behind every dark cloud—a brilliant star is shining! Remember . . . no champ ever lost a fight by being knocked down. Only by *staying* down!"

I reached for my watch. My hand touched a glass straw, and I remembered. Whenever I'd thought about a blind man it had only been "It must be rough never to see a sunset or a movie or a beautiful chick." I'd never thought about this part of being blind, not even being able to look out the window to tell if it's day or night.

The hospital was very quiet. There was an occasional pair of rubber-soled shoes making its own quiet sound down the hall. I felt around on the night table, hoping they hadn't taken away my cigarettes, but they had. I heard the day nurses coming in. That would make it seven o'clock.

The vibration I'd had in my stomach since I awoke increased as the hospital sounds picked up momentum. I visualized Dr. Hull coming in for the big dramatic moment . . . I'm sitting up in bed smiling, Will and my father are waiting. Finally Dr. Hull has all the bandages off. Then comes the great movie cliché: he passes his hand in front of my face but the eye doesn't flicker. He and the nurse and my father and Will are all looking at each other. Nobody knows how to tell me. I'm still smiling like an idiot. "Come on, Doc, let's go. Take off the rest of the bandages." Then I hear the silence and I catch on just before he tells me. "They *are* off, son." How would I play it? Do I shrug, "Well, just get me a white cane, Doc"? No. There'll be no bitter bits. I'll play it Charley Brave like the world has never seen.

The nurse was taking away the breakfast tray when my father and Will burst in.

"Aren't you guys up a little early?"

"Mose Gastin, we've been outside over an hour waiting for them to let us in. We got news like you never dreamed about."

"Poppa, what would you like to have more than anything in the world?"

"Oh, come on, Dad."

"No kidding!"

"I'd like to have my goddamned career back."

"Read it to him, Will."

"Sammy, this is a telegram from the Sands Hotel in Las Vegas, Nevada." He cleared his throat. "It says, 'Firm offer for Will Mastin Trio Featuring Sammy Davis, Jr. *Twenty five thousand per week,* first available date, please advise.' "

"They must be crazy."

My father was almost hysterical. "Crazy like a fox, Poppa. Will called the Morris office and they say clubs all over the country are breakin' their necks t'get us. With all the publicity and everything, they're offerin' money like we never even heard about. The Frontier's tearin' up our old contract to meet this price. We'll be lightin' cigars with what we used to make. We can write our own ticket across the country and back and all the way to London, England!"

I heard the window shades being pulled down. The nurse said, "Dr. Hull is on his way down the hall."

"Poppa, just relax yourself and get ready for when the bandages come off, 'cause Will and me'll be standin' right here with this telegram and you'll have something beautiful to see."

I'd planned to be pleasant and maybe throw a little joke at Dr. Hull when he came in but I couldn't think of one. My hands were clutching the tightened muscles of my legs under the blankets. There were five of us in the room but it was so quiet that I could hear my father breathing and the sound of the scissors cutting through the gauze, strand by strand. Then I heard the scissors being placed on a metal table. My father whispered, "Easy, Poppa." It was still dark but I knew I was okay as long as I could feel Dr. Hull's hands moving around my head, unwrapping the gauze layer by layer.

Suddenly light appeared on the right side of my head. It kept growing stronger as he unwrapped more and more, and as he removed the last layer, I had to put my hand over my eye, shielding it from the glare, uncovering it little by little.

I saw Dr. Hull's arm. My father and Will were at the end of the bed. I was shaking with laughter. I didn't know what to look at first. "Doctor . . . thank you." I leaned against the pillow and caught my breath. The nurse mopped my face with a piece of Kleenex. "Do you wanta know about a cat who ain't gonna take his sight for granted no more . . . Massey, you'd better call Vegas and tell 'em to get our name back up."

Dr. Hull smiled. "Not so fast. You've got to learn how to use your one eye, first."

"What do you mean?"

"It'll be a while before you get back your senses of balance and distance. For example, you'll have trouble pouring water into a glass, objects will appear flatter than they did before. . . ."

"Doc, I don't care if *Marilyn Monroe* looks flat just as long as I can move around a stage. Hey, can I have a mirror?"

I stared at my nose. It was flatter than ever. This third break had really collapsed it, and there was a big gash across the bridge. "Oh, now wait a *minute*, Doc. I was never exactly a debutante, but this is ridiculous!"

He took the bandage off my left eye. I'd expected to see a hole, but the lid had been sewn closed like a Boris Karloff make-up job. I put the mirror right down.

"We took thirty stitches inside and outside the lid."

I forced myself to look again. I could see how the lid had busted, like a paper bag, and all the ragged ends that must have been hanging loose had been sewn back together to make one piece. In the midst of that grotesque piece of flesh I had long eyelashes. Dr. Hull explained that he'd slit open the edge of the lid and stuck the hairs in one by one, like putting toothpicks into an orange, so that I'd have something there until the new eyelashes started growing.

"Maybe I'll break into pictures yet, Doc. I can play Frankenstein monsters."

The nurse was motioning my father and Will to leave the room with her. I turned away from the doctor but he put his hand on my shoulder. "You're entitled to a little self-pity. Just don't let yourself enjoy it too much. It won't bring back your eye but it will undermine the strength which has carried you through this so well. I'll be back tomorrow. Feel free to get out of bed, but move carefully."

I listened to him walking away. It hadn't been so bad until he'd taken off the last bandage. I was so high from being able to see that I hadn't been prepared for it—but if it was covered with a patch, or with make-up . . . I saw the telegram propped against the dresser mirror. I'd thought I'd be able to see half what I used to see, like when I'd had two eyes and closed one. But it was less than half, almost as though they'd built a wall over my nose that blocked out everything to the left of center. I stood up, but I got dizzy and fell back against the bed. When the dizziness passed I started walking slowly across the room toward the dresser. I reached for the telegram but my hand passed right by it and touched the mirror at least three inches away. I slid my fingers across the glass until I had it. I felt dizzy again and I started back to bed. As I turned, something struck me in the hip. A chair had been right next to me on my dead side. As I got to the bed the steel rim banged into my knees and I fell across the mattress. The telegram flew out of my hand. I groped in the air trying to catch it, but it fluttered to the floor.

The nurse walked in and helped me under the covers and I lay there exhausted and embarrassed, wondering how much she'd seen. "Don't let it get you," she said, "it's natural." She picked up the telegram and held it out to me. I shook my head. I didn't want to look at it. I could just picture myself doing my stumbling act in Vegas. And getting a nice big round of pity.

Why the hell wouldn't she stop looking at me like she was so damned sorry for me? I tried to think of something to talk about. I pointed to the adhesive tape on the palm of my right hand. "Hey, isn't this kind of a strange place for me to get a cut? I mean I was holding onto the steering wheel with both hands."

"That didn't happen in the accident." She opened the night table drawer and handed me a gold medal the size of a silver dollar. It had St. Christopher on one side and the Star of David on the other. "You were holding this when you went into the operating room. We had to pry your hand open to make you let go of it. You were holding it so tight it cut into your flesh. It's going to leave a scar."

I'd never seen it before, but I had a vague recollection of Tony and Janet walking alongside me as I was being wheeled down a hall, and of Janet pressing something into my hand and telling me, "Hold tight and pray and everything will be all right."

I gave it back to the nurse and lifted one end of the bandage and looked at the cut. It was a clear outline of the Star of David.

My father came in carrying a magazine. He seemed upset as he handed it to me. It was *Confidential* and the headline on the cover was: "WHAT MAKES AVA GARDNER RUN FOR SAMMY DAVIS JR.?" The cover was a picture of us together. I turned to the story. The same picture was captioned: "Ava and Sammy cheek-to-cheeking it in her 16th floor suite at New York's Drake Hotel."

"Poppa—just between us—I mean, is there anything to that?"

"Dad, are you losing your mind?" I skimmed through it. "Some girls go for gold but it's bronze that 'sends' sultry

Ava Gardner . . . Said Sammy after his first meeting with Ava, 'We just dig each other, that's all . . .' Ava sat glassy-eyed through a gay tour of Harlem with Sammy. Said a bartender, 'Another round and she would have been plastered.' " They'd based the whole thing on the night she'd come up to the Apollo and on the *Our World* story her studio had written. They'd capitalized on its title "Sammy Sends Me," but they left out "as a performer," and slanted all her quotes like "exciting, thrilling, masculine" about my performance onstage to make them sound like she meant in bed. Then they wrote in some smirks and left the rest to the reader's imagination. And they'd done it so well that if you didn't look carefully it sounded like Ava and I were having the swingingest affair of all time.

My father was watching me, still not sure. If he'll believe it even after I told him then I don't have a chance. Everybody'll believe it. I called the nurse. "When you went through the telegrams and letters was there anything from Frank Sinatra?" She shook her head. "It's very important. Are you sure?"

"Positive." She motioned toward a pile of mailbags. "I still haven't been through those."

"It wouldn't be a letter. He'd send a telegram or flowers. Or he'd call."

"Definitely not. I'd certainly remember if there'd been anything from Frank Sinatra."

I fell back against the pillow. Here's a man who's been nothing but good to me. For him to have to see this, even if he knows it's not true—it's inexcusable to have put her in a position so that this could happen to her.

I called the publicity man at her studio, but he argued, "Sammy, Ava's ignoring it. If you sue you'll only bring more attention to it."

"But I've got to clear her. I'm at least going to demand a retraction."

"Please, be smart, forget it. Let it die by itself. Nobody reads retractions."

"But we can make them print the original picture. Don't you remember when it was taken? You were standing in it 'til they cropped you out."

"I remember. Why do you think I was standing there? I

also remember the 'gay tour of Harlem' was a quick drink in a bar near the theater. But the best thing is to forget it. By the time they can print your retraction it'll be months from now and it'll be forgotten. You'll only revive it."

"Well, will you at least get word to Ava how sorry I am."

"Sammy, forget it and ride it out. She knows it's not your fault."

Will had come in while I was talking. He was reading the story and shaking his head. "How'd a thing like this happen, Sammy?"

"Please, Massey, I'm too tired to think about it any more."

"You've got to be more careful in the future." He tossed it onto a chair. "Well, probably not too many people read this junk anyway."

Only the world! I stared at the ceiling hoping to draw a blank. If they hated it when Eddie Cantor just put his arm around me, they'll throw rocks at me for this.

I tried to get involved in what my father and Will were saying. They were reading the damned Vegas telegram for the thousandth time and Will was nodding his head, ". . . proves what I always believed. If you know your business and you give the people what they want, then the day is going to come when they'll just have to push you into the big money."

My father sighed in agreement. "We had our schoolin' for more'n twenty years. It's no more'n right it's paying off."

Can they really believe that? Don't they know that without me they'd never have made it? Can't they see that *I* made them, that *I'm* responsible for everything they've got? Or don't they want to see it?

Will was smiling nostalgically. "I'm glad for the big money, Sam, but I still wouldn't trade away the old days we had. That was real show business! Why, when we played for Minsky . . ."

Can't they see that the only good thing about their "old days" is that they're gone? Why can't they forget them? Why do they love to talk about when they were failures? Dad, put down the damned bottle! Why does he need that? Does it lift him out of always being the second man? Will was always the boss, now I'm the star. Is that why he needs it? I looked away. I didn't want to judge him or Will or anybody. I just wanted to figure out how we could stay in the business. Why couldn't they talk about today and tomorrow instead of yesterday?

My father was standing in front of me, glass in hand, laughing. "You're mighty quiet, Poppa. Hey, remember when we was stranded in Lansing? Remember that do-gooder who put us out of work all through Michigan? Guess she never figured that little kid she run off the stage would be makin' twenty-five thousand a week."

"But for how long, Dad?"

"I believe it said four weeks. That right, Will? Tell y'the truth, Poppa, I thought I had this business learned backwards, but I'm damned if I ever hoped I'd live to see the day when they'd pay that to *anybody*."

"It's simple, Dad. They're buying the Will Mastin Trio featuring the World's Only One-Eyed Dancer."

"Sammy, don't say things like that . . ."

"Face it, Dad, it's true. I'm a curiosity. But have you and Massey wondered how I'm gonna do impressions and get laughs with only one eye?"

"Well, I . . ."

"All right, forget that. Even if I stink, the publicity and the shock value oughta carry us for one time around. But once everybody's had their look, how do we stay in the business? What'll we do for an encore?"

Will stood up. "Sammy, you've got it all wrong!"

"Have I, Will? Then maybe you'd better explain it to me."

He walked toward the bed slowly, giving himself time to think. "Well, you're making it out like a freak show, but it's only—well, with the publicity and all, we turned into a name the people heard about. Add that to the fact that we've always been a top act . . ."

"Massey, do you believe we're seventeen thousand dollars a week better today than we were last week?"

"Well, you can't look at it like that. It's not exactly we're a better act . . ." He was reaching desperately for an answer he couldn't possibly find.

"Massey, we've got a bitch of a gimmick if we play it right. If we can get twenty-five thousand for one lousy eye, then next year when they're tired of that I'll just hack off something else. The Will Mastin Trio oughta be worth at least forty thousand featuring the only one-eyed, one-legged dancer in the world. . . ."

"Poppa, for God's sake—please!"

I had the same careening, out-of-control feeling I'd had in the accident. I saw the horror in my father's eyes but I could no more stop the words than I'd been able to stop the car. "There's no limit to it. Just think of the billing each year. Instead of 'Bigger and Better' it could be 'There's less of him than ever before, folks!'"

My father was crying and Will had turned away from me. Why had I wanted to hurt them like that?

I felt a hand on my shoulder. "Poppa?"

"I'm sorry, Dad. I'm sorry, Massey."

"Maybe you'd better get some sleep, Poppa. Just get your rest and we'll be right here lookin' after you."

They were half-smiling, confused, giving me every ounce of what they had, but I was still "Poppa" and "Mose Gastin." I was dying to talk to them about what was ahead of us. I needed them to give me some concrete answers, a little logic, a plan—something. But they couldn't give answers to problems they didn't see. They were so used to thinking only of getting booked, getting our price, and doing our show, that it hadn't occurred to them to wonder: what do you have to do on a stage to begin to justify twenty-five thousand dollars a week? And what happens if you can't do it? I couldn't get through to them. I could reach an audience of a thousand strangers, reach them on any level and make myself understood, but I couldn't reach my own two fathers. I couldn't turn to them for help any more. I fell back on the pillow and stared at the ceiling, never so alone.

"Poppa? You sleepin'?"

I heard him and Will tiptoeing up to the bed. I turned around. "Hi."

"How y'feelin', Poppa?"

"Fine. How 'bout you guys?"

They smiled and nodded. My father said, "Look, maybe Will and me been lookin' at this thing all wrong. I mean we been talkin' and all we wants in this world is to see you okay. Sure we likes the money and spendin' it and all that, but . . . well, we don't want it if it's comin' outa your heart, Poppa.

I guess we was so damned glad you was alive and gettin' better, and then that wire come in and, well, we just never stopped t'think maybe you don't wanta go back and . . . what I'm gettin' at is, you don't have to lay there thinkin' you gotta get up and start workin' again 'cause Will and me's waitin' to go on. We've been thinkin' maybe we oughta quit the business while we're on top. It would be damned good show business. You know what I mean? Hell, we don't have to break our necks t'perform no more. Why, with the connections and the experience we got maybe there's some other end of it we'd like better. The one sure thing is we'll always make out at whatever we does and we'll always take care of you like we always done." Will was nodding and my father was trying to smile. "Whattya think of that idea, Poppa?"

"It's beautiful, Dad, Massey. But it's not for us. Look, I'm the one who was wrong yesterday, not you guys. Don't worry. We're going back. Maybe they'll think they're coming to a freak show, maybe it'll be curiosity, but they'll be there, I'll have a crack at them. Maybe I won't be able to do it, maybe they'll laugh at me, but at least I'm going to try. I'm not about to just let go like 'Okay, I lose, here's where I get off, and thanks for the ride.'

"I'm going to sing and I'm going to do impressions and I'm going to dance. And I'll do them all better than I ever did. I've got one good eye and I've got my legs, and this isn't going to stop us."

Eddie Cantor sat by the side of my bed doing jokes and talking show business with me for an hour. He smiled. "I see you're still wearing your mezuzah."

"Mr. Cantor, the only time I didn't have it on was the night of the accident. I'd taken it off to shower and I was twenty miles away before I realized I didn't have it. My friend searched the room and found it on the floor behind the dresser. It must've slipped off . . ." As he listened, I suspected that for one moment a question crossed his mind as it had my own, but when I finished he went on to another subject, like myself, refusing to dwell on it.

Eventually it was time for him to leave. "Mr. Cantor, the whole hospital knows you're here, and if you don't stop by the wards, there's gonna be an uprising and a mass hanging of nurses and doctors. I hate to impose on you but if you have time the other patients would get a tremendous kick out of seeing you."

"That's not an imposition, it's a privilege." He stood up and as we shook hands his face became serious, almost paternal in its expression. "Sammy, you've got a tough fight ahead of you. But you've also got a great strength. Never forget what an enormous gift God gave you when He gave you your talent. Treat it as you would anything that is rare and precious. If you protect it and use it well it will carry you wherever you want to go."

I stared out the window thinking about what he'd said. It *was* a gift . . . the best I could ever hope for.

There was a knock on the door. A rugged, athletic looking man in a khaki suit and a button-down collar introduced himself as the rabbi from a nearby congregation.

"Oh, now wait a minute. You've gotta be kidding. A football player, yes, but not a rabbi." I suddenly realized I was doing bits with a minister. "I'm sorry. Please come in."

He smiled and pulled up a chair. The image of a rabbi with a long beard and a silk coat and the big hat which I'd retained from my days as a child around Harlem was in total conflict with this man. He'd come by on his rounds to comfort patients, as other clergymen had, and after a while I said, "Rabbi, we've been talking for an hour about shows, politics, people, everything, right? Now, can we talk a little business? I'm not Jewish, but can you give me some answers anyway?"

"I'd like to try."

"Well, before you came in I was lying here thinking I've been given something. Talent. And the way it's worked out, my talent has been a fantastic edge in life. Now on top of that, I had an accident last week and by all rights I should have been killed, but instead, I came out of it with everything except one eye. I'm up to my ears in flowers and beautiful prayers from thousands of people I never met or heard of, it's like I've got the whole world pulling for me. I'm getting offered more money than I ever saw in my life . . ."

He was smiling. "What's your problem?"

"I don't know . . . maybe I should just take it all and run like a thief, but I figure there's a reason for everything, and things just don't add up. On one hand God gave me talent.

Why? Why me instead of some other guy? Very few Negroes have been given the chance to see what I've seen and to go where I've gone. Why was *I* given this free ticket to a good life? Now on the other hand, He puts me in this accident and when I heard that crash I figured it's over for me. Then I wake up and I'm not exactly better than ever but I'm here and I'm in pretty good shape, so I start thinking, why did He put me into the accident and then save me?"

"Sammy, this talent you speak of is undeniably an extraordinary gift—I've had the pleasure of seeing you on television —but as to why God gave it to you in particular, I can't tell you. Nor can I tell you why He kept you on earth. At best my conclusions would not serve you well. The real answers will only be found within yourself."

"You don't think maybe you could give me a little hint?"

"Do you want answers like 'God saved you because you are one of His children'?"

"I keep thinking maybe He's trying to tell me something. Did I do something wrong, did I let Him down somewhere along the line? And if the accident was a hint that there's something I'm not doing right, then I'm not anxious to wait around for Number Two."

"Sammy, you look upon your accident as a warning or a threat. I can only speak to you as a Jew and interpret it according to our philosophy. We don't believe that goodness should stem from threat of punishment. We worship God in love, not in fear. In the Talmud, which represents many centuries of Jewish thinking, it is written 'Whom the Lord loveth He correcteth.' Therefore, 'Should a man see suffering come upon him let him scrutinize his actions.' We believe that a 'warning' such as you have had comes not to punish you for wrongs you have done but to shake you up a little and perhaps stimulate some spiritual progress—exactly the kind of thinking you're doing now. You're wondering what you might have done wrong. Turn it slightly. Have you done as well as you might have with what God gave you to work with? We believe that man is made in God's image and therefore is endowed with unlimited potential for goodness and greatness. Thus, his most important responsibility is to live up to whatever is within him to be. But only you can know your

210

potential. Only you have the knowledge of where you have succeeded and where you have failed, where you've quit when you shouldn't have. Only you can know if you have been remiss, just as it is only for you to know how good or even how great you might be. All you should be concerned with is, are you falling short of what you might accomplish, what you might be?"

"Rabbi, do you know what the big shake-up is in this whole thing? Until I had this accident I never gave God much thought at all. I mean, I believed in Him but I've got to admit that religion was never exactly uppermost in my mind. But I'll tell you something, I've got a mental picture of myself out on that highway that would scare an atheist into church. It was the most desperate floating-in-space kind of helplessness I ever knew when I fell to my knees and begged God not to let me go blind. Here I was turning to Him and I had no right to even hope He was listening."

"So, do something about it. When you leave here give time to your religion, understand it, develop the faith that you have every reason to have."

"Can I be totally honest with you? On one hand I'm scared to death I'd better find an answer, I'd love to have a complete and unswerving faith in God, and I know what it would mean to me to have it. But on the other hand, down deep at the level you don't even want to admit to yourself, I know that if I had it to do all over again, as much as I'd like to have religion, I'd still get a bigger kick out of 'making it' and having the kind of life I was just starting to have. Do you know what I mean?"

"Certainly. Candy always tastes better than nourishing foods, until we develop an appreciation for the nourishing foods. When that happens you'll find you can take the candy or leave it."

"How do you figure I'm going to find your kind of answers in another church?"

"Sammy, we have no monopoly on the truths of life. The Talmud states: 'The righteous of all nations are worthy of immortality.' There are many mountain tops and all of them reach for the stars."

"That's beautiful." I grinned. "But you won't tell me what I've been doing wrong with my life, right?"

"You asked for a hint. Here's the best I can offer: if throughout a man's lifetime he only breathes the air and enjoys the sun, there will be no sign of him. If he plants a tree—that will remain. 'The greatest use of life is to spend it on something which will outlast it.'"

"What's your way?"

He smiled. "For one thing, trying to help you to help yourself."

"Ah hah! In other words you aren't gonna give me any answers, right? A Jewish fella ain't gonna help a poor colored fella who's laying in bed, an eye missing, with wondering what the answer is. I ask you a question and you give me a do-it-yourself kit, right? Okay, I'll fix you. I'll figure it out myself just to show you I don't need you. . . ." He was helping me already.

It was a strange sensation to know that a flashlight was shining into my eye but I couldn't see it. Dr. Hull snapped off the light and smiled.

"Do I get the new eye soon?"

"The socket is too sore for us to put in anything as large as an eye, but we can begin preparing you for it. During the operation we set a little plastic disc in your socket, about the size of a thumbnail. Your new eye will eventually rest on that. But first we'll use a much smaller plastic ball to accustom you to having a foreign substance in there.

"Don't be surprised to find that you have no control over the lid. It'll flop closed because its muscles were shattered. Eventually it will be held open by the force of the large plastic eye, but until you build up to that you'll need to wear the patch. The drooping lid won't be attractive."

"Let me ask you something about my good eye. I don't see as much as I expected I would."

"There are two factors involved in vision: depth of focus and the area of sight. Try to think of the eyes as a pair of lenses. You understand how 3-D is based on the principle of two eyes looking at an object and giving it roundness? Well, you lose that roundness, or depth of focus, with only one eye. It will never be the same as before but it will be slightly better than it is now. However, the eye compensates. Your area of sight will, in a short time, begin to expand like a wide angle lens until eventually you'll see more with one eye than you could when you had two but closed one."

"Doc, I hate to sound like a starlet, but once I get the plastic eye and I take off the patch, what happens when I look to the side with my good eye? I won't be able to make the false one look that way, too, will I? I mean it'll just stare straight ahead?"

"In the beginning, yes. But in time you'll train the outer muscles to move the plastic eye and you'll be amazed at how much movement you'll be able to get. As I told you a few days ago, the time will come when only you will know that you do not have two natural eyes."

As Dr. Hull neared the door to leave, a nurse came skidding into the room and collided with him. "Oh! Excuse me, doctor!" She was looking past him to me. "*It's Frank Sinatra!* He's on his way up!"

I could hear the excitement in the halls accelerating until it was almost a roar. Nurses were running from room to room gasping, "He's here, in the hospital! Frank Sinatra!" They were going out of their minds, with dropping thermometers and grabbing for lipsticks. . . .

Frank was standing in the doorway, smiling. "Hi'ya, Charley." He came in, flipped his hat onto a chair and looked at me, carefully. "You're going to be all right." He said it emphatically, like he'd just gotten the word from "upstairs." He embraced my father and Will. The nurse was rooted to the floor, staring at him, so flustered that she didn't think to give him a chair. He smiled at her. "H'ya, honey." She nodded like a drunk, with the grin and the glazed eyes.

He pulled up a chair and straddled it, arms resting against its back. "Well, what's happening with the eye?"

"I'll have to wear a patch until the socket heals, then I get a new eye." I shook a cigarette out of a pack and held up my lighter, but the flame missed the end of the cigarette. When I finally got it lit Frank smiled. "You're full of little party tricks, Charley."

"Stick around. For an encore I light my nose."

He'd lit a cigarette, too, and was holding it cupped in the palm of his hand. "How long do the docs figure it'll take you to straighten out?"

"They say maybe three months, but they're not sure."

"Have you still got the place in the Sunset Colonial?"

213

"Yeah. I've been keeping it."

"Well, we've got to get you out of there. That's for openers. You can't live there any more. You should have a house."

"I tried to get one, but it's . . ."

"You'll have a house in the hills where you can get some quiet and still not be in the Yukon." He looked over at my father. "I'll be in touch with you on it." He turned back to me. "We'll get you something small, a rental until you know exactly what you want. You should have a couple of guys living with you until you're on your feet. Do you know when you're leaving here?"

"A few days, I think."

"Why don't you come out to my place at the Springs and spend a couple of weeks with me? Hey, what the hell are you crying about?"

"Frank . . . I can't tell you what it means to me for you to come here . . . I thought maybe the magazine thing. . . ."

"So what else is new?"

"But . . ."

"Forget it, Charley. You don't even have to mention it. Have you decided where you want to open?"

"Well, that Vegas money looks awfully good, but I've got a funny kind of a feeling about our first date. Herman Hover can only give us five thousand and though I hate to go for the short money, well, I've been thinking maybe we should go back to Ciro's where it all began for us."

"You're definitely right. The important thing is to start strong, and in L.A. you'll be home where you know you have friends around you. The Vegas money'll still be there." He looked across the room. Will nodded. "Meanwhile, Charley, get your health back. Rest, don't rush."

"I wish it was that simple. Let's say it takes three months. By then, all this fantastic publicity I'm getting won't mean beans—I'll have blown all this momentum. On the other hand, obviously I can't come back too early, coming on like I'm stumbling around for sympathy."

"First of all you've got no choice. You wait until you're ready! Secondly, don't worry about the momentum. They'll wait for you. The day you go back to work you'll be as hot as you are today."

"I wish I could believe that."

He raised an eyebrow and half-smiled. "You want to talk about comebacks?"

He stood up and picked up his hat. "I'll see you at the Springs." He walked over to the bed and put his hand on my shoulder. "Relax. You're going to be bigger than ever, Charley. Bigger than ever."

Flash bulbs were popping all over the room and a guy with a newsreel camera was walking in close to the bed. I turned slightly so he'd get a good shot of the patch, and gave him a Charley Brave smile.

"Hey, is that the morning's mail, Sammy?" He was pointing to the three tables of letters in the corner of the room. "I hope you at least got some money in all those letters."

"Have you read 'em all?"

"Hey, fellas, I've only got one eye, remember?" It got a laugh.

"Sammy, is it true that Jeff Chandler offered you his eye?"

"Yes. Jeff offered a cornea for transplantation, and I understand that I've had nine other offers since then."

"Why do you think Chandler offered to give you his eye?"

"He's my friend, and that's just the kind of a man he is."

"Sammy, tell us your side of the story on you and Ava Gardner." He winked. "I mean, confidentially."

Everybody laughed. "There's nothing to tell. It's totally false. The guy who wrote it should win a prize for fiction. Like ten years in jail!"

"You mean there's nothing to it?"

"Baby, will you please take another look at this kisser of mine? Now you *know* I ain't about to get *that* lucky!"

"Isn't Frank Sinatra a friend of yours? How'd he feel about it? I mean with her being his ex-wife?"

"He came to visit me yesterday."

"Did he mention the story?"

"No. I brought it up but he wouldn't even discuss it."

"Isn't that kinda strange?"

"No. To discuss it would be like saying there was a possibility it was true and that would conflict with his belief that if you have a friend then he's your friend and you believe in him and that's *it*. If he'd thought about me to the contrary he just wouldn't have shown."

"Have you heard that because of what happened to you the Cadillac people are redesigning their steering wheel? They're inverting the thing that sticks up in the center."

"Sammy, now that you've had almost a week to think about it what's your feeling about what happened to you? Have you wondered, 'Why me?' "

"Baby, all I can say is that God must have had his arms around me. He really did or I would have been killed. I understand there was an identical accident in Oregon just two days ago and everybody in both cars was killed instantly. So if there's any 'why me' it can only be why did He let *me* live?"

"How do you think it'll affect your career?"

"That's entirely up to the public. If they still want me I'll be there." I pointed to the letters. "It's gonna take me a long time to answer them all. In the meantime, you guys could do me a big favor if you'd mention how grateful I am for the fantastic support they've given me."

"Y'mean the mail gave you something to lean on?"

"Baby, I can't begin to describe what it's like to have total strangers take the trouble to send little prayers and to tell you they're rooting for you. I'm having all those letters bound in books 'cause I don't ever want to be without them. Anytime I feel unlucky I'll just take them out and read how wrong I am."

"Sammy, are you trying to tell us you feel lucky?"

"I hate to do the great movie cliché where the guy says, 'I lost an eye, my face is scarred, my career is shot to hell but I'm lucky to be alive.' I know it's awfully cornball but I really mean it. This may sound ridiculous, but I'm beginning to think that as awful as it was maybe it was the best thing that ever happened to me."

"How so?"

"Well, if you'll pardon the expression, it opened my eyes." They were writing down every word. I was swinging.

When the room had cleared, I noticed Will standing in front of the window, and I was suddenly aware that he'd been there through the entire press conference. I had a mental picture of him looking at the reporters . . . but nobody had asked him anything. Okay, they were mostly interested in the accident, but we'd talked about the act and they hadn't noticed him. Nor had I. He'd just been there in the corner, the forgotten man. Now he was looking out the window, his face expressionless and still except for a single muscle moving in his cheek. He didn't know I was watching him and what I saw in that unguarded moment was completely unlike the man I'd known all my life. I'd seen many sides of him—serenity, stubbornness, his own kind of quiet arrogance, kindness, wisdom, all the facets—but never before had he appeared to be lost, almost helpless. Even during our worst days, when we'd been locked out and hungry, he'd been in control. I couldn't stop watching him and for a moment I was afraid he'd catch me intruding on his privacy, but I turned away a second before he looked up and smiled. "I'm going downstairs for some coffee, Sammy. I'll be back soon."

I nodded and watched him leave. Will isn't the type that goes for coffee. He has it with his meals and he doesn't have anything in between. He was going to take care of something he didn't want me to know about, probably paying the bill. He did those things quietly, never making a big thing out of it to remind me I should have saved my money. If he wanted to do that he'd come right out and say, "You should have saved your money." He'd never try to make me feel beholden to him. I could appreciate the quiet, sure way he'd taken care of everything all week. I remembered a lot of things I'd often forgotten. Despite our arguments and problems, Will had always been there when I needed him, in the way that he could be there. And I'd needed him a lot.

What could be going on in his mind? Isn't he happy that maybe we're about to move into the real big time? Had I been wrong? Did he fear the same things I did? Even so, that couldn't bother him this much. He's been on a seesaw for fifty years. He must be in his sixties and at least fifty of them have been spent hoofing in every broken-down toilet from one coast to the other. I remembered him telling me Bill Robinson made $3500 a week, as if it were all the money in the world. Now, at an age when logically an act should decline, Will's moving into a bigger big time than he could ever have imagined. So, why isn't he happy? Maybe it doesn't mean as much to him as it does to me and my father. He doesn't spend his money. He doesn't care about big hotel suites or a new car. What *is* the big time to him? His pleasure has always come from the business itself and from being respected in it. I think if he had his choice of a million dollars a year working in a store, or room and board in show business, he wouldn't give it a minute's thought, he'd put on his shoes and start dancing.

He'd been completely thrown by the new Vegas offer. He'd thought there was a mistake in the telegram and he was insulted that they were offering us only twenty-five hundred. He'd checked with Western Union and then with the Morris office before he'd been able to believe it was really twenty-five thousand.

Had I hurt his pride with that horrible scene the other day? Has he begun to feel insecure now that I'm carrying him? Does he think I could possibly forget all the years he carried me? Is he wondering if someday I'll say, "From now on I'm doing a single," and he'll be back in the three-a-day again? Except there is no three-a-day any more.

How can he possibly enjoy his new position in the business if he's worrying that any day I might squeeze him out? And he has every reason to fear it. We have no contract, no blood ties, there'd be no way he could stop me, nor would he try. He'd keep his dignity and say good-bye. But it would kill him.

The injustice of it was overwhelming. To work your whole life for something and finally get it, but with a string attached, a string that could yank it away from you at any time— he'd earned far better than that.

He came back, smiled hello and walked over to the window. "Massey?" He turned around. "Massey, I've been thinking. We're moving into a new phase of our careers, you know, the offers we've been getting . . ." His shoulders tensed, almost as though he were thinking, "Here it comes." That wasn't what I'd wanted. I hadn't meant to scare him. I'd intended to make a nice little speech but now I had to rush it. "We should have a contract, Massey. You, me, and Dad. We'll split everything three ways, like always, and you're the manager like always with the same billing and everything, but we should have it in writing."

He spoke slowly. "We don't need a contract."

"Massey, it should be in writing."

He didn't answer right away. "Are you sure that's what you want, Sammy?"

"That's what I want."

He walked to the side of the bed and I saw the look of

gratitude and relief from the tremendous fear that good man had been carrying. It flashed across his face and he turned away for a second. But now he was looking straight at me. He put out his hand and the touch of it, the feel of his strength, carried me back through all the years we'd been together.

I turned my pillow for the tenth time. When its cool freshness had become warm and soggy I sat up in the dark room and lit a cigarette. Would we really be bigger than ever, or would we go down the drain? I listened to the sounds of the hospital, the sure, everything's-going-to-be-all-right sounds, the anesthesia for reality. Hospitals are so safe. You're exposed to no one but well-wishers, friends who come loaded with pocketsful of optimism, doctors and nurses who speak in carefully worded encouragements, and who can stop the pain of almost anything but the future. It had been so easy to decide I'll perform like always, so pleasant to daydream that we'd be bigger than ever, that I'd be better than ever, so easy to be a hit while I was safely in bed where all problems hung suspended and harmless and where success could be enjoyed just by planning it. I'd been so sure I could go out and just walk onto the stage and dance my head off, I'd already heard the applause. Now I was afraid to sleep, dreading the passing of every hour that was bringing me closer to the moment when I'd have to step outside and do it.

Dr. Hull came by early in the morning to say good-bye. "I want you to drive the car yourself at least part of the way to Los Angeles. You'll be afraid, particularly when you can't judge distance as well as you used to. But you can drive safely if you're careful, and you must conquer the fear. In all things. The driving is only symbolic. You must walk out of here a whole man."

I dressed slowly and tried the patch over my eye at different angles. Arthur walked with me while I said good-bye to all the other patients I'd gotten to know. I did bits with the nurses, like, "Anytime you wanta be in pictures, baby . . ." That kind of humor. They laughed, but they knew I was scared. Maybe it happens to everyone who walks away from death.

There was no way to stall any more. I walked downstairs and out the front door. My father and Will were sitting in the back seat of a new Cadillac convertible, a duplicate of the one I'd smashed up.

I sat in the driver's seat. The upraised knob in the center of the steering wheel looked so harmless. I tapped it with my finger. "Well, here we go, folks. Double or nothing." Nobody laughed.

I turned the key in the ignition. My hand trembled as I put the car in gear. I looked at the car parked ahead of us. It seemed to be about fifty feet away, but I couldn't be sure. I took my foot off the brake and the car started moving forward.

15

"CAN SAMMY RUN AGAIN?" ALONGSIDE THE STORY WAS a two-column picture of me wearing the patch. "Sammy Davis, Jr. is scheduled to begin a four week engagement at Ciro's in mid-March. The announcement by Herman Hover causes one to speculate as to whether the Sammy Davis, Jr. who'll open at Ciro's can possibly bear any resemblance to the dazzling figure of perpetual motion whose career only two months ago loomed as one of the brightest in show business. . . ."

The rehearsal room was empty except for some chairs, a long mirror across one wall and an upright piano with a record player on top of it. I didn't want Morty or anybody around so I'd brought some records. I wasn't too worried about the singing or the impressions. My balance and sense of depth had become pretty good for normal things but dancing was going to be something else. I put "Fascinating Rhythm" on the machine and lowered the needle onto the record.

It was as if I'd never danced before. My legs shook, I had almost no wind at all, every turn brought a knife-stab to my eye, the tempo seemed faster than it had ever been and I was fighting to keep up with it. I kicked myself in the leg and tripped. I saw myself in the mirror, sitting on the floor, one hand protecting my eye, gasping for breath, my shirt wet and clinging to me. I pictured myself falling like that in a club. I'd have landed on somebody's table. I can't come back like, "Gee, isn't it great how hard he's trying." That's death. When I come back there can be no "He's almost as good as he ever was." I've got to be *better!*

The needle was scratching on the label of the record. I got up, picked out a slower record and started dancing again. My eye burned and throbbed but I didn't dare stop.

After a few hours I drove home to the house my father had rented for me, with Frank's help. It was a small house in the Hollywood hills, and I'd gotten Dave Landfield, a kid trying to get started in pictures, to move in with me. My father's car was parked outside.

He was pacing the living room. "Poppa, I don't mean to push you but me and Will's been waitin' for you to call a rehearsal. It's only a coupla weeks off now and we knows you hates to rehearse and all, but . . ."

"Dad, I just lost an eye!"

"We knows that, Poppa, and the last thing I wanta do . . ."

"What's the matter? You guys afraid I can't do it any more?"

"Now you knows better'n that . . ."

I lit a cigarette and blew out a long, steady stream of smoke. "Look, you and Will Mastin just worry about yourselves. When the time comes, I'll be on that stage and swinging."

I saw Ciro's lights from a few blocks away on Sunset Boulevard, and as we drew closer I could see a line of people extending all the way around the block. "They're waitin' for you, Poppa." He turned the corner and pulled up to the stage entrance. He came around to my side, opened the door and reached in to help me make the move. "You're gonna tie 'em in a knot, son." He was looking at me hard and straight, trying to give me the strength he knew I needed. "Come on, Poppa, we're goin' back into show business. And this time we're stayin' there." I couldn't answer him. I put my arm around him and we went into the club.

The dressing room was so crowded with flowers that we could hardly get in. I changed out of my clothes and into a robe and started putting on my make-up.

"Hi'ya, Charley." Frank was smiling into the mirror at me. "I just wanted to let you know that I'm going to introduce you out there." He gripped my shoulder. "The patch is dramatic as hell. See you in the wings."

People were filling the dressing room—close people—talking, laughing. I had to be by myself. I went into the bathroom and closed the door. I looked at my face in the mirror. Can they possibly relax and enjoy the act with the patch there to constantly remind them I've got no eye?

I leaned against the wall, waiting, wondering what it was going to be like.

There was a knock on the door. "Poppa? You ready to go?"

My father, Will and I were taking the same walk we'd taken a thousand times in a thousand clubs but I felt like I was ten seconds behind every step I took.

Frank was speaking to the audience. Then he was coming toward me, holding out his hand, and I was walking onstage to meet him. The applause began and out of the corner of my eye I saw people starting to stand up. Frank hugged me hard and whispered, "Don't let 'em throw you, Charley. Tonight you're the only star in the room."

I looked out into the audience. From one end of Ciro's to the other were the giants of the motion picture industry—the Cary Grants, the Bogarts, the Edward G. Robinsons, the Spencer Tracys, Gary Coopers, Jimmy Cagneys, Dick Powells—standing and applauding. I saw tears rolling down June Allyson's cheeks. People were shouting "Bravo" and whistling. I didn't know how to stop them and I didn't want to. Their faces held expressions of warmth and elation that you expect from your own family, as though they were taking personal pride that I was back, like it was their joy as much as my own. The curiosity I'd expected wasn't there at all, nor anything that resembled it. Never had I felt so

much a part of show business. All that it had given me ma-
terially was nothing compared to the kinship I felt for all
those people, strangers who'd come out because somebody
in the business had had a rough time. I felt that they weren't
there to see me entertain as much as to root me home. I saw
Frank at his table, applauding, smiling and nodding, and
Mama sitting at the ringside seeing this happening to me.

The applause kept on and on, building until I almost
couldn't breathe, and I knew that if I didn't start performing
I wouldn't be able to. I put up my hands asking them to
stop, and little by little they sat down and the room became
quiet. Morty was waiting for the cue. I wanted to say something to them first, but could I do lines like "You'll never
know how grateful I am for this reception" or "I'm thrilled
to be here"? They were the right words, but they'd been
canned and used to death in the standard, everyday "show
business sincerity." I nodded to Morty and at the sound of
the first chord all my strength and confidence was back as
though I'd never been away. I finished "Black Magic" and
they were out of their seats. I turned and bowed to Morty
for the arrangement he'd done. The second I started my
turn back toward the audience I realized I was spinning
toward my blind side, but it was too late to stop myself
and my head slammed into the microphone. There was a
horrible, loud crack! The audience gasped. The pain was
as though a burning cigar were being ground into my bad
eye. A thousand hands that had been applauding froze in
mid-air, and the room which had been exploding with
sound became deathly quiet.

I reached out, patted the mike and smiled. "Sorry, Frank.
Didn't see you come in, baby."

There was a split second of even greater silence, then a
scream of relief and I was doing the Jerry Lewis strut
around the stage—half to keep the laugh going until they
could relax and half so I could have a breather until the
pain in my eye subsided. I cued Morty for another chorus
of "Black Magic," and as I finished it I waved, "So long,
folks, gotta go do a Hathaway shirt ad."

I leaned against the wall in the wings listening to their
roars for more. All my fears had been for nothing. They'd
go whichever way I played it: if I went for the sympathy,

I'd get it—until I was sympathized right out of the business; or I could brush it off, kid it, and eventually they'd forget everything except my performance.

I hurried back on and did everything I could think of—every song, every dance, every gag I could invent or remember since I was five years old. I did Danny Kaye which I hadn't done in years and I did half the people in the room. All the show business rules of "leave 'em wanting more" fell by the wayside because it was I who could never get enough of what they were giving me.

I'd been on for over two hours, done three closing numbers and run out of excuses to stay on. I bowed a long last thank-you and when I looked up they were standing and applauding; Herman Hover was walking onstage followed by every waiter, bus boy, every cook and kitchen helper in the club. They formed a semicircle around me, the band began playing "Auld Lang Syne," and they were singing to me—led by the Chinese chef holding a long spoon for a baton. The audience fell apart . I fell apart. I just stood there crying like a baby, not just little tears, but deep, racking sobs.

Marilyn Monroe and Milton Greene were waiting for me. I'd read in one of the trades that Milton was ". . . financing and masterminding MM's break from Fox . . ." I'd been dying to meet her, not for the boy-girl jazz, just for the kick of knowing Marilyn Monroe, so I'd asked Milton to bring her to the opening. When the dressing room cleared, he asked, "You want to go back to my place and have a drink?"

"Not on your Rolleiflex, Milton, old buddy. I've had it with the Garbo bit. You and I are going to take Marilyn to the Mocambo, then it's a definite see-and-be-seen at the Crescendo . . ."

The smell of freshly percolated coffee came drifting into my bedroom, waking me up. Dave Landfield was in the kitchen eating breakfast and reading a newspaper. He handed it to me. "You don't have to bother opening it. You're on the front page."

There was a picture of Marilyn Monroe, Milton, Mel Tormé and me, at the Crescendo. It was captioned "FIRST NIGHT OUT." "Baby, I'd like to be Charley Blasé about this, but you've gotta admit that when a guy who hasn't killed somebody gets his picture on Page One, then it means he's pretty important, right?"

"The whole thing is fantastic. The phone's been going like a madman all morning." I poured myself some coffee and he handed me a pile of telegrams. I opened the top one. "Never dug you before. Dug you last night. You the man. Marlon."

Dave was pointing to an item in one of the Hollywood columns. ". . . Guess which double initialed, blonde movie queen and Sammy Davis, Jr. are mmmmmmm. . . ."

He looked at me. "They must mean Marilyn Monroe."

"Baby, they don't mean Myrna Malted."

I knew the columnist so I called him. "Look, if someone told you there's something between Marilyn Monroe and me, it's a lie. You've gotta retract it. There's not even a thought of anything."

"You were out with her, weren't you?"

"I was in her party. The picture is in all the papers, and you can see that Milton Green and Mel Tormé were with her, too."

"What do you think of her?"

"What can I think? She's tremendously exciting to be with. My God, she's *Marilyn Monroe*."

The "retraction" read: ". . . Sammy Davis, Jr. admits that blonde movie star is 'tremendously exciting to be with' . . ."

The next morning's paper had another blind item about us. I went down to Jess Rand's office. "Baby, you've got to do something. This kind of publicity is death. The public's not going to stand for it. Not on top of the Ava Gardner thing."

He tossed a magazine across the desk at me. "Hot out of the sewer today."

It was a new scandal magazine and it had separate pictures of me and Zsa Zsa Gabor on the cover but with a headline linking us romantically. "I never even *met* this woman."

"What're you, a stickler for accuracy? *Confidential* created a thing with you and a white movie star and it turned out to be their biggest selling issue so this one is following

225

the same formula." He shrugged. "There must be something about you and white chicks that people want to read, so you'd better prepare yourself to keep seeing it until the people are tired of it."

"Are you telling me I should just sit still while some guy goes passing the word around, 'Hey, you wanta sell magazines? Link Sammy Davis with a white movie star and you're in business'? I don't need this kind of trouble."

"Wait a minute. Okay, it's no bundle of laughs, and we're certainly not going out and looking for it, but exactly what kind of trouble do you mean? The fact that *Confidential* destroyed you to such a point that a guy has to slip somebody a hundred bucks to get anywhere near the ringside at Ciro's? The fact that they could fill the Hollywood Bowl with your overflow every night? The fact that last night they had to turn away *Rock Hudson?*"

I dropped the magazine onto his desk. "Yeah, how *about* that?"

He grinned wryly. "Everybody I handle should have your kind of trouble."

I stood up. "Well, look, shouldn't I at least sue them?"

"Chicky, the damage is done, and they probably don't have anything for you to win anyhow. Forget it. All it can do is make you a little more famous."

I heard a horn tooting, and looked out the window. My father was stepping out of a brand new Fleetwood Cadillac. I opened the front door and he floated in. "Just got delivery on her an hour ago. Now ain't she a hummer?"

We stood in the doorway gazing at it. "You trade your other one against it?"

"Hell no. This one's for dressy wear. Listen, whattya think about us goin' down to the showroom tomorrow? They're gettin' the new model convertibles in and I've always had it in mind to have me one of them."

"Dad, you must be losing your mind! What're you gonna do with three cars?"

He was giddy. "Poppa, I don't care if two of 'em stays on jacks. I'd just like t'know I owns thre Cadillacs."

His car horn was honking and a guy in the front seat called out. "Hey, Horse, it's gettin' late."

I stared at my father. "*Horse?*"

He nodded. "That's kinda a name some of the boys got for me. It's in honor of where my money goes." He smacked me on the back. "See y'later, Poppa. Gotta go look after my investments!"

Humphrey Bogart opened the dressing room door and looked in. Will rushed over to shake hands. "How'd you like the show, Mr. Bogart?"

"The show was great. But you're too damned old for the business. Why don't you retire? The kid's the whole show!" The smile froze on Will's face. He'd been expecting a pleasant compliment but he'd asked the wrong man. When you asked Bogart a question he assumed you wanted his honest opinion and he didn't do Dale Carnegie answers. "Look, I don't mean to hurt your feelings but why don't you face reality? You and the old man are doing less than you did the last time I saw you here and you weren't doing much even then. The nostalgia's wearing a little thin, y'know. The people have stopped saying, 'Isn't it nice they're still together?' and if you're half the showman I know you are, then you oughta see it."

Frank led me into his den, chose an album, adjusted the volume to the level he wanted and poured a drink. There'd been so many people around us at the club that it was the first time we could really talk. "You're doing great, Charley. There's nothing I can tell you about the dancing and the impressions, but about the singing: you've got to get yourself your own sound, your own style. It's okay to sound like me—if you're me. I'm only flattered that you like what I do well enough to be influenced by it and your ear for making other people's sounds isn't helping any, but it's a dead end. No matter how good it is, no copy of anything ever sold for as high as the original."

It was almost light out as I started up the hill but as I pulled up to the house it was all I could do to find a parking space. The place was swinging with performers from clubs all over town. I made my entrance. Some of them were drinking, listening to music, some of them were half asleep —but they all were waiting. I moved around the room. "I'm awfully sorry. I got hung up, couldn't help myself."

They waved away my apologies like they understood. Dave was careening around the room doing charming-bits with half a dozen of the best-looking starlets in town. As he passed me on his rounds he gestured across the room. Jimmy Dean was huddled crouched in his usual corner, legs crossed under him, glasses down on his nose, wearing an old sweatshirt, levis and sneakers. "He doesn't talk much but you've gotta admit he dresses good." He lowered his voice. "What's *with* this kook?"

"Why ask *me?* Ella Logan brought him backstage, he's breaking into pictures, he did *East of Eden* and I think he's making another one." Jimmy saw me looking at him and smiled and waved.

Dave whispered, "Hey, folks, it moved. Another week in that spot and he'll take root. He doesn't even make a move for a chick." He sighed. "Oh, well, all the more for me." A couple of new girls came in the front door. Dave winked. "Take two, they're small," and zoomed toward them.

I turned up the hi-fi set and played my bongo drums. I looked around because I felt somebody staring at me. It was Jimmy, giving me the over-the-glasses jazz from the corner. I walked over and sat down next to him. "Hey, lemme ask you something. What the hell are you watching every night? You never talk to anyone, you don't look like you're having laughs . . . what're you doing always sitting in the corner watching people? Why don't you get a girl or something? Have a little booze and *be* somebody!"

"Man, the only thing I want is to be an actor."

"So be an actor. But you don't have to be dead the rest of the time. You a little shy? Is that it? You want me to fix you up with one of the chicks?"

He smiled pleasantly but shook his head. "Man, all I want is to be a good actor."

"Whoops. This is where I came in. See y'around." I got up, buckled on my quick-draw holster and walked over to one of the guys who was working in TV westerns. I did all the fancy moves and spins with the gun and dropped it into the holster.

"Sam? Can I try your gun?"

"Jimmy, *anything* just to stop you doing that creepy peepy bit." He buckled on my holster, pushed his glasses up on his nose and tried to draw. "Don't go for the speed. Just get it right, first."

He tried and dropped the gun. It hit the floor, hard. I folded my arms, Oliver Hardy style. "Every move's a picture!"

Dave grabbed me by the arm. "I don't know how I forgot this! You got a call from Judy Kanter. She wants to throw a party for you Wednesday night."

"Crazy. No, wait a minute. She'll have to make it Thursday. Thursday between five and eight."

"Sam! Her husband's a vice president at MCA and her father's the president of Paramount Pictures. Don't get her angry. They could make me a star."

"Sorry, old buddy, but I happen to be very big on Wednesday. I've already got two parties being thrown in my honor."

He was looking at me wistfully. "It must be fantastic to make it like this."

"Yeah, I've gotta admit it. The world is my oyster, and I'm the little black pearl!"

He didn't speak. He just stood there, not conscious of the way he was smiling at me, transplanting himself into my life, enjoying a glimpse of what he wanted so badly.

"Listen, Dave, I've got a wild idea. I mean if you'd be interested. Why don't you come on the road with me as sort of a secretary-buddy? I need somebody who's hip and who I can trust. You'll be able to make some money, you'll be around the business, maybe you'll meet somebody who'll do you some good—I'll certainly help you with anything I can. At least you can put off going back to the blouse business. And we'll have a million laughs besides."

"You just hired a secretary-buddy. When do I start?"

"Right now." I gave him a shot on the arm. "The first thing you can do is take care of our rooms in Chicago. It's your home town. Get us the best two-bedroom suite in the best hotel there."

"Hey, that runs into money."

"Dave. You're working for a star! And if we ain't goin' First Cabin then the boat ain't leavin' the dock."

I sat on the floor in the center of the crowd. Somebody handed me a coke. A couple of chicks were giving me smiles but I couldn't have been happier that Dave was keeping them busy. I was so tired I couldn't even concentrate on the conversations going on around me.

Someone was shaking me gently. "Sammy, you'll catch a cold sleeping on the floor." I looked up. "No, I'm fine. Thanks, baby." One of the chicks was saying, "Maybe we oughta leave?" Dave took care of them for me. "He's happy. He's just catching a few winks." ". . . We should put a blanket over him or something." ". . . Take that glass away so he can't roll on it and cut himself."

The hi-fi set was going softly and someone was playing along with it on my bongo drums, the laughter and the talk and the party sounds surrounded me and I felt myself sinking deeper and more comfortably into the floor.

part

III

16

THE ROOM CLERK SHUFFLED THROUGH A STACK OF reservations, glancing at them in a way that you knew he knew he wasn't going to find what he was looking for. He smiled weakly. "I'm terribly sorry, Mr. Davis, but there's no reservation for you. And we're entirely filled up!"

Dave didn't catch on. "But I wired you two weeks ago."

"Well, uh, we tried to notify you—but we didn't have the address."

Morty glared at him. "Why didn't you try sending it to 'Sammy Davis, Jr., U.S.A.'?"

I sat in the cab between Dave and Monty, looking straight ahead while the doorman put our bags into the trunk. I thought this was all behind me. I really did. There was a sharp crack. The sunglasses I'd been holding had snapped in my hand.

"Take it easy, Sam."

I looked at the cracked lens and a trickle of blood coming out of my palm. "I *am* taking it easy."

We stopped at a drugstore and Dave got out to call another hotel. I rubbed the skin over my knuckles, watching the color lighten under the pressure of my thumb and then come back to normal. Morty sat next to me, silent. I stared up at the ceiling of the cab.

I'm a star. This isn't supposed to happen any more.

Dave was bustling around the suite anxiously, like a hostess. "This is great. Beautiful. Aside from all this space—and not to mention that it's the Presidential Suite—plus the fact it costs less and it's almost walking distance to the club.

And we don't have to be so worried if maybe we spill a drink or something. . . ."

I waited until he was all through. "Thank you very much. Now come on, let's get out of here and *be* somebody."

We found a great men's shop on Michigan Avenue and I went through it like a giant suction machine. I thought I'd covered everything when I spotted a gorgeous silk robe on a store dummy. "Now how'd I miss seeing *this*?" I felt the richness of the silk. "Yeah, this baby's gonna be wrapping its arms around me tonight."

"I'll get one in your size, sir."

I caught a look at a discreet price tag. $250. "Oops. I'd better check my cash. I've only got a thousand or so with me. How much have I spent already?"

Embarrassment swept across his face as though I'd ripped the brass buttons off his coat and drummed him out of the corps. "Please, Mr. Davis, we'll be offended if you give it even a moment's thought. Your face is your credit card here."

When we got outside Morty was in a cold sweat. "How much did you just spend in there?"

"Baby, I'm no bookkeeper. What's the difference? It's not how much you spend, it's how good you feel."

"Don't you think you should take it a little easy?"

"No, Morty, I *don't* think I should take it a little easy. And if you're gonna be a drag I'm not taking you shopping with me any more. Look, we'll be in Vegas soon, for a whole month. That's a hundred thousand dollars. Now you know I didn't spend *that* much."

In the dressing room my father said, "I'm sorry about what happened with the hotel."

Will nodded. "I'll make arrangements for your room in Frisco. I suppose you'll want a suite."

"Thanks, Massey, but I'm staying at The Fairmont."

"Now, Poppa . . ."

"Sammy, what's wrong with where we always stayed? It's a good hotel."

"There's nothing wrong with it, but I'll be playing The Fairmont and I'll be living at The Fairmont, because it's better than our old place, it's more convenient, and if any other star were playing there, there wouldn't be the slightest question where he's staying."

"Poppa, you saw what happened here."

"It's not going to happen at The Fairmont. If they don't want to give me a beautiful suite, then they're going to have to get on the phone and call all the people with reservations and tell 'em, 'Don't bother coming over, 'cause there ain't no show.' "

Will was shaking his head. "You can't get happiness out of forcing yourself on people."

"Massey? You think you're not good enough to live at The Fairmont?"

"It's not what I think, it's what they think."

"Well, they're wrong. And I'm not about to help convince 'em they're right. If I stay away from where I want to be and where I've got a right to be, then I'm as much as saying, 'Yeah, I agree with you. Colored people shouldn't be here.' "

"Poppa, you're knockin' your head against a stone wall. You're the same now as when you was a kid and they broke your nose at that hotel up North."

"Well they're not breaking my nose any more. Thank God I'm too big for that jazz."

"You ain't too big for 'em to break your heart givin' you dirty looks when you walk across their lobby all by yourself. I was hopin' maybe you'd learned to protect yourself. We've got everything comin' our way now. Why don't you get a little peace for yourself? Why let 'em hurt you?"

"Dad, don't you see, there's nothing they can do to me that'll hurt anywhere near as bad as if I help them to do it. I'm not choked up about the looks and knowing maybe they don't want me, but if the day ever comes when I can get first best, and I willingly settle for less just so I can 'live in peace with others' then I'm not going to be able to live with myself.

"Look, I know you guys are only trying to spare me trouble, and I'm hip to the fact that I'm approaching life differently than the 'rules' demand, but this is America and I'm going to live in it like anybody else! I'm going to go as First Cabin as my income, my sophistication, and my fame rate me. I worked for it, I earned it, I'm entitled to it, and I intend to have it."

The cab stopped in front of The Fairmont. Morty and Dave got out, and I took my time paying the driver, watching the doorman who was hurrying toward us. I got out and handed him a five. "Will you take care of our bags, please? My man will be along with them in another cab."

He tipped his hat. "Yes, Mr. Davis. Thank you."

Dave had gone in and Morty was motioning for me to go ahead. I gave him a little push. "After you, baby."

As my foot touched the floor of the lobby, I felt as though I were starting to cross a minefield. A short, thin little man, like a Donald Meek movie character, was gliding across the lobby toward us, hand extended while he was still twenty feet away. "Oh, Mr. Davis, welcome to The Fairmont. My name is Frye. The assistant manager." He snapped his fingers viciously at a bellboy. "Mr. Davis' overnight bag!"

"Mr. Frye, this is Mr. Stevens, my conductor, and Mr. Landfield, my secretary. They'll be staying with me."

"Splendid." He was looking at me like he would at his boss's kid who'd just barely got over the measles.

I started toward the front desk. He stopped me. "We can go directly upstairs. You're already registered, sir." He led me through the lobby to the elevators.

Is he trying to get me out of sight, fast? I felt the looks and the nudging I was causing all over the lobby. Why shouldn't they look? I'm a celebrity.

Mr. Frye was beaming at my camera case. "So you're a photographer, too! Does your well never run dry?" He poked at the elevator bell, impatiently glancing up at the floor indicator. "So sorry to keep you waiting." The elevator doors slid open, he smiled me in ahead of him and ordered the operator, "Express to the top." He turned to me. "We've certainly been looking forward to your arrival. Your engagement will be mammoth. Absolutely mammoth. We had to move the bandstand to create space for more tables. But I daresay that's an old story to you."

"Well you know what they say, the old jokes are the best."

He slapped his knee. "Oh, that's charming, charming."

The doors slid open and he bowed us off the elevator and ran to catch up with us. "Ah . . . here we are." He flung open the door like Loretta Young. "We've chosen one of our roomiest suites for you. We do want you to be comfortable. There's a television in every room, we've put in a small refrigerator . . ." He fluttered around showing me where the couch was. "Now, if there's anything at all that you should want, don't forget, the name is Frye. Just think of fried chicken, and think of—*oh!* Oh dear, I . . . well, good day, gentlemen." He fled.

I flopped into a chair.

Morty grinned. "You wanta do ten minutes on Mr. Frye?"

Dave asked, "Anybody hungry? I'm starved."

"Call room service for some menus, baby."

"Crazy, Sambo."

It hit me from behind like a rabbit punch. I went out the door and rushed for the elevator.

People recognized the patch. The fresh air and the smiling and waving at me felt good and I was annoyed with myself for letting Mr. Frye get to me. At least he was trying to be nice. And poor Dave. He'd have called me Sambo if I were white. I had a mental picture of him in the hall as I'd left, standing a safe distance away from me, arms outstretched, gaping at me.

I stopped at the jewelry shop in the hotel, picked out a gold watch and gave the clerk three hundred dollars. Dave leaped out of his chair as the door opened, like a string had been connected between them. "Hey, look, I don't know what I said or did . . ."

I tossed the watch to him. "Do me a favor, Dave, put that on your wrist, because that chrome job you've got doesn't look like you work for a star."

"I guess it wouldn't be a benefit if we didn't get creamed chicken."

The man seated next to me on the dais laughed. "Don't complain. I do this almost every day." He put out his hand. "My name is Alvin Fine. I'm Rabbi of the Congregation Emanu-El."

He got up to make the opening speech and without a wasted word or an idle thought; with just logic, sincerity, and dignity, he completely wrapped up the audience. He wasn't much older than I, but an old-world wisdom poured out of him in combination with the most modern terminology, almost hip. As he sat down I said, "Thanks a bunch. Y'know, I'm not exactly choked up about following you."

He smiled. "Thanks, but I'm not worried about you."

When I returned to my seat I said, "Rabbi, I had an automobile accident a few months ago, and while I was in the hospital I met a rabbi who talked a lot like you do, and I really liked what he said." I reached under my shirt and showed him my mezuzah. "A friend of mine gave me this. I wear it for sentiment, not as a religious thing, but I'm interested in Judaism, or maybe you'd call it curious. Are there any books you'd suggest that could give me the general idea? I don't mean to sound like I'm asking for Instant Judaism, I realize it's a big subject. . . ."

"If you'll excuse an anecdote, years ago a man challenged the great Hillel to explain all there was to know about Judaism, while standing on one foot. Hillel stood on one foot and said: 'What is hateful to thee, do not unto thy neighbor.' In those ten words which we know today as the Golden Rule he had recited the basic principle of Judaism. Naturally, there's a great deal more, but that's the core of it."

"Well, nobody can argue with that kind of thinking."

He smiled. "We've been getting arguments for thousands of years." He wrote some titles on the back of a menu. "I hope you'll find these to be interesting reading. And this is my phone number. If, after you've read the books, you'd like to discuss them, I'd be delighted to see you when you're in San Francisco again."

Our cab moved slowly through the downtown traffic, past the Golden Nugget, Horseshoe Club, Jackpot, and onto Highway 91. Dave was Charley Tourist, twisting around, looking out of all windows. "Hey, is this the Strip?"

"Yeah, baby. This is it."

"Wow, what a wild-looking town! What's it like in those places?"

I didn't answer.

I stopped off at my father's room to say hello. "Any word from Mama and Peewee, Dad?"

"They called from a gas station less'n an hour ago. Oughta be here by six."

"Great. I'll arrange a table for the dinner show."

"Hey, Poppa, you sure maybe you're not pushin' the horse a little faster'n he can run? Colored people sittin' out front in Vegas?" He was shaking his head. "I just hope you ain't stickin' your neck out too far."

"I'm not sticking my neck out. But I ain't pullin' it in like a goddamned turtle, either. My grandmother is gonna sit and watch me perform or there ain't *nobody* gonna sit and watch me perform." I picked up the phone and asked to be connected with the Venus room. "Hello, this is Sammy Davis, Jr. . . . fine thanks. I'd like a table for six for my family, at the ringside, for the dinner show tonight."

"Well? What'd they say, Poppa?"

"They said, 'Have a great opening, Mr. Davis.'"

"Hell, don't give *me* that poker face. I taught it to you."

"Dad, they couldn't have been nicer and they're holding a table at *center* ringside. I'll invite Dave to sit with them, that way they won't feel like they're alone in the world." I stood up. "Catch you later."

Morty, John, and Nathan were waiting for me in the living room of my suite. Charley was holding the phone, his hand over the mouthpiece. "It's Sunny. From the line." I shook my head, he told her that I hadn't come in yet, and handed me a stack of phone messages. I dropped them on a table.

"Look, guys, the pressure is on. Now, we're going to be here for a whole month and we'll have all the laughs and relaxing we want, but for just a few hours a night let's not forget what we're here for in the first place. Charley: be sure you check the props."

"I already checked 'em."

"Well check 'em again."

"What're you so nervous about? Hell, they'll be standing in line to get in."

"Charley, after you've checked the props *again* I want you to go over all my clothes. Not just the tuxedos, but all my personal stuff, the suits, sport jackets, sweaters, Levi's . . ."

"You're going to wear Levi's on stage?"

"I'm going to be switching my clothes for every show, so

keep everything ready, 'cause I won't know if it's a tux, or Levi's and a sweater until I'm ready to get dressed.

"John: see that they kill the air conditioning when I do a ballad. I'm not competing with the hum. And when Morty's working with the band, will you please run through all the light cues. I mean a physical run-through."

"Hell, Sammy, I know them damn cues backwards."

"Yeah. And on closing night in Frisco that's exactly how you did 'em. Okay, we all make mistakes, but we can't afford to have no goofs here. Look, guys, it's ridiculous for me to tell you check this and check that, you know your jobs, all I want to do is remind you that the act is getting paid twenty-five thousand dollars a week! And the people know it. They're going to be expecting a lot of show and I intend to give it to them!"

The living room was jammed and I went from group to group, saying hello, soaking up the flattery. I sat down next to Mama. "You have a good time tonight?"

"Just seeing what people think of you and how they're treating you is a good time for me, Sammy. I'd better be getting my sleep, though. And don't you stay up too late neither. You need your rest."

I walked her to the door. "Don't worry about me, Mama. I never felt better in my life."

There were still about a dozen people left. I sat down, Charley handed me a coke, and I lit a cigarette and relaxed into their conversation. Dave said, "Hey, whattya say we start at one end of the town and hit every place along the way?" His face, turned toward me, was still reflecting the excitement of the evening. "I hear there's a wild lounge act over at the Desert Inn. We could start there and then . . ."

"Baby, we're comfortable, it's late, we've got everything we want."

"It's only four o'clock. Come on, let's really celebrate."

"I don't know about those places, Dave." He looked at me, not understanding. "Baby, this is Vegas. It's one thing for me here where I'm working, but I'm not so sure about those other hotels. Now do you wanta see a lounge act, or a lynching?"

Somebody else said, "Are you doing modest bits or don't

you *know* how big you are? They'll roll out a red carpet anywhere you go."

Dave said, "He's out of his mind and I'll prove it." He picked up the phone. "Maybe years ago it was one thing . . . hello, may I have the Desert Inn, please."

Conversation stopped. Dave lit a cigarette, crossed one leg over the other and blew smoke rings at the ceiling. "Connect me with the Lounge, please, darling. . . . Hello, I'd like to reserve a table for about twenty minutes from now for Sammy Davis, Jr. and a party of . . ." The burst of red across his cheeks was as though he'd been slapped. He lowered the phone back on the hook. "Sam . . . I did it again. I'm sorry."

I shrugged. "Let's not make a ninety-minute spectacular out of it." I could feel everybody looking at me, embarrassed for me. There were murmurs of "Well if that's how they are then who the hell needs 'em . . ." "They're a hundred years behind the times . . ." The party was lying on the floor dead.

I stood up. "Charley, get hot on the phone with room service and have them bring over twenty steak sandwiches, and tell them we'll need a case of their best champagne, quick-style. Morty, do me a favor. Swing by the casino and find Sunny and the kids. Tell 'em it's a party. Invite everybody you see that we dig." I turned on the hi-fi set, loud. Within ten minutes the crowd of kids pouring in was drowning it out, and the room came alive like somebody'd plugged us in.

Dave came over to where I was standing. "You okay?"

"Thanks, baby. I'm fine."

I had the feeling of having waited all my life to own a raincoat and when finally I got one it wasn't working, the water was coming through.

I had to get bigger, that's all. I just had to get bigger.

Dave was having breakfast at a room-service table in the living room. I turned on the TV set and went around the room looking for an ash tray that had an inch of space left in it. I emptied one into a half-filled glass. "Damn, we'd better get us some buckets the way those people smoke." I sat down and took the cardboard cap off a glass of orange juice.

Morty came stumbling in from his room. "It smells like a saloon in here." He pushed open a couple of the windows.

"Hey, easy on that air, baby. That stuff'll kill you." He collapsed into a chair at the table and sat there, eyes closed, holding his head up with the palm of his hand. His complexion was somewhere in the vicinity of moss green. "Morty, you look like the last eight bars of 'Tiger Rag'."

He raised his head just enough to find me. "It's these parties. Every night—people. In my bathroom, in my closet . . . I haven't slept since we got here. I can't cat-nap like you do. I've got to get six hours. Or at least four. Look." He held out his hand, trying to keep it steady.

Dave grinned. "That's just a little case of the Vegas-Early-Mornings."

"If my folks ever saw me like this they'd kill me." He reached for his juice, spilling some into the cracked ice, took a slug and looked at me pleadingly. "I know I never had it so good. But it's killing me."

Dave buttered a roll and mopped up the egg yolk on his plate. "I feel great." He finished off the rest of the roll with some strawberry jam and poured some more coffee. I put down my fork and watched his hand circling over a basket of coffee cakes until he'd chosen exactly the right one. He polished that off and reached for a jelly doughnut.

"Dave! Put that down!"

His hand stopped in mid-air. "What's wrong?"

"Are we storing up food for the winter?"

"I'm hungry."

"Okay, baby, but in case you're still thinking about getting into pictures—they're not searching the streets for Sidney Greenstreet types."

He dropped the doughnut. "Hey, wait a minute! I'm not exactly Sophie Tucker. I've got a thirty-two-inch waist."

"Mine's twenty-eight but I'm not going for forty. Show me a man of thirty-five who's got a pot, and I'll show you a man who started that pot with bad eating habits when he was twenty-five."

He looked at me suspiciously. "Y'mean you diet?"

"No. But I don't stuff myself like a nitwit, either. It's my

business to look good on a stage. When I take off my c
I can't afford to have a goodyear hanging over my belt. I
love desserts as much as the next guy, but did you ever see
me eat one? And if I have potatoes one night I won't have
them again for two months. I eat until I'm not hungry any
more and if there's still food on my plate I leave it. And if
I have ham and eggs and a roll I don't follow it with coffee
cake *and a jelly doughnut!*"

He was staring at me, dumbfounded. "What'd I do to get
this lecture all of a sudden?"

"I was just trying to help, to be a friend."

He nodded, gazing at the jelly doughnut as though he
wanted to marry it.

As we approached the suite after the second show I could
hear the hi-fi set and the people laughing from all the way
down the hall. Morty groaned. "It sounds like half of Las
Vegas is in there."

Dave rubbed his hands together. "Don't knock it. We've
got the line from the Sahara tonight." He opened the door
and I watched him surveying the room, trying to decide
which piece of candy looked best. Then he spotted her,
hesitated, working on his opening line, touched me on the
elbow, and grinned. "Excuse me, durling. My fudge is burning."

"Dave, you ain't never gonna quit this job, right?" He
was gone before I'd finished saying it.

My father was standing near the bar. "Sammy, can I talk
to you a minute?"

"Something wrong?"

"Let's go into the other room where it'll be quiet."

The bedroom was jammed. "Come on into the bathroom,
Dad. No one'll bother us there."

He locked the door and took a newspaper clipping out
of his pocket. "Maybe you better give this a look; that's
not nice things they're sayin' in there."

The headline was: *"Is Sammy Ashamed He's A Negro?"*
I sat down on the edge of the tub.

"Sammy Davis, Jr., who recently sparkled like a 14-
carat gold star on the stage at the Fairmont, was a rare
pleasure to us as a reviewer and a pride to us as a Negro.

But, unfortunately, persistent reports of his offstage performances leave much to be desired. During his stay in San Francisco he never once came by the neighborhood where he stayed in days before he was able to make the move to the less dark, more glittery side of town. Clearly, Mr. Davis is doing nothing to discourage rumors that success has erased his memory for friends who knew him 'when.' His all-night, all-white, orgy-style parties are the talk of Las Vegas, where he is currently appearing. We are sorry to be the ones to remind Mr. Davis of his obligation to the Negro community, but even sorrier for the necessity to do so."

"I don't get it. Why should they want to write lousy stuff like this about me?"

"Well, the fact is you never did come by the old neighborhood . . . you had a coupla buddies from around there."

"And every last one of them was at the hotel with me almost every night. They came to me, so what was there for me to go across town for? Ask Charley. He was there every night. He can tell you there were as many colored cats as ofays, maybe more."

"Well, this newspaper didn't hear about 'em."

"Hold it. Am I supposed to send them a guest list every time I wanta have some people over? Should I mark the names 'colored, white, colored, colored, white'?"

"Sammy, you gotta go along with the fact that . . . well, right there in the other room, just look who you got around you. There ain't nothin' but ofays. Now if one of them writers was to walk in here . . ."

"Dad! Where in the goddamned hell am I going to find colored people in Vegas? Y'want me to invite Mrs. Cartwright? Should I go over to Westside and find cats I don't know and invite 'em to a party just to dress up the room? Or maybe you'd like me to send a plane into L.A. for buddies so this paper'll be happy?"

"Well, maybe you could cut down on the parties some."

"What else am I supposed to do? I kill myself on that stage every night, I drain myself dry. Don't I have the right to unwind? Okay, I can't do it like everybody else; I can't

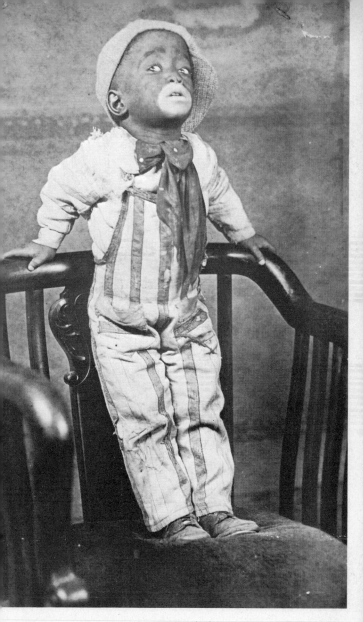

1929

Above: With Ethel Waters in *Rufus Jones for President*
Below: As Rufus in *Rufus Jones for President*

1933

1938

Above: Mama and my father
Below: My father, "my uncle" and me

Will
Mastin

Nathan
Crawford

The Will Mastin Trio featuring
Sammy Davis, Jr., 1950

The late forties

Sam Davis, Sr.

photograph by
Sammy Davis, Jr.

With Frank, at the Capitol Theater, 1947

With Will, Jeff Chandler, and my father.
Jeff was like a big brother to me

Top: Morty Stevens. It was always easy with Morty
Bottom left: Murphy Bennett
Bottom right: Arthur Silber, Jr.

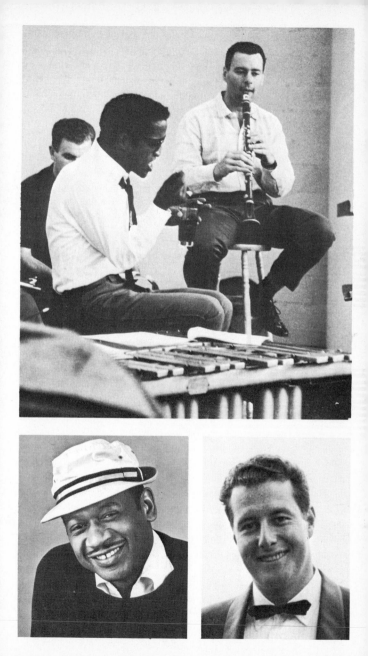

Mickey

The act. At Ciro's, after the accident   **Life Magazine**

My mother, Elvera Davis

Martin Luther King

Jane Boyar

photograph by
Sammy Davis, Jr.

Burt Boyar

photograph by
Sammy Davis, Jr.

Tony and Jeff

**Photo by
Jerry Lewis**

Above: Jane Boyar, George Gilbert
Below: The Bogarts in the dressing room at Ciro's

Jim Waters
James Cagney

Dave Landfield

go around town doing drop-ins at the Desert Inn, and 'Hey, let's catch the new Lounge act at The Sands.' I'm not complaining, but let's not forget I'm on an island here at the Frontier. I shouldn't have to draw pictures for you why I bring people over."

He didn't fight me and my anger turned to a rotten, hollow feeling. "They don't mention that because of me, colored people sat out front in a Las Vegas hotel for the first time in history. Not a word. Just that I have parties."

"Well, Poppa, they just don't know all the facts of what's behind everything."

I stared at the paper that was face up on the floor. "I don't get it. I swear to God I don't. I'd have thought they'd be happy every time one of us breaks out and lives good."

I took the towel from Charley as I came offstage, and wrapped it around my neck. "There's no party tonight. Let everybody know."

"But I've got fifty sandwiches."

"I hope you're hungry."

I hung around the casino for a while and then went back to my room. The door opened and Morty stuck his head in. "You feeling okay?" I nodded. "Y'mean . . ." A smile of hope was tentatively spreading over his face. ". . . no party tonight?"

"That's right, Morty. And stop grinning like that or you'll tear your mouth."

Dave rushed in, "Hey, where *is* everybody?"

"It's a quiet night at home for old Sam, baby. Why don't you take a look around the town?"

They both sat down and watched me tuning in the television set. I looked around at them. "What're you guys, a couple of nitwits? *You're* always looking for a good night's sleep, and *you're* always saying how you want to see the town. Well, this is that great come-and-get-it night. Go on, you don't have to sit around with me. I appreciate it but I really don't need a nurse."

They closed the door and I caught a local disc jockey. ". . . dynamic. I don't know where he gets all the energy. And he's the same offstage. Always going, always moving. Came up from nothing and now he's sitting on top of the

world . . . the greatest Negro performer to come along since
Bill Robinson. . . ." I turned the station. "Looking for the
best odds in town? Try the Lucky Buck on Fremont Street.
Every player's a winner." I turned it off and went into the
living room. Charley'd left the booze and the glasses set up.
I took one of the sandwiches back to the bedroom and got
into bed.

I opened a new book about the Nuremberg Trials, but
the Negro press rap kept running through my mind. Isn't it
my life? Why should I have to live by other people's rules?
Who am I living for—me, or some guy who sits behind a
desk and wants to tell me how to live? What makes his
rules better than mine? Why should I let myself be forced
into a mold? I've worked all my life toward the day when
no white man could tell me how to live—now the colored
people are trying to do it. I looked through the door, at
the empty living room. I had no desire for it to be empty.
What was the point of making it if I've got to wind up
sitting alone in a room like an outcast? I didn't have to become a star to accomplish *that!*

I telephoned Charley's room. "Baby, come on over to the
suite, will you please? I'm going to have some people coming over and I'll . . . what's the difference what time it is?
. . . yeah, right away."

The room was swarming with people laughing under the
wail of the hi-fi set. Morty was standing in his doorway,
hair rumpled, wearing candy-striped pajamas and a stunned
look as a chick rode by on a room service table. The word
had spread from hotel to hotel down the length of the Strip
and the kids were arriving like volunteer firemen, all but
climbing in the windows.

The train swerved sharply and Morty muttered, "Sonuva-
bitch!" He caught my involuntary smile at the slash of ink
his pen made across the music he was writing, and grinned
like thanks-a-bunch. He looked at the cover of the book I'd
been reading. "You gonna become Jewish?"

"Baby, I'll do the jokes and you write the music." I continued reading, but I could feel him watching me, dying to
say something. I put the book down. "Okay, Morty. What
is it?"

"Can I ask you a straight question?"

"You're gonna ask it anyway, right?"

"Seriously. You've been hung up in that all day. You thinking about converting to Judaism?"

"Morty, I'm interested in guns, but I didn't become a cowboy, did I?"

He shrugged. "I don't dig. When I read that stuff it was like dullsville."

"Baby, you'd better read it again. These are a swinging bunch of people. I mean I've heard of persecution, but what they went through is *ridiculous!* There wasn't anybody who didn't take a shot at 'em. The whole world kept saying, 'You can't do this' and 'You can't do that' but they didn't listen! It's beautiful. They just plain didn't listen. They'd get kicked out of one place, so they'd just go on to the next one and keep swinging like they wanted to, believing in themselves and in their right to have rights, asking nothing but for people to leave 'em alone and get off their backs, and having the guts to fight to get themselves a little peace. But the great thing is that after thousands of years of waiting and holding on and fighting, they finally made it."

He was looking past me, reaching back to his Sunday school days. "I don't remember any of that."

I slipped on the tweed patch that matched the suit I was wearing and it was a definite kissing-the-mirror. It did away completely with the medicinal look of the plain black one. I set the elastic band at the most rakish angle I could find and went over to Lindy's to find someone to try it out on.

Milton Berle was just paying his check. He waved me over. "Come on to the Friars Club with me and take some steam. It'll help get rid of all that flab."

Jack E. Leonard was sitting around the Friars shmoosing with some other comics. He walked over. "It's nice to see you again, Sammy—but I think I should tell you, your tweed beret slipped down over your eye." He gave me his glare. "Either that or you've got lint on your monocle." He turned on Berle. "Hello, Milton. I saw your show last night. Keep it up and one of these days you may own your own gas station!"

Berle nodded. "That's very funny, Jack. Will you stand still please. We were going to the gym but we'll just take a walk around you."

"That's funny, too, Milton. You've got a very familiar style. *Mine!*"

When they'd finished they smiled pleasantly at each other; Jack went back to the comics he'd been sitting with and Milton showed me around. "We're getting a new clubhouse soon. Y'know you really should become a Friar."

"I'd love to—but can I?"

"Why the hell not?"

"Milton, this isn't exactly a *sunburn* I'm wearing."

He grabbed my face with one hand and slapped me lightly with the other. "Repeat after me: 'I do the singing, and Milton does the jokes.' . . . Once again . . . Okay, that's better. Now, let's go upstairs and find Carl Timin. He runs the club and he'll get your membership started."

When I got to the dressing room at the Copa and told them about it, Will shook his head. "They never had a colored member before, and if they wouldn't have Bill Robinson and Bert Williams, then where do you get off thinking they'll have you?"

"Massey, there's gotta be a first time for everything. And with Milton Berle and his manager Irving Gray sponsoring me—"

"Just don't get your hopes too high on it. Oh, I know Milton means well, but there's enough of the others who won't let it happen. They'll smile and be polite to you but all of a sudden they won't be taking new members. You'll see, they'll think of something. You can't get in there."

Dave turned off the television set. I put down the Cleveland *Plain Dealer*. "Who told you to turn that off, Dave?"

"But you weren't watching it. You're reading."

"I don't have to be watching it. I catch glimpses, I hear it, and it all goes into me like I'm a sponge. I absorb everything, then discard what I don't want."

"Hey, sponge. Look at this." He was looking at a large picture, in the *Courier*, of a line of girls all wearing white ball gowns. "I didn't know there were colored coming-out parties."

"Baby, we're not all dancers and bootblacks!" The door

opened and Morty came in. He seemed upset. I asked, "Rehearsal go okay?"

"The band was fine, but when I left, Will was having a big argument with the guy who owns the club. I think it was over the sign out front. It just says 'Sammy Davis, Jr.'"

"You mean *only* my name? Oh boy." I went into the bedroom and started dressing.

Dave followed me in. "Y'know, I don't want to butt in . . ."

"But you're going to anyway, right?"

"Well, I was thinking that from a purely business point of view maybe the club is right. After all *you're* the attraction, not the Trio."

"Baby, from a purely business point of view the club is dead wrong because the contract they signed says the billing will be Will Mastin Trio, 100 per cent, Featuring Sammy Davis, Jr., 75 per cent."

I looked around for Will but couldn't find him. The owner of the club was standing near the dressing room. He waved me in and closed the door. "Sammy, am I glad you're here. I don't know which way to turn any more."

"What did you say to my uncle?"

"Look, I admit the old contracts always said 'The Will Mastin Trio Featuring Sammy Davis, Jr.,' so for sentiment that's how we're still signing them, but times have changed, the act has changed, so I took it upon myself to give you the billing you deserve." He shrugged. "Sammy, I've got to sell what the people want to buy. Isn't it foolish to be selling Sammy Davis and have to advertise Will Mastin Trio?"

"You still haven't told me what you said to my uncle."

"Who could say anything? He flew into my office and he says, 'Change the sign or we don't go on,' so I say, 'I'll change the sign.' That was our big discussion. The painters are on their way over, but Sammy, before they do something we'll all be sorry for, tell me, isn't it ridiculous? You're the act. Sure, they each do a dance with a few of their tricks and who could love the old show business better than me?—but then they spend the rest of the show standing behind you keeping the beat. Look, don't I know they're great guys? They're troupers and I love them for it, but we have to worry about you, too. Maybe you don't hear what people are saying, but you wanta be smart? Listen to me. I've been in this business since the year One and I know whereof I speak. I'm only thinking of you. Before I change the sign, maybe you should have a nice talk with Will and your father. Maybe you could explain it so he'll see a little reason. . . ."

I listened to him trying to steal from a man in the name of reason, labeling cold business as sentiment, when we both knew there was no other way he could have gotten us except as The Will Mastin Trio. Our entire engagement was already sold out, but he was trying to squeeze even a few more dollars out of it. But ugliest of all was the attempt to cut Will's throat with my ego.

"So, Sammy? You're the star. Tell me what to do. I only want to do what's right."

"Change the sign, sir."

"But, Sammy, those guys—"

"Do you mean my father and my uncle?"

"All right, I'm changing it. But at least do me a favor. Tell Will I didn't mean to hurt his feelings. I'm just trying to keep my head above water."

I stared at the door as it closed and then swung open. Will came in, his eyes blazing. "What'd he say?"

"He said I should tell you he didn't mean to hurt your feelings."

"He didn't hurt my feelings. I just want what's mine, and that's all I ever asked a man to give me in my whole life."

"I know that, Massey. He was dead wrong, and he knows it, too."

"If he don't want to live up to his end of the contract, then we don't play. It's that simple."

"Come on, Massey. It's not worth getting annoyed over. He had no right to do it, and it's being changed."

"You bet it's being changed. The name of this act is The Will Mastin Trio and that's the name it'll always have. We come up from nothing with that name. It was a good name in show business long before he ever built this place. The damned fool."

"Brother Mastin? You swearing in front of me?"

He'd been pacing the room letting off steam, convincing himself, but he stopped, embarrassed. "I guess that's the first curse word I ever used around you, Sammy."

He sat down, lost in thought, and I had the feeling he

was terribly lonely for the old days. I put my hand on his arm. "Don't let those bastards bother you, Massey."

He looked straight at me for a moment and his smile gained confidence. He nodded and stood up. "I better get moving. We've got a show to do."

Jack Eigen reached out to shake hands with me as I sat down in front of his microphone. "Sammy, welcome to Chicago and thanks for stopping by. Ladies and gentlemen, I'm speaking to the dynamic star of the great show here at the Chez Paree. Sammy, it's a pleasure to meet you . . ."

I glanced across the room at my father. He winked and threw me a circled thumb and forefinger.

". . . this young man just finished his first show of the engagement and literally turned the Chez upside down. It was pandemonium, they wouldn't let him off the stage, they were jammed in like sardines but they kept calling him back . . ."

He was reporting it like Clem McCarthy doing a Kentucky Derby, screaming the winner past the finish line. I looked at my father again. He made a motion of dealing cards, bridging the years, and I smiled back at him.

". . . Sammy, how do you feel about what's been happening to you lately?"

"Jack, I'd have to be out of my mind not to be thrilled and very grateful. And I'm particularly happy to be a guest on your show."

"Thank you, Sammy, I'm certainly happy to have you."

He thought it was just show biz Glad-to-be-here folks. "I really mean that, Jack. When I was a kid, there was a time when we'd pawned everything except our radio, and we held onto that just so we could listen to your show from the Copacabana. I'd sit in our apartment playing cards with my father, and we'd hear you talking to Jimmy Durante, Joe E. Lewis . . . well, maybe it'll sound a little cornball, but I dreamed and prayed that someday I'd get a little closer to all that excitement."

"And here you are not only closer to it but generating it. Sammy, it's been a long road, hasn't it? Would you say it might have happened faster for you if you weren't a Negro?"

"Jack . . . I'm not that good a guesser. But I do know that

when I was a kid and we had to scrounge for work, my uncle, Will Mastin, and my father and I used to go to the booking offices and we'd sit there alongside some awfully good white performers who were pretty hungry too. Some of us got lucky, and some didn't."

"Ladies and gentlemen, in case you tuned in late it's my pleasure to sit opposite the most talked about, most talented, most versatile Negro performer . . ."

I was aware of the warmth of my arms and legs taking the crispness out of my suit and wrinkling it.

"Sammy, we're all familiar with your great energy and your great talent. Let's find out a little more about you. Is there anything missing, anything further you'd like? How about motion pictures?"

"Well, sure. I'd love to make one someday."

"How is it you haven't done a picture already? I mean now that it's out in the open, do you feel that your color has prevented you from doing a movie?"

"Wait a minute, it's not 'out in the open' because it's never been a hidden subject. The way things have been going for us I haven't had time to even think about it, but I can tell you that the opening we had earlier this evening was everything I ever dreamed about. We'll be doing the second show soon and if the people are as fab—"

"But isn't it true, Sammy, that when a young singer has a hit record and starts getting hot, he almost automatically gets pulled right out to Hollywood?"

"I don't know, Jack. I really don't. I doubt it."

"You've had several big hits and you're a great performer . . ."

I pressed my hands against the cloth on the table and glanced at my watch, hoping it was almost show time.

"Have you had any offers from Hollywood?"

Why did he have to ruin a beautiful evening, why cut it out from under me like this? "We've been booked solid in clubs, Jack, it would have been impossible to make a movie."

The room was quieting down to listen more carefully, they were looking at me differently. I was colored again.

"But have you had any offers?"

I leaned against the back of the chair. "No, but that doesn't prove anything because neither did anybody come up to me and say, 'We aren't calling you to make a picture because you're colored.'" I lit another cigarette. The delicious taste was gone. He had asked me something but I'd missed it. I looked at him, knowing he'd repeat it.

"But they're not calling you."

"Jack, it can't be a racial thing unless you can tell me that Sidney Poitier is trying to pass." One of the ribs of the chair was sticking into my back, but I just didn't feel like bothering to move away from it. Across the room my father was staring at the floor.

"Sammy, do you feel that despite the fact that you're the most exciting Negro performer to come along since Bill Robinson . . ."

The last thread snapped. The beauty of the evening was long gone, but over and above that, words I'd heard and hated a thousand times, words I'd accepted without answering, words I'd forced to bounce off, stuck and stung me to response. "Why do you compare me to Bill Robinson?"

"Well, Sammy, I, uh, I don't believe I understand your question."

"Jack, I want to make it clear that you are not the first person to do it. I hear it all the time and I see it in the papers and in magazines, and obviously nobody means it as anything but a compliment and I'm enormously flattered by the comparison—but it's a wrong one!" He was looking at me with curiosity. "I don't kid myself that I could even begin to dance on the same stage as Bill Robinson. I haven't a touch of his greatness. But aside from that: we are not the same kind of performers. Sure, I dance, but my style is totally different from his, plus the fact that I also sing and tell jokes, do impressions, play the drums and the vibes, and act like a nut. Mr. Robinson didn't do any of those things. So if you're talking *performance* it would be much more logical to compare Fred Astaire to Bill Robinson, but I never heard *that* done."

"Well, now that you mention it . . . well, I just know that Robinson was the greatest Negro performer of his time and you're the greatest Negro performer to come along . . ."

"Hold it, Jack. Maybe it'll seem like I'm touchy, but I take exception to that too."

"To what?"

"You called me a 'Negro performer.' I'm a Negro and I'm a performer, but I don't think of myself as a 'Negro performer' any more than you think of yourself as a 'white disc jockey.'

"Why do people want to label *me* when they don't label other people? I never yet saw a newspaper refer to Milton Berle as 'the greatest Jewish comedian.' Sure, he's Jewish and he's a comedian but he doesn't do Jewish comedy any more than I do Negro humor.

"Race shouldn't come into it when people are speaking or writing about me professionally. Read the papers tomorrow and see if they don't call me the most talented Negro performer in the business. Now I realize it may sound greedy of me to knock that kind of a review but frankly I'd be happier if they wrote, 'Sammy Davis is an excellent performer' or a 'good performer' or whatever they think of me. I'll take less, if necessary, but without the label. When I walk onto a nightclub floor the newspaper guy is automatically comparing me to everyone else he's seen headlining on that same floor. I'm competing against *all* performers, so if I get a rave I don't want it to be qualified, like I'm good compared to only one small section of the business. I'll take the knocks if I have to, but if it's good then I want all that's coming to me.

"When I played Florida about a year or so ago I was staying in the same hotel as Jackie Robinson, and he happened to see some of my reviews. They were raves but they all had the 'Negro performer' bit in them. He said, 'I had it all my life. I was always the "Negro ballplayer." Occasionally a hater would throw a black cat on the field and yell the names at me, but most of the time people bent over backwards the other way. If I missed a ball or struck out they didn't boo me like they would a white guy. Then, all of a sudden one day it changed. I don't know how or why, but it did. I could argue with the umpire and shake my fist at him and the crowd started booing me, but I knew it wasn't racial. The greatest day of my life was the day I was thrown out of a game. I went into the locker room and cried like a kid 'cause I was finally just a plain "ballplayer" like any other guy.'

"I guess what it comes down to, Jack, is that I want to be looked at by the world not as Negro, white, or polka dot, or put in a category with anybody. Good, bad, or indifferent, like me or hate me—but measure me by the sum total of what I am as an individual."

My father was waiting as I stepped down from the platform. He put his arm around my shoulder and we walked back to the dressing room. "How *about* that, Poppa?" He smiled. "The Jack Eigen Show." He was saying the words, but they didn't have the ring of the kind of happiness he wanted to get out of them. He was shaking his head, reaching for the nostalgia we both wanted to feel. "You got it all now, just like you always wanted." The last few words were hardly pronounced, as if in denial of their own statement.

I gripped his shoulder. "Not yet, Dad. I've got to get bigger. I've got to get so big, so powerful, so famous, that the day will come when they'll look at me and see a man—and then somewhere along the way they'll notice he's a Negro."

17

"SAMMY, IF YOU WERE WHITE YOU'D HAVE BEEN IN pictures a year ago."

"Hold it, Lenny. That's what I hear from the cats on the street. I don't need it from my own agent. Now I've *got to have* the importance of motion pictures. I've got to expand. I'm not doing 'the clown who wants to be a serious actor' bit. I need this. I can't be Charley Nightclubs all my life. I need extra dimension. I can't stay in a box; I've got to break through the barrier of being a singer-dancer-comic, and you've got to help me."

"Well, it's not easy. Most pictures just don't have parts for Negroes. And when they do, they couldn't begin to meet your price."

"What's my price?"

"Well, I don't know, after all, you're a big star . . ."

I leaned across his desk. "My price to make a movie is fifty dollars! You hear what I'm saying? *Fifty dollars!* And I'll take a cut if necessary."

"It's not that we aren't trying for you . . ."

"You're not trying hard enough. I'm not exactly a secret in the nightclub business and I've had a couple of hit records. Big ones. But I haven't even been called to make an eight-by-ten glossy."

His phone rang and he grabbed for it, holding one hand over the mouthpiece and extending the other to me. "Sammy, we'll do the best we can. I'll bring it up at the next meeting."

I went down the hall to the television department and introduced myself to the guy who was supposed to be handling me.

"Sammy, the truth is we just haven't been able to find a dramatic role for you. But you can have all the variety shows you want."

"I've done all the variety shows."

"Right. And they still want you back. At top money."

"Fine. But that doesn't mean I can't do dramatic television, too. Out of all the thousands of shows being done every year how is it possible that you can't come up with one little half-hour script for me?"

"Well, these programs have small budgets."

"Baby, I just went through that in the picture department. All I know is everybody's getting rich in movies and on television but as soon as my name is mentioned, suddenly everything's got small budgets. Okay. I'll work for box-tops!"

"Well, in addition to that we have the problem of finding a role you can play. For a star of your importance we have to find the right vehicle."

"Don't give me the vehicle jazz. I'm not asking for Rolls-Royce parts. Find me a little used Chevy. It doesn't have to be a lead. It could be even one scene if it's the right one. Let *me* be the one to say, 'No, it's too small.' "

"Sammy, what're you knocking yourself out for? Why risk bombing in dramatic television? You're a first-rate Sammy Davis, Jr.; why be a second-rate Sidney Poitier?" I held onto the arms of my chair, telling myself: don't make an enemy, you need him, you need him. "You're a great entertainer, but that doesn't mean you're an actor. Maybe if you took some dramatic lessons, like the Actors' Studio, something that'd give us a little background to work with."

I stood up and ground a cigarette into his ash tray. "You want some background? How's twenty-four years in the business? How's *eight hundred thousand dollars* a year, of which you guys get ten per cent? How's the fact that I'm a star that you don't have to lift a finger to get booked in clubs, all you have to do is answer phone calls. But I'm asking for your help on something important to me. Please, let's stop kidding each other. The problem is racial!"

"Well, it *is* awfully touchy. Do I have to tell you that on certain networks Negroes are banned except if they appear as servants?"

"Look, we both know they aren't running around town hoping to find colored actors. But I'm a name. Maybe I can draw a rating, right? The door isn't locked. It's just closed and there must be a way to get it opened."

I walked toward the parking lot knowing I'd accomplished nothing. They had the power to swing it if they wanted to, but they were taking the easy way out, avoiding the extra work of selling me, taking the attitude: "who needs problems?"

Will stepped back to let me into his room, showing concern over what could be urgent enough to bring me to his hotel when in a few hours I'd see him in the dressing room.

"You've got to help me, Massey. You've got to go to bat for me and talk to the top echelon guys at the Morris office about getting me dramatic television or a picture. You're the one they deal with, maybe they need it to come from you. I tried and it was horrible. Like I was an unknown sitting in a casting office hoping for an audition. They're not lifting a finger. But if you were to let them know that maybe we'll move over to MCA if they don't come up with something . . ."

"No sense telling them how to run their own business. We're doing fine as is."

"Sure we are but we haven't made it just by being a hit in one medium. We can't go higher in clubs so we have to spread out into other fields until they combine to make us bigger and bigger and bigger!"

"That don't add up. Nobody's going to make more than

twenty-five thousand a week in Vegas, not year in and year out. You want to give up a date like that so's you can piddle around on some cops and robbers TV show?"

"We won't give up any Vegas dates. But the more fields we're in, the less chance there is of burning ourselves out in clubs. If we have something else going for us then we don't have to go back to the same places so often, and the less we come back, the better business we're going to do. And the extra prestige will only prolong our big money dates."

"Can't see how anybody ever prolonged a winning streak by breaking into it." He shook his head. "I've gotta go along with the Morris office's thinking. They know what's best in these things."

I closed his door behind me. How can he not understand? He's too smart not to see the value of it. How can he be blind to something so obvious?

In the dressing room at Ciro's, I spread albolene on my face and began covering it with powder. Dave was watching me. "Sam, how come you use that dark powder?"

I let the powder puff drop to the table. "Oh! You're out of line. You're so out of line you're like a bowl of spaghetti."

"Seriously. I'm working for you, I oughta know these things."

"Baby, it's for the lights. It cuts down the glare. What should I use, white powder? You want me to look like I've been rolling in a flour bin?"

I noticed Nathan helping my father into his jacket in the other room. I'd never seen him do that before. As he slipped his arm into the sleeve his face contorted in pain. I got up and went in. "What's wrong, Dad?"

"Nothin' wrong, Poppa." He was holding his right hand behind his back.

"Let's see it."

He showed it to me, reluctantly. It was swollen to half again its normal size. "It don't look too good but it ain't broke, just sprained." He smiled, "I kinda bumped it into a guy's jaw last night."

I shook my head slowly, putting him on. "Dad, I've warned you about those bust-out joints with the half-dollar doubles." I kept needling him, but I noticed that although he and I were laughing Nat and Will weren't. "Hey, is there something I don't know?"

Will said, "Sammy, you might as well know the facts. It happened 'cause Sam heard someone insulting you."

My father looked away. "No need makin' a big thing outa nothin', Will."

"What happened, Dad?"

"Oh, I was at this bar and some guy didn't know I was your old man and he happened to mention a joke they're tellin' about you, so I stepped over and told him, 'Y'know, you got a lotta mouth.'" He stopped and winked at me. "And the fact is, Poppa, he's got lots more mouth today than he had last night." He sighed, "I'd sure hate to be wearin' his jaw right now."

"Which joke was it?" I kept looking at him, but he wasn't going to tell me.

Will's voice was quiet. "Sammy, I'll tell you the joke, because it's not the first one like it . . . about you trying to be white. And I think you ought to know about it." The dampness of his face gave away how much effort it was taking for him to pronounce the words. "It's a joke about you sitting in Danny's Hideaway in New York when some guy looks at you and calls out: 'Nigger, nigger, nigger!' and you jump up and yell: 'Where? Where? Where?'"

"Thank you, Massey." I put my hand on my father's arm. "I'm sorry."

I slowed down outside of Warner Brothers so the guard could recognize me and I gave him a Charley Star smile as he waved us through. Dave and I wandered around the sets and were watching a fight scene being rehearsed when I felt a hand on my shoulder. "Y'lookin' for work as an extra?"

"Hugh! Whattya say, old buddy? And cool it with the 'extra' jazz 'cause I ain't had no better offers. Hey, y'doing any pirate shows? Maybe y'need a small colored fella to hang from a yardarm? I've even got my own patch. Excuse me, do you know Dave Landfield? Dave, this is Hugh Benson."

Hugh said, "We're screening *Rebel Without a Cause*, the Jimmy Dean picture. You interested?"

"Sure. He's sort of a friend of ours." Dave gave me a look.

As I sat in the screening room watching Jimmy Dean's

performance, it suddenly hit me: "Holy God! This guy's a genius."

The traffic was bumper to bumper back to L.A. I didn't say a word. All I could think was how I used to see him sitting in the corner of the room literally absorbing people and all I figured was he must be some kind of a kook. A sensitive, talented guy sat in my house every night for a month, reaching out for my friendship, and all I gave him was bits like "Are you here again, Jimmy?"

"Whattya say, chicky? How's the cover boy of the scandal magazines?"

"You're a bundle of laughs, Jess." I pulled a chair up to his desk. "Listen, is there something happening at Disneyland tomorrow?"

"They're having the big pre-opening thing for celebrities and their families—you know, 'Mr. and Mrs. Famous at Disneyland with their little monsters.'"

"How come I wasn't invited? I'm not exactly an unknown."

He raised an eyebrow. "Well, right off the bat I can think of two reasons. First, you've got no kids. Second, they're going for the wholesome, family kind of publicity, so if there are three guys in the world they'd make a point of overlooking, chicky, it would be Rubirosa, Errol Flynn, and you."

"You're a very funny man, Jess."

"Hey, I was just doing bits." He took a manila envelope out of a filing cabinet and handed me a stack of clippings. "Maybe you don't read all this stuff but it's my business so I have to."

The top one, a scandal magazine, another of the dozens of imitators of *Confidential,* had me and June Allyson on the cover. "Do you realize what a horrible, unfair thing this is? Here a woman was kind enough to come backstage on my opening night at Ciro's, with her husband, for one minute to say, 'Hey, I liked your show.' So for that they smeared her. That's all she did. The only time I ever met her." I dropped the magazine into a wastebasket.

"Chicky, face it: you're a sex symbol."

"You're sick."

"Come on, cheer up. Look at the bright side of it: at least they're not calling you a fag."

"Jess . . this'll kill you, but I don't think of myself as somebody who can't be seen around decent people. It's not exactly what I worked my whole damned life for."

The phone was ringing as I got to my suite in the Garden of Allah. Dave grabbed for it. "Hello? Oh! . . . yes, *sir*. One second please, he's right here." He held the phone out to me like it was hot, his face blanched of its color, and mouthed the words: "It's Frank Sinatra."

"Hi'ya, Charley, listen, you dig all this Donald Duck jazz. You want to go to a thing at Disneyland tomorrow?"

His children were leaning out of the back window waving to me, and the sight of them almost threw me. It had seemed impossible that he'd be going to Disneyland without them, yet, knowing how he protected them like all the gold in Fort Knox, I'd wondered if he'd let them be seen with the town monster.

The radio was on and as we drove a disc jockey said, "Now, the number one record in the country, Sammy Davis, Jr.'s 'Black Magic'!"

"Turn off that record, Charley. Get another station."

"Oh, sure, Frank. Gee, I wouldn't want to make you jealous, I mean a man with an Oscar and all . . ." I turned to the next station. "Here it is, folks, number one, Sammy Davis, Jr.'s 'Black Magic.' "

Frank smacked the steering wheel. "For crying out loud, I can't listen to anything on that radio but you!"

"You want me to change it, baby?"

"I'll baby you! Leave it."

When it was over he turned off the radio. "The records are good, Charley, but you're not singing yet. You're performing. You're doing them like you do them in clubs, but on a record you don't have the physical moves going for you, there's only one dimension to work with—the voice. On this one it comes across, but on some of them you don't. I don't mean they're not good, but they don't translate unless people can see you, so you're cutting down your percentages for a hit. But I'm not worried about you. One day you'll be singing."

The guard waved us through the gates at Disneyland, we

pulled into the parking lot, and the photographers crowded around before Frank could open his door. I stayed in the car while he and the children got out. I turned my face away from the mob and tried to keep busy tying my shoelaces. I could hear them yelling, "One more with your arms around the kids, Frank?" . . . "Can you move closer together, please?"

There was a knock on the window. Frank was beckoning me with his finger. "Hey, Charley, did we come here together or not? Let's go, let's get into these pictures." He pulled me over and put one arm around his children, rested the other on my shoulder, and the photographer began shooting. I looked at him smiling at the world through those cameras, as much as saying, "In your ear. He's my friend."

We walked around the park looking at the rides and saying hello to almost everyone we passed. Frank hadn't invited me just for fun. He'd known there would be newsreels, wire services, that almost everyone in the industry would be there, and he'd wanted to give me the value of association so that some of his tremendous public favor might rub off on me. I turned to watch one of the rides and when I looked up Frank was a few feet ahead of me talking to someone. He had one arm around Tina and Frank, Jr. and his other hand was unconsciously stroking Nancy's head.

He walked over to me. "What're you looking at, Charley?"

"I don't know, I was just thinking about you and the kids. Frank . . . thank you for bringing me here."

He brushed it off. "Come on. Y'wanta be late for Donald Duck's party?"

The man at the Morris office leaned across his desk. "Mr. Davis, have you any idea how much money you owe?"

"Is *that* all you wanted to see me about?"

"But Mr. Davis, it's—"

"Look, Mr. . . . uh . . ."

"Marcus."

"Mr. Marcus. I know it's your job and all that jazz but I'm really not that interested." He seemed hurt. "Look, I appreciate what you're trying to do, but I'm only in town for a few more days and well, life's too short."

"You'll find that when you owe money you make it a good deal shorter."

There was something about the way he said it and the way he was looking at me, like it meant so much to him. I decided to humor him. I sat down. "All right, how much? Twenty? Thirty thousand?"

He slid a piece of paper across the desk to me. It was blank except for "$106,050."

I scanned his face. He wasn't the type to do bits. Too square. I said, "Pardon the old joke but how successful can you get?" He didn't laugh. "Hey y'know, there should be a thing called Spenders Anonymous, like a switch on the old joke? When a guy's a spender he joins S.A. Then when he feels close to trouble he calls up another member and says, 'I've got a horrible urge to go to Tiffany' and the other guy says, 'Sit tight, I'm on my way over.' Then they go out and booze it up. Heh, heh . . . uh . . . well . . ."

"Mr. Davis, have you any idea how much money you must earn in your bracket in order to pay your debts?"

"Listen, as long as you brought it up—and I'm not kidding now—just what the hell *is* a tax bracket?"

"I'll explain it in detail later. But first I must make you aware of the fact that because your earnings are so large you pay a tax of approximately ninety cents on every dollar, and therefore, in order for you to personally accumulate $100,000 you must earn one *million* dollars! Or, to put it more dramatically, you are in debt for the next million dollars you earn."

I stood up. "Look, if this is some kind of a joke I don't get it and I'm leaving 'cause I don't dig your humor and I didn't owe any million dollars when I walked in here!"

"Please, Mr. Davis, sit down. I realize it's a shock, but it's long past time for you to treat your finances seriously or you'll be in debt for the rest of your life. Now, I sympathize with your position. I'm aware of how easy it is to fall into the trap of knowing that your income averages $15,000 a week and that when you see a car you might automatically think, 'I can afford it, it's only a third of a week's salary.' In your case, you split your income three ways, so perhaps you think, 'I make $5000 a week, it's only a week's salary, I'll buy it.' But that kind of thinking will be your destruction.

"You must entirely forget the amounts you earn because the largest part of it will never touch your hands. You must learn to think only in terms of the money you will actually receive. By that I mean your salary of a thousand dollars a week from the Trio."

"Look, without the details, obviously I'm in trouble. Can I get out of it?"

"I believe so. And, we can help you, if you'll cooperate. Now let's go over these bills from George Unger, Saks Fifth Avenue, Abercrombie and Fitch, Sulka, ad infinitum. I want you to show me which items are personal and which might be considered business expenses."

An hour later we were shaking hands and he was saying, "If you don't spend in excess of your salary, we'll be able to straighten you out in a reasonable amount of time. But remember, we can only do it if you have large income. Although you're making a great deal of money today, there's no guarantee that in two or three years you'll still be doing this well, so you dare not let this get further out of hand."

I walked a few blocks, mulling it over. The poor guy had been so solemn, he'd seemed so worried that I couldn't resist doing a bit with him. I bought a gold cigarette case and had it engraved: "Thank you for the advice. Gratefully, Sammy, Jr." What the hell, so I'd owe a hundred thousand plus another six hundred.

Mama was sitting on a chair in the front hall, wearing her hat and holding her umbrella. Her suitcases were standing near the door. "Sammy, I've got my carfare and I'm going back to New York to a furnished room."

My father and Peewee had adopted two little girls, Sandy and Suzette, and when we'd gone on the road Mama, Peewee, and the kids had moved into my house.

"Mama, what's wrong?"

"There's nothing wrong that you've done, but I can't live here any more. If it's not the children screaming then it's Peewee having her friends over for company. I don't blame her. I know it gets lonely for her with Sam on the road and all. And when he's home they're always having parties and people come up and I don't know what anybody's talking about and I can't hear the television. Last night Sam was all

juiced up and I just can't take it any more so I'm leaving.
It's the only thing I can do to get some peace and quiet.
I'm an old woman, Sammy, and I need my rest."

As she spoke I realized that as much as I loved her, I hadn't
taken the time to really look at her in years. Sure I'd kissed
her and hugged her and listened to her words, but I'd missed
the most important part. The history of her lifetime was in-
delibly etched into her face, and there was no disguising it
with a new dress or a smile. It was all there: the hard work,
the struggling, the years of hoping the relief check would
arrive on time—I could see what it had cost her to buy me the
drums, and the food she would never have bought for herself,
to never have a day in all these years when she didn't worry
about me. But I hadn't taken the time to worry about her,
the one person in the world who never stopped thinking
about me. I sat down next to her. "Mama . . . I'm sorry . . ."

"Sammy, you've been good to me, and I know you've done
everything you could."

"Mama, please, don't leave me. I need you." I took the umbrella out of her hand. "Give me three days and I'll have a
house for you. A home like I always said we'd have. Please.
Now come on, give me your hat and don't worry. I'll get
you a house. Just don't go back to New York." I kissed her
and rushed out to the car.

Dave was in our suite at the Garden of Allah. "Baby, how
much have I got in the bank?"

"Goose egg. You *had* about six thousand but I wrote
checks for those bills you were going to pay."

"They'll have to wait. I've got to buy a house."

"But I thought you were going to cut down."

"That's all fine and good but I'll have to start next week."
I sat down and made a list of club owners. Julie Podell at the
Copa, Dallas Gerson and Dave Dushoff at The Latin Casino
in Philadelphia. . . .

Dave was looking over my shoulder at the names and the
figures next to them. "What happens if they say no?"

"They won't."

The problem was going to be the racial thing and I didn't
have that kind of time to lose. I'd have to ask Herman Hover
to help me.

I stood at a window in the living room stunned by the sight of Los Angeles spread out for miles below.

The broker was aghast. "Are you *sure* you don't want to see any others?"

"I don't have to. This is *it*. Can you wait here for fifteen minutes?"

Mama was watching television. "I've got the house, Mama. Let's go see how you like it."

"I'll change my clothes."

"Don't bother about that. You look beautiful."

"Sammy, stop dragging me. You're getting me out of breath. If the house won't be there long enough for me to see it without running, then it can't be much of a house to live in."

I got her into the car and zoomed up the hill. "You're going to love it. It used to be Judy Garland's. It's on three levels 'cause it's built on the side of a hill. I figured out how you could have your own private apartment. We've got about five acres of land—there's no swimming pool, but we've got plenty of space to build one someday."

"Well, that's good, Sammy. You know how I need my swim every day."

I opened the front door and led her into the living room. She broke into a smile. I took her from floor to floor, I was racing ahead of her, in one room and out the other. "Now in here's where I figured we could . . ." I looked around. "Mama? Where are you?"

"Sammy." Her voice was coming from outside. "I'm out in the yard, Sammy." She spotted me in the window. "How'd I get down here?" She started laughing so hard the tears were rolling down her face.

Two days later, I walked into her old bedroom and turned off the television set. "The house is yours. We're moving in tonight."

"I can't move in tonight. There's no furniture and the electricity has to be put on and . . ."

"Mama, I'm leaving town tomorrow and I want to spend one night in your new house with you. You've got bed linen and Dave and Arthur'll help me bring over your bed, and I can sleep on the floor."

I helped make her bed and I rolled myself up in a blanket alongside her.

"Sammy, how're you going to sleep at this hour?"

"I'll sleep fine." I turned out the flashlight. Neither of us spoke. We just enjoyed the feeling of the new house and the glow from the lights of Los Angeles far below.

"You happy, Mama?"

"Yes. I'm happy. I love my house."

"You don't want to leave me and go back to New York anymore, do you?"

"No, I don't want to go back to New York. But now you're going to be leaving this beautiful new house you just got. Do you feel bad about leaving, Sammy?"

"Yes and no. I'm always leaving *some* place."

"Well, someday you'll miss it. Someday when it's filled with your wife and children. You've gotta have reason to stay home. And that can't be me. The Lord didn't make it for children to love their folks the same way their folks love them. Don't ever feel badly I miss you, Sammy, 'cause missing you is part of loving you and I'm as glad for one part as the other. I'm as happy as I can be."

"As you can be?"

"Someday I'll be happier. When you've got someone to miss. That's when I'll know you're happy. Good night. And thank you for my house."

I was sailing down the road doing forty around the curves when I spotted a Porsche coming up the hill, honking its horn. It was Jimmy Dean. He had Ursula Andress with him. We skidded to a halt in the middle of the road and he jumped out of the car looking like he was in costume for *Giant*, with the Levi's and a cowboy hat and a rope in his hand. "Hey, Sam, I gotta show you something I learned in Texas." In two seconds he had the rope spinning.

"Hey, that's a gas, Jimmy."

"And I'm getting a little faster with the guns."

"But you still have no chance against me, no chance at all, right?"

He grinned. "I just got back for re-makes and dubbing, I'll be here for a couple of weeks. Can I come over?"

"I'm leaving town in an hour. We open Chicago tomorrow night."

He let the rope fall. "Oh. Okay . . . see you, Sam."

Some cars trying to get up the hill were honking their horns at us. "As soon as I get back we'll get together. I've got something I want to tell you."

"Then I'll call you when I hear you're back."

"Please do, Jimmy. I really want to talk to you."

We got back in our cars and it was *rrrrrrrr* and away we went trying to see who could kick up the most dust.

Dave opened the dressing-room door. "There's a Finis Henderson outside."

Finis, a buddy since our early days around Chicago, stood in the doorway, holding back a smile. "Mr. Davis, I presume?"

I played it angry. "Finis, where in the damn hell have you been? I've been in town since yesterday."

He held up his hands. "Please. Don't raise your voice at me 'cause I don't need you. I'm poor but I'm proud."

"You silly nut, come on in here. Listen, this is Dave Landfield, my secretary, and you know Morty. Hey, where're the rest of the guys?"

He looked away. "Oh, I guess they're busy or something . . ."

"*Busy or something?*" I turned him around to face me. "What the hell is *that*? On my opening night? You're lyin' through your teeth, Finis. Now let's have it. We go back too far for you to do mysteriosa bits with me."

"Well, you know . . . maybe they're a little mixed up. They figure you're living over here with the ofays, when you oughta be over there instead. They think maybe you've gotten a little snowblind."

"Hold it, Finis. Look at my face. I've had my nose broken too many times to hear I'm an Uncle Tom."

"Well, they don't understand. They read all the stuff in the papers and . . . well, they figure it must be true what people've been saying."

"And just *what* have people been saying?"

"Oh, come on now, daddy, don't put me on the rack. I

268

came over here to see my buddy. If I want a third degree I'll rob a store."

I pulled on my jacket and jammed a silk handkerchief into the breast pocket. "Boy, that's beautiful. Wouldn't you think they'd say, 'Go, man! You're makin' it and you've got the strength swingin' for you so *live like you wanta live! Fight it for the rest of us.*' But instead, the immediate reaction is 'Hey, whattya think about Sammy livin' white?' Instead of sayin' here's a cat who might make it a little better for all of us, they turn against me and I become an outcast. I don't hear 'Hey, crazy! Maybe I can follow him through that door.' All they want is to drag me back to the gutter with them. Well, man, I ain't comin' back!"

The door opened and my father looked in. "Sammy, can I see you a minute?"

"Finis, we'll talk later at the hotel. Go on out to the table."

I followed my father into his dressing room. He closed the door. "Sammy, maybe this ain't the best time . . ."

The expression on his face was terrible. "What's wrong, Dad? You all right?"

He nodded. "I'm okay; nobody's sick or nothin' like that. I just wanta ask you to help me out with something." He opened a drawer and took a magazine out from under some shirts and pointed to the last line of a review on our Ciro's run. "Although there is no telling what heights young Davis may reach, it is a certainty that Will Mastin and Sam Davis, Sr. will go down in show business history along with Gummo and Zeppo Marx, Irving and Morris Ritz, and the third Dolly Sister." I shook my head, "Man, they're after us all; you, me and Will." I kept looking at it, stalling until I could decide what to say to him.

He sat down on the bed. "Poppa, that guy's laughin' at us. What I was hoping is maybe you could talk to Jess Rand or somebody so maybe they wouldn't write that stuff."

"Dad, Jess can't do anything about this." The hope fell from his face. "Look, leave it to me. I'll think of something. I promise you I will." I put the clipping in my pocket. "They just don't understand. Come on. Hey, betcha I can make you laugh."

He looked at me, a smile on his face that his eyes didn't know about.

"Ladies and gentlemen, as most of you know I don't usually do special material, like 'Hello, hello, I'm back in Chicago!' But there's something important I want to say and I have to do it in the way I know best. It's been a long road that brought me here and I didn't travel it by myself." The music started lightly behind me. "I'd like to tell you about the two gentlemen you see here with me, my father and my uncle: two men whose presence on this stage gives me more class than I could ever have alone." The music swelled and I started singing.

"Everything I know they taught me,
Everything I do they did.
Everything I own they bought me,
Guess I was a lucky kid.
When I was a tot,
I sang before I talked,
Believe it or not I danced before I walked.
Mama squawked, but my dad and uncle taught me—
They taught me everything I know.
So I dug their licks,
Grabbed their tricks, and what I got was for free . . .
The future looks grand,
United we stand,
My daddy . . . my uncle . . . and me . . ."

I bowed to my father and Will. The audience was applauding them, warmly, sincerely.

When we got off I saw Freddie Robbins standing in the wings—a buddy from New York, one of the first disc jockeys to play my records, when I'd needed it. I walked over to him, smiling.

"Great show, Sammy. Wonderful. Hey, Jimmy Dean just died." I searched his face for a sign that it was a joke. "It just came over the air. Car crash. He was . . ."

I went into the dressing room and closed the door. Dave was standing in front of the radio, his face ashen, listening to the report of how it had happened.

I never got a chance to tell him. I never gave him the pleasure of hearing it. And he didn't have that many people who told it to him.

They started the commercial. A jingle. I ripped the plug out of the socket and the sound died.

I sat down and looked at Dave. "We had him and all we did was brush him off. I did to him what I wouldn't want anybody to do to me. I tolerated him. I treated him like a kook."

"But he never knew that."

"Of course he knew. He was a sensitive man. He felt everything. And I made jokes about him."

How could *I* have judged a man before I knew what he was all about? Me, who's suffered from prejudgment. Oh, God, I just hope—as corny as it sounds—I hope he knows I mean it, that I wish I'd said to him, "I know you were my friend and I wish I'd been your friend, too."

After the second show, I borrowed a car and went for a drive by myself, circling through the winding road in the park, trying to shake the guilt that was ripping at me like an iron claw. I'd been so busy being Charley Star that I hadn't seen a guy who was reaching out to be my friend. Even on the hill when I could have said *something*—I could have yelled, "Hey, you were great"—I'd wanted the pleasure of telling it to him just right.

Why don't you tell someone you appreciate them while you still can?

The Chez was packed, and as I walked onstage, I scanned the room as I had every night since the opening. When I got off I sent for Donjo Medlavine, one of the owners. "Don, a straight question: are my people getting treated okay? I mean, your guy at the door isn't giving them a hard time or anything?"

"They're treated the same as anybody else—when they show up. Last year there wasn't a show we didn't have a couple of tables . . ."

"Thanks, Don. I'm sorry I asked. I should have known better."

The man behind the rich mahogany desk didn't like me one little bit. He stood up and motioned for me to sit down, studying me as I'd been studying him from the moment I'd entered his office. He didn't ask why I'd called for an appointment. He waited.

"Mr. Johnson, why are you turning my people against me?"

The faint smile disappeared. "We're not trying to turn anyone . . ."

"I didn't say 'trying.' If I thought it was deliberate, I wouldn't be here. But you're *doing* it. Not so much in *Ebony*, but your guys on *Jet* have been bum-rapping me with little zingies in nearly every issue. I've been convicted of taking turn-white pills but I was never invited to the trial. Between your magazines, and the papers like the *Defender* and the *Courier*—all of them—you've been holding America's first all-colored lynching. Now what I want to know is: why?"

"Mr. Davis, you are the one who *makes* the news. All we do is print it. When you don't like what you see published about yourself, please try to remember that it is only a reflection of the image which you have created."

"Well, there's been a little distortion, folks, a little crack in the mirror."

He laughed unpleasantly. "Can you seriously be telling me that you haven't gone out of your way to indicate a complete disavowal of racial ties, to disassociate yourself in every conceivable . . ."

"Mr. Johnson, I didn't come up here to do two choruses of nobody understands me. You've been printing your point of view. All I ask is that you listen to mine."

He settled back in his chair and smiled, not bothering to conceal his contempt.

"A few weeks ago a Broadway column ran an item saying I turned down $25,000 a week in Miami Beach, because I refused to live in the colored section of Miami. Now the fact is I *won't* live there, but that's not why we turned it down. We were offered our own suites in the hotel that was trying to book us. We turned it down because my father, my uncle, and I have one firm rule: we don't play where they won't open their doors to colored people. The columnist obviously didn't know about the suites, so the item came out sounding like I hate colored people so much that even for $25,000 a week I won't live with them. Nice, huh? Okay, it's bad enough when an ofay columnist does this—I can't expect him to care enough to find out if maybe there's something more to it—but when I see it picked up and run in the Negro press too, when I see it published by people who should be hoping and praying it's wrong, when I hear the reactions and see I'm marked lousy and suddenly I'm not getting Negro customers where I'm playing—well, that hurts. I can't say it ran in any of your magazines but I saw it in three Negro newspapers. Now I'm not looking for togetherness, but that's inexcusable."

He sat forward slowly, frowning. "You're perfectly right. It's a story that should have been checked out with you just in the hope that it was wrong."

"Mr. Johnson, when I get to a town it's not exactly a secret. There's always a sign saying: 'He's in there.' But my phone didn't ring. I've never yet had one guy call me and say 'Hey, Sam, this true what I hear?' Not one."

"Well, as a newspaperman I can guess what happened with that particular item." He leaned back in his chair again. "Whoever heard it was aware of your overall racial image, the item seemed to be in character . . ."

"Wait a minute. Before you talk about my image like *that's it*, lock the box, that's what I'm here for. What did I do to get that image? Let's go down the list A, B, C.''

"If you insist. Offhand I remember an item we ran recently about your conductor. How do you, a prominent Negro, justify the use of a white man when you know how scarce good jobs are for Negroes?"

"Mr. Johnson, Morty Stevens is one of two white men out of seven people who travel with me, he's the best man I know of for the job, he's arranged three hit songs for me and he's one hell of a conductor. I'm not buying his color, I'm buying his music."

"And you couldn't find as good a musician who's a Negro?"

"Maybe I could. But none of them have come to me looking for the job and even if they did I'm not about to fire Morty and hire them just 'cause they're colored and he's white. Should I be prejudiced and do exactly what we hate when people do it to us? Aren't we praying for the day when there's no discrimination? Should we practice it ourselves? And don't think the Negro community had a monopoly on giving me a hard time about Morty, because every time he walks onstage there are white customers nudging each other and whispering, 'Hey, look, he's got a white man working for him.' Now my job is to make those people like me, and I'm hip to the fact that it's not exactly endearing me to some of them to see a colored guy have a white guy working for him. It bothers them. But I can't worry about anyone who wants to look at me and find fault. All I've got to worry about is: am I right?"

"Fair enough. But one's image is formed by many things: you live in hotels not open to the average Negro; you bought a house in a restricted area of Los Angeles . . ."

"Right! I've got one of the best houses in Hollywood—and incidentally, the neighborhood's not restricted any more. I'm a liberal, and I decided it would be wrong of me to boy-cott one of the best neighborhoods just because the people who live there are white." He was smiling. "And about the hotels: they haven't yet figured out how to build one as good as I want to live."

"Sammy, there's no arguing with this kind of thinking, but you must see that it contributes to the impression which the average Negro has, that you have removed yourself from Negro life and have turned away from him."

"I haven't turned away from anyone or anything except living in the gutter."

"But your way of living, your associations . . . the man on the street can only interpret them as—well, they'll certainly never conclude that you're *proud* of your race."

"Why do they have to conclude anything? People I never even met sitting around deciding what I oughta do! They're out of their minds. The white cats are saying 'He oughta live there' and the colored cats are saying 'He oughta live here' and it always ends up with both of 'em saying 'Hell, he thinks he's white' and 'Yeah, he's ashamed he's colored.' *Bull!* If I was ashamed of being colored would I present myself at the best hotel in town and expect them to let me in? And I don't exactly go into those places figuring I'm going to pass! ·

"Last year I made three quarters of a million dollars in an industry that's ninety-five per cent white. Now seven hundred and fifty thousand dollars ain't exactly a shoeshine boy! And while I'm raking it in I'm taking extra glory in the fact that I'm a Negro and I beat the odds—I made ten the hard way. I'm not so damned thrilled over the unnecessary problems I've had because I'm a Negro; that I had to work harder because I'm a Negro, and that I had to be better at what I do than if I were white. Sure, I've suffered because I'm a Negro, just like you've suffered, and a lot of us have, but I have never for one breath of my life been ashamed that I'm a Negro.

"I'll tell you this though, I'm plenty disappointed in the kind of support I'm getting from a lot of our guys. It's lousy enough when I walk into a hotel and I've gotta feel a white guy looking at me, thinking 'Why does he want to push his way in?' and I'd love to sit down with him and ask 'Why should I *have* to push my way in?' But when I'm convicted by *my own people,* who should know better, what kind of acceptance can I hope for from the rest of the world?

"I want my people to like me. I really do. It kills me when I pass a colored cat on the street and he gives me a look like I'm Benedict Arnold. But I can't win him wrong. I'm not about to live by his rules or anybody's. I refuse to be put in a bind and told 'this is right and this is wrong' by any group of people. If a guy says, 'You gotta eat dinner at six o'clock,' I want to know *why* do I have to eat dinner at six o'clock? Why can't I eat at ten if I feel like it? 'Well, that's the way everybody else does.' Bull! Who is it that makes these rules to run my life? And what makes him better than me? Sure, I obey laws made for the well-being of all people, I hurt no man except myself and I ask no man to hold his dinner hour until ten just to suit me. He likes to eat at six? Crazy. Let him eat at six. And I observe the customs of kindness and decency like holding doors open for ladies and lighting people's cigarettes. But I refuse to recognize rules that try to tell me *where* to eat and *whose* cigarettes I'm going to light." I pulled a wad of bills out of my pocket. "Y'see this money? It's *mine!* Nobody gave it to me, Johnny, so there ain't nobody gonna tell me how to spend it.

"I'll tell you now. I'll be playing the Copa in New York later this year and I'm not going to live in Harlem any more than I'm going to live in New Jersey. I know now they're gonna fight me on it. The guys on the papers'll start the whole thing about me trying to be white, and the cats on the street'll read it and say, 'Yeah, how come he don't live up here where he belongs?' But Johnny, there ain't a one among 'em that wouldn't move downtown, and into the Waldorf-Astoria if he had the money and if they'd let him in.

"I'm not going to run up to Harlem and hang around to keep up appearances, either. And I know now what's gonna happen. The mass Negro's gonna bitch, 'He's not a corner boy.' And they're right. I don't go up to Harlem and just hang on the corner of 125th and Seventh. I never did it when I was a kid and there's no reason for me to do it now. I'm not about to con my own people into liking me by making regular visits to Harlem and hangin' around like 'Hey baby— I ain't changed. I'm still old Sam. Still colored!'"

The voice that was coming across the desk was warm, friendly. "Sammy, when a fireman goes into a smoke-filled, burning building he wears a gas mask, helmet, rubber coat, and asbestos gloves. As long as you have no intention of changing your approach to life, if you continue to say, 'I believe I'm right and I'll stick to what I believe in,' then at least you should equip yourself accordingly. A magazine or a newspaper seeks the unusual, and in combination with a celebrity, the unusual cannot hope to go unnoticed. If you are the first Negro to move into an all-white neighborhood, it is going to be printed, and the public will react to it; they will reach conclusions and formulate opinions. That is the nature of the beast on all sides of the color spectrum, and we're not going to change unless we stop thinking and communicating with each other.

"All I can do for you is promise that in my publications what is reported about you will be done so accurately and fairly. But, it will be reported, and people will approve and disapprove. Some will understand your motives and appreciate them, but some will prefer not to understand. This is the price you must expect to pay for being an individual. As long as you do not run with the pack, as long as you move off in a direction not generally accepted, you will continue to be a controversial figure. You are choosing the road, you should know where it leads."

18

BETTY BOGART CALLED ME AROUND NOON. "SAM, I KNOW it's short notice, but we just heard you were in town and we're having a few people up for dinner tonight. Slacks-style. Bring a date if you'd like."

"Thanks, Betty. I'm not going with anybody in particular. I'll come by alone."

It was just Frank and a date, Judy Garland and Sid Luft, the Bogarts and me. After dinner I sat in a corner of the living room with Bogie. He said, "You think you're pretty jazzy with the glen plaid patch."

I grinned. "Bogie, let's face it, either you're suave or you ain't. I mean, you've gotta admit it *is* just a little distingué, don't you?"

He just looked at me. Abruptly he asked, "How long you gonna keep the goddamned patch on your eye?"

"Well . . . I don't know, it's only nine months or so and the new eye still doesn't look very good."

"You got the eye underneath it now?"

"Yeah."

"Lemme see it."

I glanced around. "Let's not scare any women and children." I lifted the patch. "I'll tell you the truth, I've been thinking I may never give it up. I kinda dig it."

"It's a big mistake. Don't get caught on it. You aren't too goddamned pretty to look at, and the patch gives you a little feeling like the guy in the shirt ad. You figure it's glamorous. But you're getting to like it too much." He smacked the table three times and the butler came in. "Fix us another drink, please." He turned back to me. "I'm telling you, take it off

277

as soon as possible. The eye'll be better than the patch. You'll be happier."

"I'm not so sure. It's becoming a trademark. I've got it on an album cover and it's fantastic. People spot it right away on the streets. I figure I've got a good thing going for me."

"Y'wanta keep reminding people about the accident? Y'trying to trade on it?"

"Hell, no, but I . . ."

"Y'wanta walk into a room and have people say, 'There's Sammy Davis,' or do you want 'em to say, 'There's the kid with the patch'?"

"Well, naturally I don't want that . . . I guess I'll get rid of it eventually, but I'm not in any hurry."

"Don't waste too much time. You're kidding yourself with that trademark crap. You're using it for a crutch. Don't fool yourself that wearing a patch over your eye gives you an excuse for not being good-looking."

There was no snow, no icicles on the trees or frost on the window, none of the seasonal things which had always been a part of it, but it felt like Christmas. I put on a robe and listened outside Mama's door. She wasn't up yet. I walked through the house, opened the door leading from the foyer into the garage and smiled at the sight of the brand new four-door white Cadillac with a red ribbon tied all the way around it. I stood back to see what kind of a first view she'd get. No good. The thing to do would be to take her outside and then open the garage door so she'd catch a look at it all at once with the sunlight shining on it.

I put a Christmas album on the hi-fi set, loud, and listened outside her door again. She was still sleeping. I opened it a little and did some stumbling and coughing until I heard her moving around, reaching for her glasses. I leaned over the bed and kissed her. "Merry Christmas, Mama." I handed her a little box containing the car key.

She was still half-asleep. "I'll open this when we have Christmas breakfast. Then I can enjoy it."

"Okay, you get dressed and I'll get things started." I tried to lay out the things she'd need to cook with. Twenty minutes later she came in. "Mama, let's just have some coffee."

"Well . . . all right, Sammy."

"*Instant* coffee!"

She was on her second cup but she hadn't made a move for the box. I picked it up and shook it. I put it down. "Sammy, you push that any closer to me and it'll be in my cup. I guess I better open it now or you'll jump out of your skin."

"No rush, Mama. Take your time."

She held up the key. "Now what's this for?"

I shrugged. "Beats me. Let's look around and see if we can find something it fits." I tried it on the kitchen door. "Doesn't fit here. Let's go outside."

"Sammy, what're you up to?"

"I'm not up to anything, Mama. It's Santa Claus."

"Don't tell me about Santa Claus, I couldn't even make you believe it after you turned three."

I ran ahead, out the front door and called back, "Maybe we can find something out here." I turned to open the garage and stopped dead. Somebody had come by in the middle of the night with a can of paint and a brush and had smeared across the front of the garage door: *Merry Christmas Nigger!*

"Sammy, you out here?" She was just coming through the front door. I spun around and grabbed her arm, stopping her before she could see it, and pulled her back into the house. I slammed the door closed and locked it against the ghoulish, dripping letters. The smile that had been on Mama's face was distorted by a stunned bewilderment. "Sammy, what happened?"

"Mama. Stay inside! Promise me you won't go out." She nodded silently and I ran into my bedroom and closed the door. I dialed and waited. "Arthur . . . the hell it is. Listen . . ." I took deep breaths to keep my voice from breaking. "I need you. I want you to come over here tomorrow night. I'll be in Frisco. Bring a gun. Get a cop, someone off duty, I don't care what it costs, I want him on the hill across the road and I want you in the window . . . and if anybody comes onto my property . . . shoot him! Kill him. If anybody comes near my house or wants to bother Mama, then *kill him!* Stay here every night I'm out of town, please, Arthur, and kill anybody who comes near my house . . . that's the law, they can't come *here*."

I hung up and sat on the bed staring out the same window I'd looked through less than an hour before. Holy God! Even on Christmas. I had to get my mind off it. I turned on a record. I reached for a book, any book I might lose myself in. I picked up *A History of the Jews* and opened it in the middle. The first word I saw was "Justice." That's a laugh. I skimmed the pages but that same word kept reappearing. I'd read the book before, but I started reading it again, from the beginning.

More than ever I saw the affinity between the Jew and the Negro. The Jews had been oppressed for three thousand years instead of three hundred like us, but the rest was very much the same. I went through page after page, reading of their oppressions, their centuries of enslavement; I traced them from one end of the world to the other, despised and rejected, searching for a home, for equality and human dignity, suffering the loneliness of being unwanted, surviving the destruction of their homes and their temples, the burning of their books. For thousands of years they hung onto their beliefs, enduring the scorn, the intolerance, the abuses against them because they were "different," time and again losing everything, but never their belief in themselves and in their right to have rights, asking nothing but for people to leave them alone, to get off their backs. I looked at the name of the man who had written the book. Abram Leon Sachar. I felt like sending him a note: "Abe, I know how you feel."

I got hung up on one paragraph. *"The Jews would not die. Three centuries of prophetic teaching had given them an unwavering spirit of resignation and had created in them a will to live which no disaster could crush."* I kept reading it over and over again, wondering what those teachings had been. What had they learned that gave them that strength?

". . . Rabbi, I don't know if I've been describing it right. I read the books around the clock and it was like 'Yeah!' and 'I'm not the only one it's happened to.' I don't mean 'misery loves company' but there was something about seeing what your people lived through that made me able to detach myself from what was going on around me and measure my problems for what they really were. I came to thank you and tell you what I suddenly got out of them. They're nothing like what I expected. Maybe this'll sound odd to you but it's not like 'religion,' like something that's a separate part of your life and on Sunday you get it over with because it's got to be done, or even if you like it, it's a once-a-week or even a once-a-day thing. It's more like basic rules for everyday living and it's odd, I'm not a Jew but so much of it is what I believe in—ideas I'd love to be able to live up to. It was all there, straight and familiar, confirming so much that I'd learned the hard way, like fight for what you believe in, suffer for it if you have to but don't let go of your ideas—'cause if you do, then you've got *nothing!*

"I love the attitude that man is made in God's image and that he has unlimited potential, and that 'In God's world all things are possible.' I love the idea that we can reach for the brass ring and we can keep stretching until we're tall enough to reach it. This has been my thinking all my life and it's a joy to open a book and see that not everybody puts different people in separate cubbyholes and looks at them like 'How dare they' if they try to break out. And there's none of the things I hate, like 'Well, it's up to fate' and 'If it's meant to be.' I admire an attitude of: it *is* meant to be if you'll go out and get it done. I love your thinking about not waiting around for a Messiah to come and straighten everything out, that the Messiah is not an individual but mankind collectively and that it's up to them to create the kind of a world that'll be like a Kingdom of Heaven right here."

Rabbi Fine poured some coffee from a small electric stove on his desk and handed me a cup. I sat back in the chair. "There was a boy I treated badly and then he died and when it happened I'd have given anything I own to have said 'Hey, I'm sorry I wasn't nicer.' But it was too late. He was dead. Gone. That night I prayed for God to forgive me. But I had the feeling that even if God would forgive me, my friend wasn't going to know anything about it. Then last week I was going through the books and one of the lines came up and whacked me pretty hard: 'God does not intervene to redeem man's duties to his fellow man.'

"I memorized certain things, one in particular, 'The difference between love and hate is understanding.' I kept thinking about it and I realized that it was something I'd found out in the Army, something I'd seen a doezn times since then, but I just hadn't known the words for it. Can you know what a hunk of truth like that does for a guy like me? If I can keep that in mind it's like a bulletproof vest. I know for a fact that when I meet someone who doesn't like me, who hates my guts, that if I sit with him for a while my chances of changing his mind are pretty good. I've just got to give him an opportunity to see what he didn't know or think about before. I realize that there are certain people who are never going to like me, not on toast or on rye. If two World Wars didn't wipe out blind hatred then I know I'm not about to. Nor do I really care that much about trying with certain guys. If I look at it calmly and think, then I know that their prejudice is a crutch, it's an equalizer that some guys need—they're getting kicked around and they've got to let it out on somebody so they find someone *they* can kick around. Okay, but when the guy calls you the name normally you don't smile and think, 'Relax, Charley, it's his crutch.' All you know is he just hit you over the head and you want to hit him back, and whether you do or not, it's exhausting. But now, let him hit me with his crutch. I'm wearing a steel hat. If I find somebody hating me because he doesn't want to understand me, then I'm not going to hate him, because I *will* understand him. I'm not going to let him insult me and then exhaust me, too."

The rabbi was laughing. "I've heard of personally applying a philosophy but you just made a pretzel out of it."

"Don't knock it, Rabbi. It's working. Y'know my friend with the gun, and the cop I told you about?"

"Yes."

"I hired a painter instead."

"Sammy, you seem to enjoy the Jewish philosophy. I didn't give you much about our theology."

"Well, there was some, and here's where you're going to think I'm out of my mind entirely, but as I read about the three levels of Judaism, the Orthodox, the Conservative and the Reform—I hope you won't take offense, but it's something like the way I do my act. I do my shows to suit each audience. I give them what I feel they want. I'm not comparing religion to show business, only the approach, and maybe you can see how Judaism does sort of the same thing. It's broken down so that the individual can have what he needs. The religion serves the man, it's there to make his life a little better, not to tell him, 'Hey, God's over here, three shows on Sunday and you'd better catch him or you blew it and you go downstairs.' I'm not knocking the others. Obviously they work for millions of people, but I appreciate the flexibility of Judaism. You don't put a guy in a box and say, 'Now here's how to worship God.' " I looked at a piece of paper I had. " 'God, where shall I find thee? Wherever the mind is free to follow its own bent.' Does that mean what I think it means?"

"Yes, but you must not oversimplify Judaism. We place less emphasis on rules of worship than on rules of personal conduct. But we have many symbols, much ritual and ceremony which we enjoy as remembrances of particular times in our history. We remember in tribute to those before us and it gives perspective to where we are today."

I hated to break the pleasant atmosphere of near camaraderie of the past two weeks but I couldn't put it off any longer. "Rabbi, we can talk openly, can't we?"

He leaned back in his big leather chair and smiled. "I certainly hope so."

"Well, I've been coming to services, we've spent hours and hours talking Judaism and I've read all the books you gave me until I was blue in the face—and y'gotta admit, with my face that's not easy—in other words, obviously I'm pretty interested, right? But at no time in all our talks have you ever once said, or even hinted, 'Hey, why don't you convert? Become a Jew.' "

"Sammy, converting to Judaism is a monumental move. Particularly for you."

"What do you mean by that?"

"Don't be sensitive. You know there are many Negro Jews and that I wasn't thinking about that. But you're publicity prone. An immediate conversion might very possibly create the opinion that you're doing this as a publicity stunt."

"Oh, you can't believe that?"

"I resent that question. You should know that I wouldn't waste my time or thought on you if I even suspected that. I know your sincerity, but there are many who won't and they'll deride you and make a mockery of something which has begun to have significance to you.

"There's no need to rush into formal conversion. For a while be a Jew at heart. You can be just as good a Jew if you really believe in it without having a document to make it official."

"Rabbi, all my life I went in back doors. . . ."

"It's not the back door. When you've had enough time to be absolutely sure, then come in the front door. But don't rush through it. When you get back to Hollywood you should look up Rabbi Max Nussbaum. He's one person I really believe you should meet in your quest for a kinship to Judaism."

He was not a man to whom I wanted to give quick answers.

"Rabbi Nussbaum, religion is something I did without for over twenty years, but in a remote way it's like a policeman or the fire department: you may not use them often but when you need them you'd better know how to find them. I don't know how much Rabbi Fine told you about how I got interested in Judaism—it was strictly by accident. But when I started getting an idea of what it was all about I kept reading and I've developed a tremendous feeling for it, and for the first time in my life I see the hope of filling the void I've always had where religion was concerned."

"Have you given your own religion an opportunity to fill that void?"

"Well, my father's a Baptist and my mother's a Catholic but I wasn't raised very close to either of those faiths."

"Wouldn't you think it advisable to examine and understand what you already have before you trade it away for something else? What's wrong, Sammy?"

"Rabbi . . . I hope you won't misunderstand this, but I want to be totally honest with you. I get a feeling that when I talk about becoming a Jew . . . well, nobody seems to get too choked up about the idea."

"Sammy, if I brought a grown man to you and said, 'He hasn't been able to make a living in real estate but he's read a lot of books on show business and he's thinking about be-

coming a performer, so I'd like you to put him in your act'—
what would you tell me?"

I felt the heat of embarrassment crossing my face. "I apologize for making an idiot of myself."

"Don't apologize. But don't be so sensitive either. Race has
absolutely nothing to do with our reluctance to rush you into
conversion. You should know that from the reading you've
been doing. I'm sure you've come across Isaiah's pronounce-
ment 'My house shall be a house for all people.' You must
have seen that one of the primary tenets of Judaism is a hos-
pitality to differences.

"Sammy, a rabbi is a teacher. I'm here to help you find
what you want, not to act as a membership committee to
accept or reject you. In your reading you must have seen that
we do not urge people to convert. Would we, of all people,
tell others 'You should think our way'? But that does not
mean we aren't delighted to find someone who does. We
cherish converts, but we neither seek nor rush them. We don't
want today's enthusiasm to be tomorrow's disappointment.

"In the case of the majority of converts—people marrying
into Judaism and wishing to be wed in a religious ceremony
and to raise children in a home which had religious harmony
—we put them through a course, teach them the essentials,
and hope that it takes. If it does, wonderful, but if it doesn't,
we realize it was a conversion for practical purposes not
motivated by the needs of the heart, therefore nobody can be
hurt if the convert does not develop a true belief in Judaism.
But yours is a much more delicate situation. You're wide
open. You come to us looking for something. You place a
trust in us and we dare not betray it. We want Judaism to
serve you, to bring you comfort, joy—everything a religion
might mean to one—but it can only do so if approached properly, with the fullest possible understanding of what it offers.
You may in a short while decide it's not all you thought it was
cracked up to be. On the other hand, and I believe this will
be the case, I think that your appreciation and enjoyment of
Judaism, your benefit from it, will be broadened by the extent
to which you understand it."

"Well, I realize I've got to do a lot more studying, but ... I
don't know, I just hate to put off doing something I feel so
sure of."

"Don't put it off. Identify yourself as a Jew. Study, attend services, associate yourself with whatever Jewish organizations your traveling will permit. When you come down to it, what *is* the act of being a Jew? It's not a secret ceremony or a special handshake, it's an approach to life, an adherence to a set of principles, to moral code, the acceptance of a standard of human ethics and behavior. Obviously much of our thinking was yours before you even met a rabbi or you wouldn't have related to it. But know everything you possibly can before you make up your mind. Read more. Take time. Come back and see me. I will always be available to you. We'll talk about what you've read and about what you think, and we'll explore what you believe in. But let me caution you not to expect to find Judaism in books. They'll only present the philosophy, its history, its evolutions; they will give you knowledge which may or may not translate within you so that some day you will come to me and say 'Rabbi, I'm a Jew.'"

The road was lined with so many trucks that I had to park a couple of hundred feet away from my house. The big CBS portable transmitter was parked directly in front.

"Person-to-Person" had been in touch with Jess Rand about visiting me. They'd worked out a date, and although we'd barely begun to furnish the house, I couldn't afford to pass up the importance of that kind of exposure, so almost overnight I had to get the house furnished.

I stepped carefully over the cables that were leading inside, and stood in the foyer. Crews of workmen were swarming around the place hammering down carpet, putting up curtains and draperies, bringing in chairs, lamps, pictures, and parts of beds, working with hectic efficiency—like they were putting together a movie set.

Mama was rushing around in the middle of it all, dusting things that hadn't been put in place yet. I kissed her hello, ducked around a CBS engineer who was stringing wire from one room to another and retreated to a big, black leather couch. I took off my jacket, opened my shirt collar and sat there doing the "Squire of my castle" bit, looking around and beaming and watching it being created in front of me.

The microphones and cameras were set up and ready to go

on the air while the last pictures were still being hung. An engineer was going through the house taking telephones off the hooks. I got the signal from the director, I saw the little red light flash on the front of the camera and Ed Murrow was saying, "Good evening, Sammy. May we come in and visit with you for a while?"

My father hugged me, lifting me off the floor. "Poppa, I'm the proudest, happiest man in the world that I lived to see this happen." We were in the way of the CBS technicians who were taking down apparatus. I led him into the bedroom and sat down on the bed. "Poppa, I kept watching the set and telling myself that's my son there talking to Edward R. Murrow, giving him that 'won't you come in, Mr. Murrow' like you was Harry Truman, and him sayin' 'thank you for letting us come visit you.' I guess I just come to take it all for fact 'cause it all come so slow, but when I saw you on the TV set and I recalled the days we was glad to find a place to rest our heads—well, it just hit me all at once how big you got, and with the whole country seein' it like that, it shook me so bad that I sat there cryin' like a kid. The way you talked, everything about you . . . it was like what you always wanted."

The phones started ringing with calls from friends who'd seen the show. Around midnight it quieted down. My father watched me tying my tie and helped me into my jacket. "Goin' out to take a few bows, Poppa?"

I picked one of the show business hangouts on the Strip where I knew they had a TV set over the bar. A guy who works for the Morris office rushed toward me. "Hey, I just saw the 'Person-to-Person' thing. It was a gas. Jesus, your house looked like *too much!* That was a nice touch having your grandmother there. And those closets you got. Man, I'd like to have a hotel room that big."

"Thanks, baby. Glad you liked it."

"Listen, y'want a laugh? It's a gag about your new house. It's a little racial, but it's so cute you'll love it. The way it goes is your grandmother's been living in the house for about a week when one of the neighbors says to her husband, 'It's the damnedest thing. I see the maid going in and out all the time but the people who live there never leave the house.'"

He was laughing, waiting for me to laugh too. As he began to realize I wasn't going to, the smile died on his face. "It's just a gag, Sam . . . hey, you know I didn't mean anything. . . ."

I'd thought I'd really accomplished something. But it hadn't registered. He hadn't seen what was on the screen, only what was already burned into his mind: Mama wasn't a lady, in lovely clothes, at home with her grandson—she was a maid. And I wasn't a guy who'd made it and bought a fine house—I was a colored guy who'd bought a house in a white neighborhood.

"Sam, if I'd known you were so touchy . . . "

I got into my car and drove away from there, away from the lights of the Strip. I was able to buy Mama a beautiful house and set her up in it like a lady. When she steps out of her house why should she look any more like a maid than any other guy's mother or grandmother? Sure, I could understand why . . . that was the horror of it. The image was so deeply carved. Here's a guy who'd have bent himself in half not to offend me, if only for business reasons. He was actually trying to be friendly with that joke. It just never dawned upon him that anybody, including me, should expect a colored woman who walks out of a decent house to be anything but a maid.

I pulled over by the ocean in Santa Monica and watched the waves breaking high over the beach, crashing to the sand, then rolling back out to sea. It had all been for nothing. I had a mental picture of the whole world split in half, with me standing in the middle, the Negroes on one side glaring at me and the whites on the other side, laughing. What do I have to accomplish before I can walk on both sides of the world in peace? With dignity?

19

I LEANED ACROSS THE DRESSING TABLE AT THE FRONTIER, in Vegas, and put on my patch, letting my hair hang casually over the elastic band, making Charley Handsome faces into the mirror. Morty and Dave came in and caught me grinning at myself like an idiot.

Dave turned to Morty. "She's beautiful, isn't she?" Morty nodded. "Gorgeous!"

"It happens to be my business to know what I look like . . . seriously, do you know of anything more distinguished-looking in this world than a well-dressed man wearing a patch? I mean it's so damned swashbuckling. Like a Heidelberg scar."

Dave nodded. "Sam, let me ask you something. How do colored people blush?"

Between phrases of "Black Magic" I caught a woman at ringside nudging her husband, pointing to her eye, whispering, "The patch is satin, it matches his lapels." Instantly I heard Bogart's voice again, *You want 'em to say 'There's Sammy Davis,' or 'There's the kid with the patch'?"* I stopped singing and signaled Morty to cut the music.

"Ladies and gentlemen, forgive me for interrupting the show. There's something I've been wearing for the last year or so and I really dig it—maybe a little too much—but I think it's starting to wear me so it's time I got rid of it. I'd better do it now while I have the guts."

I slipped off the patch and tossed it to a corner of the bandstand. A woman at ringside closed her eyes and groaned. There was a gasp throughout the room. They were probably expecting to see nothing but a large hole.

"I hope you'll bear with me. I don't know if it looks too good but I can't wear that thing for the rest of my life. I waited a whole year and I still haven't gotten one free shirt from Hathaway." I cued Morty for the impressions.

The audience was coming out of its shock; the applause began growing, and they began standing, table by table. The people were much too high for the impressions. I had to overpower them, steamroller over them to regain control. I snapped my fingers fast, cueing Morty for "Fascinating Rhythm." The first notes burst over the heads of the audience, but it was hopeless, the music couldn't begin to climb over the continuing, growing roar.

The Frontier's publicity guy burst into the dressing room. "Sammy, why didn't you let me know? I could've had photographers, wire services . . ."

"I'm sorry, but I couldn't tip you off 'cause it wasn't planned. There was no 'I'll go and make a dramatic thing out of it.' It's the last thing I expected to do."

He was looking at me with disgust. "Well, at least let's set up a shot now of you taking it off and throwing it away. I guess I can still plant it with one of the wire services."

"Baby, it won't work. It'll be phony and it'll look like it."

"Sammy, please, I know what I'm doing."

I checked the morning papers. There were stories but no pictures. I called Jess to see if the picture had broken in L.A. It hadn't.

Dave asked, "What's there to look so happy about?"

"I'm happy to know I was right. That picture shouldn't have run. It was posed and phony and the newspaper guys smelled it. The audience got hung up on the drama of the moment because it was real and they knew it. When you're selling emotion then it better be real, daddy, or you ain't gonna sell it. The picture was dishonest. And the cat who thinks he's gonna fool the people is gonna wake up someday and find he's out of the business."

Jule Styne came into the dressing room, shy, yet bristling with energy. "Sammy, I saw your show. Fantastic! You're a great talent but you can't play nightclubs forever. You'll suffocate that talent in saloons. It's out of the question. You've got to expand, spread out. You need dimension . . ." His enthusiasm was dizzying. "The place for you is Broadway!"

I sat him down in a chair, careful not to interrupt him.

"You should star in a musical. You *must!* You can sing and dance and do everything you do in clubs. I'll produce it and we'll get some good writers to do a modern musical comedy. We'll build the story around whatever kind of a character you feel you could play best. Look at what you do to audiences every night on a bare stage and imagine what'll happen when you have three hundred thousand dollars' worth of scenery and lighting and costumes going for you. They'll die over you on Broadway. You can't possibly miss. And the stature and prestige would be enormous for you."

I was staring at him like he was Charley Messiah. "Jule,

keep talking. But keep your distance or you may get a kiss on the lips."

"Then you like the idea?"

"I love it."

"Great. We'll get together tomorrow and discuss it. In the meantime try to think of the kind of a character you feel you could play best."

He left and I found myself walking around the room, smiling at the walls: if television and movies don't want me, to hell with them—there's *nothing* that can match Broadway for stature and dignity.

I had a lunch table set up in the room and I'd put a "Don't Disturb" on the phone when Jule arrived. "I think I should play someone like me. A performer. Let's face it, that's the kind of a character I really understand, plus the fact that it gives us a built-in excuse for me to sing and dance."

"I like it. He could be a kid who's trying to make it against the odds, the racial thing . . . he's alone in the world . . . he's got nothing but talent going for him . . ." Jule's face took on a dreamy, faraway look—he was leaving me. ". . . maybe he's too sensitive to fight the race thing here so he goes off to Europe—Paris! He finds himself a little Left Bank club and he becomes the chic thing to do. . . ."

I didn't touch the food on the table and neither did Jule. I listened to him ad-libbing a show, speaking with child-like enthusiasm—the truly creative man, completely forgetting past triumphs, involved deeply and only in the thing of the moment. I was swept up in his excitement and the ideas flew back and forth across the table.

We took a breather and I said, "Jule, I'm not going to try to be a writer but I do have one strong feeling about the overall idea of the show: it's got to say something racially. And, as you said, we should do a 'modern' musical. That means an integrated show with a mixed chorus."

"Naturally."

"I mean *really* mixed. Not like the typical thing where they have eight dancers and one of them is colored and the producer goes around saying 'we have an integrated cast.' That's bull. Nobody's ever done it right and we of all people can and should be the first ones."

"I'm with you all the way. Now, we should do it first class right down the line. For choreography let's get Gene Kelly or Agnes De Mille . . ."

"Jule, people like that are fabulous, but when they choreograph a show you don't even have to look at the program to tell who did the dances—they've got their own styles, and they're great, but not for me. I don't want my audiences to watch me work and see Gene Kelly or Agnes De Mille dancing; I want them to see Sammy Davis, Jr. And I have the same feeling about the music. I'd like to use my own conductor, Morty Stevens. He's young and he's never done a Broadway show, but he's good. I mean really good. Know now, I want guidance in the areas where I've got no experience, but in certain things I could never have anyone dictate to me. I've got to dance my way and do songs my way."

Jule nodded approval. "There's a very bright fellow who works with me, his name is George Gilbert. He'll be my co-producer. You'll like him, he's young too, but he's very astute, he has great taste, he's creative and clever."

"Crazy. Jule, what about my father and Will Mastin? Do you think there'll be anything in it for them?"

"No. Not a chance. When you first come to Broadway you have to overcome the image of a nightclub guy—not that it isn't great, I'm not putting it down—but when you walk onto a stage in a show, you want the audience to be able to accept you as the character you'll be playing. I know you'll be great and within five minutes we'll have no problems, but anything that would remind them of you as a nightclub performer would be disastrous to the illusion of the show. If you came in with your father and your uncle . . . oh God, I can see Walter Kerr now: 'Sammy Davis, Jr. arrived on Broadway with everything except the scotch-and-soda and cigar smoke.' It would be terrible. He'd kill us with things like, 'A funny thing happened to me on the way to the theater last night. I wound up at the Copacabana.' Do you see what I mean?"

"Well . . . I guess so."

"Fine. I'm doing a musical for Judy Holliday so I have to leave for New York on Tuesday. As soon as I get there I'll sign the writers and get things in motion."

Will strode up and down the living room. "Sammy, who's the manager of this Trio?"

"Oh come on, Massey, don't play games with me. What's wrong?"

"Nothing. Only that the Morris office called me about some story in *The New York Times* that you're planning to go on Broadway, that's all. And I didn't enjoy sounding like a fool telling 'em I don't know anything about it."

"Massey, I'm sorry. I really am. I didn't mention it to you because I didn't know if it was just talk or not. I'm sorry that it was in the papers before you knew about it, but that wasn't my fault."

"You telling me it's true?"

"Well, yes, now that I see he's serious. Massey, will you please stop shaking your head until I explain it?" He sat down and folded his arms. "Now try to forget that I'm the kid you brought up and used to bathe in the sink. I'm Sammy Davis, Jr., I'm twenty-nine years old and after all these years I've got to know *something* about this business. Now it's wonderful that we're a hit in clubs and that we're making big money 'cause nobody needs it more than I do. But we need dimension, prestige, and there's *nothing* that can give us that prestige like a Broadway musical. . . ."

"Prestige is how much money you've got in the bank."

"Fine. But I'm talking about something that'll only be better for us in the long run."

"This *is* the long run. We've gotta make it now while we can."

"That's true. But, statistically an act has a three-year life expectancy, and if we let ourselves stay in the category of 'nightclub guys' the heat *will* come out of us, but being on Broadway would not only help us build to even bigger than we are now but it would keep us there."

He was shaking his head again. "Variety is variety, and acting is acting, and I don't see why you think you can act all of a sudden."

"When I stand on a stage and I sound like Cagney and Brando, I'm not doing it with mirrors. Massey, I'm not saying there isn't a whole world of acting I don't begin to know anything about—but I learned to dance by dancing, I learned to sing by singing, and I'll learn to act by acting."

293

He stood up. "Sammy, you can talk 'til tomorrow and I'll listen if you want but I'm dead against it. It'll break up the act."

We both stiffened at the sound of the words. His mouth moved soundlessly, as though he were trying to recapture them, but they had been said and their meaning hung revealingly, irrevocably, in the air. He sat down, letting his body sink into the chair, accepting at least the relief which accompanied the pain of an admission he hadn't intended to make, probably even to himself.

All the illogical statements from a logical man, his inability to see the obvious, his refusal to help me get into pictures and dramatic television—everything was explained. How could any argument make sense to a man who had to interpret it as "Let's start changing everything you waited all these years to have, because I want more." It wasn't as simple as "Take a year off, we'll still split the money, relax, enjoy a vacation." No matter how beautifully it was painted, to Will it would mean the beginning of the end.

I turned around. "Massey?" He brought his head up, facing me, his eyes coming up last. "Massey, why should it have to break up the act? I'm going to play a performer. The script isn't written yet. Why can't he have a father and an uncle?"

His face began brightening. "Well . . . it *would* be kinda nice to be in the legit." He smiled. "You think I'm too old to go to acting school? Of course a thing like this presents a lot of problems."

"Sure it does but we can beat them. Look, Jule's still in town. Supposing I get him over here tomorrow? We can sit down and talk it over. Nothing has to be decided. It'll be strictly a preliminary talk."

Twenty minutes later Jule was in my room. "What's wrong?"

"No problems. It's just that I was sitting here thinking about the character we discussed, and he's great. To tell you the truth I'm really thrilled with the whole thing."

Jule beamed. "I'm very excited about it myself."

"And, what I was thinking is . . . it would be sensational, I mean it would be a great natural tie-in, I mean as far as identification goes and all that jazz . . . well, if we wanted to make the kid really come to life it occurred to me he should have a father and an uncle."

Jule soared out of his chair. "That's the *worst* idea I ever heard! It's terrible. Out of the question. Forget it—"

"Jule, cool it. We're in trouble."

He was pacing the floor. "It'd be hokey and horrible. Impossible. We discussed it, I explained why it would be no good, I thought we agreed . . ." He stopped walking and looked at me. "What do you mean we're in trouble?"

"Baby, you agreed and I agreed, but *they* didn't. Now it happens that I've got a contract with The Will Mastin Trio and if they ain't in the show, then legally I ain't in the show. But even more important, I can't walk out on my father and uncle just because I want to do a play." He groaned and sat down. "I'm sorry to lay it on you like this but in all the excitement I just didn't think it out."

"There's no way out?"

"None."

He sat on the couch, holding his head. "Well, we'll just have to work it out then, that's all." He stood up. "I'll have the writers send up a father and an uncle."

"Now you're talking."

"As a matter of fact maybe it's not such a bad idea after all." He did a little walking, hands behind his back, nodding, thinking, nodding, until he was almost excited. "The more I think about it the better I like it." He looked at me. "It's great." I watched him, amused that he, like me, was turning it, accepting the inevitable, then urging himself to enthusiasm so that he could live with it.

I sat back in a corner of the room and watched the action. Will asked, "Mr. Styne, assuming we can work things out so we can do this show, how's the billing going to be?"

"Don't worry about a thing, Mr. Mastin. Sammy's name'll be over the title of the show."

Will smiled. "The name of this act is 'The Will Mastin Trio, featuring Sammy Davis, Jr.' Then comes the name of the show."

Jule leaped out of his chair for about the third time in half an hour. "It's impossible. Out of the question. There isn't enough room on the marquee . . ."

Will gave Jule a half-yawn and the sweetest smile in his repertoire. "Then either you get a bigger marquee or have a smaller cast."

Jule collected himself and tried another approach. "Mr. Mastin, you must understand that the more space we can give Sammy's name on the signs and in the ads, the better chance we have to sell tickets. If we were to do it the way you suggest . . ."

"I'm not suggesting. I'm stating it plain."

"But, then in order to make Sammy's name big enough we'd have to make everything else bigger in proportion and we wouldn't have enough room left for the name of the show."

"That'll be okay 'cause there won't be no show to have a name for."

I stepped between them. "Look, guys, it's not important. All that really counts is that we're doing the show, we'll be on Broadway—personally, I don't care where my name is."

Jule was out of his chair again. "Well *I* do! It's Sammy Davis, Jr. that'll sell tickets." He seemed suddenly to remember that Will was there. "I'm sorry, Mr. Mastin. I apologize. But I'm sure you'll agree that it's Sammy's name that's widely known from the records and the accident."

"Mr. Styne, I think you should come by the New Frontier tonight around seven-thirty and look at the line of people waiting to get tables to see 'The Will Mastin Trio Featuring Sammy Davis, Jr.' Incidentally, how much do you figure we can make out of this show?"

Jule leaned back in his chair, smiling with renewed confidence. "We'll work out a minimum weekly guarantee against 10 per cent of the gross."

"How much do you figure this show can gross?"

"Well, we'll get the biggest musical house available, which means we can plan on about $60,000 a week." He beamed at us both, pleased.

Will nodded. "I see. In other words if we have a hit show that sells out every night then our cut is six thousand a week?"

"That's right."

I got very busy retying my shoelace.

"Mr. Styne, we can make that in any dinky little club."

"But Mr. Mastin, I'm giving you the best deal possible. The Morris office'll tell you that. You'll be getting the same kind of a contract as Ethel Merman or Mary Martin."

"Can they make $25,000 a week here, and average $15,000 a week in clubs across the country fifty-two weeks a year?"

Jule Styne against Will Mastin was like sending in a tiger to fight a sphinx. And as every minute passed the sphinx was getting less choked up about being on Broadway. I moved between them again. "Massey, I know we can't make much actual money out of it . . ."

"Hold on, Sammy," he smiled sagely, "the way you call it 'actual money' you make it sound like there's two kinds."

"Massey, haven't we been through all this? We can't just keep playing nightclubs forever. We're past that now."

"You mean we're too big to make money any more?"

"I mean we need the respect and recognition we can get only from a legit show. Being in legit is—oh, come on, Massey, you know what it is. You wanted it all your life, didn't you?"

"But I never figured on leaving $25,000 a week in clubs to try for it."

Jule stood up. "Perhaps you'd prefer to discuss it by yourselves."

Will said, "I'm not saying we shouldn't do the show, Mr. Styne, but I think we've got to look into it some more. I'll talk it over with the Morris office when we get to L.A. I'm glad to have met you and I'm glad we had this preliminary conversation."

Jule looked at him with the kind of respect the challenger has as he pulls himself up off the floor and looks at the champ, and tried valiantly for a smile.

"Sammy, are you willing to pay half a million dollars in order to do a Broadway show?" The man behind the desk at the Morris office said, "The difference between what you can make in a play and in clubs comes to exactly $518,000 in one year."

"How do you arrive at that?"

He picked up a sheet of paper. "Assuming you sell out on Broadway for every single performance, the most you can earn is $6,000 a week. That's $312,000 in twelve months.

Thus, you are trading a *sure* $830,000 in firm nightclub contracts for a possible $312,000. At best, you sacrifice half a million dollars." He dropped the paper on his desk. "You can see that it's out of the question."

Will spoke gently. "Sammy, they've looked into it carefully but it's like I was afraid of."

The Morris guy said, "It's a monstrous financial loss. You can't possibly afford it."

"Forgetting the money for a minute, do you agree that it's important for us in terms of career?"

"No question about it. If the play is successful it will give you substantial longevity elsewhere."

"Then the fact is that at this stage of our careers, the prestige of a hit show could be considered more important than immediate money." I turned to Will. "How about if we compromise? Supposing we limit our run to one year?"

He answered quietly. "Can't you see that the prestige we'd get isn't worth what we'd have to pay for it?"

"Massey, I'm not looking for prestige just to have prestige. I want to invest one year to grow, to build something."

"That's fine. But you can't afford to spend $500,000 to do it."

The Morris guy nodded. "He's right. You can't forget that you're over $100,000 in debt, and you have to keep earning big money if you're ever going to get out of the hole."

"Okay, that's *my* problem. But what about you, Massey? You don't think you could live on a third of $300,000? I mean, do you live that good that you can't swing it on a hundred thousand a year?"

"Let's forget about me. Let's figure how you're going to get free and clear of what you owe. It can't happen from being on Broadway. Now, I'm manager of this act, I've always decided what's best for us and I'm deciding on this, too. I'm sorry to say it, but it's out. I won't go along with it."

"That's it, huh?"

"That's it."

"In other words, I'm the junior partner, right? My ideas, my opinions, maybe what I want—that means nothing?"

"When you're wrong you're wrong and you oughta be glad I'm here looking after your interests."

"You're not willing to lose a little money this year to make sure we'll be making it five years from now? You won't gamble that this'll pay off in the long run?"

"I don't gamble. I put my money on sure things and it's a sure thing that we've got over $800,000 coming to us in clubs this year."

I stood up. "Well, then I guess there's nothing more to discuss. I guess it was just another of my silly ideas. You're the boss, Massey, but you'll excuse me if I don't hang around here. You don't need me to help make your decisions where I ought to play, so good day, gentlemen."

I stopped at the end of the room. I couldn't indulge myself in a dramatic walk-out. I took my hand off the door knob and turned to the Morris guy. "I'd like to speak privately to Mr. Mastin. Will you excuse us for a few minutes, please?"

The door closed and I walked slowly across the room and leaned against the desk, facing Will. "Massey, let me ask you something. What is it you want out of life?"

"I don't know what you're getting at."

"What I mean is: you love the business and you like having your money safe in buildings and banks and things like that, right?"

"That's right."

"You've seen a lot of show business, Massey, good times and bad, and you've got a few investments going for you, haven't you?"

"Enough to carry me the rest of my life."

"And I'm glad you have them. We may not be flesh and blood, but we're as close as we can get other than that and I'm glad you've gotten what you want. You worked for it and you deserve it. Now I'm going to tell you what *I* want from life. We talked about this a long time ago but you didn't listen to what I was saying or if you did then you don't remember. I don't want 'nigger' written on my door. I don't want to be a buffoon because I bought a beautiful house." I took out my wallet and showed him a card I'd had sealed in plastic. "You said I'd never get this. Read it. Tell me again that they'll never let a Negro into the Friars

Club." He stared at my membership card, shaking his head slowly. "This is what *I* want out of life, Massey, and I know how to get it. I'm willing to cut down on everything. I'll drop Dave. I'll live in a furnished room—anything, but I've got to do this show. You've got yours. Let me get mine. Please. Don't stand in my way."

20

JULE STYNE WAS SMILING AT ME FROM JUST OUTSIDE THE gate to the field—there was a fellow with him: about my age, a little taller than me, horn-rimmed glasses, Italian raincoat.

Jule said, "This is George Gilbert, Sammy."

"Hello, George. Glad to meet you after all the talk on the phone. You look different than I pictured you." I hadn't pictured him at all but I wanted to make it warmer than how-do-you-do.

As we shook hands, humor flickered across his eyes. "I recognized *you* immediately."

Jule gave my baggage checks to a chauffeur, and we walked through the terminal building. I waved back to the Sky Caps and the reservations clerks; a woman coming toward us made a hurried search through her handbag and came up with a scrap of paper. "Would you, Sammy?" Others came over with pencils and papers, and I let a crowd form. "You in town for *Mr. Wonderful*, Sammy? My whole family's waiting for it. We wouldn't miss you." Out of the corner of my eye I watched Jule and George soaking it all up, beaming happily. I pointed to them. "Those two gentlemen are my producers. I'm sorry but I can't keep them waiting any more or they'll fire me and get maybe Harry Belafonte." It got a laugh, the crowd opened for me and I quickened our pace so we wouldn't be stopped again.

The limousine was waiting directly out front. I looked at Jule. "In a No Parking zone, Gracie?" He smiled, pleased that I'd noticed. "Jule, I'll tell you right now, if the people like us as much as I dig your style then we're going to be the biggest hit of all time." He smiled again, still seeing the crowd around me, and the three of us settled back contentedly against the cushions of the limousine as it rolled out of the airport and onto the parkway to New York.

The lobby of the Gorham Hotel on 55th Street, between Sixth and Seventh, was small, with a tile floor and furniture which had limped through the years barely making the transition from elegant to homey, and the elevator man was wearing one of those uniforms which you know wasn't bought especially for him. "Penthouse B" was a freshly painted large room with a bar at the end near a small kitchen. The bar and kitchen had been thoughtfully stocked.

"You do this, George?"

He gave me a self-conscious nod and pointed quickly to a pair of couches. "They open into beds. And this whole terrace is yours." I looked through the glass door leading onto a terrace that was bigger than the entire apartment. I smiled. "I'll use it for sunbathing."

He blushed and walked toward the door. "Well, I'll be going. I hope you like the apartment—it isn't exactly the Plaza."

"Baby, I've lived in worse, and for $400 a month it's beautiful."

"Anyway, I live downstairs and if there's anything I can do . . ." He grinned, "Like if you need a recipe or something."

I laughed. "Thank you for everything, George. Catch you tomorrow."

I unpacked the outfit I'd chosen for the first rehearsal: a new pair of levis—they'd cost $3.98 plus $22 for the alterations, but the fit was worth it, a red alpaca pullover under a double-breasted alpaca sweater, a little cashmere polo coat—and they'll know a star is coming to work.

I looked around the living room of Jule's suite in the Bellevue-Stratford in Philadelphia, at the director, writers, our press agent, the producers, manager, general manager—all linked together by a common bond: panic. One by one they'd come in, glanced at the others, tried brave smiles and taken seats, all with the self-consciousness of entering a funeral chapel. There was a room service table with sandwiches, coffee, and a few bottles of liquor, and occasionally somebody stood up and browsed disinterestedly through it to spare themselves the necessity of speaking.

Jule looked sick as he called the meeting to order. "Well, we're in trouble. We got one good one out of three. Sammy's personal reviews are fabulous so at least we've got that going for us. And they liked Jack Carter and Chita Rivera. But on the other side of it two of the papers slaughtered us on the racial thing. . . ."

Somebody in the back of the room ventured, "Maybe they're right. Maybe it's something that doesn't belong in the theater." The one voice triggered the others: "It's dangerous." . . . "Like they say, let Western Union deliver the messages." . . . "Yeah, the racial thing should be softened." . . . "It's touchy." . . .

I stood up in the middle of the cross-fire. "May I say something? If we take the racial theme and just sweep it under the carpet, then what'll we have left?"

"An entertaining show. That's all we need."

"Well, God knows I want to entertain people, but this isn't a nightclub, it's a play, and it's got to say something or it's got no reason to exist. I mean . . . isn't that true?"

"Sammy, if nobody comes then who'll hear what we say? Our first concern must be to sell tickets. And apparently we won't do it with the racial angle as is. You know we all feel as you do, that it's worth saying, but it's too hot."

"But if we're the first ones to come out with a hard-hitting story like this—isn't that good?"

"Sammy, maybe the reason it's never been done before is that nobody wants it."

"But there's got to be a first time. . . ."

The room sank into a fuzzy silence of uncertainty and indecision. A voice broke through. "I think that if we change the basic story line we take the heart right out of the show." It was George Gilbert and his words cut through the air with the true ring of logic, making hard straight lines. "As Sammy said, we'll have no reason to exist if we don't have a point of view."

The room burst into action again: "Our point of view is to stay alive." . . . "Sammy, you're new to the theater, it's a different art form." . . . "We know what the critics will buy." . . .

I felt the helplessness of a man getting mugged by a gang.

Jule turned to me consolingly. "Sammy, we're not going to throw our theme away entirely, but maybe we should bring it down a little, take some of the heat out of it—without losing our ideas or changing them. Let's see what we come up with."

I looked at George. He was young, too, and the others had a lot of shows under their belts. "Okay. I can't argue with your experience."

The voices that had been peppering away at me became a chorus of assurance: "Sammy, we really do know what the critics want." . . . "Leave it to us, we understand the theater."

I sat down, nodding acceptance, but uncomfortable in being completely dependent upon other people's knowledge instead of my own. After a lifetime in show business I was a beginner again.

Someone was saying, "Now the big problem is, we can't have him afraid because he's a Negro. We could solve everything by moving Charley Welch out of Paris. Let's kill the expatriate thing and make him a rock and roller working in New Jersey when Freddie Campbell finds him and wants him to come to New York."

George gasped, "New Jersey? Giving up the great life he has in Paris and coming to America on a 'maybe' is our conflict. If he's big and he's already here then where's our story?"

"So, let's not make him big. Let him be a local hit in a jukebox joint. But he's a big man around his own bailiwick."

I stood up alongside George. "But if he's not a hit anywhere except in one lousy little club then what's he got to lose by going to New York and trying for success—bus fare? If it's not racial then why else would he be afraid to make the move?"

"Well . . . he's afraid because he's afraid. Don't worry

about it. It's a detail. Right now the thing is to get him out
of Paris. We can build our story from there."

Jule said, "Bringing him to Jersey would mean new songs,
a new set, new costumes—the French stuff can't be used in
Union City."

Someone offered, "Why not? Why can't it be a French-
type nightclub?"

George groaned. "Are we all going crazy? How can an
American rock and roll singer in a small-time gin mill that
has a jukebox, possibly do a number like 'Jacques D'Iraq,'
wearing the French costumes with the billowing sleeves . . .'

We rehearsed every afternoon, played the show at night
and then had meetings in Jule's suite. Everybody's agent was
in town trying to get more lines and songs for his client, and
new scenes were being put in and thrown out in the same day.
I was in the dressing room, trying to memorize the eighth new
set of lines they'd given us, when I heard people arguing in
the corridor. I shoved the door closed with my foot. It swung
open and Will stormed in: "That line's gotta come out. I don't
intend to argue. It's plain out!"

"Hey, what's going on?"

He didn't even notice me. Jule was right behind him. "Mr
Mastin, it's only a play . . . it's make-believe."

Will sat down in a chair and folded his arms like he was
going on a hunger strike. "It comes out. It's a lie. *I* did it.
I'm the one—not Jack Carter."

George was standing in the doorway. I slipped out of the
room. "What the hell's going on?"

He gave me a nervous smile. "You know the line where
Freddie Campbell says, 'I'll make this kid a star. I'll teach
him everything I know.' Well, when your uncle heard that he
jumped up and said, 'Nobody taught Sammy anything but me.
I'm the one who taught him.' "

"Baby, do me a favor. Will you and Jule cut the line? This
show won't be a hit or a flop because of it."

I followed Will into the dressing room. "Massey, do we
really have to have another meeting? We've had one every
night this week and I can't imagine what could be more important than giving me time to learn my new lines."

He closed the door. "We're a Trio, and there's Trio busi

ness to be talked over." My father and I sat down. "Now the first matter is about the Trio becoming a corporation."

"We already agreed on that, didn't we?"

"We did. But we should go over the details again."

"I don't get it. Maybe I'm crazy, but I've been rehearsing all day, I've been with the newspaper guys, I just finished a show, I've got new scenes to memorize for tomorrow—it's panic-in-the-streets, and you want me to sit here and shoot the breeze about something we already settled?"

"There's no shoot the breeze about it. No point being in a show if you don't know what's happening to the money. Now, as I was saying, the way we agreed to set it up . . ."

As he spoke, I kept trying to understand why he was rehashing it like this. We'd always had meetings, but never so often and never about unimportant things. There was something in his face, something I hadn't noticed was missing until I saw it reappear. He had the look of a man in control, a man exercising authority to which he was accustomed, and he was enjoying it. He was his old self and I realized how unlike his old self he had been during all the days of rehearsals.

"Now the next thing we should take up . . ."

I'd been too wrapped up in the show to see what should have been so clear to me. He was the manager of the Trio but there was nothing to manage—all decisions were the producer's to make. And he had little or nothing to do on the stage. He was neither the star, nor the manager except in name. He was in the same position my father had always been in, and it was eating away at him, so he was calling meetings, making issues out of situations he'd never have bothered with six months before, repeating things that had been settled— anything to give himself purpose, to hold onto the position he'd earned and held all his life, until I had taken it away from him.

It hadn't been enough to say, "You're in the show and you've got the billing and we still split the money three ways." No one knew better than he how little reason he had to be on the stage or to have his name up. By accepting the awkward, embarrassing situation, he was giving me more than everyone thought I was giving him. And he was keeping his bargain of a year on Broadway. When the reviews had come out bad he could have used them as an excuse to say, "You see? It's a mistake. Let's quit while we still can." But he hadn't even hinted at it. He was sticking to his word, trying to live with something that was killing him.

The stagehands were striking the scenery and hauling it into New York-bound trucks before we'd taken our last bow. I changed clothes and George and I waited for Johnny Ryan, our stage manager, and his assistant, Michael Wettach, to finish seeing the last of the stuff onto the trucks. Then the four of us and Johnny's wife, D.D., went for supper at our usual place, a little Italian restaurant a few blocks from the theater.

George was staring into his plate, quietly humming something from *Pal Joey*. I glared at him. "At least you could hum one of *my* hits." Johnny made a whole production out of breaking a bread stick exactly in half and buttering the end of it like he was painting the Mona Lisa. D.D. said, "Sammy, as soon as we're in New York I'll get you some of that verbena soap I was telling you about."

I nodded ruefully and looked from face to face. "In other words, nobody wants to discuss the corpse, right?"

Johnny said, "It's not that bad."

"Baby, it ain't good. Do you realize what's happened, what we're bringing to New York? Instead of a story about a sophisticated, sensitive guy who doesn't want to live with prejudice, Charley Welch has become a shnook who doesn't have the guts to try for success. Why spend $300,000 to do a show about *that*?"

George cocked his head. "Shnook? You're getting to sound more Jewish every day."

"No joke, they're completely out of their minds. They threw out scenes and put new ones in so fast that nothing in the whole show makes sense any more."

"Don't complain. At least no one suggested they call in Donald O'Connor to play Charley Welch."

"You don't want to be serious, right?"

"Well, I don't *want* to be, but if it'll make you feel any better the fact is we've still got something left—"

"I'll tell you what we've got left, baby: the last half hour of the show, the Palm Club scene—a $25,000-a-week night club act that I'm now doing for *six* thousand."

306

Nobody argued with me. We finished eating and started back toward the hotel, walking in bleak silence, all of us knowing that the story was shot, morale was shot—that we were nothing more than a patched-up mongrel held together by string.

We passed a theater where workmen were pulling down the signs for *My Fair Lady*. "Do you think this show's as good as they say?"

George shrugged. "We'll see soon enough. They open a few days before us in New York. I know that they didn't have anywhere near the advance we had here."

I stopped in front of the Latin Casino. "The last time we played here you couldn't get in with a shovel and a wedge. There were people piled up on the sidewalk. I must be losing my mind. I actually gave up all that for this." We continued walking. "What the hell am I doing a show for? Certainly not for the money. If nobody can possibly respect what we're trying to do then why the hell am I doing it?"

George buttoned his overcoat tighter around the neck. "Please. I've got my own troubles. I own a beautiful hotel in the mountains, the Raleigh. I can take all winter off and be in Florida, instead of freezing my . . ."

"Cheer up, you guys." Johnny put his arm around my shoulder, "We've still got better than a fighting chance. The fact is that in addition to the Palm Club scene we've got lots of entertainment, lots of flash, some good songs, dances, jokes. . . ."

"Yeah, Johno—everything but integrity."

On opening night the chorus kids were all but skipping through the stage door of the Broadway Theater, carrying flowerpots, curtains, and framed pictures to decorate their windowless little dressing rooms. With two previews under our belts the word around town was "*Mr. Wonderful*'s a smash" and the cast was settling down for a long run.

At seven o'clock I started making the rounds of the dressing rooms wishing everybody luck. They were drunk on optimism and the corridors rang with kid-yourself lines like "They screamed at everything we did last night. Our trouble is we're so close to it we don't see what great entertainment we've got." I played it Charley Optimist, smiling back, trying to keep the morale up where two previews had miraculously raised it.

George looked into my dressing room fifteen minutes before curtain time. He'd been making the rounds, too, and he still had the Happy Hypocrite smile on his face, as I did. He put out his hand. We nodded. He said, "I'll see you after the show. I'm going to stand out front at intermission to listen for comments."

I stood in the wings, waiting. The kids were hurrying into position onstage, the stagehands were moving to their places ready to raise the curtain and the lights. Jack Carter was standing off in a corner by himself, blotting his face with a handkerchief. The music rose to a peak as the overture neared the end and the screaming, gorgeous brassiness of it suddenly overwhelmed me with the immensity of a Broadway musical. I watched all the pieces of the living machine preparing to swing into line, all these people straining forward, waiting for the moment when they would contribute themselves to the hugeness of it all. And, abruptly, I understood that even as the star I was only one part of it. A red light flashed, two stagehands grasping a steel cable heaved their weight onto it, the curtain rose, and the chorus rushed on. I leaned against the wall, chilled by the finality of the realization that it wasn't entirely up to me—I was confined, tightly imprisoned by the design of the show, and if I saw I wasn't making it with the audience, if I wasn't touching them, I couldn't just slip Morty a cue and switch into "Birth of the Blues."

The clock on the Paramount Building showed 3:00. In a few hours the whole city would know we were a flop. I looked out at the buildings, most of them dark except for occasional lighted windows, and I wondered if the people inside near those lamps were reading our reviews. George was sitting at my bar. He poured himself another scotch and stared at the bottle. He picked it up and started reading the label. Our eyes met but there was no reason to speak, we'd said it all: the cliché cop-outs like "They didn't understand what we were trying to do" when both of us knew too well that they *had* understood. Maybe the techniques were different on Broadway, but it all boiled down to the one thing that worked anywhere—honesty. I gazed blankly out the window at the past weeks, seeing myself so awed by "theater" and "Broadway" that I'd sat back and let myself fail on other people's decisions. I'd put my career in other people's hands—the career I'd built. I'd gambled my past and my future on other people's opinions and judgments, letting them override my own. I'd known enough of right and wrong to become a star but I'd chickened out and permitted other people to tell me, "We know best." At least one thing was sure: if it meant doing my shows on street corners I'd never make that mistake again. I was so disgusted with myself for seeing the inexcusable wrong of it—but too late. I'd had the greatest opportunity in the world and I'd blown it. The lights of the city became hazy as tears began filling my eyes. I was aware of George watching me and I hid behind a Garfield bit. "Sure, sure . . . y'see those lights up and down Broadway? Well, I'll give 'em to you for a necklace, I'll have this town on its knees." I shook my fist out the window. "Big town, I'll get you yet!"

I heard George blowing his nose. He'd seen that movie, too. "If you'd done that onstage maybe we'd have been a hit."

I turned, amused by his boundless irreverence. "George, you're rotten. You're rotten to the core."

He lowered his eyes, pleased by the compliment. "I know." He picked up the reviews but lost heart for reading them and looked away from them, despondently; then remembering that I'd been watching him, fearful that he'd been caught admitting that something was beyond joking, he spun around on the bar stool, holding his knees up with his arms like a kid taking a ride, and dropped the papers, sighing "All gone." He made about two turns and let the stool slow to a stop, his attempted abandon gone. He poured another drink.

"Man, them mothers didn't use up *any* of their good words, did they?" I read aloud: " 'If you want to see "Mr. Wonderful" we suggest you get over to the Broadway Theater this week. He won't be around very long . . .' "

"Well, thank God at least *you* got great personal reviews."

There was no point explaining that I could find little

309

satisfaction in seven critics discovering I do a good night-club act; that I'd come to Broadway to accomplish something and I'd been told, "Stay in nightclubs where you belong."

"I suppose you'll be going back to clubs."

"I signed a contract to be on Broadway for one year, and I intend to stay for one year." I crumpled the reviews into tight wads. "The votes aren't all in yet."

"Sammy, even if the afternoon papers are good . . ."

"I don't mean the critics. I'm talking about the people."

He was looking at me sympathetically. "I know how you feel, but it's impossible. You can't beat the critics. Nobody ever did—except *Hellzapoppin'* and that was only because Walter Winchell decided to plug them every single day. He made them a hit, but we don't have him and . . ."

"Baby, I know everything you're going to say, so don't bother. I'm hip that when the critics come out against you everything changes—all the heat comes out of you. I'm hip that where just last night we could call our shots with the press, now we'll have to fight for every inch of space we get."

He nodded. "The world hates a loser."

"The world doesn't hate losers, George, it just has no time for them." I walked over to him. "But did you ever see a guy get beaten bloody and then get up off the floor and start fighting? Did you ever see what happens to the crowd when he starts *winning?*" I felt the cool edge of excitement biting through the sogginess of failure. "Ten things that should have finished me in the business, didn't: the accident, the scandals, the constant 'white girl' bit—each of them should have been disaster, and if *they* didn't finish me then you'd better believe that I'm not about to lay down dead with my feet in the air just because a handful of critics say I should. Our show is going to run. I came to Broadway to get something and I'm not leaving without it."

He sighed, negatively. "I only wish it could be true but the chances are a million to one."

"Baby, hock your shirt and take those odds. I'm going to beat them."

The kids began straggling into the theater at around

seven o'clock. They weren't due until "half-hour" at eight, but when you're a flop there's no fun in hanging around the show business bars. At the theater, they had refuge from the embarrassing sympathy of friends, and the smug looks from people who are glad there's no reason to be jealous any more. By the second night of a flop you're tired and sick like you've got a hangover, and there's no one you want around except maybe someone else who has one. I could picture them sitting around in those pathetically gay little rooms they'd fixed up, like people who'd bought ice cream and paper hats for a party and then nobody showed up.

I asked Johnny Ryan to have the cast gathered onstage at ten minutes before curtain. I deliberately didn't change into my first act costume which was designed to make Charley Welch look like a loser. I wore my own clothes, my own jewelry. I wanted them to see success talking.

They were standing around like lost souls, clustered in little groups of defeat. I walked to center stage. I remembered a scene from *The Great Dictator* in which Hitler made Mussolini sit in a very low chair so that he had to look up at Hitler and subconsciously got the feeling of looking at strength. I motioned for them to sit on the floor in front of me.

". . . I've got no plans to be Charley Flop Came to Broadway. But either we play like we're the biggest hit in the world or we're going to die, because with the people pre-sold against us we're only as good as what we give every song, every line, everything we do on this stage for every audience. Now, nobody can keep the people away from what they like and want to see. And they like *me* or they wouldn't pack the nightclubs to see me. I can bring them into this theater but I can't entertain them without you. So if you give me the word, if I can count on you, I'll go out and get us audiences with my bare hands; I'll go on television and radio, I'll use every friend I've got, I'll do every interview, from the network blockbusters to if there's a cat on Broadway and Fiftieth with a megaphone, I'll be his guest. The people will come to see me and if we work a mile over our heads, if we kill ourselves to entertain them, they'll talk about us and I guarantee that we'll run . . ."

One of the boy dancers jumped up. "We're with you all the way." Another was on his feet. "We'll work our heads off . . ." The mood swept through the crowd, catching them up in it until all of them were standing and cheering. It was straight out of an MGM musical. They were shouting and waving their fists in the air, a pack of losers changed into fighters. It had turned into a cause.

I'd just finished doing the impressions in the Palm Club scene, when a woman in the audience stood up and shouted, "The critics are crazy. We love you, Sammy." I threw her a kiss. "So tell your friends!" The audience cheered. It was eleven-fifteen and I was ready to go into the last number but I cued Morty and I did an extra thirty minutes.

Mike Goldreyer, our company manager, was waiting in the wings, wringing his hands. "Sammy, it's no good. It's no good. We can't keep the stagehands so late. We have to pay them overtime. . . ."

Jule Styne burst through the fire door between out front and backstage. "Sammy, that business of 'tell your friends.' It's terrible. *Terrible.* It's not 'theater.' You can't do it."

I closed the dressing room door behind us. "Jule, for the last few months I've listened to everybody telling me how to do a show: writers, directors, producers, chorus boys' parents, out-of-town critics—everybody! But that's all over. From now on I do it *my* way. Maybe I didn't do the chic thing out there but I didn't see anybody walk out, and I sure as hell heard a lot of people yelling bravo when we took the curtain calls. So don't tell me about overtime or 'theater.' I'm not in the 'theater' any more. I'm back in the entertainment business!"

The elevator opened into the reception room of the Morris office. I waved to the girl behind the desk, "Darling, will you tell Mr. Bramson I'm on my way in, please." I smiled at the performers waiting to see their agents, pushed the double doors open and walked down the corridor to the television department.

"We've *been* talking to Sullivan, Sammy. We knew you'd want that exposure for your show . . ." Sam Bramson looked down. "But, he doesn't want you."

"You're joking!"

"It's not exactly that he doesn't want you . . . look, why don't you speak to him yourself? I'll get him on the phone."

Ed said, "Sammy, I can't use your father and your uncle. Naturally, I'd love to have you on the show, but I want you alone. I'm sorry, I really am, but if I buy you and put aside eight minutes for you I don't want that time split up. You're what my audience will tune in to see and that's what I want to give them."

"But Ed, we've always been a . . ."

"They're dead weight, Sammy. I can understand your loyalty to them and it's wonderful and there's no reason why you still can't split the dough with them if you want to, but from a strictly show business point of view it's lost its value, and frankly, it's becoming uncomfortable."

"You don't understand . . ."

"No, Sammy, I'm afraid it's you who don't understand. When Babe Ruth was playing ball you didn't see his father and his uncle on the field. Maybe they helped put him there, maybe they trained him, but when it was game time he walked out there alone. You're not the first performer who had a situation like this. It was the same with Willie and Eugene Howard, and Al Jolson and his brother Harry. Al had the big talent, so Al worked alone. But it wasn't easy for him. You'd go into a town where an Al Jolson movie was playing and across the street from it there'd be a vaudeville theater with a marquee saying 'Jolson' in the biggest possible size, then over it in little tiny letters it said 'Harry.' I'll never forget the day I bumped into Harry Jolson and I said, 'Isn't it great how well Al's doing in the movies?' Harry looked at me like I was crazy, and said, 'Ed, that son of a bitch is making such lousy pictures that I can't even get booked.' All I'm trying to point out is that Al had his problems too, but he never let them interfere with what he did on the stage. I understand your situation, Sammy, it's a sympathetic one and I apologize for saying as much as I have, but I wanted you to see my side of it."

When I hung up, Sam Bramson said, "Steve Allen's been after us for you. He's fighting hard to compete with Sullivan and he's offering $10,000 instead of Sullivan's top of $7500."

"No. Sullivan was the first network show I ever did and

he's always been a gentleman to his fingertips. I can't just run for the money. Keep trying. Maybe he'll change his mind."

When I got back to the hotel, there was a telegram for me: "WELCOME TO NEW YORK. PLEASE DROP IN AND VISIT US. ED WYNN, THE HARWYN." I called George at his office. "What kind of a place is the Harwyn?"

"East Side supper-clubbish. It's the hot place. Whatever *that* means."

I read him the telegram. "That's damned nice of them."

"Well, really! You *are* the star of a Broadway show."

"Baby, I admit I'm one of the great stars of our time. I even admit that I'm adorable. But I'm not exactly in demand around the chic nightclubs." As I spoke, the tone of his voice caught up with me and I realized that he'd understood; I could picture him smiling, but he was considerately playing it cool. "Anyway, the least we can do is accept the man's invitation, right? Will you have your secretary make a reservation for me for twelve-thirty, baby?"

"Sure, *baby*."

"And call Johnny and D.D. and Michael and tell them we'll all go over to Chandler's after I get off tonight—I've got the Barry Gray show—and then we can swing over to the Harwyn and be chic and East Side-ish."

"Is that little *schvartza* going to sit with us?"

The words, whispered contemptuously, cut through the restaurant sounds, zinging their way to me as I walked into Chandler's. It came from a club-date comic sitting at the performers' table. I scanned the room for somewhere else to sit but the place was packed and the captain was at my side. "This way, Sammy. Barry's expecting you."

The comic looked up, feigning surprise at seeing me, smiling big, arms outstretched, long-lost-brother style. "Sammy, baby, great to see you again."

"Hello, Jackie." He was in his forties but still Charley Almost, just another stand-up comic off an assembly line, using everybody's jokes, everybody's style, with no change or improvement in his act for fifteen years—but watching with bitterness the young, inventive guys who offer something fresh and make it big. He represented the great para-lox of the business: a failure who earns $1500 a week.

His face had the strained, desperate look of a man beginning to understand he's never going to make it, a man aware of his positive and final classification in the business as a second-rater. He didn't hate me, he hated himself. He resented everybody's success, but the fact that a colored guy had made it devastated him.

"How are you doing, Jackie?"

He shrugged. "I'm still the best-paid secret in the business. You know the bit: I play Boston during Lent, Miami in July, and in Vegas I play roulette." It was an old joke, but his genuine bitterness, the built-in apology for failure, killed any possibility of humor. He leaned forward anxiously. "Listen, Sam, I don't like to impose on our friendship but you could do me a favor. If you were to ask for me when you go back to clubs, like Vegas or the Copa . . . I mean if you said you wanted to use me on the bill with you . . ." His ingratiating smile was the picture of a man committing moral suicide.

I heard my name and saw Barry waving for me. I stood up. "I'll be in town for a year, Jackie. Keep in touch."

Barry Gray gave the show an enormous plug as he'd been doing every night since we'd opened. Then we got down to the interview. "Sammy, do you mind if I get personal with my questions?"

"Anything you like."

"Is it true that you've become a Jew?"

A hush fell over the restaurant. The people were leaning in, listening. "Yes, Barry, I am a Jew."

He extended his hand. "Welcome aboard, lantzman. When did this happen?"

"I think I have always been a Jew in my thinking and my own undefined philosophies which I found so clearly spelled out when I began reading about Judaism a few years ago."

"How do you think people will react to Sammy Davis, Jr. being a Jew?"

"I guess everybody will react differently, if they're going to react at all. And judging from the past—they'll react. I don't think my departure will set Christianity back. As for the Jewish community, I'm aware of the possibility that

315

they might be offended by a Negro becoming a Jew. Maybe it'll turn them against me, I don't know. It's a pretty frightening thought, because they make up more than 50 per cent of my audiences. But I've found something in Judaism, and I'm not about to give it up. I have to believe they'll accept me according to Jewish law and custom which sees no color line or any lines other than between belief and non-belief."

"I've heard it said that you wanted to be a Jew because all your friends are Jewish."

"Barry, Frank Sinatra is my closest friend and I never yet saw him wear a *yamalka*. I'll admit he eats a bagel every now and then . . ."

"I read a joke in one of the columns that said you were playing golf on Long Island and the pro asked you for your handicap and you told him, 'I'm a colored, one-eyed Jew —do I need anything else?' How do you feel about the Sammy Davis, Jr. jokes?"

"They're a hazard of the business and the fact is you're glad people know your name well enough to do jokes about you; but some I despise because they are destructive and insidious."

"Can you remember—or would you rather not remember —any you'd classify that way?"

"I'm not about to forget them."

"Would you tell us one?"

"Yes. But in order for it to serve a purpose I'd like to say a few things first so that maybe you'll be able to see this kind of humor as I see it. I was reading a book about Judaism and I came across a statement: 'The difference between love and hate is understanding.' The understanding is obstructed by the images which are embedded in people's minds. Obviously it's not the dark skin that's unattractive to white people or they wouldn't spend a hundred dollars a day in Florida trying to get it, right?"

"In other words, Sammy, you believe that what separates people is a lack of knowledge of each other?"

"Isn't that the definition of the word prejudice, Barry? Pre-judgment without due examination. Wasn't there a time when people thought all Jews have horns? Now, the only

Jew I ever met with horns was a Jewish bull I got to know in South America once. But he's the only one."

He smiled, "So when you saw that all Jewish people don't have horns you became Jewish?"

"Right, Barry. And as long as we're discussing it I don't mind saying it was a pretty big shake-up that after I decided to become a Jew only *then* did I learn the Jews don't really have all the money. When I found out Rockefeller and Ford were *goyim* I almost resigned.

"Anyway, I believe a very large chunk of the racial thing is a question of changing the images that remain in people's minds and *certainly* not contributing to them. You've noticed that there are no Step 'n' Fetchits any more, no more Parkyakarkases, none of the characters which were caricatures of entire groups? It didn't happen because they weren't fine performers, but pressure groups went to work and they asked Hollywood, 'Hey, don't use a Step'n'Fetchit any more. Let's not have any more kids growing up thinking of Negroes as slow, lazy, shuffling characters.' Groups like the American Jewish Committee fought against stereotyping Jews as greedy, grasping, and money-mad, just as the NAACP got Little Black Sambo, and all those damned pancakes he ate, out of the school books and out of our lives.

"Now, getting back to me and the jokes: I get myself to the point at which I'm able to own a beautiful home, we keep our house and grounds looking well, and although I certainly didn't buy the house as my contribution to racial harmony, it's a beautiful extra to know that the neighbors can see a colored family and they've got to say, 'Gee, it's not really true they live eighty of them to the room.' The next thing I know a guy tells me a joke that's circulating: One of my neighbors tells her husband, 'Strange about the house next door: The maid comes and goes all the time, but the people who live there never leave the house.'

"Now, I'm not so hard-nosed and bitter that I can't see the humor in a well-constructed joke. But I have to detest humor predicated on the assumption that all colored women are maids. My grandmother *was* a maid, and a lot of guys dug ditches until they became president of the company or until their families made it and pulled them up with them.

There comes a time to forget humble origin. Mr. Armour isn't a butcher anymore, right?"

"Sammy, did you rap the guy in the mouth, I hope?"

"No. He wouldn't have known why I was hitting him. Most of the people who tell these jokes are not haters; they'd never yell a dirty name, they'd get sick if they saw a mob throwing rocks at a colored kid trying to go to school, they'd be repelled by racial violence, yet—intentional or not —they are perpetuating the legends which perpetuate the prejudice which causes the racial violence.

"Charley Joke-teller doesn't understand that violence is the smallest part of prejudice. He's standing in the middle of a social revolution, telling his little jokes, thoughtlessly assuring people that we all carry knives and steal and lie, until it's hardly any wonder that when we try going to school with you, some guy who's been convinced is ready to crack open our skulls to prevent it.

"As awful as violence is, at least it's out in the open where it can be recognized and handled and eventually it's ended. But the jokes keep on, quietly, subversively, like a cancer, rotting away the foundations of hope for the Negro, stealing the dignity on which we can build respected lives.

"And as bad as the jokes, are the words—the put-down words like 'nigger,' 'kike,' 'chink,' 'wop,' 'spick.' I hear them used between buddies, good-naturedly, but anyone who thinks he's above prejudice, so he can use them affectionately or humorously, is missing the point: If a person sincerely desires to stamp out a sickness he can't keep a few of its germs alive just for laughs. Before we can reach a Utopia in human relations those jokes and those words and the legends which they perpetuate must die.

"You can pass legislation for desegregation, but you can't legislate people's minds and that's where the progress must finally be made, in people's minds and in their hearts. Opening school doors and job opportunities is the first step, but it's like hacking off the top of a weed: After we do it we've got to get down and pull out the roots so that it won't keep growing. We've got to get to the source of racial intolerance, of prejudice—the ignorance, the clinging to long outdated legends which continue to distort the picture of the American Negro. When people reach the point at which they examine the facts then there'll be little or no need for laws that say colored kids can go to school with white kids because I really believe there won't be anyone suggesting that they shouldn't."

"Sammy, this Utopia you mentioned, do you think it will ever come?"

"I'm sure it will. I'm sitting here talking to you on the radio about it, right?"

"It's remarkable that despite the racial abuses you must have suffered, you haven't turned around and hated right back. You're really an optimist."

"I have a right to be. I don't want to do Pollyanna bits, I've been knocked down by white people—but I'm not about to forget that every time it happened the hand that was reaching out to help me up again was white. But more important, I'm not a bigot. No Negro can intelligently lump all white people together like 'They're all no good.' Wouldn't that be everything we don't want people to do to us?"

In the cab to the Harwyn Michael looked at me. "And where did all *that* come from? My God, you sounded like Harriet Beecher Stowe."

I nudged George. "And what about our producer? Doesn't he have some kind word for his star who just turned out to be a public speaker?"

"I was trying to remember if I've ever told a racial joke."

"Baby, the fact is, half the racial jokes I hear I get from colored guys. Who sits around twenty-four hours a day wondering 'What've I done for the racial situation?' But the beautiful thing is when somebody *starts* thinking about it, then he's not about to go out and tell any more racial jokes, right?"

"Racial jokes! I'll even be afraid to listen to Amos and Andy from now on. When I think how much I used to like Step'n'Fetchit and Willie Best . . ." He sighed. "Little did I know what I was doing. Every time I laughed I probably sank a ship."

The Harwyn's doorman held open the cab door. "Nice to see you, Mr. Davis." He moved quickly to open the front door for me. I let Johnny, D.D., George, and Michael go in first.

As I took off my coat, a tall, good-looking man extended his hand. "Sammy, my name is Ed Wynn. Thank you for coming in."

The dance band started playing *Mr. Wonderful;* people all over the room were smiling and waving at me; Ed led us to the only unoccupied table in the room and called over the table captain. "Mac will see that you have everything you want." A waiter brought a bucket with champagne bottles in it. "Compliments of Mr. Wynn."

I leaned back against the soft banquette and smiled at the group. "That's how it is when you're with a star, folks. It's a definite First Cabin all the way."

Mac was handing out menus. I could see they were in French. I waved it away. "Thanks, but I know what I want, a steak about an inch thick. . . ."

A vaguely familiar-looking guy, one of those faces you see around Vegas and New York, came over to the table. "Whattya say, Sammy?"

"Hi, baby. How y'doing?"

"I'm gonna come by and see your show."

"I hope you will. And be sure to come backstage and have a drink with me."

"Hey," . . . he smiled. . . . "Thanks, Sam, I will. How's Thursday?"

When he'd left George asked, "Who's that?"

"I don't know, he's a guy."

"And you're going to have drinks with him?"

"I'm not going to spend the night with him. But what'll you bet he'll be at the box office tomorrow? And what'll you bet he'll bring friends? Now, am I Mr. Wonderful or not?" He looked pleased. "You see, George. Colored people aren't really lazy."

When I called for the check the waiter said, "Compliments of Mr. Wynn."

I leaned toward George. "Baby, give me a twenty for the waiter and ten for the captain, will you? I'll catch up with you Friday."

Ed walked me to the door. "Thank you for coming in, Sammy. Now come back soon. Please. Think of this as your home."

We left Johnny, D.D., and Michael getting a cab and

George and I started walking toward Park Avenue. When we were far enough away from the club I grabbed his arm and hung on it like a half-hysterical nitwit. "Do you want to know about a small Negro lad from Harlem who just saw his first chic supper club and the owner told him, 'This is your home'?" I did a few Bill Robinson steps up the stoop of a private house.

George shrugged. "Now really. What's the big deal?" But his face was bursting with concealed pleasure for me and I danced back down the steps and gave him a shot on the arm. "You rat fink, take that."

"Ow."

"I'm a star and it's in my contract that I can hit my producer any time I feel like it."

"Listen, if it's going to affect you like this you'd better stay home from now on. And let's get a cab, my ears are freezing."

As we pulled up to the Gorham the meter read fifty cents. I whispered, "Give him a deuce." He looked at me, shocked. I nodded. "A deuce, baby. I'm a star."

The elevator stopped at his floor and he said, "Well, thanks for walking me home."

"Hey, it's only two-thirty. Come on up, have a nightcap."

George sat down at my bar, shaking his head. "I actually gave that cab driver a dollar-fifty tip for a fifty-cent ride."

"I'm sorry, baby. It's a little brokesville. I'll straighten out with you."

"I don't care about that. But that cab driver, Mr. Mancusi, he'll be tailing me from now on." He became serious. "Do you really mean to tell me that you're broke? Sammy Davis, Jr.?"

"Well, I didn't exactly *mean* to tell you. But it's not so unfathomable. While we're doing the show, all the Trio can afford is a $500-a-week salary for each of us. And I've got a few old bills hanging around, so before I get my five it's gone."

After a while he said, "Do you realize you've got a bill at the box office for nine hundred dollars' worth of tickets? I can't imagine why *you* should be paying for all those tickets."

"Most of them are for people who can do us some good but who don't come under the heading of press. Somebody calls and says, 'Hey, I'd like to see your show.' Let's say it's the president of a picture company. Am I going to be a piker for eighteen dollars? You can't be a star only when it's autographing time."

"But why don't you let it come out of the Trio?"

"Baby, Will Mastin won't go for spit. I mentioned it once and his great answer was, 'What's a movie company got to do with us?' "

"But . . ."

"George, I can't let myself get bogged down by these things. I've gotta worry about getting out on that stage and being adorable. Now let's talk about something nice. Do you want to do ten minutes on how five different people come over to say, 'Hey, I've got to come and see your show'?"

"Well, we can use them. We're selling out the balcony and the mezzanine but we still have seats in the orchestra. And that's a switch."

"You've seen what happens when we walk down a street: the cats who wave and yell hello are the guys driving trucks and cabs. My fans are the people, the man on the street, which happens to be the best thing that can happen to a performer."

"Well, I wish you had a few fans who own limousines."

"Hold everything, 'cause if that's your problem old Sam can fix that, too." I reached under the bar and deposited a stack of invitations in front of him. The top one was an invitation to a cocktail party at Park Avenue and 68th Street, being given for me by one of our investors. I showed him the Tiffany & Company engraving on the inside edge of the envelope. "Baby, there was a time when I used to go to parties where all the booze and the food and the furniture put together didn't cost as much as this invitation." I shuffled them like a deck of cards. "Yes, it's a definite socializing with the upper crust and filling up the limousine section for you."

"For *me*? When I walk down the street nobody calls *me* Mr. Wonderful."

"And as long as I'm going to be Charley Social Lion with

the personal appearances, tomorrow we'll go to Cye Martin's and work out some sartorial splendor—something a little suave, a little distingué—for old Limousine Section Sam. And I'd better open an account at the Harwyn 'cause it's a definite every other night drop-in there."

He poured himself another drink. "But let's bring along somebody else to leave the tip."

George put on his sunglasses as we left the Gorham and we started walking briskly toward Seventh Avenue. A cab driver waved, a guy unloading a Horn and Hardart truck on the corner smiled hello. George waved back and mumbled, "All these people staring at me . . . my public." We crossed Seventh, over to Broadway and turned downtown. A man with a gait like he was in a walking race—arms pumping, long strides—was a few yards ahead of us. George hurried forward and fell in step a few feet behind him—arms pumping, taking the same long strides. He tired of that, and tapped on the plate-glass window of an automobile showroom. A salesman left a customer and came to the door. George smiled. "The cars look lovely. You're a credit to Broadway," and kept walking. He stopped at the corner and waited for me.

"Baby, I'm a star and you're a nut. I can't be seen with a nut. It could get in the papers."

"Oh, speaking of *that* . . ." He reached into his coat pocket and held out a column from one of the afternoon papers.

"Do you really believe that a big star should be seen standing on Broadway in broad daylight reading about himself?"

"Well, I thought you ought to see this." I glanced at the item. ". . . Who's the luscious blonde Sammy Davis, Jr. was tch-tchatting with at the Harwyn? . . ." He was peering at me through his dark glasses, disturbed. "Why would anyone want to make it sound like you were with a . . . a blonde date?"

"The word is 'white,' baby. They've got me down as Charley White Chicks Chaser, and *that's it*, so just get used to the fact that every time I sneeze, there's somebody gonna say 'And a white girl gave him a handkerchief.' "

When we got to Cye's, I walked to the back of the shop and sat down where Rocco was working. "I've got some ideas and I know now it's going to be a definite shake your head and argue with the customer but do me a favor: humor me, treat me like I'm a nut." He nodded, already looking at me that way. "Thank you. Now I want my jackets to have four buttons down the front."

"You're going to walk in the streets with four-button suits? Like from the old days?"

"Rocco . . . remember, I'm a nut. The suits will be like in the old days, but I'm going to wear them now. The main thing is the pants. How many inches around at the knee are my pants now? I mean what's normal?"

"Maybe twenty-two to twenty-four. For you I'd say twenty-two."

"Make them sixteen inches at the knee."

"You said sixteen inches?"

"Maybe less. I have to see it before I can be sure. The point is I don't want yards of extra material flapping around me. I want a sort of modern Edwardian suit. If you make the jackets very trim they'll be distinctive, they'll have my own look. And I want the pants so tight that I can barely sit down in them. You get what I'm trying to do?"

"Sure, now that you explain it."

"Wonderful."

"What you want is a flannel suit with leggings."

We left and walked down Broadway. "Now I've got to have shoes made that'll work with the suits. Something that'll disappear under the cuff so there's an unbroken line, and my socks won't show when I move."

George shrugged. "I always thought it's sexy to show a little sock."

I gave him a look. "A high shoe, but not with laces or buttons, sort of a modern Congress gaiter like Lincoln used to wear."

"That's a very nice tribute. After all he did for you it's the least you can do." He looked at his watch. "Well, it's a little late, folks. I'm going up to the hotel for the weekend and I've got to pack a few things."

I stopped walking. "You mean you'd leave your star in the middle of the street . . . well, don't worry about me, baby, Johnny and D.D. invited me over for Sunday dinner, so you go right ahead and have fun in the country. I have other friends who'll be looking after me."

"My God, I'm only going away for thirty-six hours. I'll be back Sunday."

"That's okay, baby. Don't give me a thought. See you in the spring if I can get through the mattress."

He got into a cab and I walked to Fifth Avenue, then up, thinking about D.D. and Johnny, remembering the surprise of seeing his name, John Barry Ryan III, in Cholly Knickerbocker, and learning that a guy who worked as a stage manager and dressed like he couldn't afford to get his name in the phone book, was Charley Social Register. He'd said it would be an informal dinner. With anyone else that would be levis and hamburgers, but with them it might be a sit-down dinner with only three forks instead of five.

I walked to Tiffany, glanced at the window display: a golf club poised in mid-air, ready to swing at a large diamond resting on a tee—and pushed the revolving door slowly, trying to get my bearings before I was inside. A store detective standing inside the entrance smiled. "Hello, Mr. Davis." The showcases sparkled as though every time a customer touched one a hand came out and polished it.

As I stepped off the elevator, into the silver department, a saleswoman approached me. "Mr. Davis, so nice to have you in the store. May I help you?"

"Thank you, yes. I'm interested in two things . . ." I selected a beautiful silver water pitcher to bring Johnny and D.D.

"You said there was something else, sir?"

"Yes . . . it's a favor I'd like to ask of you. Just between us, I don't know the first thing about the different kinds of silverware and I want to learn. I thought about looking it up in Emily Post but then I figured that she must have learned it *here*."

She laughed, pleased, and lowered her voice. "You wouldn't believe how many people don't know an oyster fork from a bouillon spoon. Come along, Mr. Davis, it will be my privilege to show you."

21

I Slept Late Sunday, Had Some Juice And Coffee, And took the package from Tiffany out of the closet. I slid the string off the outer wrapping and opened the large blue box. The pitcher was in a flannel bag. I rewrapped it exactly as it had been. A few dozen roses would be more appropriate for one dinner, but Johnny and D.D. had been great to me on the road and I wanted to give them something nice. I could always play it as though it were in return for the books on fine art they'd given me. I dressed in a gray tweed suit, an eggshell shirt, and a black knitted tie, put on a vicuña polo coat, and left the apartment.

A strong gust of wind from the East River almost knocked the box out of my hand as I stepped out of the cab in front of River House. I gripped the box securely against me and walked toward the building. As I reached the front door, a doorman stuck his head out and pointed to the left. "Delivery entrance is up the street." He closed the door.

My phone was ringing as I got home. When whoever it was gave up, I called the desk and asked that no calls be put through. George was back and had asked them to let him know when I came in. I told them to ask him to come up, "But be sure to tell everybody else that I'm out."

George breezed in. "Am I crazy or weren't you supposed to be having dinner with Mr. and Mrs. John Barry Ryan III, cha, cha, cha."

"Something came up, baby."

He sat on the couch and glanced idly at the box that was with my coat on a chair. "Who lives in *there?*"

I put it into the closet. "It's just something I bought." I

looked through my mail and autographed some pictures. After a while, he stood up and walked toward the door. "I'll see you later. I don't dig funerals."

"Come back here, you nitwit."

He grinned. "Oh? We're feeling a little better, aren't we?"

"George, you're rotten to the core."

"That's more like it." He came back and tapped an empty glass on the bar. "Scotch."

He was peering across the bar at me, smiling owlishly. "Well? What happened to Mr. Wonderful?" He twirled his glasses around by one stem, like a yawn. "I'm only asking so I'll look interested. Is there anything we want to tell Sergeant Gilbert? They say—whoever 'they' are—that these things feel better when you tell them to somebody . . . I mean, you tell it to me, and I'm not even listening, but you hear how unimportant it is . . ." He mumbled self-consciously, "Whatever all *that* means!"

I poured a coke. "I learned a long time ago that if you've got a problem and no one can help you with it, then keep it to yourself." I looked up and was touched by the tenderness in his face. "Baby, if it was something you could do," I smiled. "Like if I needed some money . . ."

"Oops, wrong number."

I smiled back at him and walked to the window. "Y'know something. Despite all my years of living with prejudice, so help me God, I'm incredulous every time it hits me in the face. I never one day of my life woke up thinking I'm colored, or I'm anything other than just a guy. And then every day somebody reminds me." I strummed my hand up the venetian blinds. "I guess I'm lucky that I can start fresh every morning."

George walked into the dressing room and did a Donald Duck take, gaping at a line of bulky sweaters hanging along an iron pipe rack. "My God. What is *that?*"

"They're for the kids."

He inspected one of them. "You bought seventy-dollar sweaters to give away? For no reason?"

"I'm not giving them away, I'm going to wear them on-stage, a different one every night, to help keep the kids from getting bored." I heard Johnny Ryan's voice in the hall. I got busy showing one of the sweaters to George.

"Sam? Are you okay? You weren't sick last night?"

I turned around. He was standing in the doorway. "No, John. I'm fine. I'm sorry about dinner, baby, but something came up."

"Oh . . . okay."

I went after him and stopped him in the hall. "Look, Johno . . . I'm sorry. I didn't forget. I just couldn't make it."

He was looking at me, not with anger, but confused and hurt. "Sammy . . . D.D. spent the whole day cooking a turkey for you. Couldn't you at least have called?"

"I'm sorry, John. I couldn't. I really couldn't."

His eyes became veiled, just as surely as if a stone wall had risen between us. "All right, Sam. We'll do it some other time." He turned and I stood there watching him walk away from me.

I smiled with satisfaction at the first line in Earl Wilson's column: "The B.W. and I had dinner with Jack Benny who is as tight as Sammy Davis, Jr.'s pants." The pants were on their way to becoming a trademark for me. I opened an envelope of newspaper clippings. The top few were from the Negro press. The first was a three panel cartoon: two colored guys were standing near a lamp post which said "Harlem." One of them was asking "Howcum we never see Sammy Davis hangin' on the corner up here?" The other was shrugging, "You crazy, man? Sammy ain't colored no more."

After a while I looked at the next one, an article: "Sammy Davis Jr. Starring in 'I'd Rather Be White.'" My thoughts kept drifting back to only a few years before, to other stories, to newspaper clippings hanging over Mr. Peterson's counter and the pride Mama had taken in me. I didn't want to think about her seeing these, but I knew she would; she read the Negro papers religiously, looking for stories about me.

I kept going through the clips, picturing the disapproval in the faces of the people who wrote and read them, unable to stop reading, like a gambler on a losing streak who stays in the game hoping the next roll of the dice will bail him out. I stopped at a Robert Sylvester column from the *Daily*

News: "Dropped in to see Sammy Davis, Jr. in *Mr. Wonderful*. Sorry, but I just can't get excited over him. Maybe it's me because throughout his nightclub act—the last scene, Mr. Davis' talents were not lost on the rest of the screaming, applauding audience."

I called Jess on the coast. "Baby, when we first played the Riviera, can you remember what Bob Sylvester said about the act?"

"Yeah . . . he said you were ugly as a shovel but you could dance like a son of a bitch! Something like that."

"Do you still have the clipping?"

"It's probably in one of the early albums. You want me to send it to you?"

"No. I'll hold on till you find it."

It was a rave, just as I'd remembered. I hung up and stared at Sylvester's name. What the hell had happened?

I lit a cigarette and watched Cliff Cochrane's face as he reread the recent Sylvester clipping. He handed it back to me. "I've read worse."

"You're wrong, Cliff. I'm in big trouble. That's the most serious thing that's ever been written about me. I need some public relations. Fast! You can't see what I see in it, but it's not a typical rap; there's nothing racial about it, nothing snide, no snipe job—just a simple, honest statement: 'I don't like Sammy Davis, Jr.' It's more than honest. The man even bent over backwards to be fair by saying that other people *did* like me."

"So?"

"If Bob Sylvester saw my act for the first time and he didn't dig it I'd say, 'Crazy, you can't win 'em all.' My act is not like water which everyone must like. But Sylvester *used* to like the act. And the act hasn't changed! You were there when we opened at the Riviera. I did everything I do now except I'm technically better today than I was then, I'm more polished, more mature. And I've got to assume that Sylvester's taste hasn't changed, either. Let's face it, he was a pro then—it wasn't like he was seeing his first nightclub act and he got carried away by the excitement. So, if the act didn't change, and Sylvester didn't change—what did? There's only one thing left. Me! My image."

"I don't see the connection. The man was reviewing the *show*."

"Cliff, there's no separating a performer's public and private life—not with a 'personality.' It all weaves together. Whatever people believe I am from what they hear and read *must* have an effect on what I'm trying to say as a performer. Obviously all the bad publicity, the constant 'wild kid' bit has been hammered at so often that it's hardened into fact and created an image so strong, so vivid and distasteful, that a guy like Sylvester doesn't like me any more.

"When he saw me on the stage in *Mr. Wonderful* he saw a better version of everything he liked a few years ago, but instead of the-sweet-kid-who-loves-his-father-and-his-uncle-and-isn't-it-nice-he-doesn't-push-them-aside, he saw a monster who bleaches his skin white, sits in bars with a bottle of whiskey and six blondes on his lap, shouting 'Drinks for the house.' And his sense of morality made him dislike me enough as a person, so that he just couldn't feel what I was doing as a performer.

"Okay, I lost Sylvester. And I know for a fact I lost Hy Gardner. When I opened at the Riviera there was nobody more in my corner than Hy. He's been a friend, in his column and personally, right down the line. Now even he's shooting little zingies at me, like he's crossed me off. That's two important guys I've lost, two that I *know* about. But how many others are starting to turn away from me? People who can't let me know it in a column, people who just stop coming to see me."

Cliff said, "I never thought it was this serious. Sure, I didn't like your lousy press but I didn't give it much thought; you seemed to be getting only bigger as a result of it."

"Baby, how could you see it if *I* didn't? When it first started happening I got scared but then I saw that it wasn't hurting me—on the contrary, it was adding something, making me more interesting. There were times I even secretly gloried in it. When all the bedroom scandals started, a lot of chicks began looking at me like: 'Let's find out what he's got!' and I didn't exactly chase 'em away. But that's over now. I can't let it run wild any more.

"The other side of it, which is horrible, is it's killing me uptown. I'm being isolated from my own people. I'm an outcast. Obviously I'm not white, but now it's gotten so the colored people don't want me, either. It's like I'm the man without a country.

"I've got to completely remake my image. The first step is to straighten out with the guys who reach the people, guys like Sylvester and Hy. I want to go about it methodically, man by man, with every paper, every magazine: the columnists, editors, feature writers—everybody! You've got the connections. I need you to set it up for me to meet every single one you can get to."

He was stirring his coffee slowly. "That's going to be a tremendous job for you."

"Baby, I eat dinner every night. Let's make use of that time. Let's make every dinner count. I'm available any time of the day and night except when I'm on the stage."

He nodded, staring past me into space, evaluating, planning. "What about the Negro press? I can't do you much good there. I just don't know them."

"I've already spoken with a buddy of mine, Billy Rowe, a top press agent. His wife is Izzy Rowe. She writes a very important column in the *Courier* and she's always been fair with me: if I do something she likes she says so, by the same token she never misses beating my brains out when she doesn't dig something. The important thing is that because of Billy, I always had a liaison with her so she could at least check with me and find out if such and such is true. I've got the same thing with *Ebony* and *Jet* because I made it a point to meet the publisher and they've been completely fair with me. That's all I can hope for, and between you and Billy maybe I can get it right down the line."

Cliff nodded. "We should hit it from another direction, too. You should start appearing at every benefit for every important cause. The new image needs that kind of dimension."

The next evening Billy Rowe met with Cliff and me at Danny's.

"I don't know where I went wrong with them, Billy. I cherished their acceptance when I had it, but I sure lost them somewhere along the way. Like Evelyn Cunningham. Cliff, this woman is our Hedda and Louella put together but with a little Dorothy Kilgallen thrown in. Now I never even met her, but for some reason I happen to be her personal choice for President of the White Citizens Council."

Billy nodded painfully. "The general impression around the Negro press is that he's got it made and he just doesn't give a damn. Maybe we should start off our campaign with the Negro press by having a little get-together. Let them see how you feel. It might break the ice a little before you tackle them individually."

I smiled at him. "Beautiful. We could do a special thing just for them—family style. No business, no interviews, none of the 'Hey, put my name in the paper' jazz. Strictly a thing for us all to relax, have a little booze, a little food, and get to know each other."

Evelyn Cunningham's column jumped up out of the *Courier* and slapped my face.

Dear Sammy,

Right off I can't think of anything I dislike about you. Not only are you one of the greatest entertainers in the world but from what I hear and what I see you also seem to be one of the nicest. In a way I'm proud of you as I am of Ralph Bunche, Thurgood Marshall and the rest of the guys who will be written about in history books.

So, when you invited me to your press party I was real tickled to get a chance to meet you. I didn't expect that you and I would get to be boons on sight or that you would even remember my name after we'd met. All I wanted was the kicks of being in close quarters with you and maybe getting a small idea of what makes you tick. You see I'm a 14-karat fan of yours. Anyway I got the most awful sinking of the stomach when I got to the party and saw at a glance that it was a press party for people on the colored papers. My stomach turned over again when I suddenly realized that it had been a long, long time since I had been through this type of all-colored press party in New York. Seems they went out with ankle strap shoes.

But I'm crazy about you. So after my stomach turned up I made excuses. I said to myself he's got something special to say to us that's exclusively for us or something really big is coming because this doesn't make sense. Nothing came. You were charming, gracious and entertaining. You hopped from guest to guest and went to the trouble of engaging in small talk with us. But you weren't happy. Neither were we. Every now and then I got the feeling that you were embarrassed, that you didn't think the party was such a good idea after all. And then you made a short talk. You said, with great sincerity, that you were deeply appreciative of the Negro press and the Negro patrons who were helping to keep *Mr. Wonderful* running on Broadway. You intimated that despite the negative reviews of the show when it opened, Negroes were in a large measure responsible for making it run. For this, thanks. But Sammy, wouldn't it have been a gasser if you had said the same thing at a press party to which you had invited people from both the daily and weekly papers? It wouldn't have offended the daily boys. In fact I've got an idea they would have respected you even more. Don't get me wrong. I don't want you running down to Montgomery and jumping on buses or yelling and screaming about your civil rights. But in many, many quarters integration is fashionable and chic and you have access to these quarters. In short I don't think the press party was necessary, but I love you anyway. Love and kisses,

E.C.

P.S. Ain't it rough being cullud? There's always something!

I got Billy on the phone. "Did you see what that bitch wrote? Did I have to throw a party for *that*?"

"Sammy, she's right and we were wrong. Read the column again and you'll see it."

"Holy Toledo. Is it against the rules to be friendly and just say hello? Isn't 'Have a drink and let's be friends' enough of an announcement? What the hell does she want from me?"

George glared at me as I got into the limousine. "Do you realize I've been sitting in this hearse for almost an hour?"

"I'm sorry, baby. I really am. But Will called a meeting."

"My God, what do you talk about in those meetings every night?"

I sat back in the seat. "Trio business."

He gestured toward the chauffeur. "Have you any idea where Jeeves is taking us?"

"Brooklyn."

He groaned. "Couldn't you have found a benefit a little closer?"

"Baby, it's a drag and I don't like it any more than you do." I pulled out the jump-seat and rested my feet on it. "It's just a quickie 'Glad to be here folks,' a song, and good-bye. But I'm going to catch thirty winks or I may not make it up the stairs to the stage."

As I turned and got comfortable, he muttered, "Don't worry about me. I'll hum to myself."

The M.C. was saying, ". . . the moment we've all been waiting for, here he is, Mr. Wonderful himself . . ."

I did two songs. The audience was applauding, calling for more. The M.C. tried to help me off. "We can't impose on Mr. Davis any longer. He has no more arrangements with him, he wasn't able to bring his own accompanist along. . . ."

Their reception had been so warm that I hated to leave. I held up my hands. "Thank you, but I like to think of myself as an 'entertainer' not just a performer, and if I can't come out here and entertain you with no more than a pocket comb and tissue paper then I should get out of the business. So, if you've got nowhere to go. . . ."

An hour later George was in the wings as I came off. "Just a quickie song and good-bye? Really." He wanted to play it chic and bored but he was having trouble. "You'd think I see you perform enough in *Mr. Wonderful*. Whatever that is."

I handed him the plaque. "Just a little something to let you see what people think of your star."

The car headed for New York and I asked the driver to take us to the Harwyn. I turned to George. "Now here's the skam: it's a little sip and sup over champagne and steak sandwiches—a definite see and be seen."

"By which columnist this time?"

"George, while you're concocting your vicious remarks old Sam is thinking, thinking—always thinking. Now, it happens that waiting for us at the Har are Milton and Amy Greene,

Chita, Michael, plus a model by the name of Harlean Harris whom I happened to meet on the cover of *Ebony* magazine." I closed the window between us and the chauffeur. "Aside from the fact that she's a very wholesome, sweet kid and one of the great-looking chicks of all time, she happens to be colored. Y'dig? Let 'em just *try* to say 'He was with a blonde.'"

"Well, just don't do any table-hopping."

"Baby, I'm going to stick so close to her that she's gonna forget she's colored and think she's *Siamese!*"

The Harwyn's doorman held the front door open; the hat check girl smiled admiringly at my plaque as I handed it to her; Ed gave me a tremendously warm hello and as I hit the main room the band swung into *Mr. Wonderful.* I waved to them and slid onto the seat next to Harlean. "Sorry I'm late. Good evening, everybody."

Mac, the table captain, asked, "What'll it be, Mr. Davis?"

"Ah, yes, innkeeper. The best champagne in your cellars and be done with it."

He bowed and played straight. "A jug of wine, sire. Any particular year?"

I gave him a little Bogart. "Whattya? One of them fresh guys? Nobody says 'jug' to Little Frenchy! Bring us the best you've got and you're on your honor 'cause I been in stir so long I won't know the difference."

Michael gave me a raised eyebrow. "Oh? You're drinking tonight?"

"Just enough to make me suave and sophisticated." Mac was pulling out the table next to ours, for a middle-aged couple who'd just arrived. I smiled at them Charley Gracious Star style. The man turned away. I heard him tell Mac, "I'd prefer to sit over there." He was pointing across the room. I looked away, but Mac saw that I'd caught it. George plunged into conversation. "Well, our 'Mr. Wonderful' here was a smash tonight . . ." Obviously he'd caught it too. I glanced at Harlean. She was chatting with Michael. George continued ad-libbing wildly. Mac came by. "The characters you run into in this business." He made a face. " 'The air conditioning is too strong.' " I smiled my thanks for his sensitivity. I glanced over to where the couple was seated. They looked away. I tried to catch the attention of someone at the next table, but I couldn't; I tried the next table, and the next, but nobody was smiling at me, and I had a punch-in-the-stomach awareness of Harlean and me being the only colored people in the place.

I slid out from behind the table and went up to the band-stand. I shook hands with the pianist. "Okay if I sit in with your guys?"

He grinned. "You kidding?"

The drummer smiled and moved out from behind the drums and I sat down and picked up the beat. The people on the dance floor began nudging each other and I heard a growing murmur: "It's Sammy Davis . . . Sammy Davis . . ." The sound was rolling toward me in waves, swirling around me, bathing away the tension, soothing every hot nerve end until I felt my arms loosening, my neck relaxed. . . .

"Mr. Davis?" A college girl was smiling up at me. "Would you sing something?" Her date, a kid with a bright face and a short haircut, said, "Would you?"

I nodded. "Thanks for asking." I waved for the drummer to come back, took the mike and began singing, standing back so it wouldn't look like a performance. The people started dancing again; the whole room was focused on me; Ed Wynn was standing in the doorway, beaming. More and more people were coming to the dance floor until it was so crowded they could only stand in place, swaying back and forth.

As I slid into my seat, George asked, "Giving away free samples?"

"Don't knock it. I could've sold a dozen tickets right from the floor." The waiter poured a glass of champagne for me. "C'mon, let's go back to my place."

I sat behind my bar at the Gorham. Harlean was across from me, Michael, Chita, and George were watching the Late Show. A pleasant drowsiness crept over me as I relaxed in the knowledge that I didn't have to be tuned in all over the room trying to catch what everyone was saying or thinking.

Jack E. Leonard spotted me entering Danny's, and made a whole production of slowly walking around me and staring at my suit. "I just want to say I like your pants, Sammy. You look like a Jewish skin diver!"

Cliff Cochrane led me to a quiet corner of the bar. He was angry. "If Billy and I are going to do you any good we can't have you working against us."

"What's wrong? What'd I do?"

He read from a column. "'Sammy Davis, Jr.'s eyebrow raiser at the Harwyn was gorgeous Harlean Harris, a top model.' Now look, I'm a press agent, not your nursemaid. If you wanta swing with white chicks then go, Daddy, but do you have to make a display of what we're working to defeat?"

"Cliff, Harlean Harris is a model for *Ebony* Magazine! Did they say she's white, or a blonde?"

"Well, no, but I thought . . . well, it sounds like she is."

"Don't be embarrassed, baby. The cat who wrote that *wanted* people to think she's white. Sammy Davis and a colored chick ain't news. It's conviction by innuendo: I don't have to do it, and they don't have to actually say it, but with my reputation people put two and two together and it comes out white. That's just why I need you and Billy."

George was waiting at my table with Burt Boyar, a columnist who'd been shooting zingies at me. He introduced me to his wife, Jane. I smiled graciously. George smiled back. "We've been getting along famously without you." It was one of his great moves that sounded harmless but which was to tell me: there's nothing I'd rather do than spend half an hour making small talk with strangers. He added, "We find we have so *much* in common."

I gave him a look to cool it. I was there to neutralize people, not to offend them. "Incidentally, baby, I just want to remind you about Sunday."

"Sunday? Which Sunday?"

I tore apart a piece of bread. "Tomorrow. Polly Bergen and Freddie Fields' dinner thing. It's seven-ish."

"Seven-ish? I didn't even know I was invited-ish."

I tiptoed along the line between not lying, yet not telling the truth. "Didn't I tell you? Anyway, I spoke to Freddie today on the phone."

"And he invited me?"

I gave him a patient look.

"Well, I'm only surprised they didn't call me personally.

It's not like we're strangers. Listen, are you sure they really invited me, too?"

"George, obviously you're not going to believe *me*, so why don't you call Freddie and make a fool of yourself by asking 'Am I *really* invited to dinner?' like nobody's ever invited you anywhere before. I'll have Pete bring over a phone, you can make the call and I'll be right here when you're ready to apologize."

He blushed. "Well, you don't have to make a three-act play out of it."

"No need to apologize. In the words of Abe Lincoln, 'A man who can't make a mistake can't make anything.'"

Early Sunday evening George called from his apartment. "Your producer is ready. I'll meet you in the lobby." I called the garage and told them to have my car ready. Nobody was going to think I was an errand boy when I stepped out of a Mark II Continental.

Walking toward the garage, George said, "Why don't we just take a cab? Why bother with parking?"

"Baby, I don't remember asking you to organize this trip."

A uniformed nurse wheeled a baby carriage across Fifth Avenue toward the park, pushing the carriage with one hand and with the other grasping a little boy bundled up in a fur-collared coat, leather leggings and a hat with ear-muffs. I drove slowly up the avenue, looking at the immaculately kept mansions and the elegant apartment buildings.

George mumbled, "I really can't understand this whole thing. I mean Polly is so proper, it just seems peculiar that she wouldn't invite me herself."

I stopped the car. "George, you're getting to be the noodge of all time. Now you're free to open that door, step out, and I'll make your apologies for you. I'll just tell them 'I'm sorry my producer is rude and so touchy that he won't go anywhere unless he gets an engraved invitation.'"

He slunk into the seat. "You're holding up traffic and you don't have to get so excited. It just seemed strange, that's all."

As we approached Polly and Freddie's building, a man in riding breeches, boots, and a glen plaid jacket stepped out of a maroon limousine and strode past the doorman who touched his cap and rushed to open the front door for him. As the car drove away I backed into a space just short of the door. The doorman saw me behind the wheel, looked at George— then back at me, and making no move to open our door, spoke through the window. "Can I help you?"

George said, "Mr. and Mrs. Fields," and opening the door himself, stepped out of the car.

The doorman rushed ahead of us to the front door, blocking it. "Are you expected?"

George glanced at me. "Yes."

"Well, I'll have to announce you." He opened the door, admitting us to the lobby. "Who shall I say it is?"

"Sammy Davis, Jr."

He went to the house phone, plugged in a wire and pressed a lever, glancing over at us as he waited for somebody to answer. I looked outside, through the glass door. I heard the phone being cradled. "You're expected." His voice was toneless, withdrawn, and I had the feeling he was thinking more about Freddie and Polly than about me, and that he was never going to feel quite the same about them.

As we waited at their apartment door, I only hoped Polly wouldn't see George and react with a "Why, George, what a pleasant surprise! Uh, come in." A maid opened the door. Polly was behind her. She saw George, and it was a falling face, then a quick catch and a smile, "Why, George, what a pleasant surprise! Uh, come in."

Even at Tiffany the table didn't have so much silver. I knew every piece, but I held up the oyster fork. "And who is *this* for? The children?" I gathered up all my silver except one fork, one knife and one spoon, handed the whole bundle to the maid, and turned to Polly. "Darling, I know I'm a big star but I'm just folks, and the only time we ever had three forks on a table is when three of us were eating."

We left after midnight. The elevator door slid three-quarters open revealing us to a different elevator man, it stopped, he recovered quickly, and it rolled back the rest of the way. The door slid closed behind us; the inner brass gate snapped across the entrance and we began the descent. The elevator man faced front, stonily erect, displaying his displeasure and distaste by the emphatically precise manner in which he was doing his work.

The doorman did a begrudging saunter-over to the door,

letting us know it was his job to open it for us but he loathed doing it. As we passed through the open door George stopped and studied him. "Doorman, did anyone ever tell you that you're a dead ringer for Hans Von Gerhardt, the great Nazi motion picture star?" He tapped him on the chest, speculatively. "Yes! I must use you in my next picture."

The doorman didn't begin to understand that it was a put-on. His face flushed with pleasure. "Thank you, sir. Thank you very much." He followed us to the car. "Uh, sir, what was the name of the gentleman you said I resembled?"

George waved him away. "No matter. He's been executed."

A brightly lighted, nearly empty bus broke the no-traffic stillness as it roared its way up Fifth Avenue. Then it was quiet again. "George, about bringing you tonight . . ."

"Well, we all have our little problems." He did not enjoy the frankness of the moment—the admission of seeing me wide open, and, eager to withdraw quickly from it, refusing to intrude by staring at the sensitivities and embarrassments which a man tries to keep hidden, he snapped on the radio and stabbed at the push-buttons. A disc jockey's voice blared: "And now a medley of those great hit songs from *My Fair Lady*. . . ." George snapped it off. "We don't need *that!*" He said, "It's only twelve-fifteen. Do you feel like a movie?"

"No, baby, I'd like to go home. We'll find Chita and Michael, and I told Jane and Burt to come by around one."

"Oh? Aren't we carrying meet the press a little too far?"

I pulled up in front of the Show Spot, George went in and got Chita and we drove over to Downey's. Michael climbed into the back seat, mumbling, "I was in the middle of a drink. I feel like I'm under arrest."

I sat behind my bar and smiled across at the group. "It's a definite be-it-ever-so-humble." George had turned off the television set. "Leave it on, baby."

"My God, even a train stops?" He picked up a package of Black Crows and raised an eyebrow. "What do you mean by *these?*"

"George, when you're finished with the racial humor maybe we can talk some business. The kids are goofing. They were just phoning it in all last week."

He put down the candy. "I already spoke to Johnny

340

Ryan about it. With the gross picking up this is no time for them to start getting bored."

Chita said, "They're not bored. It's more like spring fever."

George scowled at her. "Oh? A word from the queen of the gypsies?"

I interrupted their banter. "You got any ideas how we can lift 'em up a little?"

He made a face. "We don't have a Morale Budget."

"Baby, I'll take care of that part of it. This is important. The fact is all the taking-them-to-the-movies, the parties—everything we've done that's made it family-style has paid off on the stage, right? You're always hearing about some show that's got cast problems with feuds and intrigue, and that kinda jazz has got to come across in the performance. Thank God we don't have none of *that* and let's keep it that way."

He thought about it. "Well, let's bring them all up to my hotel. We can have a 'Mr. Wonderful Weekend at the Raleigh.' We'll hire some buses, leave here after the Saturday night show, and stay until Monday afternoon. . . ."

Jack Carter shouted, "Everybody out of the pool!" He flopped down on a lounge chair next to me and groaned. "Oh . . . a youth I'm not. That softball game . . ." He closed his eyes, "Help. Seltzer!"

As our kids began jumping in and out of the pool, I watched the regular hotel guests. Nothing but smiles. They were diving in, joining the party.

George gestured toward a boy dancer standing on the diving board, and spoke quietly. "I never told you this but the first day of rehearsals he wanted to quit. He hadn't realized it was a mixed cast and he didn't feel he could work with colored people. Anyway, he decided to stay—obviously—and this morning he came to me and said he was embarrassed over what he'd said that first day, that he loves the show, the cast—he was like apologizing to me. And I'm not even colored." He looked blankly into space. "Maybe I am."

Joe E. Lewis gazed around the jam-packed ballroom

of the Delmonico Hotel. "It's wonderful being up for lunch . . . actually I'm not really up, but it feels nice." He had the mike against his mouth. "I sound like the all-clear signal at a floating crap-game."

Walter Winchell heckled from his seat on the dais. "Speak into it. Don't kiss it."

Joe E. continued, "I don't want to interfere with the fun. I'll just introduce my fellow Friar, one of the greatest entertainers of all time, Sammy Davis, Jr."

I stood up. Red Buttons shouted, "Sit down, you shmuck!" He stalked over to Joe E. "You're supposed to introduce *me!*"

Joe E. nodded. "Gentlemen, I wasn't supposed to introduce Mr. Davis—you're catching me on a losing streak. I want you to meet Mr. Davis' nephew, Red Buttons."

Red took the mike and gestured toward me. "We're gathered here to honor this runaway slave. . . ." He waited for quiet and spoke seriously. "It's a happy thing for the Friars to be throwing a luncheon for someone we love and who has accomplished something important in our business." He looked at me. "Don't get a big head, you bum." He smiled at Winchell. "Walter, it's nice to see you take a few minutes off from fighting with people. I have a few telegrams here. This one is from Adam Clayton Powell: 'Sammy, if you vote for Adlai Stevenson you'll never play The Apollo again.' Here's one from *Confidential* Magazine: 'Dear Sammy, You made us what we are today.'

"For our first speaker, I want to introduce Eddie Fisher, one of the finest singers to come along in three or four months."

Eddie took the mike. "Gentlemen . . ."

Jack E. Leonard shouted, "I trust that will be your closing remark!"

Eddie composed himself. "As I was saying, before I was so rudely interrupted . . ."

Jack Carter heckled, "Work without the mike, Eddie. You're better off."

Eddie grinned. "I'll try again."

Jack E. called out, "I want to wish you luck with your comeback!"

Joe E. groaned, "Three-to-one he won't sit down."

Eventually, they let him say a few words to me, then Red took the floor again. "I'd like to introduce some members of the press who are in the room . . . and Earl Wilson the great columnist from the New York *Post*." Red looked nervously at Winchell. "Walter, I'm sorry, but I've got to do these things. . . . All right, he's *not* such a great columnist." Still getting no smile from Winchell, he threw out his hands. "The hell with this. I'm quitting the business."

Jack E. was on his feet. "I've got a big shock for you. You were never *in* it!" He took the mike and looked from Winchell to Red. "I just want to say, Red, I certainly enjoyed watching the end of your career today." He stared defiantly at Winchell. "Mr. Winchell: I like Ed Sullivan! Seriously, Walter, you're doing a great job on your TV show and you're a very clever fellow but I just want you to know that soon you'll be off the air with the rest of us."

Alan King began his turn at the mike: "I have nothing bad to say against Mr. Winchell because I'm just getting started in this business whereas all these other guys are through. . . ."

The hilarity of the afternoon could not, at least for me, overwhelm the warmth which motivated not only the jokes, but the presence of the men who were telling them. As they heckled and insulted me, I remembered the night Jack E. and Red had come backstage at the Riviera. I looked around the room and up and down the dais remembering a kindness with almost every face, and I could think of no greater satisfaction, no sweeter pleasure, than the approval of my own kind of people, show people.

The luncheon was drawing to a close, the heckling ended and Walter Winchell took the mike. "Sammy, I join all the others who have saluted you and honored you here today with quips and insults. You know we are all devoted to you and respect your art and talent. Damon Runyon once wrote that the word 'Class' is difficult to define. But, once you see it you recognize it, and once you've recognized it you'll never forget it. Class, he said, was something you might find in the grace of a ballerina, the lift of a thoroughbred's hoof, or the flip of a champion's glove. Gentlemen, Damon must have meant—Sammy Davis, Jr."

As I walked to the microphone the entire assemblage

was standing, applauding me, and I looked toward the table where my father and Will were sitting with George, Michael, Burt, and Charley Head. My father smiled at me and so did Will, but there was confusion in Will's eyes, and I could imagine the turmoil within him: the tug of war between wanting to enjoy what he'd never believed he would see happen, to believe it was real and okay, with no strings attached, and the fear that something would happen to prove it all a lie. But the layer upon layer of emotional scar-tissue which had taken a lifetime to develop was impenetrable, and I knew he could never see it as I did and enjoy it as tangible proof that a Negro could gain acceptance at least somewhere in a white world.

At dinner, dozens of people came by my table at Danny's to congratulate me. When there was a break George groaned, "I feel like I've been sitting through the same movie twenty times."

I smiled. "And the night is young, baby. After the show it's a definite out-on-the-town for your friend the Friar to take a few more bows . . . Michael, incidentally, is that blazer and those slacks the only clothes you own? I mean I understand about being broke but you're working steady—you must have at least one suit. After all, we *are* going to be celebrating."

He smiled, embarrassed. "I'll wear a suit."

He left the table a few minutes later and George looked at me. "Don't you know who Michael *is?*"

"What do you mean don't I know who he is? Who should he be?"

"His mother's a Guggenheim."

"Then what's he doing working as our assistant stage manager?"

"He likes the theater."

When he came back I put down my fork. "Michael, do you mean you've got money coming out of your ears and you've had the audacity to go sneakin' around here looking like Monday night on 125th Street—and stop blushing 'cause it won't help you. What is it with guys like you and Johnny Ryan? You with the dollar-ninety-eight khaki pants and him Charley Undernourished with the frayed collars? The two of you look like: 'Send These Kids to

344

Camp.' Well, the party's over. Tonight we're starting a new game called 'Give the check to the assistant stage manager.' Now, here's the skam: we'll start our little celebration by letting you take me, George, Chita, Jane and Burt to Sardi's after the show. I'm a Broadway star and it's time I made an appearance there."

He smiled agreeably. "Okay."

"Then we dash over to the Copa to catch a little Joe E. from the ringside and on to the Harwyn. And consider yourself lucky that I'm anxious to see Sardi's because I might just as easily have told you I'd like to go to Romanoff's. In *Hollywood!*"

I didn't have to know the room to know we'd been seated in the back of the bus. "Well, it's another 'Welcome to Broadway' for old Sam by the chic theatah people."

George said, "Sammy, I forgot there was an opening tonight. If Richard Rodgers walked in here at this hour without a reservation . . . I mean there's nothing they could do if they don't have a table."

If I were Richard Rodgers it wouldn't matter. I sensed heads all over the restaurant turning and staring at us like "Hey, look where they stuck Sammy Davis, Jr." Somebody from the show that opened must have walked in because there was a burst of applause. The savory show business atmosphere floated rich and desirable all around us and I hated myself for caring where my damned table was.

Michael said earnestly, "If you look around the room, the fact is the really important people are sitting back here."

I shook my head. "Michael, you may not be poor but you lie beautifully, baby."

"Well, anyway," he said, "when people see you sitting here they'll assume the chic section was moved. Just think how uncomfortable you're making all the little nobodies who thought they had good tables up front."

Chita asked, "Would you feel better if we left?"

"Darling, you've got a lot of talent and a big heart but you've got a few things to learn about being a star; we play it with smiles and chic talk like we couldn't care less 'cause our every move is being watched—like the man said: 'The curtain never falls.' Also we don't order anything

345

that'll keep us here too long. One drink, then a casual exit, and home sweet home."

Michael asked, "What about the Copa and the Harwyn?"

"Another time, baby. Old Sam's had it for tonight. We'll go back to the hotel. We can sit around, get to know each other better. . . ."

George groaned. "My God, how much better can we know each other?"

I turned on the television set and sat behind the bar. "I admit we don't have caricatures on the walls, but we have records, television, books, magazines, and guns for those who wish to practice their draw. Now, the first thing we'll do is make a little call to The Stage and get some delicacies sent over. . . ."

Burt said, "Here's that pass you wanted for your father."

"Thanks, baby. He'll get a big kick out of this. I'll go down and give it to him now."

My father smiled at the words "Working Press," fanned the little slips of paper for each day of the racing season, and hung the pass on the lapel of his pajamas, beaming. "Poppa, I'll be the first man standing at the gate in the morning." He winked. "Wait'll some of my pals sees me with *this* hangin' from my jacket."

I got out of the cab in front of the Gorham and said goodbye to Jane and Burt. "Catch you guys at Danny's. Six-ish." As they drove away, my father pulled up in another cab. While he paid the driver, I made a whole production out of checking my watch and giving him Oliver Hardy looks through the window. "Oh, no. Oh . . . I don't believe this. You ran out of the money by *three o'clock*, Gracie?"

He stepped out of the cab, looking brokenhearted, like he'd lost his shirt. "You have a bad day, Dad? You drop much?"

"No. I just didn't feel much like stayin' around."

He started to walk into the hotel but I held his arm. "I don't get it. Why?"

He hesitated. "Y'know that pass you gave me?" Tears started coming to his eyes. "Well, when I got to the gate the guard looked at it and then at me—and he made me take it off." He shrugged like that was all but obviously it wasn't and I kept looking at him waiting for the rest, not realizing how he'd not wanted to tell it to me until he sighed resignedly, looked away, and continued, "Anyway, he wouldn't let me in. He kept the pass. He said, 'This ain't yours. Ain't no nigger reporters on the New York papers.' His shoulders sagged as he pronounced the last few words and he kept looking past me up the street, avoiding any contact with me that could only be a final twist of the knife that had slashed into his sense of pride, a knife placed there not by the white man, whose hatred could never be a surprise to a middle-aged Negro, but by the necessity for a father to stand before his son degraded, stripped of all dignity, beaten in a fight which never took place, helpless to do anything but admit, "This is all I am —the man who dreamed you'd look up to me."

I put my arm around him and we went inside. "Look, Dad, the guy was a bastard. Burt'll get you a new pass and he'll speak to the track so it can't happen again."

He was shaking his head. "Thanks, Poppa, but don't bother. What the hell. I appreciate it and all but I don't think I'd wanta try usin' it . . . it wouldn't be no fun any more. . . ."

I stayed with him at his apartment for an hour or two, then went upstairs to dress for dinner. I was tired and I dressed slowly, waiting for the usual adrenalin, the charge of excitement I could always count on to surge through me at the prospect of meeting new press guys and beating their preconceptions, neutralizing them, winning them over. It was always there for an audience, for an interview—the greater the challenge the greater the extra voltage—but it wasn't happening, and I had to drag myself downstairs and into my car.

As I checked my hat at Danny's, Cliff Cochrane put his arm around my shoulder. "We got a bad rap in the *Amsterdam News,* a thing about you always eating here instead of going uptown. Billy set up a dinner with the editor for next week. At least he's willing to meet with us and get to know you."

"Great. Thanks, Cliff. I appreciate it. What else is new? I mean with you personally?"

He looked at me strangely and I realized I was just stalling, standing back from the moment when I'd have to sit down at the table and be on. He said, "I'm fine. Couldn't be better," and filled me in on who was waiting for me at the table. I started toward them, trying to remember the names he'd just told me, trying to get myself in the right frame of mind. George and Burt and Jane were already there. I shook hands with the people, sat down, and started smiling.

I did ten minutes of chitchat to loosen everybody up, then somebody asked, "Sammy, you live on Fifty-fifth Street, don't you?"

"Yes, ma'am."

She tried to conceal her surprise at something she had known but couldn't really believe. "Well . . . isn't that interesting . . . I mean it's much more convenient for you."

A little girl was tapping me on the shoulder, holding out a piece of paper and bashfully looking at the floor.

"Of course, darling." I kidded with her for a minute, her shyness was replaced with confidence and she giggled happily, and ran back to her table to show it to her parents.

My guests were smiling with approval.

"Children seem to like you, Mr. Davis."

"I guess that's 'cause they can sense how much I like them. I'm going to have a house full of them if I ever get lucky and find someone who'll marry me."

They laughed, they were trying to be nice, to keep it social—but they were testing, weighing, judging, and with every answer another layer of doubt seemed to fall away from their faces, and I knew that soon I'd see the look that would say, "Gee, he's a human being," and I resented my eagerness to see it, to be so goddamned glad to get what should have been mine to start with. A guy across the room was staring. I'd been aware of it from the moment I'd sat down. It wasn't idle curiosity with a quick turn-away when I looked up—he was doing a real stare-down. I turned back to the people I was there to meet, but I could feel his eyes still on me. Why doesn't he eat his dinner and get off my back? If he doesn't like seeing me then why is he looking? Or why doesn't he leave?

George and Jane and Burt were helping me carry the ball.

They had to be bored to death but they were going along with it for me, playing it charming and interested. Why did I have to impose this on them? Why should it be necessary for me to use my friends as props and scenery?

"Sammy, I've been curious about your becoming a Jew. As a matter of fact when we first read about it my wife said, 'Doesn't he have enough troubles?' I mean what with having one eye and being . . . uh, a member of the—" he lowered his voice, "Negro race."

"Well, sir, the truth is I never *did* get invited to be in the St. Patrick's Day Parade. Now they've got two reasons."

I could feel people all over the room looking at me, and I was aware that as usual I was instinctively watching myself, making all the right moves so nobody could point a finger and say, "Well, what do you expect?" I was so tired of being tested and judged, of doing the right things, for the wrong reasons. Why couldn't I have good manners because I *want* good manners? Not because I *need* them because I'm colored. Why must I always keep proving myself? Nobody else has to. Why me? Why must I always prove what I'm not before I can prove what I am?

The son of a bitch across the room was still staring. I looked around our table, from face to face; the woman was completely won over, her husband was on the fence, skeptical, but one more question and answer and I'd have him on my side, too. I turned to him. I could feel the hate-filled eyes from across the room still boring into me as I heard my own voice being charming, sensible, witty, humble. . . .

Is all this doing any good? Am I accomplishing anything? When does it end? I can't meet the whole world, I can't neutralize everybody one by one. I can't even make a dent. What am I doing here? Fighting, always fighting, always begging people to like me. The faces at the table came into focus again and I saw them looking at me like I was supposed to say something. They were waiting and I remembered somebody had asked me something but I couldn't remember what it was. Everybody at the tables around me was talking, the whole room was talking, but I couldn't hear what anybody was saying, there was just a great big drone like a car horn that was stuck and wailing at me, growing louder, droning on, screaming, screeching, surrounding me, pushing me. . . .

I was standing in the middle of the room and Pete had his arm around me. "You all right, Mr. Davis?" "Yeah, fine, thanks . . ." Danny was in front of me, worried. "Hey, maybe you'd better sit down. You feeling okay?" I stepped around him. "I've got to get out, Danny. The walls are closing in on me."

My new car was in front of the door, a Cadillac Brougham, $14,000 worth of automobile, the most expensive American car built. I got into it and started driving uptown.

Maybe in Harlem I'd be able to breathe, to get a reprieve from the grasping for quicksilver acceptance, from the constant looking over my shoulder, the listening, waiting—the endless vigil. I had to come down off the tightrope, to break the spasm of suspense.

I tore my collar open and kept pushing uptown, stopping at lights, not aware that the car had lost its motion until they changed and I was surging forward again, straining to get there. I passed 110th Street—I was actually beginning to feel better, looser. I turned west on 125th and drove slowly over to Seventh Avenue and parked.

I walked over to the corner. This is where they want me. Okay. It's easy. I'll hang on the corner. Anything. I let a crowd form around me. They were shoving to get near me, excited, calling down the street to their friends. But they didn't give a damn that I was Sammy, that I was home, standing on the corner. I was just another celebrity, that's all they saw—that and my car and my clothes. They were shoving and crowding and their voices were getting louder and louder—the same mass of noise as downtown. I broke through the circle, pushed my way through them and got back into my car. I drove further uptown toward Mama's old place, speeding, suddenly afraid it might have been torn down.

I stared up at the window over the candy store, remembering Mama watching for the truant officer; shaking her head at our old heaps and making us park around the corner so the neighbors wouldn't see them. The door of the Brougham slammed shut with its rich, heavy, solid sound, and I walked across the street and into the building.

I put my hand on the banister, trying to feel as I had when Mama was in the kitchen and I could race up the stairs and inside for dinner. The rich warm smells of the food Mama was cooking, the home smells, used to be all the good things in the world to me. I looked around me at the walls, the stairs, the banister—not really surprised at finding it no different, but not the same. I thought of going upstairs and standing in front of our door. Somebody'd come by and say, "Aren't you Sammy Davis, Jr.?" and I'd nod, "I used to live here." They'd ask me in and I'd sit in the easy chair next to the window and the whole family would come in and watch me. "That's Sammy Davis, Jr., he used to live here, right here in this room." They'd be poor like we were, and when I left I'd find the landlord and pay up their rent for a year. But I knew that I was only torturing myself, romancing my unhappiness, playing a corny scene from any one of a thousand old movies—that I didn't even feel like I was home.

I got back into my car and took a last look at Mama's window, wishing I could cry, but knowing I wouldn't. Only by seeing what I had come from, had I been able to see how far I'd gone. Perhaps I didn't belong at Danny's yet, and Mama's place was yesterday, but I'd made my choice a long time ago and the years and all they contained had closed the doors behind me.

I shifted into gear and headed downtown to the theater. I had to keep playing it the way I'd set it up. If it worked out, then someday I could stand on the corner or sit in Danny's—I could be anywhere and still be home.

GEORGE DID A MOCK GROAN. "MUST WE SIT UP SO close? I feel like I should get up and sing or something."

I gave him the glare he'd been expecting. "The biggest

opening in ten years, but you couldn't possibly just say, 'Hey, Sam, this is a wild table.' There's got to be a zingy, right?"

He blushed. "That's my policy."

Jane asked, "Did you see Earl Wilson's column today?" I'd seen it. "What'd he say, darling?"

"He said, 'If you want to see Sinatra at the Copa you'll have to speak to Sammy Davis, Jr. He's got a ringside table for ten every night.'"

I touched my father on the shoulder. "I'm going back and say hello to Frank." I passed Sugar Ray squeezing through the crowd on his way back to my table. He shook his head. "They usually put four ropes around me when I fight." As I moved through the club it reminded me of the night at Ciro's —a famous face at every table.

When I got to the dressing room Hank Sanicola told me that Frank had gone out for a walk, by himself. If ever there was a time for a performer to be alone, this was it. The strength to face that fantastic audience could only come from the same place that he'd drawn the power to attract them. I went back downstairs, not envying him this hour. It's great to know that the world is out there waiting for you, but who could know better than Frank how easily you can close your eyes to bask in the flattery and the admiration of millions of people and then when you open your eyes they can be gone. It's great to be the absolute hottest thing in the business but how do you live up to being a legend?

As I sat down at my table a man seated behind us tapped my shoulder. "Hey, Sammy, you just see Frank? It's wild up there, huh? Broads and booze . . . he don't care about nothin', right? How about him! He's some guy . . ." The man's face was bursting with delight. The rest of his party were smiling excitedly, enjoying their own mental pictures of the I-don't-care-guy, eagerly waiting for me to confirm all that they'd read about Frank. I smiled and nodded, and their faces reflected an ecstatic satisfaction.

As Joey Bishop came on to open the show, my father whispered, "Like the man said, Poppa: I wouldn't give that spot to a leopard." I nodded. The audience was looking at him with polite indulgence, accepting the presence of a relatively unknown comic as nothing more than a sign that when he finally left Frank would be next.

Joey stood in the center of the stage, making a big thing out of looking around the tightly packed, glittering assemblage, and shrugged modestly, "You think *this* is something? Wait till *Frank's* following shows up." They laughed and shifted toward him a bit, mildly curious. Joey shook his head, puzzled. "I don't know what all the excitement's about. It's the same act I've been doing for years." The room exploded with laughter and I relaxed for him, admiring the brilliance of what he was doing. Obviously he'd come in with brand new jokes, worked on and polished, but having the most valuable thing a performer can possess—the understanding of his audience, the ability to judge what they would accept and what they would not—he knew that his prepared routine couldn't possibly have drawn the people's attention off the subject of the evening, that no matter how funny the jokes might normally have been they would have died. He threw away his act and began ad-libbing, working with all the things the people were thinking, helping them to enjoy the excitement all the more, riding along on the momentum of the evening instead of trying to buck it, and he went off on bravos.

The lights lowered and a single spot shone on the microphone in the center of the stage. The music started, only the brass and the drums, like a signal, an announcement. I glanced toward the stairs. Frank was standing motionless, looking straight ahead, waiting.

It was all there: the sound, the confidence, the distinctive hands, the shoulders, the cigarette cupped in his palm, the slight stretching of his neck—everything, and within three songs he'd more than lived up to the legend, he'd surpassed it. As he rolled from song to song dictating every emotion of his audience, the ability to judge what they would accept in '53 or '54: the same man, walking by himself, hands in his pockets, coat collar turned up—nobody recognizing him. To see him come back from that, not only a better performer but bigger than ever, was a sight to behold. And he'd done it alone. A-lone. When everybody had said, "He's finished," when they'd said, "Forget him, he's a used-up nothing," then, with nobody helping him, he fought his way back on sheer guts and talent.

I watched him working—the consummate performer: in fine voice, mature, precise, totally in control, delivering everything his name had promised. But it was more than just his performance that was causing a sort of mass hypnosis. The women were gazing at him with greater adoration than ever, and now even the men were giving him a beyond-envy kind of respect, leaning in to him, approving, nodding like *Yeah!* because Frank was the guy who was living, being, doing, accomplishing it; he was the guy with the guts to walk alone, the guy who'd fought the odds and won, the man who stands on his beliefs "Like me or not" but he stands on them, who professes to be no god, from whom there is no "Look at me, I'm a pillar of society" but who is a man, and like a man, all the mixtures are there: the good guy, the bad guy, the actor, the father, the businessman—every known facet of his off-stage personality had fused with his perform-ance, and his atmosphere was lifting everyone to that peak of nearly hysterical excitement which surrounds a performer as he stands on the ultimate plateau.

I moved slowly with the crowd up the stairs toward the lobby. The group had drifted ahead of me in the stream of people and they were in front of the hatcheck room. A semi-name singer was holding the coat he'd just been handed and smiling ingratiatingly at George. "You like the show?" The smile twisted into a smirk. "I saw you sitting down there —in Africa."

The crowd pushed past me. I watched George's astonish-ment build to an anger of which I hadn't thought him ca-pable. He said something and turned away. The singer's face blanched. He reached for George's arm. "Hey, Georgie, what're you all excited about? Hey," he feigned a laugh, "how can I not talk to you? I'm opening the season for you at the hotel."

"You just got canceled."

George was climbing into our limousine. I drew him aside. "Thank you." I could see him thinking, remembering I'd been way behind him. I smiled. "Baby, I may have only one eye but I *hear* everything."

On Wednesday morning I read with sadness the grim,

giant headline: "HUMPHREY BOGART DIES." Frank wasn't taking calls. I left word that if he needed me for anything I was available.

I got a call from Julie Podell. "Sammy, Frank can't go on tonight. I've got Jerry Lewis for the first show. I need you for the second."

I was back in a nightclub again. I didn't have my father and Will on the stage with me, there was no chorus, no supporting cast, no story; I was alone—making it on my own again, and it was glorious.

Frank was back the next night and I was at ringside again. As I cut into my steak a voice behind me snarled angrily ". . . little nigger in front of me." I continued cutting my food and without raising my head shot a glance around my table. They hadn't heard it. The voice demanded "Waiter, let's have the captain over here." Then he was sayig, "You got any authority around this place?"

"Is something wrong, sir?"

"Damned right there is. I want a table without such a lousy view." A woman was trying to quiet him down. Jane glanced past me, then at me, smiled nervously, and went back to her food. George took a shot glass of scotch in one swallow and closed his eyes in pain as it seared through his chest. The captain must have signaled up above because I heard Bruno asking, "Can I help you, sir?"

I kept cutting away at my steak.

"Maybe you can do better than your flunky here. You look like a man who knows right from wrong." The voice softened, becoming fraternal, conspiratorial. "It's obviously some kind of a mistake. I come in here thinking I'm spending my money in a first-class place, so you can understand my surprise when I find my wife and I seated behind that little jigaboo. Now I'm sure that you . . ." The words ended in a gasp. George was staring past me, his face chalked by shock. I turned. The table was empty. Bruno and the captain had the man under each arm and were already halfway out of the room with him. A woman was hurrying after them. People all around us were leaning together, whispering, looking toward me, speculating on what might have happened.

The group was sitting in their chairs, limp. They were

doing self-conscious smiles of relief, not knowing if they should look at me or away from me, and I felt the sympathetic stares burning into me from them and from behind like I was caught in the headlights of a dozen converging cars.

A hand was on my shoulder. Julie Podell was looking at me sympatico. "The bum is out on the street where he belongs."

The kids were starting to get their wind back and they were talking, but their voices were like a record being played at the wrong speed. Michael had said something to me. "I'm sorry, baby, what did you say?"

He blushed. "It wasn't worth repeating. It was just something insipid, like 'keep a stiff upper lip, things'll be better someday.'"

I sympathized with their impossible position, but I hated my own. "Baby, if you'll excuse a little well-earned bitterness: colored people don't really have big lips, we just look that way from *keeping* them stiff for so long."

The lights had dimmed and Joey was onstage. I looked up and put a smile on my face because people would be watching me as they always watch celebrities. Joey looked at me curiously. "Don't I know you from somewhere, sir?" The crowd roared, and I played the scene of enjoying myself, laughing, stamping my feet hilariously.

As Frank sang I thought: if I can make myself remember the first time I ever came in here, how I felt watching him from that table in the back room, if I can appreciate how far I've come . . . I looked at the brochure on the table, forcing myself to stare at the picture of me wearing the Copa Bonnet with all the other stars. I *did* it. It took fifteen years but I did it. I'm not in a corner any more. I'm a star. It's all different now. So much has changed.

But nothing had changed. Not really. And I had the sensation of slipping helplessly backwards through the years, hearing my father's voice despairing, "You ain't gonna get away from it till you die."

The meeting started the same as all the others: my father and I sat down and Will closed the door and began dragging up subjects. But I had a feeling it wasn't just another meet-

ing; there was something in his face, something he was holding as a surprise or a trump card, and as he covered a half
dozen issues I sensed even his own impatience to get past
the preliminaries and into the main event. He finally laid it
on me, very casually. "By the way, Sammy, tonight Big Sam
and me left the Palm Club scene fifteen minutes before you
finished." He said it as though it were an afterthought and I
suddenly understood that he hadn't been holding it for last,
he'd been hoping I'd noticed and would ask him about it, or
better still, complain.

"I was going to bring that up when you were finished,
Massey. How come?"

He shrugged. "No special reason except that's what we
felt like doing. No need for us to be there anyhow, no one
notices us. . . ." He was steaming himself or trying to steam
me but when I heard the driving unhappiness in his voice,
the anguished defeat, I lost track of what he was saying,
recalling the same voice twenty or thirty years before: "Mose
Gastin, we're booked and I got an advance." . . . "Here's
your meal ticket too, Sammy." . . . "Now the first thing to
remember about show business—" . . . "Never let 'em know
they got to you. . . ." The man now speaking merged with
the man who had been a tower of strength, who'd owned the
name Will Mastin and had earned the unwavering respect of
people working for and around him, whose reputation had
gotten us work so many times when our talent hadn't. I was
focused on the same man all these years later and I saw what
had happened to him through no fault of his own, and as I
listened and saw what he was doing to himself I had to restrain myself from shouting: Why don't you retire? Quit,
Massey! Retire. The words were formed in my mind:
Okay, this is it. You still keep your cut but no more performing. I'm doing a single. Can't you see that it degrades you to
stay in the act? It's for your own good!

". . . and tomorrow night we may not show at all. How
do you like *that?*"

He was challenging me and all I had to say was "Well,
if that's how you want it." They wouldn't be able to back
down and from then on I'd be doing a single. It would be
that easy. They were watching me, anxiously, waiting, and I
saw how badly Will needed me to shout back and fight him

as I used to when we'd had something to fight about—when I'd needed him. He was starving for the importance of being fought, but if I did it I'd only be sweeping everything under the carpet. Why prolong their agony? I was trapped between the impossible premise that something good could come from something wrong, and my absolute belief that if it's for their own good, then it's their decision to make, that I have no right to tell them how to be happy.

They were waiting.

My fist crashed into the dressing table catapulting make-up in every direction. "Goddammit, Massey, if you guys can't be there to give me the support I need, if you think I'm going to do it *all*, you're out of your minds. I'll walk off the lousy stage with you . . ."

Tears began welling in his eyes.

I pounded the table again. "That's it. I won't discuss it. You'll *be* there!" I slammed the door behind me and ran into my dressing room, locked the door and sat down and cried.

"Oh?" George exclaimed. "Are they wearing pajamas to chic parties these days?" I said hello and went back to my juice and coffee and the Sunday *Times*. He helped himself to some coffee. "Didn't you say we were due there at four o'clock?"

"They'll still be there at five, baby. Unfortunately."

He raised an eyebrow. "Hmm. The bloom is off the rose?" I began dressing. He asked, "If you don't want to go, then why bother? I mean, going to parties isn't exactly compulsory." He mumbled, "Except for me: the Jewish Monty Woolley."

"And what, exactly, does that mean, George?"

"Only that every hostess in town looks at me like I'm bad news. They invite you and they get me—I'm America's Guest." He looked at me seriously. "It would be one thing if at least *you* enjoyed them."

"Baby, if people are nice enough to say, 'Hey, I want to throw a party for you,' what am I supposed to do, be Charley Boor and tell them no?" I jabbed a cuff link into my shirt. "Do I have to tell *you* that it also happens to be good business? I'm getting seen around town and it's showing at the box office, right? I mean the limousine jazz. But most important, I can't live in a vacuum. I can't spend my time only with hippies. I need diversity. I've got to be tuned in to everybody."

I closed the door and pressed the elevator button. "We don't have to stay eight hours. Just a drop-in, a little being charming until it's time to meet the kids at Danny's."

I spotted the doorman from a block away: another Concentration Camp Gerhardt, in full dress uniform. I let myself get caught on a traffic light and watched the cars headed the other way, down Park Avenue. I was tempted to make a U-turn and go back to the hotel.

"I'll take care of it for you, Mr. Davis." He was smiling as he opened the car door. He rushed ahead of us and held open the front door, then he ran ahead and bowed me toward the elevator. I smiled, "Thank you."

He turned to the elevator man. "Mr. Davis and this other gentleman are going to the penthouse."

I hadn't said where I was going. He hadn't recognized me and been courteous out of respect, he'd been expecting me, I was getting "safe conduct": someone had warned him, "Sammy Davis, Jr. is coming here. He's colored. Watch for him and don't embarrass him."

There was only one apartment on the floor and the party sounds floated through the open door. The host hurried over. "Sammy, welcome, welcome, welcome." His eyes tensed. "You didn't have any trouble . . . finding us, did you?"

"The number was right on the building. This is George Gilbert, my producer."

"Glad you could make it, George." He put his arm around my shoulder. "Come on in, Sammy, everyone's dying to meet you." He walked me around the living room introducing me to attractive people who were smiling, being courteous. A group formed around me. Somebody said, "I saw *Mr. Wonderful* and you really are. You were just marvelous."

My host said, "He's only the finest performer in the business, that's all." He put his arm around my shoulder. "Let me get you a drink, Sambo. What'll it be?"

I took out a cigarette. "I'll have a coke, thanks." Before I could reach for my lighter somebody had one flaring in front of me. "Thank you very much."

"My privilege. I'll light your cigarettes any time. I wish I knew where you learned to dance the way you do."

A woman interrupted. "Oh, Biffy, don't be ridiculous. No one *learns* to dance like that. Some people are . . ."

There was a death pause and I tried to take them off the hook. I smiled. "Well, you know what they say about colored people having rhythm."

Biffy wouldn't take the out. He was looking at me blankly. He couldn't imagine what I was talking about. Not the foggiest. "Oh? I'm surprised I never heard that."

I shrugged. "It's just an old cliché."

"Say, that's very interesting. I mean, do you think there's anything to that? I mean, about colored people . . . do you think that the Negro people"—he lowered his voice as he said the words "colored" and "Negro"—"really do have rhythm? I mean, now that I think of it I do recall hearing something about the background of jungle life. Naturally I'm referring to centuries ago. . . ."

George mumbled, "I *hope* so," and wandered off to the bar.

"Uh, what I'm trying to get across is . . ." He was staring into my eyes, afraid I'd think he was looking at my skin, talking like a man struggling to get out of quicksand. Beads of perspiration were forming around his forehead.

The merciful thing was to play it straight. "I doubt it. I know some Negroes who can't dance the foxtrot. On the other hand there are people like Fred Astaire, Gene Kelly, Donald O'Connor. . . ."

Someone said, "I'm going to look at the buffet table."

I smiled. "But don't eat anything. Just look!" They roared, relieved, the pressure released.

A man with a plate in his hand said, "Sammy, my name's Endley. Funny that I should meet you. My kid goes to school with Ralph Bunche's son."

"I haven't had the pleasure of meeting Dr. Bunche."

"Well, neither have I, actually. But his son's a fine lad. I've never exactly met him but I hear nothing but the finest things about him . . . the finest things."

It was a dead end. I excused myself and walked over to the buffet table. It was beautifully laid out. There was a large silver chafing dish of Lobster Newburg, something elegant looking like pâté de foie gras, a tin of caviar resting on shaved ice, and a platter of fried chicken.

The hostess came over to me. "I do hope you can find something you like. I didn't know . . . I wasn't sure what you like to eat."

I smiled. "Anybody who can't find something to eat here just plain ain't hungry."

She picked up a chicken leg between two fingers and smiled. "I adore this. Just adore it."

Her husband came by. "Come on, Sam, I'll give you the fifty-cent tour."

He took me from room to room. "Sammy, c'mon and say hello to our cook. It'll be the biggest kick in the world for her." He brought me into the kitchen. "Sarah, I guess you know who this is, don't you." He stood back beaming at us.

She smiled and wiped her hand on a towel. "I'm glad to meet you, Sammy," and shook hands. Harry Host put his arm around her, elaborately. "Sarah's a member of the family, aren't you, Sarah?"

She nodded and smiled. "Yes, sir."

As we left the kitchen he said, "Great woman."

His wife joined us and we went upstairs. I said, "This is a fantastic setup. I wish I had something like it myself."

The wife said, "Uh, well—uh, maybe there's something available in the building—we can check if you're interested . . ." She was rushing on, trying to convince me she hadn't noticed I'm colored. Her husband said, "Of course vacancies are pretty rare. . . ."

"Look, I was only talking. I've got a home on the coast that I haven't spent a full week in, and I'm usually not in New York enough to make it worth while."

She leaped for the out. "Believe me, you're just as well off. The city's ruined . . ." Oh, God, she'd done it again. She tried frantically to recover. "It's those damned *spicks*. Ever since *they* started coming over here . . ."

The car doors slammed shut, first one then the other, sealing us off safely from the rest of the city. I rested giddily against the soft leather seat. "George if you ever wondered how come colored people's hair is kinky—it's from going to parties like that one."

"Did something happen I don't know about?"

"Nothing special." I turned the key and started the engine. "But before I accept another of those invitations it's a definite half-gainer into the river."

I sat behind my bar grinning at George as if somebody were rubbing my back. "Baby, your star is home from the wars and he ain't about to leave this room unless someone yells fire."

"Have you forgotten that Jane and Burt and Michael and Chita are going to be meeting us at Danny's in an hour?"

"A great star never forgets." I called Danny. "This is your old buddy Sammy Davis, Jr., known to his close friends as just plain Mr. Wonderful. . . . No, baby, I'm dead on my feet, but the buddies'll be looking for me in about an hour. Will you tell them there's been a change in plan and there'll be a Carey car for them and to just get in it and come over to the Gorham? And Danny, give them a couple of jugs of spaghetti and some of that veal-pajamas and maybe a little shrimp marinara . . ."

George was puzzled. "I still don't understand what happened. I admit the people were a little square . . ."

"Hey. Hold it. You know I've never put anyone down 'cause they're square." He was waiting. I sat back against the curve of the bar, lit a cigarette, blew the smoke out and looked up. "George, did you happen to notice the platter of fried chicken?"

"Well, yes . . ."

"Do you think they serve that at all their parties? With the caviar?"

"Well . . ." He took a slug of his scotch. "They were trying to be nice."

"Baby, I'm not saying they weren't trying. And I love fried chicken, I could eat it all night. But I also eat other food—like anybody else. It's not like they invited a rabbit so they had to have a head of lettuce on the table for him. Let me put it this way: how would you like to be the only Jewish cat invited to a party and you look at the food and it's lovely and then over in a corner of the table you see they've got a little side order of gefilte fish for you?"

"Well, now that you mention it"—he couldn't resist

smiling—"I did wonder when they were going to start your crap game."

"You see? You did catch it."

"Well . . ."

I leaned across the bar. "Listen, y'know the old cliché 'Some of my best friends are colored'? It's been up-dated. Now it's 'My kid goes to school with Ralph Bunche's son'."

He smiled slightly, holding back, knowing that his complete reaction would only steam me. He shrugged, trying to minimize it. "Well, I don't want to do a cliché, too, but you've got to remember that to most people," he made a face, "particularly that crowd today, you're the first Negro they ever met socially and they just don't know how to handle it."

"Baby, if that's the case, and it probably is, then they'll have to get somebody else to practice on. Let them go out and hire some colored kid who needs the dough. Let them sit down and talk to *him* 'cause I've had it with running classes for learners."

"Well, I can understand that it's not exactly kicks, but at least you know their intentions are good. You know how they feel about you. They certainly wouldn't be throwing parties in your honor if they were prejudiced or anything."

"I know exactly how they feel about me. The trouble is *they* don't know how they feel about me. Let's not celebrate National Brotherhood Week just because a woman throws a party for me instead of keeping me out of school. They wanted to show off to their friends that they know Sammy Davis, Jr. Fine. I'm only flattered. But let's carry it a little further: here's a woman who adores herself for being a liberal and having 'a colored man' to her apartment, right? But do you want to do about ten minutes on what a shake-up it would have been if instead of you I'd brought Charley Head with me? Or any colored guy who dresses well, who makes a lot of dough and has been around—but isn't famous. I'd have set back her personal integration movement by fifty years. There'd be lorgnettes dropping all over the place, with mumbling, 'Well, we like *him* but did he have to bring his friends?'"

"I don't know why I'm defending her, but as long as I'm involved, how can you be so sure she'd react like that? Okay, they tried to do something they weren't experienced at and they blew it, but that doesn't mean . . ."

I came out from behind the bar. "Look, you're talking to Charley Optimist. I don't just casually jump to the conclusion that people are prejudiced. I'm hoping and praying I won't see it. Further, if I expect people to give me the benefit of the doubt then obviously I've got to give *them* the benefit of the doubt. But when a woman says to me, 'I like the colored people. It's the spicks I hate,' *this* is a prejudiced woman. Here's an educated, presumably intelligent person lumping a whole group of people together—millions of them in one swoop—and judging them. It doesn't occur to her that if her Negro maid didn't come in one day you don't go around saying Ralph Bunche, Sidney Poitier, and Thurgood Marshall are unreliable. By the same token there is nobody justified in hating all the Puerto Ricans 'cause nobody has *met* all the Puerto Ricans. But this woman wants to believe that she prejudges one group without prejudging another. Impossible. Either you see people as *individuals* or you don't. My God, you can't even say, 'All of last year's string beans were lousy' so how can you do it with *people?*

"Then another cat tells me, 'I've got ten Negroes and six white men working for me.' Here's a man who's counting people by color, but he makes a trip across the room to brag to me that he's a liberal. Do you realize that the only cliché I escaped is: 'Oh? I didn't even notice you were colored.' "

"Small world. Somebody said that to *me.*"

"George, you're rotten to the core."

He frowned, pleased. "I know."

"Now, Act Two: I'm reaching for an hors d'oeuvre and a man smiles broadly at me: 'I want to shake your hand. You're a credit to your people.' Here this phony all-too-liberal is telling me colored people are rotten but *I'm* okay and he's waiting for me to say thank you.

"How do you fight someone like this? The worst thing in the world is when you're up against people *who don't know they're prejudiced.*

"They bring me to their homes, put their arms around my shoulder and walk around the room insulting me, patronizing me, hurting me just as much as a hater would, maybe even more, but *they* expect me to say 'Thank you.' They go to bed puffed up with the satisfaction of being humanitarians, patting themselves on the back: 'I'm not prejudiced, I even had one to my home,' and they fall asleep counting colored people coming to their parties."

I stood up and gave a bar stool a little spin with one finger and watched it wobble slightly as it turned. "I'd be the last person in the world to say that anybody *must* be anything but what he wants to be. And even if he decides he wants to wear the badge of liberal I'm not asking him to turn over his income to the NAACP, or to go ride Freedom Buses—but he's got to know there's more to it than not throwing rocks."

George was looking into his glass, turning it slowly, troubled, seeing something he'd seen around him all his life but which had to look different from the inside.

The doorbell rang. He looked up, and as surely as if he were putting on a different coat I could see him getting ready to hide again behind the façade of sophistication. He grinned. "Your fried chicken is here."

When I noticed the Paramount clock showing 4:30 I closed the blinds so the kids wouldn't notice it beginning to get light outside. I put the tape recorder on the bar. "Okay. Chita will be Leticia Vanderveer, Washington hostess whose salon is, in reality . . ."

"Lamont Cranston."

I gave George a look. "Whose salon is, in reality, a hot-bed of undercover agents . . ."

"Hot bed? Hot bed? What do you mean by *that?*"

An hour later the tape ran out, the loose end ticking each turn around the spindle. I jumped up to change it.

Michael yawned. "It's just as well. I'm so tired I can't see."

Chita was putting on her coat. "I'm crazy. I've got a class tomorrow at eleven. How can I possibly dance with no sleep?"

I shrugged. "I know someone who's the star of a Broadway musical who manages to do it and people don't exactly hiss and boo me."

Burt said, "We've got to get home and do the column."

"And why are you pulling up your tie, George? You're only going downstairs."

He pulled it open. "That'll show you how tired *I* am."

365

I turned off the tape recorder. "Then that's it, folks, right? It's a definite run-out-on-old-Sam."

Michael asked, "Have you ever tried sleeping?"

"Okay. Don't let me keep you. All of you do what you feel you should. I'll just stay here alone—with all my friends."

George said, "Now really, it *is* five o'clock."

"No need to apologize. Get your sleep." I handed out a set of Shakespeare books. "Tomorrow night we'll have Hamlet readings. I've got a benefit so we won't meet here until one. You've all got until then to learn your parts. You don't have to know them by heart but it'll be much more fun if you're familiar with your lines."

I snapped my book closed and rolled on the floor hysterically. "That's it, folks. That's *it*. Michael—I'm sorry, baby, but we're all family here so I can say it—Polonius you ain't!"

Chita yawned. I glared at her. "It's only three o'clock, Chita. If you start in with that dance class jazz again . . ."

"But I *do* have a lesson and I was rotten today."

I stood up. "Never let it be said that I hampered anybody's career. It's too bad, though, that I went to the trouble to think up things that might be amusing for the few people I care about . . ." They were watching me curiously, defensively, as I unwrapped a Monopoly set.

Chita picked up the racing car, then she inspected the other tokens. "Are these real gold?"

"Quite." I smiled bitterly, disappointedly. "I thought it would be a pleasant change for my friends to play Monopoly with solid gold instead of little pieces of tin."

At around six-thirty George stood up. "Why am I still playing? I hate this game."

Chita looked at me beseechingly. "I've really *got* to go."

I lifted the board carefully and placed it on the bar. "Okay, we'll finish tomorrow night. Everybody remember what they are."

I stood at the door while they waited for the elevator. "So, the buddies are running out on me again, eh? A man has to write a column—maybe that I can understand, he's got a deadline. Although I don't see why you can't bring your typewriter over here. But you, George, and Michael, and you Chita," I gave them the tragic look, "I suppose it never occurred to you to skip your class just once and help bring joy to a poor soul who, this evening alone, has entertained thousands, a man who's brought happiness to total strangers and asks nothing for himself but to be surrounded by his few close friends." As she stepped into the elevator I called out, "I hope you get great big muscles in your legs!"

I watched the door slide closed and went back into the apartment. It was getting light outside. I washed my face, purposely using warm water so I wouldn't wake myself up. The lid of my bad eye was hanging one-third closed, the sure sign I was tired. I opened my bed, but I had no desire to get into it. I sat at the bar and looked at the Monopoly set, embarrassed by it and by the Shakespeare books—the traps I'd used to keep friends with me until I'd turned them into prisoners. I stuffed the money, the deeds, and the gold tokens into the box, gathered up the books and put them in the closet.

As my head touched the pillow it was as though I'd hit the lock on a giant Jack-in-the-Box which sprang open and out flew the clown, jeering, sneering, shattering the quiet of the room, razzing me with words and images that belonged in the past, but that I could only keep locked away through the warmth of an audience or the security of friends. My pillow was hot and I turned it. I tried to ignore the sounds, to concentrate on the good things: the audiences, the people at benefits looking at me with approval, as though color didn't matter, as though they didn't know there were such things as scandal magazines and gossip columns. I strained to remember, to nourish myself on their affection—but by memory, the hatred and anger was stronger, louder.

Eventually the first rays of the morning sun were streaming through the venetian blinds, casting shadows, like prison bars, on the walls of my room.

I sat behind my bar looking through the mail, autographing pictures, occasionally glancing up to see how George, Chita, and Michael were doing. The bell rang and Michael opened the door for Jane and Burt. I waved. "So the wandering journalists have returned home after another glittering night of gathering tomorrow's news today, eh?"

Jane slipped off her shoes and walked over to glance at herself in the mirror. George asked, "And where were Mr. and Mrs. Manhattan *this* evening?"

"The usual." Burt's voice came from the closet. "There was an opening at the Plaza . . . we looked into Morocco . . ."

"Don't knock it," George grumbled. "These four walls."

I listened to them talking, realizing that it had been weeks since we'd been anywhere except Danny's for dinner. It was always the benefits, maybe a drop-in at Barry Gray's show, then straight back to the apartment, to the island I'd created, to the few people I'd allowed to live on it with me—like a recluse, avoiding aggravation. Not only had I given up everything I'd come to New York for, but by doing so I was giving sanction to the idea that I had no right to it. It was frightening. I was the guy who comes home from the office and goes for a dip in the ocean, closing his eyes, luxuriating in feeling the tensions and pressures easing—unaware that he's drifting from shore, further and further . . .

"Burt."

"Yes, Sam?"

"What's it like at El Morocco?"

He thought about it for a moment. "I guess it's about the best place of its kind in town, probably in the world. It's gay, sophisticated type crowd, glamorous . . ."

"But you're never going to take me there, right?"

"Just say when."

"It's only one o'clock. Let's go tonight?"

Chita jumped up. "You really mean it, Sammy?"

"How long will it take you to get home and change your clothes?"

She rushed for her coat. "I'll be back in less than half an hour."

Michael was already out the door and ringing for the elevator.

When the door closed I told Burt, "Maybe you'd better make a reservation . . . tell them I'm in your party."

He dialed a number. I opened a window, got a camera and started making shots of the lighted buildings, appreciating the tripod which kept the camera steady, concentrating on the methodical clicks of the shutter that cracked across the room like gunshots until they were drowned out by the sound of Burt's voice, angry, pinched, straining to be calm, but vibrating with emotion. I glanced around quickly and saw the skin pulled tight around his jaw, the muscle in his cheek throbbing; Jane started going through her purse, George picked up a photography magazine which he'd already looked through earlier in the evening. I heard the phone being set slowly on the receiver.

"They don't want me, right?"

He sat down, stunned, his face totally drained of color, chalky. I walked over to him and gently pinched his cheeks. "Baby, it's okay to be white but you're overdoing it." I sat behind my bar. "Well, I went for broke and I got it." I looked at Burt. "Well, let's hear it, don't leave me in the dark. Oops. What do I mean by *that?*"

He was shaking his head slowly, staring at the phone, holding a cigarette in one hand and a lighter in the other, not moving to bring them together. He looked at me blankly. "It was unbelievable . . . he started to say they didn't have any tables but he didn't go through with that—he knew I'd know that's ridiculous at this hour. Then he said he wanted to speak to John Perona—he's the owner. I don't know if he actually did or not but he came back in a minute and said, 'We'd rather not.' I told him we weren't asking if they'd rather or not. Then he asked me what you looked like."

"What I look like?"

"He said . . . 'He's very black, isn't he?'"

"You're kidding!"

"I wish to God I were. Then he started copping-out by saying, 'I mean he's not light-skinned, I mean it's awfully dark, isn't it?' Then he asked me to hold the phone again and came back with a new idea. He said you've been in *Confidential* and the scandal magazines and that's the reason they don't want you—because they don't want to encourage people like that. . . . Sam, I should have mentioned a dozen of their steady customers who've been in those magazines, to say nothing of Bob Harrison who publishes *Confidential*— he's there almost every night . . ." His voice lost its momentum. "But I was so dazed I . . . I just hung up."

"Did they actually say, 'No. He can't come here'?"

"No. They know better. That's against the law. They just

said you're not welcome and that you won't be treated nicely if you appear there."

I ground my fist into my hand, drawing my fingers tightly over the knuckles, watching my skin changing color under the pressure, overwhelmed for the millionth time by the great goddamned difference people saw in it, disgusted by my incredibly naïve optimism that had survived so many moments like this and had, again, inexcusably, suckered me into going for the rare chance that maybe this time it would be different.

"Sam?"

I looked up. Burt's face was racked by the hurt and bewilderment of someone who'd always known fire was hot but now the first searing touch of it had shown him how hot it really is. He smiled grimly. "As he was saying you weren't welcome, just as I hung up—the dance band was playing 'Mr. Wonderful.'"

"Well, folks. It's a small world. Particularly if you're colored." I stood up. "Okay, let's forget it. It was a bad idea and it ain't gonna get any better with you guys giving me the June Allyson smiles." Nobody could think of anything to say. I looked around the room at Jane, Burt, and George. "At least you've got to admit this is the first funeral parlor you ever saw with TV, hi-fi, and booze." The doorbell rang.

George groaned. "Oh, God . . ."

Nobody was making a move for the door. I stood up. "Well, somebody's got to answer it."

Chita was framed in the doorway, dressed to the teeth, posing *Vogue* magazine-style. She yawned, "I left my *large* diamonds in the vault." Michael was behind her, all smiles.

I bowed them in. "This way, dear friends. Services will begin in a few minutes."

The strip of street lights that ran up and down Broadway went off, a second later they went off at Seventh, then Sixth, Fifth—as if somebody were running across town pulling switches. I sat in front of the window and sifted through a batch of newspaper clippings—the reading of the public pulse, the sum total of what I'd accomplished: fair, fair, lousy, rotten; judgments, indictments, jokes that didn't even pretend at good humor, pictures of me and white girls that had been taken at cast parties in complete innocence but were published dripping with innuendo. I looked at an item from the Negro press: "The Negro girls at Sammy Davis, Jr.'s dinner party at Danny's Hideaway last Tuesday were only there as cover-ups for the white woman who was really his date." My date had been Ruth King, an old friend and a top Negro model. But whoever had seen us, ten of us, had automatically assumed I was with a white woman. As if it was impossible I'd be with a Negro. It was only the ultimate in the same old story.

Billy Rowe's voice came over the phone, heavy with sleep. "Sammy? What's wrong? What time is it?"

"I don't know what time it is, Billy, and I only called to let you know you can stop working 'cause we ain't never gonna make it."

"What in the hell are you talking about?"

"Just my gorgeous image. It's set in their minds that my face is The Picture of Dorian Gray and there's nothing gonna change it. I don't even want you to try any more."

"Sammy, I don't understand, what happened?"

"Nothing happened, Billy. *Nothing*. You and Cliff did everything anybody could do but they don't wanta know any different than what they always knew and that's fine with me, 'cause from this moment on I'm living my life and they can report it any mothery way they see fit. I'm not coming to them on my knees any more; let 'em pour it on, let 'em tell the cat on the street what he wants to hear 'cause I don't care *what* he thinks any more. If he wants to take out his troubles on me then crazy, let him hang around uptown bitching about how I live and who I live with, but I've had it with apologizing and explaining myself and feeling guilty 'cause I made it. It's over.

"Baby, I want you to do just one thing for me: every time you meet a colored cat who works on a paper or a magazine and he's been rapping me I want you to tell him, 'I've got a message for you from Sammy!' Tell 'em they're creating their own monster. Ask 'em how come they don't want pictures of me when I'm with a beautiful girl like Harlean Harris or any other of the colored girls I'm dating. It's not copy, right? They wait till they see a picture of a white chick and they say, 'Who they got here with this chick? Sammy Davis?

Crazy!' They complain about it and they rap me for it, but that's really all they want because that's copy. Well, you make sure they know they're every bit as bad as the white cats who do it. Worse. When one of our guys who thinks he's fighting for equality starts belting me 'cause I live downtown—laugh in his face, Billy—tell that handkerchief-head he's cutting his own throat."

I hung up, hearing the sound of my own breathing, feeling my chest heaving, pumping the heat of my body up through my shirt collar. In the mirror behind the bar I saw my wet face, and beneath it a bronze plaque, and the words "Brotherhood," "For Humanity" . . .

. . . I was holding a bent, twisted piece of bronze, trying to focus on the long wooden splinter that was sticking into my thumb like a dagger. The wooden back of the plaque was smashed and the corner of the bar was broken.

The cab let me off at 125th and Seventh. The street was silent, still. Iron gates were drawn and locked across the store-fronts. A woman turned the corner and passed by without looking at me and I was grateful for the acceptance. I pulled the collar of my leather jacket close around my neck, put my hands into the pockets of my levis and started walking. I looked to my left and to my right at the empty sidewalk, concentrating, until I could see the kids falling in alongside of me, staring up at me, happy just to be walking with me, and I heard the words "You're Sammy Davis." A statement of fact. I kept walking, to the barbecue stand. I leaned my back against the locked door and closed my eyes, seeing the faces, hearing the questions . . . reaching for the past.

23

WHEN I GOT UP I CALLED GEORGE. "COME ON. LET'S go spend some money and *be* somebody."

"Sammy, I'm in the middle of a meeting."

Above: Fred Astaire and Ed Sullivan
Below: "The Summit" at The Sands, Las Vegas

My wedding to Loray White, 1959. Donald O'Connor, Harry Belafonte (my best man), Joe E. Lewis, Loray, Jack Entratter

Opposite:
Top: Sidney Poitier
Bottom: Peewee and my dad

As Sportin' Life in *Porgy and Bess*

Above: With Eartha Kitt in *Anna Lucasta*
Below: Sergeants Three

Doing Chaplin on the Nat Cole Show, NBC-TV

Opposite:
Above: Ocean's Eleven
Below: There was finally a Negro cowboy, and for luck in playing it, John Wayne gave me the hat he's worn in all his pictures. (In the playhouse at my home.)

Grant Lyons Studios, Ltd.

Above: Our wedding day. My father, my mother-in-law and father-in-law, Mr. and Mrs. Ernst Hugo Wilkens

Below: A few minutes before the ceremony. In the living room of my home. Peter, Frank, Rabbi William Kramer.

Gunnel von Essen

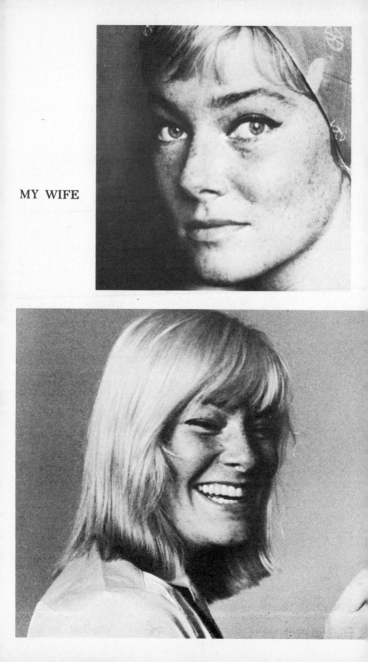

MY WIFE

photographs by
Sammy Davis, Jr.

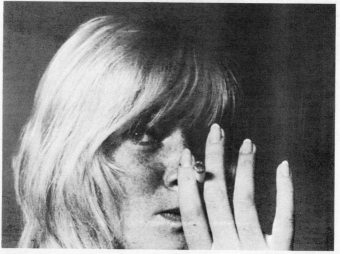

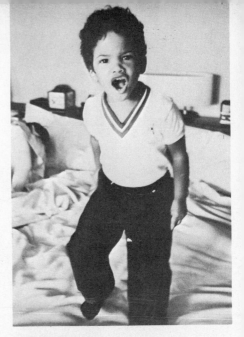

Our son,
Mark Sidney

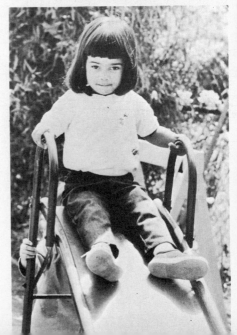

Our daughter,
Tracey Hillevi

photographs by
Sammy Davis, Jr.

Bengt Erwald

"Don't tell me your troubles, baby, 'cause I'm colored and I've got my own. Now, if you're not in the middle of this lobby in half an hour your star may get so upset he'll develop laryngitis."

As we walked across town I stopped at an antique-silver place and gazed through the window at a large silver goblet resting on a piece of red velvet. "Hey, George. Dig."

He shrugged. "I guess it's okay if you're Henry the Eighth."

"It's just right for Sammy the Second, too. C'mon in while I have them send it."

We walked to Madison Avenue, and at Lefcourt's I showed Lloyd, my salesman, the shoes I wanted to see. "In black and brown."

George murmured, "What do you mean by *that?*"

Lloyd, a Negro, shot a glance at him, but said nothing. When he left to get the shoes I looked at George. "Your face is so red I can't even see your lips."

He was frantic. "It slipped. I should apologize. Or would that make it worse?" He slumped into his seat.

"Baby, Lloyd's the peaceful type so you're lucky, but some of our guys are Mau Mau's: they cut first and ask questions later." He groaned. I leaned in close to his ear. "You keep making mistakes like that and someday you'll really put your foot in it and you'll hear somebody asking, 'Hey, man, cat got your tongue?' and then you gonna hear another voice, mean and angry, saying, 'Yeah, daddy, I got it right here.' "

When at least a dozen boxes of shoes were piled alongside me George said, "My God, isn't that enough? Even a train stops!"

"Baby, do you mind if I get a little pleasure out of life?" A crowd was forming outside the window, watching me. I swung the show into high gear. While Lloyd was trying a shoe on me another salesman was on the run for more styles. The crowd kept growing and so did the pile of shoes until I was almost hidden by the boxes.

We walked up Madison Avenue. George said, "I thought you were so broke."

"I ain't half as broke as I'm about to be. Now just up the street, with a little turn to the left and a turn to the right, we have A. Sulka and Company where you will see a truly creative man destroy himself. Then we follow the yellow brick road to Gucci."

George was almost punchy as we left there. "Six suitcases for like a hundred dollars apiece—and you're not even going anywhere, Sammy, I'll see you later. I really can't stand watching you in these stores. It's like letting Ray Milland loose in a distillery. You're doing *Lost Weekend,* but with money." He hesitated. "Look, I'm not trying to be staff psychiatrist, but whatever your reasons are you're only causing more trouble for yourself with all this."

"I know."

"You *know?*"

"I've been making big money for a long time, I'm not exactly drunk on the novelty of it. Baby, I know everything wrong that I ever do—and I don't need a psychiatrist to tell me why I keep doing it."

"But if you know it's wrong . . .?"

"I'm not looking to be right. I'm just looking to be happy."

He was shaking his head. "You're too smart to mean that."

We were at the corner of 52nd Street and I saw a song plugger I know get out of a cab and waltz into "21" like he owned the place—and I knew that no matter what I ever accomplished I could never hope to go into one of those places and feel like that. It was all so stupid, so unimportant—except for the fact that I knew I would never be able to understand, to really grasp it, and that after all these years of looking in a mirror and seeing a man, I finally had to accept that it might as well be a trick mirror. I half wished it were. I looked away. "I don't know, George. I'd like to be as wise as I am smart—but I just can't swing it."

Because we'd stopped walking, a few fans appeared and offered me pieces of paper to sign. One of them stared at George with curiosity. "Are you anybody?"

He scowled. "I'm a famous madam."

I steered him away, and we continued walking. After a while he said, "I guess it's none of my business, and I know it's not a Lucky Strike Extra to be colored, but if there are a few places and a few idiots . . . well, how can you let them bother *you?* I could understand if the average 'colored cat'—whatever *that* is—complains, but you're a big star, people stop you on the streets, you can go almost anywhere and wherever you *do* go you get treated better than most people ever hope to be treated." I didn't answer and he continued, uncertainly. "I mean you've got to admit that it *is* a lot better for *you.*"

"Yeah, baby, being a star has made it possible for me to get insulted in places where the average Negro could never *hope* to go and get insulted." I was surprised by the edge of bitterness in my voice, but I liked it. "Things are so beautiful for me that maybe by 1999 I'll even be able to rent an apartment in one of those buildings where they throw parties in my honor. But, all things being equal—and they never are—until then I'll keep reminding myself I'm a star in the only way I know. And if you're going to be a drag then go back to your meeting 'cause if I need a drag I'll call an agency."

We kept walking down Fifth Avenue, neither of us speaking for several blocks. As we reached Saks he looked at the windows and mumbled, "My God, when I think what a wardrobe I could have if only I were colored."

I laughed. "You're catching on. But baby: where would you wear it?"

After the show George came into the dressing room. "There are two limousines downstairs. One says he's supposed to take you to a benefit in Great Neck and the other one says you're supposed to be somewhere up in the Bronx." He was looking at me like: they're not *both* right?—*are* they?

"Tell the guy from Great Neck to follow us to the Bronx. He can wait for us and then take us to Great Neck."

"But this makes ten benefits this week." His voice had the sound of a man helplessly asking a friend: Do you realize you're drinking yourself to death? He was looking at me with compassion. "Sammy? This afternoon—all the money you spent—didn't it help?"

I laughed, to get it light, "It's like a Chinese dinner, baby."

As I put my feet on the jump-seat he gave me a vicious look. "Oh? Settling down for a long winter's rest?"

I loosened my collar. "Yes, said the little brown bear."

As I fell asleep he was muttering, "Where does he get all the energy?"

I finished the show in Great Neck, got back into the car and held the second plaque against my shirt sleeve. "George, do you think these are too big for cuff links?"

"Well! The little brown bear certainly revived himself."

"I guess *that's* where 'he gets the energy.' Driver, you can drop us in New York at the Harwyn, please. But don't drop us too hard because I'm pregnant."

George fell back against the seat. "The *Harwyn?* At this hour?"

"We've gotta swing by there for a quickie. I've got a few people meeting us."

George gaped at the twenty-foot-long table running down the center of the back room. "What did you do? Run a call for a general audition?"

"Baby, bear with me. They're just some kids from *Bells Are Ringing* and *Fair Lady.*" I sat down at the head of the table. After about thirty minutes, I spoke quietly to George, Michael, and Jane and Burt. "Let's split and go back to the apartment."

Burt said, "Sam, I think we're going to go home."

"Hey, it's only four o'clock . . ."

"Well, I've still got the column to do and we're getting up early tomorrow to be at the record session."

"Holy Toledo, baby, I'm not worrying about it and I'm the one who's got to sing."

Jane said, "Sammy, don't you think you should get some sleep, too?"

I gave her the withering stare. "No, Jane. I *don't* think I should get some sleep. But far be it from me to keep you guys up one second later than you want to be. See you at the session tomorrow." I turned to George and Michael. George said, "Well, it really wouldn't hurt you to get some sleep." Michael yawned and started to make an excuse but I cut him off. "Don't even bother. So the family's deserting me again. Okay, get your sleep. See you all when you have time for me."

I tapped my glass with a fork. "Drink up, everybody, and it's a definite move—the party over to the Gorham.

My eyes felt gritty, and my throat was tight. I finished the hot tea I'd sent out for and walked over to the mike in front of the window of the control room. Milt Gabler pressed his talk-back button and spoke into the studio. "Let's go for it this time, Sammy?"

A photographer who'd been shooting pictures for some magazine kept flashing the bulbs in front of me. I waved him away. I cleared my throat. The red light went on. The orchestra started playing and I waited for my cue, my right hand cupped behind my ear to catch the sound of my voice, hoping the tea had done it some good. But one cup of tea can't beat only three hours of sleep and I barely climbed in under the big note.

While the band ran through the next number I walked over to a bunch of the kids who'd been at the apartment the night before. "Sammy, that was fantastic. Beautiful." . . . "If that's not a hit then I never heard one." . . . "Great sound . . ."

"Thanks, kids. We'll see what the public wants to buy." I went over to the group. They all smiled at me.

"It was very nice."

"Don't strain yourself, Michael." George made one of those faces which says: I hated it but I don't want to hurt him so I'll look pleasant. I turned to Burt and Jane. Burt gave me a George Gilbert look.

"And what about *you*, Jane? What's *your* opinion?"

"Well . . . I've heard you sound better. You *are* tired and I could hear it in your voice."

"Everybody's a critic, right? Well, it's very strange that *you* didn't like my voice because the president of Decca Records is inside that control room and *he* didn't seem to mind it."

George murmured, "That's show biz."

I glared at him. "What's that, George?"

"I said, 'I'll have a gin fizz.' "

I called out to the other kids. "It's a definite one o'clock at Sam's place tonight."

Burt said, "Sam, you look kinda beat. Don't you think you oughta get some rest tonight?"

"Hey. I don't remember asking how I look. And I have no desire to get some rest."

I sat behind my bar watching all the action, digging the party sounds. One of the chicks from *Bells* was wearing levis and she had my twin holsters slung low on her hips. She wasn't trying to draw, she just dug walking around, flinging her butt out as she leaned her hands against the guns. One of the other chicks was on the phone rounding up some of her friends. The group was sitting at the bar like there was nothing going on around them.

Jane watched me pouring a coke into my silver goblet. She said, "What is *that?*"

"That, my dear lady, is my glass. I'm a star, and I don't drink out of the same sort of a glass that the common people use."

"Oh. Well, I'll settle for some ginger ale in a common glass." She walked behind the bar.

"Jane! Get out from behind my bar." She looked up, surprised. "That's right. Out out out! You can have anything you want, but just ask for it." I poured a glass of ginger ale for her.

George said, "That's his toy; you know you're not allowed to play with it."

I nodded, sipping from my goblet. "You can go to El Morocco; I sit behind my bar. Now, if my friends, the inner circle, are through finding fault with me . . ."

The door bell rang and George glanced vaguely over his shoulder at the throng of new arrivals. "Anyone you know?"

I looked away from him. "Michael, it's time for a little Stage. Order about forty roast beefs and corned beefs, will you, baby?"

He blinked. "You don't mean you're going to *feed* all these people?"

"Michael, please, just order the sandwiches, like a buddy? Don't give me any raised eyebrows, no 'Well, really!' Okay?"

George came over to me as I was doing gun tricks for a group of kids. He said, "Well, it's '30' for tonight. The Big Producer is going to sleep." Within fifteen minutes, he, Jane and Burt, Chita, and Michael had gone.

I sat behind the bar watching the chick with the holsters slithering toward me, smiling.

"Darling, whatever you're auditioning for—you're hired."

I skimmed through some fan magazines, then called Arthur Silber on the coast. "I didn't wake you, did I, baby? . . . Crazy. Listen, Arthur, I'll be back in L.A. soon and I don't have a swimming pool. Will you get moving on it for me? . . . Arthur, what in hell do I know about swimming pools? I don't plan to hold the Olympics in it, but on the other hand I don't want a bathtub. . . . Fine. And figure on a little cabana, too. You know, out-of-their-slacks-and-into-a-bikini, right? As a matter of fact you'd better make two dressing rooms with showers, one for the guys and one for the chicks. Y'know, baby, the more I think about it, we ought to make it like a Playhouse, a self-sufficient unit, so when I have parties I won't need to worry about the kids running all over the house bothering Mama. We could do a thing where the dressing rooms are at one end, y'dig, and the rest of it is one large room, as wide as you can make it and maybe thirty feet long so we could even show movies. . . . Arthur, what am I working for if I can't have a little joy out of life, the niceties. Now look, put a bedroom in there too, so in case it's late at night and I don't want to go back to the house I'll be all set. Or I can use it for a guest room. . . . Well, then build a second floor. Hey, that's wild. Put the bedroom over the dressing rooms, and make the main room studio-style—two stories high. And you'd better give me another bathroom upstairs so it's a complete suite. . . . Hey, let *me* worry about that, please! I'll get it from somewhere. As long as we're going to do this, let's do it right. You'd better get a pencil and write all this down: put in a slate floor and a bar with a refrigerator and all the jazz with maybe six comfortable stools, with backs and arms and leather padding, right? And you'd better use cork walls so if we're a little noisy we don't get heard all over the hills. And about the movie set-up: I want it so I can sit on a big curved couch in the center of the room, in a smoking jacket, press a button and zzzzzz a screen comes out of the ceiling; I press the next button and the lights go out; I press another button and the guy in the projection room starts showing the movie. And get two projectors, hooked up so we go directly from one reel to the next. I don't want one of those Mickey Mouse setups like when you're at a guy's home and you're watching a picture and you have to wait around for ten minutes between reels. And find the best sound system that we can wire into every room, including the three johns, and give them each their own volume control and turn-offs . . . You know the kind of stuff I dig. Make sure the johns all have full length heaters in the wall so when people get out of the shower it's not goose pimple time. . . . What's the difference? If you're gonna be a star be a star! And make sure the pool lights up at night."

When I hung up I beckoned to the chick with my holsters. "I dig you. What's your name?"

I woke up around noon, went to the kitchen for some tomato juice, and almost broke my neck on a high-heeled shoe some idiot had left behind. I opened the blinds. The sun spotlighted dozens of half-filled glasses with cigarette butts floating in them, used coffee cups and little pitchers of cream with wrinkled yellow skin on top. There was a scotch bottle on the floor under a stack of my record albums that had been strewn around like old newspapers, and everywhere I looked there were overflowing ashtrays and twisted pieces of bread. The place smelled like a garbage pail. I stood there looking at it all. It hadn't seemed that bad when I went to sleep.

Cliff called. "Sammy, have you seen the columns today?"

"What is it this time?"

"'Sammy Davis Jr.'s long unpaid bill at a midtown book shop now totals $1,460.' It's none of my business but—"

"Cliff, you're right, it isn't any of your business. I don't mean to be rude, but between Will Mastin and the Morris office I've got all the damned managers I need."

"Look, spend your money any way you like, but don't be surprised if a lot of this kind of item starts to break. I've been hearing it all over town for months. It's like a mark of distinction. People love to say 'Sammy Davis owes me . . .' "

We hung up. Once it started becoming public it would destroy the illusion, the atmosphere of a star.

I pulled a suitcase out of the closet and began opening the hundreds of bills I'd stuffed into it as they'd come in. I put all the dangerous ones in a pile and totaled them. The very least I needed would be about forty thousand. I called the Morris office and told them to set up Steve Allen and all the variety shows they could. Then I got busy on the phone with a few out-of-town clubs and lined up $25,000. I dialed the Copa and waited for Julie Podell. I was clean with him and borrowing money now would mean committing myself to play there in the spring, only a few months after we closed the show. After so much exposure on Broadway I'd planned not to play New York for a full year. But I had no choice. Better to have to fight to draw crowds than to have a lousy name to do it with.

The night man at the desk called out, "Mr. Davis, your father said to tell you to stop off at his apartment no matter what time you come in."

Peewee and the kids had gone to bed. He was sitting in the living room, wearing a bathrobe and slippers, waiting for me. There was an almost empty scotch bottle on the table next to him but he was cold sober. "Sit down, Poppa. I've got something to say."

"You okay, Dad?"

"I'm fine. Sit down."

I took off my coat and pulled up a chair.

"I'm leavin' the show, Sammy. I'm quittin' the act and I'm retiring." He looked straight at me. "Don't you think it's time, Poppa?" There was no sympathy seeking, no hidden hope that I would deny it—just the calm of a man offering the intimacy of honesty. "Poppa, I wish I could go to Will and tell him: Let's both quit, and we could do it right, maybe take an ad in *Variety* sayin' how we're puttin' you out on your own—that'd be good show business and I'd love to go out that way—but you know Will and you know he's got the same damned sickness I had all these years only he's got it worse: he's gotta be on, gotta see his name up." He paused. "Maybe when he sees me out of the act he'll get the idea and quit, too. But I know if I was to tell him I'm quitting, he wouldn't let me, he'd talk me out of it. So I've got it in my mind how I'll do it but it's best you don't know. Only reason I'm telling you is so no matter what you hears about me in the next coupla days, you don't worry . . ." While he was talking I noticed that the scrapbook of our press clippings he'd been keeping since we first went on tour with the Mickey Rooney show was open. He must have been going through it earlier in the evening.

He looked at me straight. "I hears the jokes about Will and me. And they're right. I knowed it the first time we opened Ciro's. I watched Will do his dance and then I did mine and I stood back thinkin' we was really somethin' else. Then I watched you and I saw what you was doing to the people and I knew we'd moved into a show business that was over my head, that I didn't have no right to be on the same stage with you, and I shoulda been happy sittin' out front or standin' backstage and lovin' you 'cause you was mine, instead of being in your way, makin' it harder for you."

He poured himself a drink, took it down straight, and slowly shook his head. "I just didn't have what it takes to quit, Poppa. I liked the fuss everybody was makin' over us and I liked the money and I figured well, I'll just hang on a little bit and enjoy bein' big for a while before I bow out. But the more I got of it the harder it was for me to walk away. You know what I mean?" I nodded. "The sun never fell on a day since then that I didn't tell myself 'Today's when I'll do it.' Then I'd think what it'd be like to be out of show business and on the side and I couldn't bring myself to do it. Then you had that song written and I let myself believe it was true—that we taught you all the things you do. Hell, if Will and me couldn't do 'em ourselves . . . well, I guess I wanted to fool myself, just like I wanted to believe the people likes seein' us still together. But deep down I always knowed it was wrong. . . ."

As he spoke, I could remember knowing it was wrong for us to remain a trio, but none of the reasons seemed important compared to the pain on his face, the longing he'd feel for our way of life, the finality of the exile to which he was sentencing himself. "Dad, maybe it isn't wrong. Who the hell knows? We're doing good . . ."

"Poppa, please. Leavin' show business is the toughest thing I ever done. Don't talk me out of it. I'm grateful you'd even try, like I'm grateful for a son that wouldn't push me out like most kids'd do. I ain't been much as a father. I shouldn't never have let you sign that contract with the Trio. I let you down there, and a hundred times since, so for God's sake let me do this much while I've got it to give. You know what I mean? It's all I can give you."

He got up and took something out of a drawer. "You know what these is, Poppa?" He was holding a pair of shoes on the palm of his hand. "The first shoes you ever wore to dance in." He sat down, smiling nostalgically. "It was back in '28 or '29, you was three years old and there was this amateur contest at the old Standard Theater in Philadelphia. . . ."

Two days later the newspapers reported that my father had suffered a mild heart attack and his doctor had ordered him to retire from show business.

A stage hand was centering cards on an easel and a cameraman was focusing on them: "Mike Wallace"—"Night Beat." I was sitting in what they'd started calling "the hot seat." I smiled back at him. You go right ahead and make it hot.

The commercial was over and he leaned into the camera. "A Negro . . . a Jew . . . the Peck's Bad Boy of show business . . . a man to whom any worthy charity can turn . . . probably the finest entertainer in all of show business. There appear to be many Sammy Davis, Jr.'s, all running at top speed twenty-four hours a day . . ." The camera swung over to me. "Sammy, in this past week, you've done eight performances of *Mr. Wonderful*, appeared at nine benefits, rehearsed and performed on the Steve Allen show, you've been on radio with several disc jockeys, you've entertained parties of from eight to twelve every night for dinner at Danny's Hideaway, and you've ended every night, or I should say morning, with gatherings at your apartment."

I smiled. "You've been checking up on me pretty good."

"We want to know the real Sammy Davis, Jr. but our research has turned up more questions than answers. I don't mean this facetiously, but don't you ever get tired?"

"Y'mean, 'Where does he get all the energy?'"

"I guess it *is* a cliché, but, where *do* you get it? What keeps you going? Is it the love of what you're doing or is it a desperation? Are you running toward—or away from something?"

"I think I'd better light a cigarette and stall a little before I try to answer that."

"All right, let's put it differently. You've already achieved more than most men ever hope for. You have fame, you earn a fortune, you wear fine clothes, drive the best cars, own a magnificent house—why can't you sit back and enjoy life? Why does Sammy Davis, Jr. remain a controversial figure?"

"First of all, I don't think of myself as a controversial figure—I know that I am but I don't *feel* controversial. I never woke up and thought: 'Today I'll shake 'em up. Let's see now . . . what convention should I defy?' I do what you just suggested: I try to sit back and enjoy the life I've been able to make for myself. Obviously that has to be done on my terms. I choose my own friends, live where I like, and do whatever I feel I have a right to do. Now, unfortunately there are people who disagree about what my rights are, so I become controversial."

"But you're not the only Negro who's ever been in the limelight, how is it the things *you* choose to do seem to become so public? Specifically, your dating of white women, your conversion to Judaism."

"Mike, I never yet went on radio or television and said 'Hi there, folks, I'm dating a white chick,' or 'Yoo-hoo out there in television land. Guess what? I just turned Jewish.' On the other hand I'm not going to go out of my way to hide what I do. I keep a book of the Talmud on my night table—I like to have it there. When friends come up I don't slip it under the pillow. They see it and I guess because it's me they mention it to other people. From time to time it's come up in an interview and I'm not about to say 'No comment' or tip the guy off in advance 'Let's not talk about that.' I'm no hero but I'll stand on what I do or I won't do it."

"But there are other Negro performers of major name value, why don't we hear jokes and slurs about *them?* What do you do that they don't do?"

"I think my problem lies not in what I do—but in my refusal to go out of my way to keep it quiet. There's noth-

ing I do that others haven't done before me and won't be
doing long after I'm gone, but I guess the difference is that
others have been more discreet. Perhaps they want the peace
of being left alone more than they yearn for the dignity of
knowing that they're doing what they feel like doing, like
all other free men."

"Sammy, is this determination to live your own life motivated by a desire to do so for the good of the rest of the
Negro people?"

"I wish I could say I live my life as a crusade, it would
be nice to get medals like 'He's a champion of his people.'
But, what I do is for me. Emotionally, I'm still hungry and
let's face it, paupers can't be philanthropists. I can't do anybody else much good until I get *me* straightened out. However, I know that my people will benefit from what I do,
because every time someone moves downtown—not just to
a hotel, but in all ways—he opens the door a little wider
for others to follow. I didn't suffer a lot of the humiliation
I might have because there were pioneers before me who
diluted the prejudice. Look what Jackie Robinson went
through as the first Negro pro-ball player. But he just dug
in and played harder. Now, I don't know who he was doing
it for but I do know that he made it a lot easier for guys
like Willie Mays to follow him. In my case, I'm totally
aware that if I break down a barrier, others will benefit,
and although I can't claim that as motivation, it certainly
gives meaning to some very unpleasant moments."

"To balance those unpleasant moments in the struggle
to be Sammy Davis, Jr., have there at least been rewards?"

"Definitely."

"Professionally?"

"Yes. I never went to school but I can stand in front of a
thousand people and just talk to them and make them
laugh, and that's something I couldn't do years ago and
wouldn't be able to do today unless I understood my audiences and could speak on their level of sophistication. I
don't have to rely on 'colored' or 'show business' topics to
get laughs. I can reach them because I understand them.
Naturally, as in all things, there's been a price attached to
it. I bought a knowledge of the rest of the world, not just

one segment, and I paid for it. I'm still paying and I suppose I always will."

"Sammy, despite your fame, do you also pay by feeling a certain amount of discrimination as you travel through what is predominately a white world?"

"I've had my moments."

"Even here in New York?"

"Mike, let's not kid ourselves that prejudice is geographic. Down South they lynch you and kill you—up North most Negroes die before they ever really lived at all. How much difference is there between preventing a man from earning the money to buy clothes, and ripping them off his back? Either way the result is he's standing there naked.

"If you steal a man's dignity, does it matter if you rob or embezzle it? The crime is the same—only the method is different. Down South they do it openly; the restaurant puts up a sign 'No colored people allowed.' Up here they use raised eyebrows to accomplish the same thing. You don't see many or *any* Negroes lunching or having dinner in ninety per cent of the good restaurants below 125th Street. And this isn't because all the colored people got together and said, 'Hey, let's boycott all the best restaurants and the best hotels in town.'"

"Could it be explained, at least partially, in terms of economics? Just the simple cost of going to these places?"

"Sure, for ninety-five per cent of the colored people that might be the answer. But what about the other five per cent, the guys who make the dough? When a Negro walks into a downtown restaurant, he's going to be watched, silently criticized—at best he's a curiosity. And when he's finished a hard day at the office he's not exactly dying to go through that jazz. It's almost like he'd call a buddy and say, 'Hey, let's get our wives and go downtown tonight and have a little indigestion.'"

"You mean assuming they'll be admitted in the first place."

"Right. So, the result is all them cats in Harlem cruise around in block-long Cadillacs complete with radio, TV, and kitchens, they wear diamond rings on every finger— and then the white cat rides through Harlem on the commuter special to Westchester shaking his head: 'I can't understand these colored people; they live in tenements like animals but you always see brand new cars parked out front.' How else can they spend it? They can drive it and they can wear it. Period. They'd prefer to eat balanced meals, but if the meat store is the only one open then they've got to make a whole meal out of steak. They can't go join a golf club and spend an afternoon shagging golf balls, or say to their wives 'Happy birthday, darling, let's celebrate, we'll catch the show at the Waldorf or the Plaza.' There's no 'Where do you feel like eating tonight?' They *know* where they can eat and it's not listed in *Cue* magazine. So they're buying all the things they shouldn't because they can't do half the things they should.

"Why does a man buy his wife a big diamond ring, Mike? Because it's beautiful and he loves her and he wants to make her happy. But, isn't it also because he wants to look at that ring on her finger and be able to feel that in her eyes and in the eyes of the world he made it, he belongs, he's somebody? But if every day of his life someone jumped up and told him 'You *don't* belong. You're *nobody*,' if every place he went he saw that he doesn't even cast a shadow—imagine how big a diamond he'd need."

He was looking at my clothes, at the gold cigarette case I'd just opened, then at my face. Leaning forward, his eyes probing mine, he seemed to have forgotten that we were on the air, and I caught a glimpse of a human being hooked on the contradiction between fact and reason, involved in it, feeling the frustration of it. He got a time signal from one of the floor men, and surfaced. "Sammy, one last question. I asked you earlier what it is you're looking for. Could it be summed up in one word: acceptance?"

"That's as good a word as any."

"You want people to like you."

"Yes, but that's the frosting on the cake. In its simplest form: I don't want people to *dis*like me before I've earned it."

24

I Poured A Coke Into My Silver Goblet And Watched a guy, his arm around a chick, swaggering toward my bar. As they reached me he gave her a little squeeze and bragged, "Here he is, Myrna. Did I tell you I'd introduce you to Sammy Davis, Jr.?"

She clutched my hand, pathetically sincere. "Oh, Mr. Davis, I'm . . ."

"Call him Sammy," he blustered, putting his hand gaudily on my shoulder, across the bar. "What's that Mr. Davis bit? He's my buddy." His other hand was crawling around her like a roach but she made no move to stop him. He winked at me and I was tempted to louse up his plans for the evening by saying, "Good to see you again . . . uh, what's your name?"

My father was easing his way through the crowd, carrying a platter with some wax paper covering it. "Here's some stuff Peewee cooked up for you. I'll put it in the icebox." He went into the kitchen and I heard the refrigerator door open and close. Then he was standing near me, surveying the room, trying not to let the disapproval show on his face.

"Have a drink, Dad?" He nodded and I poured him some scotch.

"Can I talk to you a minute, Sammy?"

I followed him into the kitchen. "What's the matter?"

"Well . . . I guess it's nothing, it's just I'm your father and I don't feel good seein' you comin' apart like this."

"Coming apart? Where the *hell* do you get that kind of an idea?"

"Ain't you? You looks terrible, you're blowing your voice

388

doin' too many benefits, you're blowin' your money on garbage like you got out there . . ."

I closed the kitchen door. "Hey, wait a minute. If I feel like having some friends in . . ."

"Friends? That crowd out there ain't nothin' to you. Hell, I betcha you can't tell me half their names. And they don't care none about you 'cept to eat your food and drink your whiskey and be around you 'cause you're big. George, Morty, Jane and Burt, Michael—maybe *they* cared some about you but you chased 'em away." He looked past me. "Why should they mix with what you got hangin' around you now?"

"Hold it. I didn't chase anybody anywhere."

"Then how come they ain't around no more, Poppa?"

"They've got their own lives. I see them but do I have to have them living with me?" He smiled sadly at having won the point. "Look, Dad, I don't need to be told how to run my life."

"The hell you don't." We stood there glaring at each other. "Poppa, I know you don't like bein' told nothin', but I just wish you didn't need all them people around you all the time."

"I don't want to talk about it any more. If I can't have some people over after I finish working and doing benefits and doing Barry Gray, without you deciding I *need* them like I'm some kind of a mental case . . ."

When he'd gone I sat down behind my bar and scanned the room. I knew *less* than half their names. I glanced from face to face. I feel nothing for them—I don't even want to talk to them—but I want them here. Somebody I didn't know was shaking my hand. "Sammy, I've got to tell you, baby, you're the greatest! I mean you're *it*, man, y'know what I mean? I've seen performers in my life, I've seen 'em all but you're the greatest, I mean the greatest . . ." I smiled, not thanking him because I didn't want him to stop. ". . . probably sound like an LP or something but I mean it, you're the greatest!" When he'd run out of words the party sounds came surging back, harsh and vacuous, and I gazed around the room, mesmerized by the scene: hoards of people swarming over my apartment, sprawled over my chairs, dropping ashes on the floor, handling my records, my books . . . I watched two girls sauntering into my bathroom like it was a public john in a hotel lobby. I was spending money I didn't have on people I didn't care about, I was hooked on them, like a junky, loathing them and the need for them, yet needing more and more of them all the time.

I tried to remember the last time the group had been up. It had been weeks. Yet how could I blame them? I picked up the phone and spoke to the night man at the desk. "Ring Mr. Gilbert's apartment for me, will you?"

"Mr. Davis . . ." He was hesitating. "I talked to him about an hour ago and he said he was going to sleep then."

"Ring him lightly. It's okay."

I heard the buzz, then the receiver being fumbled with. I held my hand over the mouthpiece, muffling the noise around me. George cleared his throat. "H'lo?" His voice was groggy.

"You sleeping, baby?"

"Sammy?"

"It's your very own star. Listen, I'm sorry if I woke you. Go back to sleep—unless you feel like a little drink or something."

There was a pause, he was listening. He said, "It sounds like you've got the American Legion up there. I think I'll go back to sleep . . ."

"It's just a few people. But okay . . . catch you around the theater."

A guy named Dick had sat down across the bar from me. He waved his hand in front of him clearing away the clouds of smoke, then opened a window and came back smiling. "Not that it'll help." He looked at me curiously. "Do you *ever* get any fresh air?"

"Sure. I had some once."

"I'm serious." He leaned forward. "Listen, one afternoon next week why don't we drive out to the country, up to Westchester. I'll put the top down, you'll breathe in some clean air, you'll look at the trees. I know a duck pond where we can sit and look at the ducks, it's better than a psychiatrist. We can stop off and have a quiet dinner at my brother's place—he's got a little restaurant up there—and be back in town by eight o'clock."

He was reaching out to be nice and I hated to tell him I wasn't especially interested in sitting around looking at some ducks. He was the only person in this whole crowd who'd shown the courtesy to bring up a few bottles of scotch and I remembered appreciating the gesture.

"Baby, I sleep late; could we make it around four o'clock some day?"

"Sure. And we don't have to overdo it with the back-to-nature bit. Just one lungful." He smiled, pleased. "It'll do you a world of good. I'll call you and we'll set a day."

I moved around the room emptying ashtrays and putting used glasses in the sink. I can stand these people as long as they're here but when they're gone I don't want to be reminded of them. I noticed one of the chicks helping me, bringing glasses into the kitchen. I knew her name was Betsy and she was with one of the new musicals. She was young and small and she had a gorgeous body. She was starting to wash some of the glasses. I turned off the faucet. "Thanks Bets, but the maid'll do it in the morning."

She wiped her hands, smiling. "I've been here three times and this is the first time I've ever spoken to you."

I laughed. "It does get kinda hectic." She made a face, her eyes looking up.

"One of these nights," she said, "well, I live alone, and if you'd like I could give you my phone number and if you ever feel like talking, I mean if you're not too busy . . ."

I glanced at her fantastic build but I felt cheap, lecherous; she was just a star-struck kid, naïve and wholesome. She was looking at the floor, blushing, and I enjoyed the flattery of the whole scene that was like out of an Andy Hardy picture. I took the piece of paper she was secretively offering and I smiled, college-hero-to-the-coed, "Thanks, Bets. That's a great idea. Love to sometime."

There was a commotion over by the couch. A couple of chicks were arguing. I'd been a little interested in one of them but now, maybe because she was drunk, she'd forgotten to hold in her stomach and her slacks looked too tight. She saw me looking and walked over. "Sammy, you settle it, willya? Who's got a better chest, I or Rhoda?" She was pushing her chest out at me, just another cow in a whole stockyard, but grinning, smug, like "Here's a thrill for you." The crudeness of it brought the rest of the room back into true focus—the faces without names, the loud laughter, impersonal as street sounds, crashing around me like empty tin cans

—it was the same scene I'd been watching for weeks and suddenly I couldn't define which night it was and I had to restrain myself from yelling, "Out. Everybody out. Please . . . go away!"

Dick was waiting in front of the Gorham. He saw me coming down the street and hurried toward me, smiling. "I was afraid you forgot. I called upstairs but the operator said you were out."

"I never forget." I smiled. "I was over at Decca, baby."

The car wound steadily up the parkway through Westchester and I sat back against the seat wrapped up in a furry blanket. It was new and I had a feeling he'd bought it for this occasion. I bundled my coat and scarf tightly around my neck, enjoying the warmth of the heater on my feet, and the cool, crisp air streaming in through the open top of the convertible. Dick glanced up from the road and smiled and I appreciated not having to talk, not having to be on. A car horn was honking repeatedly; a little boy was waving out the window. I waved back, pleased at realizing that I hadn't been looking for anyone to recognize me. I wrapped the blanket tighter around me and closed my eyes, lulled into a delightful feeling of well-being.

The car was slowing down and turning off the parkway. "You getting a little hungry, Sam?"

"Whatever you like, baby."

He drove through a small town and stopped in front of a restaurant. There was a sign in the window: "Sammy Davis, Jr. Day."

Dick smiled, embarrassed. "That's my brother for you. You know how it is, he's proud that I know a celebrity." He looked at me anxiously. "I hope you don't mind all the people."

As the crowd swarmed around me from every direction, from tables, from the bar that was packed three deep, I saw a man taking down a poster—not quite fast enough: "Admission $5.00 per person." He stashed it in a corner, face against the wall, and pushed his way through the crowd. "Sammy, I'm Dick's brother. Welcome." He was pumping my hand. "When Dick told me he'd get you to come up I thought he was crazy! But he's some kid, that brother of mine, huh?

He's nuts about *you*. Come on, we've got a seat waiting for you over here with the family . . . it's beautiful of you to do this for us."

George leaned against the wall of my dressing room. "We're going to gross $59,000 this week." He dropped the words like a jeweler spreading diamonds on velvet. "The word is all over town that you've single-handedly beaten the critics."

I let myself sink back against the chair, floating on the pleasure of the moment. "We did it. We really goddamned did it." The countless interviews, the television shows, radio shows, the handshaking, the appearances at parties and clubs, the month after month of pushing uphill—all the strain of it was washed away in that one glorious moment.

"Can you appreciate what this means? It's like *for the first time!* You've really made Broadway history." He sat down, smiling. "When you said that you were going to beat the notices . . ."

"Yeah . . . remember that night? God, they really knocked the wind out of us, didn't they?"

He nodded and we sat in silence, remembering that night and all the nights that had brought us to this moment.

"Hey, look, I've got no benefits tonight. I'm clear. Whattya say we get Chita and Michael—we'll find Jane and Burt and we'll go some place and celebrate. I'll have the elevator guy at the hotel get rid of everybody. We'll really make a night out of it."

"Michael's already left with some people. And I know that Chita's got some boy she's going with . . ."

"Well, how about you? We can take a walk down Broadway. Look, I know it's corny but I just feel like doing it."

"Well, I have . . . wait a minute, maybe I can cancel an appointment I've got . . ."

"Never mind, baby. Look, it's not such a big deal."

"Sammy, I . . ."

"Hey, we're grown men, right?" I started putting on my shoes. "Look, if it could've worked out it would have been pleasant but it's not life and death."

I took extra long signing autographs at the stage door, doing bits with the people until I was afraid they'd begin to notice that I was giving them too much attention. On Broadway I saw Hal Loman and his wife Barbara standing in front of our theater holding hands and staring up at his name on the marquee. When they saw me watching them they blushed like tomatoes. I shook my head. "Of all the corny things I have *ever* seen: two grown people, pros, stand in front of a marquee with gaping and staring and holding hands? Now let's be honest, I mean you don't think maybe you're just a wee bit sickening about it? And you could at *least* stop holding hands while I'm talking to you!" I grinned and gave Hal a shot on the arm. "You two are beautiful. Hang onto what you've got." As I watched them walking away holding hands again, and as I stood there under my own name twenty times bigger, I got a creepy feeling that I personified the lonely star cliché: "his name in lights but nobody to look at it with." I hurried away from there, toward the Gorham. I stopped. I couldn't face that crowd, not this early. I turned and headed downtown. At least I could kill a few hours at a movie.

"We can up the year's gross by $30,000, if you'll accept this Miami offer . . ." Sam Bramson sat across the table from me and Will in the board room of the Morris office, holding a sheet of yellow, lined paper with penciled-in dates, names of clubs and figures, plans for after the show closed. His voice was tentative. "They've agreed to a beautiful suite . . ."

"What about letting colored people in to see the show?"

He looked down at the paper, avoiding my face. "Well, that's the only problem, Sammy. It's not that they don't want to go along with you but the custom down there . . ."

"The custom stinks. We've been through this before, Sam. I don't play to segregated audiences."

Will nodded. "That says it for me, too."

Sam held up his hands. "I'm with you a hundred per cent. I'm just telling you what the offer was. Now, Julie Podell says you've agreed to go in there in the spring."

Will grunted disgustedly. "Sammy, the dumbest thing you could've done was to go borrowing money from Julie Podell and committing us to play for him this spring. That's hardly three months from now. Who's going to come and see us?"

"I know, Massey."

"We shoulda stayed away for a year. Six or eight months at least. Here we're gettin' offered the best money from clubs that we've ever got—and I credit the show with that— but what good is it if we can't cash in? If Julie Podell'd had to come to us, we could've sat down and set a new price with him just like we're doing with everybody else—not countin' those clubs you used for banks."

"Massey, I've already said you're right. Can we forget it, please? It's done and it'll work out."

"Maybe it will and maybe it won't. Either way it's time you stopped leaning on your talent and used your head."

I stared at his indignant, angry face. "Yeah, Massey. You're right. I really should use my head."

One of the Morris guys said, "Sammy, the fact is, your uncle is right. But it's not just borrowing money, it's a lot of things. I don't know if you're aware of it but the publicity you've been getting, well it hasn't been good. You really ought to do something about it. For your own good . . ."

Another chimed in. "And it was a terrible mistake to overexpose yourself on television . . ."

Will nodded, annoyed, grumbling. "That's right. Here we waited out this whole dead year, but instead of lettin' them build up interest from not seein' us you've been jumping into their living rooms every couple of weeks."

"Hold it, Massey. I was just being told my publicity was bad. Do you think it's a good idea for people to read I owe this one and that one? Now, how did you expect me to get the money to pay off?"

"Sammy," another Morris guy was speaking gently, pacifying, "we can certainly understand your personal money problems, but you haven't done the over-all picture any good."

"Another thing you've got to stop doing . . ."

I didn't look up or even bother trying to associate the voice with any of the faces surrounding me at the table. I stared out the window, hearing them planning where I'd work, when my voice would need a day off, how long it would take them to ship me from Pittsburgh to Detroit—figuring the best things to do about me: how to package me and sell me so everybody'd get the most out of me. They were feeding on me —hacking away at me—cutting me up like a goddammed melon, carving their slices and telling the melon it was for his own good.

What would it be like if I just disappeared, ran away from them all . . . a runaway melon? At least I don't have to sit here and listen to it.

As I closed the door behind me their conversation continued, unbroken. They hadn't even noticed I'd left.

I wandered over to the Stage Delicatessen, pushed a door marked "Pull" and sat down at a table.

Jack E. Leonard came over. "Hello, Sammy. I didn't recognize you all by yourself." I smiled, not enjoying the joke, and asked him to join me. He became serious. "Your old man's okay now, isn't he?"

"He's fine, Jack. Thanks for the flowers you sent him."

He nodded, then shrugged slightly. "Things work out. What the hell, let's be honest, it's time you were doing a single."

"Well, it's not exactly a single. Will's staying with the act."

He looked up. "You mean, just you and him?" I nodded. "But it's still the 'Will Mastin Trio'?" he asked knowingly. I nodded. "I see." He gazed into his coffee cup. "Well, that's a very interesting Trio, Sammy: you, your uncle, and your talent." He shrugged. "Who the hell knows? Like they say: the *Saturday Evening Post* comes out on Wednesday and they're doing okay."

I'd been so tired, so glad to see everybody leave, but now I wished I'd told one of the chicks to stick around. I tried to think of which one I should have kept but I couldn't remember any of their faces. They'd all evaporated into air like the laughs, leaving nothing behind.

I looked through a drawer in the kitchen and found the slip of paper that kid Betsy had given me, and propped it against the phone. Why couldn't I call her and have her come up, just for company, or take her for a walk—the city's beautiful at this hour.

Her voice sounded sleepy and I'd have hung up but I didn't want to frighten her. "Betsy, this is Sammy."

"Sammy who?"

"Sammy Davis, Jr." I could all but see her: sitting up, smiling. . . .

I opened the door and she walked past me into the apartment.

"Hey, I told you I'd meet you downstairs. What if I'd had some chick up here?"

She smiled. "Then you wouldn't have called me, would you?" I took a windbreaker from the closet. "Sammy, it's much too cold for walking." She opened her coat. She was wearing nothing but a bra and pants.

"You're out of your mind. Now stop being silly and cover yourself up." She'd dropped the coat to the floor. I picked it up and put it around her shoulders. "Thank you very much, I appreciate the gesture, but you're not the type for this kind of jazz." She stood helpless and vulnerable, the coat hanging from her shoulders, gazing at me blankly. "Now, listen, Bets, I didn't mean to hurt your feelings, you're a gorgeous kid and I dig looking at you, I like it better than golf—it's taking every ounce of strength I've got to stay away from you—but you don't have to impress me that you're a swinger. Now, be nice. You're young, you've got a lot of living ahead of you . . ."

She tossed off the coat. "Sammy, I voted last year. And I'm not sorry for anything I've ever done. Now, may I have a drink? Scotch and water, please."

I mixed it for her and stayed behind the bar. She sat across from me, caught a look at herself in the mirror behind the bar, and smiled, satisfied, then raised her glass. "Well, here we are."

I smiled, looking straight at her face so as not to encourage her by letting her see me enjoying the sight of her body.

She asked, "You won't be in New York much longer, will you?"

"Just another month or so."

"You can play any club you want to, can't you?"

"Yes."

"I read in *Variety* that you signed a million dollar contract with the Sands in Las Vegas. They must want you pretty badly."

"Well, if you read the story you saw that it's over a period of five years. . . ."

She finished her drink, came behind the bar, stood in front of me and put her hands on my shoulders, flexing her body, posing, inviting. "Sammy? I'd just love to work in the line at the Sands: the girls make great money out there; if you even mentioned my name to Jack Entratter I'll bet he'd give me a job. I'll never get anywhere on Broadway; I know I haven't got any talent. But I've got the looks for Vegas, haven't I?" She stepped closer and put her arms around my neck.

At least when a drunk gets rolled he has an excuse.

As I turned away from her I saw my face in the mirror: the nose, the scars, the dead eye, the features jammed together—it looked so vastly different than I had felt.

I tore my gaze away and was confronted by her face again, the looking glass in front of which I'd primped and pranced, gorging myself on the joy of playing Sir Galahad, Lancelot, and Walter Raleigh, all rolled into one big clown.

I lifted her arms off my neck, walked past her, out from behind the bar, and dropped her coat over her arm.

She looked at it as if it belonged to somebody else. "You don't want me?"

"Some other time. I'll take care of Vegas." I walked to the door.

"You're mad at me."

"Darling, I love sirloin steaks but I don't have to consume every one in America. I'm tired. It *is* seven o'clock in the morning, right?"

She put on her coat and closed it around her, smiling like she'd made the phone call and gotten her dime back, too. "Okay, but whenever you're in the mood I'll be available. Aren't you going to take me home?"

"I never take anybody home. Here's twenty for a cab. I'll let you know about Vegas."

The door closed softly behind her.

I poured a coke and watched the foam rise above the edges of the silver goblet, hang in mid-air, then run down the sides and form a puddle on the bar. I touched my finger to it and wrote "Sammy Davis, Jr." on the bar top. I sat there staring at it. It no longer seemed like the name of a person.

I could see the chick's underpants outlined against her slacks as she walked toward me and plunked herself down on my lap. "What's wrong with poor Sammy?" She cooed,

"Such a long face. Everybody's having a good time except him, and it's his party."

"Darling, why don't you get yourself another drink? You're wrinkling my suit."

She stood up, pouting, playing it hurt. "I was only trying to be friendly."

"There's a time and place for everything." I glanced at my watch. "For you the time will be five-thirty sharp. That's when I want you ringing my doorbell. Go out and have a cup of coffee while I clear the room."

She blinked, stupidly. "But the party's just getting started . . ."

"That's right, and it's in my honor. Now if you don't want to play the home team's rules—there's the door."

"Well . . ." she stalled, "you could at least be a little bit of a gentleman about it."

"I don't *have* to be a gentleman. I'll see you at five-thirty."

"Well, I don't know . . . we'll see." She was trying to gather her dignity.

I laughed. "You ain't never gonna find it."

"Huh?" She blinked. "Find what, Sammy?"

"Skip it." I tapped my watch. "Five-thirty."

I pulled a fall-asleep on the couch and got rid of everybody. I checked my watch against the *Times* clock. In twenty-five minutes the doorbell would ring and a woman would arrive to go to bed with my name. She'd smile and say, "I decided to give you another chance even if you are awful." But as she took off her clothes she'd be telling me. "You can have anything you want because you're a star. You insulted me but here I am anyway. It doesn't matter what you do, how you act, because it isn't you I care about at all, it's Sammy Davis, Jr."

I set a stack of my own albums on the record player. I put on a silk robe with a large "SD Jr." monogrammed across the breast pocket. Then I walked behind the bar and faced myself in the mirror; I ran my finger slowly along the scar which circled the bridge of my nose, I touched the eyelid that was drooping like a dope addict's. "You're ugly. You've got nothing going for you except your talent and the fact that you're a star. You didn't see any chicks running after you when you were hungry and you haven't gotten better

looking since then. They want to hang around you because
you're a star and they dig being around success. That's all
they care about. So take what you want without ever looking
back. They're getting theirs and you don't owe them nothing!
Just never kid yourself why they're here. Say it every day:
you're *ugly*."

I sat down at the bar, propped my watch against an ashtray and watched the sweep second hand wiping the minutes
away. At exactly six seconds after 5:29 I heard the elevator
door slide open at my floor, and the bell ring. I looked in the
mirror. "You see?" I poured a coke and the bell rang
again, timidly. I took a long slug of my drink, holding the
goblet in the air, savoring the nectar of arrogance. I saw my
reflection in the silver, staring back at me, the smile twisted
and broken by the design of the goblet. I stood up and took
my time walking to the door.

As I passed through the bar at Danny's, Jack E. Leonard
nodded toward the other room, "Your *team* is waiting in
there for you."

I made my entrance and sat down at the head of my table.
The guy who had the seat next to mine looked at his watch.
"Sammy . . . we've been waiting an hour." He softened it
with a nervous laugh.

"Baby, I'm not the Pennsylvania Railroad. I don't run on a
schedule."

He panicked. "Gee, don't get me wrong, Sammy. I was
just worried you wouldn't have time for your dinner. I mean,
I know you need time to digest it before you go on . . ."

Pete came over and I said, "I'll start with some scampi,
then a sirloin—with spaghetti on the side in honor of the
fact that you're Italian." I stood up. "Excuse me, everybody."

Marty Mills was at another table.

"Where've you been, Marty? How come I don't see you
anymore?"

"I've been around but you're kinda busy . . ."

"Hey, don't give me that jazz. We go back a few years, remember?"

"*I* remember."

"Come on, Marty, don't do hurt bits with me. You know
how busy I am with the show and the interviews and with

record sessions, but you could've picked up a phone and called me."

"I've called you, Sammy."

"I swear I never got the message."

"Well, what's the difference? You've got a million guys around you all the time, you're a big star now . . ."

I walked around the restaurant looking for anyone else I knew, table-hopping until my food was on the table. Across the room Marty was talking to his friends as though he didn't know I was there, like he'd crossed me off. I called Pete over. "Baby, put Marty Mills' party on my tab. When he asks for his check tell him 'X-2 took care of it.'"

The scampi smelled good but I didn't feel like eating. The guy next to me said, "What's wrong, Sam?" He was wearing expression #17: Sincerely Concerned. "Everything okay?" The guy next to him nudged him and whispered, "Anything wrong?" The first guy made a worried face. "He seems a little down." Then they both looked at me, Concerned, and it moved down the length of the table like a row of swimmers peeling off into a pool. I was glum, so they looked glum. I smiled. They smiled. They're a bunch of idiots. I went from face to face, playing the friendship game: this "friend" figures if he hangs around I'll leave the Morris office and let him bring me over to his agency; this friend wants me to record his songs; now, what the hell is *this* friend's angle? He just digs being around "names," for his social position and his sex life; this friend's been bugging me to do that benefit way the hell out in New Jersey so he can be big with his in-laws. . . .

But do they have to lay it on so thick? Where's their flair? How about a little artistry?

As my glance swept the table they grinned, winked, and smiled at me. I signed the check and stood up. "Well, friends, I've gotta go meet the public, catch you all at the apartment later."

I began putting on my make-up. Charley Head was packing the things I wouldn't be using again, putting a year of my life into boxes. George came in and looked around the dressing room at the stack of telegrams, the flowers, the table of little gifts from the kids, and the *World-Telegram* that was opened to our "Last Performance" ad. He leaned against the wall and spoke to my reflection in the mirror. "I hear some of the brokers were getting a hundred dollars a pair for tonight."

"That's a pretty nice send-off for the unwanted child." There was a silence in the room. I looked up. "You're coming to the Harwyn, aren't you?"

He seemed hurt as he said of course he was and I was sorry I'd asked, but I'd wanted to be sure.

He smiled nostalgically. "I'll have to hire someone to call me in the middle of the night and wake me up."

"You're not going to change, are you, George?"

He stared at the floor. "I'm rotten to the core."

As I waited in the wings to go on for the last scene, to close the show, there was a gasp of surprise from the audience and I looked onto the stage. The Palm Club set was packed with tables of celebrities, stars of other Broadway shows and of every important nightclub in town. Walter Winchell was seated at "ringside," next to him were Judy Holliday and Sydney Chaplin, Jerry Lewis, Tony Bennett, Shelley Winters. George, dressed in the headwaiter costume, was ushering a customer to a table: Jule Styne, wearing Ruth Dubonnet's mink coat.

In the middle of my act the entire choruses of *Fair Lady*, *Li'l Abner* and *Bells Are Ringing* arrived from their theaters and seated themselves on the stage; Edward G. Robinson who was appearing in *Middle of the Night* down the street walked on with his cigar, the slouch hat, his hand in his pocket, Little Caesar style. He took the mike out of my hand, cased the stage. "Kid, you're making a big mistake, see? Y'got a good setup here, see? Lotsa dames. Of course we got dames over at my place but they're all old married dames." Jerry Lewis sprang from his seat and began dancing around the stage, still wearing his make-up from the Palace where he was doing his first "single." It was the hottest ticket in town, the talk of the city. I waved. "Hi'ya Jer. What're *you* doing in town?"

It got a laugh. He gave me a smug look. "I just finished my show at the Palace. And Sam," he paused for emphasis, "*I'm* not *closing!*"

The audience screamed and he did his strut around the

stage heckling everybody. I could ad-lib with Jerry because he could hit back. I folded my arms, Jack Benny style, and watched him with mock impatience while I was looking for the right line. My father had come back to the show for closing night and he and Will were in their usual places. I motioned toward them, "Jer, I've still got *my* partners."

Shelley Winters got up from a table and took the mike. "Ladies and gentlemen, all these people sitting up here came over after doing their own shows to pay tribute to a great performer and it's been a lot of fun but you'll have to excuse me for adding a serious note because there's something that should be said. Sammy made something important happen on this stage for the past year. *Mr. Wonderful* is more than just a hit show. It's the first show in which both Negro and white performers worked together on the same stage and after five minutes nobody cared or even noticed the difference."

As I finished my closing number—row by row, like waves popping up on an ocean, sixteen hundred people stood, applauding. The cast gathered around me, we took twelve bows, and the audience was still applauding and shouting "Bravo" as the curtain fell on *Mr. Wonderful* for the last time.

"You really did it, Sammy." ". . . fantastic personal triumph." ". . . tremendous accomplishment!" ". . . you really made it." I moved from table to table through the Harwyn, which I'd taken over for my closing night party. From person to person the words hardly changed as the people kept smiling, patting me on the back, asking me to sit with them —showing and telling me in every way they could that I'd made it. But I couldn't feel it. "How about *The New York Times*, Sammy? They buried you a year ago but they finally had to list you under 'Hit Shows,' right? Beautiful." I smiled and nodded, wishing I could feel something more than an empty satisfaction at having done what I'd said I'd do, wishing I could feel the kind of exhilaration I knew should be the payoff for making a show run for a year. "What a night, Sammy! Those names on the stage, I never saw anything like it. What a closing!" A waiter walked by with a bucket of champagne, the orchestra played "Mr. Wonderful" again and everybody turned to me, applauding, as they had when I'd walked in. I smiled back at them, seeing them all celebrating, happy for me, and I kept moving around the room trying to feel some of the excitement, too. They stopped me at every table to tell me I'd made it but the words wouldn't fill me up, they kept running out, leaving me hollow. The higher the hilarity rose the more impossible it seemed for me to reach it. I kept moving, playing host, trying to soak it up and feel it as everybody else could, trying to open myself to it, hoping that if I heard it over and over again it would numb the doubt, and the joy of the evening would flow into me too, and I'd be able to taste what they were all telling me was mine. . . .

Jane and Burt were getting up from my table to dance. I spoke quietly. "Let's go to El Morocco."

"*Now?* In the middle of your own party?"

"Just for a little while, then we'll come back. Will you take me?"

I told our chauffeur, "El Morocco," and I sat back in the seat. Here we go, daddy. It's either the frosting on the cake or a pie in the face.

We were approaching the blue and white awning I'd passed so many times, and the doorman, dressed like a guy from the French Foreign Legion, symbolizing the gaiety inside. Burt, Jane, and I did a wordless grasping of hands. The doorman opened our car door, we stepped out and went through the revolving door.

Two headwaiters stood at the entrance to what seemed to be the main room. Burt smiled pleasantly. "Good evening, Joe, Angelo. We're three tonight."

They didn't look at me but at Burt, and there was a wordless, momentary pause, a vacant look in the eyes of the two men, a look conveying the hurt of betrayal.

"This way, please."

Time and sophistication had refined the moment. At another time, another place, it might have been "I'm sorry, do you have a reservation?" At still another time and place it might have been "Colored people can't come in here." Or it could have been more brutal.

It was a hollow voice saying, "This way, please," offering no welcoming warmth—but at least the words were right. At least they hadn't embarrassed me, and I was walking to a table at El Morocco.

The motion with which the room was alive seemed to veer and change course and accelerate into a more frenetic kind of action; heads were spinning as if they were tops and my entrance had just pulled the strings. I walked behind Burt, looking straight ahead, but seeing the nudging and leaning, the blinking and staring, the simple surprise at the presence of someone with my color skin who wasn't wearing a turban. Then smiles began breaking out here and there like beacons across a dark field and I got little four-finger waves, and a "Hi, Sammy" murmured discreetly as I passed a table of six. I looked to see if I knew the man who'd said it but they were all strangers. I kept walking, experiencing an awareness of myself that I'd never felt before an audience of five thousand people. As the maître d' led us past the dance floor, the people swayed back and forth, keeping the franchise of being there, maneuvering for better looks at the drama of the moment.

The maître d' stopped at a table against the wall, drew it out, and the three of us slid behind it. He bowed slightly and left. It was no moment for "stage waits" and the three of us plunged feet-first into conversation. "Did you enjoy the crossing?"

Jane tossed her head back. "Oh, rather. I do prefer the Italian ships though, the English are so stuffy, don't you think?"

"Quite."

"How is your dear Aunt Agatha?"

"Haven't seen her of late. Dead, y'know."

"Really?"

"Rather!"

A table captain took our drink order. Waiters were going out of their way to walk past our table for a look at me. The guys in the band hadn't broken into *Mr. Wonderful* but they were welcoming me secret-service style, playing all the other songs from the show. People at other tables smiled, and although the three of us were still playing "Oh dear, Morocco again? Such a bore," the tension began softening under my awareness of the incredible fact that I was actually sitting at a table in the place I'd read about for years as the most sophisticated club in the country.

When the waiter had served our drinks I leaned closer to Jane and Burt and spoke quietly, "Hey, this is *okay*, isn't it? I mean they're not even doing the slow service bit. Let's be fair. I'll admit they didn't toss flowers at old Sam but it's a lot better than the last time, right?"

Burt smiled. "Yes. It's fine," but the muscle in his cheek was working itself back and forth.

"Baby, if something's wrong I think you'd better tell me."

"Nothing, Sam. Really."

I looked at Jane.

"Okay, fellas, let's have it."

Burt hesitated, then said, "It's not important, it's just that we're on the wrong side of the room. The tables they consider best are on the other side of the dance floor. It's ridiculous but the idea of it . . ."

We all knew that in this case it was not ridiculous, that it was the stone wall between acceptance and rejection. I had thought that they'd resisted me by habit but once I was there, once they had seen me, they'd accept me. But they were fighting me on their own terms: the nuance, the veiled insult. Everyone in the room had known I was being insulted, that even a semi-name would immediately have been given a table on the other side. Everywhere I looked I found my hands fumbling with something. I took out my pipe and tobacco pouch to use as a prop, and I filled the pipe slowly, deliberately, trying to appear as though that was all I was concentrating on in the world. As I struck a match the maître d' seemed to materialize in front of our table.

"We don't allow pipe smoking."

I put the pipe down quickly. "I'm sorry, I didn't know." He smiled, like: Of course you didn't.

Burt said, "Casually turn your head to the right and look at the swinging door, the one to the kitchen. That's John Perona."

The owner of El Morocco, a legendary figure in international society, the epitome of so-called sophistication, was hiding behind that door, staring out at me through a little window as though trying to figure out what I was.

I looked away. "Do you think we've been here long enough so we can leave?"

When our limousine door closed, Burt told the chauffeur to take us to the Harwyn.

"Baby, do me a favor. Drop me off at the Gorham. Pay my respects at the party, and I'll see you guys at the apartment whenever you can get away."

Jane put her hand on my arm. "Sammy . . . you worked a whole year for this . . . it's your party. Don't let this ruin everything for you."

They couldn't understand that there had been nothing to be ruined, that Morocco had only failed to contradict what I had known: I hadn't gotten what I'd come to New York for. The people at the Harwyn were celebrating the fact that I'd made a show run for a year but that was not what I had wanted to celebrate on my closing night.

"Darling, I'm fine, really. I'm just shot. It's been a long day." I smiled. "In the best tradition of Mary Noble, Backstage Wife: The marquee is out and so is he."

The apartment was dark except for a haze of light coming in through the windows. I sat on the couch, too tired to unbutton my overcoat or to reach for the lamp only a few inches away from my hand. I hadn't done it. I really hadn't. And now I was at the end of a long, long road, standing in front of a stone wall a whole world high and a whole world wide.

25

As I Passed Through The Kitchen On My Way To the wings, a waiter carrying a tray with bottles of scotch and setups went out of his way to walk alongside me. "We missed you like a son, Sammy, welcome home." I nodded and he hurried away to his station. Sure, welcome home. They love you *better* than a son. You're Santa Claus come to deliver the big tippers. Just don't let the deliveries slow up. The chorus kids had just come off and as they passed me one of them stopped, winked, and swung her satin-covered bottom at me. "Rub it for luck, Sammy."

Will was already standing in the wings. He nodded happily to me, then turned back to the audience as though magnetically drawn to them—unconsciously lifting one foot and buffing the already gleaming leather shoe against the sock of his other leg—waiting to go on with all the ready-to-go of a Major Bowes contestant. I looked away from him.

The announcer's voice blared: "The Chez Paree proudly presents The Will Mastin Trio starring *Sammy Davis, Jr.*"

Will rushed on.

I watched him doing his old-hat number, selling it as though it mattered, smiling confidently, "giving the people what they want," and my distaste for the ludicrous picture became mixed with resentment toward my father for leaving me with this. Instead of just once standing up to Will and saying, "It's over. I'm quitting and so are you," he'd taken the easy way out. The one time I'd needed him to come through for me he'd come up empty. All I'd gotten was a dramatic scene, a lot of tears, and a pair of baby shoes.

I walked on, took the handmike and began singing over the applause:

"Hello Joe, whattya know
I just came out of a Broadway show
and it feels wonderful . . .
It feels *wonderful* . . . to be back in
a nightclub again.

"Give me a saloon every time.
Maybe it's hokey but I like it smokey,
tell me I'm choosey but I dig it boozey,
show me a guy with a broad . . .

"Seriously, folks, that song speaks for how I feel. Sure, we had an interesting year on Broadway and I won't say it wasn't a joy beating the critics, but I don't kid myself I'm Rex Harrison: Let's face it—I'm a saloon guy." I paused for the applause. "With your very kind permission I'd like to make mention of a gentleman who isn't with me tonight as he has been all my life. That gentleman, of course, as most of you know, is my father who was taken ill during *Mr. Wonderful* and was forced to retire to California where he's enjoying a well-deserved rest from a lifetime of supporting me on this stage . . ." I smiled Charley Good Son during the applause, then switched to Charley Modest. "I just hope that my humble efforts may satisfy you as well in his absence as when he was here to help and guide me every step of the way." I held my hands up, preventing more applause. "If I may impose upon you just a bit more may I say that the gentleman to the right of me is the man whose wisdom and show business teachings are so much a part of everything I do on this stage, the man who has given so generously of his vast experience and taught me all the tricks of the trade which he knows so well, and which in my humble opinion account for whatever small success I may have had. I wish you'd help me thank him for his kindness and generosity in remaining on with me, providing me with the support I need so much . . . ladies and gentlemen, my uncle, my teacher, and my friend: Mr. Will Mastin. Take a bow, Uncle Will." I led the applause and turned smilingly toward him, respectfully, devotedly, thinking: you ridiculous figure.

I waded through the crowd in my suite at the St. Clair and found George and Jane and Burt. George waved to the crowd, smiling derisively. "Hello, Chicago."

I folded my arms. "Okay, let's have it, George. You know what they say: only his best friends'll tell him."

He shifted uneasily on the couch. "Well, if you must know, I could've lived without that 'saloon' song." He glanced at Jane and Burt, like they'd all been talking about it, then he faced me and shrugged. "Aside from the fact that I think you're far beyond the point where you need special material opening numbers—"

"You don't have to soften it, George."

"Well, I just think that song is in the worst possible taste. It's phony and patronizing. I kept waiting to find you were kidding, but the whole show had the same attitude, all those little remarks and digs about Broadway—I don't

know about the rest of the audience, but *I* don't go to nightclubs to have the performer put me down."

"Baby, you don't understand. You're taking it personally
but I need a song like that; it breaks the ice for me. I'm
back in clubs and I can't have Charley Square feeling like I
think I'm so goddamned chic now that he can't be in the
same room with me. The second I walk onstage he's got to
know I'm gonna tummel around like the Sammy Davis he
always knew."

He looked at me dubiously. "It's a little hard to believe
that you have to do anything except be a good performer."
He shrugged. "But what do *I* know? Nobody's standing
in line to see *me!*"

"Right, baby. So, you produce the Broadway shows and
let *me* worry about the nightclubs."

His face flushed and he reached for his glass. "I'll tell
him when he comes in."

A comic playing one of the other clubs pushed his way
through the crowded living room toward me. "How's the
skinny Farouk?" He gazed around at the girls, playing it
awestruck. "How am I going to adjust when you're gone?
Every night with women hanging from chandeliers, with
stuffed under sofas . . . hey, she's got to be joking with
those footballs under her sweater." He grinned at me. "This
is a regular Fort Knockers! I asked a cab driver where I
could find a girl and he brought me *here.*" He scanned
the room. "You cornered the market on 38's."

"Help yourself, baby. Excuse me." I called Charley aside.
"Get 'em all outa here, will you? But y'see the one standing
next to Morty? With the boobs. Tell her to stick around.
And the one next to her—the red satin with the long
swingin' legs—have her here tomorrow at noon."

"Twelve o'clock?"

"That's when noon usually is. Unless somebody changed
it."

"But you know you won't be getting up 'til three or four
o'clock. Why have her sit around for nothing?"

"Charley, if I feel like keeping some money in the bank
do I need your okay?"

I slipped out of the room and into three a.m. on Dearborn

Street, relieved to be away from all the fun I wasn't having, the laughs that were gloss and veneer, that underneath were only mechanical and blah, like a second helping of dessert. The weeks had dragged by, a mass of days without definition, their one-ness broken only by the hours I was onstage. Between those periods of oasis, I shopped, had parties, dinners, interviews, let crowds gather around me on the street for my autograph—all the things that had always been the ponies on my personal merry-go-round which I still kept spinning, although it wasn't very merry any more.

There was an empty table in a corner of the Latin Casino. My glance kept being drawn to it throughout the show. There was another one the next night. And the next. Then it got slightly worse. The dinner shows were strong but there were always three or four empty tables at the late shows.

It didn't figure. I'd been away from Philadelphia for over a year.

The Copa was filled for the first week, but by the middle of the second, Julie Podell was closing off part of the room for the late shows so the people who did come wouldn't realize how empty it was. I wasn't getting the repeat business I'd always been able to count on, the familiar faces that come back three and four times during a run, and Will was giving me I-told-you-so looks every night as we came downstairs and saw the dance floor wider than it had ever been for us before. Okay, there was a logical reason for it in New York. But what had happened at the Latin? Was Philadelphia so close to New York that the year on Broadway had hurt me there too?

The last weeks at the Copa dragged mercilessly as I waited to get out on the road again and see what was waiting for me.

Arthur came into the dressing room. "It's like a morgue downtown. There's nobody in Vegas except a crowd of Texans on a convention. You're doing all the business in town. Everybody else is dying."

He was pressing to sound casual, trying to give me a good

reason why I wasn't doing capacity business, but nobody ever figured out a good *enough* reason. Or a cure for an unidentified sickness. And night after night the symptoms were there, grim and threatening: I was playing Vegas for the first time in over a year, I was at a different hotel and I should have been bigger than ever, but something was choking off the customers just short of capacity. Neither Will nor the club owners paid any attention to what was only a slight dip in business, but if they couldn't see it as the start of our decline I could. To me those few empty tables represented not the dozen or so people who weren't there but the hundreds who had not been turned away; the difference between an act that's on the way up or on the way down.

Like the young, athletic-looking guy who's indulged himself in all the foods he knew were wrong until finally he looks in the mirror and can no longer kid himself about the jowls and stomach he's built slowly and surely by piling one layer of fat onto another, I had to face the fact that I'd stretched my luck and talent too far, and all the mistakes had begun to catch up with me: my lousy press, the lunatic spending that had caused the debts which everybody in the world seemed to know about, and the need to make desperation moves like wrong bookings and grabbing for quick money from every variety show on television—until every time anybody turned on his TV set, I was standing there doing Louis Armstrong.

I started to call the Morris office but it would be more dramatic, more effective to fly to L.A. and see them in person.

Sy Marsh sat on the edge of his desk. He was about my age, which was young for top man in the television department.

"Sy, don't book me on any more variety shows for one year."

"That's a hundred thousand dollars you're throwing away. Can you afford it?"

"No." I lit a cigarette. "Neither can I afford to blow eight or nine hundred thousand a year from clubs. And if the Morris office can't see what *must* happen at the rate I've been doing variety shows at least I can: the day's gotta come when I'll get to a town and instead of people breaking the doors down, the reaction'll be, 'Oh, him. Why pay to see him when we just saw him sing, dance, and do the impressions on television last week?' "

"God forbid."

"I'm hip." I stood up. "Sy, you weren't with the office when I used to come in here begging them to get me dramatic television, so we'll start from scratch: Get it for me or I'll get an agent who can. It's chips down time! I've got to protect my nightclub business so I'm cooling it with the variety shows, but I can't become America's Secret; I still need a medium that brings me to the public. I can't let the people in Chicago and Philly and all the towns I play wonder whatever-happened-to-Sammy Davis until I get there once a year or I ain't gonna do they're-lined-up-in-the-streets kind of business. That means I *must* have the importance and the impact of major exposure and that can only be one of three things: a big record? We know that's the maybe of all time. A motion picture or dramatic television? We forget pictures 'cause it's been like we've got the Ku Klux Klan running the motion picture department here. Obviously they figure I'm not as big or as talented as *Tab Hunter!* Okay. I've never made a picture so I can't argue with them about box office. But when it comes to television I've got a history of accomplishment going for me. It's right on the record that I lifted the rating of every show I was on. And those ratings were in the South as well as the North so there's no sponsor who can intelligently say I'm not one bitch of a good buy." He was staring silently at his desk. "Sy, one thing: don't tell me it's touchy."

"Screw *touchy*. It's plain goddamned stupid that you're not on a million shows right now. Here they're fighting like dogs over names half as big as you. . . ." He shrugged. "Well, I guess we both know that the heroes are *on* television, not *in* it. But I'm sure there are guys in the business who won't go along with that crap." He picked up a manuscript from his desk and dropped it, thoughtfully. "The one tough thing'll be to find parts for you. I'll talk to some of our own writers."

"This'll kill you, but how about a Western?"

He nodded. "You were right. It killed me."

"Baby, I'll play anything except an Uncle Tom, but don't brush off the Western thing so fast. Aside from the fact that I happen to be better with the guns than most of the Schwab's Drugstore cowboys they're using, it also happens there were a lot of colored cowboys."

"You serious?"

"The guys who wrote the history books happened to be white, and by a strange coincidence they managed to overlook just about everything any Negro did in and for America except pull barges up the goddamned Mississippi. But I've got books on the early West, I can sit here and do an hour on authentic stories about Negro cowboys, an entire Negro regiment in the Civil War, dozens of things that have never been used—a wealth of fresh stuff. But let me ask you something: why do I have to play the part of a Negro?"

He looked at me, blankly.

"I'm dead serious. Why do I have to play a part that depends on color? Why can't I play something where the fact that I'm a Negro has no bearing on the script in any way? Why must a special part be written for a Negro? Or else, an entire script switched so they do *Abie's Irish Rose* with an all-Negro cast? Y'know something? I *die* every time I read in the papers about some cat on Broadway who says, 'What we need is integrated theater. Authors should write in more parts for Negroes.' That's not integrated theater. *Really* integrated theater will be when an actor—colored or white—is hired to play a part. Period. Not when a Negro actor is hired to play the part of a Negro who's in the story strictly *as* a Negro, like when they're doing a scene in a Harlem bar and the producer tells Casting, 'Send up one Negro bartender, one Negro bar owner, and some Negro extras for customers.'" I pointed to a script on his desk. "For example: who's the central character in that?"

He smiled. "An aging film actress."

"Okay, baby, what about the one underneath?"

"A mobster."

"Why can't I play *that*? Is there anything in the script that makes it necessary to the story line that this guy is white?"

"No."

"Then isn't it wrong that they'd never think to call a Negro to play him? Or a cop, or a doctor, a soldier, a judge, or a lawyer—with no emphasis on color, no mention of it? I don't say do illogical or far-out things like showing a Negro doctor making a house call to a white family—although God knows it would be beautiful—but certainly if there's a scene in a hospital and you have doctors and nurses walking around, why not cast it as *is*, with colored doctors and nurses too? If you're doing a hospital *do a hospital!* But they don't. According to dramatic television there are almost no colored people in America. And that's about a twenty-million-person difference with what the census shows. How's *that* for being overlooked?"

"It's ridiculous. But I guess the reason is that the sponsors aren't going to stick their necks out and take a chance on jarring customers in the Southern markets."

"Baby, have you any idea how jarring it must be for about five million colored kids who sit in front of a television set hour after hour and they almost never see anybody who looks like them? It's like they and their families and their friends just plain don't exist."

About an hour later we were shaking hands and he was saying, "I'll really try for you. Somehow we'll get you on," and I was dying to believe that maybe I'd finally found a guy who'd go to bat for me.

I called him from Vegas the next night. "Y'know what you were saying about how tough it is finding parts for me? Well, I was just watching *Twilight Zone* and I've got a story idea that if Rod Serling liked I think would work."

"What is it?"

"The central character is a hater, the bigot of all time; he doesn't even like *movies* in color. He's a big man in a small Southern town where he's head of the Klan *and* White Citizens Council. Scene one: he's making a speech at one of their meetings—we bring the camera right in on him and he's screaming for a lynching or a bombing and you all but see the venom oozing out of him. Scene two: he leaves the meeting and on the way home he has an automobile accident. Scene three: he wakes up in a hospital, he's cut and burned and his arms are bandaged like a mummy. He's lucky to be alive but he's not getting the attention he wants;

he's yelling how important he is but nobody gives a damn. He decides he'll go out in the hall to raise hell. He drags himself out of bed and as he passes the dresser he stops dead in front of the mirror. He's colored! The same guy, the same face, the same everything—except he's colored and there's nothing he can do about it for the rest of his life. He's in the Twilight Zone."

Sy gasped. "It's a bitch. It's beautiful. I'll get on it right away. And maybe I've got something else that looks pretty good. I talked to a guy, a director who's only done pictures but he's going to be doing a half-hour anthology series and he's very interested in you. He wants to have dinner with you the next time you're in town."

I knew as he was telling it to me that before he could sound excited over an untried director and a series that wasn't even on the air yet, he must have struck out up and down the line. This was the consolation prize and it wasn't exactly Playhouse 90. "Look, Sy, let's not take a chance he'll cool off. Why don't we invite him down here for the weekend? You think he'd come?"

"Well, sure, but . . ."

"If he's married invite his old lady, too. I'll wire you the dough for the plane tickets."

I sat up in bed. "You're calling to tell me I was so charming he wants me to do all the old Arlene Francis shows, right?"

"Sam . . . I'll give it to you straight. On the plane back to L.A. last night he opened up and told me he didn't think he could get you past the sponsor. 'Too touchy,' he said."

"Son of a bitch."

"I guess the whole thing was just because he wanted to meet Sammy Davis, Jr. I'm sorry, Sam. I'll make it up to you. I promise I will."

"It's not your fault. Forget it. Let me know when the *Twilight Zone* thing falls through."

There was a pause. "I got word this morning. The network turned it down."

I couldn't think of anything to say.

"Sam? Look, it's not entirely dead. Serling loves the idea and he wants to do it as a special someday. He has more

416

control of specials than he has over the series. It won't be right away but we've at least got that iron in the fire."

"Sy, the only iron in the fire is the one they use to mark me lousy." I knew as I spoke that I wasn't making it easy for him, that he'd never imagined the wall would be this high and this wide, that he was probably more stunned by it than I. But he could be stunned and walk away.

I hated for Frank to see me doing anything short of landslide business. As he watched me from ringside, his face changed from relaxed-and-laughs to curious as he sipped his drink and observed me clinically, smiling at all the right times, but watching, studying me.

He closed the dressing room door behind him, sat down on a wooden chair and lit a cigarette, holding it cupped in the palm of his hand the way he does when he's tense or when something's bothering him. I wiped off my make-up and kept talking but I could feel him watching me. I glanced at him through the mirror. His eyes narrowed slightly, causing lines to appear at the edges of them. "What the hell's eating you, Charley?"

I slid my tie up to my collar. "Everything's swinging, Frank." I turned around slowly. "I'm a little tired, maybe. Why? Did it show?"

Slowly he shook his head, then, as though he'd tried a door, found it locked and walked away from it, he said, "This won't do you much good right now but I'm making a picture in about a year or so, and I want you in it. It's a thing called *Ocean's 11*, about a bunch of guys who try to heist Vegas. I hadn't planned to talk about it yet, but you can count on it. As soon as I clean up some other commitments, we go into the movie business. I'm going to pay you a hundred and twenty-five thousand."

He tossed it off like "Here's a scarf I picked up for you." There was no "We'll have to do a screen test." None of that jazz. He didn't know if I could say hello on film and make it sound convincing, yet he was willing to lay his money and his picture on the line for me. And he knew he could have gotten me for $1.98.

From town to town the dance floors grew larger and the

aisles between tables—aisles through which waiters once had to walk sideways—became broad avenues criss-crossing the clubs, linking New York, Philadelphia, and Vegas, to Reno, San Francisco, Detroit, and L.A.—a string of nearly-filled nightclubs, of people not breaking down doors to get in. And of endless wondering: why? I was stretching the shows from the usual hour and twenty minutes to an hour and thirty, forty, sometimes two hours, staying on until I was drained, doing everything I knew how, hoping that maybe word of mouth would start filling the gap. I think I stayed on, too, because wondering if they were ever coming back, I hated to let them leave.

Then, when finally there was a break in my luck, when Max Youngstein, president of United Artists, called me in L.A. while we were playing the Moulin Rouge, offering me the male lead opposite Eartha Kitt in *Anna Lucasta;* when miraculously this lifeline appeared, I could grab for it with only one hand. The shooting dates for *Anna* conflicted with our next run at the Sands. I never wanted anything as much as I wanted to cancel Vegas but my debts were somewhere between a quarter and a half million dollars—there was no counting them any more, it would have taken a month to even figure out the fantastic borrowing from one guy to pay another and then from another to pay him, the complex web of advances from clubs, record companies, unpaid taxes and corporate debts—and there was never a day without at least one pressure thing, at least one guy who wouldn't wait any longer. My piece of the $100,000 from Vegas was already promised to eight different people and my third of the $50,000 movie salary just wouldn't be enough. The shooting dates couldn't be changed so the only solution was to do the picture and play Vegas at the same time. I'd have to leave Vegas every night after my second show, sleep in the car, and arrive in L.A. in time for the morning call. Shooting would be over by five and I'd grab a plane back to Vegas to be there for the dinner show.

The last thing in the world I wanted was to commute back and forth like a madman, making my first picture without being able to devote myself to it. But here it was again, more damaging and wasteful than ever: my future irrevocably owned and controlled by my past. At a time when I needed everything going for me my mistakes were in control. Money made the decisions, out-voting knowledge and judgment, and I had no choice but to go in the direction of the road I'd paved with my own stupidities.

Will was standing in the doorway of my dressing room at the Mou, dressed for the show, wrist in the air, eyes riveted meaningfully to his watch. I walked past him. "Don't you know that's a cliché, Massey?" My father, seated on the couch, winked, "By a nose, Poppa." "Hello, Dad." I handed my jacket to Charley and started undressing, fast.

Will followed me in, angry at something that hadn't happened. "In another few minutes I'd've had to tell them to hold the show."

I tossed my shirt and tie onto a chair. "You ever know me to miss a performance?"

"Where were you?"

"Vegas."

"*Vegas?*"

"Vegas."

"Since last night you been there and back? You must be crazy."

"Poppa." My father was shaking his head, slowly, as though the things I did were beyond human comprehension.

I sat down. "Look, Dad, Massey, I went to Vegas to talk to Eartha, to make sure she's happy. God knows it's going to be tough enough without having *her* fighting me. So big deal: I sent her some flowers, flew down, we had dinner, I played it like 'You're a pro 'cause you've made pictures and I'm just an amateur,' she dug it, I asked for her help, she was flattered, I'll send more flowers, blah, blah, blah—she's in my corner. Now is there something wrong with that?"

"What's wrong is you're running yourself ragged like a fool, making special trips to Vegas to talk about a picture you've got no right to be doing in the first place . . ." His voice droned on, repeating all the things he'd said a dozen times since I'd told him I was going to be doing *Anna.*

I spread albolene on my face and began putting on the powder. "Massey, I've got no time to talk now."

"You mean you don't *wanta* talk."

419

"Whatever you say."

"I say you're crazy, that's what I say. You'll be wearing yourself down to nothing."

"Will's right, Poppa. You gotta look after your health. You're stretchin' yourself too thin, tryin' to be everywhere at once."

I looked at him and he nodded, pleased with the fatherly advice he'd given, like the advice I never stopped getting from Will, advice that wasn't for me but for them, to assuage their consciences. My father wasn't saying "I'm sorry I blew all my money and I can't help you." Will wasn't offering "I'll sell a building and help you." Neither of them was volunteering "We'll take less than our regular cut 'til you straighten yourself out," or even "We've got nothing to do with the movie so you keep the whole fifty, that'll cover what you need and then you can cancel Vegas." They didn't want to give anything except advice. But they both wanted me to thank them for their concern.

"Sammy, what's wrong with you? Can't you see this is no way to make a start in movies?" Will was walking slowly up and down the room, enjoying the role of the wise old showman straightening out the novice with pearls of wisdom. "I'm surprised at you not knowing you can't do your best in the movie this way, plus you won't be giving your best on the stage . . ."

As though independent of my control my hand slammed down on the dressing table and the powder burst out of the open box and onto my pants. I tore them off and glared at Charley through the mirror. "Godammit, Charley, don't just stand there gaping. Get me another pair." I turned to Will. "I don't need you to tell me how good I'll be. I'll do the best I can. And not you or anything in this world is going to stop me from making that picture."

"Your health'll stop you."

"If you're so worried about my health then how the hell come you don't tell me to cancel Australia? How come I don't hear you saying that thirty-six hours in a plane each way and ten stops in ten nights isn't worth the $70,000?"

"Don't you raise your voice to me."

"I *have* to raise my voice because you must be deaf! Or you're blind. Can't you see anything but what you *want* to see? Can't you see past your name out front? Don't you know what's happening around you?"

He blinked, confused. "What's happening around me?"

I stared at him, examining his face. "Get out of here, Massey. I've got to go entertain the people. Or would you like to do it alone?"

He looked at the floor for a moment, then turned and left. My father stood up, touched me on the shoulder and walked to the door. "Poppa, I'll leave you alone."

I always *am*. Except on payday!

I walked in a circle around the room, trying to relax. As I passed the mirror over the dressing table I saw the skin pulled tight across my jaw, the good eye blazing with so much resentment that it made the phony look more dead than it had ever seemed. As loathsome as the face was, it so perfectly matched what I felt. I heard the opening act's music and I laughed out loud at the thought of myself on-stage, being Charley Nice.

I'd done an hour and fifty minutes, I'd had no sleep, and I was exhausted but I couldn't bring myself to leave the stage. The taunting snow-white tablecloths, combined with a strange kind of incompleteness I'd begun to feel at every performance, drove me to do more. I called for John to bring out the vibes and drums, did a twenty-minute jam session and then cued Morty into "Birth of the Blues." As I reached for the big note a searing pain cut across my torso, like a hot wire suddenly drawn tightly around my back and my chest and I knew I was having a heart attack and I thought, "Oh, God I'm going to die."

I knew I should stop singing and walk off. I knew it was ridiculous but I had the dramatic picture of myself collapsing onstage and the papers reporting, "He died as he lived: performing. Death took him from the people he loved: his audiences." As corny as it was, if I had to go that's how I wanted it to be. My head cleared, I heard the music behind me and I reached desperately for the strength to finish the last bars.

As my feet touched the stone floor backstage I felt myself falling. . . .

I was on a couch in the dressing room, rigged up in an electrocardiograph machine. A doctor was sitting next to me.

"I'm Dr. Weiss. How do you feel?" I nodded. My father and Will were standing back, watching me. The doctor explained that I'd had a mild heart attack, "a warning that you've got to be careful." He was looking at me reproachfully. "With an athletic heart you can't keep burning the candle at both ends as I understand you do . . ."

When he'd left my father closed the door and sat on the edge of the couch. "Poppa, this tears it. You've gotta cancel out Australia and you gotta take your choice of *Anna Lucasta* or Vegas. Will and me'll go along with either one but you can't do 'em both. Truth is you really oughta take a month's time and do nothin' but sit around the house gettin' your strength up." Will nodded.

I gave them a round of applause. "Beautiful MGM musical, folks: the performer gets sick, takes time off, and the whole world stops 'til he's ready; music, curtain, have some popcorn. But I'm not Dan Dailey, I need the picture, I need the money. If either of you have any better ideas I'll be glad to take a month off for an ocean voyage."

They both stared at the floor, not an idea between them. Will began pacing. "At least you gotta cut the shows back to normal, maybe even down to an hour." He nodded in agreement with himself. "An hour's plenty."

"Is it?"

He stopped walking. "Sammy, I don't want to fight with you." His voice was quiet, his face a combination of compassion and confusion. "I know that anything I say is going to be wrong but I see you onstage for over two hours breaking your back to do everything you know how," he looked right at me, "going past good showmanship, making mistakes you knew better than to make when you was a boy. I watched you tonight and I didn't know you. In all my years I never saw a performer trying to eat an audience alive like that. You couldn't find enough to do for 'em, like you wanted to open up your veins and give 'em your blood, too. Don't take my word for it. Big Sam here'll tell you. And you're acting like that movie's the last one that'll ever be made; and as far as your debts go, you know I don't approve of owing money—I never did and I never will—but paying bills don't come before staying alive." He hesitated. "All I mean to say is you can't keep on like you've been doing, or you're going to kill yourself."

My father nodded and I looked from one to the other. All they saw was "debts" and "he wants to be in a movie." They didn't begin to understand.

"Massey . . . the only time I'll kill myself is when there's nobody out there waiting for me to go on."

Tony Curtis came over to me in the wings at the Beverly Hills Hotel as I was waiting to go on at a benefit. We hugged hello and he whispered, "How was Australia?"

I knew he wouldn't fly to *Las Vegas.* "You've *gotta* go see for yourself. You're very big down there."

"No kidding?" Then he gave me a look. "Very funny. Listen, come on by the house later, we're having some people over for booze and coffee."

I knew almost everybody at the party and Janet was introducing me to the few I hadn't met before. She led me over to a group in a corner of the living room.

Kim Novak held out her hand and smiled. "I'm awfully glad to meet you. I admire your work tremendously."

Tony sat down on the floor with the group of us and nudged me. "Big deal. So you flew to Australia."

"And, baby, I did it the *hard* way. I came back by way of Africa."

Janet asked, "Seriously?"

I nodded. "Yeah, Sapphire, I thought I'd drop in on the *old* country." It got a laugh. "Actually, what happened is: we're in Sydney winding up the tour and I get a call from Frank. 'Can you do me a little favor, Charley? I promised Jack Kennedy I'd be in New York for a benefit his family has every year for retarded children, but I'm hung up on location. Can you come back to the States by way of New York and stop off at the Plaza and appear for me?' Naturally I say 'Sure, Francis, tell the Senator I'll be there' and I hang up and tell our travel guy to re-route us. Now, the plane lands in Africa and I figure, 'Hot damn, I'm home. I'll go out and see the family.' I start down the ramp and I see two rows of chieftains in their tribal clothes. I give 'em my smile and wave 'Hey, baby, here I *am.*' Well—them cats started mumbling and looking at me with such hate that I turned right around and got back into my *safety* belt! Hell, Mississippi is rough but them cats in the Congo—they're mad at *everybody*. They don't *never* smile. They're still mad at us from old Tarzan pictures.

"But the shake-up of my *life* was earlier. I was in my seat doing one of the great sleeps of all time when the stewardess announces, 'We're re-fueling in Karachi. You have thirty minutes before we take off.' Michael Silva, my drummer, starts pulling on my sleeve. 'Come on, let's see what's happening.' I tell him to cool it, there ain't *nothing* going to be happening in Karachi or it wouldn't still be in Karachi. But he won't let up. 'Come on, Sammy. How many times we gonna be here?' Well, there's no arguing with *that*, and he's not *about* to let me sleep, so, scene two: he's got the cameras slung all over him, we're walking across the field to the terminal building and I see all the cats working around the field smiling and waving like 'hey, baybee . . .' but not just to *me* like they know who I am—they're waving to *everybody*, there ain't a frown to be seen. Then I notice there's something strange about the air. I look at Michael and he's sniffing too, like he can't believe it. He looks at me. 'That what I think it is?' He shakes his head like a drunk. 'It can't be.' I said, 'Well, it sure smells like it . . . nah, it's impossible.' Now we go into the building and the smell is un-be-*lievable!* It's everywhere. I run over to the ticket counter and I ask the guy, 'Hey, what's that stuff?' He gives me a smile like 'That's right, baby' and points out the window behind him and so help me there's a bunch of cats with rakes in their hands, burning an entire field of marijuana. But I mean *a whole field of it* going up in smoke. The stuff is legal there and it grows so fast that they have too much of it, so like every month they have to burn it up. The scene is not to be believed: the entire population standing around stoned, three feet off the ground, sniffing and grinning, whacked out of their skulls. . . ."

The next afternoon Arthur came into the Playhouse and sat down at the end of the bar. I nodded hello, listening to one of the new sides I'd just made for Decca. When it was over he said, "I never thought you'd hold out on me like this."

I slipped the next side onto the turntable. "Like what, baby?"

His grin broadened into a mysteriosa smile. "You know what I mean. Come on, you don't have to do bits with *me!* It's all over town."

"*What's* all over town?"

"You and Kim Novak."

He was staring at me, first realizing that I hadn't known what he was talking about. He asked, "Didn't you see the papers today?"

"Certainly I saw them, but they didn't say nothing about me and no Kim Novak."

He showed me one of the columns. ". . . Kim Novak's new interest will make her studio bosses turn lavender . . ." I'd skimmed past it earlier, never imagining it meant me. I started to tell him that we'd hardly spoken twenty words to each other, but as I looked up and saw the admiration in his face I smiled, shrugged noncommittally and turned on the record machine.

When he left I got her home number and called her. "Kim, this is Sammy Davis, Jr."

"Hi. How are you?"

"Well, frankly I'm feeling horrible over a rumor that's going around."

"I heard it."

"I'm calling to say I'm sorry as hell and I hope you know I didn't have anything to do with it."

"Of course I know that."

"We can handle it any way you think best. I realize the position you're in with the studio."

"The studio doesn't own me!"

"Well, but they'll probably feel—"

"Don't worry about what they'll feel. *I* don't. Listen, I'm cooking some dinner. It's not much, but would you like to join me?"

I called Arthur and told him to come back, and I was dressed in levi's and a leather jacket when he got to the house. "Now, just so you won't think I'm holding out on you, here's the skam: I'm going to Kim's house for dinner." I caught his smile of satisfaction. "Obviously I can't

425

leave my car parked in her driveway, so I need you to drive me over, in your car, to play it safe."

Half a block from her house I said, "I'll get out here. Now, check your watch with mine. At exactly ten o'clock—to the second, I want you pulling up in front of her place. I'll be running out of there on schedule and I don't wanta have to stand around on the street and get picked off by no photographers or neighbors. And have the car door open for me." I pulled up my collar, slipped out of the car and ran the last half block, ducking behind trees and slinking across her lawn. I rang the bell. Instantly the door opened. I slipped inside and she closed it.

She'd made spaghetti and meatballs and as we were eating I thought: wouldn't the papers give their eye teeth for an 8 x 10 glossy of me having dinner with Kim Novak.

She smiled conspiratorially. "About an hour after I spoke with you I got a call from the studio. They wanted to know if we'd ever met."

"What'd you tell them?"

She seemed pleased with herself. "The truth. I said, 'Yes, I met him at a party. He's such a delightful man.' "

I laughed. "Then what?"

"Then there was what the scripts call: a moment of stunned silence while the studio gathers itself together and, in a voice tensely casual, asks, 'Is that the only time you've seen him?' I told them we hadn't met since then." The amusement left her face. "Oh, how I loathe people interfering in my life. Do you know what I mean?"

I laughed. "Sort of."

She smiled, sympatico. "Well . . . at least you don't have an entire studio checking every move you make. I mean they must really believe they *own* me."

"I guess it gets to be a drag sometimes but let's be honest, it's not *all* bad."

She sighed. "You're not much fun, are you?" Then, looking at me, dramatically, "I'm using you. You're a wall of wet paint."

"And all the signs say 'Don't touch.' "

She nodded, pleased.

I'd known it the moment she'd invited me to dinner. Through me she was rebelling against the people who made rules for her. And wasn't I doing the same thing? We'd spent a few hours in each other's company at a party, and when we'd said good night there'd been no slipping of private phone numbers, no thought of getting together again. I was impressed by the glamour of a movie star and she was impressed by my talent, but she hadn't thought about me any more than I had thought about her—until it was forbidden. Then we became conspirators, drawn together by the single thing we had in common: defiance. I'd sensed it on the phone and in the way she'd been waiting behind the door, playing the scene like it was a B-movie, and I was aware that I, too, had been doing everything but wear a cloak and mustache.

At exactly three seconds before ten I opened the door and dashed to the street. Arthur had timed it on the button and was just pulling up; the car door swung open as I reached the curb and before he'd come to a full stop I was inside and we zoomed away. Even he was caught up in the intrigue, playing it like he was driving a get-away car.

All I could see were the red lights at the tip of the wing and I had the feeling that it would be glorious to sit out there, my legs hanging over the edge of the wing, peacefully riding through space, the clean, fresh air bathing away all the problems.

"Look at this." Arthur was pointing to an item in one of the papers we'd picked up at the airport in Detroit. ". . . Guess which sepia entertainer's attentions are being whispered as The Kiss of Death to guess which blonde movie-star's career? . . ." He showed me others, shaking his head in amazement. "Imagine if you hadn't been out of town for the last three months?"

I opened a scandal magazine and skimmed "The Real Story Between KIM and HIM," a re-hash of all the rumors and gossip items. The real story *I* saw was the deep insult to me and to all Negro people. I wondered about the men who wrote these things, and the columnists. Didn't it occur to them how it might feel to hear "A woman's career can be ruined just by association with you"? Didn't they understand that's what they were saying? Didn't they care? Worse —they didn't think. They couldn't feel anything that might *make* them think because their sensitivities were covered by a big, thick callus that it had taken three centuries of stupidity to develop.

I rested against the seat. The stewardess came by. "Would you like a pillow, Mr. Davis?" Her eyes flicked to the magazine, then back to my face, and she maintained her smile, making a business-like attempt to camouflage the condemnation in her eyes.

As she moved down the aisle Arthur opened an envelope of clippings and leaned over to me, reading, " 'Advice to Sammy Davis, Jr. before it's too late: Sammy, I consider myself your friend so I'm speaking up to beg you to show some sense. Don't damage a promising career, and probably your own, too. Wouldn't it be more fitting for a man of your prominence to be a credit to his people, instead of one whose life is scandal, scandal, scandal? Think it over, Sammy, you're too smart for this.' "

I sat motionless in the seat, gazing blankly out the window. Arthur asked, "What are you going to do?"

"About what?"

"Well, I mean . . . are you going to keep seeing her?"

"Why the hell not?" I turned and looked at him. "Because 'everybody says so'? Can you begin to know how sick I am of being watched and judged and criticized and told what to do? Do you realize that even the goddamned stewardess on this plane has an opinion? *She's* ready to cast her vote how I oughta live. Well, lotsa luck to 'em all. Will Mastin ain't gonna tell me how to live, my father ain't gonna tell me, the damned Morris office ain't gonna tell me, or the papers—nobody. You hear me?"

"I'm not telling you what to do." He looked around frantically, afraid somebody was listening, and he spoke softly, pacifying. "I only meant maybe you're letting yourself in for more trouble than it's worth. She doesn't mean anything to you and you don't mean anything to her . . ."

"You can't drop it, right, Arthur?"

"But do you really think it's smart to keep it going?"

"No, but I'm going to."

"But with the whole world saying the same thing . . ."

I looked away from him. "If I'd listened to what the whole world says I'd be in Harlem shining shoes."

I rented a beach house at Malibu so we could meet secretly, and Arthur was driving me there for the sixth night in a row. As we got within a few miles of it I said, "Baby, it's still light out so pull over and let me get in the back. I'd better stay flat on the floor and under a blanket 'cause the way the rumors are flying, them cats on the papers may have movie cameras set up all along this road."

The floor smelled lousy. There was a clump of dirt a few inches away from my head. From one second to the next the game ended and it was as though I was standing back, seeing myself huddled on the floor of a car, hiding, like an animal. For what? So I could say "I showed them." What was I showing them? I wasn't making my own rules, I was sneaking around theirs, doing everything I'd thought I'd always refused to do. They were saying "You're not good enough to be seen with a white woman." And I was hiding on the floor of a car, confirming their right to say it.

Arthur whispered, "We're almost there."

I couldn't answer him.

"Hey, I said we're almost there." He looked in the rearview mirror and saw me sitting up in the back seat. He jammed on the brakes. "You crazy? It's broad daylight."

"Keep going. Don't stop at the house."

He glanced quickly up and down the street. "You spot somebody?"

"Just keep going."

The car started moving again. "Okay, but I don't get it."

"Drive downtown—any place." I rested against the back of the seat.

As we drove through the skid row of Los Angeles we stopped for a red light and a bum with a week's growth of beard and filthy, torn clothes staggered up to the car. He looked at me and then asked Arthur, "Buddy, can y'give a guy a little help?"

I started to reach for some money but I stopped. Why should I? Underneath all that filth his skin is white: he'd been given a pass through the world and he'd blown it. I stared at the mass of wasted life holding out his hand and I had a weird, ridiculous picture of her arriving at a movie premiere, dressed to the teeth, escorted by this old rummy wearing the same clothes and no shave and everybody smiling and applauding as they walked in. He could be a pimp or a dope peddler but still he'd be okay. There's nothing he could ever do to get himself as low as me.

"C'mon, buddy, be a pal," he whined at Arthur, "whattya say, just a few cents?"

I took a hundred dollar bill out of my pocket, folded it and rolled down my window. "Here." He turned, stared at me, hesitated, then took the money. "Thanks a lot, mac. Damn white of ya." He stuffed it into his pocket without even looking at it and stumbled away. He probably thought it was a single. He'd put it on a bar and get change for a dollar. The stupid bastard would never know what he'd had in his pocket.

The usual crowd was jamming the Copa dressing room when I got upstairs between shows. I went into the bedroom, "Charley, get out there and close that goddamned window. And make sure the radiators are up."

"But, you've got people out there . . ."

"I didn't ask for a guest list. I said close the window."

He was shaking his head. "I can't keep up with you. You always said I should make guests comfortable. Well they were too hot."

"Don't try to keep up with me 'cause you'll never be able to! Now I want it *hot* in these rooms. That's how I like it, that's how it'll be. Right?" I put on a robe and went into the next room, poured a coke, turned on the TV set, and sat down in a chair facing it. I could see some of them were disappointed. Tough. If they want entertainment let them go downstairs and pay for it.

After about twenty minutes one of the guys said gingerly, "Sam, it's kinda warm in here." He'd opened his collar and his neck and face glistened with sweat. "Y'think we could open the window for a minute?"

"I'm sorry, baby. The heat's good for my throat."

"Oh. Sure! Of course."

"But you go downstairs if you're uncomfortable. I'll catch you in the Lounge after the second."

"No. It's not that bad. Really. I don't mind at all."

I watched him cross the room and explain it to his girl. Her face fell. She caught me looking and smiled over. I lit my Sherlock Holmes pipe and watched them out of the corner of my eye. They're unbelievable. I'm ignoring them, their hair is curling from the heat, their clothes are getting wrinkled, they're actually suffering, but still they don't leave, they just sit here staring at me. It's fantastic. They're like moths around a flame. They get singed, burned—but still they come back for more.

As I opened the second show, a cloud of cigar smoke billowed toward me from the table at center ringside. I smiled at the guys boozing and making out with chicks while I was performing. A few tables away a man had his back to me and was eating his dinner. It's your money, buddy. I cued Morty for a ballad to quiet the room, to lure attention, but the conversations kept humming over the sound I was making. . . .

I stood in the wings waiting for the applause to build before going out to take a bow, remembering the bursts of sound that had always snapped me back, the banging on tables, the heads turned watching the spot where I'd re-appear. I mopped my face, stalling, and as I heard the sound diminishing I knew I couldn't leave them on *that*. I ran on, taking no bow, as though the show hadn't been over. I cued Morty. The guys in the band gaped and hurried to re-open the music. I glared at them and smiled to the audience, "We'll now do a few bars of that popular song 'The Search.'"

I started with a jam session and began building, selecting numbers carefully, using only the sure-things, trying to lift them out of their seats if only by sheer strength, digging down deeper than ever before to entertain them, to get them involved, to get response—but it was as though I were playing handball with an orange. No matter what I did I couldn't find the power to gather them all up in one lump the way I'd once been able to. I was aware of the tension behind me on the bandstand, and I could feel the guys watching me, knowing I wasn't going to make it. I'd done an extra hour and twenty minutes, the longest show in my life, when I finally cued Morty for "Black Magic." As I roared through the number, straining every muscle and nerve in a last effort to reach the people, searching their faces for a touch of the excitement that used to be there, I saw a man looking at his watch.

Will was in the wings as I came off, his face a mask of bewilderment. As I was passing him he put his hand on my arm to stop me. "Sammy . . ." it was half-gasp, half-whisper, "you did two hours and thirty minutes."

"You don't like it? You're the manager. Fire me!" I started walking but I turned back. "And you can tell Morty Stevens that I don't need him to second-guess me. Until his name is out front he'll let *me* decide when the show is over."

I lay on the bed in the dressing room, still dressed, staring at the ceiling. Big John opened the door a crack, came in, and closed it behind him. "Sammy, y'know what I was thinkin' you oughta have?"

"A lock on my door?"

"No fooling, Sammy, I was thinking you should have a clause in your contract sayin' the waiters can't serve while you're on. Hell, all the big stars got it. They don't have to put up with guys dropping glasses and bangin' knives and forks around while they're performing . . ."

This big gruff man was looking at me with sympathy he couldn't conceal, trying to make it sound like something he'd thought of for no particular reason. I was grateful for the loyalty that had brought him to my defense. "Thanks, John. I'll give it some thought."

"You really oughta, Sammy. No reason for you to have to put up with drunks talking and calling for more booze —hell, you're a great artist, you're too big for that." He smiled awkwardly. "Well . . . see you tomorrow night, boss."

"Good night, John."

I lay still, wishing the answer could be as simple as a clause in a contract but knowing that the audiences had to write that clause themselves, that you can't *make* people listen to you. So many times I'd seen comics begging attention with panic lines like: "Just keep eating, folks, I'll still be here when you look up," and "I know you're out there 'cause I can hear you breathing," lines that are not only corny in their own fashion but they're a death rattle.

Once you have to say "Hey, please listen to my act," then it's too late.

I lit a cigarette and sat on the edge of the bed remembering all the years they'd been so engrossed in my show that it had never occurred to them to eat or drink while I was on. Then, I reheard the lack of excitement downstairs, and for the hundredth time in a month I reviewed every move I'd made onstage. Point by point I was as good a technician as I'd ever been, maybe as I'd grown older I'd become even better. But I wasn't touching them any more.

I called John back into the room. "Tomorrow night I want you to tape the act. From the beginning to the end. I'm planning a special kind of an album and I want to hear some of the off-the-wall stuff I do. As a matter of fact, do both shows."

He gave me the tapes the next night. I went straight back to the Warwick, alone. I threaded the machine. I poured a coke, lit a cigarette, and stared at the "Play" button until I gathered up the nerve to press it.

"Ladies and gentlemen, I'm thrilled to be back at the Copa . . . the one place I really think of as home . . . your kind attention to Mr. Mastin whose teachings and unerring advice . . . and now our humble offering of . . . with your very kind permission may we beg your indulgence during our humble rendition of . . ." I sat dead still, stunned, repulsed by what I was hearing. It went on and on—the nauseatingly humble this and humble that until even an idiot would know it was pure arrogance, reeking of insincerity, of "Charley Star" putting the audience down. I was doing the one thing I knew could never succeed on a stage: being totally dishonest.

I listened to the second tape, finding it impossible to associate myself with the mechanical man gushing sentimental statements without a shred of real sentiment attached to them. Every word sounded tinny, every emotion was a pretense, a sham that screamed of guile. I waited painfully for the songs and dances as reprieves from the fraud, hoping that after each break it would change course, but the voice kept coming back in a relentless drone of "show biz sincerity," out and out phoniness, that cut through me like a knife. I heard myself doing lines that should have reached out and caught their hearts but nothing happened; I lost most of the hushed silences I'd always been able to create; jokes that were clever and funny got laughs—but not the screams you get from people who really like you. The beautiful one-ness which had existed between me and the audience, the ability to touch them, was buried beneath layer upon layer of dishonesty.

I pressed the re-wind button and as the spools jerked and reversed, pulling back the words, my mind raced back over the past year, to all the audiences who'd heard this, who'd come to see somebody they like and had been cheated, offered a fiction, a counterfeit man. When they could no longer find what had first made them like me, then I had nothing going for me but my physical performance. And that's not enough. Once the novelty of any performer has worn off, once he's been around a few times and the people have seen what he does, then he's on the way down the moment he hits the top—unless he has that extra thing going for him, the intangible that makes his audiences care for him. Jerry can do the same jokes, be the same idiot kid, because the people see something that makes them love him. Frank has it in a different way—the strength, the independence, the unbending "right or wrong this is how I am" kind of honesty.

Obviously the audiences couldn't put their fingers on what was missing as I could, they wouldn't analyze it and say "Hey, this kid's a phony," but they didn't have to know *why* they weren't excited or *why* they weren't telling their friends "You've got to get over to the Copa and see Sammy Davis."

All the desperation for dramatic television and movies was like giving vitamin pills to a man who'd been cutting his own throat.

I rewound the first show and turned it on, listening to it clinically, stopping the machine and writing down every hokey or insincere line.

I taped the shows the next night and locked myself in my room to hear them. The sound of my voice hit me like a wet towel: whap! All the phony things I'd memorized and been careful not to say were gone, but unwittingly I'd invented new ones.

Night after night I threaded the machine, pressed the button and out poured the same hollowness. No matter how many words and phrases I eliminated, they were replaced by other words, other phrases, equally phony and equally damaging. No matter how carefully I guarded against them, no matter how sure I was that I'd succeeded in stamping them out, the tape caught them, saved them, and threw them back at me. It wasn't my act that had changed, it was me. It wasn't the words that were wrong but the attitude which continued to create them. It wasn't something I could operate on and cut out like a piece of business or a speech affectation; it had dug in far deeper than that. It was a malignancy throughout my whole personality.

I'd become a Jekyll-and-Hyde character. And I could see the history of it.

Whatever happened offstage, I looked forward to my shows like another man waits for the weekend or a summer vacation, knowing that when I was in the wings waiting to go on, I'd first begin to feel whole and that finally, in conjunction with the audience, I would come alive. When I walked onstage, when I stood amidst my audiences and I saw their faces and knew I was home, where they liked me, I could relax—it was as though I could take off a coat. Then, when I had to leave that warmth and acceptance, when I had to leave the stage, I put on the coat again.

But no one can remain two distinct personalities. No one can sneer at people all day long and then for a few hours a night separate them and say "But these are 'audience' so they're different." You can only con people if you have no respect for them, and the more you con them and get away with it the less respect you have for people in general. The saloon song I'd had written after *Mr. Wonderful* was proof of how it could not be confined to the streets or to the dressing room crowd. Phoniness, the lack of respect, had become a habit, a reflex, and there had been a transition within me, a shift of balance so slight that I hadn't seen it happening and the "con man" began creeping onstage until gradually but inevitably he overpowered the honest performer and I was no longer able to take off the coat. I had stopped playing the role and become the character.

I remember becoming aware that I wasn't the "nice kid"

that had always been my stock in trade. I knew that I had to make the audience believe that I was nice, humble, warm —any number of things which once I had been but was no longer, and to accomplish it I'd reached for everything that had worked for me in the past: they'd always liked the relationship between my father, Will, and me so I'd grabbed for it, using the same words; I played "the kid," I flattered the audience—I did a dozen things I'd done when we were coming up and I did them exactly the same as I'd done them when they'd worked, when the emotions had been real. But as I acted them out, as I recited words remembered, the people recognized the difference, and all the statements and sentiments I utilized for effect, all the words which once I had meant, fell hollow, like all echoes.

I did my shows, straining to be nice, to *feel* nice so I could come across nice, but the tapes kept proving the lie. I tried to change, to make it real. I heard about a bellboy in the hotel whose wife needed an operation and I gave him a thousand dollars. Will hadn't been feeling well so I flew a specialist down from Boston to examine him. I made a list of people I knew cared about me and I called them all over the country just to say hello. But even as I did these things I knew they were pointless: nothing I could think to do was for anybody but myself, no compassion I felt was for anybody but me and each audience was perceptive enough to recognize and refuse to accept a kind of honesty that wears a mask. And I had no choice but to wear a mask because they would never accept what I really felt.

Night after night there was nothing I could do but sit by myself after the shows, staring at the foot-high stack of tapes—the coffin of anything good I had been—listening to my own voice destroying everything I'd built. Show by show it got thicker and deeper and the more I tried to struggle out of it, the more honest I tried to be—the more dishonest it came across. It had grown onto me like a barnacle and it was eventually going to pull me under.

I threw no party on closing night. I stayed alone in my $100 a day suite wondering how long before I couldn't afford this kind of luxury, looking through the penthouse window, immune to the majesty and beauty of the city below, trying to anticipate the future like a man who's been told he's got two years to live. If I was lucky and if I played my cards right and didn't come back to the same places too often maybe I could even stretch it into three. It wouldn't happen overnight—I had too much name, too much momentum—but it had to happen.

I didn't need to play the tapes anymore to hear the tinniness, I could see it in every face at every club at every stop along our swing from New York to Los Angeles. I unpacked some of my books on Judaism, books I hadn't looked at in almost a year. "Humility depends upon both thought and action. A man must be humble at heart before he can adopt the ways of the meek. Whoever wishes to conduct himself humbly without being humble at heart is only an evil pretender and in the company of those hypocrites who are the bane of mankind." It was like a finger wagging at me, telling me what I knew was wrong, but not how to fix it.

Rabbi Nussbaum asked, "Why, Sammy?" and as I heard his voice I was aware that it was the first time he'd spoken for at least an hour.

"There're a hundred reasons."

"Give me just a few."

"I want to make a change in my life, in my thinking—a complete overhaul."

"And you sincerely believe that conversion would be the thing to do it for you?"

"Rabbi, it's *got* to!" I was embarrassed by the loudness of my voice—the desperation it revealed. "Rabbi, I'm not going to bore you to death with my problems but I've got to have something to grab ahold of, something solid that I can depend on." I stood up and leaned across his desk. "I know what I am and I don't like what I am; I know what's in the books and I *like* what's in the books. I want to change but I can't do it alone. I've been trying to be a Jew in my heart but that's not enough. I can't stay on the outside looking in. I've had that all my life, Rabbi, and I just can't go that route anymore. I've got to get on the inside where I can feel it and participate in it. I know there's more good in people and in life than I can see and I've got to find a way to see it, to make contact again. I've read and I've studied and I've called myself a Jew. Everything you said. I've tried to feel like a Jew, I really have, but I know it can't work until I know I really *am* a Jew. Please. Don't turn me away."

I sat down and leaned my head against the back of the chair, staring at the ceiling. There was a long silence, then I heard the desk drawer open and close. He wrote something on a sheet of paper and slid it across to me. It said: "Sammy Davis, Jr. is a Jew." He'd signed it. He wasn't smiling or waiting for me to laugh, as if it were a gag, yet obviously it wasn't the real thing. I read it again, stalling, trying to understand. "I don't get it, Rabbi."

"Do you feel any better? Different? Does this solve any of your problems?" He crumpled the paper and dropped it into a wastebasket. "I hope you'll forgive the dramatics, Sammy. I was only trying to illustrate that I cannot make you a different person merely by signing a piece of paper."

"Then it's a turn-down, right?"

For an instant his eyes showed pain. "Sammy, try to understand that you're as much as asking for a diploma instead of the education it represents. If I let you delude yourself into believing that you have found what you need then you'll stop looking and it will never be yours to serve you as we both believe it can. You're grasping wildly for something to keep you afloat and I want urgently to give it to you. I'll clear my calendar to suit your needs, I'll give you all the time you need, I'll do anything to help you, but I will *not* give you a meaningless piece of paper and let you walk out of here believing it to be your lifeline. I will not encourage you to hold onto something which has no substance and cannot possibly support you."

"Well, that's all fine and I appreciate what you mean but it's not like I just read a pamphlet on Judaism and I came over and said, 'Hey, I wanta be one of these.' This has been going on for years with me. I've read the books by the dozens, I believe in the ideas—I can recite them to you."

He stood up and looked out the window for a moment, then turned to me. "The first time we met I told you not to expect to find Judaism in books, I warned you they would give you the philosophies and the theology but that it was up to you to translate them into religion. Do you remember?"

"I think so. I'm not sure."

"Well, I'm sorry to say that it hasn't happened. Further, you're looking to Judaism as a quick cure for your problems. You're coming to me for a bandage to cover a sore, a crutch to lean on, a pill to remove a headache. But Judaism is not a symptomatic cure. It cannot be taken internally like a tranquilizer. On the contrary, it must start from within and work its way out. Judaism is a philosophy, an approach to God and to life, a way of thinking, a state of mind. As a scholar of that philosophy I can help you to understand our principles, I can lead you to them, but only you can adopt them as your own. A rabbi is only a teacher. I don't speak to God any more than any man can speak to Him. I can't put religion into you. All I can do is help you to find it and then sign a paper attesting to the fact that in my opinion you have found this particular approach to life. But I cannot make you a Jew. Only *you* can do that. And you have not yet done it."

"But I think I have."

"Sammy, that is your desperation speaking, not your intellect. You didn't walk in here and say, 'Rabbi, I'm a Jew because I think and feel as one.' You didn't ask me to certify something which has already taken place within you, you've asked me to make it happen."

I avoided his eyes, knowing he was right, that I'd kidded myself it could work and taken a wild stab, like everything I'd been trying. It was embarrassing and I tried to laugh it off but the sound I made wasn't pleasant. I didn't feel very pleasant. "Well, I guess that's it folks. It's turn-in-the-books time."

His voice softened. "Sammy, it's entirely your choice, but you have such a feeling, such an understanding for Judaism that it would be a pity to have come this far, and then abandon it."

"Rabbi, I don't have much time left." I hated the melodramatic sound of that. "What I mean is I leave for Vegas in a few days. You don't suppose we could swing it by then?"

He sat down behind his desk. "Isn't it time for you to

stop fooling yourself?" I looked away. "Sammy, think back over our conversations. You've told me about friends you have but have not, about happiness you should have but have not. We've talked for hours and you've itemized all the points of your life, ticking them off one by one.. And what do they add up to? A twenty-four-hour-a-day vacuum with the single exception of your career. Hasn't it yet occurred to you why your life is like this? Isn't it likely that your career is the only thing to which you have given of yourself, that your audiences are the only people you have ever placed before yourself? By your own admission you've bought most of your friends and you've never had a relationship with a woman that was based on anything but carnal desire. You've built a gaudy house of cards and now you look around in surprise at seeing it topple. You see chaos but I can be more objective. I see justice. You've worked hard at your profession, you've been true to it and you became a star. But you gave no thought or consideration to anything else, so you have nothing else. Should I let you approach Judaism in that same way? Would I be doing you a favor if I were to help you create another pitifully vacuous experience? And this one would be the worst of all. Where would you turn when your last resort has failed?"

"I've got a better question. Where do I turn now?"

"To yourself."

I stood up. "I've been there. There's nobody home."

"Try again. You're the only person capable of shaping your life. Don't just read the books. Practice them. Don't just come to services and say prayers which are pointless unless they reflect a life which emulates the ways of God. I shouldn't have to tell you these things. You know them. If you believe in our philosophy then follow it, give it a fair opportunity to serve you."

"Rabbi, there's nothing I'd like better. I've been trying for years but it just doesn't seem to take. I guess I must be in pretty bad shape."

He stood up and walked across the room with me. "There have been worse. There have been men who didn't know they were in bad shape. There have been men who didn't have the power to alter their thinking." At the door he said,

Neither I nor Judaism would suffer if you tried it and it failed. Only *you* would lose."

"I was going to ask you when you think I'll be ready but guess that's a ridiculous question. It sounds like I'm trying to cook a chicken."

He smiled. "You'll know before I do. You'll become a Jew long before I put a piece of paper in your hand. And although I look forward to that day, you will not be the slightest bit better a Jew than you were the day before. As a matter of fact when you know you're ready you won't even rush in here to get the certificate. You won't need it then because you'll have what it represents."

The car seemed to be moving up Sunset on its own. What was I supposed to do until then? I'd stopped for a light and found myself staring at graying walls and the unlighted front of a building on which a cheaply painted sign advertised: *Available for Bingo and Banquets* and as the haze of thought cleared I realized I was looking at Ciro's. I tore my gaze away, not wanting to see the club dead but was too late and I saw the phantoms of a great couple of years: people who had once stood in line along that block, the image of myself on that stage, a figure with hope, strong and alive with the vigor of success, energized and propelled by the love of being loved. The light was still red but I pressed my foot on the gas and as the car roared away the image of what I used to be was joined by a Halloween-like figure jerking convulsively up, down, sideways, pacing furtively in a circle which kept growing smaller and smaller. . . .

My father was shouting and staggering around the living room, loaded again. Peewee was on the couch, crying. Another argument, another fight, the same atmosphere I'd felt a hundred times. He turned from Peewee and started toward Mama, his hand raised.

"If you touch her I'll kill you." He looked up, shocked by the roar of my voice. I was on top of him before he could open his mouth and as big as he is he might have been a piece of paper I was shoving toward the front door of the house, "Get out of here, get out of here." He looked at me and ran out the door. I followed him to the street still screaming as he went down the road. "If you come back

I'll break your arms . . . don't ever raise your hand to Mama as long as you live!"

I went back into the house. Mama was crying, Peewee was crying, Sandy and Suzette were crying. It was horrible and ugly. How could he pick on Mama? On Mama of all people. I picked up a table that had been knocked over, slammed the door to my bedroom, and sat on the bed shaking. If it wasn't my father, it was Peewee and Mama fighting over who'd use the kitchen. I'd built Mama a separate kitchen but it didn't help. There was always something. I lit a cigarette and just sat there smoking, trying to calm down. After a few minutes I threw the cigarette into the fireplace. Peewee was alone in the living room. I patted her on the arm. "I'll go get him." The road was dark except for the small street light. I started running, afraid he might walk into a car coming around a curve.

He was sitting on the curbstone at the bottom of the hill crying, "I didn't mean it . . . I didn't mean it . . ."

"Dad, come on. Let's you and me go for a walk, huh?"

The air was cool and clean smelling and I could hear him breathing deep, trying to collect himself as we walked up the hill. "Poppa, all the fights . . . all that stuff . . . it's all my damned fault. I knows I got a good life but I wake up every morning and I got nowheres to go, nothin' to do . . . hell, I don't even come up with the house money the way you're still splittin' with me and Will."

"Dad, that's ridiculous. Lots of men retire."

"But on money they put aside for themselves, Poppa. I'm not my own man. I wasn't going to tell you this but while you been on the road I been goin' down to the Playhouse every day, workin' out, gettin' back in shape. I got the idea watching television, seein' they don't dance today like we used to. I worked out a good routine for a single and thought up the name Sam Time—after how you never *could* do a time step." He smiled nostalgically, "Anyway I put this little act together and I figured some of the places we used to work might give me a break as an opening act. I called the ones I knew to be friends and told 'em I had to use the name Sam Time 'cause I didn't want to trade on your name, plus I didn't want people to say you cut me off and damned if I didn't set up my first date in Minneapolis

442

Five hundred a week, two weeks, with an option for two more. I planned the way I'd tell you was I'd send you a copy of the newspaper ad for 'Sam Time' and I was gonna mark it 'That's me, so stop sendin' the checks, son. I'm off your hands.'

"Anyway, I got to town and went over to the club and there was this sign for 'Sam Time' but underneath in foot-high letters it said 'Sammy Davis Jr.'s Father.'" He looked away, "I took the next train home."

I put my arm around his shoulder and we walked in silence, then he said quietly, "All I knows is show business, Poppa. I goes to the track to kill the day and then I gets drunk to forget all the money I lost and it goes 'round and 'round and I guess I takes it out on Mama and Peewee and even the kids. God knows I don't mean to . . ." He stared blankly up the road. "I guess there ain't nothin' can help a man when he's seven'd out."

26

THE DAY WE GOT TO VEGAS WILL TOLD ME, "SAMMY, I'm quitting the act. I had another examination in L.A. and the doctors say I can't keep it up. Truth is they told me I should stay home and rest but I'll keep traveling with the act as manager."

I'd expected it and I'd planned we'd open an office in L.A. or in New York and save the $20,000 a year in travel expense for him and Nathan. "Massey, maybe you should listen to what they say. If they think you should stay home . . ."

"No. Doctors don't know everything about a man. They don't take into account that if I had to stay away from show business I'd have nothing to live for . . ." Abruptly he snapped himself out of it. "Everything'll be the same as always. We're still the Will Mastin Trio except I won't be on the stage. You'll be doing a single."

It should have been the greatest day of my life, despite the ludicrous billing, but no outside force could make things better or worse, no pleasure I might have had could survive the constant question: But for how long?

I was starting to drink. For the first time in my life I was using hard liquor, trying to get drunk. I tried Frank's drink, Jack Daniels, and it was working. If nothing could help me make it with the audiences at least there was a way to forget them, to remove myself from the pressure of shows which I couldn't make come alive no matter what I did.

I was in the middle of a dance when my legs felt tired and I had to switch to a comedy piece to give myself a rest. It happened because I'd stayed up all night but it made me feel I was getting old; going without sleep had never affected my performance. A few nights later I was doing a jump-up onto a piano—it was just a baby grand, only about four and a half feet high and I'd always made an "effortless" leap in the middle of "Me and My Shadow" and finished with a soft-shoe on the piano top. I went for the jump and my toes landed barely an inch or two past the edge and I had to dig in to stay up there. I was lucky and made it look graceful and nobody noticed it, but I knew how hard I'd strained and that there'd come a night when I'd miss. I cut it out of the act.

Age catching up with me was frightening because I'd created my own monster—perpetual motion. I'd thrived on "Wow, where does he get the energy?" Now I had no choice but to slow down the act, and it was the ultimate threat; if I didn't die one way I'd be devoured another.

And the papers kept grinding away: "Sammy Davis, Jr. has been warned by top Chicago gangsters that if he ever sees that blonde movie star again both his legs will be broken and torn off at the knee." . . . "The boss of a certain moom pitcha company has a photo of SD Jr. on his office wall. Flings darts at it." . . . "Sammy Davis owes—"

The rumors and innuendos trailed me across the country, but these things, which would have bothered me at another time, were like mosquitoes buzzing around a man being pulled down by quicksand. Everything was drowned out by the drone of the tapes as they continued telling the only story I cared about, "Sammy Davis is losing his talent . . . losing his talent . . . losing his talent."

Mickey Rooney was at a black-jack table. He didn't see me. I stood back waiting for the seat next to him to open up, remembering the good times we'd had together, how he'd really started it for me eight years ago. Eight years. It seemed so very much longer. A woman seated next to him gathered her money and walked away. I put my drink on the table and dropped a $25 chip on the line. "Hello, Mick."

He looked up from his cards, there was a flash of pleasure at recognition, then it was subdued and there remained just the trace of a smile. "Hello, Sam." He continued playing his cards.

I touched his shoulder. "It's great to see you, Mick."

He nodded. "I see you've started drinking."

"Yeah. Hey, how long've you been in town?"

"I came in a few days ago."

"You're joking. Why didn't you call me? Let me know you were here? That's a hell of a thing to do."

He took a slug of his drink. "What the hell, you've been busy . . . I know how it is."

"Busy? You've gotta be kidding. Too busy for *you?*"

He smiled, tentatively. "I called a few days ago but I guess they didn't give you the message." He took another card from the dealer, went over, turned his down-card up and looked at me.

"Mickey, I swear to God I never got a message. I didn't even know you were in town until I saw you sitting here."

He shrugged. "It's not important." And as I played my cards quickly, to get it over with, I caught a glimpse of my wrist watch, the platinum gleaming out from under the rich silk cuff of my shirt, and I could feel Mickey looking at my clothes, my jewelry, at the pile of big chips in front of me. When I turned to him again he was smiling at the corners of his mouth, nodding his head slowly, his eyes seemingly removed from the moment. "Remember the old days, Sam? When we used to pal around together?"

His voice lost the softness of nostalgia. "I read a story about how you got your start. Funny, I didn't see my name. Well, you're a big star now, you've got important friends . . . you don't need me any more." He hid behind the mock-hurt bit, "It's okay, Sam. It's great. I'm happy for you. Glad to see you doing so well . . ." He was playing it like a joke and there were people around so I laughed—but I wanted to cry. There were new cards in front of me but I couldn't play them. I excused myself and went outside and walked around the pool. How could I have let this happen to me and Mickey? Here was a *friend,* a man who'd fought for me with his position as a star as well as with his fists, yet during all these years when I'd been aware of the troubles he was having I'd never thought to pick up a phone or send him a post card just to let him know, "I remember all the good and kind things you did for me." With his talent he'd always land on his feet, he didn't need me, but it might have been comforting occasionally to hear "you were my friend and I'm yours." I looked down into the water of the swimming pool and stared at my reflection, seeing ugliness that no mirror could reflect.

My father had come in from L.A. for the weekend and I knew by the way he closed the dressing room door that it wasn't going to be: Great show, son.

"Poppa, I've gotta show you what they're writin' about you in our papers. Mama saw this one and it made her feel real bad."

"Sammy Davis, Jr., once a pride to all Negroes has become a never-ending source of embarrassment. The legend of Mr. Davis' amours trips gaily from one bedroom to another, leering out at us from the covers of endless scandal magazines, dragging us all through the mud along with him. Perhaps Errol Flynn can prosper from this sort of publicity but on one of us it doesn't look good. Mr. Davis has never been particularly race conscious but his current scandal displays him as inexcusably *un*conscious of his responsibility as a Negro. Look in the mirror, Sammy. You're still one of us."

I dropped the paper. "I don't need a mirror to remind me I'm colored. There's *nobody* in this whole goddamned world who'll let me forget it."

Will stood up and glared at me. "All my life I did a clean act, but the way you're rolling around in the mud there'll come a day when people are going to stop bringin' their families in to see us." He walked out of the room, shaking his head.

"Poppa, I . . ." there was a long silence. Then, "Hey, whattya say we go get us a little somethin' to eat? Maybe some Chinese food, just you and me?"

"I'm not exactly hungry, Dad."

"Well . . . I guess I'll stop by the casino. . . ."

He was standing at a crap table. His face brightened. "Glad t'see you, son."

"You're sure it's okay for me to be in here, now? I mean you don't think maybe the papers'll get upset and call me Uncle Tom or nigger rich?"

"Sammy . . ."

"Catch y'later, Dad." I wandered over to the cashier's window. "Baby, let me have five thousand." I sat down at a black-jack table and put $500 on the line.

At least fifty people were gathered around me, groaning as I went down hand after hand. "Baby, you'd better send over for another five thousand for me." I signed the slip and kept playing. It all seemed so silly: I go to a window, I sign my name, a man gives me a stack of chips, I put them on a table and another guy takes them away. "You'd better get me another five, baby." A cocktail waitress came by, "Coke, Sammy?"

"That's last year's publicity, darling. It's Jack Daniels now."

I walked over to the crap table and tapped my father on the shoulder. He turned around and smiled. "I thought you'd like to know, Dad. I just lost thirty-nine thousand dollars!" I waited for him to be shocked or get angry but he just looked sad, his eyes got watery and I wanted to kill myself. "I'm sorry, Dad." I touched his arm and walked away.

I did my second show, got boozed up in the lounge, and

stumbled into my car half-stoned. When I didn't feel like driving any more, I got out of the car and looked around. The lights were blazing, music was coming at me from all directions, I was in front of the Silver Slipper.

I pounded the bar top. "Innkeeper! Wine for my horses and nothing for my men!" Oh, fine—I was in rare form, using lines from the act.

The bartender grinned, "What'll it be, Sammy?"

"A little Daniels, old buddy, a little double Daniels for old Sam to make up for lost time."

The show had ended and the girls were coming out front. Hmmmmmm, which wench will ye have m'lord? . . . One of them was walking toward me. The body looked familiar . . . but I couldn't place the face.

"Hello, Sammy."

I tried to focus on her but she kept moving. I was bobbing my head back and forth trying to get in rhythm with her. "Don't I know you . . . I *know* I know you . . . oh, for God's sake, hello Loray, what're *you* doing here?"

"I'm working here. I hope you didn't drive over in the shape you're in."

"Nobody was driving, officer, we were all in the back seat singing. How've you been, Loray honey?"

"Fine, Sammy. How about you?"

"Swingin'. Crazy! Don'tcha read the papers?"

"I've been reading about you for years."

"I'm a big star, huh, Loray?" She nodded. "I'm 'bout as big as anyone can get, right?"

"Just about."

"Have a drink, Loray! Whattya drink?"

"I'll have a glass of champagne."

"That's right. Now I 'member. Barkeep! Champagne for the lady, and more red-eye for old Sam." I grinned. "Hey, where've you been, Loray?"

"Right here at the Slipper. I played some places in South America . . ."

"Rio, or Mississippi? Oh God. C'mon, we'll find a table in the lounge and get comfortable. Y'wanta gamble?"

"No, Sammy. I don't think you should gamble either."

"Hey! Hold everything. No one tells *me* when to gamble. I'm a star, remember?" I took out a roll of bills. "Y'see this? Thousands!" I winked at her. "I feel lucky tonight." I gotta be lucky, tonight. Something's gotta be going for me. I gave her a handful of bills and steered her over to the crap tables. "Let's *be* somebody."

I got on a winning streak right away but I couldn't get interested. "C'mon, Loray, this is a bore."

She gasped. "You're crazy. You're *hot*."

"I'm hot and hot-blooded." I gathered the chips that had piled up in front of me and stuffed them into my pockets. I looked down at my legs. "Goddamned tight pants bulge." I took out some and handed them to her. "Buy a hat." She gazed at the money. "Tut tut, wench. A mere farthing. I've a thousand acres of the finest cattle land, as far as the eye can see. . . ."

We went back to the bar. "Y'know, you're a beautiful girl, Loray. You're one swingin' chick, y'know that? How come we stopped going around together?"

"That's something you know better than me, Sammy. You just disappeared."

"Yeah, I remember. What a lousy thing to do to a nice chick like you. We had a good little thing goin' for us. Nothing fantastic—but it was kinda nice, right?"

"*I* thought so."

"Sure . . ." Oops! It suddenly came back to me. She *had* thought so. She couldn't play it for laughs and catch-you-next-time-around. I'd smelled a cottage small by a waterfall and I'd run like a thief, left town without even calling her.

Maybe that was stupid . . . maybe a wife's what I'd needed all the time, maybe that's what I need *now*. If I had a wife, I'd belong. I could relax, the papers would get off my back. I looked at Loray. She's beautiful. Better looking than ever. Hey, this is a beautiful chick, Charley. She understands the business, she's a lady, she knows how to dress. I bet she still digs me.

"Y'know, Loray, if I had any sense I'd marry you. Hey, this is no joke! Y'think I tell that to everyone I meet? Y'know I don't have to do this jazz to get a chick. I've got 'em comin' out of my ears. Never been more serious in my life. Just 'cause I made a mistake once doesn't mean I have to keep making the same one all my life, does it? Does it?"

"I don't mean to be ungracious but you're drunk, Sammy."

"Sure I am, but I know what I'm doing. Whattya think I came in here for in the first place? Hey, have another drink, Loray. What're y'drinkin'?"

"Still champagne."

"Waiter, some champagne for the lady and booze for Sam. Cert'ny Loray, honey. Whatsa matter, they don't have booze at the Sands? I didn't exactly have to come here to buy a drink, y'know."

"Please, maybe this is laughs for you, but I don't want to play."

"Hey, cool it! Did I ever ask you to marry me before?"

"No, but—"

"Answer the question. Did I ever ask me to marry you before?" I knew I'd screwed up the words, but I hoped maybe she wouldn't notice it.

She smiled. "Okay, I'll go along with you. I accept your proposal."

"You do?"

"Yes."

"Hey, that's pretty crazy." I leaned back to focus on her. This is a natural. Just what I need. A nice girl to come home to, someone I can be proud to introduce as my wife; I'll come across to the public as Charley Straight. They'll drop the "wild kid" jazz in the papers. And the Negro press'll go out of their minds; they'll eat it up like a hundred yards of chit'lins. There'll be hugging and kissing and front pages with come-home-son-all-is-forgiven.

I stood up. "C'mon. We'll announce it." I led her over to the bandstand and waited for the guys to finish their set. The whole idea kept getting better all the time. The music ended. Here goes Charley Single. I took Loray's arm. "'Scuse me, guys. Got a li'l announcement to make." The room quieted down immediately. "Ladies and Gentlemen, your 'ttention, please, if I may . . ."

The club's press agent pushed his way through the crowd around us. "Is this on the level, Sammy?"

I put my arm around Loray and smiled at him. "Sure is, baby."

"Will you stay around 'til I get a photographer? Please? Just a few minutes." He was panicking. I nodded and as he turned to dash away I nudged him, "Congratulations, baby."

People were pulling us to their tables to offer us drinks. This is beautiful, everybody loves it. Sam, baby, you did it again. Another great move. "Let's have 'nother drink. A li'l booze f'r th' happy couple, huh? How often does a guy get married? What're y'drinking', Loray, honey?"

Arthur was standing close to my head, "Sammy? You up?" What the hell's he whispering for? If I'm awake why doesn't he just talk? But if I'm sleeping then leave me alone. "Sammy? You awake, baby?" I turned over and waved my arm at him, but he wouldn't go away. "Sammy, your father's on the phone. He wants to know about your engagement to Loray White."

Oh God. I started to sit up but I grabbed my head and fell back onto the pillow. I sat up, slowly. "I'll call him back. And Arthur, gimme a Coke, with a lot of ice." I rested, trying to piece the evening together. "What'd my father say? How'd he hear about it?"

"It was on the radio at five o'clock this morning. That's when I first heard it, and it's in all the papers today. Front page here in Vegas. When'd you start seeing Loray again?"

"Baby, cool the questions. I've got to think."

"Whattya mean? Isn't it true? What happened?"

"Arthur, how the hell do *I* know? I asked a girl to marry me. I got drunk and made a complete, total fool of myself. That's what happened."

"You're joking. But you haven't seen her in years. Not that she isn't a hell of a nice girl . . ."

"Arthur, she's a lovely girl. So is Eleanor Roosevelt, but I'm not in love with *her* either."

"Then you're not going to marry her?"

"What do *you* think? You know Loray and I were all over two years ago. Do you really think I'm about to *marry* her now?" My head killed me when I yelled. I lowered my voice. "Don't be an idiot with ridiculous questions when I'm trying to figure out what in the hell I'm supposed to tell her."

"Maybe it's not so serious. Loray's a smart girl. She's probably waiting to see if you still mean it now that you're sober."

"I'd like to believe that." I looked up. "Maybe you're right. She knows I was gassed out of my mind. . . ."

451

He gave me a stack of phone messages. "You'll have to think up a statement. All the L.A. papers have been trying to reach you. There's a guy outside now from one of the wire services, waiting 'til you get up. The Negro press has been on the phone every ten minutes. *Jet*, the *Courier*, some woman in New York—someone Cunningham."

"*Evelyn* Cunningham?"

"Yeah, that's her. They're all excited about the wedding and when it'll be and when'd you meet Loray."

I flopped back on the pillow. That's it. This does it with the Negro press. Even if Loray lets me off the hook they'll wrap this around my ears: He was just using her for publicity, he doesn't want her because she isn't white. Before they're finished there won't be a colored cat in the country who'll talk to me.

Arthur was answering the phone. "Yes, he is, Mrs. Cunningham."

I hissed, "I'm still sleeping."

He put his hand over the mouthpiece and whispered frantically, "But I already said you're awake."

"What the hell did you think I was waving my arms at you for?"

"But she's already called three times."

He knows I don't know which way to turn and he puts me on with the toughest columnist in the whole Negro press. I shook my fist at him and took the phone. "Hello, Mrs Cunningham, so nice to hear from you."

"Hello, Sammy, I believe congratulations are in order."

She said it as if it was a test question. All I'd need is to say: Congratulations for what? I took the plunge. "Thank you very much, Mrs. Cunningham. Very kind of you."

"Then it's true?" I could feel the phone warming up. "You and Loray White *are* engaged?"

The nails were in the coffin. "Yes, ma'am. We became engaged last night."

"Well, congratulations!" This time she really meant it. "This is wonderful." It was as though she was thinking: could we have been wrong about him? "When will you be married?"

"We haven't set the date. Soon though, I hope."

"Will Loray keep up her own career? Or will she travel with you?"

"Well, we haven't discussed it, but if she wants to keep up her career, I certainly won't object—she's a very talented girl, you know."

"Perhaps she'll want to do an act with you."

Oh, fine. *Another* partner. "Well, that's certainly an interesting idea, something to think about. Of course nobody could ever replace my father and my uncle."

"Sammy, I think this is a wonderful thing. I'm really very happy for you. Sometimes a man needs some responsibility."

"Yes, ma'am. Thank you."

Arthur was gaping at me, mouth open, as I hung up. I nodded viciously and bowed. "And thank *you*, Arthur. You did it again. One of the great, *stupid* moves of our time."

"Sammy, I'm sorry. I know how important those papers are to you so I thought you'd want . . ." He shrugged helplessly.

The phone was ringing again. "Go ahead baby, you can't bury me any deeper."

I was flopped out on the bed listening to him chat with Loray, "Arthur, if I'm not intruding, you'd better tell her to come over here this afternoon around five."

He hung up, "She'll be here. What're you gonna do?"

I couldn't breathe without causing waves of nausea. "I'll explain the whole thing and ask her to go along with me. We'll get married, we'll make it look good for a while, and then we'll get divorced."

"Do you think she'll go along with it? Y'know you didn't treat her so well that she oughta be looking to do you any favors. And, another thing, once a chick becomes Mrs. Sammy Davis, Jr., she's not going to let go so easily."

"Arthur, may I assume this is *all* the good news you have for me today?"

"What I mean is, maybe it's not worth it. You've been in trouble with the press before."

"Of course it's not worth it! But this is one time I can't afford trouble with them."

"Why now more than ever?"

"Baby, just know this: if I back out now, I'm dead."

"I don't know . . . it just doesn't seem right, I mean going into marriage like this."

"Arthur . . . is that your considered opinion?" I got out of bed and started dressing. Will arrived. He cocked his head to one side. "This true, Mose Gastin?" He hadn't called me that in years. He looked confused, which, all things considered, was about as good a way to look as any other.

"It's true."

"Do you love this girl?" He searched my face. "You get her in trouble?"

"Not the kind you're thinking of."

"Then—"

"Massey, I got drunk and I asked her to marry me. It's that simple. What's worse, I had to get up on the stage at the Silver Slipper and make sure everybody knows."

"Well, then, you gotta come out and say it was all a mistake."

"Sure." I turned on him. "I'll take full page ads in *The Defender, The Amsterdam News,* and *The Courier:* 'Sorry, folks, it was all a mistake. Old Sam got loaded. Heh, heh, heh.' Massey, I've thought it over very carefully. There's no other way to handle it." I walked into the bathroom to get away from him but he followed me in with Arthur right behind him.

"Sammy, nothing is as bad as if you marry someone you don't love." He was trying to control himself, speaking carefully—like I was an inmate at a mental institution.

Arthur nodded. "I agree with Will, Sammy."

I glared at him. "*Do* you, doctor?" He backed up. "Now look, you guys, it's my life. Whatever happened was my fault. Mine. *I* did it and I've gotta straighten it out."

Loray sat stiffly erect on the couch, waiting, expecting me to tell her, "It's all a mistake," and I almost enjoyed the dramatic moment. "Loray . . . I need your help."

She didn't move a muscle. "You don't have to marry me, Sammy."

When I'd finished explaining it to her, for about three long minutes she just stared at me, then she stood up. "Fine."

"Great. I can't thank you enough. Now look, don't leave town, I'll call you as soon as I need you."

My father tried to talk me out of it; the phone kept ringing all day; everyone was butting in, all of them certain they knew exactly what was best for me. I made arrangements for the ceremony. The sooner the better.

On the night of the wedding I did only one show at the Sands. Loray was at ringside. I introduced her and did all the shtick the audience expects from a guy who gets married: the bedroom humor, with a leer and "Well, folks, I've gotta get back to the room."

I had a few shots of bourbon with some of the people who'd come to the dressing room, but I couldn't keep up the front any longer, I had to get them out. I sent them ahead to the party with Loray. I don't know why they thought I wanted to be alone, but they winked and grinned and left. The unbelievable lunacy of the whole thing had reached its full proportion. I locked the door. I couldn't have taken it to see them nudging each other, "Look, he's so happy, he's crying."

I read a few of the telegrams that had been pouring in from all over the country, from people who were wishing something good for me. How cheap could I get? How many people could I feel, using their warmth and their affection against them, letting them put themselves in unflattering positions like this?

The party was in a saloon on the West Side and it was going full blast when I got there. I emptied a full bottle of Jack Daniels into an ice bucket, then added a few Cokes and I drank from that. All the guests thought it was hysterical; the "family" didn't. They'd never seen me like this before. Who had? Who went around getting married to make other people happy? Me. Beautiful goddamned me.

I'd wanted so badly to be married to the right girl and have a home and kids and a life in the community. I was married now, drinking out of my loving cup—a cardboard ice bucket in a broken-down saloon, letting photographers pull me all over the room for "a shot of the happy couple." I kept drinking and posing for pictures, my arm around Loray, and walking around the room with my ice bucket.

Arthur was trying to take the bucket away. "Sammy, maybe you've had enough."

"I'm okay, baby . . . just wanta find a wife . . . just want people leave me alone . . ."

He had his arm around me. "Come on, I'll drive you and Loray home. Can you stand up okay?"

I got up. I was dead but I just wouldn't fall down. I took a last look around. This was my wedding night, *the* night in a man's life.

I was in the front seat with Arthur. I wanted to break something or tear something. I was clawing at his sleeve while he was trying to drive. Loray reached forward to stop me. I'd forgotten about her. Loray. She was in the back seat, and it was all her fault; I grabbed her by the throat. Arthur was pulling me away from her with one hand and trying to drive with the other. I nudged him. "Hey, y'got a little congratulations for old Sam? Huh, baby, old buddy? A little kind word f'r old Sam who finally came through? Now everybody's happy, right?" He didn't answer. He was trying to drive the car and he was crying and trying to hold my hands down. "Hey, what the hell are you cryin' for, huh, Arthur? You cryin', baby? . . . somethin' wrong?"

The car had stopped moving and Arthur was standing at the open door, holding out his hand. I leaned back against the seat. "I don't wanta get out. I wanta stay here. Hey, whattya say we spend the night here, like in the old days— you still got your sleeping bag, Arthur? Remember when I used to sleep on the floor at your folks' place? Remember? That was beautiful . . . hey, how're your folks, old buddy? Gee, I haven't seen your folks in so long."

"Come on, Sammy. Take it easy. The bridal suite's all set up for you. Come on . . ."

"The bridal suite? How 'bout that? Hey, Loray, they gave us the bridal suite. That's touching, huh? Gets y'right here. The bridal suite for good old Sam and his bridle. 'Sure, what the hell, give 'em the bridal suite. We can throw away the furniture or send it out to be cleaned after he leaves.'"

Arthur was carrying me into the hotel in his arms. "Arthur, put me down. I'm no goddamned baby."

The tears were pouring down his face. Loray was there

and she was crying . . . why the hell is everybody crying? . . .

27

FROM THE DAY OF THE WEDDING EVERYBODY KNEW IT was a phony. They didn't know why or how so they grabbed for the nearest, most obvious reasons and the papers broke loose like I was World War III: "A blonde movie star just lost 20 lbs. No diet. Simply begged the love of her life to marry another to save her career and now she misses him. Boo-hoos herself to sleep every nite" . . . "The facts: Mrs. Sammy Davis, Jr. has a six month contract with her husband. The deal: a flat $10,000 and no options." . . . "SD Jr. moved his new wife into a new house on a hill overlooking Hollywood. Close friends say he overlooks her too." . . . "Insiders say Harry Cohn paid $50,000 to guess which song-and-dance man, to take the heat off Columbia's top box-office property."

Almost everything I read about the marriage was wrong except for the single underlying truth, that nobody was fooled by it. Despite a wedding, announcements and pictures of "the happy couple," the people sensed it was a phony, they could smell the hoax. It was the absolute proof of how impossible it is to accomplish anything through dishonesty.

But the complete shock was that as I moved across the country, the crowds grew bigger than ever. I was *hot* again. I taped some of the shows. The false humility was still there, it just wasn't coming through as strong because the drama was covering it. I was riding the crest of a controversy and there was no way to kid myself that I had anything but a reprieve that was limited in life by its own nature. The important thing, the shows, were abominable, and the new interest in me would fade with the rumors.

For the first time in my life I dreaded facing audiences. Whatever they were thinking or guessing, whatever opinions they had about me and the marriage, it was humiliating to have to stand before them to be inspected, it was degrading to know I was selling a performance but they were buying a display. Invariably as I walked onstage there were women at the ringside looking me up and down, like: What's he got? and the guys were grinning and winking like I was the swinger of all time, even more than they had after the Ava Gardner story. I was so genuinely miserable that I couldn't begin to hide it, and that was probably the first honest emotion I'd communicated to the audience in at least a year. As I sang, my fists would clench and I'd pound my leg or my side, and they connected the songs to Loray or to the rumors or to unhappiness in general—whatever they were thinking it brought tears to their eyes while I performed. That was the final, sick joke: to touch them but for the wrong reason.

I started drinking as soon as I woke up, kept a glow going until after the last show and then drank hard until I could pass out and sleep. Then in a few hours I awoke to face another day and another night of waiting to learn the excitement's dead and this is the night they stop showing up. But they kept coming back, filling the clubs, and the longer it dragged on the more menacing and depressing they were.

Sam Bramson was tremendously excited when he reached me by phone in Toronto. "The Eden Roc in Miami Beach has met your terms: $30,000 for ten days, suites for you and Will—and the doors are open to everybody. I never believed it could happen. You've broken down a tremendous barrier."

Big John came into my suite and I waited for him to react to the lavish ocean-front layout. "Sammy, I just come over from Miami—I dropped my clothes off at the Lord Calvert—I figure you oughta know what's happening."

"Such as?"

"What they're saying. Coupla guys I know caught me in

the lobby and they said, 'Howcum Sammy's not stayin' here? What's he doin' livin' over there on the Beach?' Then this other guy says, 'You kiddin'? He thinks he can pass.'"

"What'd you tell 'em?"

"Wasn't much I *could* tell 'em." He shrugged. "Fact is you're over here and all . . ."

"It's always gotta be something, huh? Well, the next time anybody says anything, you tell them what *I* say. Tell them I'm living *free* in a suite that would cost anybody else eight hundred dollars a week! Tell them I've opened the door for them and if they haven't got the guts to come over here then I don't have the stomach to go over there."

He nodded slowly and spoke quietly, "Sure, Sammy. Whatever you say. You're the boss." He stood up. "I'll tell 'em."

I watched him walking away, knowing he was my friend, knowing they'd probably said worse than he'd passed on to me. "Baby, check me into the Lord Calvert. Take a nice suite there."

"You gonna move?"

"No, dammit. Why the hell should I when I can live in the best hotel in town? But get the suite. It'll keep up appearances."

He nodded, pleased, protective. "You don't need 'em chewing you to pieces, boss." He shrugged and left to take care of it. I knew it was a futile gesture, even patronizing, but it was worth it if I could stop even one guy from perpetuating the "He takes white pills" talk.

My suite at the Eden Roc was crowded with people who'd been to the opening. I walked over to Harry Mufson, the owner of the hotel. He was sitting with his wife and some friends. He said, "It was fabulous, Sammy. We'll be packed for the entire run."

"Thanks, Harry. And thank you for what you've done by bringing me down. I know how hard it was."

I drifted into the crowd, wishing Will had come to the party or that my father had come in from the coast for the opening—someone who'd understand and look at me and say "Well, you did it." I'd have given anything for somebody close who could appreciate the broken barrier, somebody who'd been with me along the way, somebody I could tell, "Yeah. We really did," and we could be excited about it.

As we moved across the country the tapes were like an X-ray, giving a clear, unwavering verdict. I still had that helpless inability to reach through to the people, as though a thin rubber wall existed between us, and no matter how hard I tried to push myself through it, no matter how thin I stretched it, it was always there, separating us, making any real contact impossible.

I slept as late as I could to cut down the hours I had to sweat out every afternoon, wondering, is this the night they'll stop coming?

Then, the ordeal of arriving at the club; the painfully casual question, "How're the reservations?" the momentary relief at hearing "We're sold out," then the nauseating awareness that tomorrow is another day, and the overriding absolute, that "tomorrow" would come in a week, in a month, in a year, that it was irreversible.

I checked into the Waldorf Towers instead of the War-wick. I closed the bedroom door so Arthur wouldn't hear me and I called the Copacabana. "My name is Hawkins. I see that Sammy Davis is playing at your place and I'd like a table for two tonight . . ."

"I'm sorry, sir, we're entirely sold out this evening." I fell against the pillow, relieved.

It was five in the morning when I finally closed the door and looked around the suite. I walked through the dining room, down the long hallway, trying to appreciate the mar-ble-fitted bathrooms and the beautiful antique furniture in the living room. There was frost on the window and I doodled with my finger trying to draw a house with a chim-ney and smoke coming out of it. I had a lousy feeling that all I ever did was sit in front of windows in hotel rooms waiting for people to wake up or waiting until I could sleep. I looked uptown, thinking about the long road to Park Avenue and 50th Street. We'd been hungry sometimes and frustrated always, but even if it had only been in a waiting room or the back seat of a car, at least we had slept. I tried to remember how terrible it had been up there, but the thoughts of everything I'd hated and escaped were overwhelmed by the memory of something I'd never appreciated, never valued, something I could never feel again—there had always been the hope that tomorrow we'd be on the way up!

The opening at the Moulin Rouge was tremendous. Throughout the first week I kept watching the faces, waiting, half-hoping they'd finally look away from me and get it over with. But they wouldn't. Night after night they jammed the club, pouring in en masse, prolonging the agony of the death vigil.

By the end of the second week I couldn't stand to hang around the dressing room between shows or after, to hear what great business I was doing, to face the invasion of the back-slappers, loud, laughing, transparent and ugly: "How's Loray?" . . . "Hey, the show was a gas." . . . "Never saw you better. Man, what drama." . . . "What business you're doing!" . . . "For a second show—on a week night! Never saw anything like it."

Their voices scraped my nerves raw. Whose dressing room will it be tomorrow? I pushed my way past them and left the club.

As I turned off Sunset and started climbing the hill to my house I could actually feel the atmosphere changing, softening, and as I made the turns near the top of the hill and saw the lights of Los Angeles miles away they seemed only peaceful and beautiful.

I pulled up in front of the house. I cut the motor, put out the lights and sat there in the dark. I could hear a dog barking, then an answer coming to him from another part of the hill. I listened to them; first one, then another, then a third joining in, like they were buddies. It was restful hearing sounds that had no meaning to me—no threat, no urgency.

I got out of the car and unlocked the front door. The racket hit me like a wet cloth in the face. My father was yelling at Peewee and the kids were crying. I leaned against the wall in the foyer. Their voices droned on, grinding each other to pieces. I'd recognize the sound of those arguments anywhere—the single overriding tone of discontent. It was ugly. Violently ugly. And the kids were right in the middle of it all, always being exposed to it, feeling all the pain and confusion that kids shouldn't feel. I listened, saddened by the same old clashing and complaining, the knowledge that nobody was satisfied, nobody was happy, and it was costing a fortune to be keeping them like that. This is my goddamned dream house. Is this what I've accomplished? To have provided money for people who can't live together in peace, who can't be happy? To be perpetuating *this*? Maybe even to be causing it? It's bad enough that *I* can't be happy. But them, too?

I stepped forward to let them all see me but nobody stopped even long enough to say hello. I backed away and ran out of the house. As I started the engine of my car I knew what I was going to do. Why not? No matter how fast I ran I couldn't get out from under the cloud that hovered over me. It kept chasing me, moving with me, always hanging over my head, and one day it was going to drop and smother me. Why wait? If I'm not doing *anybody* any good then why keep running? Who'll miss me? Who'll really give a damn? Why not go out while people think I'm still on top? Why suffer through more months, maybe even years, of sinking into oblivion, and then endure the rest of my life as a loser? Better to go out now.

The perfect spot was off the side of the cliff past Rising Glen where an eagle sits on top of the hill. There's an empty space between the houses and a sheer drop of at least five hundred feet.

I was gunning the motor, roaring around curves at sixty miles an hour, then sixty-five, steadily pushing my foot down further, gripping the wheel with both hands, planning to hold tight to it as I went over the cliff, imagining the feeling of nothingness beneath me as I'd ride out the drop. The wheels were screeching around the curves. I pressed more gas into the engine until the pedal touched the floor and I kept it there, watching the road growing shorter ahead of me and the needle reaching just past seventy as I got to Rising Glen. I braced myself, turned the wheel sharp and held on.

The car stopped, like I'd hit a wall! I kept my foot on the gas, gunning and gunning and gunning the engine: I could hear the tires screaming over the roar but the car wouldn't budge. It was as though a huge hand had reached out and was holding it, preventing it from going over.

When I opened the door the smell of burnt rubber gagged me. I turned on a flashlight. The transmission had snapped in half and was jammed into the ground like an anchor. The front wheels were sunk into the lip between the sidewalk and the dirt.

Let anyone hit this spot at any other time and it would positively fling them over the cliff. It had to.

God had had his arms around me again. Nothing else could have saved me.

An hour or so later I walked back to the house. There was a single night light on in the living room and my father was asleep on the couch. The kids were in bed and Mama and Peewee must have been in their rooms. I went to my own room and closed the door. I looked out the window at the lights of Los Angeles, then up at the sky. Dear God, I don't know why you gave me another chance. I don't know why you want me here or why you gave me this talent. And I know I haven't used it the way you must have intended for me to use it. But I want to. Honestly I do. Please show me what to do. I know that I just seem to do all the wrong things. I know I must be a disappointment to you but I don't want to be. I know I don't pray except when I need you. Please forgive me. I can't seem to do anything right. But I'll never again question why you put me here, or try to leave here until you want to take me. I'll try to live as I think you would want me to, and to do the things I think you want me to do. But please help me. Just once more. Please God, help me. . . .

How had I come to love life so little as to want no more of it? What had I wanted and failed to find that had been more precious than life itself?

Each question drew a response too quick, too automatic to trust, and as I held them against the light of logic and fact they began opening like the petals of a carnivorous plant revealing the skeleton of the phantasy in which I had tried to live.

I was the man who'd committed the monstrous indignity of becoming a star to become a man; who'd waited and worked, planning to surprise Hatred by proving I was its equal. I was the man who'd looked to the magic of stardom

463

to religion, to everything but the absolute of my own worth.

I was the man who'd missed the smiles of a thousand, obsessed by the sneer of one; who'd listened for drums and never heard the concerto; who'd focused on the faces of Hatred in close-up, a hundred times their size; who'd tried to find everything I desired by searching for everything I did not.

There had been no harm in the dream of a boy—until it hardened and fastened itself onto a man as a necessity, blinding, obstructing maturity, preventing re-evaluation. No white man could ever have been the enemy to me that I had been to myself: he was often guilty of unkindness and stupidity, but I had wasted my life and my talent to win a victory over that stupidity. I was the man who'd opened the door and let Hatred come in, and presented my case to a madman.

I was the man who'd paid tribute to Hatred with every breath of my life.

Rabbi Nussbaum said, " 'It is difficult to make a man miserable while he feels worthy of himself and claims kinship to the great God who made him.' "

I smiled, "Lincoln."

"Yes. Sammy, life is not designed for 'no problems.' But there are men who cringe from their problems and others who face them, as you have begun to do, looking toward the satisfaction of surmounting them. Look at the design of life. When a man makes a mistake, he loses what he had tried for but at least he gains wisdom. If he's young and he breaks a bone it heals and becomes stronger than before. You're still young, Sammy—"

"But, Rabbi, do you know how many mistakes I made?"

He smiled. "Imagine how wise you must be. Don't dwell on your mistakes. Correct them. And don't hold a grudge against them; they've taught you almost everything you know.

"Man is a thinking being. He has the power of reason. He can move into any shaped house he wishes to build. There are tools, helps, but he must do the building himself. If he works steadily toward his goal, eventually he accomplishes it.

"When a man sets about to construct a new home he gives great time and thought to how it will look, how long it will stand and how well it will serve him. He chooses woods from dozens of samples, he learns about various stones, he shops for the best of everything within his reach. Isn't it sad that so few people take the same care in constructing their lives?"

I stretched out on a lounge alongside the swimming pool, feeling as though I'd come home after a long, hard war. I looked at the scar on the palm of my hand, the Star of David. It had faded and it would probably disappear someday but my need for Judaism was permanent and I was grateful now that I'd been prevented from rushing into it. I knew that the comfort and self-detachment it had already given me was only the beginning, and I was eager for it to develop slowly, but well. There was so much changing for me to do, within me, but I felt ready and able to do it and somehow time was not so imperative. It didn't matter how long it might take before I could approve of myself thoroughly, without reserve. All I wanted was to know that next year I was going to be better than I was last year.

After a while I went inside and sat at the window dissecting, until I understood, mistakes I could never make again: the using of color as a cop-out for any impulse I'd felt like indulging; the incredible lack of human understanding—from *me* who wanted to be understood; the scorning of people's weaknesses, using them; the grabbing, taking, drawing everything I wanted out of everything and everyone who came near me; accepting kindness and generosity as though they were owed to me.

And what I'd done with my talent—milking it for whatever I'd wanted, hiding behind it, using it to fill my closets, caring only that it was there, never asking why God had chosen my body in which to place the awesome gift, never seriously trying to understand what I was supposed to do with it. I remembered planning to think about it when I'd come out of the hospital and it was frightening to look back and see that once the panic had passed, as soon as things had started swinging again it had been strictly: I've got talent, I'm a star—and I'd just grabbed it all and run without looking at the price tag.

Maybe it was too late. Maybe I'd used it all up, milked it dry. But if I still have another chance what do I do with it? . . .

The ultimate mystery is one's own self. In the days that followed, days I dared not waste, I pondered and probed through what had passed, and came up with some answers. I knew they were not the whole story, just as I knew that no one can know himself so well as to say: Here I am. Entirely. This is me.

But it was a beginning, and if nothing else, an end to so many years of disastrous self-deception.

part
IV

28

SAMUEL GOLDYWN STOOD IN THE DOORWAY OF MY DRESSING room at the Moulin Rouge, his hand extended. "Mr. Davis, you are Sportin' Life. The part is yours."

Frank, Jack Benny, George Burns—a dozen top people had tried to interest him in me but Goldwyn's reply had been "Sammy Davis? He's a singer or something?" The guys in the motion picture department at the Morris office had been breaking their necks for me and striking out completely. Finally Abe Lastfogel told them, "I'll take over." He'd made his pitch for me and Goldwyn had groaned, "All right, Abe! Sammy Davis, Jr. is coming out of my ears already. Let him make a screen test." Mr. Lastfogel had refused. "He doesn't make screen tests. You want to see film on him? Run *Anna Lucasta*. You want to see him perform? I'll take you to the Moulin Rouge, we'll have dinner, and you will see a consummate artist." The Goldwyns probably go to a nightclub once in five years. Only a man of Mr. Lastfogel's stature could have brought them there.

The Morris office pushed back all my nightclub dates that fell during the six-month shooting period. I came in off the road and the picture began moving on a clockwork schedule. The day after I finished recording the soundtrack I was due for costume fittings at the wardrobe department.

Irene Sharaff handed me a suit she'd created for Sportin' Life and as I started toward the dressing room she called out, "I don't want anything underneath those pants. Nothing!"

I stopped walking. "Miss Sharaff—I've got to have a little *something* . . ."

"Nothing!"

As I started to close the dressing room door she held it

open with her foot and gave me an Eve Arden cynical grin, "You won't mind if I make sure, will you? I don't want anything underneath those pants except your skin."

"You're joking. You mean you're going to stand here while I—"

"Put on the pants."

"Look, Miss Sharaff, I don't wanta be Charley Modest, but . . ."

"Relax." She waved her hand, bored, "I've seen half of Hollywood undressed. Just put on the pants." She was standing there arms folded, foot in the door.

"Okay, but I feel like a stripper."

She grinned, "Tell me the truth. If I wasn't standing here like a cop, you'd try to sneak in a little pair of jockey shorts, wouldn't you?"

"Well, I'll admit it crossed my mind."

She nodded. "Put on the pants!"

They fit like skin. It was all I could do to close them. "Y'know, I wear tight pants, but this is ridiculous."

She called the tailor. "Make them tighter. I want those pants so tight that you'll see him move all over his body." She handed me a coat which buttoned down the middle and closed completely in front from top to bottom. She shook her head. "No good. Split the coat at the bottom. I want them to see everything he's got."

I broke up. "You've got to be kidding. I've heard about this jazz with the glamor girls—but with *me?*"

Mr. Goldwyn sat forward at his desk and peered at me over his glasses. "You're a *what?*"

"I'm a Jew, Mr. Goldwyn, and I can't work on the high holy days."

"You mean it? It's not one of your little jokes?"

"No. I'll do anything in the world for you, Mr. Goldwyn, but I won't work on Yom Kippur."

"You're a real Jew?"

"Yes, sir. I converted several months ago."

"You know what it'll cost to suspend production for a day? We can't change the schedule, it's too late. Twenty-five thousand. Maybe more."

"I just learned today that I'm scheduled to shoot on Yom Kippur, sir. I came up as soon as I heard."

He threw out his hands. "Sammy—answer me a question. What did I ever do to you?"

"Sir, you've been wonderful and I feel terrible about the problems I'm causing you, but I've gone to temple a lot less often than I would have liked because people still look at me like they think it's a publicity stunt or like they can't understand it, but I must draw the line on Yom Kippur. It's one day of the year I won't work. I'm sorry. I really am."

He took off his glasses. "Sammy, you're a little so and so, but go with your yamalka and your tallis—we'll work it out somehow." He sighed, like now he'd seen everything and as I left his office he was behind his desk talking to the four walls, "Directors I can fight. Fires on the set I can fight. Writers, even actors I can fight. But a Jewish colored fellow? This I can't fight!"

Charley Head had tired of traveling, and quit the job after *Porgy*. As it came time to go on the road again I hired a man named Murphy Bennett. I led him into the bedroom and he gazed at the array of camera cases, pipe racks, guns and holsters, tape recorder, twelve suitcases, a six-foot-high trunk and clothes piled high on the bed and on every chair. "I'll need the lightweight stuff in Florida and the heavier things for the rest of our swing—New York, Toronto, and Buffalo." He nodded dazedly and I couldn't help enjoying the way he was looking at everything Alice-in-Wonderland-style.

Jim Waters looked into the room. "Will Mastin and the people from the Morris office are waiting for you in the Playhouse."

I smiled at Murphy. "It's all yours, baby."

Jim, a tall, good-looking actor, had come to work for me in his spare time. He was an intelligent, responsible man; we'd taken four rooms in an office building on Sunset Boulevard and I'd turned all of my business details over to him. I said, "Grab the phones for me while I'm down there, will you, Jim? I wouldn't want anything to interrupt the fighting."

I'd gotten a cable from London: "STILL MOST EAGER TO BOOK YOU HERE. NAME YOUR TERMS. AL BURNETT." It was at least the tenth contact he'd made with me in three or four years, inviting me to play his club the Pigalle, and I'd had as many offers from the Palladium. I'd given cliché turn-downs like "We're booked solid" but the fact was, I was afraid of it. What did I know about England and what did they know about me? I'd seen too many important English performers come over here and die like dogs because our audiences hadn't understood them. Sure, it would be great to have the prestige of being a hit over there—but what if I didn't make it? Within twenty-four hours the word would be all over American show business. But now my fears of London were balanced by the possibility of making a fresh start there. Maybe if I totally changed my surroundings, if I started from scratch with new people, with new audiences, I might be able to make contact again.

Sam Bramson was in town from New York and I'd asked him and Will and a few others from the Morris office's nightclub department to come by. He sighed patiently, "Haven't we been urging you to do it for years? But not in a *nightclub*. You've got to be presented *properly*, with the prestige and stature you rate. The Palladium can give that to you, but the Pigalle . . ." he shrugged and the others nodded agreement.

Will said, "Sammy, here some of the world's greatest experts on show business are telling you: play the Palladium. Judy Garland plays there, Danny Kaye plays there, Jack Benny plays there . . ."

"Massey, I respect the experience and the judgment of everyone in this room. But I'm the world's greatest expert on Sammy Davis, Jr. After the decisions are made and the contracts are signed, eventually it's opening night, and you'll be here in the States and you'll all send cables 'Good luck, Sammy' and that's beautiful—but then Sammy has to go onstage and do it. *You* don't go on, Massey, Sam Bramson doesn't go on, Abe Lastfogel doesn't go on—it's just me. The music starts, I wait for my cue and I walk onstage alone. So, when that moment comes I want to know that I've got everything going for me that my thirty years of experience can provide.

"Every word you say about the Palladium is true. But those are the exact reasons I *don't* want to play there. Look, we all agree I'm not going to London for money, so the only important thing is: what can I *accomplish* over there? Danny Kaye did as good as any man is going to do at the Palladium —ever! And Judy Garland did it for the women. I'm not going to top them. Nobody is. My one chance for individuality is to come into London differently. By playing the Pigalle I'll stand out and be judged on my own.

"I have another reason. I want to create my image for London in the area where I can control it best, my own medium—a nightclub. At the Palladium the headliner comes on, does an hour or so and closes a big show. Well, if I'm going to make it with people who've never seen me perform I want to know I've got as much time as I need, to do all the things I want to do for them. Maybe it'll be an hour and a half, maybe two hours—I have no way of knowing 'til I'm over there. But I can't be limited. I've got to be sure that each audience goes out of there having seen me as I want them to see me. Then maybe I'll get lucky and they'll like me and they'll say 'There isn't nobody gonna be that good in a nightclub as Sammy Davis.'"

I looked around my suite at the Eden Roc and went into the bedroom to begin unpacking. "Murph!" He didn't answer. He was sitting on a chair in the living room, crying.

He looked up and smiled, embarrassed. "I know I look foolish, Sammy, it's just that I never thought I'd see the day I'd walk in the front door of a Miami Beach hotel. When I gave the bellmen the tip," his eyes flooded with tears again, "they said, 'Thank you, sir.'"

I felt myself starting to go under with him. "Murphy, you're working for a star and we go first cabin all the way. Now go down to your room and get into some comfortable clothes and let's get this jazz unpacked so I can do a show or we're gonna be *living* in a cabin!"

I'd told the stage manager not to announce the act in order to avoid the ludicrous moment after: "the Will Mastin Trio starring Sammy Davis, Jr.," when only I appeared.

Morty hit the first few bars of *Mr. Wonderful* which had become a signature for me, then a fast rhythm thing, an exciting mixture of drums and brass. He kept repeating it, building suspense, and because there was no way of knowing when I'd be coming on, the audience was forced to keep watching the wings. I walked on. I didn't wait for the applause to stop. I started singing right over it.

I was in the middle of the show, taking a breather, chatting with the audience; I'd just done Louis Armstrong and I was still holding the oversized handkerchief that I used as a prop. I dropped it over my head like a hood and spoke through it. "And there'll be *another* meeting tomorrow night!"

Laughter started tentatively in the back of the room and gathered momentum as it rolled toward the stage completely stopping the show.

When they'd calmed down I said, "I love Miami Beach. I really do. And such nice, friendly people: only this afternoon I went by the pool and guys stuck their heads out of cabanas and shouted, 'Hi'ya, Sam. Beautiful tan y'got baby.'"

They screamed.

Will burst into the dressing room. Murphy left, fast, and Will locked the door. "Sammy, now I *know* you're crazy."

"What's wrong, Massey?"

"Don't what's-wrong-Massey me. You tryin' to get yourself lynched? In all my years around show business I never heard a colored man stand in front of a white audience and do *those* kinds of jokes. Never!" He looked at me, aghast. "I can't believe I really heard you doing jokes about the Ku Klux Klan. And in *Florida!*"

I pulled a chair over to him. "Take it easy, Massey. Sit down. You want a drink or something?"

"Sammy, what got into you? How'd you even *think* to say those kind of jokes on a stage?"

"I never thought about it at all. The lines came to me while I was onstage and I thought 'why not?' so I did them" I sat down next to him. "Look, during the show you were watching *me* when I did those jokes, but I was watching the audience. Those lines weren't the funniest in the world, but they screamed. You heard them. And there was no race riot. On the contrary. Maybe it's because Little Rock is on the front pages every day and the racial thing is all anybody talks about, but the fact is that by bringing it out in the open it was like I'd bridged a gap that had been between us like it *always* is between *any* colored guy and white guy until one of them acknowledges that there's something standing there between them."

"All right, Sammy, you did it and it can't be undone, but promise me one thing: no more."

"I'm sorry, I can't do that. There's something I've got to try."

"What's that? Get yourself run out of town?"

"Massey, to two thousand people a night I'm not colored. Sure, they know I've got brown skin but they don't think of me like 'Colored people? Keep 'em out.' I'm not *that* kind of being colored . . ."

He looked at the floor, resentfully, "How many kinds they think there are?"

"That's the point. Obviously they don't *think* about it *at all*. But they see me onstage, speaking to them on their own level, the guy they played gin with out at the cabana. I'm the guy they invite to their homes, to play golf at their clubs —they know me, they feel close to me, some of them even love me. They hear me sing and watch me dance and they think 'Isn't he adorable!' and that's my moment—and I have to *do* something with it, I can't waste it—that's when I have to show them: But remember, I'm colored.

"I *must*. I want to make them equate 'colored people' with *me*, an individual they know and maybe understand, instead of with a formless, mysterious mass they instinctively fear and hate."

He left the dressing room still puzzled and frightened for me and I sat by myself trying to evaluate what had happened. I liked the idea of not in any way glossing over the fact that I'm colored, and I felt an enormous satisfaction at having broken the eternal gentleman's agreement: the I-know-I'm-colored-and-you-know-it-but-let's-not-notice-it.

I began adding more racial humor to the act, offering my point of view through my humor, and they were accepting it, giving me standing ovations at almost every performance, and each time it happened, each time I watched those people standing to applaud me I wondered if maybe things are happening faster than we can see from within all the chaos. Granted the audience had only a small percentage of native Southerners but still—it was happening in Florida and it couldn't possibly have happened five years ago.

I sang, "Georgia . . . Georgia . . . ain't goin' there."
The laughs kept building. "No sir, if them cats in the sheets
want *me* then they gonna have to come and *get* me.

"Ladies and gentlemen, if I may be serious for a moment
—thank you for being able to laugh with me at these
things. Maybe there are some people who'll say 'Hey, how
can he kid about a serious situation?' but I think you feel as
I do, let's bring it out in the open where it can be seen for
how ridiculous it is. Let's not hide it in a corner pretending
we don't know it exists. Hatred won't die of old age. But
it can't stand light, it has to breed in secret, like cancer, like
every disease and evil that grows undercover and survives to
destroy the people who look away from it."

The audience applauded their agreement, like they understood what I was doing, that the jokes weren't just to get
laughs. I smiled, "*However,* needless to say, I ain't goin' to
Mississippi to do this." They screamed.

"I mean it! I'm not even on the maybe list. Martin Luther
King is not only a man I admire to the fullest possible
extent but I have the good fortune to call him my friend.
I had a few days off after I finished shooting *Porgy* and he
was in L.A. and he said, 'Look, why don't you take a rest, a
little change? Come on home with me. You'll spend a few
days with me in Atlanta.' I almost *hit* him!"

A man at ringside drawled loudly, "I'll say one thing for
you, boy, you've got a sense of humor."

"Thank you, sir. I need one." Despite an occasional guy
like that, oddly enough the people who laughed the hardest
were Southerners.

"This has been a wonderful year for me professionally. I
just finished my second motion picture and I did my first
dramatic television show. You all know what a nut I am
with the guns and the quick-draw quiz. Well, my big am-
bition is to do a Western. I mean it. I'm not sure if Hollywood'll ever let me play a cowboy, but if they do, *that'll* be
the time the Indians win!

"I watch television all the time. I'm a nut with it. And do
you know what bugs me? Howcum I ain't never yet
seen no colored people on *The Millionaire?*" I paused, "I
can just picture that cat who walks around giving out the
checks. He goes up to my old neighborhood, 140th

Street and Eighth Avenue, he climbs the stairs, it's nine in the morning and he knocks on the door. 'My name is Michael Anthony . . .' The colored cat looks out at him, 'You better git outa mah face wakin' me at no damn nine o'clock.'"

The breaking of my speech pattern and dropping into the "illiterate" worked beautifully for me. I could get away with saying, "Well, yeah, Kingfish—" and the colored guy sitting in the audience didn't resent it because he'd already heard me speak good English, plus a minute later he heard me using the same formula with a heavy Yiddish inflection. The Jewish guy in the audience didn't object because I turned around and did a stereotype of the Negro with an Amos 'n Andy dialect and lines like, "Sapphire . . . if every woman in Texas looks like your momma—then the Lone Ranger's gonna be alone for a *long* time!"

I wanted to do impressions of Step'n Fetchit and Willy Best and I found a way to work them in so that they might say something. "Ladies and gentlemen, we've made wonderful progress racially. Organizations like the NAACP asked the movie studios, 'Please don't always show the Negro as a slow, lazy, shuffling guy,' and Hollywood stopped using the Step'n Fetchit-type characters. Now, on a personal level I'm very happy about it, but professionally I miss them. They were wonderful performers . . ."

With that kind of an introduction I had told the audience that it's not logical or right to think of Negroes only as the old-fashioned stereotypes, and I'd indicated how even Hollywood has helped to stamp out these racially sneering things. Without direct lecture, without pleading or protest, a seed was planted.

I finished the impressions and cued Morty for a ballad. As the music started I walked over to George Rhodes, my pianist. "George, I know how sensitive you are, but would you mind playing on some of the *white* keys?"

From a performing standpoint every comic or humorist must have a point of view. Mine was, for me, the most satisfying part of the shows. I had been given access to ears that would listen, and through the racial humor I was telling them exactly what I believed in, and they were accepting it—giving me an important reason for standing on that stage.

29

I Drove Out To Fox To Have Lunch At The Commissary. With two picture credits and a third ready to start shooting in Vegas in a month I wasn't looking through the candy store window any more. One of the kids at the table was an actress, Barbara Luna, whom I talk to like a kid sister. She was working in a remake of *The Blue Angel*. We were eating and talking when a tall girl with long blonde hair walked in and sat down at a table by herself. She was in costume and wearing make-up from a picture. Her hair was very straight and I dug the dramatic way it framed her face, which was unbelievably beautiful. I nudged Barbara. "Oh God."

She followed my gaze across the room. "That's May Britt."

"Now that's a girl! Yeah. I mean that's a *girl*."

"Forget it."

"I saw her in *The Young Lions* and she was wild looking, but in person she's unbelievable."

"Forget it."

I looked around at Barbara. "Hey, wait a minute. Whattya mean 'forget it'? A beautiful girl walks in and I just . . ."

"I mean: for-get-it! I see her on the set every day, she's a nice girl but she doesn't do anything but work. She goes nowhere with nobody!"

A few nights later I was in my Jag, heading down Santa Monica not sure where I felt like going for dinner. I stopped at a light. May Britt was walking across the street. There was no missing the style of her hair. She was wearing a bluish-gray skirt, a button-down collar man's shirt and a jacket. She stood very straight and walked with a driving energy. There was an older woman with her, probably her mother. I watched them buy tickets at a movie theater and go inside.

There was a loud knocking on the roof of my car. A cop was leaning in my window. "Shall we dance, Sammy?" The light had changed and the cars behind me were honking their horns. "Excuse me, officer." I grinned like an idiot and drove away.

I pulled into the parking lot at Patsy's Villa Capri. Maybe I'd bump into Frank or some of the buddies. I looked around inside. Nobody I knew. I took a booth and sat by myself, talking to the drink I'd ordered: How's this for being a star? A whole city of people and I'm sitting here with *you!*

I saw Judy and Jay Kanter coming in and waved for them to join me. We'd been buddies for years and we were close enough so that I didn't have to be "on" with them. I sat there with my head hanging into my drink.

Jay asked, "You got troubles?"

"Nothing serious, baby, just a case of the humbles. I just feel like sitting here and having a little booze with you guys."

Judy asked, "How's your love life?"

I answered her through clenched teeth. "Listen, I saw a girl tonight . . ."

Jay got interested. "Who'd you see? Who is it now?"

"It's not a who-is-it-now. Her name's May Britt and she's . . ."

Judy threw out her hands. "Forget it."

"Hey! What's this 'forget it' jazz? Every time I mention her name it's like I'm Robespierre plotting to swipe the Queen's diamond studs."

Jay was shaking his head. "You haven't got a prayer. She's so straight that nobody even goes over to say hello to her. And the best have tried. She's not interested in dating, parties, nothing! She's strictly work. She's getting a divorce from some kid who's got millions and she won't take a nickel from him. Sam, this is an unusual girl."

"Now *you* hold it. You don't think maybe you're exaggerating just a *little* bit?"

They wouldn't even bother to answer me. They gave me you-poor-fool looks, smiled at each other, shrugged and turned back to their veal parmesan. I sat there watching them eat, trying to think of some way to open the conversation again. I took the fork out of Jay's hand. "Baby, let's talk sense. I've been around this town a few years, too, right? Now there just can't be a chick that looks this good that ain't swingin' with *somebody!*"

He gave me the blank stare and shook his head like: You wanta be an idiot? Okay. Be an idiot.

I got back to the coast again about three weeks later, and had some kids over to the Playhouse. Rudy Duff, a man I'd hired to drive for Mama and to look after her, was making drinks and running the movies and it was one of those pleasant kind of evenings. Barbara Luna came by with some kook she'd run into at Schwab's Drugstore and I watched her dying of boredom with him. Her date meant no more to her than all the nameless chicks had ever meant to me. I felt sorry for her, like we were both on the same island.

I took her aside. "Barbara, let me ask you something. You ain't never gonna introduce me to May Britt, right? I mean you don't want to arrange anything for old Sam, do you? Maybe help a pal . . ."

She looked surprised. "I know May Britt. I worked with her in *Blue Angel.*"

"Nut! I was in the commissary with you, remember? And by the way, I caught a screening of the picture and it stinks. But she was good. And she looks—well, she looks like *too much!*"

"Yeah, she's great looking. What'd you have in mind?"

I sat down next to her. "I just want to meet her. That's all. Simple, innocent, nice. Listen, I'll make up a party for Dinah Washington's closing at the Cloisters next week. Then we'll all come over here afterwards and . . . well, we'll just let nature take its course."

"Great. I'll give you her phone number and you can invite her."

"No good. I need an opening. With this girl if I call her cold it's a definite turn-down and maybe even a hang-up of the phone and a broken eardrum. You've got to call her for me."

"Well, if you wanta make a whole thing of it," she shrugged, "all right, I'll try to get in touch with her."

Three days passed and no call from Barbara. I got her on the phone. "You didn't do it yet, right?"

"What's wrong, Sammy?"

"Wrong? Who said anything's wrong? I just called to tell you I'm receiving the Celibacy Award at the Hollywood Bowl next week and I hope you can attend the ceremony!"

"Oh gee, Sam, I forgot."

"You *forgot*?"

"I'm sorry. I've been so hung up with things. You know how it is."

"No, I *don't* know how it is."

"Okay, get off the phone so I can call her." She called me right back, "Well, I spoke to her."

"She can't make it, right?"

"It's not that. She said, 'If he wants to talk to me why doesn't he call me himself?' "

"Whattya mean?" I knew exactly what she meant.

Someone answered, briskly, "Tell me!"

Tell me? What the hell is *that*?

Again the voice said, "Tell me."

How Swedish can you get? "May I speak with Miss Britt, please."

"Who's calling?"

From her voice *alone* I wished I had on a heavy sweater. "This is Sammy Davis, Jr."

"Oh, hello there." Some of the chill disappeared. She was still a little crisp, but she didn't sound angry that I'd called.

I gave her the Orson Welles voice, resonant, full of timbre: "Miss Britt, you don't know me . . ."

"I know that." Oh, swell. I needed this. She said, "But I've seen you perform. At the Moulin Rouge. I thought your show was marvelous."

Hey, this is going to be all right. She didn't have to say that. "Miss Britt, I'm having a little party—I mean a large party, at the Cloisters, Thursday night, and I wonder if I might have the pleasure of your company." I rushed in with a little protection. "Barbara Luna will be there."

"I'd like to come but my mother's visiting me from Sweden."

481

"I'd be delighted to have you bring her along, if you like."

"If you wouldn't mind. Thank you very much. That will be fine."

I spent the next few days planning every move, inviting just the right people to dress up the party. I invited no attractive single guys. I cast it like a schoolgirl setting up her sweet-sixteen party.

I went through my wardrobe and decided on a nice little double-breasted dark blue mohair. The double-breasted jazz would give me just a touch of European flavor while the mohair would keep it American. I looked through my cuff links. A simple gold pair with no stones. Small and conservative. No ring. And the flat, gold cigarette case with the rubbed finish and the lighter to match.

I had to split the party into two side-by-side tables for ten. Barbara arrived early. I wanted her next to me to help me carry the ball and I earmarked the two seats across from us for May and her mother. But it didn't work out the way I'd planned. They were all good friends so I couldn't tell them "don't sit there," and within fifteen minutes the two seats were taken.

The show was about to start when I saw her walking in. I nudged Barbara, "Your friend sure has a strange-looking mother." She was with George Englund, who'd produced *Odds Against Tomorrow*.

I walked over to greet them. She looked unbelievable. I put out my hand, "So nice to see you."

She smiled, "My mother was tired. Do you know Mr. Englund? I hope you don't mind my asking him."

"Mind? Of course not. Delighted to see you again, George." If you'll believe *that*, you mother, you'll believe anything. I walked them to the second table. "Do you care for champagne?"

She smiled, "I hate it."

"Oh. Well, how about some vodka? Scotch? Bourbon?"

"No, thanks. I don't drink. I'll just have a plain tonic, thank you."

"Schweppes or Wildroot?" She didn't answer. "Well, heh, heh, heh, . . . those are the jokes, folks." She looked blankly at me, not understanding what in the hell I was talking about. Very smart, Charley. "Well, enjoy yourselves . . . catch you later." I retreated to my table.

After the show I danced with Dinah and with Barbara but I kept watching May and Englund at the other table. They had their backs to me. Beautiful.

If she were dancing I could cut in but I wasn't about to risk walking over there and getting "I'm sorry. I don't dance." When the party was ready to break up I went over to her. "Everybody's coming to the house for a nightcap. Would you like to join us?"

"Nope."

"Well, don't let anybody tell you you're not direct."

She smiled and put out her hand. "Good night. Thank you for inviting me."

I sat in a corner of the Playhouse, hating her. One of the buddies who'd been at her table sat down next to me. "Are you interested in what was going on between May Britt and George Englund?"

"No."

"Okay." He started to leave.

"Like what?"

"Well, after you went back to your table he told her, 'I think he's making a play for you.' She said, 'Do you really think so?' and he said, 'It's obvious.'"

Oh? I hadn't thought I was so damned obvious. I walked over to Barbara. "Well, what do you think? Should I call her again?"

"I don't know. Use your own judgment."

"Thanks, Barbara. That's what friends are for."

I waited a few days and called her. "I'm having some friends up to the house tonight—running a few movies—would you like to come by?"

"I'm sorry, I'm going out for dinner."

"Well, how about after dinner?"

"Give me your number and I'll call you when I'm through."

At ten o'clock I sat down at the bar near the phone. "Rudy, relax and enjoy the movie. I'll take the calls." It seemed as though everyone in Hollywood had chosen this night to call me. I kept clearing the line as fast as I could.

By midnight I suddenly saw myself as I was: an idiot

sitting in front of the phone waiting for it to ring. I got up from the bar and sat down on the couch in the middle of the room. Nobody's *that* good-looking. The phone rang. "Rudy! Will you answer the goddamned phone!"

He put his hand over the mouthpiece, "Do you know a Miss Britt?"

She said, "Hello there. I'm coming over now. Will that be all right?"

I hung up and dashed for the bedroom in the Playhouse, where there are two walls of mirrors, and checked my clothes. I was wearing dark blue jeans and a shirt with three buttons on each sleeve and a bright red sweater. I gave myself a little shot of after-shave lotion and started downstairs. If she's got another guy with her. . . .

Fifteen minutes later she buzzed from the gate.

Before Rudy could call up over the intercom to ask who it was, I pushed the button to open the gate and ran out of the Playhouse and up the steps to meet her. She was alone.

Now it got to be like a party. Barbara was there, which was good, and she knew a few of the other kids, too. She was wearing slacks and I wondered if she'd gone home and changed specially, or if she'd been someplace casual for dinner. I could've spent the whole night just watching her move. She walked like an athlete, but oh, was she a *girl* athlete!

It was time for me to stop calling her Miss Britt. "Would you care for a drink, May?"

"What do you have that doesn't taste like whiskey?"

"Do you like oranges?"

"I love them."

"I've got just the thing. Orange brandy. It's very sweet and fruity tasting."

"I hate sweet drinks."

"Hey. Cool it! Don't hate it till you taste it." I poured a small shot for her. She sipped it, smiled, held out her glass and I poured a little more.

She said, "This is darned good. I love it."

I looked across the bar at her. "You either hate or love *everything*, right? I mean, there isn't anything that's just in-between?"

She lifted her head and smiled. "Nope."

I wondered how old she was. Twenty-three maybe. There was something about her that made me feel very mature. She was so definite, so sure of everything. It was such a youthful, attractive thing. She took another slug of the orange brandy. "You know what else I hate?"

"What's that?"

"I don't mean to embarrass you."

"Go right ahead. Please."

"You called me May."

"Oh. Well, I beg your pardon. I'll call you Miss Britt and you can call me Kato." Oh, God. Green Hornet bits!

She gave me the blank look of all time. "All I mean is that it's spelled M-a-y but it's pronounced 'My' not 'May.' My real name is Maybritt Wilkens. In Sweden Maybritt is a common name. I shortened it to May Britt, for films."

"I'm sorry, I didn't know."

"That's okay. I hope you don't mind my telling you."

"No. Not at all. I'm glad you did. I really am . . ."

We got hung up on it and started laughing. Her glass was empty again and I filled it. For a chick who doesn't drink she was belting the hell out of my orange brandy.

Rudy started the second movie. In the middle of it she excused herself. She came back, watched a little of the movie, and then left the room again. I began to get the picture.

I have always hated women who drink and get sick, but she was no boozer, she'd just fallen for the taste of the orange brandy. She was obviously miserable but trying not to let on, like a kid who'd had too much to drink the first time—and instead of turning me against her it endeared her to me.

I whispered, "I'll take you home." She smiled gratefully.

I walked over to Arthur's kid brother-in-law, Pepe. "Baby, do me a favor. I'm going to drive May home in her car. You follow us in mine and bring me back."

I drove May's Thunderbird toward the beach. She sat next to me, silent except to give me directions. She guided me through Malibu Colony to a large estate on which she rented the guest house.

We walked through a creaky wooden gate into a large garden. There wasn't an electric light anywhere. We were surrounded by what seemed like a jungle of foliage. I looked

485

up at the full moon and saw, against the sky, the silhouettes of gigantic trees, bent and leaning, like they'd been standing there for hundreds of years. There wasn't a sound except our footsteps on the grass. It was exactly the spooky sort of a setting where you'd expect a mad scientist to jump out from behind the bushes and leer, "Come to the laboratory with me. I need your brain."

"The pool is a few feet to your left. Be careful."

I wanted to kiss her good night but I knew it couldn't be like with other chicks with grabbing and squeezing and what-could-I-lose? Do I ask, "May I have a kiss?" like Andy Hardy? She stopped at her door. I held out my hand. "Thank you very much for coming tonight. I hope you feel better."

"Thank you."

"I'm going to Las Vegas the day after tomorrow . . . may I call you?"

"I'd like that very much." As she smiled she cocked her head in such a way that the moonlight shining on her face lit it so beautifully that I felt a weakness pass over me. She had freckles and her skin and hair looked more lovely than anything I'd ever seen or imagined. I felt a shimmering glow within me like nothing I'd ever experienced, as though by looking at her I'd become transfused with her warmth and serenity. The moment was something apart from all moments through all the years of my life. She lowered her eyes, turned and went inside.

30

THE SIGN IN FRONT OF THE SANDS WAS A CLASSIC, AS marquees go, for nightclub shows:

FRANK SINATRA
DEAN MARTIN
SAMMY DAVIS, JR.
PETER LAWFORD
JOEY BISHOP

A few months before, when we'd made our plans to shoot *Ocean's 11* and play the hotel simultaneously, the newspapers had been filled with stories about Eisenhower, De Gaulle, and Khrushchev planning a Summit Conference, and Frank had joked, "We'll have our own little Summit meeting." One of the papers printed it, others picked it up, and it stuck.

Within a week after our "Summit" was announced there wasn't a room to be had in any hotel in town. People flew in from Chicago, Los Angeles, New York—from all over the country—weeks before we got there, to be sure their rooms weren't sold out from under them. We'd been in Vegas for a week, and still plane, train, and busloads of people were pouring into town, arriving without hotel reservations, sleeping in lobbies, cars, anywhere, hoping to get rooms.

All of Vegas was affected by it but the Sands was the hub and you could hardly push your way through the lobby and casino. Hundreds of people crowded the entrance to the Copa Room, fighting for tables with money, connections, or both.

I was in the middle of a dance when Peter wandered on-stage. I switched to a soft-shoe and motioned for him to join me. He fell in alongside me and grinned, "I'm not prejudiced, Sam. I'll dance with you." I smiled cynically, "But will you go to *school* with me?" Frank and Dean came on wheeling a room-service table loaded down with booze. They poured drinks and Dean did a few minutes of staggering— the only cold-sober lush in show business. Suddenly Frank turned to the band. "Cut!" He beckoned to me. "You! Over here."

I played it with nervous looks at Peter and Dean who shrugged like: You'd better do as he says. I crossed the stage and stood in front of him, head hanging, meek.

Frank folded his arms and looked at me like I was a worm. "Look at what Peter's wearing. Look at what Dean and I are wearing." They were all in dinner suits. "Now look at yourself." I made a whole thing out of inspecting my blazer, silk ascot, and gray flannels. I smiled a thin, Stan Laurel smile. Frank snapped, "Where do you get off coming on this stage in that little toy suit? Just where do you think you are?

On your *yacht?*" I hung my head, taking it, playing my role of "the Kid." He glowered. "Now you go get yourself into a regular grown-up tuxedo like the rest of us. Go on. Get out of here. Get off this stage."

"Hold it!" I sneered, "What're you, *Esquire* magazine? You don't tell me what to do! Y'hear that, *Mister* Sinatra?" The audience egged me on: Yeah! Tell him Sam. Attababy! I poked him in the chest with my forefinger. *"Nobody* tells me what to do." I crossed my arms arrogantly. "What're you, some kind of a big deal? Not to *me!"* I strutted around the stage taking bows while the audience cheered. I stopped in front of Frank again, looked up at him, and flicked a piece of lint off his lapel. "I'll change my suit when I'm plenty good and ready!"

He spoke quietly. "When'll that be?" He was smiling, beady-eyed.

I did a sickly grin. "I'm ready, Frank."

After the shows we sat in the lounge while the crew set up cameras so we could begin shooting when daylight broke. Frank's presence in the hotel created its own atmosphere. Everybody was having a better time, looking for laughs, kicks, almost as though they felt they had to live up to his reputation. The hotel kept eight security guards around him to prevent the crowds from turning into a mob scene. Almost anyone else would be at his wit's end because of the money involved in the picture—his money—and all the details and aggravations plus the two shows a night. But he was doing jokes with me and the other guys, the same kind of bits we'd have done if he'd come down for a weekend just for laughs. I felt someone tapping me on the shoulder. A woman in her forties glanced timidly toward him. "Sammy, could you please get his autograph for me?"

She was about the eightieth person to ask me that week. "Darling, he's right here. Why don't you just ask him?"

She shrank back. "But I've heard . . ."

"Don't go by what you've heard. Go by what you see with your own eyes. He's not going to hurt you."

She tapped him on the shoulder so lightly he didn't feel it, then looked at me helplessly. I nodded reassuringly and she tried again. He looked around. "Hello honey."

Her hands sprang to her face. "You called me honey!"

He smiled and gave her his autograph and she tottered dazedly into the crowd.

The bad guy image which had grown so immense bore no resemblance to the man, but the legend of Frank Sinatra was uncontrollable and a wall of fear had been built around him. The day we arrived in Vegas there was a television show being filmed on the hotel grounds and somebody took it upon himself to say "No shooting today. Clear the hotel. Frank Sinatra's coming in." If Frank had known, he'd have been furious. Never would he stop a performer from working. But people are always hovering around, over-protecting him, biting their nails, fearful that he'll blow up and walk out. Certainly he wants the respect and attention due his stature in the business. Professionally he wants the best musicians, the best lighting and sound equipment; he's in a position to expect them and he has the temperament to refuse to be imposed upon: if a club owner hasn't provided the right microphones, Frank might very well refuse to go on and the story "Sinatra walked out" would get passed around, distorted, like "That's how he is all the time." Obviously, a man does not attain Frank's success and *keep it* by doing irrational flounce outs.

Never would he even desire a restaurant to be "cleared" because he's eating there. Wherever he plays he makes the whole town rich and if he wanted privacy he could say "I want a tunnel dug from my dressing room to my suite" and the bulldozers would be working in an hour. He could say "I'm in my room, send up Connecticut" and the management would try. But he's a warm guy who likes people and he loves to get out and sit in the lounge, have dinner in the dining room or go to a friend's restaurant and pay his respects. He never has been to Atlantic City without dropping into the bar where my mother works. Even if she's not there when he comes in, he'll stay and have a drink, knowing that within minutes the word will spread, the place will be jammed and my mother will get credit for it. Countless times a friend has been in trouble, or in a hospital, and the phone has rung and it's Frank from halfway across the world and he clowns with the guy to cheer him up, and the hospital tab gets picked up, quietly. Stories like this are legion but they aren't the ones which circulate.

We finished shooting around four every afternoon and the five of us met in the steam room at six when it was officially closed for the day. Frank came in one evening, carrying a bundle of newspaper clippings and we sat there passing around soggy clippings, from England, France, South America—everywhere, astounded by the incredible worldwide attention we were getting.

Peter said, "Listen to this one: 'The quintet of Sinatra, Martin, Davis, Lawford and Bishop moved into Las Vegas in the form of an attack force with Sinatra as the nominal leader of their clan.' "

"I don't want to be the leader. One of you guys be the leader."

Peter jabbed the paper with his finger, "Sorry, Frank, but it says here *you're* the leader."

"Hold it," I said. "I wanta go on record that I ain't belongin' to nothing that's called a *clan*."

Dean sighed, "I don't know, pally," he nodded toward Frank, "you'd better discuss that with the leader."

I shook my head. "Maybe he's *your* leader but *my* leader is Martin Luther King!"

The papers had been developing "The Clan" and "The Rat Pack" image of us as five guys who buddy around, have laughs, and in their spare time make a movie and do shows at The Sands. We were amused by it but no one could understand better than we how silly it was. I never discussed it with Frank but he, being an astute showman, must have thought: Dean's good box-office, Sammy does great in clubs, Peter has a television following—why not make a picture utilizing the combined drawing power?

It was not unlike what was done years ago when Hollywood teamed stars like Katherine Hepburn and Spencer Tracy, Walter Pidgeon and Greer Garson, William Powell and Myrna Loy, Cagney and Raft; and although each had been tremendous on his own, when they came together in a picture it virtually exploded at the box office. In the last ten or fifteen years the studios had stopped doing it, but now Frank's idea had so captured the public's imagination that movie theaters all over the world were ordering a picture that wasn't even finished. Recognizing the potential in our combination he formulated what he called The Five Year

Plan: assuming things continued as it seemed they would, we'd make five pictures together, one a year.

When we'd settled into our shooting schedule, I called May.

"Tell me."

I smiled at the already familiar greeting.

She said, "I hear it's fantastic there."

"How'd you like to come down for the weekend and see for yourself?"

"I'd love to. But do you think you can get me a hotel room?"

I played it like the King of France wandering through Paris in disguise—the classic scene in which the loyal, deserving subject whose wife is wrongfully imprisoned asks hopefully, "But do you think you can possibly get my case to the attention of His Majesty?" and the King smiles behind his disguise and chuckles "I believe I can manage it."

I was so delighted with myself it was practically incest.

She was the fifth person out of the plane. She paused at the top of the ramp and I couldn't decide if she was playing "Mary Moviestar Arriving in Las Vegas" or if she was looking for me. As she came through the gate she smiled and her face was like sunshine. She put out her hand. "Hello, there."

"Hello, there, yourself." I took the make-up bag she was carrying. A lady was standing behind her and I had a sudden horrible moment of recognition: it was the same woman who'd walked into the movie theater with her in L.A. and there was a definite family resemblance.

"I'd like you to meet my mother, Mrs. Wilkens."

I did one of the great recoveries of my life with an eighteenth century bow that had all the flair of: Charmed, m'lady. "I'm so glad you could come, Mrs. Wilkens." For that statement alone, my nose should have grown twelve inches.

"My mother is going back to Sweden next week and I thought she'd enjoy seeing Las Vegas before she leaves."

They went to their rooms to relax and unpack, and I headed toward the health club. *Now* she brings her mother. To a party in a nightclub—*then* she doesn't bring her. No. She waits for a weekend in Vegas!

Frank was alone in the steam room. I sat down next to him. "Will you do me a favor?"

"Sure, what is it?"

"I invited May Britt down for the weekend. She's got her mother with her, but with all the press in town I want to be absolutely sure nobody connects us. I don't want to louse her up with her studio, so will you cover for me? Would you let it be known that she's your guest?" As I was asking I realized that I was imposing upon him, but he just looked at me with a penetrating curiosity.

"Sure, Charley, she's my guest."

I introduced May from the stage with the other celebrities, and her mother beamed with pride. I met them in the lounge after the second show, we gambled a little, had a bite to eat with Frank and the guys. I didn't have any scenes the next afternoon so I took them sightseeing, showing them downtown Vegas and everything I could think of that her mother might like to see. As we drove back across the desert from Lake Mead, May said, "My mother's a little tired. I think we'll have dinner in our room so she can go to sleep early. Can I come to see your second show alone?"

"Of course. I've got a permanent table. There'll be some of my friends there so you won't have to sit alone."

As soon as I got off I sent Murphy out front to escort her backstage.

"Hello, there. I liked your show." Murphy did a sneakyfoot out the door like one of the discreet men of all time, and we were alone.

She was wearing a bright yellow dress. She had a sunburn which highlighted her freckles, and her hair was hanging long and golden over her shoulders. We smiled wordlessly at each other.

"Would you like something to drink?"

"No. Thank you very much. But you have one if you like."

"No, thanks. I don't feel like one either."

"The club was really packed."

Yeah . . . things sure are swinging. . . ."

The inane chitchat was coming out of our ears. I was desperate to make conversation, but I'd never really *talked* to a girl before. It was always laughs, jokes, and pow! into bed or not. She walked over to the TV set and stood there, her eyes glued to it. I stared at it, too.

It was impossible to believe. Here's a girl I could get drunk just from looking at, she's just seen me do the show of my life, she's in my dressing room, the door is closed—and we're standing like idiots watching a twenty-year-old movie. A minute later we were both pretending to be hung-up in the commercial.

I looked at her beautiful face. She glanced up as she sensed me staring at her. The haughty look she'd had in *The Blue Angel* and when we'd first met was completely gone, her cheeks were flushed, and she seemed self-conscious. I walked the two steps over to her, put my hands on her shoulders and kissed her.

She was a little tall. I asked, "Would you mind taking off your shoes?"

She laughed and kicked them off. I kissed her again.

Suddenly it was easy to talk. I remembered the closed door and opened it and as I turned I caught the trace of a smile of satisfaction on her face.

The airline was announcing her flight over the loudspeaker. I said, "Thank you very much for coming."

She put out her hand. "Thank you for asking me." She tilted her head a little. "So long." She turned abruptly and started toward the plane, walking with the brisk, purposeful stride which was so distinctly her. As she started up the ramp, I realized I was still holding her overnight bag. I ran onto the field. "May!"

She turned, saw me waving the bag in the air and came back for it, annoyed with herself. As I handed it to her, I grinned, "Too bad, it was a beautiful exit."

Her eyes caught mine, she blushed, then let herself laugh. "Oh, well."

As the ground crew locked the door and rolled away the stairs I had a sense of relief. From the first minute to the last it hadn't worked the way I'd expected it to. I'd asked her down like, "Here's a crazy-looking chick and I dig having her around." But it hadn't been that superficial. I'd done forty-eight hours of keeping doors open and inviting people to be with us; I'd looked forward too eagerly to seeing her every day; I'd been too willing to just sit quietly and look at her and listen to her Swedish accent; I'd been making all the high-school moves hoping to please her mother, and I'd taken pleasure in them.

I sat in my car watching the plane taxi down the runway, then circle Vegas, gaining altitude heading west toward the mountains, and I urged it on in its crawl against the sky as though every inch of the way was drawing me that much further out of the involvement. I felt as if I'd been walking backwards and turned around just in time to see that in a few more steps I'd have fallen over a cliff.

I went back to the hotel and wandered through the casino. I didn't feel much like gambling and it was too early for the steam room. What I needed was a chick. I called an old stand-by, one of the kids from the line, and she came right over. But as soon as she got to the suite I sent her away. I didn't feel much like that, either.

31

I HUNG UP THE PHONE BEFORE SHE ANSWERED. I WALKED around the Playhouse and looked out at the pool. There wasn't a ripple in the water. Everything was quiet and orderly.

I could have affairs with a thousand chicks and walk away from them without thinking to ask their names, but every time I even thought about May I could feel myself getting drawn in deeper. To let myself get hung up on her defied all logic. Where could it go? I'd have to be a lunatic to leave myself that wide open.

I bummed around town with the buddies, forcing myself to stick out each night until I was tired enough to fall asleep. I was in the middle of planning how to kill another evening when I pulled myself up short. I'm out of my mind. Here I've got the first really free time I can remember in years—nothing for two weeks, and I'm wasting it. I've been making too much out of the whole thing. If I'm careful, if I play my cards right, why can't I keep it free and winging with May? Nobody forces anyone to get involved.

From the moment she said "Tell me" I felt like a different man. I invited a bunch of people over to the Playhouse and while they were watching a movie May and I sat outside near the pool, talking.

"What's your next picture going to be?"

"Fox hasn't assigned me another yet."

"Well, they will soon, don't worry."

She smiled. "I couldn't care less."

"Y'know, I've never *yet* gotten an answer from you that I expected."

"I like making films but oh boy do I hate all the other stuff that goes with it! The fuss, the press things you have to do, getting pushed into crowds and being nice to people you can't stomach—it's such a lot of baloney!"

"You mean you don't care about being in pictures?"

"Not particularly. My sister is a nurse in Sweden. That's what I wanted to be."

I looked at her suspiciously. "You sure you're not giving me the jazz from the studio bio?" She shook her head. I laughed. "It would never have worked. A guy would come in with high blood pressure, he'd be in bed, resting, you'd walk into the room and it would be *over!* You'd be more dangerous around a hospital than a staph germ. Within six hours doctors would be running up and down the halls shouting, '*Get rid of that nurse.* Fire Britt!'" She was smiling. "The best thing you ever did was to give up nursing. How'd it happen?"

"I was working as a photographer's assistant in Stockholm when Carlo Ponti came by to see the man I was working for, looking for a girl for the lead in a new picture. He asked me if I wanted to test for it. It sounds like the corny Hollywood drive-in story, doesn't it? Anyway, I got the part and my mother and I went to Rome. She stayed with me for a while, then she went back to Sweden—my father works in the post office there. I stayed in Italy and made twelve films. I did *War and Peace* over there and then Fox offered me a seven-year contract and the part in *The Young Lions.* . . ."

Arthur had come out of the Playhouse. He stopped a few feet away, "Am I busting into something?"

"Well, you're not exactly vital, but sit down, baby."

He rushed over the rest of the way. "I just got the greatest idea you ever heard. Look, you've got about ten more free days, why not use them for a real rest? Let's hire a boat and take a cruise down to Mexico."

"Arthur, what in hell would I do on a boat for ten days?"

"You'd rest. Look, I know of a 110-foot sailing yacht, with a captain and crew. We could keep it down to 'family': me and Nita and Pepe, Luddy and Jim, Shirley and George Rhodes . . . it's got a big living room so we could bring a projector and show movies at night."

I turned to May. "You're not shooting, so you've got the time. And before you answer I'll tell you this: if you don't come then there ain't gonna be no boat trip and everyone'll be mad at you." I played it like I was kidding but I knew that I wasn't about to spend my vacation away from her.

The sun was shining gloriously through the porthole, the boat was rolling—not so gloriously. I got into my bathing suit and went upstairs or up "the ladder" or whatever the hell it is. Arthur was the only one on deck. We were dueling with some cutlasses, doing all the boat shtick: "Avast me hearties" and "Blast these landlubbers" when May appeared. She was wearing a one-piece suit that covered her like a tent. She smiled. "Hello there."

I dropped my sword and glared at her. "Do you mean to stand there in those overalls and tell me that I chartered an entire boat and the best I get is a one-piece suit? I thought Swedes don't like to wear clothes."

Her face turned stony, "I've never heard that." She walked away.

I watched her sit down in the sun and turned to Arthur, "Only *I* would find the one modest Swede in the whole entire world, right?"

As we approached Encinada to pick up some fresh water Pepe said, "Why don't we go ashore and go horseback riding?"

I could picture the column items: Sammy Davis, Jr. and May Britt seen galloping along the beach at Encinada. "Pepe, we have a *boat* this week. We can go riding in L.A. anytime. But you go if you want to."

He looked around. "Anyone else?"

I was stunned by the sound of a Swedish voice. "I'd love to go."

The two of them rushed below to get dressed. I turned to Arthur. "I bring her all the way to Encinada so she can go horseback riding with your brother-in-law?" There wasn't much I could do about it, however, except be a little nasty. As they ran down the gangplank I called out, "It's now eleven-thirty. The boat sails at two o'clock. With or without you."

May looked over her shoulder, like Harriet Haughty. "We'll manage to get back to L.A. if that happens."

At ten minutes to two there was no sign of them. I could see the whole picture: May was going to be late, just to show me. She'd come waltzing back at two-thirty and give me a wise-guy grin and "I'm sorry we're late." I stood on the deck steaming, looking at my watch. She picked the wrong banana for *that* kind of jazz. At exactly two o'clock I called up to the bridge, "Okay, Captain. Sail away."

Arthur was standing next to me. "Listen, they probably couldn't get a cab . . ."

"I warned them, baby. You were standing right here and you heard me."

After an hour and a half I told the Captain to turn back and we got in at around five o'clock. They weren't there. The dockmaster shouted up, "A boy and a girl were waiting for you but they went back to town."

Jim looked at me, unsmiling. "Well, you did it again, eh, Sam?" Luddy shook her head in disapproval. Shirley patted me on the back. "Beautiful move, Sammy. You really showed *her*." She turned away from me.

I glared at Arthur with disgust. "Someday remind me to do ten minutes on how much I need your brother-in-law, the horseback rider!"

We located them at a police station. Without money they'd had no place else to go. May didn't say a word in the cab back to the boat and I played it Charley Silent right back at her. When we got on board she went straight for her cabin. I called after her, "Dinner's in twenty minutes." She didn't answer.

Half an hour passed but she didn't appear. I told the others to start eating and walked downstairs and knocked on her door. "May?"

No answer.

"May, it's me . . . Captain Shnook! I'm sorry. I really am."

No answer.

"Look, come on out and we'll go upstairs and I'll tell everyone I'm an idiot."

No answer.

"May . . . I'm going upstairs for dinner now. . . ."

I sat on the stairs watching the knob on her door. I had a feeling that she was carrying it further than she really wanted to, that she needed an out. I sent dinner down to her but I deliberately didn't include a fork on her tray so she could have an excuse to come upstairs. Then I could apologize and convince her to stay.

Two hours later I knocked on her door, "May, we're starting the movie now—it's a great one, *The Mummy's Hand*."

She didn't come out until the next morning. At breakfast she laughed and joked with everyone else, then sat in the sun with Shirley and Luddy, as far away from me as possible. It was the same thing at lunch and dinner. I wasn't getting much of a play from the others either. I was the creep of the boat. What the hell is this? I don't have to spend the one vacation of my life like *this*. I told the Captain to turn around and head back to Los Angeles. Then I went back to the living room, "Well that's it, folks, the party's over." I looked at her profile. And it's the best thing that could have happened.

On the morning of the last day I was on deck, taking pictures, when I heard "Hello, there." My reflex was to give her the same treatment she'd given me. But I didn't want that. I smiled, "Good morning."

She smiled back and put out her hand. "How about forgetting it, okay?"

It was a gorgeous, sunny, balmy day. We talked about our fight and laughed over it. I'd offended her by expecting her to wear a bikini, as if because I'd hired a boat I was entitled to free looks. She also hadn't been too choked up about the cliché that all Swedes are nudists. I, of all people, should have known better than to do that.

After lunch she came on deck wearing a two-piece bathing suit. It was far from a bikini but I appreciated the gesture. We stretched out in the sun. It was a pity to have wasted all that time, but that one glorious day made the whole trip worthwhile.

I woke up at around eleven, put on a robe and went into the kitchen. I drummed a few beats on the stove, and gave Etheline, my housekeeper, the W. C. Fields voice, "Yes, yes, m'dear, how about a little liquid libation for the master of this household. . . ."

After a few slugs of coffee I ran the shower good and hot, did a chorus of Pagliacci, made the big note, and started dressing. It was mid-March and May's birthday was on the 22nd. We were shooting interiors for *Ocean's* and this was the only day I had free to go downtown and buy her a present. I knew it was going to be a piece of jewelry but I wanted plenty of time to select just the right thing. I'd invited her over for dinner on the 22nd, only the two of us: a little candlelight, a jug of wine, and I'd hand it to her when her birthday cake was served.

The front doorbell rang and I heard Etheline talking to Berney Abramson, the photographer who does my dark-room work. I pulled on a pair of pants and shouted, "Be right out, Bern."

He was in the living room holding a package of enlargements. "Your yachting pictures, Commodore." He grinned and tapped the package, "That May Britt's a wild-looking chick!"

I pulled it out of his hands and walked into the bedroom. He followed me in. "Sammy? What's wrong?"

Berney'd handled pictures of countless girls I'd photographed. Maybe a hundred times he'd made similar, friendly remarks and I'd only been pleased. How could he know it would steam me this time when I wouldn't have known it myself? I gave him a friendly shot on the arm. "Everything's fine, baby. No problems. Thanks." I walked him to the door.

I separated May's pictures from the others and spread them out on the floor. I'd had them made up 11 x 14 and they were incredible. From every possible angle she was beautiful. I picked up the nearest one, to study it more closely, and as I held it I was struck by the contrast of my thumb against her arm.

I put the picture down and went into the bedroom. I forced myself to look in the mirror at my broken face, at my bad eye, the scar across my nose . . . I thought of her beauty, of the hundreds of desirable men she could have. Still, she wasn't telling me to go away, she'd come to Vegas, she'd made the boat trip . . . Sure, Charley, she needs *you!* You want to fool yourself that you're Charley Dapper, Charley Star? Well, you go right ahead, keep forgetting you're colored and you're short and you're ugly—until you get reminded. Better still, throw yourself in front of a truck! It's quicker and it'll hurt less.

I couldn't cancel our date for her birthday, not without giving a good reason. The thing to do would be to go through with it, playing everything down, and let it taper off until I could bow out gracefully.

On the 22nd when we broke for lunch I called Etheline and told her to pick up a birthday cake. There was no point in being rude. We finished shooting early and I headed home. I felt rotten having no present for her. She had no family over here . . . what the hell, maybe I'd get her something silly, something that doesn't mean anything. I drove to Beverly Hills and browsed through the Toy Menagerie, looking at joke-type presents like a giant stuffed giraffe. But I didn't want to give her a giant stuffed giraffe.

I walked a few blocks, stopped at Si Sandler's and looked at the beautiful rings and clips and pins in the window. I'd never wanted anything like I wanted to give her one of them. But she was no "chick" who'd accept an expensive gift from a guy she wasn't really serious about. She'd hand it back and feel bad about embarrassing me. And that would be it.

I stared into the window. What could I lose? Who was I kidding? I was in so deep that I couldn't walk away from her any more. She'd have to send me away.

I raised the lid of the box and set it down on the coffee table in front of her. It contained a simple diamond cocktail ring, one that couldn't possibly be mistaken for an engagement ring. "Okay. You can open your eyes now."

She looked at it. She didn't speak or move.

I shrugged, "Look, not everybody likes jewelry, so I won't be offended . . ."

She lifted the ring out of the box and put it on her finger. Her voice was a whisper. "Thank you."

After dinner she said, "The studio gave me some rotten news today. They assigned me a new picture. *Murder, Incorporated.* I can't afford to go on suspension so I have to take it." She looked away. "I have to go to New York next week. We'll be shooting most of it on location there."

The story of my own life was the constant moving from town to town, pretending not to mind leaving behind the things you can't pack in a suitcase, so I was able to accept the fact that she had to go, but I couldn't bring myself to ask for how long. "Do you know where you'll be staying?"

"The Sherry Netherland. I'll have to be there for a month."

We spent every possible minute together for the little time that was left and on Sunday I drove her to the airport. As we pulled up in front of the TWA building, she said, "I hate saying good-bye." She got out of the car, ran inside, and was gone.

I drove back to the house, had a quiet dinner with the family and killed the next few hours going over my lines for Monday morning's shooting, until I knew she'd be at her hotel and I could call her. I knew I couldn't give my name. Maybe because it was Sunday I thought of the characters in "Peanuts," the comic strip we both liked, and when the hotel operator asked who was calling, I said, "Tell her it's Charlie Brown calling Peanuts."

May was laughing as the connection was made. "Tell me, Sharlie Brown, are you somebody I just left a few hours ago?"

I kidded her about the way her accent slid over the "Ch" sound, softening it to "Sh," and, maybe to take the emphasis off the fact that I had to use a code name, I laughed a little harder than it was worth.

When we finished shooting on Monday I browsed around a flower shop for almost half an hour. I enjoyed choosing what I thought she'd like, and it occurred to me that since I'd been a star I'd probably sent out ten, twenty, maybe even thirty thousand dollars' worth of flowers, but this was the first time I'd ever been in a florist's shop.

We spoke on the phone as often every day as we could. I had scenes to shoot all week and at night I forced myself to go to sleep early. On Sunday I called to say good morning and we spoke until afternoon. Neither of us had anything to do all day long, but there were three thousand miles between us.

I bumped around the house trying to get involved in books, television—anything to help pass the time. I went down to the Playhouse to straighten out my record albums. I rolled out the first drawer of the cabinets in which Jim had them filed and cross-indexed, trying to find some out of place, but they were all exactly right. I pushed the drawer shut, fixed myself a drink, and sat down on the couch. It was fantastic that with all the things I'd done, all the people I knew, one girl with a funny Swedish accent, who answered the phone "Tell me" could, by herself, fill my life—or leave it so empty.

I knew that if I had a brain in my head I'd get busy on the phone and have the place swarming with chicks. But I had no eyes for all the chicks in Hollywood put together, it was too late for that. There was no suddenly saying "This is the woman I love," yet it was impossible to imagine the day I'd ever stop seeing her, and I knew that compared with what was coming, I'd never had a problem in my life.

What do I do when she becomes aware of how much I love her and she says, "I'm sorry. I like you, maybe even love you, but I . . . well I never dreamed you were thinking of marriage."

Even as the world's greatest optimist how can I hope for anything else? Let's say she loves me. It's one thing to have quiet dinners together, go on private boats, come to Vegas with her mother and with Frank covering for her. But marrying me brings it out in the open. There'd be no secret-service style, no being surrounded only by close friends. She thinks she doesn't care about her career, but how will she feel when they take it away from her? How can I expect her to face the world and her family and say, "This is my husband. He's a little dark, folks. . . ."

Night after night I placed my calls to her, like an

alcoholic watching the bartender pour his drink, waiting anxiously while the operator connected us and then, finally, relaxing as the warmth of her voice spread through my entire being, restoring resilience to my overstretched emotions, suspending my fears. Then, after each call, as the phone touched the receiver, the fears and the doubts gripped me again and I lay stretched out on the bed, staring at the ceiling, hating myself for breathing life into a relationship which I'd known was condemned before it was born.

After shooting on Thursday I went to Romanoff's with Frank, Dean, and Peter. Right after dinner I excused myself and went back to the house.

We'd been on the phone for almost an hour, she'd been telling me how she hated being away, we'd counted the days she'd been gone and I just said, sort of wistfully: "Wouldn't it be great to be married?" The instant I heard my own words slip out I hurried to make a joke of it, "Listen, at these prices on the phone two could live cheaper than one."

She said, "It sure *would* be great, wouldn't it?"

I was unable to continue talking. I told her I'd call back and we hung up. I sat on the edge of the bed, my hand still on the phone, hearing her answer over and over again.

But she was in New York and I was in California and she couldn't see my skin through the phone. Had she considered that after marriage comes children? And with us they might be colored? Was she prepared for that?

I let go of the phone, trying to break contact, forcing myself to face some reality. Did she know what she was saying? Had she thought seriously about it before, or had she answered too quickly?

I walked around the room thanking God she hadn't said no, but knowing that I couldn't accept her "yes" so easily. I couldn't let myself go blundering happily on until a month or who knows when from now when we'd talk about children and she'd say, "I guess I didn't really give it enough thought." I owed it to her and I owed it to myself, now, once and forever to be sure she understood what she was doing.

I called her back an hour later and after we'd talked for a while I said, "You know how I love kids. Won't it be great when we're married and have lots of little brown

babies?" I said it gaily, but I meant it to be clear and realistic.

"I'd love to. Lots of them. Sammy? . . . Sammy, are you
there?"

"Yes."

"Don't *you* want little brown babies?"

I had to fight to hold the phone to my ear. I couldn't
speak. The tears were running down my face. I don't know
exactly what I'd feared—a deathly silence, or words that
would cut me in half. I'd dreaded being one inch from
heaven when the gate swings closed. But then to have all the
fears miraculously disappear like a horrible dream from which
you've just awakened and the sun is shining and it's a beautiful day and you know that it *always* will be a beautiful day
—the relief was paralyzing. A few hours earlier I hadn't
even known that I was going to propose to her, yet if she
had turned me down, if she hadn't wanted my little brown
babies, I knew then as sure as I stand on God's earth, I
would have hung up the phone and blown my brains out.

I asked Frank, "Can I have a few days spare? I want to
go to New York."

"Sure, Charley. See you Monday."

I told Jim to book us on a flight to New York with a
return Sunday.

"Us?"

"Baby, I can't go walking into the Sherry Netherland like
'Hello America: Sammy Davis and May Britt are an item.'
Jane and Burt are in Florida and they gave me their apartment—it's right around the corner from the hotel. I'll need
you to pick May up and bring her over and I want you to
stay there like a chaperone so if anybody *does* get hip at
least I can always prove this is no 'Hey, they're having
secret love trysts.' "

I called May and told her I'd be in New York the next
morning.

"Oh, Sharlie Brown, that's marvelous. I can't *wait* to see
you. By the way, a journalist called me about us. You'll
probably see it in the papers tomorrow. He wanted to know
if it's true I've been dating you. I said yes, and he wanted to
know 'Is it serious?' "

"What'd you say?"

"I told him, 'Any time I see a man more than once I consider it very serious.' "

"Darling, that was a beautiful Mary Moviestar line but do me a favor, don't talk to any more press guys until we can discuss it."

"Okay." Her voice was touched with disappointment because I wasn't thrilled with her statement. She asked, "When is your plane coming in? I'll meet you at the airport."

"No. Stay in your hotel and wait for me."

"But I *want* to. I'll rent a car."

"Darling. You'll wait in your suite. I'll call you when I get in."

"Boy oh Boy, I didn't know I was marrying a dictator."

"You're marrying somebody who loves you and who's asking you to do what's best. Just bear with me. Okay?"

"Okay."

Her picture was on the front page of the New York *Journal American,* captioned, "Going Steady?" I knew that as soon as it became known and confirmed that we were going together the opinions would start flying, and with them would come pressures and stares and antagonism that was pointless to subject her to for a single day longer than absolutely necessary. It was almost mathematical: the moment it's known, the furor will start building, it will reach its peak when we get married, then lose its heat and begin dying down. I can't prevent the furor but I can spare her some of it. I put down the paper. "Darling, I've been thinking that with your divorce not final until September, we have five or six months before we can be married, so we've got to cool it with letting it be known we're going together. No more cute-ums bits with the press. We've got to let them forget us. We can't be seen together—"

"You mean we can't be seen together for six months?"

"I'm afraid so."

"You mean I've got to duck journalists and give them phony answers? Why can't I just come out and tell them, 'Yes, I love him and I'm going to be his wife'?"

"Please, take my word, it's better this way. God knows I'd love to make an announcement and say, 'This is the girl I

505

love and we're going to be married.' But if we do that then there's going to be six months of a whole publicity free-for-all, with will-they-or-won't-they, and you certainly don't want that, do you?"

"Oh boy, no. I'd hate it."

"Then that's it. We cool it." She nodded agreement. "Darling, do your parents . . . do they know about us being serious?"

"Yes. I've written them all about you. And I know my mother has told my father how much she liked you."

"That's great but I'd like to meet him in person and give him a chance to know me and make up his own mind. I was thinking, I'll be playing London in June and you mentioned you might visit your folks in Sweden around then—is there any chance you could come over to London with your father? That way we could meet and get to know each other. It would be beautiful if we could get his official consent."

"Hey, that's a great idea."

We watched television, cooked some steaks, and talked. I gave her a complete run-down on my money situation. "It's pretty disgusting to know that after earning maybe six million dollars, I haven't got at least a million dollars put away. All I can do is tell you that I'll start right now toward becoming solvent and building something for you and for the kids we want. Money has a meaning, a value that it never had before. I've been in touch with Joe Borenstein in Chicago. He's my lawyer. He's a nice, nice man and he's been giving me good, sound advice, which I haven't had the sense to follow. But now we're going to start doing all the things he and Jim Waters have been noodging me to do for years. I hate like hell to begin marriage on an economy drive . . ."

"Sammy, I've sold stockings and washed dishes. I like luxuries but I can take them or leave them. Also, my salary is two thousand dollars a week. We can put our money together and be paid off that much faster."

"No. I appreciate it but I've got enough coming in so that we can be cleaned up in a few years. All I have to do is cut out the waste." I told her about the setup with Will, my relationship to Mama, Loray—everything I could think of.

"Sharlie Brown, I feel a little pushy listening to all this.

What you did before we met is your business, and although I'm glad you're telling me these things you certainly don't have to."

"I know, darling, and I appreciate it, but there's a lot of little things that should be said now. Let's not have any fine print in the contract. I want you to know what you're getting into. This kind of relationship is a first for me and I'm not sure if I can have a marriage in the fullest sense of the word. I really don't know if I can be half of two people instead of all of just one."

"But you want to, don't you?"

"Yes. But it's not that simple. First of all I don't begin to know what marriage is going to be like. Not only have I never gone steady with a girl, I've never even done light housekeeping." She looked puzzled. "That's an expression for when a guy has a girl and he pays the bills. What I'm saying is, I've never had a day-to-day relationship with a woman, to the extent that I've never even spent a whole night in bed with a woman."

"Seriously?"

"Never. When it was time to sleep either they'd go home or I'd fall asleep on the couch or on the floor. I haven't slept in bed with anyone since I was a kid and my father and I used to share a bed on the road. I don't begin to know how to be around a woman like a man is around his wife or some-one he cares for dearly. For example, I remember once I was going to an opening with a married couple. It was two blocks away and I felt like walking. We were in evening clothes and the husband said, 'We'll take a cab and meet you there, Sam.' I thought he was a nut and only later did I learn that he was hip to the fact that it was a damp night and it was going to ruin her hairdo. A thing like that makes me realize there must be a million and one little things I've never even *begun* to think about. Plus the fact that I've never in my adult life had to think about anyone's desires but my own. I could make my mistakes without affecting anyone except me. I've never had anybody I'd tell 'I'll be home at six.' And, if I was with fifty people and felt like bringing them home I'd bring fifty people home. I may start off as the inconsiderate husband of all time so you'll have to bear with me. I've had thirty-four years of one-way living—

on the other hand I've waited thirty-four years before I fell in love with somebody so have no fears about how much I love you and how much I want to be Charley Married, but there's a danger: I don't know how much I *dare* to change."

"I don't understand."

"Look, I make a lot of money and I'm big in the business because of three things: I've got talent, I've worked hard, and every bit as important, I have let myself remain an individual. That doesn't mean I've been a non-conformist deliberately making myself different, but neither have I been Charley Chameleon who permits his own ideas and tastes to be overwhelmed by the 'accepted way' of doing things until finally he blends into the masses and he ain't never seen or heard from again. We're all born as individuals and in a million and one little ways I've managed to remain Sammy Davis, Jr. I don't go by a slide rule and a set of plans. I go by what I see works best for me. I do things on a stage that defy the common-sense rules of the business: I stay on too long, I do too many things—and if there were a book on how to be a hit it would definitely say *'Hold it! Don't do these things!'* but the book would be wrong because I don't stay on too long for *me* and I don't do too many things for *me* and the proof is in the audiences. Whether the people know it or not, my individuality is part of what they're buying when they come to see me. What I'm saying is, I know I'm not perfect but whatever I am in sum total, my faults and my virtues have combined to make me one-of-a-kind, and it works for me. Somewhere in the over-all scheme of things everything has its value. Maybe if I'd had an education I wouldn't have had the desire to do all the reading I've done, maybe if I'd had a little more religion as a kid I'd never have gone out and found one I could really sink my teeth into. If I'd been born white, things would have been easier but maybe I wouldn't have tried so hard and made it as I have. Who can say? All I can know is that I've got a winning combination and I dare not mess with it.

"Something has stayed in my mind since the first time I read *The Picture of Dorian Gray*. Oscar Wilde had a theory that when you love someone it must take away from you as an individual. I never before loved anybody enough to feel they're as important as I am or more important so for their happiness I'll change. But now that I'm in that position I can see that I've got to be extra careful. I've seen so many marriages where the husband or wife blended into each other until there's no way to tell them apart except he buttons his coat from left to right and she buttons hers from right to left. One has changed the other and maybe it's fun—but for me it would be death. I live in dread of the day I turn around and find I've been made over and I've lost my individuality."

The wisdom of a sensitive woman is a marvelous thing. I could see as I was telling her these things that she already knew them. Or at least she understood.

"Darling, if my business weren't so closely related to my personal life I wouldn't worry about it. I'm sure it's nowhere near as serious as I'm making it out to be. I'm deliberately exaggerating it so that I'm positive I don't make the mistake of unconsciously slipping into a different personality."

"I can certainly understand that you can't afford to be changed and I wouldn't want to change you anyhow. I must say I don't want to be blended with anybody either so that I just come out like a piece of macaroni with no shape of my own.

"Sammy, do you think you'll hate losing your independence?"

"I was never independent until I met you."

The seriousness in her face yielded to a smile. "Is that really true?" She clasped her hands behind her neck and leaned back against the couch, sighing contentedly, "Boy oh boy, I must be a wonderful person for you to love me so much."

I smiled. It didn't exactly require an answer.

"Sharlie Brown? Why do you love me?"

"Darling . . . ask Elizabeth Barrett Browning."

"Seriously. I don't mean the usual stuff like I love you and you love me. I mean what do you like about me?"

"You're really going to put me through this, right?"

"Come on. Be a sport."

"Your honesty, independence. . ."

"You think I'm honest?"

"Yes."

She nodded, like she was caught and had to admit it. "You're right."

"I dig the idea that you're beautiful."

509

She thought about that for a moment. "When you look at me do you think 'oh boy, she's beautiful'—or do you accept it automatically, because I'm in films?"

"Darling, Edna May Oliver was in films but I didn't ask her to marry me. I may only have one eye but that's all I need."

"Well, if I weren't beautiful, would you still love me?"

"I don't know."

She gasped. "That's a *terrible* thing to say."

"Why? Being beautiful is a part of what you are. It's not *the* reason I love you but it's one of them. I also dig the idea that you're an exciting personality, I mean commercially like 'Hey, there's May Britt.' Let's be honest. I'm a showman first, last, and always, in everything I do, and I've got to admit that I dig the kick of the combination of personalities so that when we walk down the street it won't be just 'there's Sammy and his wife' but it'll be 'there's Sammy Davis and May Britt' and there's an extra excitement to it. I love you for all the dozens of things you are—and being May Britt instead of Maybritt Wilkens or Maryjane Smith is a part of what you are. By the same token I expect you to love me, in part, for my professional self, I spent my whole life trying to become a star. I started off in the world as fat, bone, and a gallon of water and I think it would be ridiculous to expect you to love me for *that* or for what I was when I was twenty. I love you as I want you to love me: for the sum total of what I've made of what I started with."

She told me some of her feelings. "For one thing I want a house that's filled with kids. And I don't intend to be one of those Hollywood mothers who stops by the nursery for ten minutes every day. Sure, we'll have a nurse if we can afford one but I want to raise my own kids. I want them to know me and I want them to know *you*."

"I couldn't agree more. And I've been thinking, even if God lets us succeed in having our own child I want to adopt children too. There are too many kids, particularly colored kids, who don't have homes, and nobody comes to give them one and they grow up hollow inside because they never had anybody to love them. I think it's inexcusable if somebody can afford it and they don't take a child into their lives, a child who's already living and breathing and who needs them.

I know that I have enough love stored up in me to lavish it on you and on all the kids we can physically handle."

"I agree with you one hundred per cent. I don't care how many we have of our own I'd still love to adopt some, too."

"Then we've got no problems there."

She said, "I realize that you'll have to be on the road a lot and when I can be with you then I want to be, but I know there'll be places too expensive to travel to for only a short time or I'll want to be at home with our children so at least when you are home I'll expect you to try to create the atmosphere of a real home. I know you have a lot of friends and business guys to see when you're on the coast but I want us to have a certain amount of privacy, too. Maybe it's corny but I'd like to sit down at a dinner table with just my husband and have dinner with him. Particularly when we have children. I want them to have the security of being able to see as many of the traditions of home life as we can possibly make for them."

"I agree completely. And I'm hoping the day will come when the debts are paid and I won't have to spend forty weeks a year traveling around the country. Sy Marsh has kicked down the door for me in dramatic television, the ratings I've gotten have been unbelievable—they definitely prove that the whole South isn't turning off its television sets the minute I come on—so eventually I should be able to count on maybe three or four good TV shows a year. That, plus a picture a year, and we'll have it made."

"You mean that? When we're out of debt, you'll be able to stay home?"

"No. I'll never want to cut out clubs entirely. I'm primarily a nightclub performer and I'll always want to spend a certain amount of time facing audiences, both to keep myself up as a performer and because I enjoy it. Besides, the clubs have enough trouble finding acts that can draw without me walking out on them, too. But it'll be beautiful to play just certain places, to pick and choose without being financially pressured to play every good offer that comes along."

We sat near a big window in the living room, eating ham and eggs and talking, watching Sunday spreading over the city.

Jim took her back to her hotel, then picked her up again around noon. At two o'clock he said, "Our plane is at three-fifteen. We'd better leave here in about fifteen minutes."

"Baby, get us on the next flight, will you?"

There had seemed, on the plane and in L.A., to be so many urgent things to discuss with May, but now the fact and joy of being together was more important than the details and problems of the future. She was wearing slacks and a bulky sweater and although the weather outside was clear and sunny and we were in a New York apartment, I had the feeling I knew I'd have had if we'd been sitting in front of a stone fireplace in New England with mountains of snow outside, lulled by the flames of a blazing, crackling fire. "Hey, let me ask you something. How come you didn't come over to the house that night after Dinah Washington's closing? Didn't I impress you at all?"

She laughed and gave me one of those reluctant compliments. "I must confess I was a *little* sharmed by Sharlie Sharming. But I couldn't just say, 'Sure I'll come up,' the first time we'd met."

"But you wanted to?"

She was embarrassed. "The next day I went out and bought your album 'Sammy Davis, Jr. at Town Hall.' I played it so much that my mother finally said, 'Don't you have anything else to play?' Then, when you said you'd call me from Vegas," she hesitated, "I really shouldn't tell you this . . ."

"Yes you should, we're engaged. Come on."

"Well, I sat by the telephone waiting to hear from you, and whenever I had to go out of the house, I made my mother swear she wouldn't leave . . . oh boy, was I mad when you didn't call right away. Then I started getting worried you weren't interested and—listen, I've told you enough. Now you tell me something. What did you think of me?"

I described the trouble I'd had making connections with her. "And let's not even discuss how I put together a whole party just to meet you and you walked in with George Englund and sat with your back to me all night. Then I left town and did a whole tug-of-war with myself, 'Should I invite her to Vegas? Maybe she'll say no.'"

She burst out laughing. "I had my bags packed for two days."

"And I want to thank you for having your mother's bags packed too."

Jim came into the living room. "Okay, kiddies, this is it. TWA is running out of planes."

The car swung down Park Avenue, to 57th Street, then west to Fifth Avenue. It was one of those gorgeous winter Sundays with people strolling Fifth Avenue in couples. At the Sherry Netherland May got out. "So long. See you, Sharlie Brown. Good-bye, Yimmy." As the car pulled away, I watched her through the rear window. She was standing on the sidewalk, waving good-bye, making a beautiful picture in a sporty, cream-colored fur coat with the collar pulled up and a large alligator purse slung over one arm—Mary Moviestar all the way.

Frank was Charley Raised Eyebrows on the set Monday morning. "How'd everything go in New York?"

I hadn't told him why I was going but obviously he knew.

"Frank, we're going to get married."

"So what else is new?"

"I mean it."

His voice was gentle. "I know you mean it, Charley."

He must have known it before I did. He'd probably suspected something when I'd asked him to cover for me in Vegas, knowing I'd never ask him to do anything like that with just another chick.

Frank is two people: one, his public image—the swinger, the legend, the idol, the "ring-a-ding-ding" and "wowoweewow" guy who says, "Let's get the broads and get the booze and *be* somebody!" The other is the serious businessman, the father, the friend. The façade of fun, the atmosphere of laughs comes off like a coat, the looking everywhere at what's going on stops dead, his attention is fixed on one thing and his lifetime of hard-earned experience comes forward. He was studying me, evaluating, balancing the factors involved, weighing one against the other, understanding—as only a friend and another performer could—exactly what I stood to gain or possibly lose by such a marriage.

Finally he spoke and the words were deliberate. "Yeah. It's a good thing. Do it, Charley. Get yourself some happiness."

There was no pontificating. Just simple. He'd thought about it and he agreed with it.

I took a last look around the living room. Jim, Luddy, Rudy, Etheline, and I had spent the morning blowing up balloons and hanging streamers around a huge sign: "Welcome Home, Peanuts."

It was time to leave for the airport. I was nervous. I yearned to be standing at the gate when she got off the plane. But someone would point "Hey, look," like he couldn't believe his eyes, or there'd be a slur, or she'd catch a hard look that would hurt her. Maybe nothing would happen—but I couldn't take that chance.

I drove my new Rolls-Royce. Jim was looking over the upholstery. I'd put all kinds of pressure on the Rolls people so that I'd have it in time to pick her up in it. He grinned, "You wouldn't by any chance be trying to impress her with this car, would you?"

I gave him a look. "I'll say this about them, Mary, they've got rhythm, and they love big cars."

He blushed. "I wish I'd had this car when I was courting Luddy." He was talking fast. "On the other hand I got her anyway . . ."

I broke up. "I've always suspected you were a hater . . . that's why I keep you working for me, so I can keep an eye on you."

He shrugged, "I'm glad you didn't say eyes, as in 'the plural of.'"

"Ah, my dear Inspector, so you are aware that one eye is false, eh? But did you also know that it contains a precision camera of infinitesimal dimensions with which I have been photographing all of your country's strategic plans and ciphers?"

He nodded solemnly. "It's all in my report to the Yard. But before you kill me, would you mind telling me how you operate it? I've known for months what you've been doing yet I've never seen your hand go near your face."

"Certainly, Inspector. Delighted. Small good it will do you now." I turned to him and raised my eyebrow. "I have just taken your picture!"

We did a few more minutes of international spy bits and

drove the rest of the way in silence. As we neared the airport, I said, "You go and get her, baby. I'll stay in the car."

I saw May running ahead of Jim toward me and it took all the strength I had not to indulge myself in the pleasure of jumping out and throwing my arms around her. She stepped into the car. "Hello, there, Sharlie Brown." She didn't seem to mind that I hadn't come out to meet her; she put her hand on mine and the gesture said, someday we'll do all these things.

At the front door of the house I told her to close her eyes, and guided her until she was facing the living room. "Okay, now you can open them."

She stood amidst the confetti and the party hats, staring at the sign, holding one of the balloons, not even trying to blink away the tears. "Nobody ever did anything like this for me before."

I dabbed gently at her eyes with my handkerchief. Through the weeks, the veneer of the beautiful but cold and haughty girl had gradually relaxed with me to a softness that was loving, yet still independent. But now, sitting on the couch pouring out her happiness at being loved, like a little girl, so soft and defenseless, it was as though she'd gained the security that permitted her to lower a final shield and admit to me how lonely she'd been.

By what miracle had we found each other and known, without really knowing, that we needed each other so much? I held her in my arms wanting to promise that I'd never let her be lonely again, wanting to tell her everything she meant to me and all the things I yearned to do for her that I'd never done or even thought of doing for anyone else. It was a moment when there was so much to say yet no words with which to say it. But at least it was also a moment when so much could be understood with no words at all.

After a while I stood up. "Okay, we've both had our little cry, now here's the skam: we'll go downstairs so you can say hello to Mama, then we'll have lunch and I'll take you home and you can unpack and get some rest."

"But, Sharlie Brown, I just got here."

"Hey, cool it. I haven't seen you, either, and I ain't all that choked up about letting you go but you're in the middle of shooting and you need your sleep. Unless, of course, you're doing a re-make of an old Marjorie Main movie! Darling, you're making a picture?—do it right!"

After taking her home, I went downstairs to see Mama again. She was sitting in her chair, her TV set off, like she'd been expecting me.

"I'm going to marry her, Mama."

"You sure that's what you want to do, Sammy?"

"Yes, Mama, that's what I want to do. I love her and I've asked her to marry me and she's said yes."

Her eyes were looking at me but seeing past me and I couldn't be sure if she was seeing the years ago or the years ahead. "I won't say do you know what's ahead of you, Sammy. I know you must have thought it out."

"Yes."

"You think *she* knows?"

"No. How could she?"

"Is she strong?"

"Yes. And I'll do everything I can to protect her."

Mama nodded. "I watched her these times she's been here. She's a nice girl. Does she know what kind of life you led 'til now?"

"Yes. I've told her."

"Well, if she'll have you, knowing everything you've done bad, you've got the right to marry her. But make her happy." Her face took on the familiar, strong, stern expression it used to have when she was fighting my father or Will in the old days. "Be good to her, Sammy. Do everything you can to make her happy. If you don't I won't like you."

"I'll try my best, Mama. I'll make her happy."

She relaxed and smiled with a grandmother's confidence that if I said it, and if I meant it, then it was good as done. "Mama, there's something else. I spoke to Dad and Peewee about getting a new place for themselves and the kids, but this house is really yours and mine and I'd like it very much if you'd stay with me and my wife."

"Do you think she'll want me here?"

"I know she will."

Mama smiled happily, "Then that'll be fine, Sammy. That's what I want. May is a nice quiet girl. I'll like that."

We went to a few parties at Frank's, and at Tony and

Janet's, where I knew there would be only close friends and I could be sure nobody was going to slip into the other room, grab the phone and do a "Hello, Louella."

Hugh Benson called. "Why don't you and May come over for dinner tomorrow night? Diane and I are inviting some of the kids, Peter Brown, Nancy and Bob Culp . . ."

I thanked him and hung up, appreciating the way he'd anticipated my thoughts and had casually given me a guest list.

Jim and I picked up May and as we neared Hugh's house she asked, "Sammy, can we tell them?" Her face was aglow like: "She's lovely, she's engaged . . ." Seeing my hesitation she said, "After all, they're friends."

"Let's see if the right moment presents itself."

She smiled happily, looked through the window and began humming. She waved to a woman waiting at a bus stop. "Hello there. Good news. I'm engaged to Sharlie Brown." She said it against the soundproof glass and I wondered if she suspected the answers she might get when the window was rolled down. She was wide open, naïvely trusting, bursting to tell them all, to share her happiness—as though we were Debbie and Eddie and the whole world was waiting to throw flowers at us with unrestrained joy—and I dreaded the moment when her openness, her trust in the goodness of people would be met with a "How nice," or a raised eyebrow or any of the signs of disapproval. It had to happen and there was no way for me to tell her that "friendship" did not always transcend a lifetime of one-way thinking; no way for me to prepare her for the few who would turn away from us, without educating her to be an outcast, turning her into a human Geiger counter like I'd been, testing and probing for the presence of hatred. Should I force her to wear a raincoat twenty-four hours a day because it may rain occasionally?

Throughout dinner the conversation seemed constantly to arrive at "kitchens," "babies," and a dozen other topics that were perfect cues for me to tap a glass and say, "I have a little announcement to make," and as each opportunity arose, May turned to me expectantly but I looked away, scanning the faces at the table, wondering. Hugh's thirteen-year-old son Jeffrey was at dinner with us and even if the adults reacted as I hoped they would it was almost a sure thing that Jeff's youthful honesty would expose an immediate reaction—a glance from May to me and the almost out-loud thinking, "But she's white and he's colored." I wanted to spare Hugh and Diane the embarrassment of fumbling for cover-up lines, and May the pain and shock of hearing them, but each time I switched the talk away from marriage I saw the eagerness fade from her face, and by the time we were halfway through dinner the bright-eyed excitement she had radiated was completely gone, shrouded by a bewilderment which caused mechanical smiles when she was talking and a near glumness when she thought she wasn't being watched.

At my next chance I said, "Look, we've been keeping it quiet because we don't want a whole publicity thing, but you're all friends so May and I would like you to know that we intend to be married."

Jeff's face brightened. "Hey, that's great. Wow . . ." and from all directions the air filled with the warmth of good wishes as people stood up to kiss May, to shake hands with me and to offer toasts. She was blushing happily and I smiled, accepting the congratulations, resting against the back of the chair, concealing my complete exhaustion.

Just before midnight Gail, the Bensons' daughter, got home from her date. Again my stomach knotted as Hugh told her, "Darling, we've got great news. Mr. Davis and Miss Britt are engaged to be married."

Her face reflected spontaneous excitement. "That's *wonderful!* That's *fabulous!*" and as she rushed across the room to kiss May, to kiss me, to kiss everybody, I looked at Hugh and Diane, my eyes watering, ashamed of myself for imagining it could have been different, filled with awe and devotion for a man and woman who had raised their children with enough love and care to overcome what kids almost can't help but pick up from others who are brought up differently.

We dropped Jim off at his house and as I drove May out to Malibu she sighed, "Boy, that was a beautiful party."

I nodded, wishing she could enjoy the depth of satisfaction I felt, yet hoping to God she never would learn enough to be able to fully share this kind of an evening with me.

Jim picked May up at the studio and as she walked in the door I took her by the arm and escorted her to the couch. She sat down, watching me, sensing I had something exciting to tell her.

I bowed low. "Mademoiselle, I take pleasure in informing you that your fiancé has this day been invited to appear at a Command Performance before the Queen of England." Her eyes widened with delight, her excitement as great as my own.

"Here I am the world's greatest nut for castles and moats and 'Ah, yes, m'liege' and 'By your grace, m'lord' and I get an invitation from Buckingham Palace." I turned to Jim, "Baby, before I forget, call Sy Devore and tell him we need a complete list of my measurements. And when you get them, shoot them right over to the Morris office so they can cable them to London."

He went to make the call. "I'll be wearing my own tux for the show but I need tails for the presentation to the Queen. They said I could bring my own or they'd supply them. And one thing I know, England is England if I get my tails from the Royal Tailor, or whoever they use, there'll be no question about looking right. I don't want no 'Hmmphs' from them cats in the bowlers."

I sat down next to her, holding the invitation for both of us to see. "'Mr. Sammy Davis, Jr. is requested by Her Majesty, Elizabeth, Queen of England, to appear at The Royal Command Performance at Victoria Palace, on the sixteenth of May, nineteen hundred and sixty. . . .'"

32

I SMILED, "THANKS, AWFULLY," AT THE BRITISH CUSTOMS inspectors. I wasn't putting on; from the second I set foot on British soil I *felt* English.

Al Burnett was waiting for me and as we walked toward the car he said, "I've taken the liberty of arranging a press conference at the club. I hope you'll oblige."

"I'll be happy to." He gave instructions to his driver, then settled back in his seat. "Your arrival has stimulated strong interest here and the press is eager to meet you personally."

I raised an eyebrow. "I'll bet they are."

He smiled, "I gather you've heard there have been occasional failings in chemistry between American performers and our press?"

"Al, every performer who heard I was coming here called me—long distance—to tip me off. 'Hey, stay away from this one 'cause he's tricky and dangerous.' . . . 'Don't open your mouth to so-and-so 'cause he twists things' and 'Don't face 'em all at once 'cause it's a rumble!' "

He became serious. "Well, if you'd rather not . . . I could make your apologies."

"No. I'm looking forward to it. I love the challenge of a good hard interview."

I gazed through the windows of the car as we moved through London. It was everything I'd expected it to be. I knew I was in England, and I dug it! Signs and billboards swept by in a montage of names and trademarks I'd never seen before—then as we pulled up in front of the club, I had the thrill of standing on a strange street in a strange country and seeing my own name.

The Pigalle was one flight downstairs, like the Copa. I sauntered into the main room and skidded to a halt at the sight of what awaited me. It seemed there were twelve million of them. I nudged Al, "Are these the reporters or the readers?"

They cleared an aisle through their midst to the center of the stage. Al introduced me, then stepped back as though removing himself from a fight, leaving me in the ring.

The questions exploded like fifty feet of Chinese firecrackers. I had to get control. I put up my hands. "Hold it. *Hold* it, fellas." I jumped up on the piano. "Gentlemen, you've got the days mixed up. *Tomorrow* is the lynching. Today we have a press conference." They laughed. I looked at one of the reporters. "Now, sir, you were saying?"

"Is there anything between you and May Britt?"

"I sincerely hope so." It got a laugh.

"Do you intend to marry her?"

They had English accents but they were no tea drinkers. I couldn't deny it or admit it. I parried. "Who wouldn't want to marry May Britt? Imagine some guy saying, 'No, I don't want to marry the most beautiful girl in the world.' Now, whether or not she wants to marry *me* is something else."

They laughed and the questions kept coming. "Mr. Davis, we in England have read of your amorous affairs with the glamorous women of the world. What do you have that makes you so desirable to these fabulous creatures? If I may say, without intending to be insulting, you know, you're not the most attractive man in the world."

I looked around the room, thinking: well, here they are, the British Press: tough, mischievous, skeptical. I gave him the Jack Benny stare, stalling. If I say why I think I'm attractive I come off like I believe I'm Cary Grant. If I say I haven't the faintest idea it has to sound like false modesty. Further, to steam me into being foolish he'd added the zingy about me not being good-looking. Who in this world doesn't see *something* attractive in himself?

I asked, "Are you married, sir?"

"Why, yes, I am."

"Is your wife pretty? I mean, is she beautiful—attractive?"

He was becoming uneasy. "Yes, I think she's attractive. *Most* attractive!"

"Well, if I may turn the phrase around—ever so slightly —y'know you're not exactly Sir Laurence Olivier. What attracted her to *you*?"

He rubbed his chin. "Jove, that's a good point." He laughed and the other reporters got a kick out of it.

A man in the rear raised his hand. "Mr. Davis, is my information correct—you're appearing here for twenty-six nights at a flat 20,000 pounds? In American dollars that would be approximately fifty thousand."

"That's correct."

"Are you aware that this is an extraordinary sum of money for a performer to earn here?"

"I've been told that. And I'm most appreciative and flattered by it."

"Do you suppose that people will pay a charge of thirty

dollars per couple merely to get inside the Pigalle to watch you? Plus additional charges for everything they care to order?"

"I have to rely on Mr. Burnett's good judgment in establishing his prices."

He smiled. "Is it true that you earn close to a million dollars a year?"

"Yes."

"Do you believe that you're worth being paid that much money?"

"I am to the people who pay it."

"Sir. How good a performer would you say you are?"

"I'm a very good performer."

"Mr. Davis, earning as much money as you do, how is it possible that you're in debt? Or is that not true?"

"It's true."

"I suppose it's due to the fact of high taxes."

"No. It's due to the fact that I was an idiot."

"Oh?" He smiled. "Might I inquire: are you still an idiot?"

"I sincerely hope not."

Another reporter waded in. "You dress very well. Are you influenced by our styles?"

"I'm influenced by good taste."

He advanced again, "Do you always wear a vest or did you do that for us?"

"I often wear them at home. I love a vest. Among other reasons, I like them because I can wear watches like this one." I took out an antique gold pocket watch.

"A family heirloom?"

"Yes, but not *my* family."

"I see you wear high-top shoes. Are those lifts?"

"No, they're dancers' shoes. José Greco and a few other dancers wear them. I started wearing them because I'm a great fan of Lincoln's. He used to wear Congress Gaiters which were a similar high-top shoe. I like them because they go well with my pants which are," I smiled, "tapered."

I was able to maintain control by making switches, turning the loaded questions around or taking the bite out of them with jokes. There's nothing in the rules that says you have to discuss anything you don't care to but my answers to their questions indicated the respect I had for them and it wound up like the corny movie scene in which the two heroes fight, beating the hell out of each other but getting nowhere, and as they lie on the ground puffing and panting, you can see that now they like each other, they've developed a strong mutual respect.

The doorman at the Mayfair Hotel opened the car door and smiled pleasantly, "Good afternoon, sir," and I had a feeling he didn't know who I was. We crossed the lobby to the front desk and as I registered I sensed politeness and cordiality. There was no bending over backwards, no special treatment in either direction.

Al took me to dinner at Les Ambassadeurs. I waited awhile before getting around to "How're the reservations?"

He answered with both eyebrows. "Enormous. Jack Benny, Judy Garland . . . virtually every American performer who's been here has added to the legend that you're quite the most extraordinary thing in America. Frank Sinatra, for one, was asked whom he thought to be the best entertainer in America and he said, "Sammy Davis, Jr.!" He smiled. "His exact words were, 'He can do everything except cook spaghetti.' And, incidentally, it was a superb piece of timing playing the Command Performance on your second day. You couldn't hope for a better introduction to England."

The morning papers had me on Page One, and the stories read like a kiss on the lips. I looked across the breakfast table at Murph. "Baby, your employer and friend has successfully run the British Blockade." I went into the bedroom to dress. I looked over my clothes for just the right rehearsal outfit . . . light gray slacks, a double-breasted six-button blazer and a white, button-down-collar shirt.

As we walked into the theater a buzzing began among the performers. Morty went backstage and Arthur and I sat in the back of the theater. Nat Cole was onstage. This was his second Command Performance. The press, most of the same guys I'd seen the day before, were shooting pictures and writing things down. They waved hello to me and I waved back and mouthed the words "Thank you."

I watched the rehearsal. It was like a gigantic Ed Sullivan show, with the biggest stars of two continents. There was a chorus of twenty boys and girls—the top popular singers in England, like Cliff Richard and Adam Faith—who did nothing but sing "Tell Me, Pretty Maiden."

A man had walked up the aisle. "Mr. Davis, my name is Jack Hylton, I'm the producer of the show and I'm delighted to meet you. We've put you next-to-closing." At any other time I'd have expected the honor of being given the star spot and accepted it with satisfaction, but right then all my cool went out the window. He was smiling pleasantly. "Liberace will follow you and close the show with a simple song on the piano." I wanted to say: Lee doesn't know how to play a *simple* song, but it was no time for jokes. He said, "You'll have nine minutes." Well, that was good. It was a minute more than I'd been told and it would mean that much more I could do to get them.

I sat back and watched an act do a beatnik sketch, and they were sensational. Bruce Forsyth, the M.C., walked onstage and started in with lines and stories and ring-a-ding-ding, and he was brilliant. Talk had always come back from London: They're old-fashioned. They're square. Like hell. They are solid, fine performers with no old-fashioned or anything connected with it. There could be no thinking: They don't have what we have. Everybody's got it. And I'm hip that if I went to India there'd be a guy there doing it, and as hip as we are here he'd be that hip there.

Arthur turned to me. "We ain't out-of-town, old buddy."

I nodded. This was show business at its best. It was Broadway or Hollywood but with all the dignity of the old vaudeville in which I'd been raised. Despite the sour grapes stuff I'd heard from guys who'd come back after dying in London I always knew that they had to have great performers if for no other reason than variety had lasted twenty years longer in England than in America, and it's still going strong.

A man onstage peered out into the audience, "Mr. Davis? You're on next, sir. Rehearsal, please."

I walked down the aisle and rather than making a leap onto the stage as I would at home I went around through the door which connects the backstage to the audience and walked onstage. Everyone, from the performers and the stagehands to the maids and cleaning women and the people from the office, the press and performers' friends, had taken seats. As I reached for the microphone the performers began applauding. I never had that kind of courtesy in my life. A performer doesn't know what courtesy is until he goes to London.

Murphy had ordered dinner sent upstairs at the hotel. I couldn't look at it. I had the colds, the hots, and I was shaking like a leaf.

Arthur watched me walking up and down the room. "Relax. You saw what happened this afternoon. You wrecked 'em."

"Baby, it's beautiful to be a hit at rehearsal, but it's a little more comfortable when it happens after the *performance*, right?" I stopped walking. "Hey! Nobody gave me the protocol on what happens if I get introduced to the Queen after the show. Baby, get moving and find someone at the theater who knows these things."

"What can it be? You shake hands. Why're you so worried?"

"Arthur, when I was a kid in Harlem nobody told me, 'Now here's what you do when you meet the Queen of England!' "

The backstage doorman said, "You're dressing on the third floor, sir. Mr. Cole asked us to put you with him." He smiled. "The best luck, Mr. Davis."

At each landing kids leaned out of dressing rooms, calling to me, "You'll be a smash tonight," "Don't worry about a thing," "You'll be magnificent!" It was that way with every performer I passed.

Nat was already in the dressing room with his man and Murphy, and George Rhodes, my pianist. I sat down and looked around. Murphy had my clothes and make-up laid out. Nat was sitting across from me, not saying a word, doing some quiet drinking. I looked at the bottle next to him. "Nat, you don't drink scotch."

"I'm drinking it tonight."

"I don't drink scotch either. Lemme have some." I poured a water tumbler full of straight scotch, and dumped it, neat. Whack! I felt it land in my stomach but it might have been tomato juice. I looked at Nat and shook my head. "I ain't *never* been this scared before!"

He said, "Take it easy, we've got three hours to kill."

Arthur burst in. "The place is packed. People are standing in the back, they're out in the streets. . . ."

The show was starting. I could hear the music. Nat was on the bill before me, closing the first half, and he started dressing. When it was time for him to go downstairs I wished him luck, and stood on the third floor landing to listen.

Nat is the personification of sophistication and calm. When he walks on, whatever nervousness he may feel stays inside of him, it never shows, and it was comforting to hear his smooth, mellow voice—like a touch of home. I started to relax. Then suddenly he cracked. "Oh, God!" Nat Cole has never cracked in his life! He has perfect control at all times, under any conditions. Even when he's hoarse, he knows how to play with his voice so that it doesn't come out rough, it becomes even more resonant, a little lower, and richer—never cracking!

He came back upstairs, dripping wet, shaking his head miserably, "I don't *never* want to do *that* no more! Not *ever!*" He collapsed into a chair and pulled his tie open. "Man, they is *out* there tonight!" He beckoned to his valet. "Give me a drink."

I was Charley Trembles but ten times worse than before, like I had a vibrating machine in my mouth and someone just plugged it in. "Whhhhh—wwwwwhattya mean 'they is out there'?"

He looked at me, "Get yourself another drink and sit down. Everybody else get out." He closed the door. "Now listen good. When you get out on the stage you *go* for it. Don't hold back nothin', 'cause they's *ready!* There ain't *nothin'* happened down there yet. You is *it!* They is waitin' fo' *you!*" He'd been talking "colored" to emphasize his point, and to relieve some of the urgency, but now he settled down to business. "When you come on, take your bows slow and easy. Don't let anything rush you. Do you remember what that cat told us before about don't look at the Queen? Forget it! *Damn* protocol. You give her a sneaky little peek out of your good eye, otherwise you'll be looking for her when you should be worrying about your song. And at the end of your act they're going to try to rush you off.

Don't let them. Just take and tear them apart!" He took another shot of scotch. He must have had a dozen in the past three hours but he was cold sober. "*And,* if you don't kill 'em, if you don't, I'm gonna take my fist and beat you to death."

He was beautiful. He knew that if ever I needed someone from home to encourage me, someone on my own level as a performer, someone who knew me well, I needed it then.

"Now, when it's over and you do your bow, bow to the Queen last. Bow here, here, here, and then give her one of them—I know you know how to bow with all that gracious bull you do—so you've got nothing to worry about."

"What did *you* do, Nat?"

He reached for the bottle again. "I didn't do *none* of that. That's how I know you should do it."

The second half of the show had started and I went downstairs a few minutes early to stand in the wings and get a look at the audience. It was like a movie scene: diamonds were dripping all over the place, almost every man there was wearing a red sash across his chest with medals hanging down and walrus mustaches—they didn't look anything like my kind of audience.

I watched Charlie Drake onstage. He seemed like Chaplin, Jerry Lewis, amd Marcel Marceau rolled into one, plus the Keystone Kops, with the pie throwing. He was doing a silent sketch, a slap-stick-vaudeville thing with balloons, and the people were falling out of their seats.

Bruce Forsyth whispered, "You're next. Walk onstage while Charlie's finishing and stand behind the closed curtains in back of him."

Charlie was in the wings and he gave me a wave like "Good luck." Bruce was onstage to introduce me. The audience was starting to buzz. I stared straight ahead at the threads of the curtain in front of me, trying to clear my mind of everything.

"Ladies and Gentlemen, Mr. Al Burnett."

What the hell is that? Nobody told me Al was going to be on. His voice came through the curtain between us. "Ladies and Gentlemen, I have been a performer and a nightclub owner for the better part of my life, and as a night-club owner I have contracted the finest entertainers available.

Three years ago I saw a young man perform in America. I wanted the pleasure of this moment, and thanks to all concerned—to Mr. Hylton, to all the people here at the Royal Command Performance, the pleasure is mine. Ladies and Gentlemen, the greatest entertainer in the world: Sammy Davis, Jr."

The curtains opened in front of me, Al stepped back to shake hands, left the stage, and I was alone.

By the grace of God I never performed better in my life. Cheers and applause roared up at me, crashing all around me and I stood limp, absorbing the beauty of it. As Bruce "carried" me offstage he whispered, "You were magnificent. Wait in the wings. You were magnificent."

Pandemonium was building out front. A stagehand screamed, "The Queen put down her fan and applauded!" Another answered, aghast, "She did. She really did." Bruce was at center stage leading the applause, motioning for me to come back on. I hesitated because we'd been strictly warned that nobody takes an extra bow. A stagehand pushed me. "He's the boss. Out you go. Can't keep the Queen waiting, y'know."

I bowed and walked off, but the audience was still calling for me and again Bruce, still clapping, reached his hands toward me and I walked to the center of the stage, took a deep bow and then the long walk back—and I did it not two or three times which would have been unbelievable, but *eight* times.

They were starting to shout "More—more—more" in time with the applause, like one voice, but I knew I didn't dare go out there again and as I closed the dressing room door I could still hear them calling for me.

Nat lifted me off the floor. "You did it, you dog, I *knew* you'd do it." He was carrying me all around the dressing room, laughing, "I knew you'd do it, I knew you'd do it . . ."

"It's over, it's over, Nat, oh, thank God it's over!" He put me down on a chair, and just sitting there was heaven. "What a night. Oh, what a gorgeous, beautiful night."

The door opened and the assistant stage manager called in, "Eight minutes before the finale."

I jumped up. "Finale? What Finale? What'll I sing? No one told me about any Finale."

Nat said, "The number we all do together."

Of course. We were all supposed to come out in our tails and top hats and sing "Strolling," a typically English song. Then there was a big production number with a ramp and stairs down which we all walk in a promenade with Vera Lynn coming down the center to close the show with "We'll Meet Again."

"Murphy, where's my suit?"

"Hanging right here, Sammy. All ready for you."

I ripped off my tux and jumped into the pants they'd sent. I didn't need to look at them in a mirror. I could feel the way they fit. I could have put a grapefruit between me and the waistband. I was flapping them in the air. "They're like ten inches too big. This isn't my suit, Murphy."

"Yes, it is, Sammy. Look. It's got your name on it." I'd never rented a suit in my life and I hadn't thought to try it on. Murphy was panicking. "What are you going to do?"

"Do I have a choice? Give me a safety pin, baby. We'll pull 'em up from behind so at least they'll stay on." We pinned them. "Well, it's not exactly my type of fit but the tails'll cover it."

He held the shirt for me. I slipped my hands into the sleeves, but they never emerged. I stood there, arms extended, not even a fingertip showing. "Rubber bands. Quick."

The assistant stage manager called in. "Two minutes, please."

Murphy was ripping the dressing room apart. "I can only find one rubber band."

I put it on my left shirt sleeve and experimented with my right arm. "If I hold my arm tight to my side maybe the cuff'll stay up. Okay, let's go with the vest." I put it on. "Horrible! All right, lemme have the coat." The sleeves dropped past where the shirt sleeves had gone. Murphy reached into a box and took out a black silk high hat. I put it on my head and it went plopppppp! Over my ears. Completely over my ears. Only my nose stopped it.

"Come on, Murphy. Give me *my* hat."

He was almost in tears. "Sammy, this *is* your hat."

"I don't believe it. I *won't* believe it. It's not true." I sat down. "I can't go on like this, that's all. It's impossible. I look like a Walt Disney character."

The door opened again. "On stage for the Finale. Onstage, everybody."

Nat said, "Here, take my hat. I have another."

It wasn't much better. I could get both hands completely under it while it was on my head. I stuffed some Kleenex into the hatband and tried it again. At least it was resting on the top of my head. I put on the gloves, which of course were four sizes too large, and I held the walking stick they'd sent. Why wasn't it six feet long? I stood in front of the mirror —baggy pants, gorilla-length sleeves, one arm pressed tight against my side, hat teetering on my head, cane held in a baseball glove—the whole thing was like a Chaplin movie: the poor soul fighting for dignity against all odds. "Hello, your Majesty. You like my outfit?"

We were singing, "Strolling, when we're strolling down the lane . . ." Vera Lynn walked down the center and began singing, "We'll Meet Again . . ." and everything was fine. The big finish to the show is when all the performers sing "God Save the Queen." Naturally when you sing this you remove your hat. We're less than a minute away from it and I've got both arms pressed tightly against my sides and I can't for the life of me remember which sleeve has the rubber band and which one leads to the hungry lion. The music strikes the first notes of "God Save the Queen." The audience is standing. I have to make a choice. I go for my hat with my right hand and as I move it from my side the sleeve falls, swoosh! over my fingertips. I raise my arm, shaking my wrist to get my hand free, the cuff slides back, my fingers appear, and I can feel the hat. I get it off my head a few seconds behind everyone else and as I swing it down to my side the Kleenex flies out of the hat, sails over the orchestra pit into the audience, and hits a man in the face. It falls to his shoulder and he plucks it off with two fingers and drops it to the floor.

I am so humiliated, so mortified that I'm praying I'll fall straight through the floor and never be seen or heard from again. We're coming to the last bars of "God Save the Queen" and I'm thinking: how do I put the hat back on? I can't be the only one standing here holding his hat.

The song is over. I put the hat on and it slides down over my ears and onto my nose. I try to tilt it back so maybe it'll catch on my forehead. I'm wrinkling my forehead trying to grip the hat with my eyebrows, but nothing helps. Only my mouth and chin are showing. All I can see is the inside of the hat but I can hear the audience starting to fall apart. They're English and they're dignified and they've been trying to hold on but there's a limit to everything and we'd passed it long ago. Even the performers, the two hundred disciplined kids behind me were cracking wide open and starting to die all over the stage. Finally we start filing out and I hear Jack Hylton hissing, "Take it off. Get the hat off. . . ."

I stood backstage like a kin of the deceased as performers and stagehands came by, tapped me on the shoulder and muttered, "Tough luck, Mr. Davis." . . . "Bad break." A red carpet was being rolled down the center aisle of the theater from the steps of the stage to the door of the Queen's car. At a signal the stars of the show filed onstage and lined up for presentation to Her Majesty, the orchestra began playing "Pomp and Circumstance" and two little girls came down the carpet dropping rose petals. Then, the Queen was walking down the aisle toward us, Prince Philip a few yards behind, with dignitaries following in strict royal procession.

The Queen reached the stage and began walking down the line of people, smiling but stopping at only one out of every four or five. You're not supposed to touch the Queen's hand unless she extends it. I saw out of the corner of my eye that when she did stop she did not put out her hand. She was four people away from me, then three, then two, then one. . . .

The Queen of England was standing in front of me, smiling warmly, offering me her hand, and I was shaking hands with her, addressing her as "Your Majesty"—a phrase, the grandeur of which one can never fully understand until one is saying it to a person who is actually entitled to it.

Al Burnett came to the dressing room to get me. I was to do a special pre-opening show at the Pigalle. He'd invited a lot of people from the Command Performance, plus press and celebrities and I was glad that I had that to do; if I'd gone straight home without being able to taper off from the excitement, I'd have gotten the bends.

The Pigalle was packed beyond capacity. Most of the American stars in London were there: Gregory Peck, Tony Quinn, Bob Mitchum, and dozens of English performers. I was onstage for two and a half hours, but nobody would leave. The audience pounded the tables for twenty solid minutes. Finally, Al had to come onstage and ask them to stop because they were breaking his tables.

I sat on the edge of my bed pulling off my shoes, savoring the incredible evening. Then, to enjoy it all the more, in vivid contrast, a montage of other, lesser days that seemed so long ago, as if they'd happened to somebody else. And, in a way they had. Show business had made me somebody else. It had taken a hungry kid off the streets of Harlem and brought him to England to entertain the Queen.

I heard Murphy and Arthur speaking low, putting a blanket over me. It would be poetic to say that as I fell asleep I also remembered myself as a child telling Mama, "Someday I'm going to sing for the Queen of England." Mama would surely have said, "Yes, Sammy, if you want to sing for her you will." But I didn't say it. As high as I had hoped, I never dreamed I'd have such a night.

The *Daily Sketch* said, "Let's start by re-naming last night's Royal Variety Show at the Victoria Palace 'The Sammy Davis, Jr. Show.' For, in eight electrifying minutes, this . . . entertainer made the word 'star' seem inadequate . . ." Isadore Green of *The Record* and *Show Mirror* wrote: ". . . Those lucky enough to see him in person at the Pigalle indeed saw the greatest entertainer in the world . . ."

I was waiting at the gate as May cleared through Customs. She smiled, surprised to see me, and I became aware of the boldness of what I'd done. As we walked toward the Rolls-Royce I'd rented, I realized that since my arrival in London I'd seen so many African students, with the bushy hair and the tribal claw marks on their faces, walking down the streets with white women, and nobody so much as looking around at them that my built-in caution had relaxed, I'd instinctively known that nobody would care.

May and her father had deliberately flown separately and we had four hours together before his plane came in. I took her to the hotel and we made a date to go sight-seeing around London together like a couple of tourists.

I was waiting in the car when she came out. Her arrival hadn't been mentioned in the papers yet, but in their own mysterious way her fans had found out that she was in town and there was a crowd of teen-age girls waiting with scrap-books and pictures for her to autograph. She started signing and as the crowd grew she gestured to me, "I'm sorry," and I waved back, "Stay. Crazy. Make it."

As she approached the car, the kids spotted me and gathered on both sides of the car shoving pencils and papers to us through the windows.

We cruised around London sight-seeing and talking, walking along Saville Row, stopping to sign autographs, experiencing nothing but warmth and kindnesss.

"When do you figure I should meet your father?"

"As soon as he gets in. The sooner the better. Don't you agree?"

"Yeah. Sure. The sooner the better. No doubt about it. Look, better still, why don't you bring him to the club for the first show and then we can go out and have supper together?"

She was looking at me, tenderly. "You don't have to impress him with your talent before you meet him."

"Oh, now wait a *minute* . . ." I was caught like a rat. "Look, I just want him to like me."

"Sammy, I love my parents, so I hope my father likes you and I hope you like him, but if you don't or if he doesn't, it won't change how I feel about you."

"Darling, that's good to hear, but you'll still come to the club first. Anything I can have going for me is just that much gravy, right? And I warn you—you're gonna see a show like I've *never* done. And at dinner I'm going to be so sweet, he may get diabetes. It's a definite 'Sammy Davis, Jr. starring in *The In-Law*.' Hey listen, what about the suite? Is it okay? You think he'll be comfortable there?"

"The suite is beautiful." She smiled, "Stop worrying so much." I got out of the car at the hotel and she continued on to the airport.

I had a four o'clock appointment with a newspaperman in

my suite, then I had an appointment in the hotel bar with a man from one of the English television networks. I dashed out of the suite, twenty minutes late, and headed downstairs. The elevator door opened onto the lobby, I rushed out and collided with a distinguished-looking gray-haired gentleman. His hat flew off his head. We both reached for it and bumped heads together. I grabbed the hat but so did he. I tore it out of his hands trying to give it back to him. When it fell again I made such a lunge for it that I crushed the crown entirely. I kept bungling and apologizing and clutching the hat, like a slapstick comic. I heard a familiar laugh and I froze, bent over, afraid to look up.

"Sammy, I'd like you to meet my father."

"No . . . it's not fair . . ."

She spoke in Swedish to the man I'd been wrestling with and he began laughing too, and extended his hand. I stared with horror at the hat clutched in my fist, destroyed. He looked at it and smiled. I wanted only to disappear, dissolve, evaporate. What in hell was going on with me and hats? First in front of the Queen of England. Now him.

We went into the bar, had a drink and made plans to meet later in the evening. I kept my appointment and then rushed upstairs to call May. "Well, your fiancé handled that with all the suave at his command, right? Only to *me* . . . with all the elevators in the world, I have to pick that one to come running out of like a madman."

She was laughing. "Relax, Sharlie Brown. He hasn't sent me back to Sweden, yet."

"He must have a hell of a sense of humor. I almost knock the man down, then I break his hat—the whole fiasco . . ."

"But you apologize so beautifully."

"Look, give me his hat size. At least I'll send up a dozen new ones."

May sat next to me at supper and her father was across from us. Throughout the meal I'd been rephrasing the question in my mind: Sir, I'm sure you know that May and I want to get married. . . . Maybe I should wait? Not push too much? Maybe let him get to know me for a few days? We were having our coffee and we'd still done nothing but chit-chat.

He put down his cup and said, "We have so far spoken of all but what we wish most to say. Sammy, we know much about you. Maybritt had written us many letters . . . we will be proud to have you for a son."

"You mean it's—it's all right?"

"I wanted to meet you, of course, but I did not come from Sweden to see you. I came to see Maybritt with you. Her mother and I wanted to know if what was in her letters was also in her face." He spoke slowly, reaching for the English words. "Perhaps you thought we would care that you have a different skin. I will speak candidly because you will be my son. When Maybritt told us her desire to marry you we had fear for the hardship such a marriage faces in America where you will make your home. But we believe that if your love for each other is strong enough then there are no important problems which cannot be overcome. Your skin is not important to us," he touched his heart, "we care what is here. The happiness we saw in Maybritt's letters is indeed in her face. And we have never seen it there like this before." He smiled warmly. "You make us all very happy."

I had to excuse myself from the table. Through all the excitement of the Command Performance and the opening, this had always been there—the wondering what he'd say, how he'd feel when he finally saw me face to face.

I hid in a hallway near the kitchen unable to hold back huge, racking sobs. I felt May's arms around me. "Sharlie Brown, please don't . . ."

I gave her my handkerchief. "Look who's talking." We pulled ourselves together and started back to the table, but her father had already paid the check and was waiting for us in the lobby.

I still had my late show to do and they were going back to the hotel. I walked them to my car and shook hands with May's father. "Thank you." He drew me toward him and embraced me, "God bless you, Sammy." Then he got into the car and drove away and they didn't see me start in all over again.

One of the London papers ran a short piece: "Is May Britt to Wed Sammy Davis, Jr.?" As the days passed people sent me others from American papers—the same sort of thing, but rough: "The gasps around London are over Sammy Davis, Jr. and May Britt and their 'we-don't-give-a-damn-who-knows-it attitude.'"

I told May, "I think the best thing we can do is announce it quickly and kill the 'are they or aren't they?' jazz before it starts in heavy. If we come out and tell 'em, 'Yes, we're engaged,' it'll get a flurry of attention and be forgotten. People love to speculate, but once they know something for sure they'll lose interest."

I took her hand. "Darling, I've also been thinking that maybe we should get married over here. Maybe the smart thing would be to come back here in October and do it quietly. That way, the story'll break in the States, they'll do all their objecting and how-dare-they and get it out of their systems and by the time we get back as Mr. and Mrs. Davis, nobody'll pay much attention to it. It's beautiful all around: it'll even save your folks the trip to America."

"Anything you like. I couldn't care less where we get married."

"We can have the ceremony right here in London. I'll play a month in the provinces and then we'll do like a two-month tour of the continent. I can book my dates with plenty of free time in between so it'll almost amount to a three-month honeymoon.

"I've hired an English press agent, Al Hunt, who's been coordinating my interviews and press things. I never had a man working for me who did a better job. I'll tell him to set up a press conference for us."

"Couldn't we just give out a written announcement?"

"No. They'll want to ask questions and it's best to answer them loud and clear once and for all."

"Ladies and Gentlemen, Miss Britt and I have been subject lately to newspaper items questioning whether or not we are seeing each other and if we intend to be married. You asked me that yourselves when I arrived here. At that time I could not properly say 'yes' because I hadn't yet met, and received the approval of, Miss Britt's father. However, I am now at liberty to tell you that I have that approval and we are engaged to be married.

"I hope to impress upon you that I would not call you all here to make this announcement as if I believe it to be earth-shaking news. You've been overwhelmingly generous to me and I wouldn't have the audacity to impose upon you for publicity's own sake. We hope you will publish it for the one reason that we are anxious to avoid any of the unnecessary and sometimes vicious public speculation. We want it to be a matter of record so that we can end all that."

They congratulated us warmly, then started asking us questions: "When do you expect to be married?"

"Probably in October."

"How long have you known each other?"

"We met in Hollywood several months ago while I was filming *Ocean's 11* or just about to . . ."

An American reporter from one of the wire services stood up. "Sammy, how do you think this'll go over in the States?"

"I don't think it's something that should have to 'go over' or not go over."

"Well, uh, whattya think's gonna happen when you get back home? Do you think you'll ever be able to work there again?"

"I can't imagine that my career is so flimsy that it could be ruined by marriage, but if it is, then it's really not worth having, is it?"

He sat down but he wasn't satisfied. Throughout the questioning by the English reporters, simple, pleasant questions such as where we'd live and how many children we hoped for, he kept sniping, shooting the zingies at me: "Are you announcing it over here because you're afraid to do it at home? Are you sort of testing for reactions?"

"No, sir. We're announcing it here for the reason I stated clearly at the beginning of this conference."

"I see . . . well, let me ask you this: what happens if you find you can't go home?"

I lit a cigarette, slowly, using the time to calm myself. "You keep asking hypothetical questions, the best I can do is give you hypothetical answers. If, as you suggest, I find there is such a harshness against what I do with my personal life then I'll pack my bags and leave because it won't be the America I know and love. But, I must add that I've never thought about such an extreme, so I can't be sure what I might do. Perhaps rather than leave my country I'd choose to stay under any conditions. If it should turn out that the stage is no longer open to me then I'd give up my career and do whatever I can to make myself and my future bride happy."

The English press elbowed him out of the way with their own questions but soon he was back again.

"Isn't this the first marriage between a Negro man and a blonde, white movie star?"

I could feel the muscles in my face tightening. "Perhaps it is. I don't keep track."

Again the English press came to my side. They'd already asked everything they needed to know and it was obvious they were just reasking questions trying to nose this guy out, hoping he'd lay off, but he wouldn't.

"Isn't it kinda rough sledding at home on mixed marriages? I mean, the chances of making them work are . . ."

"Wait a minute. I don't know what America *you're* talking about, but I know something about mixed marriages. There are many of them and eighty-five percent of them work. Eighty-five percent. That's higher than among people who are so-called 'suited' for each other racially and religiously. They work better because nobody who's faced with it would step out of his or her race to marry unless the love was so great that they felt they could not be happy without it."

"Well . . . what about the children?"

One of the English reporters said, "For crying out loud, he's already said they hope to have many healthy, happy babies. If you missed the exact wording I'll be delighted to give it to you. This isn't a trial, you know."

I wanted to hug that sweet little Englishman.

The guy said, "But he still hasn't told me what I want to know about the kids . . ."

Out of at least fifty reporters he was the only one who had been attacking, chipping away, looking for trouble, and I felt a mixture of deep dislike for him as well as embarrassment that it had to be an American. "What *about* them? Exactly what would you like to know?" Everyone in the room was glaring at him.

"Well . . . what about them? . . . you know what I mean . . ."

He was gutless, and I wasn't about to make it any easier for him. "Exactly what are you driving at?"

"Well—I don't know. I mean, well . . ." He looked at the floor. "What do you figure they'll look like?"

An English reporter murmured, "Oh, now really!" and a heavy silence settled over the room.

I said, "We expect them to look like babies."

"No, you know what I mean . . . do you have some kind of preference about color?" He finally squeezed the words out, "Uh . . . how would Miss Britt feel if her kid turns out to be black—you know what I mean?"

"Buddy, I've known what you meant for forty-five minutes. Now as far as our children are concerned it would not matter to us, in terms of our love for the child, if it were white, brown, or polka dot. We don't think in terms of color. All we care about is that if God graces us with a child it will grow up to be healthy and love us as much as we'll love it from the moment its life begins."

"Yeah, I guess we all want that, but . . . they'll have a pretty rough time of it, won't they? Isn't it kinda rough for mixed-marriage kids to grow up?"

"Because there are people who'll dislike our children even before they're conceived, we'll fortify them with every spiritual and emotional security that we can provide. We'll give them all the love and affection parents can give, and buddy, you can bet your typewriter that when the day comes for our child to leave our home and make it alone, he or she will have enough love to lean on to support the weight of every bigot in the world."

David Niven was the first person to send us a wire. He was in Europe making *The Guns of Navarone*. His wife is Swedish. He said, "Good-o, old chap. Lucky you, to have found a nice Swedish girl."

May and I were having lunch in my suite, reading the newspaper stories and the wires that were coming in, when the hotel operator rang up. "I have an overseas call for you, Mr. Davis. Mr. Hugh Benson in Hollywood, California."

I smiled to May. "Hugh Benson." I played it English. "Davis, here."

"Sammy, why in hell did you have to say you don't give a damn if you have polka-dot children? It's all over the front pages."

"What are you talking about? Read it to me."

" 'Sammy Davis, Jr., Negro entertainer, announced today he will marry Swedish blonde actress May Britt. Asked about children Davis said, 'I don't care if they're polka dot.' "

"That's *it?* That's all they say?"

"Yes. Just a few lines with a big, lousy headline."

I read the original statement to him, out of the English papers. He cursed, sadly. Then, "Look, they're making a big fuss out of this thing. It ran in all the papers here, probably all over the country. The way it reads you come out pretty lousy and there's no way of knowing what's going to happen. But whichever way it breaks, you can know that you've got friends; I've got the official okay from Jack Warner and Bill Orr to tell you that you can count on a picture or two a year with us and at least a couple or three television shows."

May was waiting to hear what it was all about. I explained. "The reporter used it out of context and changed its meaning into the most vile-sounding statement in the world." She was deflated, bewildered, like a child who'd been punished but couldn't understand why.

We read several of the English papers again and without exception they had printed it exactly as it was said and meant. Nobody in England got the idea that I didn't care if I had polka-dot children. Only in my homeland were the readers offered that choice bit of dishonesty.

May's shock was turning to anger. She strode up and down the living room. "What a rotten thing! What do you think we should do about it?"

"Nothing." She looked at me, surprised. "Darling, it's done. Smashing this guy's face won't change anything. Maybe I could call somebody and get him fired but it won't erase that quote from the millions of minds that have already absorbed it, right?"

She nodded, reluctantly. "But I sure do hate that guy."

I had the sensation of an emotional paralysis at the sound of the word "Hate"—a four-letter word that had directed the course of my life. Like a person who has seen death by gunfire and can never look at a gun again, I could never take up hatred as a weapon of my own. That emotion was dead in me—not by design or by logic but by simple overexposure to its evil and waste.

I walked over to her and took both her hands in mine. "Darling, I'm not going to do wise-old-man bits but don't exhaust yourself hating that guy. He earned it, but what you and I want is not going to be found by hating him or anybody. There's just no such thing as happiness endowed with hatred."

The phone rang. It was Frank, consoling, reassuring. After we'd talked for a while, he said, "Let me say hello to your old lady."

As she listened she was nodding and smiling and I saw tears forming in her eyes. When she hung up she said, "Can you imagine Frank and Hugh . . . to call us overseas. It's *so* beautiful, Sharlie Brown."

I put my arm around her. "I don't want to do Pollyanna bits but look at how even out of something lousy and rotten something good emerges."

I was leaving the hotel to do some shopping when I felt Arthur staring at me.

"Arthur. What in the *hell* are you looking at?"

"I'm not quite sure. You'll think I'm putting you on, but since you've been over here—you've become good-looking."

Murphy said, "He's right, Sammy. I've been noticing it myself. You look different. You really do. There's something about your face . . ."

I had an idea what they meant and how it had happened. I had stopped thinking of myself as a Negro. The awareness wasn't there because the constant reminders were gone: there were no El Morocco's I couldn't go to; I wasn't invited to "the best private clubs which accept

Negroes," I was invited to the best private clubs, period. I could go anyplace that was open to the position I'd earned in life, and without the automatic evaluating: Do I dare? Is it worth the aggravation? I could walk down a street with May and enjoy the simple pleasure of feeling her hand in mine and knowing that I was walking down a street with the girl I love; there was no wondering who was revolted or infuriated, or frowning, or tolerating us. There was no looking for the security of a friendly face. Without the presence of disapproval I had stopped searching for approval.

The weeks in London had been a vacation from fear and tension, a chance to take a breather and refurbish and rebuild my moral fiber. It was as though all my emotional mechanisms had been sent out, dry-cleaned and put back again. And I'd reacted to it physically. My face wasn't tight. The jaw had relaxed. The skin lay smooth on my face. I hadn't been aware it was happening. It just sneaked up on me like a gentle sleep for all the nerves and reflexes.

When we finished shopping I went on alone to the Dorchester to keep an appointment with some picture people at the American Club.

It was like stepping out of an air-conditioned room into the heat of the outside. The moment I entered I felt the old familiar atmosphere. The awareness returned. I sat there watching them watching me. They weren't cold, they were friendly, but they were appraising, measuring, discussing me and I was listening over my shoulder again, on guard, defiantly uncaring of what they thought. I'd merely walked through a door and I was back in the vise.

And this was only the road company. In a week I'd be going back to the heart of it, back to the cooker, back to the constant anticipating of problems that might or might not materialize—the eternal war of nerves. And suddenly I thought: why should I? Why drag May through pointless agonies? Why not live in London and be treated magnificently? Why not travel half the world free of unnecessary burdens? I can accept any one of countless English offers, stay over on an extended visit and return to the States for a few months every year—nobody'd even realize what I was doing. I projected to the day when we'd have our first child. I knew I could provide a high wall of love that would block out most of the problems, but no wall is high enough or strong enough to keep out everything. Why sentence children to a life of built-in scorn and hatred? Why pass as close to hell as man can get when there's another road?

When I was able to make an exit from the club I hurried to the street like a man groping for air. A workman in a pit popped up, "Oh, I say . . . would you mind terribly if I asked for an autograph?" I gave it to him, thanked him and continued down the street, smiling back at people who recognized me. An English bobby stopped me on the corner. "Mr. Davis, may I impose upon you, sir? Saw you on the telly." "Congratulations, Mr. Davis. When's the happy day?" "Have a big family, sir. That's the best kind." "No offense, sir, but your fiancée Miss Britt is such a beautiful lady." . . .

I burst into the living room. "Murph! Get busy on the phone and place a call to Will. Tell him I'm not coming home. Tell him to cancel out everything. I'm staying in London."

He nodded slowly. "Okay, Sammy."

"Well, don't just sit there. Get hot on it."

"Sure, Sammy. I'll take care of it right away." But he didn't move off the sofa. He just smiled like Charley Philosopher.

"You son of a bitch. You think you know me pretty damned well, don't you?" I slammed the door to the bedroom and sat down near the window.

It had felt good to get it out of my system, to rebel, but I knew I was far from ready to put my country down to adopt another. As much as I loved being in England it is not Utopia, and the colored cat who goes there thinking he's walking into heaven is going to be disappointed. Despite all the problems, America is still the best country in the world. Even with all the tensions, the equality which is still only a technical thing—despite these things I became a star. With everything going against me I was able to make it in America. It could never have happened for me in England. I don't know of any Negro who started with nothing and made it there. Social equality is all they have for the Negro there. In America, although we have far less social equality, we have constantly expanding *opportunity*, and that has to be the best. Social acceptance is delightful, but it's only ice cream and cake—opportunity is the meat and vegetables.

I looked through the window at the garden of the hotel where I'd thought May and I would be married. If I got married in England I'd be running, just as surely as if I moved there permanently. I couldn't start off by ducking the first problem that faced us or it would be one compromise after another.

At Siegi's, after we'd ordered dinner, I explained it to May. "I want to get married in America. I want to stand up in my own country and be married like anybody else. I want us to have a real wedding, with close friends and family."

"That's what I always wanted until you said it would be easier to do it over here quietly and come back as Mr. and Mrs. Davis . . ." a smile spread across her face. "Hey—I like the sound of that."

I saw the trust in her face and I felt tears welling in my eyes for love of her. "Darling, try to be serious for a minute because I want you to understand what it involves. I don't know what to expect at home. Maybe they won't want me any more and I'll go down the drain professionally. There's a chance of it. But one thing is positive: there can be no sneaking around, no cop-outs, no code names.

"Aside from personal reasons, when I got out of the Army I did a lot of shouting 'Let me live like I want to live' but nobody heard me. Today I whisper it, and millions of people read it the next day. Now, it's beautiful to hold this position, but with it comes responsibility. I owe it to my people never to let anyone say, 'Sammy Davis knew he shouldn't be marrying May Britt so he sneaked out of the country to do it.' And I owe it to my country, too. I've gotten a *lot* out of America—more than anybody has the right to even hope for—so the very least I can give back is a show of confidence. I can't be an expatriate. I won't let the rest of the world say, 'Hey, a colored guy had to run away from America to marry the girl he loves.' I believe in the integrity and fairness of my country as a whole and I have to back my beliefs by putting everything on the line."

As our car approached the club the chauffeur said, "There seems to be a commotion outside the Pigalle."

A truck with loud-speakers on top of it was in front of the club. Pickets wearing swastika armbands were carrying signs: "GO HOME, NIGGER." . . . "SAMMY, BACK TO THE TREES." . . . "GET DIVORCED FIRST, SLAG." . . .

The chauffeur said, "Mosley's men."

"Who's Mosley?"

"He's got the Nazi party here."

"I didn't know there *were* Nazis any more."

May asked, "Do you know what they mean by the word 'Slag'?"

I shook my head.

She asked the chauffeur. He didn't answer immediately. "I'm sorry, ma'am, it's a slang word for a white woman who associates with Negro men."

The sound-truck driver spotted us and followed our car to the stage entrance, his loud-speakers blaring savagely, venomously.

In the dressing room May picked up a magazine, sat down and began to leaf through the pages. "Have you got a Salem, Sammy?" I gave her the cigarette and lit it for her. "Thank you, Sharlie Brown." She continued reading.

"May?"

She looked up.

"Don't you care about what happened out there? Doesn't it bother you?"

"The only thing that bothers me is that maybe it bothers you. Did it?"

"It could have been worse, I guess."

"Okay."

She was smiling as she read, but I saw the moisture around her eyes. She was playing a beautifully corny scene, trying to give me support. She had all the guts in the world, and it was all the more pathetic to know that she had absolutely no preparation for this, no experience to help her through it.

Cassandra, the most widely read columnist in England, ran a front page editorial in the *Daily Mirror*:

CASSANDRA WRITES
A LETTER TO SAMMY DAVIS, JNR.

Dear Sammy Davis,

I don't know you. You don't know me. I have never seen your show and I assume you have never seen mine. All I know is what I read in the papers.

But this is just to tell you that the beastly racial abuse to which you were subjected outside the Pigalle Restaurant, when Mosley's louts followed you waving banners with the words "Go Home, Nigger," has nothing to do with what English people feel and think.

I, and maybe I can speak for a few others (say 51,680,000 minus 100 of the population of this country), feel revolted, angry and ashamed at what happened.

Yours sincerely,
Cassandra

Dozens of others of the English press came roaring into the fight, indignant and embarrassed by the pickets. Letters and telegrams came avalanching in by the thousands from all over England from people who felt personally affronted by the Nazis, embarrassed that an American or any foreigner might think, "So this is England." The English people rallied toward us en masse. In every restaurant and shop, down every street I walked, I received apologetic looks and disgusted head shakes, and as I found the club overflowing every night and the lines growing longer I saw that like so many other problems or handicaps I'd encountered throughout my life, Sir Oswald Mosley was working for me instead of against me.

On closing night, the Pigalle was so jam-packed that tables had to be put onstage. The waiters stopped serving drinks and the cooks came out of the kitchen to watch the final show. I came onstage wearing a bowler and carrying a cane, hoping to make the audience understand what I felt for them—what I had experienced within myself by being there.

I did a two and a half hour show, dreading and delaying the end, until finally I'd run through everything I could remember or invent. I cued the band for my closing number and I sang the song Vera Lynn had done at the Command Performance: "We'll meet again, who knows where, who knows when . . ." But I couldn't sing more than a few words and the audience rose to its feet and picked up where I'd been unable to continue. I could hardly see them through the prism of tears, but I could hear them and I could feel them as surely as if they had wrapped their arms around me. I dropped my head and bowed to them with all the gratitude and love a human being can feel.

I saw May off on a plane to Sweden and a few hours later boarded my own plane to the States. As we taxied down the runway I settled back in my seat and tried to anticipate my return home and the reception there. I was fully aware that my intended marriage seriously jeopardized everything I had worked for, but I'd achieved all the golden dreams and they'd far from fulfilled the promise. If club owners said, "Sorry, we can't book you any more," there would be no decision for me to make; if it meant packing all my gun-belts and my records and tape machines and moving to another country, I'd do it.

The Mosley thing was a forecast. For me hate held no unknown quantity. It might take a different form but essentially there was nothing they could do or say that hadn't already been done and said, and above all I had the experience of surviving it. But could May withstand its pressures? She'd shrugged off the friends who'd stopped calling, she'd absorbed the Mosley thing, but would she be able to absorb constant disapproval, suddenly closed doors, expulsion from movies? Sure, she's a strong girl with a mind of her own but no man no matter how strong he is can step into the ring for his first fight and take on the heavyweight champion. I had to protect her from as much of it as possible. I had to keep every ounce of my strength and experience constantly at her side. I had to be thinking ahead of them, running interference, blocking, shielding, anticipating, softening anything that might be waiting. But ultimately, her ability to endure, the final measure of her strength, would be in the extent of her love and need for me.

The huge engines were roaring to their peak, the pilot released the brakes and we began hurtling up the runway. I looked out the window, glad for the chance to delay my involvement with the problems of the future and dwell for a few moments on the happiest weeks of my life. As we climbed into the sky I watched London grow smaller until it resembled a fictional place in children's storybooks, a setting for fables which describe the beauties of the world and overlook the realities of harshness and unkindness. Ten thousand feet below me I'd left the hurt of Sir Oswald Mosley and a wire-service reporter, and as our jet moved into the clouds and London disappeared I took with me only memories of a fairy-tale city.

33

THE THOUSANDS OF DELEGATES IN THE JAM-PACKED CONvention hall applauded wildly as Frank's name was called and he stepped forward. One by one we were introduced—Peter, Tony and Janet, and the others who'd been invited to appear at the Democratic National Convention in Los Angeles to make a show of allegiance to John F. Kennedy. My presence on that stage brought the extra satisfaction of knowing that through television and the thousands of newspapers focused on the moment, millions of people from Los Angeles to Moscow who'd been exposed to race riots in Little Rock were also seeing democracy proving its definition.

My name was called and I stepped forward. The applause rang out clear and loud across the hall. Then there was a loud "Booooooooooo. . . booooooooo . . . booooooo . . ." My head snapped upward involuntarily and almost every head in the hall turned with mine, searching. It was the Mississippi block. Four or five men were standing, hands cupped around their mouths, still booing me, the sound cutting grotesquely through the applause.

I finished my bow and stepped back. I focused on a flag in the back of the hall and clung to it, standing there, torn to shreds inside, hurt and naked in front of thousands of people, in front of the world. Frank, looking straight ahead too, whispered, "Those dirty sons of bitches! Don't let 'em get you, Charley." The tears exploded in my eyes and cascaded down the front of my face, blinding me from everything but a haze of color and light. I gouged my nails into the palms of my hands but the tears kept pouring out. "Hang on, Charley. Don't let it get you!"

"It's got me, Frank. What'd I do to deserve that?"

A voice on the public address system boomed across the hall. "Ladies and gentlemen, our National Anthem." I sang "The Star-Spangled Banner," humiliated, fearful that I'd hurt the very thing I'd flown three thousand miles to help; if I might have swung a few votes toward Kennedy, how many might I be costing him?

Thousands of voices roared across the hall: ". . . what so proudly we hailed at the twilight's last gleaming . . ." And as I sang the words I could hear my own voice telling reporters in London, "This could never happen in America."

". . . and the rocket's red glare . . . the bombs bursting in air . . ." The whole world is watching what's happening here today. How can anyone hate me so much that they'd let the rest of the free world see that the men who might be selecting the next President of the United States are men who feel racial prejudice?

". . . the land of the free . . . and the home of the brave."

As we stepped off the stage reporters swarmed around me. "Why do you think they did that, Sammy?" I excused myself and found Frank and told him I wasn't going to stay for the rest of the ceremonies.

"Okay, Charley." His hand was on my shoulder. I could feel the tension in his fingers but his face showed nothing, like a man who couldn't be surprised by people any more.

I stood on the street in front of the convention hall, looking for a cab, hearing bursts of applause from inside.

A cab pulled up. I'd planned to spend a few hours with May before going back to Boston but she'd been watching it all on television and I couldn't face her sympathy. I told the driver to take me to the airport.

I closed Boston and had a week free on the coast before opening in Washington at the Lotus Club. As I walked through the TWA gate I saw May running gaily toward me. I hugged her quickly, "Come on, darling, big stars don't hang around airports." She clung to my arm as I hurried her through the terminal building.

"How come Jim didn't come with you?"

"I told him to meet us at the house. I was dying to meet my fiancé alone."

"Where's Rudy?"

"In the car. Out front." She was holding a piece of paper. "Guess what this is?"

I saw a woman nudging her husband, motioning for him to look at us. He gaped, shaking his head, like "How dare they!" May hadn't caught it. Her face was flushed with excitement. "It's our wedding invitation. It's only the sample the printer sent back but boy it's beautiful! Look."

I took it from her and put it in my pocket. "When we're home, we'll look at it like ladies and gentlemen, right? Let's save it and enjoy it." I could feel the attention building around us and I kept her moving quickly through the hum of whispers, of conversations breaking off in the middle of sentences, faces staring openly, accusingly, like: if we had any class we'd break up to make them happy.

As we came to the luggage counter May slowed down. I pulled her along. "Darling, your fiancé is much too big to stand around waiting for his luggage. Rudy'll come back for it. I mean, if you're going to be a star be a star." As we cleared the front doors I saw, gratefully, that Rudy was parked directly in front of the entrance.

At home I sat her down on the couch, "Darling, it was beautiful of you to meet me and I dug it, but I don't think you should do that any more. Let's wait a while."

"But it's not a secret now, we have nothing to hide."

"I know, but let's keep attention on us down to a minimum. The other day Lee Mortimer ran a thing about 'Hey, it's just a publicity stunt, folks.' What do we need that for? The less they see of us until after we're married the less of that jazz we're going to get."

She nodded, like a kid. "I guess you're right." Then she perked up, "Can we look at it now?"

I took the invitation out of my pocket and held it for both of us to see.

550

Mr. and Mrs. Ernst Hugo Wilkens
request the pleasure of your company
at the wedding reception of their daughter
May
and
Sammy Davis, Jr.
on Sunday, October Sixteenth
Nineteen hundred and Sixty
at six o'clock in the evening
Beverly Hilton Hotel
L'Escoffier Room

"It's beautiful. Incidentally, I spoke to Frank and asked him to stand up for me."

"What did he say?"

"He knew it before I asked him. It was just a formality.

"Y'know," I said, "I've been thinking, we should redecorate. Let's face it, it's not exactly feminine around here."

"What about our economy drive?"

"I think this is important. I won't feel that the place is yours if we leave it this way. I think we should at least do the bedroom, the living room and the kitchen. I can pay it off in a year with no problems."

"You don't have to do that. This will be my wedding present to us."

"Hold it. *I* pay the bills around here. Maybe I'll be a little slow but I'll pay them."

"Holy Toledo! Who cares whose bank account it comes out of? And the few thousand dollars it'll be isn't a drop in the pail compared to what it's going to cost you to support me all my life."

"Darling, it's a drop in the *bucket*."

"Right, so what do we accomplish by getting more deeply in debt when we have the money?"

"I know, but . . ."

"In the words of Sharlie Brown 'there's no buts.'"

"Look, I realize I sound like an idiot doing the 'no woman will ever support *me*' bit because obviously you're right, but frankly, I'm pretty shook . . . no woman ever gave me *change*."

She hugged me. "Oh, thank you." Then, gazing at the

area in front of the windows, "Do you know what I'd love? A dining set right there so we could have dinner and look out at L.A. With only six chairs so we can't possibly have great big dinner parties. I hate it when there are so many people that there are ten conversations going on at once."

"I'm with you on that. The crowd scenes'll be in the Playhouse. Up here we'll keep it strictly family and the few really close buddies." I walked over to the bedroom. "I'm not going to sleep in here again until we're married and we move in together." I liked the romantic gesture, myself. "I'll use the Playhouse or I'll stay at the Hilton."

"Boy," she sighed, "that's beautiful." She was looking at me like I was D'Artagnan.

I had a bunch of people over for a Sunday afternoon. A long-time friend grabbed me by the arm, "I have to talk to you." He steered me upstairs to the bedroom of the Playhouse, into the bathroom and closed the door. "Are you and May Britt really on the level? It's *not* a publicity stunt?"

"You know I don't do publicity stunts."

He clutched his head with both hands. "You don't know what you're doing." I waited for him to say something else, not wanting to accept what I had heard. Not from a friend. "Sammy . . . you're out of your mind. You can't do this. It's no good." He was holding me by the shirt. "You'll ruin your life! And what happens when you have children? Have you thought about that? And you're just getting started in pictures. Why ruin everything? She's just a kick. You'll get over her. If you want to get married, find yourself a nice colored girl. Can't you see what I'm trying to tell you?"

"I see it. Thank you for telling me."

I watched him going back to the party. How could I have known him for so long but not at all?

I glanced through the morning papers. Louella Parsons had: "His best friends have been unable to talk Sammy Davis, Jr. out of the May Britt marriage. The reception will take place at one of the Hollywood hotels."

We were in almost every column. Approval and disapproval were cropping up all around us. It's a strange thing to find that your engagement is a case history, something to which each person was attaching his own significance—ten different things to ten different people, each starting from the point of seeing it as an interracial marriage, each viewing us as either hero or villain, none seeming to grasp the basic point: you can hate by color but you can't love by it; that I'd asked May to marry me, I had not said, "Will you intermarry me?'"

Rudy brought in the mail. In it was the usual assortment of letters from strangers—the few who took the trouble to write and let us feel their support, and the familiar-looking envelopes with no return addresses, the hate letters. One was addressed to both of us and I wondered if May was getting any of them at the studio.

"Rudy, while I'm out of town, May is going to be coming in and out of here with the decorator. Please check the mail carefully. Make sure none of this filth is lying around."

I had the day free so I called May, to ask her to come over but there was no answer. A few minutes later she called. I laughed, "I just called *you*. Where are you?"

"Sammy, guess what? I was passing a store on Wilshire and there in the window was exactly the kind of dining set I was telling you about. Six chairs. It's *beautiful!* I'm in the store now. How would Sharlie Brown like to drive over here so we can look at it together?"

"Darling, I'd love to but I can't . . . I've got a heavy day. But if you like it then go ahead and order it."

"No, I want to be sure you like it, too." Her excitement had paled. "Do you think maybe you could make it tomorrow?"

I hesitated, despising the situation that was forcing me to refuse her such a simple pleasure, stealing what any engaged girl was entitled to. But what could be gained by giving her the pleasure of looking at some furniture if in the middle of it somebody cuts her in half with a lousy look or an out-and-out insult? There was enough attention, opinion, and snipes at us without me putting her in the line of it by doing "engaged couple" bits all around town. "Darling, I ll tell you what. It's in the window, we'll run over there tonight and take a look."

"Okay." There was a pause, then "Hey, that's a *great* idea!" Her voice was overcheerful. "Oh boy, I like that idea *much* better. If we do our window shopping at night we can have privacy, we won't be bothered by a lot of autograph jazz. Gee, I've got a brilliant fiancé."

I hung up heartsick from the realization that she was beginning to catch on, that it was inescapable, that the atmosphere of fear and caution and compromise, of walking on eggs, was surrounding her, slowly dragging her into the web, stifling all that love for life—forcing it into the prison of my skin.

Will stopped by a while later and we discussed some Trio business, some dates that had to be firmed up. Then I braced myself. "Massey, the wedding is on the sixteenth and I'd like to take off a few days before and then a week after. I'll need some time around here for last minute things and I'd like to have at least a full week honeymoon."

He nodded. "I was thinking that myself. We can't move the date of the Huntington Hartford one man show 'cause they're already selling tickets or I'd say you should take off a month. But we can cancel the two weeks before in Detroit and play them next year. I'll take care of it. And, you're going to be having more responsibility so I think you'd better start drawing an extra five hundred a week expenses."

We sat silently across from each other. It was the first glimpse in a long time of the man I'd begun calling "Massey" so many years before, and I felt a flicker of the unity we'd had when we were starving but pulling in the same direction trying to keep each other alive.

"Massey? What the hell happened to us?"

"I don't know, Sammy." He shook his head slowly, sadly. "I guess when people put their hands on something new they've got to be extra careful not to drop what they already had . . . I don't know. . . ."

I tried to remember when all the fighting and arguing had started. It was when we'd started making it, when things should only have been better.

I walked across the room and put my arms around him. "Thanks, Massey." Whatever the reason, or whoever was at fault, I was glad to have that warmth and friendship again.

One by one all the details had been handled. The decorator had been at the house every day, a dressing room was being built for May, a TV set had been suspended from the ceiling so we could watch from bed, and a large marble fireplace was being built in the living room. I had only Washington and Vegas to play before the wedding.

I went down to see Mama. I'd said good-bye to her like this a hundred times but for some reason this time it reacted on me. It wasn't as if she groaned and said the was having trouble with her legs as she sometimes did, she was smiling happily, "Get your sleep, take care of yourself, Sammy," but as she was saying it, it was like a Zoomar lens that goes shoooom, close-up! and you see things you didn't see before, that were always there for you to see. I looked at her face and it suddenly hit me: she's not going to be around much longer. She has to die someday and the older she gets the sooner it's going to be. It could be any day. I thought of all the times I'd known I should go downstairs and sit with her and talk awhile but hadn't because I was too tired or involved in something, or because I had nothing in particular to say. I kissed her and hugged her and held onto her and I managed to say, "Good-bye, Mama, see you soon." But when I left her room I fell apart.

I drove slowly around the curves of the hill, watching the road, May beside me, each of us with our own thoughts.

"Sammy? How come you never asked me to convert? To become Yewish?"

"Well, for openers if you keep giving it that Swedish 'J' I don't think they'd even *take* you."

She was smiling, pleased with herself, as she handed me a piece of paper. I pulled over to the side of the road. It was a certificate of conversion from Temple Israel in Hollywood. "I was always very satisfied being a Lutheran. But when you were on the road I started thinking about the children we want and I decided that whatever extra unity and support we could provide for them would mean just that much more emotional security built-in. So, I went to see your rabbi. We can be married in a religious ceremony, now."

"Darling, there's no nicer present you could ever have given me."

"Then you wanted me to convert? Why didn't you say so?"

"I didn't feel I had the right to. I knew that if you thought I wanted it you'd convert and I didn't want you to unless you personally had the desire to do it. You know how much

I've gotten out of Judaism—for me it's everything, but I'd be the last person in the world to say: Do it my way because my way is better."

"Well, I must say that I started looking into Judaism strictly because I wanted our kids to have the same religion as the two of us, but now that I've studied it, I'm getting to really love it."

I took her hand in mine and kissed it. "Thank you."

34

CONVERSATION IN THE CAB DIED OFF. BIG JOHN WAS STARING through the windshield, straining to see ahead as we moved through traffic, toward the Lotus Club. Murphy and I followed his gaze and saw them. Nazi storm troopers picketing me in the middle of Washington, D.C. They were wearing khaki shirts with swastika armbands and carrying signs: "WHAT'S THE MATTER, SAMMY? CAN'T YOU FIND A COLORED GIRL?" . . . "GO BACK TO THE CONGO, YOU KOSHER COON." They had a little black dog walking with them. He was wearing a swastika and they'd attached a sign to his back: "I'M BLACK TOO, SAMMY, BUT I'M NOT A JEW." Another sign said "MARRIAGE TO MAY BRITT WILL BE AN IN-JUSTICE TO THE NEGRO RACE." It was not being carried by a Negro.

I'd anticipated this, thought about it a hundred times, but when it finally, actually hit I could only stare at them, thinking: This is happening. It's really happening. Thank you, God, for not letting May be here to see it.

My first impulse was to pull up in front of the club and walk through their midst even though normally I'd use the stage door, but that's just what they wanted. They didn't expect that their picket line would keep my customers away; they were hoping for an incident that would, combined with my name value, land them on page one, draw attention to them, help them spread their doctrine and get new recruits.

Big John put his powerful hand on my arm. "Sammy, you know I'm not afraid of them mothers, and I'm with you in whatever you do, but if you swing at them then I'm going to break a few of their skulls, and we'd only be playing their game. A riot's what they want."

"I know, John. Thanks."

As I walked onstage the audience, as a body, rose to its feet, applauding, shouting: "The hell with 'em, Sammy. We're with you."

"Thank you. Thank you for what you've given me. I'll make a quick statement and that's all because I don't think they deserve any more of your time. They're idiots. They don't bug me. I hope they don't bug you."

The wire services carried the story and the phone didn't stop ringing with calls from buddies all over the country. The local papers all took the attitude of Harry MacArthur of the Washington *Star:* "That self-appointed Nazi leader should live so long as to make as many people happy in a lifetime as Sammy Davis does in one night. . . ."

Murphy put down his paper and looked across the table at me, his face a study in bewilderment. "What I don't understand is that those Nazis can get a license to do this."

"The law works for everybody, baby. I guess they've got a right to their opinion." There was a knock at the door. "I'll get it."

"No, I'll get it, Sammy, it's just the mail. I called down for it." He rushed ahead of me.

I laughed, "Hey, I admit I'm a big star but I can open a door, right?"

He stood back reluctantly as I took the mail from the bellman. I sat down at the breakfast table and opened the first envelope that didn't have a return address. "Dear Nigger Bastard, I see Frank Sinatra is going to be best man at your abortion. Well, it's good to know the kind of people supporting Kennedy before it's too late. (signed) An ex-Kennedy Vote."

"Sammy, why do you bother to read those lousy things? I can take care of them for you. . . ."

"Baby, if you thought it would hurt me you wouldn't tell me, right?" He didn't answer. I handed him the letter. "Have we gotten many of these?"

"They don't mean anything. They don't even sign their names."

"They don't have to sign their names when they vote. Now I appreciate the fact that you were trying to protect me but please don't keep things from me. I have to know what people are thinking. Do me a favor. Find an out-of-town newsstand and get a dozen or so papers, particularly from the South and the Southwest."

The first mention I saw was: "Show business and politics have merged more heavily in this election than ever before. Notable (and noisiest) among the vote-swayers is Frank Sinatra, who'll give you an autograph if you'll vote for Kennedy. The crooner, a close friend of JFK, will take time off from politics only to serve in the coveted capacity of best man at the wedding of Negro entertainer Sammy Davis, Jr.—another Kennedy booster—to blonde movie star May Britt." I combed the papers every day. The already stale news that Frank would be my best man continued making the front pages and too often by "coincidence" right next to it were stories about Frank campaigning for Kennedy. The Broadway and Hollywood columns were alive with jokes and political rumors: "If Kennedy's elected his big problem is: should he appoint Sammy Davis, Jr. Ambassador to Israel or the Congo?" . . . "Public opinion experts say that when Frank Sinatra appears at pal Sammy Davis, Jr.'s interracial marriage it will cost Kennedy as many votes (maybe more) as the crooner has been able to swing via his immensely successful JFK rallies." . . . "Insiders hear that Frank Sinatra has informed Sammy Davis, 'I can't be your best man. It's too hot.'"

I tried to scoff at the idea of my friendship to Frank being able to affect a national election but a bigot's vote counts as much as a liberal's and the smear experts were hungry for weapons like an interracial marriage. There were thousands of people stumping for votes and obviously too many of them were willing to drive their man to the White House in a garbage truck if necessary.

I hadn't been in Vegas twenty minutes when I got word that the bookmakers were offering three to one that Frank wouldn't show at my wedding.

Frank, Dean, and Peter had come down for the weekend and I was in the steam room with Frank. He asked, "How's she standing up under all the garbage?"

"So far so good, I guess. But the momentum keeps picking up as we get closer to the date and I dread the day when somebody's going to think up a little zingy that'll penetrate her outer layer of strength. At least if I could be with her to balance it off, but I figure the less we're seen together until the wedding the less they'll have to work with. I'm deliberately bringing her down here for only one weekend. Fortunately, she's busy and excited getting things ready."

He nodded. "She'll be all right. She'll have her moments but she'll make it."

When I spoke with May between shows she said, "Frank called me a little while ago. Just to say hello and find out how I am."

I saw him the next afternoon as he and the guys were leaving. "I talked to May last night, Frank. Thanks."

"See you at the wedding, Charley. I'll leave Hawaii on the fourteenth and be back a day early to make sure I don't run into weather."

One of the Hollywood columns said: "Fox is sitting out May Britt's contract until it runs out in July." I suspected that it was one of those carefully planted "leaks" intended as a last-minute warning to her. I'd expected it just as surely as I knew that the next day the studio would release a complete denial saying it was "a totally unfounded rumor" and they're busily looking for scripts for her. I didn't mention it on the phone, nor did she.

I met her at the airport Friday afternoon. "Now here's the skam: get unpacked and comfortable in some slacks and we'll have dinner in my room. It'll be the only time we'll get to talk until late tonight because I've invited some people over after the second show. I've got a lot of friends here and they haven't stopped with 'When am I gonna meet her?' "

When she got to my suite I sat beside her on the couch. "May. Did you see the Fox thing?"

Her face blanched and she nodded. She reached into her purse for a cigarette not noticing the open pack I'd put in front of her. She asked, "How do you feel about it?"

"Horrible. I just don't know how to tell you how sorry I am." I looked at the floor and the silence hung thickly between us, a silence of barriers despite all that had grown between us.

She said, "If I do get dropped by Fox I can always make Italian films. Of course I realize they won't have the same impact so maybe we won't have quite as much of the 'May Britt and Sammy Davis, Jr.' jazz . . ."

"I don't dig."

"You said it was one of the things you liked about me."

I looked up. "You mean that jazz about the combination of personalities?"

She nodded.

"You're not seriously worrying about *that?* I only meant that it's a pleasant little extra, a kick, but it never had any importance."

She studied my face before she spoke. Her voice was quiet, urgent. "If I ask you something, can I get an honest, no-kidding answer?"

"Yes."

"Would you love me as much . . . if I weren't in pictures?"

"You've got to be joking with a line like that." She shook her head. I reached out and held her face in my hands. "Darling, I'll love you if you never even go to *see* a movie."

"I'm serious, Sammy. Have you thought about it?"

"I don't *have* to think about it. I love you like I don't even love myself, and you know that's *love.* If I seem depressed about this Fox jazz, and I am, it's because of the way it happened. If you'd said to me, 'Hey, I'm bored with pictures, I'm quitting,' I'd say, 'Crazy,' but I don't want pictures to quit you. I realize that right now the last thing in your mind would be to do a picture. That's natural. But things are going to calm down and there may come a day when you look at a fan magazine and you see some kid on the cover and you think, 'Gee, I'm better looking than she is and I'm a better actress,' and maybe you'll wish you were able to go back and do one-a-year. Let's be honest, you don't exactly hate being Mary Moviestar and you've earned your career, you've worked hard and you've got a great start and," I forced myself not to turn away, "I don't want you to look up one day and think, 'What a heavy price I paid to marry him.'"

The color was coming back into her face. "Well, if you were only bothered about how *I* felt then we can forget it. As long as you love me then there's nothing else I want. I couldn't care less about being in pictures. I'd *much* rather stay around the house with our babies and be just plain Mrs. Sharlie Brown."

I held her in my arms, grateful for the way it had worked out. I thanked God that she'd had the strength to absorb it, but I knew there'd be other things, and because she had all the guts in the world she'd keep trying. She'd made it this time, she'd make it the next time and maybe even the next, but would she eventually crack under it?

While the waiter served dinner, she brought me up to date. "The acceptances are pouring in. The carpet is down and the fireplace is gorgeous . . . it looks just like we pictured it would." Then she became serious. "Sammy, I want to ask you something but I don't want you to think I'm complaining. It's about the party tonight. I guess I'd feel pretty rotten if you didn't want me to meet your friends, but is it always going to be like this? Are there always going to be crowds of people around?"

"Look, darling, I'll admit it wasn't one of my most brilliant moves. I didn't think it out very well when I invited them and by the time I realized I should have waited at least 'til tomorrow it was too late to change it. Just bear with me on this one. I've had it with the days of thirty and forty people swarming in and out of the Playhouse all the time. But you've got to understand that those people were there when I needed them so I can't just brush everybody off like 'I don't need you any more so beat it.' It's going to have to be a tapering off process until they get the idea that I'm married, that things have changed and it's not a free-for-all at Sam's every night."

"That's all I want. I don't want to be rude or hurt their feelings either, and I can wait as long as necessary if I can feel I'm not always going to be sharing my husband with a pack of people who knew him before I did. Naturally I want to hold on to whatever real friends we have."

When I got to the dressing room I looked through the mail. Somebody had sent me a clipping from one of the hate sheets, a two panel cartoon. The first panel wa sa picture of me dressed like a butler, grinning and serving a platter of fried chicken and watermelon to John F. Kennedy. In the second panel I was sitting at the table eating it with him. The caption was: "Will it still be the *White* House?"

The party was at its height when a comic came over to May and me. "Hey, Sammy, is that on the level about Dean instead of Frank?" May sat forward. Seeing her interest he explained, "There's a thing in one of the columns today, something about Dean Martin understudying Frank as Sammy's best man just in case Frank suddenly gets 'ill' and can't show." May sat back, noncommittally, and he turned to me, shaking his head angrily, sympathetically, "Man, that's pretty lousy of him."

I said, quietly, "It's not lousy because it's not true. If you're going to believe everything you read I'd better tip you off also that Little Orphan Annie isn't really still eight years old."

I wondered what May must be feeling, constantly hearing that her wedding was something so terrible that the presence of a friend as best man could create this kind of an uproar. I didn't have the guts to discuss it with her and by the time I saw her off at the airport on Sunday afternoon we'd talked about everything else in the world, but not that.

When I got back to the hotel I called the switchboard operator, "I'm not in to anybody except family and long distance." It seemed impossible that one wedding could cause such a cross-fire of emotions, such problems. And for so many people. But, right or wrong, fair or not, my wedding was giving the Nixon people the opportunity to ridicule Kennedy and possibly hurt him at the polls. And every survey showed that he couldn't afford to lose a single vote. I could imagine the pressure Frank must be under. He must have eighty guys telling him, "Don't be a fool. You've worked hard for Kennedy, now do you want to louse him up?" He must be getting it from all sides. And the worst of it is it's understandable. If Frank is identified with Kennedy strongly enough to help draw votes then it follows that if he stands up for me at a controversial interracial marriage only a few weeks before the election there must be some votes he'll lose for Kennedy. And the innuendo and publicity it's gotten so far is only a hint of what'll happen after he appears at the wedding and they have a piece of hard news to work with. They'll wrap it around his ears in almost every paper in the country.

How can I call myself his friend when in the name of friendship I'm keeping him in this kind of a bind? If he's holding out for me like this how can I not be equally his friend and take him off the spot?

But, aside from the fact that I couldn't imagine being married without him there, at this point if Frank did *not* appear it would be almost as bad as if he *did*. It would backfire, they'd make it look as if the rumors had been true, that somebody on Kennedy's staff had suggested it. Maybe he'd regain the bigot vote but he'd lose some of the liberals and a lot of the Negro vote.

There was only one way to take the pressure off everyone concerned. Postpone the wedding. I knew he was back in the States for the weekend, at the Springs with Peter and some of the guys. I placed the call. His man must have answered it in the den and while I waited for him to come to the phone I could hear music and people laughing, then I heard the phone being picked up.

"Hi'ya, Charley, what's new?"

"Frank, I won't keep you because I know you've got people there but I just wanted to let you know that we're so up to our ears getting the house ready and all that jazz that we're going to have to put the wedding off a couple of weeks. You wouldn't believe the problems a poor soul has trying to get married: there's a hitch getting the Escoffier Room for the reception, the rabbi can't make it 'cause he's already booked for a bar mitzvah . . . anyway, I don't know when it'll be but I'll give you plenty of notice."

"You're lying, Charley."

YES I CAN

I hesitated, but it was pointless. "Look, what the hell, it's best that we postpone it 'til after the election."

There was a long silence at the other end of the line. Then, "You don't have to do that."

"I want to. All the talk . . ."

"Screw the talk."

"I know, but it's better this way."

When finally he spoke again, his voice was almost a whisper. "I'll be there whenever it is. You know that, don't you?"

"I know that, Frank."

"You know that I'd never ask you to do a thing like this. Not your wedding. I'd never ask that!"

"That's why it's up to me to be saying it."

"You're a better man than I am, Charley. I don't know if I could do this for you, or for anyone . . ."

"You've been doing it, haven't you?" There was a long silence, then I heard him put down the phone. A few seconds later Peter was on the line. There were no jokes. None of the usual insults we do with each other.

He said, "Frank can't talk any more."

If he got that choked up now—if he could break down in the middle of a phone call then the pressure on him must have been even greater than I'd imagined.

"Charley?"

"Yes, Peter?"

"Charley, I . . . it's beautiful of you."

"Thanks."

We hung up. I'd died a little inside, not from the decision I'd finally made; it had happened when I'd realized the necessity of making a decision.

May would be getting to her house soon. Somehow I'd have to make her understand. I stared at her picture on my night-table. What can I say to her? "We're postponing our marriage because it's so repulsive to some people that they won't want to vote for Kennedy. You understand, don't you, darling?" How does a man explain this to the one person in the world above all others from whom he wants respect and admiration?

I got into my car and drove aimlessly around downtown Vegas, racked by the picture of her excitement of the past

564

few weeks, the rushing around and getting the house ready, waiting for her parents to arrive from Sweden, sending out the invitations, fitting her dress . . . the sooner I faced it the faster it would be behind us. I went into a drugstore and sat down in a phone booth.

Her excitement soared through the phone. "Sharlie Brown, our first presents arrived over the weekend. There are six of them here. One is from George and Gracie Burns, the others must have their names inside and I haven't touched them. I can't wait 'til you get home so we can open them together."

"May, I have something important to tell you, but before I do I want you to know that this is the first and only thing that concerns us both that I'll ever do without consulting you. But I had no choice this time. It's a decision I had to make myself. . . ." As I explained it, I knew by her silence that she was hurt and saddened. "Darling, it boils down to this: over a period of almost twenty years Frank has been aces high, aces up—everything a guy could be to me. There's nothing in the world he wants from me, nothing I can do for him except be his friend. Ninety-nine per cent of the others come and go and you act nice and help them if it's convenient, but Frank is a *friend*, and now he needs something from me, so there can be no evaluating, no hesitating, no limit. It's got to be to the end of the earth and back for him if he needs it."

"I understand. And I agree with you. There was nothing else to do."

"I'm sorry I didn't speak to you first."

"I know it's not easy to suddenly start thinking differently than you always have, and I know you're trying. When do you think we can get married?"

"Well, the one-man show opens at the Huntington Hartford on the 26th and closes November 12th. The election'll be over so why don't we get married the next morning, Sunday."

"Fine."

"I guess you realize that this means we can't have a honeymoon, either. It's too late to juggle dates around. I have to open in San Francisco on Tuesday the 15th."

"Don't worry about that. It's not important at all."

"Look, maybe it won't be so terrible. I'm only doing one

show a night in San Francisco so it's not like I'll be stuck in a club till three in the morning. I'll get the Presidential suite at the Fairmont and at least we can have the next best thing to a real honeymoon."

"That sounds great."

I could only whisper into the phone. "I'll make it up to you, darling. I swear to God I will."

When we hung up I slammed my fist against the phone with all the strength I had, and it hurt. I hit it again, and again, and again. Dear God, will it ever end? Will I ever be able to be like everybody else?

The next morning we sent telegrams to everyone who'd received an invitation: "THE WEDDING OF MISS MAY BRITT WILKENS AND MR. SAMMY DAVIS, JR. WILL BE POSTPONED UNTIL SUNDAY, NOVEMBER 13TH. WE SINCERELY HOPE YOUR ATTENDANCE WILL BE POSSIBLE FOR THE WEDDING RECEPTION AT THE BEVERLY HILTON HOTEL ON THIS DAY AT 4:00 P.M. RSVP 9057 DICKS STREET, LOS ANGELES 46, CALIFORNIA. MR. AND MRS. ERNST HUGO WILKENS."

I'd signed with Rogers and Cowan, a large Hollywood publicity office, and they sent an announcement to the press: "The Sammy Davis, Jr.-May Britt wedding has been postponed due to legal technicality in Miss Britt's Mexican divorce from her previous husband."

That was the lie and that's how we told it. We let nobody in on it.

I checked into the Beverly Hilton Hotel, and started rehearsals for the one-man show at the Huntington Hartford.

On the evening of the opening I took a nap on the couch in the dressing room. I was awakened by a knocking on the door. The stage doorman put on the light. "Mr. Davis . . . I'm sorry to wake you . . ." He was trembling.

I sat up. "What's wrong?"

"I've been getting phone calls. I didn't want to upset you, but . . ."

"What kind of calls?"

"Well, the first one was this morning. He said, 'We've got guns and hand grenades and we're coming to blow up the place.' It sounded like a kid so I didn't pay much attention to it. But then an hour later there was another one . . ." He looked away from me. "They said, 'Is that so-and-so bastard still gonna open there? There's a bomb in the theater right now.' I called the police. They've been going over every inch of the theater and they haven't found anything so far. But I just got another call and this one said, 'We'll fix him and we'll get his so-and-so girl friend, too.' I figured you should know, so you can take precautions."

I called May. "I think you shouldn't come to the opening tonight. I know it's the last minute and I'm sorry. You might as well know this from me before you hear it on the radio or on television . . . we've had some threats and I don't want you around."

"What kind of threats?"

"Just idiots. It's probably nothing, but I'm not about to take chances."

"Are you going to do the show?"

"Yes."

"Then I'll be there."

"May, it's out of the question."

"Don't argue with me, Sammy. Nobody is going to frighten me away from you."

I sent for Murph. "Where is May going to be sitting?"

"In the third row with Jim and Luddy. The first three seats on the aisle."

"Now, listen carefully. Take her tickets back to the box office and tell them I want *five* seats in the fifth row, not on the aisle but in the center. I also want the four seats directly in front of her and the four directly behind her. You got that?"

"Yes, but it's impossible. They're sold out."

"I want her boxed in by people I can count on, and I want her where it'll be the toughest for anybody to get to her. If they give you any argument just tell them if I don't get those tickets I don't walk onto the stage."

I called Pete Pitches, Sheriff of Los Angeles County. "Pete, I want to hire ten of the best private detectives in L.A. I thought you might know some guys who used to be on the force . . ."

Somebody from the manager's office came in. "Don't

worry about the tickets. We'll work it out. Let's just hope the papers don't get ahold of this."

"No, baby, we've got to warn the people what they may be walking into. They have the right to make up their own minds if they want to come here or not. It's too late to get it printed but we definitely should try to get it mentioned on radio and television."

Murphy came in and gave me a folded sheet of paper. His hand was shaking. "Somebody slipped this under the stage door. Sammy, you shouldn't go on."

A bullet was drawn in the center of the paper. Underneath, it said, "I'm going to shoot you dead during your show. Guess when?"

The threats were obviously from cranks, sadists, all seeming alike—yet among them could be the one that might materialize. How do you guess which one? How do you anticipate the workings of a man's mind when obviously he himself isn't in control of it?

It was almost seven o'clock. "Murph, take my car and beat it over to the house and tell Rudy to give you my black double-rig holsters and a box of .45 caliber ammunition."

"Bullets?"

"Let's not waste time discussing it. And make damned sure May doesn't know about this or about the guys we've got around her."

I was dressed when he got back. I buckled on the double rig and checked the gun on the right, the one I'd use for the tricks. I looked into the openings of the cylinder and saw the paper wadding at the tips of the blank cartridges. From the gun on my left, I removed the blanks and replaced them with lead-nosed .45 caliber bullets.

Murphy had been watching me silently. "Sammy, you're not going to go on the stage like that?"

"Well, you'd better believe that I'm not about to let myself get shot by some fanatic climbing onto the stage and then for my big satisfaction as I'm dying somebody says, 'Don't worry, the cops arrested him.'" I unbuckled the holsters. "Unfortunately, I can't walk on and do the opening numbers wearing guns but have this ready 'cause I'm going to move the gun tricks up early and then I'll just not bother to take the holsters off. Now do me a favor and go get May's tickets, baby."

I was putting on my make-up when he returned, shaking his head sadly. "The Nazis are picketing us again." Steve Blauner, Bobby Darin's manager and a dear friend of mine, came in behind him, chalky-faced and out of breath, his tie pulled away from his collar. I jumped up. "What happened?"

Murphy said, "I'd just picked up the tickets when I saw these guys with signs and a crowd standing by watching them. Then here comes Steve and he grabs the sign from one of them and breaks it over his knee. The guy starts to argue so Steve raps him in the mouth. *Now* the crowd started closing in and it's a good thing there were cops around or there'd be a bunch of dead Nazis out there now. The police took them away into protective custody."

I looked at Steve. "Thank you. That was beautiful of you." I straightened his tie, appreciating the affection for me that had turned a gentle, nice man into a street fighter.

At eight o'clock May came in with Jim and Luddy. Her face was drawn tight by worry. "Sammy, do you think you should go on?"

"You're making a whole thing out of nothing. I admit I was a little concerned when I called you, but let's be realistic. When someone really intends to blow up a theater he's not likely to warn you so that you can stop him, right?"

"But why don't you put the opening off for a few days so the police will have time to be sure?"

I put my hands on her shoulders. "Darling, know now: I'm not doing hero bits, with reckless and dramatic and the show-must-go-on. But I can't let myself be chased off the stage by anyone who makes a threat or I'm going to spend the rest of my life running from shadows."

She nodded reluctantly. "I guess you're right."

"Of course I am. Now you guys go to your seats and relax. I'll see you at intermission." I held her face in my hands and kissed her forehead. "You look beautiful."

I walked to the wings. Policemen were stationed in pairs all over the backstage area. I looked through the curtains. She was in her seat, talking to Jim and Luddy, and

I got some comfort from seeing the men unobtrusively surrounding her.

I scanned the faces around the theater. How do I entertain them while wondering if a bomb will explode? How do I do two hours of singing, dancing and jokes, distracted by the thought that at any moment a lunatic might shoot me?

Morty started the overture. Murphy was standing right behind me. He knew I wouldn't need him for at least fifteen minutes, but he was there with the holsters, his hand gripping the butt of one gun.

The audience was applauding, waiting for me.

May was gazing at the wall next to the dining table, her arms folded, eyes focused on something that wasn't there but which I had a feeling was going to be. She began nodding, agreeing with herself. "Do you know what we should have? An old-fashioned bell-pull. Do you know what I mean?"

"Sure, like Vincent Price always has."

"That's right. I hate ringing a bell at the table like a village crier, or stabbing around under the table with my foot trying to find a buzzer under the carpet." A shade of doubt crossed her face. "You don't think it might be a little showy?"

"Only if after you ring it there ain't no butler to come out."

The decorator stuck his head out of the bedroom. "The carpet is down in the bathrooms, Miss Britt."

She beamed. "Come on, let's look."

"Darling, I love everything you're doing, but I'm getting out of here this second 'cause I'm hip it starts with 'Isn't this beautiful?' but it ends with that cat telling me, 'Stand in the shower and see if it's comfortable.'"

As she walked me to the door I said, "You're taking your folks to Romanoff's tonight, right? I called Mike and he's expecting you."

She took my arm. "I must say I like being able to give them such a good time. They've never had a vacation like this in their lives. Especially my father."

I kissed her on the forehead. "Call me at the dressing room."

She sighed. "I sure wish it was tomorrow morning." Her

eyes flashed with excitement. "Can you believe that we're actually, really, honest-to-goodness going to get our marriage license?"

I gave her a look. "Darling, there isn't a chance I wouldn't believe it. You've mentioned it eight times in the last hour."

She blushed. "What time do you think we'll go?"

"No rush. They're not going to run out of licenses. We'll get our sleep, meet here around noon, have some coffee and we'll go do it."

I called Rudy outside. "Do we have any of the paint we use on the garage doors?"

"Not that I know of."

"Then get some. And a large brush."

"You gonna start painting doors?"

"Rudy, just have it here, please. I want you to check the garage door the first thing every morning and if anybody's written anything on it you be ready to cover it up fast."

I went over to the office to see Jim. He said, "We can't swing it. I spoke to Pete Pitchess and I spoke to the head of the marriage license department. Everybody has to go to City Hall personally. No exceptions. Even if you were the mayor."

"If I were the mayor I wouldn't have to worry that some lunatic might take a shot at my fiancée." I sat down.

He looked at me consolingly. "Writing hate letters and picketing is one thing, but I don't think many people would actually cause unprovoked violence."

"Baby, it only takes one nut to do it. Well, what we *can* do is have the applications filled out in advance and at least cut down the time we'll have to hang around there. Send a messenger downtown to get some and bring them to the house in the morning." I reached across his desk for the phone and called Pete Pitchess.

"Sammy, I'm sorry."

"Thanks, Pete. Jim explained it and I understand."

"What time do you plan to get there?"

"Around noon."

"Make it ten-thirty so you can be in and out before the lunch hour crowd is on the streets. I called and they'll be expecting you so you won't be delayed. And, I'll have officers around the front of the building."

I told Jim, "Be at the house at nine. We'll fill out the forms and leave at ten. In the Cadillac. The Rolls is too conspicuous. You'll drop us at City Hall, cruise around for fifteen minutes and then come back."

May arrived at the house radiant and smiling at nine-thirty. I held out the application blank and a pen but she didn't take them.

"Aren't we going to City Hall?"

"Sure we are." I led her across the room to a table. "I just thought it would be more pleasant to fill out the forms in comfort. Also, it'll be just that much less time we'll be pestered for autographs, right?"

She looked at the form, then at me. "Good thinking." She sighed elaborately. "I'm definitely not in the mood to sign autographs today."

When we were ready to leave I went into the bedroom and slipped a revolver into the waistband of my trousers. Jim had followed me in. "Sammy," he spoke quietly, "I'd feel a lot better if when we get there I could go upstairs with you."

"Thanks, baby, but we're covered. I've got two of the guys I had at the opening. They'll stick with us 'til we're back in the car."

"Does May know?"

I shook my head. "They'll stay back. What's to be gained by frightening her?"

He nodded, his eyes riveted to the area of my waist. "If it came down to it do you think you'd really use that? And maybe kill somebody?"

"If you saw a poisonous snake coiled and ready to strike at Luddy would you think twice about killing him?"

He winced. "It's a hell of a way to have to go for your marriage license."

I gave him a shot on the arm. "The big trick when you're carrying one of these is, when you're sitting down, you shouldn't hiccup."

As we drew up to City Hall I scanned the street, concerned that a license bureau clerk might have leaked word to the press, but there was no sign of any photographers, no crowd. Pete's officers were spread out around the outside of the building. May squeezed my hand excitedly as I helped her out of the car. We entered the building and my two private detectives left their positions on either side of the doorway and followed us across the lobby.

The elevator stopped at our floor. "To your right, Sammy. Best of luck to you both."

Halfway down the corridor May increased her pace and in a controlled voice whispered, "I think there are two men following us. I saw them in the lobby."

I hadn't counted on her being so aware. I whispered back, "You better believe they're following us. They work for us."

"You mean *bodyguards?*"

"Just to keep the crowds away, that's all. . . ."

We gave our applications to the clerk, who was obviously expecting us. May glanced behind us.

"Darling, sign your application."

"I only wanted to see if my bodyguards were guarding me."

Word that we were there had swept through the area and by the time we got downstairs people were swarming into City Hall, crowding around us like it was a movie premiere. The sheriff's deputies broke a path through the mob to the car.

As Jim was driving away May looked behind us. "What happens to my bodyguards?"

"They have to guard somebody else's body now."

She frowned. Then, "Hey, that crowd was nice, wasn't it?"

I smiled, "They couldn't have been nicer."

"Sammy, would you give me a light, please? If I've got bodyguards then I'm much too important to light my own cigarettes."

I held my lighter for her. She inhaled deeply. I put my hand on hers and felt it cold and trembling. Her mouth was curved in a smile. But in her eyes there was fear.

The audience was calling me back but Murphy grabbed my arm. "Jim's on the phone. He says it's important." I waved to the stage manager to ring down the curtain and rushed for the phone. "Yes, Jim?"

"Sammy, I'm at May's house. You'd better get over here."

I ran to the parking lot, grateful that I was a minute or two ahead of the theater crowd, and tore across to Santa Monica and out past La Brea.

It had to happen. It had to. I'd been so damned afraid to alarm her that I'd left her wide open. If I couldn't keep her locked up or have her followed around stores, at least I should have had some guys guarding her house. I pushed the speedometer up to 80. A siren wailed and a red light was flashing in my rear-view mirror. I pulled over quickly. The cop stopped in front of me cutting me off, and got out of his car fast, hand on his gun. I stuck my head out the window. "Officer, I'm Sammy Davis, Jr., my intended wife is hurt, I don't know how badly and I'm rushing to see her. I know I was speeding but could you possibly let me have the ticket later? I give you my word I'll come and get it whenever you say."

He'd flashed a light on my face. He snapped it off and his hand fell away from his gun. "Where does she live, Sam?"

"About eight blocks from here." I told him the address.

"Let's go." He hurried back to his car and led the way, lights flashing, cutting the traffic out like an end making room for the fullback. In front of May's house, he circled around and called out, "Hope everything's okay, Sam. Give our best to the lady."

A doctor was shaking down a thermometer and May was up to her chin in blankets. She made a disgusted face. "Hello there. I've got the flu."

I sank into a chair, falling apart like I'd been held together with a string and somebody had pulled it.

Jim was standing over me. "Maybe you've got it, too. You look like hell."

"Baby, hy didn't you say it was only the flu?"

"You hung up before I had the chance. I called right back but you were gone." He shook his head slightly. "You're honed pretty thin, friend."

The doctor was saying, "Mr. Davis, as I told Miss Britt, she should be well enough by Sunday to stand up for your wedding ceremony, but I strongly advise against her attending the reception. She's been hit hard by this virus and she'll be extremely susceptible to germs. The excitement of a party, going in and out of air-conditioned rooms—she really shouldn't even go to the ceremony, however, I can understand. . . ."

May started to fight him.

"Darling, put the thermometer back in your mouth. It's a shame to miss the party but it's really not important."

The next afternoon she was sitting up in bed going over guest lists and keeping track of the presents that had come in. I took the papers from her. "I have an office with a typewriter and a girl who's paid to sit in front of it all day long and go plink, plink, plink. Let *her* worry about these things. You rest." I drew a chair up alongside her and told her that the wire services, *Life* magazine, the papers, were taking the position that we were unreasonable not to let them in to the wedding.

Frowning, she said, "Don't they understand that people would like some privacy at their *wedding?* Just a few little hours . . . why can't they forget about it?"

"Darling, maybe we should be glad they can't. It's beautiful to say, 'This is my wedding and it's sacred,' there's nothing I'd like better, but nobody has the right to expect the comforts of anonymity at the same time he's raking in the rewards of fame. I've got a house, a swimming pool and a Rolls-Royce because people are interested in me. And I'm not so sure that I have the moral right to say, 'Sorry fellas, this is *my* day, no press,' ignoring the fact that they have a job to do and that by doing their job through the years they've done me a lot of good. Okay, maybe they've been a little rough lately but if I look at the record since I started making it I've got no complaints."

"Well . . . I guess that's true."

"And, from a practical point of view, they're going to write about it whether we let them in or not. If we keep them out we'll antagonize them so that instead of reporting it simple and nice maybe they'll throw in a few zingies and stir up trouble for us."

She sighed, acquiescing. "Will they be there during the ceremony?"

"No. The ceremony is *ours* and we'll keep it that way. When it's over, we'll invite them in, have a round of champagne, answer some questions and let them take a few pictures." I put my hand on hers. "Darling, weighing the good against the bad, thank God that the people are enough interested in me so there's even a question of should we let the press in."

Frank took the mike and waited for all the guys to be quiet. "Okay . . . now you've all come to hear some dirty words and to say a little *kaddish* for one of our boys. You're all chums who respect and love him—otherwise you'd be out in the parking lot. Now, this first fella who's going to sing for you only dumped the next President of the United States to be here. You can't show more friendship than *that!*" Peter got up and did a duet with Tony Curtis and for half an hour they and the others kidded me mercilessly. Milton Berle sauntered in dressed like May on the *Blue Angel* posters with the black net stockings, the strapless top and high heels plus a fantastic blond wig and make-up job.

Frank took the mike again. "Well, nobody's going to follow *that,* so we'll close the evening by letting our buddy know how we really feel about him. Come on up here, Sam."

He put his arm around my shoulder and sang, "*Goodbye Sammy . . . goodbye, Sammy . . .*" The guys all joined him, "*Goodbye, Sammy . . . we're sorry to see you go . . .*" They were smiling at me, standing in a group, in strength, singing to me, as much as saying, "Here we are. We're your buddies and we're behind you." I'd planned some bits for this moment, some sharp lines—but I didn't feel sharp, I just felt grateful. "I'm sorry if I'm getting a little sickening. I just never knew that so many guys gave a damn about me . . . thank you very much."

Frank followed me out of the room to an empty corner table and sat with me while I pulled myself together. "Charley, about our deal for *Soldiers Three.* I'm changing it so instead of the straight hundred and a quarter in salary you'll be getting $75,000 in cash and seven per cent of the profits. After a while that seven per cent piece should be worth over a quarter of a million. You can sell it for a capital gain. You're going to have a wife and you want kids and you've got to build something for them. To hell with your own self; you can't let them down, Charley."

He stood up and smiled, "I'll go see if there's any drunks to throw out."

I dressed slowly, then drove leisurely across to Sunset Boulevard. There was no final, sentimental reflection on my bachelor days, no nostalgic last-looks. I felt only relief at leaving them behind.

People were leaning out of windows all the way up the hill, with telescopic lenses trained on my house, and hundreds of them were crowded onto the porches of the houses above us as if they'd bought tickets for a ball game. Reporters and newsreel men clustered in front of the door. Photographers were perched in trees to get a free line of sight to the doorway. I waved and spoke to the press guys for a minute, then slipped past them into the house.

I walked down the outside stairs and into the Playhouse and as I saw the guys waiting there a wave of sentiment swept through me. Their presence was like a gathering of the good things I'd acquired along the way.

Frank was completely in character, a cigarette in one hand, a glass in the other, intense, yet with a casual air in the way he punctuated his sentences with the familiar Sinatra hand gesture. I thought of him at the theater in Detroit: "Hi'ya, my name's Frank." I watched him, thinking what it took for him to be my best man. It's easy enough for others who sit in a relatively obscure corner of fame to say, "It's only right for him to be there, he's your friend, isn't he? He *should* be there!" But it's not that simple. He's also a man who commands the absolute top money in everything he does, and he depends on the hater as well as the liberal to keep him in that position. With all his independence, still he knows where it comes from, and how quickly a career can go down the drain on the whim of the public. For him to publicly say, "This is my friend and in your ear if you don't like it," means putting in jeopardy everything that he'd lost once and regained and must fight to hold onto, not only for himself but for his family. It was not a minor thing for Frank to be my best man, nor for Peter and Pat, the President's sister and brother-in-law, to be in th ewedding party.

One by one my beginnings with each of these men flashed before me, and as I remembered things that had passed I knew that it had all contributed toward bringing me to this day, and even the bad moments were marked paid-in-full.

Rudy called on the intercom. "They're ready to start the ceremony."

I took my place in the living room under the canopy of flowers which had been built in front of the wall of windows. Frank was at my side. Peter was next to him. Mama and my father and Will—all the "family" were gathered around us.

May appeared from the next room with her father, walking toward me. She was every fine and lovely, precious thing that God ever put into a woman. Her father kissed her and smiled at me as I stepped forward. She put her arm in mine, we turned, and the rabbi began the ceremony.

"Almighty God, supremely blessed, supreme in might and glory, guide and bless this groom and his bride.

"Sammy and May, you are standing in front of me to join your lives even as your hands are joined together, and custom dictates that I, as your rabbi, give you some advice.

"Your marriage is something more than just the marriage of two people in love, and it is most certainly that or I have never seen two people in love in twenty years of the ministry. But, as you come together as man and wife something more is involved. You are people without prejudice. You represent the value of the society that many of us dream about but, I suspect, hesitate to enter. As such, because you are normal in an abnormal society—society will treat you as sick. To be healthy among the sick is to be treated as sick as if the others were healthy.

"Through no fault of your own except your love, because both of you are greater than the pettinesses that divide men, you become not simply a symbol of marriage, but because you both have accepted Judaism equally as your own you become representatives of Judaism because you are in the public eye; you are part of that from which the public gets its response and its value systems—either by acting along with or reacting to.

"Also, because of the circumstances of your love, there is a symbolic representation to the fact that you are of different racial stocks originally and that now you merge your love as in a sense all mankind is merging its genes and chromosomes to the oneness which is inevitable. It's not really fair that your love should have so much imposed upon it but it must

578

be a mark of the greatness of your love to know that you must not only continue to love each other because you do love each other, but because circumstances beyond control, and all circumstances involved in real love are beyond control, make you representatives of Judaism and marriage to a world that watches with curiosity, with eagerness, almost with a will to see failure rather than success.

"An additional pressure is on you in knowing that because of the different racial backgrounds you are a symbol, too, of the success that must come from such unions. If you are true to the story of your love then your social role in our times will be an important one. Important for the future of the amity of races.

"What I pray for you, May, and for you, Sammy, is the strength that you may fulfill either the public role or the private role, because if you can do either you will be doing both. If you are true to that which you have called upon yourselves or which has been thrust upon you by society, then your love will be a love story to join the immortal love stories of the ages.

"May the blessings of the patriarchs and the prophets, may the blessings of God Almighty be upon you and may you be worthy, my dear friends, of an historic trust and a great love.

"Standing here in the presence of God the guardian of the home, and in the hearing of these the witnesses and your dear ones, answer the question which I now put to you. Do you, Sammy, of your own free will and consent, take this woman, May, to be your lawful wife? Do you promise to love, honor and cherish her throughout your life?"

"I do."

"Do you, May, of your own free will and consent, take this man, Sammy, to be your lawful husband?"

"I do."

"Praised be Thou, oh Lord our God, who has blessed these children of Israel with holy matrimony. And now I take in my hands the cup of wine and pronounce over it the blessing of our people . . .

"Sammy, take this cup, offer a sip first to your bride and then partake of it yourself.

"As together you have shared this cup of wine so may

your lives be entwined, may you always be aware of the Presence Divine, may you always address each other and each other alone, 'Thou art mine.'

"This cup of wine which you have shared is a symbol of life's twin cups. One is a cup of joy, the other is a cup of sorrow. Sammy and May, when you share together the cup of sorrow, because you are two become one may your sorrows be cut in half, and please God, through the magic of a good marriage when you share together the cup of joy, because you are two become one may your joys become doubled.

"Now take this ring, a symbol of holy wedlock, and place it on the finger of your bride. Help him, May, like a good wife. Face her, Sammy, and repeat after me: 'Be thou made holy unto me by this ring as my wife in accordance with the laws of Moses and the faith of Israel.'

"May, take this ring and place it upon Sammy's hand. Face him and repeat after me: 'Be thou made holy unto me by this ring as my husband in accordance with the laws of Moses and the faith of Israel.'

"Now, Sammy, with your foot break the glass which I have wrapped in cloth and placed on the floor. It is symbolic of the destruction of the temple and of the sorrows of Israel. By tradition, the breaking of the glass in the midst of your great happiness serves to remind the bridal couple of the sorrows of life and of your responsibilities.

"Praised be Thou, oh Lord, who has blessed these children of Israel and all mankind with the covenant of holy wedlock beneath the canopy of marriage.

"And now, you have said the words, you have performed the rites which bind your lives together, the one to the other. Therefore by the power vested in me under the laws of the State of California, with the blessings and good wishes of our mutual friend, Doctor Max Nussbaum who so wanted to be with you today, I, Rabbi William Dramer, as a rabbi, preacher, and teacher of Israel, do declare you the members of my congregation in Temple Israel to be groom and bride, and I now pronounce you man and wife and ask that you bow your heads for the blessing.

"May the Lord bless you and keep you, may the Lord make the light of His countenance shine upon you and be gracious unto you. May God grant that you find within your hearts love, that you find in your fulfillment toward each other, peace. May your marriage prosper in a world where the nations are at peace and where peace and amity come among all groups of mankind."

The street looked normal again, the house was quiet and May was propped up in bed when I returned from the reception. She pressed the remote control button on the television set, cutting off the sound. "I've been watching the news reports. We've been on all of them."

"How are you feeling?"

"I'm feeling rotten that I couldn't go to my own wedding reception. When I think of all the silly parties I went to in the last year . . ."

"Look, it was a rough break but that's it." I sat on the bed beside her and told her all about it. "There was an air of happiness that you could almost hold in your hand. I'd figured I'd have a rough time getting away, but even people I hadn't seen in a year, people who'd flown across the country, who'd come all the way from London, from South America, were telling me, 'Go home to your wife. That's where you belong. You don't have to sit with us.' It was beautiful."

There were tears in her eyes. "Poor Sharlie Brown had to go alone to his own wedding party."

I held her in my arms. " 'Alone' is a word I've lived with since I went into the Army, for over fifteen years it was an inescapable state of mind, but it has no claim on me any more. Do you know what I mean?"

Her eyes were closed and she was smiling. "I think so. But tell me anyway."

35

"Do You Think I'll Need This Dress?" She Was Holding an orange wool dress against her, waiting for an opinion.

I put down the camera I'd been cleaning. "Darling, I'll make a deal with you: you won't ask what clothes you should wear and I won't ask what numbers I should sing."

"But you're my husband. What if you don't like something?"

"Your clothes didn't stop me from falling in love with you, did they? Now, I believe in togetherness but just 'cause we're married doesn't mean we should throw away that great thing of when we're getting dressed to go out and I don't know what you're wearing and all of a sudden you appear and it's like 'Yeah.' Isn't that more exciting than if we stand around and brush our teeth together till there aren't any surprises any more? Let's keep a little of the mystery swinging for us." She nodded begrudgingly and went over to the suitcase and pushed the clothes down, testing for space. She went back to the closet, got another dress, hid it under her robe and did a whole comedy number of sneaking it past me. I gave her a round of applause and turned back to my camera, but out of the corner of my eye I saw her racing back and forth between the closet and the suitcase like a madman, dropping dresses into it like she was in a potato race.

I jumped up. "You've got to be joking. We're not *moving* there, we're just visiting!"

I took her by the arm and led her to the bed. "What you wear in San Francisco isn't nearly as important as the fact that you're still not a hundred per cent and you're knocking yourself out. Now, we've only got a few hours before the plane and I think you should get some rest." I drew the blinds. As I was tucking her in, the phone rang. I kissed her on the forehead. "I'll take it in the other room. Sweet dreams."

Rudy had his hand over the mouthpiece. "It's the manager of the Geary Theater in San Francisco."

"Mr. Davis, I don't mean to alarm you but you have the right to know that in the last few days we've had a number of bomb threats and threats against your life. It's probably just cranks, nevertheless the police are rounding up every known arsonist and bomber in the city. As for yourself, we've arranged for complete protection at the theater. . . ."

When I hung up Rudy asked, "Trouble?"

I nodded. "Make me a drink, will you please, baby?"

Obviously there could be no more hoping that the commotion at the Hartford was merely a flurry before the wedding. This was the tipoff that they'd be waiting for me all across the country, that it was going to be toe to toe all the way.

I stared into the glass, at the water the ice cubes had become. I opened the bedroom door quietly. The blankets were covering all but the top of her head. I looked at her suitcase packed and ready to go.

She sat up. "I'm too excited to sleep."

I closed the door and sat on the edge of the bed. "Darling . . ." She stopped smiling, sensing something serious. I forced the words out. "I'm sorry, but you can't come to San Francisco."

"You don't mean because of the flu?"

I shook my head and she listened without interrupting as I explained what was going on. "We can say it's wrong, it's lousy, but that's not going to change it. In the days of chivalry and King Arthur, or the days of the Romans they'd accuse a guy of something and they'd have a trial by ordeal: they'd say 'We'll put him in with a hungry lion,' and if he survived he was set free. It's going to be something like that with us. The first year will be the tough one. If we can survive that then I think we'll have it made."

"Do you really believe it will take a whole year before they'll leave us alone?"

"I don't know. I'm sure that in some cities we'll have no

trouble at all, in others we'll have to be careful. But I do know that until they get off our backs I have to protect what I hold dear. We'll have to adopt a routine, a strict procedure that we'll follow until the pressure is off. You will not arrive in any city with me. I'll get there first and get a feeling of what's up, the atmosphere. If it looks safe I'll wait a few days to be sure and then I'll be on the phone telling you to grab the first plane."

"Okay."

"Meanwhile, I've hired someone who'll move in and stay here while I'm gone. Naturally, Rudy'll be here, too, but it won't hurt to have another man around the house."

"A guard?"

"He's a private detective."

"Do you think . . . do I really need that?"

"Frankly, no. By the same token I don't expect the house to burn down but I carry fire insurance against the remote chance that it might."

"That's true."

"And if by being here he does nothing else but ease your mind, it's worth it. We'll take every precaution and when it turns out we didn't need them then crazy, we spent a little money and effort for a lot of peace of mind." I looked at my watch. "I'll go downstairs and say goodbye to Mama." I stopped at the door and walked back to her. "May? Thank you for not making a fuss over something I can't change." I took her hand in mine. "I want you to know how sorry I am about all this and how much I appreciate you."

She smiled, embarrassed, "Do you think I'm marvelous?"

I gave her a look. "I think you know how to take a simple compliment and milk it into a three-act play. Let's face it: I'm going to San Francisco, not Australia by paddle boat."

When I got back to the bedroom she was dressed in slacks and a sweater. "I'll go with you to the airport."

"No. Let's not take any unnecessary chances. Get your rest so that when I call and tell you the coast is clear, you don't have to say I'm back in bed with the flu. We'll say good-bye here."

"Sammy . . ." her face was losing the façade of cheerfulness and her voice was starting to quaver. "I'm afraid I'm not going to be so marvelous . . ." She was trying to fight the tears. "This is so darned rotten." I held her in my arms stroking her head while she got it out of her system. "A fine Joan of Arc I turned out to be." Her ears became red and suddenly, abruptly, she pulled herself together and strode briskly across the room. "Okay, that's enough of that." She faced me. "I'm sorry. That's the last time I'll ever do that to you. I promise. I won't make it harder for you than it already is."

I knew that she meant it, that she'd ache with pain before she'd ever again let on how it bothered her. I knew that as we parted time after time she'd earn medals for guts and bravery. But I couldn't begin to understand why it should be necessary.

The applause increased, kept growing louder, but I could only think of it as an ideal shield for the sound of a gunshot. And as I worked I knew that my physical performance was not as good as it should have been. The one thing that had remained constant all these years had finally succumbed to divided attention. Despite the plainclothesmen spread all over the theater, despite every possible precaution, I found myself unable to devote myself as fully to each song, each dance; I was looking for hints of trouble, studying hazy faces in the back of the theater. As I did the impressions my mind's ear wasn't tuned entirely to Cagney or Robinson, and as I sang only half of me was absorbed in the words of the song while the other half was praying that somebody hadn't left a window or a door unlocked at the house. I was afraid. Somewhere out there, in this audience or in the next, was the guy who'd make trouble. Or, worse still, was he in Hollywood, creeping up to the house, planning some horrible thing against May?

I left the stage exhausted and waited at the phone in the dressing room until I got her on the line, until I heard her voice. I told her I'd call again later when I got to the hotel and we could talk. I sat chained to the chair by fatigue, too tired to get up and change my clothes. Murphy was straightening out the make-up table. He lifted the Kleenex box and looked at a stack of hate letters I'd left under it. "Those are the violent ones, baby. Find the local FBI office and get them over there tomorrow like they asked."

There was a knock on the door, he turned quickly, leaning his head close to it. "Who is it?"

"Paul Newer."

Paul came in and locked the door behind him. He looked more like a young schoolteacher than a detective. He was tall, wore glasses, and his suit was loose so that his gun and holster wouldn't bulge. He said, "I moved you into a different suite."

"You're joking. What was wrong with the old one?"

"As long as we're going to be together for a year, you should be familiar with basics. You will always occupy a different hotel room than the one in which you're officially registered."

"Baby, isn't that a little pointless? Eighty room-service waiters and maids'll know where I am."

"Percentages. We keep the odds as low as we can. You will not answer a door even if you think you know who it is. Obviously all packages and mail will be left at the desk, never delivered directly to you. I'll pick them up and bring them to you."

"The bellboys are gonna love *that*."

"We're not worried about the bellboys. You won't leave the theater or the hotel without me. Ever. I'll enter every building or room ahead of you. It'll be annoying, maybe awkward sometimes, but I'll be with you from when you wake up until you go to sleep," he smiled, "and when you're sleeping I'll be in the adjoining room."

"In other words I ain't never going to be able to shake you, right?"

"Till death do us part."

Murphy looked up, "Watch your language."

The threats didn't let up, the pickets kept coming back to the theater—I dared not have May join me.

I sat at the phone knowing that from the moment we'd start talking she'd be waiting for me to say "Pack your bags and come on," that I'd stall, hating to tell her, yet hating to keep her in suspense. What's she getting out of marriage besides being made a prisoner?

I called Burt in New York. "Baby, I need a favor. May digs the Sherry Netherland but I don't know anybody there and I'm not sure how they might feel about me. I'll appreciate it if you find out and if possible get me their best suite for the month I'll be at the Copa."

When he called back and told me I had it and there'd been no resistance at all I called May. "Darling, your husband might just turn out to be one of the great idea men of his time. Instead of you coming all the way over here where there's still some pressure—and the fact is there's nothing to do —I'm booked on the flight to L.A. right after the show Saturday night. I'll get to the house by one or two o'clock, there's no show on Sunday so I'll be able to stay home until late Monday afternoon. I'll do the same thing the next weekend," I rushed on, "and in-between I figure I can do a few quickie trips over like Tuesday and Thursday. If I didn't have certain interviews and stuff that I've got to do here I'd commute every day."

"Hey, that's great." Her voice didn't falter.

"And what's your favorite hotel in New York?"

"The Sherry Netherland."

"Well, I reserved a gorgeous suite for us there, facing Central Park."

When we hung up an hour later I glanced through the papers. One of the Broadway columns said, "The S.D. Jr. marriage is rumored wobbly already. Two days after the ceremony he went on to Frisco and left her at home in L.A."

I fell into the strict routine Paul had set up. He came everywhere with me, he was introduced as a friend, but he was always facing the entrance, always sitting between me and the door.

As the time came to leave for the road, I looked back over the empty threats, and was tempted to tell May, "Come on, we'll go together and take our chances." But I resisted it, reminding myself that the extra weeks together weren't worth risking the years beyond them and as I kissed her good-bye after spending two beautiful days at the house I found it more difficult to leave her than ever before; almost impossible to explain away as merely "a precaution" the expensive need for constant security, to do it with a laugh, to play down my longing for her, yet make her know that I didn't want to go anywhere without her, and to expect her to accept indefinitely the fact that we had to wait for the

YES I CAN

future before we could enjoy the simple pleasure of being together.

I moved through Idlewild Airport counting the smiles, the hard looks, weighing them all, one against the other, conducting a private poll. From city to city I'd been measuring reactions of cops, cab drivers—everybody, wondering how much business I was going to do; would they stay away because of the marriage? Have I gone over the line this time and done something they just won't be able to accept?

I went directly to the Copa on the pretense of wanting to check the lights, and casually asked, "How do the reservations look?"

Bruno grinned, "We haven't had anything like this all year. The boys are going to pay their mortgages on this month."

I walked around the corner to the Sherry Netherland. The man at the desk slid the registration pad toward me and extended his hand. "A pleasure to have you with us, Mr. Davis."

Waiting for the elevator a young couple smiled. The door opened and a dowager-type saw me and did a double take, like she hoped she was wrong.

Murphy was at a desk in the living room, separating the mail into two piles. I glanced at one of the letters. "Many of these?"

"No, Sammy, just a few. Really. Maybe one out of twenty. The rest are beautiful. Some of them even have little poems wishing you happiness."

"When May gets here don't even bring the mail upstairs. Take it to the dressing room and screen it there."

Standing backstage I felt more than the usual opening-night tensions. Bob Melvin, the comedian I'd been using on the bill with me, was on the floor and I stood near the kitchen listening, trying to feel the way the crowd was going to be.

Julie Podell came over to me. "Sammy? Have a drink?" He rapped the service bar with his pinky ring. "What're you drinking?"

"Nothing, thanks. I'll just stand with you."

He raised his glass. "To the Mrs." He downed his drink and, gesturing toward the audience, growled, "They're killing me for tables. I had to yank the production number.

588

How in the hell can I get eight girls on a floor the size of a postage stamp?"

The lights went down and John and Nathan rushed onto the darkened stage to arrange my props. George Rhodes and Michael Silva moved quickly and efficiently to their places on the bandstand. I stood in the back, taking a last few drags on a cigarette, holding it cupped in my hand, letting the heat of its ember penetrate the chill that had swept over me. There was a hush, then the first sound of music, and the lights went up on the stage I had to fill. The applause began, I saw the heads turning, straining toward the spot where I'd appear. I waited, listening to them calling for me—then I was on the floor, standing among them, hearing their welcome grow stronger.

I stood motionless, looking at the familiar faces. We were old friends who'd seen a lot of years together, good ones and bad, and it was a glorious thing to see them rising to applaud me, nodding, smiling, even before I'd begun dancing or singing.

As I swung through the first few numbers I knew that whatever had afflicted my personality had passed, gone as unexpectedly as it had come. And the reason was clear: I'd taken a stand in life, not through courage but out of necessity. I had opened the only door available to me and I'd walked through it with May into the limelight or into oblivion, whichever it might be, but together. There'd been no compromise, simply, "I have done what I believe in and here I stand, good, bad or indifferent, I hope you will still like me but if you don't, I will regret it but I cannot change." I wasn't hedging any more, trying to please everyone, and my missing rapport with the audience had returned with all the intensity it had ever had, perhaps more.

I looked out at the people jamming the club. I'd prepared myself to find them gone, but there they were, en masse, as much as saying, "Yeah, Sam, go. Do what you want to do. We like you any way you play it."

When you look at people and you feel the great good fortune of what they have done for you, and you realize that here you are by their grace and here you may stay by their grace you begin to understand the meaning of humility. All the books I'd read, the philosophers, the poets, all the careers I'd studied, the plays, the movies, all these never taught me. I guess you can't learn it that way. It just happens to you one lucky day when God gives you pause to appreciate what surrounds you. Suddenly you see the beauty and the cooling shade of a tree instead of the fact that leaves fall and have to be raked up.

When it happens to you the word "humility" is thrown away. You can't use it any more, certainly not commercially, for effect on a stage. It becomes something felt deep inside you which may transmit to the people in its own unspoken way.

I moved around the tightly packed dressing room saying hello to the people who'd come upstairs. As the crowd shifted, making room for new arrivals, I walked over to where George Gilbert was sitting with Jane and Burt. I lowered my voice. "Shall we discuss how a small, colored, Jewish lad has become the darling of the 400?"

"It's wonderful," muttered Jane, squashed into a corner, "but must you have them here all at once?"

I saw Evelyn Cunningham at the door and hurried across the room to greet her. She introduced me to her husband Cam. We talked for about fifteen minutes and when they were ready to leave I said, "Evelyn, I appreciate you coming up here like this." I smiled. "I never exactly enjoyed being an outcast."

As we shook hands she said, "I'd love to meet your wife. Why don't you bring her up to our apartment some night next week?"

Her visit and the invitation to her home seemed to crystallize the approval I'd been sensing from areas where I'd never before had it. It seemed incredible that marriage to a white woman would bring the Negro people so solidly behind me. Yet, the same person who'd battered me bloody in her column for as long as I could remember seemed to have been trying to let me know, "I don't care who you married as long as it's on the level." Certainly not all of the white or Negro people believed in what I had done, the only logical answer was that they respected the honesty of it and, at least, *my* right to believe in it.

May said, "Sammy? What is it you want more than anything else in the whole world?"

"I want you to get your Swedish fanny on a plane and get here, fast."

"What else?" She was stifling a giddiness that kept creeping into her voice. "Something we want *so* badly . . . ." I could almost see her smiling through the phone.

"Darling . . . do you mean little brown babies?"

"That's what I mean, Sharlie Brown. I knew about it this morning but I wanted to tell it to you when I saw you so I didn't say anything the other times you called but I just couldn't keep it to myself any longer."

Her plane landed at seven in the evening. I drove out with Jane and Burt, and Paul, to meet her. It was close to show time as the car neared the city. I said, "Darling, you'd better drop me at the club. Paul will go back to the hotel with you and Jane and Burt; you can get comfortable, rest, and I'll come over between shows."

"But I was hoping I'd see your second show tonight."

I tensed, "Well . . . I figured you'd be tired after the trip. . . ."

"Sammy, I haven't seen your show since we've been married. Don't you want me to see it?"

"Of course I do." I'd been completely wrapped up in the excitement of seeing her and the happiness of a baby coming, but now there was the sobering realization that subconsciously I'd been hoping to avoid her coming to the club. I was dying to have her sitting out front, but lurking behind that pleasure was the question of how the audience would treat her when they saw us in the same room. It was one thing for them to say, "Wonderful. Be happy," but it was something else for them to actually see us together. That's the part that even some of the liberals couldn't take, the contrast. That's what bothered them.

"Well, then, do it this way: Jane and Burt can drop you and Paul at the hotel, swing back to their place and change clothes, the car can wait for them, they'll pick you up and you'll all come to the dressing room. You'll sit with me 'til I'm ready to go on and then you'll go downstairs."

"And at eleven forty-five we'll have shuffleboard on the Promenade Deck."

"What's that, Jane?"

"What's that, Jane?"

When I got to the club I called downstairs to Bruno, "Baby, hold a center ring for my wife for the second, please. For four. And Bruno, do me a favor, be sure you know exactly who's sitting at the tables to the left, right, and directly behind her."

At 11:45 I walked them from the dressing room to the elevator and watched the door close after them. *Please, God.*

I called Bruno again. "Baby, she's on her way down with Burt and Jane and my guy Paul. Will you make sure she doesn't get caught in a crowd? Can you have some of the guys escort her to the table?"

"I've had two captains waiting at the elevator for the last ten minutes. Relax. Khrushchev couldn't get to her."

Murphy had filled my cigarette case and was holding it out to me. I put it in my pocket and stood in the living room, staring unseeing at the television set.

Murphy called out, "Sammy, it's Bruno."

I grabbed the phone. "What's wrong?"

He was shouting over the crowd noises in the background. "Nothing. I just thought you'd like to know that when she came in the audience applauded her."

"What do you mean?"

"I mean the people applauded the missus as she walked to her table. They stood up and gave her a hand. In all my years I never saw it happen. Except for DiMaggio."

The second I hit the stage I could see the audience glancing from me to her and back again. Despite the protection of Paul and every captain and waiter in the room, seeing her in the midst of a crowd was even worse than when I'd known she was at home on the coast. I went through the act, leaning on professionalism—watching, looking for pressure spots, dreading the moment somebody would have one drink too many and say or do something he might not do if he were sober. I did an hour and ten minutes and left the stage, drained, exhausted by the impossible chore of trying to be an entertainer and a bodyguard at the same time.

I told the room service waiter to put the table in front of the window overlooking Central Park. When May was seated I stood back a few feet and adjusted the view-finder, getting her into focus.

She frowned. "Are you going to take my picture before breakfast?"

"Yes. I want to get a picture of my wife sitting at a breakfast table, no make-up, pregnant, and the most beautiful sight in the world."

She beamed. "Do you really think that?"

I caught that smile and put down the camera. "Yes, I do. And that's the last compliment you're going to get until three o'clock this afternoon." I sat down across from her. "Do you wanta know what a thrill it is after thirty years on the road to look across the table in a hotel room and see you instead of Murphy Bennett?" She smiled happily and began opening a boiled egg. I said, "I don't want to do expectant-father bits, but what kind of a diet did the doctor say you should be on?"

"Just good food." She looked up. "Do you have to go anywhere today?"

"Nope. Today it's a definite sit-around, lazy-style, just me and my wife. We'll watch a little television, read the papers . . ."

"Boy, that sounds *great*." She smiled, "Mr. and Mrs. Sharlie Brown at home." She tapped the second egg with her spoon, and studied it. "I'm really not too dying to have this egg. I sure wish I hadn't ordered it . . ." She stared at it, spoon poised indecisively. She put down the spoon. "My husband makes twenty-five thousand dollars a week. I don't have to eat this egg." She pushed it away. "Boy, I'm sure glad to get that off my neck."

I stared at her. "You're really going to do ten minutes on that egg?"

"I won't say another word about it." She glanced across the table. "But I hope I haven't hurt its feelings."

"You're a nut. Now, here's the skam for tonight: around five-thirty we'll dress, Jane and Burt'll be here at six-fifteen, then it's a little dinner at Danny's. At seven forty-five I'll cut out and do the show while you guys take your time over coffee and brandy. When you're finished you'll come by the dressing room between shows and keep me company. There'll be no crowd scene, just the four of us."

"Can we catch the second?"

"Of course."

The phone rang and she answered it. "I'm wonderful, thank you, Murph. Here's my husband."

I took it from her. "Murphy, I'm *trying* to have a little breakfast with my wife."

"I know, Sammy, and I've been taking all the calls but I think you'd better take this one. It's Sid Robinson at the Copa and he says it's important."

"Put him through." I waited while the call was transferred to my line.

"Sammy, we just got word that the Nazi party got a license to picket us tonight . . ." May was gazing out the window. I held the phone tightly against my ear. ". . . Julie tried to block it but the law says the bastards can picket. I thought you'd want to know. It's a damned shame, particularly with everything else going so beautifully. We couldn't take another reservation tonight if it was for the Mayor himself."

May was watching me. I smiled into the phone. "Well, if he comes in you can give him my table. Thanks for calling, Sid. I appreciate it."

When I hung up she asked, "Is anything wrong?"

"That was Sid Robinson. He's Julie Podell's brother-in-law and second in command at the Copa. We're sold out to the rafters."

"That's marvelous." She motioned for me to look out the window at an ice skating rink. "Sammy, how do you feel about our child learning to ice skate?"

I sat down at the table again. "Gee, I'm glad you mentioned that because just yesterday I went to buy ice skates but I didn't know if I should get them in pink or in blue." She blushed. "Darling, I want our baby to do anything and everything any healthy child can and should do. And, speaking of health I think maybe you shouldn't come to the club tonight. It's going to be a crowd scene and somebody could bump into you by mistake. Why take chances? Besides, professionally, I don't want it to get around town 'May Britt is at ringside every night' like it's our bit."

She nodded, disappointed. "Well, I can understand that . . . I guess."

"And as long as you're not going to be coming to the club then it seems pointless for you to get all dressed up for dinner. We'll make Danny's another night. I'll tell Jane and Burt to come over here slacks-style, and we'll have room service."

"Okay. But can we come to the dressing room in slacks?"

"Darling, it'll be jammed with people doing drop-ins. What do you need it for? It's cold as hell outside. Stay here where you'll be much more comfortable. You can watch television, sit around and talk . . ." I picked up the phone. "May I have the bell captain, please?"

"Sammy, I don't care about the crowd if I can be with my husband. And it'll feel like a weight on Jane and Burt if they have to stay in just because I do."

"Darling, they won't mind. They're friends. Please, don't fight me on this. I know what's best . . . hello, this is Sammy Davis, Jr. Will you send up all the papers, please."

I was slamming through the *Journal-American* and May had the *Post*. She gasped excitedly, "Would you like to see something so beautiful that it's unbelievable?" She was pointing to Earl Wilson's column: "The Sammy Davis, Jr.'s are expecting. If it's a boy they'll name him Mark Sidney, and Tracey if it's a girl."

I looked at the words, but the pleasure of having the news be known was muffled by the awareness that from the moment the newspapers hit the streets our troubles would increase. May was clutching my arm, smiling with all the gaiety of champagne bubbling out of the bottle. "Tell the truth, now: you've seen your name in the papers plenty of times but this is pretty darned marvelous, isn't it?"

I drew her close. "Darling, it's beautiful. It really is."

For several days I didn't look at the mail, not wanting to let it intrude on my pleasure. But more than a hundred unsigned letters had piled up in the dressing room and they had to be got rid of. As I skimmed through the predictable threats and obscenities from the haters and fanatics, I was aware that I felt only tired of them. I'd already been as afraid, as humiliated, as hurt, as disappointed as I could be, so that now, after all these years, these people and their hatred had become little more to me than a big fat bore.

There were some, however, that disturbed me. The thinking behind them was unfathomable. "God will strike you down for what you are doing. You have sinned against God's will," I read, finding it impossible to understand how an obviously religious person could accuse God of hatred —a pettiness invented by man.

"He will make you pay for what your children will suffer. You have thought of yourselves but have you thought about your children?" Letter for letter asked the same cliché question: "What about the children?"

Don't they understand that they who are so "concerned" for the welfare of my future children, they who are actually angry at us for our intention to bring children into such "unhappiness"—they are the ones who are going to cause the unhappiness? The same people who ask, "What about the children?" could solve the problem as easily as they have created it. All they have to do is *forget about our children* and there won't *be* any problem. They don't have to go out and do anything, all they have to do is *nothing*. But it won't work that way. They'll ostracize them: they'll be inwardly suspicious and openly unkind in exercising every one of the current day's methods of discrimination. If there's a school party maybe they'll forget to invite my kid. I don't know the form it will take, times change, but I do know that as the years pass they'll make my children cry. Then, those same people will shake their heads and say, "How *dare* they bring children into the world to face such unhappiness."

And if I'd married a Negro woman, would they treat my children any better? With more kindness? No. My baby would have it tough no matter what, until *no* baby would have it tough no matter what.

I heard a knock at the door, May's slippers on the foyer floor and the knob turning before I could call out to her not to open it. I grabbed for my gun and was out of bed as a room service table was wheeled past the half-open door and into the living room. I recognized the waiter and relaxed. When he'd left May came in. "Good morning, Sharlie Brown. Breakfast is ready. Surprise."

I nodded. "You almost gave that nice man a much *bigger* surprise." I slowly took the gun out from behind my back. "Darling, you do *not* open doors."

She spoke through her fingers. "Did I frighten you?"

"I wasn't exactly planning to go out and shoot a bagel for breakfast."

She pulled back the window curtains. "Look. It must have snowed all night." I put my arm around her and we stood at the window admiring it. "Sammy, can we go walking in the snow?"

"Darling, may I tell you something?"

"Sure."

"That's the *worst idea I ever heard!* A woman takes a singer who dances—a dancing singer—and wants to turn him into a ski instructor? First of all, have you any idea what happens when a small colored fella like me goes walking around in snowdrifts? Right away people point and yell, 'Hey, look, it's a penguin, it's a penguin.' "

When we'd finished breakfast I asked, "Don't you need some clothes?"

She shook her head emphatically. "I brought plenty with me."

"But most of your stuff is for warm weather. I think you should spend the day around the stores and get some dresses, maybe a pair of ski pants, that kind of jazz. I've got a meeting up here with the Morris guys and there are a few other things I have to do. . . ."

"I'll wait while you have your meeting. I don't want to go shopping. I want to be with my husband."

"Darling, togetherness is beautiful but we're not two peas in a pod. Now, you haven't been out of the hotel in over a week. There isn't another woman in the world who spends ten days in New York City and hasn't bought even a handkerchief." I took five one hundred dollar bills out of a drawer and gave them to her. "It's pointless for you to wait around 'til I'm free because out of the whole day I'll have maybe ten minutes to spend with you, if I'm lucky. Why don't you call Jane and look around the stores?"

While she talked to Jane I stood at the window watching the snowflakes swirling through the trees in Central Park, wishing I could take her out and we could run around like a couple of nitwits. I yearned to take her window shopping along Fifth Avenue and maybe go into some of the stores and buy things together. I wanted to take her to the theater to see

Camelot, or to a movie. But I didn't dare. I knew that if we went to a movie theater the time would come, maybe not the first time, maybe not the first ten times, but eventually I'd hear somebody behind us saying, "Isn't that the nigger who married the white woman?" And I wouldn't be able to walk away from that. I'd have to save face in front of my wife. I'd have to confront him and he'd either back down or we'd start swinging at each other. I had no physical fear. Even if it became a mob I always have my gun. But the best I could hope for is to break even. And for what? So we could see a movie together? We'd had dozens of nice invitations I didn't dare accept. Even the idea of taking her to Danny's where it was as safe as any public place could be—still, the hotel and dressing room were safer. Nobody could insult her there or do icy stares from across the room.

When Jane arrived I got her aside. "I want to get May a mink coat. Who's the best furrier in New York?"

"Maximilian."

"Do you know anybody there?"

"Ask for Mr. Dix. Mr. David Dix."

"Don't mention a word of it but do me a favor and try to get her back here at five o'clock, okay? No later, no earlier."

I was in the hotel lobby at five when she and Jane pulled up in the Rolls I'd rented for them. May had a cloth coat wrapped around her and she shivered, "Boy oh boy it's cold. Hey, how come you're down here?"

"I was just getting some cigarettes and waiting for you."

She looked at me suspiciously. "You never go down to get your own cigarettes . . . heyyyyyy, is it just possible you missed me, Sammydavis?"

I gave it a Ned Sparks reading. "I missed you, I missed you. How'd you do around the stores?"

"Nothing."

"You mean in the entire city of New York you couldn't find a single dress to buy? Where did you look? In hardware stores?"

"No. We went to Bergdorf, Bendel, Elizabeth Arden, and we stopped at the store Jax has here." She opened her handbag and gave me back the money.

"And there's wasn't a single dress?"

She shook her head, "Nope." But I knew that if we were free and clear she would have found some dresses. "All right, you're out of your mind, but let's go upstairs."

I opened the door to the suite and let her in first. The living room had wall to wall mink in every color it comes in, each one deeper and more luxurious looking than the next. She turned to me and her mouth moved but no words happened. A gentleman was walking toward us from the other end of the room. "Darling, this is Mr. Dix."

She shook hands with him, then excused herself, pulled me into the bedroom and whispered, "Sammy, we can't afford it. You don't have to buy me a coat. I love you anyway."

"May, be gracious about it. When I want to buy you a present you have no right to take that pleasure away from me." I took her by the arm, "Let's not be rude and keep the man waiting."

I had brought Finis Henderson in from Chicago as co-ordinator of a benefit for Martin Luther King at Carnegie Hall. Frank and Dean would be flying in from the Coast to do it with me. I had a drink with Finis in the Copa Lounge and he brought me up to date. "The tickets are completely sold out but our souvenir program is death." He smiled wryly. "I know you wanted me to send you a list of who bought ads but I was hoping to get a few more so I could use up the minimum words Western Union allows."

I scanned the list he handed me. "It's a little damned embarrassing to have a benefit for Martin Luther King and to have almost no ads from colored people."

He nodded. "They didn't come through with a black-eyed pea."

"I'll call you and we'll spend an afternoon uptown. We'll go from door-to-door if we have to, but we'll come back with ads."

As I opened the door to the suite I saw Paul standing behind it. I nodded, appreciating his professionalism. "Okay, Punjab. Daddy Warbucks'll take over."

May was fast asleep. The lights were blazing and she was sitting on the bed, propped against the pillows, wearing lounging pajamas, her make-up freshly put on since I'd last seen her. In the living room there was a room service table, set for two, with ice and sandwiches and hot coffee. I draped a napkin over my arm and rolled the table to the bedroom. "Room Service!!"

She sat up and did two minutes of "I just dozed off for a second." I pointed to the television set, "They went off the air at two-thirty. You dig watching patterns? I love having you wait for me like this but it's ridiculous. You're going to be a mother and it's important you get your sleep." I flung her a few scowls but it was pretty thrilling that someone cared enough about me to wait up that late just to say hello before we both went to sleep.

"How was the show?"

"Would you believe that you are married to a man who had the *audacity* to stand in front of Sir Laurence Olivier and do *Hamlet?*"

"You're kidding."

"He came in with Tony Quinn. I did Tony—the thing from *Viva Zapata*—and then I had the colossal effrontery to say, 'Ladies and gentlemen, there's a man in the audience that I dig so much that I'm about to make a complete and utter fool of myself by doing him.' Well, it was fantastic. He applauded like crazy and he made a little speech and he was just charming."

"I never saw you do *Hamlet*."

"I haven't done it for maybe a year."

"Oh, then if you did it before you weren't worried it would bomb."

"Darling, nothing happens on that stage by mistake. There was no question I could do it but the kick was doing it for *him*."

I told her about the problem we were having with the benefit. "But as heartbreaking as it is on one hand, it's beautiful that a guy like Julie Podell turns out to be the biggest single contributor to Martin Luther King. He bought the highest-priced full page ad plus three boxes at $800 apiece. Whenever we have problems with the racial thing and we wonder if it'll ever change we should remember this is the same man whose policy wouldn't let me into his club."

She whispered in disbelief, "He wouldn't let you in?"

I'd drifted into a feeling that we'd always been married, that there'd been no other life before her, forgetting how much of the early years she didn't know. How remote, how unbelievable they seemed even as I said it. "Ten years ago when Frank was playing the Copa I had a date with some friends to go over and see him. When we got there they wouldn't let me in."

"At the *Copa*? It's incredible."

"It's not incredible. That was the custom in those days. That was Julie's policy just like it was all over town. But somewhere along the line he reversed it. And I'm sure it wasn't easy for him. He's so set in his ways that he makes Will Mastin look fickle. So it's pretty thrilling when a guy like this comes over to your side."

"Sammy?"

"Yes?"

"Boy oh boy I'm going to hate going back to the coast without you."

"You're not going to hate it as much as I'm going to hate being in Camden and Pittsburgh and Windsor without you. But they're short jumps and by the time I could look around and send for you it'll be time for me to go on to the next one. We both understand it so that's it."

"But how about Florida? You're going to be there for two weeks."

"Darling . . . don't be a noodge. Take my word for it. I really don't think Florida's the place for us."

"But we haven't had any trouble here. Okay, I know the South is different but after all, how different can it be?" A hurt kind of puzzlement was crossing her face. I knew that the statement: "Darling, it's the South," just didn't mean enough to her. Sure, she'd heard about it in school, with the plantations and the slaves and then Lincoln freeing the slaves and everybody dancing around singing "Swanee River." But she could have no real understanding of what the South meant in 1960 to a Negro who would not ride in the back of the bus. And I couldn't bring myself to make the humiliating explanations and subject myself to pity from my wife.

I'd gotten up from the table and walked across the room. I turned and faced her. "Listen, I've got a great idea. How about if tomorrow afternoon we go to a movie? Just you and me together."

Her face surged with excitement. "Seriously? Do you mean that?"

"Yes. Would you like to see *The Misfits?* It just opened."

"Oh, boy. I'd like to see *anything* with my husband."

She was rattling around the bedroom dropping things, humming, looking out the window so the sunlight would get past the shades and wake me. When she heard me sitting up she called room service. "Hello there, this is Mrs. Davis. My husband is awake. You can send our order up now."

I showered. As I dried myself I looked out the window at the street and at the people. It was beautiful to sit in our suite and blow up pretty balloons but we had only to take the elevator downstairs and go through the revolving door to be plunged back into reality. I was afraid again. I pictured somebody sneering, insulting her. Sure, it had to happen someday, but not yet, not during her pregnancy.

I stirred my coffee slowly, planning how I'd break it to her. There was no way to soften it. "Darling, I'm sorry, but I won't be able to make the movies this afternoon. . . ." Surprise and disappointment flicked across her face. "I don't know how I forgot but I've got to go uptown with Finis and drum up those ads. There's a deadline and I've got to do it today or we blow it with the printer."

"Oh. Well, it's pretty cold out today, anyway. Hey, listen, I hope you have some luck up there."

"Here's what we'll do. I'll have a movie projector and a screen sent up here and right after the second show we can see two, even three, pictures if we feel like it instead of just one."

I called Finis, and kissed May good-bye. Paul was putting on his coat. I gave him a look. " 'And wherever little Mary went,' right?"

"That's it, daddy."

I did a slow turn-around. "A former San Francisco policeman, a square with flat feet, gives me a *'That's it, daddy'?* You're getting pretty hip for only a month in the business." I smiled. "Stick around here, baby. I don't exactly need you where I'm going."

The broad smile of welcome from the owner of the large laundry, the delight that all his employees had seen me coming to visit with him, paled when he heard what I wanted. "I'm sorry, Sammy, I'm not in a position to make a contribution."

"I don't understand . . . don't you approve of what Martin Luther King is doing?"

"Of course I approve." He shrugged uncomfortably, "I suppose what it comes to is they have to fight their own battles down there. I'm up here and I've got my family to worry about. I've got my own problems."

He owned a fleet of taxicabs. He shook his head, "I've got no money to send down South. Hell, let them send some up here." He gave me a wise-guy grin. "Then I can tip the headwaiter at the Copa and get a good table."

"What's that supposed to mean?"

"It means what you know it means. Like last week I was fool enough to tell my wife, 'Hey, let's go down and see Sammy. That place must be okay if he's there.' Like, they waltzed us in and hustled us back to where we needed a telescope t'see you. Like, I looked to see who was up front and there was no chocolate there, daddy. None. So, when your Dr. King gets finished in the South tell him our equality can use a little repair work, too. Maybe then I'll have a few hundred to spare."

"You ever been to the Copa before that?"

He laughed. "Never before and never again."

"But you figure that when you walk in they should put you at the ringside, right? You go down there to spend your big fifteen dollars and you expect to get what they give the man who comes in once every week and spends maybe five thousand a year in there? Why? 'Cause you're colored? You want kid-glove equality? 'Hey, treat him carefully 'cause he's colored.' "

"I'll try a few years of that."

He owned a five-and-ten. "History, son, read your history and then tell Dr. King he's a fine man but he's wasting his time. Just look around you. The Irish came over and the door opened wide. The Italians came over and the door opened wide. The Germans, the Russians—*everybody* came over and the door opened wide. And who opened the door, son? *We* did, smiling 'Yassuh.' "

He owned a trucking company.

"But it *is* your problem, sir. Just like it's *my* problem. He's down there fighting for us as a people. Isn't it unthinkable that we don't support him as a people? Can't you see that Martin Luther King is to us what Moses was to the Jews?"

He smiled, but it was plastic. "Why don't you get it from them?"

"Don't knock 'em. I've been up here for hours trying to get money from colored people to help colored people, and I can tell you there's plenty we could get from the Jews, and not just money."

He smiled unpleasantly. "Like what?"

"Unity. Pride of heritage. They believed in themselves. They didn't just sit around complaining, 'We're as good as anybody else,' they went out and proved it. And there's less of them than us so how come we're flat on our backs and they're up and swinging?"

"Supposing you tell me."

"For one thing they helped each other. You read a lot about Israel, but how do you think it happened? When Hitler burned six million Jews the lucky ones in America and in England didn't say, 'I'm up here and they're down there.' They built Israel for Jews who needed it, people they'll never meet. I've been to their fund-raising dinners and I've seen them stand up and pledge from fifty dollars to as much as half a million from one man, and raise millions for a cause that was far from their homes, but, mister, it was close to their hearts."

"You comparing being Jewish to being colored?"

"Don't look at me like that. Obviously we can't match them in money, but we can match them in sentiment. And that's all we need. I'm talking about a theory that's as basic as 'united we stand, divided we fall,' as sure as breaking a hundred matchsticks one by one between your fingers but being unable to break them with a hammer when they're bound together. How can we be so stupid as to let ourselves be hated as a race and not at least fight back as a race?"

He owned a nightclub. All he'd give was complaints.

"In other words you wanta sit around and bitch but you won't help the man who's risking his life to improve things for colored people all over the country?"

"Colored people never did anything for me. All I ever got outa being colored is more room on the subway 'cause white people didn't wanta sit next to me."

He owned a large bakery. "Why should I give money to a hopeless cause, Mr. Davis?"

"How can you call it hopeless when in the last ten years there's been more advance in human rights than in the hundred years before?"

He looked at me patiently—as though he were explaining something to a white man. "How can you hope for human rights when you know they don't figure us as human?"

"But that's exactly the point Dr. King is making. Every time a redneck pours ketchup on the head of one of the sit-ins somebody who never cared one way or another leans a little closer toward us. I've seen it in my own life. People get you to the ground and kick you and kick you—but eventually some of the people who stood by watching it step forward and say, 'Hold it. Get off his back. Nobody can be *that* bad.' And then they're thinking in your direction, they're open to you."

"I must say you're very persuasive."

"Isn't it a pity that I should have to be?"

"But I'm afraid you're also an optimist. You're counting on people feeling bad when they see what's happening to us, people whose ancestors came over here looking for freedom and the first thing they did was go out and get themselves slaves."

He owned a wholesale meat company. He stood behind his desk and leaned toward me. "No, I *do not* approve of what he's doing."

"Are you telling me you don't want integration?"

"Not the kind he's goin' around beggin' for." The man's eyes narrowed. "Smarten up, Mr. Davis. The only integration you'll ever see in this country is when ofay blood runs in the gutter and mixes ith good colored blood."

I felt an un-funny laughter building up in me. Only *I* would walk in on a Muslim and ask for money to support Martin Luther King. I stood up. "I think you're dead wrong but you're entitled to your opinion."

He laughed. "You think I'm a Muslim, don't you?" He shook his head. "The Muslims are wrong. They want their own country, but I say *this* is our own country. So I'm not looking for separate states where we can set up shop by ourselves." He smirked. "And you *know* if this government ever did give us our own state they'd give us Alaska." He sat down in his swivel chair. "Before I owned this business I worked for one like it and I broke my back for six days before I got a week's pay. And I never figured I owed my boss a thank-you when he handed me the envelope. You read me? Well, that's how it is for rights. I don't want no goddamned white man sittin' around in an office my taxes are helping pay the rent on, deciding if maybe he should give me what the law says is mine. If the good Reverend wants to get on his knees and pray-in and sit-in that's his privilege, but I'm not paying for it. You want money from me? Then come up here some day and tell me you're putting together a black army to *fight* for what's ours and I'll show you the kind of money you never even dreamed about."

He owned a hotel. He smiled uncomfortably. "Sammy, I'm the first one to say something should be done. . . ."

"But by somebody else, right?"

He owned a supermarket. He was an old friend and he was embarrassed. He struck back defensively. "Where do you get your nerve coming up here telling me how to be colored? Why as far back as I can remember you've been ashamed to death that you're colored."

"You're wrong."

He laughed in my face. "Sure. You were *proud* of it."

"No."

He stopped laughing. "You admit it?"

"What's there to be proud of? Do people with green eyes

walk around being proud of it? If they do they're idiots. There's nothing to be proud of just 'cause your skin happens to be brown, white, or polka dot. But I'm going to be proud of it someday, when we find something more important to draw us all together than just mass hatred of the white man."

"Name me something better."

"The respect for ourselves that we want from other people. We don't have it, but when we make ourselves heard and felt as one solid force saying, 'We helped build this country, we contributed to all the arts and sciences. . . .' "

"Sure," he was nodding bitterly, "we carried bricks into every building in America. That's a lot to be proud of, being America's pack mules."

"Someday we'll take pride even in that. There's no glory attached to being born in a tenement. Not while you're living there. Only when you can look back on it from a penthouse. When I lived up here I hated it. But I don't mind talking about it now. It glorifies me to say, 'That's where I started, but look where I am.' That's how it's going to be with our people. Someday it's going to get written in history, in big letters: 'These are the people who beat the odds. They started from behind but they pulled together and here they are.' "

"You're dreaming."

"You're wrong. It's starting to happen now. We've got a Martin Luther King going for us and he's going to light up enough lunch counters 'til we can all see what he's doing, and then we're all going to get behind him so solid, so strong that there'll be an honest to God social revolution. We'll start sticking together, pulling each other up, and when we do we're going to raise ourselves so high that it's going to be impossible for anybody to see us by looking down.

"Someday the whole world is going to look at the mass Negro and see him on a financial, educational, and social level with the white cats who had it all handed to them. And if I don't live to see it, at least my kids will. They're going to walk down the street wearing their brown skin as a badge of honor."

He spoke softly. "Do you really think it can happen?"

"We have to believe it will."

I'd talked myself hoarse, walked from one end of Harlem to the other and all I'd collected was a crowd. As the cab headed downtown Finis said, "It's inexcusable."

"It's horrible and it's heartbreaking, but I'm not sure how inexcusable it is. Losing gets to be a habit, baby. People need success." I looked out the window at what we'd come to accept after three long centuries of disappointment. But, every lunch counter and bus stop was arguing that there *can* be light where thirty million people had come to believe only in the certainty of darkness. The day was coming when we'd no longer be strangers to hope, when there would be no shame in having been the laborers of yesterday because we'd be the architects of our own tomorrow.

I was sitting on the floor in the living room, watching a Laurel and Hardy picture and cleaning my pipes. May picked up a magazine and put it down without opening it. She picked it up again and opened it, obviously trying to get interested but in a minute she put it down. She lit a cigarette and sat back on the couch and I could feel her concentrating on Laurel and Hardy, forcing herself to watch as if she were bound to the couch by a seat belt. As though I could hear the fibers tearing I sensed the moment before she stood up abruptly, crushed her cigarette into an ashtray, leaving part of it still burning, and strode out of the room.

When I walked into the bedroom she was putting on her boots. "I'm going for a walk around the block. I've got to get out of here for a while."

I glanced out the window at the falling snow that was being blown into deep drifts on the sidewalk. She was putting on a coat. "Darling, don't you like your mink coat?"

She was startled. "Of course I do. I love it."

"Then how come you haven't worn it yet? You certainly ought to wear it today. It's cold out there."

She shook her head and seemed surprised that I didn't understand. "I'm saving it to wear with my husband." She kissed me goodbye. "I won't be long."

I wiped some of the frost off a window and caught sight

of her as she turned the corner at 59th Street. Paul was a few yards behind her. The frost was re-forming on the glass, blurring the outside, reducing the world to the rooms of our suite. It had been more than ten days of confinement to the club and the hotel and her only breaks from that routine were when she went out with Jane. This walk had been the first sign she was cracking. There'd been some casual questions like "How come we don't go to Danny's?" and "What's the Harwyn like?" and I'd covered with trumped-up reasons why we had to be at the hotel: an interview, exhaustion—always something, but I was afraid she was beginning to suspect that I was deliberately not going anywhere with her, that we were in hiding.

She stamped the last of the snow off her boots, her face pink from the cold, smiling, as though she'd opened a safety valve and all the pressure and tension had been released. I helped her off with her coat. "How was it?"

"*Beautiful.* There's hardly anybody on the streets and the snow is so fresh . . ." She saw the hot chocolate I'd ordered for her. "Heyyyyyy . . . I was just thinking I could use something like that to hit the spot. "

I felt the handle of the pitcher, wrapped a napkin around it, and poured some for her. I scooped up a huge bunch of whipped cream on a spoon and flipped it onto the top of her hot chocolate. She finished one cup, poured another and went for some more whipped cream. I said, "Easy on that stuff. It sticks. If you're worried about keeping your figure after the baby is born, don't make it tougher than it has to be. Would you rather have an extra spoon of whipped cream or look good in your Jax slacks?"

She stared at me accusingly. "You think I'm getting fat!"

I stared back, stunned. "Darling, am I crazy or did you *ask* me to help you diet?"

She put down the spoon. "Boy oh boy it's rotten that you're always right. Why can't I be right sometimes?"

"While you were out I got four tickets for *Camelot* for the matinee tomorrow."

She sat back in her chair, savoring the moment. "You mean my husband and I are really honest-to-God saying to heck with meetings and stuff and going to a matinee? And of *Camelot.*"

I woke up afraid. I felt it physically, like whirring motors in my stomach, down my legs, and an ache in my heart for her when she finds out she's not a beautiful girl going out to a matinee with her husband, she's a "nigger lover." It was out of the question to risk it. I knew I couldn't keep her a prisoner forever but I had to wait until I could be sure that she was emotionally prepared for whatever we might run into, until I was certain that we have enough background together so that the threads of our marriage can absorb the shock of the kind of abuse that was waiting for us outside. She was moving around quietly, believing I was still asleep. She'd washed her hair and had a towel around her neck. I didn't move. I heard her open the bedroom door then close it softly behind her.

Her mink coat was hanging outside the closet door. Under it was an orange dress and pink beads. Her boots were on the floor directly under the coat. It was one o'clock. It seemed like a long time before I heard the door opening.

"Sammy?"

I rolled over. "Mmmmmmmmmm?"

"It's one-thirty."

"Give me five minutes, darling, just five minutes."

I heard the phone ring in the other room. "Sammy, that was Jane and Burt. They're on their way over. They said the traffic is very heavy and we should be downstairs or we'll miss the overture."

I rolled over, keeping my eyes closed. "Five more minutes . . ."

"But Sammy, if you don't get up now we'll miss the show." I could smell her perfume. I didn't want to look at her and see her all dressed and ready with her make-up on. "Well, if you're this tired you'd better sleep for another hour or two. We can see the show some other time." I was aching to tell her, "Darling, I don't want to sleep away my day. I love you and I want to see you happy. I don't want to keep your beauty locked in a closet. I'd give anything to be able to take you to the show as we'd planned, to take you everywhere, but I don't dare."

I stayed in bed long after she'd left the room, certain I'd done the best thing, yet, what was it costing? Incident by incident, disappointment by disappointment, would it become so unpleasant for her that eventually, layer by layer, it would wear away the love?

I stood in the doorway of the living room, wearing a robe and pajamas. May got up from an arm chair and hugged me.

I held her tight, then kissed the palm of her hand. "I'm sorry." Jane and Burt were on the couch. "I'm sorry, boys. I just couldn't have gotten out of bed if my life depended on it."

Burt shrugged. "We saw it once. You're the ones who missed it."

"Look, I've been doing two shows a night and three on weekends without a day off for months and I plain ran out of strength."

May poured a cup of coffee for me and looked at Jane and Burt. "Coffee?"

Jane smiled. "No, thanks. We're already awake."

"Hey," May said, "he's my husband and if I'm not angry at him then you guys have no right to be."

They didn't care about the show. They were annoyed and puzzled by the way I was treating May. There was no way they could understand without my telling them and it was better that they didn't understand and couldn't pity her. I said, "I've got a swinging idea for dinner tonight. Instead of ordinary room service we'll have a full-dress dinner party. We'll really make an occasion out of it. The guys'll wear black ties and the girls'll wear long dresses . . ."

"And you'll be sleeping, right?"

"I'll ignore that, Jane. We'll order caviar, lobster cocktails, champagne, steaks or maybe some duck . . ."

"What if I don't like caviar?"

"Then you can sleep through it, Jane. Don't ad-lib with me. Where was I?"

"You were cooking a duck."

"Right. Now for dessert we can have a soufflé or baked Alaska, cordials with our coffee—we'll do it banquet style for like two hours and we'll keep a waiter and a captain here to serve the whole meal. We'll be so chic we'll hate ourselves."

Jane and Burt left at four-thirty to get dressed. They sent flowers and arrived at six. I had music playing softly in the background. I'd ordered a magnum of champagne and I poured drinks for the four of us, offered a toast and we sat down for dinner. It went off with the luxury I'd planned, but all I'd accomplished was to raise the level of the prison.

A gust of Miami heat swept through the doorway of the plane as I stepped aside to let Jane and Burt off ahead of me. Paul Newer's partner, Ray Wilson, who was replacing Paul for a while, said quietly, "No autographs, no stops for anything. Let's get out of the city of Miami as fast as we can."

I moved through the terminal building flanked by Jane and Burt and Harold Gardner, the head of the Fontaine-bleau's publicity department, on one side, and Ray and Murphy on the other. The car was waiting in front of the nearest exit and the chauffeur started rolling the instant the doors closed. Ray pressed down the locks.

Some of the pressure eased as we rolled off the causeway over Biscayne Bay and onto Miami Beach. I smiled at Harold. "Thank you for meeting us. I appreciate it."

"You've got a beautiful suite in the new building," he said.

Jane asked, "Is that the controversial one that blocks the sun from the Eden Roc?"

I looked at her. "Why bother to ask? Wouldn't you know that if there's a controversial building I'll be in it?"

May's voice over the telephone was heartbreaking. I told her, "I miss you, too, darling. I really do."

"Are Jane and Burt there?"

"Yes. They asked me to send you their love and they'll call you tomorrow. Harry's playing next door and Augie and Margo are on the bill with him."

"Who are Augie and Margo?"

"They're the best dance act in the business and they're good friends of mine. I've known them for years."

"Everybody's there but me."

"Darling, let's not talk about it, okay? We've been over it a hundred times and there's nothing new we can say, right?"

"I guess so. Do you *really* miss me?"

I sat on the bed long after we'd hung up, still hearing the semidoubt in her voice. When someone doesn't understand the real reasons for something they begin analyzing and they have to come up with the wrong answers. I was afraid what those answers might be: "Is he more concerned with his career, afraid a few people might stay away because of me?" She could be thinking anything and I realized that in order to spare myself humiliation I was causing her the needless anguish of doubt.

She answered the phone on the first ring.

"May . . . I want to explain this Miami Beach jazz."

"Well, as long as you mention it, I must say I don't understand, although I sure would like to."

"Okay. Try to understand that we haven't only committed the cardinal sin of the South. It's not that simple. Florida has a state *law* against miscegenation—a white person mixing with a colored person. They could put us in jail for a year if they wanted to."

"It's against the law?"

"That's right."

"But we're married . . ."

"Forget it. Down here I don't have the right to even walk down the street with you despite the fact that we're married."

"I didn't know."

"Darling, I have to have a special police card or if I go out on the streets at night I can be arrested. I need a police card so that a taxi driver will take me . . . look, it's an old-fashioned thing but the law still stands. It's changing but it still hasn't changed enough."

When she spoke there were tears in her voice. "Oh, God, I feel rotten making you tell me that . . . I'm so sorry."

"There's nothing to be sorry about. You couldn't know."

I invited some friends up to the suite a few days after the opening. As it thinned out leaving Jane and Burt and Augie and Margo, Big John stopped by. "Can I talk to you a minute, Sammy?" I followed him into the bedroom. "They keep asking me over in Miami what you want to do about your suite this year."

"Baby, tell 'em thanks but I don't need it. I work at the Fontainebleau and I live at the Fontainebleau. That's *it*."

"You know what they'll start saying."

"That's their privilege." He frowned apprehensively. "John, I can't beat people into liking me and I can't beg 'em for it, either. And isn't it long past time I stopped trying? Frank doesn't keep a suite in the Italian section of town just to show 'em he's still one of *them*. They can like me or hate me but it'll be on the basis of what I am. I wouldn't be helping any cause by living over there, or in Southside, or Westside, or in Harlem. The one thing the Harlems of the country do not need is more colored people."

He smiled. "I'll give 'em the message."

It was so ridiculous that I was embarrassed I'd ever done it at all.

As I walked into the living room Burt asked, "Anything wrong, Sam?"

"No, baby, I was just musing over something I used to do when I was young—last year. What've you guys been talking about?"

"Your show," Augie said. "We think you're better than you ever were."

Burt nodded. "We noticed it at the Copa and even more here. I can't put my finger on exactly what it is but your performance has an extra dimension."

All that had changed was "attitude." I wasn't "the kid" anymore. I was working just as hard, but not as wildly, not wasting anything as I used to. I was making everything count.

Jane said, "You're not dancing as much."

"Do you miss it?"

"I love seeing you dance, on the other hand you're doing more humor, and it's great. I never heard straight comedians get such laughs."

The changeover had been coming on gradually. It seemed as though God was helping me; as my energy diminished He replaced it with more wit, more insight, more maturity on the stage and, as a result, an even greater rapport with the audience. I'd dreaded the day when I wouldn't have the strength and the energy which had always been the very heart of my act, but when time finally forced the necessary changes the "irreplaceable" had been replaced, and by something even better.

Things seem to level off and work themselves out. At

thirty-five I couldn't possibly go out there with the physical strength and speed that I had at twenty-one. But maybe if I'd still been able to do the go-go-go stuff the audience would have grown tired of it after all these years. Perhaps the newness, the changing personality, had a sustaining quality built into it.

"Augie," I glanced between him and Margo, "are you holding your wife's hand because you love her or are you afraid she's going to hit you?" I looked at Jane and Burt. "Only *I* have to sit here alone, and like an idiot."

Jane looked at me unsympathetically. "All you have to do is call her and tell her to come down."

Things had been quiet, there were no indications of trouble and if we stayed within the hotel grounds maybe it would be all right. The Fontainebleau was like a city in itself, with shops, restaurants—there was nothing we'd have to go outside for.

When I told her she sounded like a kid. "Do you really mean it? I don't want to be pushy like the other day."

"Darling, I miss you terribly. Ask Jim to get you on the first plane he can tomorrow. Have him tell Arthur I'd appreciate it if he'd keep you company on the trip. I won't meet you at the airport. Ray'll come down in Ben Novack's car."

I was up early the next morning getting weather reports, and stocking up on things she liked. On my way downstairs to the florist shop I passed an open door to another suite. It was only partially furnished but it was gorgeous.

I called Ben Novack, the owner of the Fontainebleau. "I just saw a suite down the hall, Ben. You've got to let me have it."

"Sammy, you're in the most beautiful one I have."

"I know and I appreciate it but my wife is coming in today and I know she'd particularly love this one. Her favorite color is yellow. . . ."

"But it's not finished yet."

"Ben, please, I know it sounds crazy but do me this favor. Put eight guys in to finish it right away if you have to. I really want it."

Two hours later I was moved in and Mrs. Novack was supervising a small army of men who were running around like a Mack Sennett movie, bringing in lamps, a coffee table, porch furniture, hanging curtains and a chandelier over the dining table. The top of the dresser was covered with about a dozen bottles of perfume I'd picked up at the drugstore. Jane and Burt came in behind three bellboys who were bringing up the flowers. She smiled, "Did we miss the ceremony?" Then she said, seriously, "It's beautiful."

I knew that while I was doing the shows May'd be with Jane and Burt, but if they were living here, in the suite, she wouldn't feel like a drag, like they were always coming up to keep her company.

I called them into the second bedroom. "Listen, I just had an idea. I can't shake you guys no matter how hard I try. I mean, we're together like twenty-four hours a day as it is, and when May gets here it'll be the same thing, right? So why don't you move your stuff in here and stay with us?"

Burt nodded, "Sounds great."

I waited for Jane to say something. I glared at her. "What's wrong, Jane?"

"It has no full-length mirror."

"I'll *get* you a full-length mirror."

She laughed, "Okay then." She hesitated. "What about May? How do you think she'll like the idea?"

"First of all, you know I wouldn't have asked you if I wasn't sure she'd love it. You're buddies, right? And now with this mirror jazz I begin to understand why. Secondly, as far as privacy goes the place is big enough so that if after a while you can't stand looking at us or if we can't stand looking at you we've got the whole living room and dining thing between us, you've got your own private entrance . . . and just so you won't feel I'm out-starring you the bedrooms are both the same size."

She grinned. "Separate but equal, right?"

"Watch that, Jane." I picked up the phone and called for some bellboys to move them.

I put a handkerchief into a seersucker jacket and looked around the living room for my sunglasses. "Where're you guys going today?"

May said, "Jane and Burt say there are some pretty good stores in Surfside, so we're going to look around there.

And we might go to see the jungle."

"Great." I looked at my watch. "It's a definite off to meet the press."

She walked over to me. "Poor Sammydavis. It doesn't seem fair that you work so hard and the three of us run around like we're on a vacation."

"That's how it is when you're a very big star." I kissed her. "Have fun and I'll catch you back here around five for cocktails." I hurried out the door and slowed down only when it was closed behind me.

Day by day I'd found reasons to be away in the afternoons—benefits, interviews, playing golf with "somebody important." I didn't dare just stay around the room with her because it would emphasize the fact that we were never going anywhere together.

I ordered huge tables of hot hors d'oeuvres to be delivered every afternoon at five o'clock and I invited everyone I thought she'd like. Harry and Julie came over a few times, Martin Luther King was in town and he came over, so did Sidney Poitier and Henry Ginsberg, who'd produced *Giant*. June Allyson was in the hotel for a few hours and she came up and had lunch with us. The economy plan went on a Florida vacation. In ten days my little campaign to brighten up hotel life resulted in a $2,500 bill for drinks and hors d'oeuvres. I was the Mad Social Director, waiting only for the day when I could walk down the street with my wife.

May cut into her steak with gusto. "I must say that I like a dining table instead of those crowded room service carts."

"It's just one of the little niceties your husband tried to arrange for his wife and friends. Incidentally, the Novacks are giving a closing night party tomorrow. And Frank got in today. He's right down the hall and I told him we'd come by after the second tonight." I beckoned for the waiter to serve my coffee. "I realize that you three have nothing to do but loaf around but *somebody* has to do some work around here." I finished my coffee and stood up. "What're you guys going to do?"

"You won't believe it, Sammydavis, but one of my old

pictures is playing in the hotel. We're going to see it. *The Hunters*."

I did an elaborate display of "aghast." "Darling, you're my wife and you're beautiful and I love you, and I'm not saying you didn't make some good pictures, but *that* wasn't one of them. Are you really going to subject good friends to sitting through that atrocity? They could divorce us."

Jane said, "I wouldn't go if I didn't want to."

I glared at her. "In other words if I said 'good morning' to my wife you'd have a comment, right?"

"Well, I would if you said it at *this* hour."

Burt said, "I'm going to stay up here and do the column."

I smiled at him, knowingly, and looked at Jane. "But you really intend to go through with this?" She nodded and I sighed like Father Flanagan at Boys' Town, "You're not *all* bad, are you, Jane? There's a little good in everybody, eh?"

It was four in the morning and the party was still going strong as we said good night to Frank and some other friends and walked down the hall to our own suite. May clung to my arm, especially pleased by something. "I never thought you'd leave a party at Frank's so soon."

"We sat with him, had some drinks, paid our respects—but he's got other guests to spend time with, and he's got his life and I've got mine."

She'd sat down on the couch and was looking at me blankly, trying to conceal her pleasure, to treat the issue academically. "But do you miss the partying you could do if you were single?"

I raised an eyebrow at the flagrant playing of tell-me-how-happy-you-are, but she had a right to know. I sat beside her. "Darling, I developed my set of values the hard way. I'm completely, totally happy with what I've got."

She nodded contentedly. "In other words, what you're saying is you don't envy Frank his freedom?"

"That's what I'm saying. Although I don't know why you need 'other words.' Isn't one set enough?"

"But do you think . . ."

"I think you've had enough compliments for one night." We sat there quietly, each thinking our own thoughts.

"Sammy? Did you have a good engagement here? Did you do as much business as you'd hoped?"

"More. It was unbelievable."

"Did you do as well as last year?"

"I never did business like this in my life."

She walked across the room and took an orange from a bowl. "Jane and Burt told me that business was great in Camden, and at the Copa, and Boston, Pittsburgh—that you broke your own records."

"I told you all that myself. Why did you have to ask them?" I smiled. "You checking up on me?"

She became very involved peeling the orange. "Well, I wasn't really checking up . . ."

"Hey, I was only kidding—but you're serious. Why would you have felt I wasn't leveling with you?"

"Well . . . you *do* try to protect me and if you weren't doing the kind of business you'd hoped, you might not tell me because I'd know it was because of me." She sighed, "I must say I'm tremendously relieved," and her smile was like that of somebody thinking back on a nightmare. "I sure would have hated it if you had to look around and see that what you built up for thirty years was falling apart because of me. I could picture you looking at me and thinking, 'What did I need *her* for?' "

I took her in my arms. "You really thought it could make even the slightest difference in how I feel about you?" She nodded, but she didn't look up. She was crying gently, unwinding after God knows how many days and nights of living with a fear which need never have existed. I stroked her head.

"May? Has it been worse than you expected it to be? I mean, rougher than you bargained for?"

She raised her face which had been buried in my shoulder. "Rough?" She was shaking her head slowly, with surprise, almost shock, at the question. "It hasn't been rough at all. I love my husband and I know you love me. That's all I want or care about."

"Darling, that's beautiful and you know I appreciate it, but let's be honest, you didn't go into this marriage thinking it was like Maryjane Smith marrying the boy next door."

"Of course not."

"How did you feel about people's reactions to us?"

"Well, I can't say I didn't feel badly at the *idea* that people can feel what they do—but there was no point dwelling on it. I loved you, I intended to marry you, and that was that."

"And you were able to just close the reactions out of your mind?"

"I tried to." She lit a cigarette. "As long as we're talking about it, frankly one thing I *have* felt badly about is that you feel you have to treat me as though I'm made out of glass, as though if somebody said something I'd just break apart."

"May, if you've thought I was overprotecting you, why didn't you say something?"

"Because I knew it was rotten for you to have to talk about it."

"I had no idea you were so completely aware of it."

"Once, after we were picketed in London, I thought maybe I would not marry you because it seemed almost a certainty that I'd ruin your career, and I understood its importance to you. That's the only real fear I had."

"Darling, if I never knew this before I know it now: if I walked out on a stage and there were only five people in the audience it wouldn't be as important as knowing that you're home waiting for me."

There was a beautifully corny, full moon shining. I opened the door to the terrace and we stood at the rail, silently, together, absorbing the serenity and peacefulness of the early morning, enjoying the caress of breezes not yet warmed by a sun that was starting to break over an ocean rolling gently, quietly onto the deserted beach. I stood next to May experiencing the miracle of happiness and contentment a man can feel when he is aware that he can encircle his whole world within his two arms.

36

"Sammy . . . I'm Having The Pains . . ." I Sat Up In bed and turned on the light. Her eyes were closed. "I'm sorry to wake you up."

I jumped out of bed and got the stop watch. "Here, time them."

She pressed the starter button. When she stopped the watch it was at two minutes and thirty-two seconds. "The doctor said I should call him when they're coming every seven minutes."

"Oh God. Don't move. Just keep timing them." I'd kept Dr. Steinberg's number handy for the last two weeks. His answering service asked if it was an emergency and he called me back within five minutes.

I hung up and helped her out of bed. "Which dress do you want?"

"My blue and white check Jax."

I dashed for the closet, got it, and rushed back to the bedroom.

She was sitting at her make-up table. "You've *got* to be *joking*. You're having labor pains every two minutes and you're sitting there putting on eye-liner? I don't believe it. I really don't believe it." I knew I shouldn't upset her so I got busy checking the small bag of things I'd had ready, the camera, film, cigarettes. I called Jane and Burt in the Playhouse. "Sorry to wake you guys up but you'd better get up here. We're going to the hospital." I called Rudy's room and woke him, too.

May was back in bed. "You know something? I think it was a false alarm." She nodded, satisfied that she was right.

"Darling, the doctor must know what he's talking about.

621

He's a *doctor*." I tried to keep calm so I wouldn't frighten her, yet I had to get her moving. "May, we dare not delay. If they're coming every two and half minutes then it's like you're almost ready to give birth. If we don't hurry it could happen in the car."

"But what if it's a false alarm?"

"It's worth the risk. *Please*, May, it's a long ride over there and you could be in agony if you wait much longer."

"Sammy, if I go and then find it's too early I'll have to stay there alone for extra days. At least if they had a room for you like we wanted, but to be there without you for no reason . . ."

"No reason! Oh God."

She gasped. "Wait a minute. It's starting again. Okay, you win. Oh *boy*, they hurt!" I handed her the dress and checked my watch. Six-forty-five. At least we'd beat the morning traffic.

She wasn't moving to get out of bed. "I think they went away again." She smiled and nodded. "Yes, definitely."

"Darling," I leaned against the wall, gnashing my teeth, "please! You're killing me." Rudy came rushing upstairs buttoning his shirt as he reached our room. I waved my arms at him. "Don't bother, Rudy. Go back to sleep, baby. Or better still, just boil some water."

He asked, "Are the pains coming close together?"

I told him. "*Only* every two and a half minutes."

"Whew. That's too close."

Jane and Burt came dashing in. I held up my hands. "Relax, fellas. It's all off. She's decided against it."

May started moving off the bed. "Okay, I'll go, but if I have to wait around there a week before anything happens—"

"Darling, let's worry about that later, huh? Rudy, start the car, we'll be out right away."

Jane asked, "Aren't you coming?"

I stared at her, incredulous. "Jane, what kind of a stupid question is *that*? No! I'm going to let my wife go to the hospital to have our baby without me. Are you out of your mind?"

She gave me one of those looks like she knew she was going to be in trouble. "Are you going like that?"

The three of them were struggling to keep straight faces. I was still in my pajamas. I shook my fist at them and ran for some clothes, feeling like a cartoon character. I was dressed in three minutes and we were ready to leave.

May said, "Let's have a cup of coffee."

Jane gasped. "Coffee? Now?"

I smiled broadly. "Of course. I should have thought of it myself. And crumpets. You'll read about us in tomorrow's papers: 'the mother and child are doing fine, the father is dead.' "

But we sat in the living room, drinking coffee, like a bunch of lunatics.

May said, "Shouldn't we tell Mama?"

"No. Let her sleep. Rudy can come back for her later."

It was eight o'clock when I helped May into the front seat of the car. "Sit in the back with Jane and Burt, Rudy. I want to know that I drove my wife to the hospital." I pulled out of the driveway and down the hill, creeping along at fifteen miles an hour, trying to avoid bumps in the road.

"Maybe you'd better go a little faster, Sammy."

"Oh, *now* you think maybe it's not a false alarm?" I turned left on Sunset and stepped it up a little, trying to keep the car at an even speed.

May said, "Oh, boy," and clenched her fists.

"Hold on, darling, we're halfway there!"

She sounded angry, "Boy! If I'd known this was going to happen today I'd have had a hot fudge sundae last night. Now I'll have to start dieting right away." We stopped at a light and she opened the window and spoke to a woman waiting for a bus, "Hello, there! I'm having a baby."

I blew three lights because the car in front of me was doing twenty miles an hour and I was afraid to weave in and out of lanes to pass him. "Just my luck to get behind an imbo in a Nash Rambler." I pulled into the emergency arrival area of Cedars of Lebanon at eight-twenty and stopped as close to the door as I could. May pointed to a sign.

"We're not parking, darling. Rudy'll move it." I helped her out of the car and we walked slowly to the front desk. A nurse was waiting for us. "Come with me, Mrs. Davis."

"How about me?"

"I'm sorry, you'll have to take care of some details down here and then you can wait in the Expectant Fathers' Room."

I hadn't expected I'd have to leave her so soon. I held her face in my hands and kissed her forehead, the elevator doors closed and she was gone.

I was shown into a small waiting room outside the maternity

ward. "You can sit here until Mrs. Davis gives birth. I'm afraid no one but the fathers are permitted in here, though, so your friends will have to wait downstairs."

I lit a cigarette and waited.

Dr. Steinberg came in. "May is in wonderful condition. It won't be long. You'll have only a few hours to wait."

"But everything's okay?"

"Everything's fine. I'll send someone out occasionally to keep you posted."

I went downstairs and sat with Jane and Burt in the lobby. Rudy came in. "I just heard it on the radio in the car."

We'd been there less than an hour. Somebody from the hospital must have called the station. "Baby, call Hugh Benson and make sure he knows and call Arthur and Jim and tell them."

I went back upstairs to the waiting room and called my father.

"I'm on my way, Poppa."

I hung up smiling at the excitement in his voice, happy that he could see this day. I dialed Will's number. "Good morning, Massey. You're about to become a grandfather."

Frank would still be sleeping. I'll wait until noon when he gets over to the set. Maybe the baby'll be born by then.

A doctor came into the waiting room and told me everything was going along fine. I looked at my watch. An hour had passed. It was ten-thirty. I concentrated with all my strength, trying to reach May through telepathy.

Dr. Steinberg entered the room. A surgical mask covered all of his face but his eyes. I was afraid to speak. He took off the mask. He was smiling. "You've got a beautiful baby girl." He was extending his hand to me. "May came through it beautifully. It was a very smooth, simple birth. I'll send for you shortly."

I sat down. I leaned back in the chair and closed my eyes, a montage of scenes swirling through my head. *"How do you do? I'd like you to meet my wife and our daughter Tracey."* . . . *"Why, yes, I just happen to have a picture here."* . . . *"That's our daughter there, the pretty one in the red convertible . . ."* I saw her growing up and going to school and I panicked because I wouldn't be able to help her with her homework . . . I saw her graduating from college at the head of her class and bringing her boy friend home for me to be jealous of . . . I was buying her things, walking hand in hand with her and May through Disneyland . . . standing on a stage singing my songs to her, throwing myself in front of a car to save her, and slipping into her room to kiss her good night every evening.

I hadn't heard the nurse come in. She was holding out a surgical gown for me to change into. Pinned to it was a big, pink button which said, "It's a Girl."

May was smiling as she slept, as though she knew how much someone loved her. The nurse gestured for me to follow her again.

A man is not complete until he sees a baby he has made, and by the grace of God I stood there looking at mine, seeing her tiny face and hands, her whole delicate self.

I watched the nurse taking Tracey away until she was out of sight. I wasn't ready to go downstairs and talk to people. I went into the waiting room and sat down near a window. I was comfortable in the belief that we were ready to help our child grow up, ready to impart everything we had learned the hard way, able to give her all the love and strength she might need—but I prayed that by the time our baby is grown she would not need all that strength, that she would live in a world of people who would not notice or care about a layer of skin. There were cracks in the wall, and they were widening, but will it happen fast enough? Are people willing to change? Are they willing yet to understand a child's innocence?

I gazed out the window, grateful for the time in which I live, for the hope it contained, grateful for the talent I had been given and because of it the thought that perhaps I could have something to do with affecting the world so that some day my children, or maybe only my grandchildren, but some day somebody of mine would be able, finally, to stop fighting.

I knew that in the years to come we would hold our children's hands, walk at their sides, guiding them, protecting them, preparing them for the day when we would have to let go of their hands and watch them step forward to win their own medals, to make their own mistakes, to experience and become all the things which combine to make a person his final, total self. I knew that whatever world tomorrow might contain our children would face it, ready, standing within it, saying words that I myself have said: "Good, bad, or indifferent, here I stand with my convictions, right or wrong, like me or don't—I exist,

I breathe, I live, I love, I make mistakes, I do some good; I have troubles and joys but here I am, my code is my code and it is responsible for the bad things I do as it is responsible for the good."

I walked out into the hall and looked for a nurse. "Can I see my wife again?"

"But she's sleeping."

"That's all right. Please, just for one minute."

I stood beside May's bed. Her face was turned toward me. She was asleep, still smiling. I knelt down beside her and put my hand on hers, "Darling, I know you can't hear me and I'll tell you this again but I wanted to say now how much I love you and thank you for everything you've given me. I'm going to build something good and strong and wonderful for us, and I'll never let you down. I promise." I stood up and kissed her beautiful face and vowed I'd never let anything take away that smile. Whatever problems and pain there had been for me in the past, they were only the measure of the serenity and happiness I experienced at that moment as I looked at my wife and thought of our daughter and the life that had so miraculously brought me to them. If this is what I have come to, then there is nothing I am or have done that I would change. Perhaps all the successes and the failures, all that I did, were necessary for me and for those I love so that now, after thirty-five years, this is really only the beginning.

THIS BOOK

ORIG... $4.50

The Great Discount Delusion

NOW ONLY

75¢

ARE YOU BEING CHEATED?

This exposé of slick marketing techniques will
shock you. It will also save you money.

by Walter Henry Nelson

75171/75¢

PUBLISHED BY
POCKET BOOKS

CHURCHILL'S HISTORY OF THE ENGLISH- SPEAKING PEOPLES

arranged for one volume by
Henry Steele Commager

99701/ $1.65

PUBLISHED BY
POCKET BOOKS